BARCODE NEXT PAGE 0247688292 £43.70

The Mental Health Industry: A Cultural Phenomenon *by Peter A. Magaro, Robert Gripp, David McDowell, and Ivan W. Miller III*

Nonverbal Communication: The State of the Art *by Robert G. Harper, Arthur N. Weins, and Joseph D. Matarazzo*

Alcoholism and Treatment *by David J. Armor, J. Michael Polich, and Harriet B. Stambul*

A Biodevelopmental Approach to Clinical Child Psychology: Cognitive Controls and Cognitive Control Theory *by Sebastiano Santostefano*

Handbook of Infant Development *edited by Joy D. Osofsky*

Understanding the Rape Victim: A Synthesis of Research Findings *by Sedelle Katz and Mary Ann Mazur*

Childhood Pathology and Later Adjustment: The Question of Prediction *by Loretta K. Cass and Carolyn B. Thomas*

Intelligent Testing with the WISC-R *by Alan S. Kaufman*

Adaptation in Schizophrenia: The Theory of Segmental Set *by David Shakow*

Psychotherapy: An Eclectic Approach *by Sol L. Garfield*

Handbook of Minimal Brain Dysfunctions *edited by Herbert E. Rie and Ellen D. Rie*

Handbook of Behavioral Interventions: A Clinical Guide *edited by Alan Goldstein and Edna B. Foa*

Art Psychotherapy *by Harriet Wadeson*

Handbook of Adolescent Psychology *edited by Joseph Adelson*

Psychotherapy Supervision: Theory, Research and Practice *edited by Allen K. Hess*

Psychology and Psychiatry in Courts and Corrections: Controversy and Change *by Ellsworth A. Fersch, Jr.*

Restricted Environmental Stimulation: Research and Clinical Applications *by Peter Suedfeld*

Personal Construct Psychology: Psychotherapy and Personality *edited by Alvin W. Landfield and Larry M. Leitner*

Mothers, Grandmothers, and Daughters: Personality and Child Care in Three-Generation Families *by Bertram J. Cohler and Henry U. Grunebaum*

Further Explorations in Personality *edited by A.I. Rabin, Joel Aronoff, Andrew M Barclay, and Robert A. Zucker*

Hypnosis and Relaxation: Modern Verification of an Old Equation *by William E. Edmonston, Jr.*

Handbook of Clinical Behavior Therapy *edited by Samuel M. Turner, Karen S. Calhoun, and Henry E. Adams*

Handbook of Clinical Neuropsychology *edited by Susan B. Filskov and Thomas J. Boll*

The Course of Alcoholism: Four Years After Treatment *by J. Michael Polich, David J. Armor, and Harriet B. Braiker*

Handbook of Innovative Psychotherapies *edited by Raymond J. Corsini*

The Role of the Father in Child Development (Second Edition) *edited by Michael E. Lamb*

Behavioral Medicine: Clinical Applications *by Susan S. Pinkerton, Howard Hughes, and W.W. Wenrich*

Handbook for the Practice of Pediatric Psychology *edited by June M. Tuma*

Change Through Interaction: Social Psychological Processes of Counseling and Psychotherapy *by Stanley R. Strong and Charles D. Claiborn*

Drugs and Behavior (Second Edition) *by Fred Leavitt*

Handbook of Research Methods in Clinical Psychology *edited by Philip C. Kendall and James N. Butcher*

A Social Psychology of Developing Adults *by Thomas O. Blank*

Women in the Middle Years: Current Knowledge and Directions for Research and Policy *edited by Janet Zollinger Giele*

Loneliness: A Sourcebook of Current Theory, Research and Therapy *edited by Letitia Anne Peplau and Daniel Perlman*

(*continued on back*)

D0236501

SOCIAL SUPPORT:
AN INTERACTIONAL VIEW

Social Support:
An Interactional View

Edited by

BARBARA R. SARASON
IRWIN G. SARASON
GREGORY R. PIERCE

University of Washington

A WILEY-INTERSCIENCE PUBLICATION

JOHN WILEY & SONS

New York • Chichester • Brisbane • Toronto • Singapore

This publication is designed to provide accurate and
authoritative information in regard to the subject
matter covered. It is sold with the understanding that
the publisher is not engaged in rendering legal, accounting,
or other professional service. If legal advice or other
expert assistance is required, the services of a competent
professional person should be sought. *From a Declaration
of Principles jointly adopted by a Committee of the
American Bar Association and a Committee of Publishers.*

Library of Congress Cataloging-in-Publication Data

Social support : an interactional view / edited by Barbara R. Sarason,
    Irwin G. Sarason, Gregory R. Pierce.
        p.   cm. — (Wiley series on personality processes)
    Includes bibliographical references.
    ISBN 0-471-60624-3
    1. Social networks.   2. Stress (Psychology).   3. Social
interaction.   4. Developmental psychology.   I. Sarason, Barbara R.
II. Sarason, Irwin G.   III. Pierce, Gregory R.   IV. Series.
HM131.S61713   1990
302—dc20   89-27301
                                                                           CIP

Printed in the United States of America

90 91 10 9 8 7 6 5 4 3 2 1   2217/12291

Contributors

Toni C. Antonucci, Ph.D.
Associate Professor and Associate
   Research Scientist
Survey Research Center
Institute for Social Research,
   University of Michigan
Ann Arbor, MI

Tracy Bennett, M.A.
Department of Psychology
University of California at Los
   Angeles
Los Angeles, CA

Paul H. Blaney, Ph.D.
Professor
Department of Psychology
University of Miami
Coral Gables, FL

Jonathon D. Brown, Ph.D.
Assistant Professor
Department of Psychology
University of Washington
Seattle, WA

Ana Mari Cauce, Ph.D.
Associate Professor
Department of Psychology
University of Washington
Seattle, WA

James C. Coyne, Ph.D.
Associate Professor

Department of Psychiatry/Family
   Practice
University of Michigan Medical
   School
Ann Arbor, MI

Christine Crofton, Ph.D.
Senior Associate
Prospect Associates Ltd.
Rockville, MD

Carolyn E. Cutrona, Ph.D.
Associate Professor
Department of Psychology
University of Iowa
Iowa City, IA

David L. DuBois, M.A.
Doctoral Candidate
Department of Psychology
University of Illinois at
   Champaign-Urbana
Urbana, IL

Christine Dunkel-Schetter, Ph.D.
Associate Professor
Department of Psychology
University of California at Los
   Angeles
Los Angeles, CA

John H. Ellard, Ph.D.
Assistant Professor
Department of Psychology

University of Calgary
Calgary, Alberta, Canada

ALEXIS ENGEL-LEVY, M.S.
Doctoral Candidate
Department of Psychology
Northwestern University
Evanston, IL

RONALD J. GANELLEN, PH.D.
Director
Neuropsychology Laboratory
Michael Reese Hospital and Medical
 Center
Department of Psychiatry and
 Neurology
Chicago, IL

RONALD GLASER, PH.D.
Professor
Department of Medical Microbiology
 and Immunology and the
 Comprehensive Cancer Center
Ohio State University
Columbus, OH

NANCY GONZALES, M.S.
Doctoral Candidate
Department of Psychology
University of Washington
Seattle, WA

PATRICK H. HARDESTY, PH.D.
Assistant Professor
Department of Counseling Psychology
University of Louisville
Louisville, KY

KENNETH HELLER, PH.D.
Professor and Director of the Clinical
 Training Program
Indiana University
Bloomington, IN

BARTON J. HIRSCH, PH.D.
Associate Professor

School of Education and Social Policy,
 and Research Faculty
Center for Urban Affairs and Policy
 Research
Northwestern University
Evanston, IL

STEVAN E. HOBFOLL, PH.D.
Professor
Applied Psychology Center
Kent State University
Kent, OH

JOHN R. HOGG, B.A.
Doctoral Candidate
Department of Psychology
Indiana University
Bloomington, IN

JAMES S. JACKSON, PH.D.
Professor and Research Scientist
Survey Research Center
Institute for Social Research
University of Michigan
Ann Arbor, MI

DAVID JACOBSON, PH.D.
Associate Professor
Department of Anthropology
Brandeis University
Waltham, MA

ROBERT M. KAPLAN, PH.D.
Professor and Acting Chief
Department of Community and Family
 Medicine
School of Medicine
University of California at San Diego
La Jolla, CA

SUSAN KENNEDY, PH.D.
Postdoctoral Fellow
Department of Medical Microbiology
Ohio State University
Columbus, OH

JANICE K. KIECOLT-GLASER, PH.D.
Associate Professor
Department of Psychiatry
Ohio State University
Columbus, OH

SHARON LANDESMAN, PH.D.
Professor
Department of Psychiatry and
  Psychology
Director, Frank Porter Graham Child
  Development Center
University of North Carolina at Chapel
  Hill
Chapel Hill, NC

MICHAEL D. NEWCOMB, PH.D.
Associate Professor
Department of Counseling
University of Southern California
Los Angeles, CA

GREGORY R. PIERCE, M.S.
Doctoral Candidate
Department of Psychology
University of Washington
Seattle, WA

RICHARD H. PRICE, PH.D.
Professor
Department of Psychology
Research Center for Group Dynamics
Institute for Social Research
University of Michigan
Ann Arbor, MI

MOLLY REID, PH.D.
Acting Assistant Professor
Department of Psychiatry and
  Behavioral Science
Child Development and Mental
  Retardation Center
University of Washington
Seattle, WA

KAREN S. ROOK, PH.D.
Associate Professor
Program in Social Ecology
University of California at Irvine
Irvine, CA

DANIEL W. RUSSELL, PH.D.
Associate Professor
Graduate Program in Hospital and
  Health Administration
College of Medicine
University of Iowa
Iowa City, IA

BARBARA R. SARASON, PH.D.
Research Professor
Department of Psychology
University of Washington
Seattle, WA

IRWIN G. SARASON, PH.D.
Professor and Chairman
Department of Psychology
University of Washington
Seattle, WA

ROXANE COHEN SILVER, PH.D.
Associate Professor
Program in Social Ecology
University of California, Irvine
Irvine, CA

DAVID A. F. SMITH, PH.D.
Research Associate II
University of Michigan Medical
  School
Ann Arbor, MI

MARY ANN PARIS STEPHENS, PH.D.
Associate Professor
Department of Psychology
Kent State University
Kent, OH

WILLIAM B. SWANN, PH.D.
Associate Professor

Department of Psychology
University of Texas at Austin
Austin, TX

MICHELLE T. TOSHIMA, B.A.
Doctoral Candidate
Joint Doctoral Program in Clinical
 Psychology
University of California at San Diego
 and San Diego State University
Department of Community and Family
 Medicine

School of Medicine
University of California at San Diego
La Jolla, CA

CAMILLE B. WORTMAN, PH.D.
Professor
State University of New York, Stony
 Brook
Stony Brook, NY

Series Preface

This series of books is addressed to behavioral scientists interested in the nature of human personality. Its scope should prove pertinent to personality theorists and researchers as well as to clinicians concerned with applying an understanding of personality processes to the amelioration of emotional difficulties in living. To this end, the series provides a scholarly integration of theoretical formulations, empirical data, and practical recommendations.

Six major aspects of studying and learning about human personality can be designated: personality theory, personality structure and dynamics, personality development, personality assessment, personality change, and personality adjustment. In exploring these aspects of personality, the books in the series discuss a number of distinct but related subject areas: the nature and implications of various theories of personality; personality characteristics that account for consistencies and variations in human behavior; the emergence of personality processes in children and adolescents; the use of interviewing and testing procedures to evaluate individual differences in personality; efforts to modify personality styles through psychotherapy, counseling, behavior therapy, and other methods of influence; and patterns of abnormal personality functioning that impair individual competence.

Irving B. Weiner

University of South Florida
Tampa, Florida

Preface

The origin of this book can be traced to a stimulating conference on social support held in Bonas, France, in 1983. A book containing that conference's proceedings was published in 1985 and reflected the significant growth in knowledge about social support that had accumulated since empirical work on the topic had begun in the 1970s. This book, like the one published in 1985, is an update of empirical developments, but its focus and the breadth of phenomena toward which it is directed are quite different. Our awareness of these changes in thinking—which have come about since the 1983 conference—motivated us to invite a group of leaders in social support research to write chapters reflecting their current thinking and the evidential underpinnings of how they currently see social support.

Attention has shifted in the social support field from the accumulation of empirical observations to a search for theories to explain the vast and often conflicting findings that link social ties to behavior and health. Everyone working on social support seems to have had the simultaneous insight that, as Kurt Lewin said, there is nothing so practical as a good theory. The themes that run through the 18 chapters of this book are steps toward the formulation of conceptual paradigms that will further our understanding of social support. We believe this quest for theory is itself the most important, most promising development in the field.

The scope of phenomena investigated by social support researchers has broadened because, even though they continue to be guided by the theme of social ties as a factor in personal development and coping with stress, the variations on that theme have become increasingly complex. Theories of social support need to go beyond the statement that social ties provide help, to specify the conditions under which social ties provide help, to recognize that they do not always help, and also to recognize that under certain circumstances they might be harmful. Social support, we are coming to realize, is a multicomponent construct rather than a unitary entity. The contributors to this book describe how these various components are now being studied and the conditions that heighten their effects. They point out that there now are new frontiers, such as the assessment of social support in children; the roles of social support in everyday life, not just under stressful conditions; the cultural context of social support; the place of companionship in social support; social support and coping with stress; and the need for empirically based clinical and community interventions that enhance feelings of social connectedness. These new directions also emphasize the theme of this book, that various aspects of what has been traditionally called social support interact between the person and the environment and that these aspects are defined by close social relationships and those related to a series of larger settings defined by persons, organizational settings, and overall cultural expectations.

These frontiers of social support offer both challenges and opportunities. We believe that this book's contributors have succeeded admirably in communicating this, and our greatest debt is to them. Our initial confidence that the book would be valuable as a guide to future research and application has been realized. Our contributors have worked with us to produce a book based on an interactional approach, with the hope of advancing the development of theory. Because of the book's distinguished, enthusiastic group of contributors, our job as editors was easy. We are indebted to the many students at the University of Washington who helped us, in a series of seminars, evaluate the current research in social support. We also are grateful to our colleagues nationwide, many of them represented here as authors, who shared ideas with us at professional and informal meetings. We also want to acknowledge the help and support provided by Betty Johnson in working on the manuscripts and all the correspondence that a book such as this entails, and to Beth Rutherford and Al Weinbarger who pitched in to handle last-minute tasks as the project neared completion.

BARBARA R. SARASON
IRWIN G. SARASON
GREGORY R. PIERCE

University of Washington,
Seattle

Contents

PART THREE   SOCIAL SUPPORT AND COPING WITH STRESS   251

10   Social Support, Stress, and the Immune System   253
Susan Kennedy, Janice K. Kiecolt-Glaser, and Ronald Glaser

11   Differentiating the Cognitive and Behavioral Aspects of Social Support   267
Christine Dunkel-Schetter and Tracy L. Bennett

12   Hardiness and Social Support   297
Paul H. Blaney and Ronald J. Ganellen

13   Type of Social Support and Specific Stress: Toward A Theory of Optimal Matching   319
Carolyn E. Cutrona and Daniel W. Russell

14   The Role of Social Environments in Social Support   367
*Barton J. Hirsch, Alexis Engel-Levy, David L. DuBois,
and Patrick H. Hardesty*

PART FOUR   SOCIAL SUPPORT APPLICATIONS AND INTERVENTIONS IN CLINICAL AND COMMUNITY SETTINGS   395

15 The Role of Coping in Support Provision: The Self-presentational Dilemma of Victims of Life Crises   397
Roxane Cohen Silver, Camille B. Wortman, and Christine Crofton

16 The Functional Effects of Social Relationships on Chronic Illnesses and Disability   427
Robert M. Kaplan and Michelle T. Toshima

17 Social Support During Extreme Stress: Consequences and Intervention   454
Stevan E. Hobfoll and Mary Ann Parris Stephens

18 The Role of Social Support in Community and Clinical Interventions   482
Kenneth Heller, Richard H. Price, and John R. Hogg

INTRODUCTION

The Road to Theory in the Field of Social Support

BARBARA R. SARASON, IRWIN G. SARASON, AND GREGORY R. PIERCE
University of Washington

The idea for this book was not to summarize the broad and growing field of research on social support. Instead, we wanted to help set the stage for the next major advance in social support research, the growth of theory.

Social support researchers are demanding theoretical development in the field, and so it is time to begin specifying the mechanisms by which social support promotes health and well-being. In addition, we should explain how social support develops, how the feeling of being supported continues or changes throughout life, and how support can be administered effectively. We have taken an interactional approach in this book in order to begin answering these questions. The authors of each chapter consider how those aspects of social support that particularly interest them may affect or be affected by other aspects of the person–situation interaction relevant to social support.

THE THEME OF THIS BOOK

The book focuses on ways to organize and integrate ideas about social connectedness, the environmental settings and individual differences that social connectedness influences, the outcomes to which it is related, and pertinent support-providing interventions. Of course, organization and integration require knowing what needs to be organized and integrated. The contributors to this book name a number of interacting social, personal, and situational factors—all studied in order to understand social support—that result in different behavioral outcomes. To ignore these interactions is to invite ambiguity and confusion in interpreting the results of empirical investigations. More often than not, characteristic personality patterns, relatively enduring social ties, developmental histories, and situational demands combine to produce the effects that, in the simplified world of a few years ago, we might have attributed to that amorphous entity, social support.

1

In order to explore our knowledge about these roles of social connectedness, we will emphasize four aspects of social support: (1) the conceptualization of social support, (2) social support in ongoing personal relationships, (3) the role of social support in coping with stress, and (4) applications of social support in clinical and community interventions.

As is appropriate to this book's theme, an interactional view of social support, its 18 chapters analyze research methods and findings from various vantage points. They examine several theoretical perspectives in an effort to clarify relevant personality variables (e.g., self-concept, hardiness), developmental processes (e.g., attachment relationships), biological factors (e.g., the immune system), and social units of various sizes (e.g., the community). In addition, they demonstrate that social support has both cognitive and behavioral components and that the experience of social support involves both intrapersonal and interpersonal processes. Several contributors point out the need to recognize that there can be both a negative and a positive side to social support, and they describe how that outcome might occur. Taken as a whole, the chapters make a strong case for better understanding the complex interactions among persons, their social environments, and challenges as they pertain to adjustment and health.

The book is divided into four parts:

PART ONE: Theoretical and Practical Implications of Defining and Assessing Social Support
PART TWO: Social Support in Personal Relationships
PART THREE: Social Support and Coping with Stress
PART FOUR: Social Support Applications and Interventions in Clinical and Community Settings

Each part approaches social support as an interactional process requiring well-defined assessment tools, observational methods, intervention strategies, and integrative theories. The four parts make clear that social support is both a consequence (a developmental product) and an antecedent (an influence over an individual's life and the lives of significant others).

PART ONE

Part One presents an overview of assessment approaches, issues, and challenges in social support research. The historical and theoretical roots of the approaches are analyzed, and several measurement techniques stemming from each are illustrated. The importance of matching concepts of social support with relevant methodological techniques is highlighted. Three major methodological approaches to the assessment of social connectedness are the mapping of social networks, the support available to people in their daily lives, and the individuals' own perceptions of the support available to them. The need to distinguish among these approaches is essential to interpreting research findings because of evidence that different ways of defining and assessing social support yield different results.

Two topics discussed in Part One have, until recently, been neglected: the ways in which recently available statistical techniques can help advance theory by allowing the researcher to see the connections among multiple variables, and the need to assess social support in both adults and children. The introduction in Part One to structural equation modeling as it applies to the assessment of social support should be useful to many researchers. Of special interest is the potential role of structural equation modeling in clarifying the contributions of specific theoretical models (e.g., the stress-buffering hypothesis) to our understanding of social support processes. Part One also provides an example of the development of social support measures that can be used with children of various ages.

PART TWO

Part Two places social support within the context of personal relationships. Supportive behaviors do not occur in a vacuum; they are a product of social relationships. Recognition of the interpersonal context leads to an emphasis on the qualitative aspects of these relationships (e.g., conflict, companionship) and on social support as a two-way street. Each of us is both a recipient and a provider of support, a fact that focuses on (1) the specific features of relationships (past, present, and continuing) that affect a person's feeling of being supported and accepted by other people and (2) interdependencies between recipients and providers. The needs and goals of two or more persons, as well as the problems and challenges each faces in meeting the other's needs, are part of social support. One of the most important personal needs is for people to affirm themselves in their social relationships. Stable, positive self-concepts aid people in organizing their experiences, guiding their behavior, and predicting the future.

In addition to identifying events and processes in particular social relationships, we should be aware of the cultural context that shapes perceptions of what constitutes support, who should provide it, and in what manner and under what circumstances providing support is appropriate. A cultural analysis of social support requires drawing on work in the areas of sociology and anthropology that cover group process, as well as the typically individually oriented worlds of psychology, psychiatry, and social work. For instance, cultural context is essential to the sense of well-being among older people. Although companionship is sometimes considered part of social support, it may be much more important to older people and have different implications for the health and personal adjustment of different age groups.

PART THREE

A major focus of research on social support continues to be its role in coping with stress. Part Three reviews the roles of specific social provisions in dealing with challenges, such as negative life events. It also explores the use of social support as a buffer against stress. If social support does have buffering properties, which definitions of support are most pertinent to these protective effects for personal adjustment and health? Measures of support perceived by the individual to be available and support that is reported to have been received will not necessarily yield similar results. Growing evidence shows that the mere presence of a partner does not necessarily protect health. On the other hand, there also is evidence that the presence of a confidant who is nonjudgmental about negative disclosures has a very positive influence. Work on the relationship between social support and the functioning of the immune system illustrates this point, as does research on how people cope with particular types of stressors. What does social support contribute to an individual's hardiness and relative invulnerability? The concept of hardiness may provide a link between individuals' perceptions of being supported and their resistance to stress.

A key question in social support research is whether certain types of social support are especially beneficial in relation to certain types of stress. If optimal support–situation matches can be identified, particular types of supportive interventions can be designed. The chapters in Part Three suggest that for certain types of negative life events, there are specific components of social support that can lead to optimal outcomes. However, for other types of negative events, a broad range of supportive components may be required. Similarly, different types of social network characteristics may be differentially effective in helping people adapt to various types of situations. For example, a less dense social network may be adaptive for someone wishing to change roles, but a more dense network may be more effective for stabilizing roles.

PART FOUR

Part Four is concerned with clinical and community applications and reviews evidence concerning the negative and positive roles that friends and family can play in trying to help individuals respond adaptively to stress and trauma. Can the needed coping skills be taught? Can social resources be provided to help individuals meet life's challenges? There is evidence that clinical interventions in cases of bereavement and serious illness may be especially useful if support providers (e.g., family members, friends) can be helped to come to terms with the negative feelings that accompany their supportive efforts. Social support may be a positive resource, a burden, or a neutral element. This fact may have important implications for special support groups and clinical settings (such as family therapy), as well as in everyday life.

Communities, clinicians, and family members are potential sources of support; yet we know much less about them than we do about support given at the individual or small-group level. This gap in our knowledge is especially unfortunate because of the potential multiplier effect across community members. The use of complex social structures in the community represents an opportunity that most social support researchers have not explored.

THE FUTURE

The major theme throughout this book is social support conceived as an interactional and bidirectional process. Thus, social support reflects the needs, responses, and perceptions of relationship participants and their mutual influence. Building on this theme, we believe that social support can now enter a new, important period of development, with a much greater theoretical focus and concern for the relationship between theory and methodology. The term *social support* refers to many constructs, defined in many ways, that play important and sometimes changing roles in our lives over time. Social support is, at the same time, a current characteristic of the individual, a historical product of past experiences, and a process. We believe that mapping these aspects of social support may be the principal research challenge of the immediate future.

Theoretical and Practical Implications of Defining and Assessing Social Support

Part One discusses the assumptions underlying current assessment approaches, the use of statistical procedures in advancing theory, and the extension of measurement approaches to assessing social support in children.

Most researchers acknowledge that social support as it is currently conceived is a heterogeneous term and that its division into meaningful components would enhance the theory-building process. Chapter 1 presents a brief historical review of the origins of the social support construct and then assesses the positive and negative aspects of three major conceptions of social support: the network model, the received support model, and the perceived support model. All of these approaches are useful in building a comprehensive theory; and so we also need a better understanding of each one's implications and how they might be fit into a more comprehensive theory.

As more user-friendly software has become available, structural equation modeling has increased in popularity as a method of testing hypotheses and theories. Chapter 2 presents a nontechnical introduction to this technique and shows how it can be applied to research on social support. The results of applying latent factor modeling to several of the social support measures mentioned in Chapter 1 are used to illustrate different approaches to the definition of social support.

Until recently, the most common ways of assessing a child's relationships were behavioral observation and parental report. But if the work on perceived support with adults is also valid for children, we should also study the child's own perspective on his or her relationships. Chapter 3 discusses the development of an assessment instrument suitable for children of widely varying ages, as well as the data generated by its use. Chapter 3 also describes the development and structure of children's social networks and the support they derive from them.

CHAPTER 1

Traditional Views of Social Support and Their Impact on Assessment

BARBARA R. SARASON, IRWIN G. SARASON, AND GREGORY R. PIERCE

University of Washington

I shall be content if [my history] is judged useful by those inquirers who desire an exact knowledge of the past as an aid to the interpretation of the future, which in the course of human things must resemble [it] if it does not reflect it.

THUCYDIDES, *The History of the Peloponnesian War, Book I, section 1*, 413 B.C.

What's past is prologue.

WILLIAM SHAKESPEARE, *The Tempest*, 1611–1612.

Those who cannot remember the past are condemned to repeat it.

GEORGE SANTAYANA, *The Life of Reason*, 1905-1906

For more than two millennia, historians, philosophers, playwrights, and novelists have reminded us that we have much to learn from what happened in the past. An understanding of why certain institutions or approaches evolved and the consequences—both intended and unintended—of this evolution can, in their view, prevent the recurrence of the same problems. Even more important, an understanding of the past can lead to a better understanding of why things happen and lay the groundwork for improved theories. Although psychology does not focus on the same wide stage and the same sweep of time as history does, a psychological understanding of the present also profits from an analysis of the past. Nowhere is this more evident than in the area of social support.

With increasing frequency, discussions of social support are focusing on the need for theory as a guide to understanding the mechanisms by which social support affects health and adjustment. In order to build such theories, it is important to understand what the term *social support* means. Although social support can mean many different things, it has become clear that it is not a unitary concept but, rather, an omnibus term. In order to divide this heterogeneous construct into more homogeneous parts, therefore, we must define those parts and also understand the historical context in which each of them came to be considered impor-

9

tant to social support. In this chapter we will highlight some of these historical roots, show how they relate to current assessment approaches, discuss the relationships among differently defined constructs, and describe some general points to consider when deciding how to assess social support or how to interpret and incorporate into a theoretical framework the research findings concerning this multifaceted variable.

Some of the earliest interest in the effects of social relationships was in clinical medicine. For instance, Charles Darwin (1872/1965) wrote about one of his father's patients who eventually died from heart disease, "who positively stated that his pulse was habitually irregular to an extreme degree; yet to his great disappointment it invariably became regular as soon as my father entered the room." Durkheim offered (1897/1951) another early idea about the importance of social relationships, that a lack of social relationships increased the probability of suicide. Although Durkheim's work certainly influenced sociological theory, work on the association between social relationships and health—conceptualized under the name of social support—did not begin until much later. When sociologists did become interested in social support, it was primarily on the effect on health outcome of embeddedness in a social network.

Two seminal papers by Cassel (1976) and Cobb (1976) launched the cross-disciplinary research field that studies what is now called social support. From an epidemiological viewpoint Cassel emphasized the social environment in general and the "presence of other members of the same species" in particular as factors in the host's susceptibility to environmental disease agents. His review of both animal and human research underscored the buffering effects of social support on stress. Cassel recognized the need to strengthen individuals' social supports, rather than to attempt to decrease their exposure to stressors, as the best way to prevent disease.

Cobb's interest arose from findings in clinical medicine. He not only explored social support as a moderator of life stress but also attempted to refine the meaning of the construct. Cobb described social support as information leading to one or more of three outcomes: the feelings of being cared for; the belief that one is loved, esteemed, and valued; and the sense of belonging to a reciprocal network. He believed that social support provided protection from pathological states, accelerated recovery from illness, and enhanced compliance with medically recommended regimens. Like Cassel, Cobb saw social support as a buffer that was used in situations of crisis rather than to produce a main effect of dramatically improving adaptation.

In addition to epidemiological research and conclusions about the effectiveness of social support from clinically based studies of stressful life events, another source of interest in social support came from community psychology. Community psychologists often saw how community-based and -supported services staffed by professionals and paraprofessionals might provide support for those who were coping ineffectively and who were not part of natural supportive networks. Research showed, for example, that the emotional support offered by health care personnel or others was beneficial to health (Auerbach & Kilmann,

1977; Whitcher & Fisher, 1979). The idea of institutions supplying support to those without adequate resources was appealing, and so researchers turned to measuring the social support that individuals received. Their efforts in part reflected findings from sociological studies suggesting that stressors were more common in economically disadvantaged groups. The political climate of the 1960s fostered massive intervention attempts directed toward primary prevention, such as the War on Poverty, as well as community support services.

Child development provided a third, quite different, orientation to social support. In particular, the work by Bowlby (1969, 1979, 1980) on attachment provided a basis for thinking of social support as a personality variable that has its source in early close relationships. This way of looking at the support variable demonstrates its stability over time, its perception as being available for access by the individual, and the relationships that can serve as support providers.

This brief history illustrates some of the conceptions and definitions that characterize the multidisciplinary area of social support. The instruments used to measure social support reflect the full range of these differences. However, because all these measures are described under the same rubric, we often assume that they measure the same thing. Until recently, little attempt had been made to determine whether the various definitions driving these measurement attempts were important to the sometimes conflicting findings from research on the effects of social support.

Perhaps even more unfortunate than the assumed equivalence of these disparate definitions is the lack of a coherent theory of social support. Here, again, a look at history is instructive. In order to understand how the protective functions of social support work, it is necessary to distinguish among aspects of the social support construct. For instance, House, Landis, and Umberson (1988) stated that a broader theory of social support must address each of the following factors: (1) the quantity of social relationships; (2) their formal structure, for instance, their density and reciprocity; and (3) the content of these relationships as it reflects social support and other variables. They further argued that in order to understand better the associations among these variables, researchers should examine these characteristics in the same study.

Also necessary for a broader theory is a better understanding of the social, psychological, and biological processes that link all these variables to health. For instance, studies of the effects on residents of the environmental stress of the Three Mile Island disaster showed that social support interacted differently with different aspects of stress (Fleming, Baum, Gisriel, & Gatchel, 1982). Perceived support served as a buffer to stress when the outcome measure was self-perceived symptoms, depression, or the ability to concentrate on a behavioral task. In contrast, when the outcome measure was somatic distress or urinary epinephrine level, a main effect of social support was produced. The fact that social support and stress related to each other differently depending on what outcome measure was chosen indicated that social support may affect health in various direct or indirect ways. Social relationships may affect health through physiological effects, by encouraging or discouraging certain health-related behaviors, providing a sense of meaning to life, and the like. We should consider both positive and negative aspects of relationships, as conflict within relationships may detract from the helpful effect of any support given.

THE HISTORICAL ORIGINS OF ASSESSMENT APPROACHES

Currently available measures of social support may be divided into three categories: (1) the network model that focuses on the individual's social integration into a group and the interconnectedness of those within that group, (2) the received support model that focuses on what the person actually received or reported to have received, and (3) the perceived support model that focuses on support the person believes to be available if he or she should need it.

Network Measures

Those network measures that we use today are not for the extended network that has been of interest to sociologists and social anthropologists. Instead, the current network tools relate either to individuals and those people with whom they have direct personal social links or to those people who through significant or important ties provide the individual with support. Network measures appear to vary less than do other categories of measures, but there are some differences among them in (1) specificity of the questions asked, (2) specificity of the network targeted, and (3) specificity of the components to be measured (O'Reilly, 1988). Some measures concentrate on particular populations, for example, the elderly, whereas others can be applied to a general population. The measures also differ in whether or not they limit the number of network members whom the respondents are asked to identify. That is, some ask for a particular number of supporters; others specify the relationships with supporters, for example, by limiting the inquiry to a list of those judged most significant in the respondent's life. Research suggests that it may not be necessary to move beyond the person's closest relationships. House and Kahn (1985) recommended that gathering data on more than 5 to 10 individuals in the subject's network yields rapidly diminishing returns.

Network measurement instruments also identify different network components. Some of them look at the network's structure and measure its relationships, size, and density. Others ask about the qualities of each relationship in terms of its durability, frequency of contact, and intensity. Still others explore the functions of each of the network members, such as the type of help he or she provides.

The specific definition of the network to be assessed is important to understanding the relationship of network measures to other types of social support instruments. If the instructions ask for "people that you see frequently" or "those who are important in your life" or some similar description, the people nominated may indeed provide support, but they may also be sources of negative feelings, conflict, and other types of stress. This problem is similar to that of using one of two categories, such as married or not married, to indicate whether or not social support is offered. Some relationships may involve close and frequent contact and endure over a period of time but contribute little to personal adjustment. For example, help or emotional support that comes from a conflictive relationship may exact such a high price that its positive qualities are overridden by its negative ones. Thus people whose marital relationships contain high levels of conflict may not adjust as well as do those who are not married at all (Gove, Hughes, & Style, 1983). Many young adults and adolescents list family members as sources of support, but they may ask for that support reluctantly because of the price they must pay in feelings of dependence or guilt that accompany its receipt (Pierce, Sarason, & Sarason, 1988).

Measures of network size and availability or adequacy of support have been shown to be only weakly associated (Seeman & Berkman, 1988). This may be because neither the size of the network nor the size of the group of network members to whom the person feels close can indicate how much support he or she actually receives (Stokes & Wilson, 1984). A curvilinear relationship has been found, however, between the number of confidants and satisfaction with support among college students (Stokes, 1983). Measures such as network size and satisfaction are not unique to the traditional network format and can be obtained much more easily by other less labor-intensive approaches such as a questionnaire.

One of the unique aspects of the network approach is the assessment of the network's density (the extent of mutual linkage among individuals). At present, this measure, besides being time-consuming to obtain, has not been a fruitful way of connecting social support to adjustment or health outcomes. That is, density may interact with the type of stress experienced so that high- and low-density networks can be either helpful or detrimental to specific kinds of situations. For instance, Hirsch (1980) investigated the effect of different patterns of social networks on the mental health of women in transition, both young women who had recently been widowed and mature women who were returning to school full time. In this study, the higher the network density was (i.e., the higher the proportion of actual to potential ties among the women's family members and the women's friends), the more likely the women were to have many symptoms, depressed mood, and low self-esteem. Gallo (1982) looked at the role of network density on well-being in a community sample of subjects aged 60 and over who were not involved in role transition. His findings, in contrast with Hirsch's, showed that network density was positively associated with well-being. These findings reinforce the proposal by Vaux and Harrison (1985) that low-density networks may help facilitate transitions and adjustment to new circumstances, and that high-density networks may be helpful when "retrenchment, recuperation, and validation is the appropriate response" to the stressor (p. 19). Although network density is an appealing variable for study, the situational factors in which the stress occurs, as well as the characteristics of the relationships in the network, must be considered when predicting whether its function as a stress buffer will be positive or negative. Indeed, we need to explore further the relationship between the density of the network and the perceptions of support associated with it.

In general, the evidence for the network measures' usefulness in studying the relations between health and social support has not been impressive compared with the more economically administered measures of social support that simply ask for the number of relationships (House & Kahn, 1985). In addition to the current absence of demonstrated relationships between measures unique to the network approach and adjustment or health outcomes, an even more basic problem is the almost total lack of reliability information for the available measures (O'Reilly, 1988; Orth-Gomer & Unden, 1987). This difficulty may be important because earlier work with social networks raised questions about the accuracy of the responses obtained from subjects who were queried about their social networks (Hammer, 1980; Kilworth & Bernard, 1976).

Network instruments appear to be appropriate to assessing the reciprocity of relationships. This may be an essential variable to consider, therefore, because when the initiation of supportive behaviors is one-sided, the results may not be conducive to adjustment (Gottlieb, 1985). Although the idea of reciprocity seems to be based on an extended time frame, at least in close relationships, an inequality that continues over time may greatly change the meaning of supportive behavior for both the recipient and the giver (Levitt, in press).

On balance, then, the traditional network measures have not proved their usefulness in the study of social support when the focus is on relating that support to a health outcome. This measurement format does have an inherent appeal, however, and it may be that an understanding of the outcome variables unique to network measures may be valuable in developing a theoretical model if we study the specific characteristics of the stressors likely to be encountered by the population under study and the relationships on which they rely for social support.

Social Integration Measures

Epidemiological surveys are likely to include questions about certain aspects of the respondents' social network, which may be described as a social network index, but these are not a network measure in the formal sense of the term. For example, Berkman and Syme's (1979) measure of social integration used in the Alameda County study assessed four types of social ties for both presence and extent, including marriage, contacts with extended family and friends, church membership, and other formal or informal group memberships. In this instrument and similar measures of social integration, these questions are used as a single scale. This approach has been useful to researchers because it consists of only a few questions, can be used easily in an interview format, and, at least in some cases, has been an effective predictor of mortality in prospective studies (Berkman & Syme, 1979; House, Robbins, & Metzner, 1982; Schoenbach, Kaplan, Fredman, & Kleinbaum, 1986).

Although this type of measure has proved helpful for very large study populations, it poses a number of problems for smaller studies. One of the difficulties is its unreliability because of the small number of items and the scale's lack of internal consistency. Another inadequacy comes from the same source as that discussed for the network measures: Just because relationships exist, it does not necessarily mean that they are supportive, or if supportive behavior does result, that the presence of conflict in the same relationships does not detract from or overwhelm the effects of the supportive behavior (Coyne & DeLongis, 1986).

Received Social Support

Much of the original interest in social support was related to the possibility of intervention. This meant that the attention was on offering support to those who were experiencing stress and/or who seemed to have poorly developed coping abilities because of some combination of personal characteristics and socioeconomic circumstances. The study of received social support looks at what people get from others. Social support conceptualized as the specific acts of others can be viewed as either *enacted support* (Tardy, 1985), in which the focus is on the actions that others perform to assist a particular person, or *received support,* in which the focus is on the recipient's account of what he or she noted as coming from others that was either helpful or intended to be helpful. One of the first things to notice about these two definitions is that they do not yield identical reports. The few studies that looked at veridicality of support as reported by the giver and by the recipient have found only a moderate level of agreement when specific veridicality was measured (a level of agreement of about 50 to 60 percent) (Antonucci & Israel, 1986; Shulman, 1976). When the studies investigated the social support given and received in any specific pair, any disagreement was caused by the givers' reports that they gave more support than the other person reported as received. This finding was consistent whether the focus was on specific supportive acts or on support at a more molar level. The perception of reciprocity was found to be a slightly better predictor of well-being than was the actual support exchanged (Ingersoll-Dayton & Antonucci, 1983). The determination of what aspects of the person and the environment influence these perceptions is important to the development of a theory about the perception of social support.

Typically, information on support given by others is gathered from the self-report of the recipient. Thus it seems that the term *received support* is more appropriate to the available data. It is clear, however, that this received support does refer to the perception of past events rather than to the perception that support will be available if needed, an aspect of social support that will be discussed shortly. A study that assessed the overall factor structure of a measure of received support, the Inventory of Socially Supportive Behaviors (ISSB; Barrera, Sandler, & Ramsey, 1981), together with a measure of perceived available support, the Social Support Questionnaire (SSQ; I. Sarason, Levine, Basham, & Sarason, 1983), found that the two measures were distinct and separate (McCormick, Siegert, & Walkey, 1987). Three of the five factors that were obtained represented the ISSB, and two represented the SSQ. The cross-loadings of the factors between measures were negligible. This finding shows that even if the measure of received support is derived from the reports of what the recipients perceive they have been given by others, it is clearly different from their perception of the support that might be available should they wish or need it.

One of the greatest problems in understanding the implications of received support as a factor in promoting health is that the supportive behavior a person receives is often a function of not only who is available to be supportive but also the perceptions by these others of the individual's need for help and support. This means that received support represents a confounded picture of support availability, the individual's apparent coping skills, and the degree of severity of life stress that he or she is perceived by others to be experiencing (Thoits, 1982). In several studies that used measures of received support (primarily the ISSB), a positive linkage between stress and social support was observed (Aneshensel & Frerichs, 1982; Barrera, 1981; Belle, 1982; Cohen & Hoberman, 1983; Sandler & Barrera, 1984). Thus a person's exposure to stressful life events may trigger supportive actions by those in the person's social network, because these others are aware of the negative event, because they see the person as in need of help, or because the stressed person actively solicits support. The last two contingencies may have an implication different from that of the first. They suggest a failure in coping, either because of the person's ineffective skills or because of the event's over-powering nature. It may be for this reason that measures of received support, or of enacted support, were found to be positively correlated with both negative life events and symptomatology (Wood, 1984).

Despite the discovery in a variety of studies that there is a positive relationship between social support and personal distress or psychiatric disorder, this relationship still seems counterintuitive. However, there is a growing appreciation of why this might be the case, especially when the measure of support relates to seeking supportive behavior from others (see, for example, Coyne, Aldwin, & Lazarus, 1981; Fiore, Becker, & Coppel, 1983). It may be that support is elicited as a result of coping failure or obvious unhappiness. Also, the receipt of such support may have a negative effect on self-esteem because it might be interpreted as verifying one's personal inadequacy. It may also produce feelings of obligation or guilt, which lead to dysphoric feelings. Finally, the receipt of help from others may have a negative effect on future coping efforts (Kaplan & Hartwell, 1987; Taylor, Bandura, Ewart, Miller, & DeBusk, 1985).

It seems clear after examining the evidence that received support has specific implications that are not associated with other types of social support measurement. It is therefore likely that many of the inconsistencies in the literature can be traced to a failure to differentiate findings using measures of received support from those using other types of social support measures. The work on received support is an excellent illustration of the need for clear distinctions among support measures according to which aspect of support they are designed to measure.

Measures of Perceived Support

Work on both network measures and received support show that what is reported by the recipient does not necessarily match the reports by others involved (Antonucci & Israel, 1986; Shulman, 1976). It seems that both what happens and differences in the perception of the events are relevant to the social support that is reported. The importance of perception in social support is evidenced in the highly consistent finding that it is the perception of social support that is most closely related to health outcomes (Antonucci & Israel, 1986; Blazer, 1982; Sandler & Barrera, 1984; Wethington & Kessler, 1986).

The focus on perceived social support meshes with and is reinforced by the current emphasis in psychology on cognitive appraisal and the influence of cognitive schemata or working models on behavior. The importance of cognitive appraisal was emphasized in the work on stressful life events and the coping process. For example, Lazarus and his colleagues concentrated on appraisal when assessing the degree of a situation's threat and the resources, either personal or from associates, that might be used to deal with it (Folkman, Schaefer, & Lazarus, 1979; Lazarus & Launier, 1978). The personal experience of stress from any event was based on this appraisal rather than on the particular characteristics of the event itself. Thus, perceptions of both the need for social support and its availability if needed affected the amount of stress experienced. The perception and individual meaning attached to events were also shown to have cumulative importance. In his work on the measurement of life events, Sarason also considered the person's perception of the positivity or negativity of the event when he predicted the cumulative outcome, rather than simply using the total number of events reported without regard to valence as a predictor (I. Sarason, Johnson, & Siegel, 1978).

The concentration on perceived social support also fits well with the early conceptualizations of social support by Cobb and Cassel. Cobb (1976) hypothesized that social support's major role is to convey information to the individual that others care about and value him or her. Thus, the support emanates from not so much what is done but from what that indicates to the recipient about the relationship. In a similar approach, Cassel (1976) examined the feedback function, because he believed that conveying to the recipient caring and positive regard was more responsible for the positive effect produced than was any specific behavior.

The majority of measures of social support fit under a loosely defined perceived support category. They differ, however, in specifics that may affect their use as predictors and certainly in their comparability to be generalized across studies. These differences can be summarized under the following headings: the use of either or both adequacy and availability; the use of global measurements of availability or those summing individuals over events, the assessment of what usually happens or what might be available if needed, and the separation of perceived support by function and a general support factor. The various measures of perceived support use different combinations of these approaches.

Availability Versus Satisfaction

Some measures of perceived support stress availability; some stress satisfaction; some combine both aspects of support in an overall score; and some keep separate scores for the two. The principal point for investigators to keep in mind is that availability and satisfaction measures are not highly correlated even when they are measured as scales within the same instrument (Henderson, Byrne, & Duncan-Jones, 1981; McCormick et al., 1987; I. Sarason et al., 1983; B. Sarason, Shearin, Pierce, & Sarason, 1987). For example, two different research groups studying the SSQ found that the Availability and Satisfaction scales represented separate dimensions (McCormick, et al., 1987; I. Sarason, Sarason, Shearin, & Pierce, 1987). In extensive work with the SSQ, we found that the correlation between the Availability and Satisfaction scales over a large number of populations is in the moderate range (.30–.40). Availability may be somewhat more closely related to social skills and life circumstances, whereas satisfaction is somewhat more closely related to personality characteristics such as degree of neuroticism (B. Sarason, Sarason, Hacker, & Basham, 1985; I. Sarason et al., 1983).

Measurement Approaches to Availability

Another difference among measures of perceived social support is the way in which availability is measured. That is, most perceived social support assessment instruments are global, with each item asking for the overall level of availability and/or satisfaction, often as a dichotomous judgment. An alternative approach that provides a more detailed appraisal uses one of two general approaches: One is to enumerate the number of supporters or the amount of social contact in a variety of situations and to sum this over situations. This is the approach used in the SSQ (I. Sarason et al., 1983). The second approach looks first at the degree of support in different situations in each of a specified number of relationships and then derives a score by summing across relationships, thus indicating perceptions of support from specific relationships (deJong-Gierveld, 1989; Pierce, et al., 1988).

The global approach to assessing support availability is not equivalent to either of the more detailed approaches (B. Sarason et al., 1987; deJong-Gierveld, 1989). For example, Van Tilburg (1986) found that the global assessment had the closest association to assessment summed over relationships if eight rather than fewer relationships were considered. But even when using eight relationships, the correlation between the two types of measures was still too small ($r = .43$) to conclude that the two approaches were measuring the same thing. Similar findings are obtained using the other summation strategy. Comparing measures using the global approach and measures summing across situations showed that they were only moderately correlated (B. Sarason et al., 1987). Pierce found that the relationship-specific measure added to the prediction of adjustment even after using a global measure of social support (Pierce, Sarason, & Sarason, 1989). Not only is the relationship between global and nonglobal approaches not robust, but also the two nonglobal approaches, summing over situations and summing across individuals, do not yield identical findings (Pierce et al., 1989).

DeJong-Gierveld (1989) argued that the global assessment method is defective as a measure of social support because it can lead to a confounding of social support with loneliness. Cutrona and Russell (see Chapter 13 in this volume) contend that social support and loneliness measures assess the same variable.

DeJong-Gierveld's criticism is also similar to the frequently expressed concern that measures of perceived social support and, particularly, satisfaction with that support are confounded with perceived stress and personality variables (Gore, 1984; Henderson, Byrne, Duncan-Jones, Adcock, Scott, & Steele, 1978). Both Henderson (1981) and Sarason (I. Sarason, Sarason, & Shearin, 1986) proposed, from somewhat different viewpoints, that perceived social support may represent a personality variable. Henderson examined social support perceptions as the inverse of neurosis. The Sarason group was concerned with the development of the perception of available support (see Chapter 4 in this volume). Lakey and Heller (1988) also suggested considering personality in the understanding of perceived social support. They believe that the generalized appraisal that one is cared for and valued may not necessarily be anchored in any specific relationship or particular supportive transaction but may instead reflect a generalized appraisal bias that has become part of the individual's personality.

Everyday Status Versus Potential Availability

Another issue in the concept of perceived social support is whether it is based on a general perception of the current state of support availability or on the belief that support would be available if one wished it. The originators of the measuring instruments have not usually made explicit this difference, and so the only way to determine the status of any particular measure is by examining the items. Indeed, the implications of these two views could be quite different. For example, if perceived support has a strong personality component, as several researchers believe it does, then it should be expected to remain relatively stable over time. This stability has been found in at least one study that assessed individuals for several years, both at the beginning of an important life transition and again at intervals (I. Sarason et al., 1986). But if the perceived support is based on experience, especially recent experience, then the perception of support may deteriorate over time if the person experiences stress and does not at the same time believe that people who are thought to constitute his or her support group are behaving supportively. Reinforcing this view, some studies showed that the experience of stress diminishes the perceived availability of social support or satisfaction with that support (Dean & Ensel, 1982; Lin & Ensel, 1984).

A General-Factor Approach Versus a Structural Approach

A final difference among measures of perceived social support is their emphasis either on dividing social support into various functions and assessing the availability of each component or on looking at social support from a general-factor point of view, which might be called a *sense of support*. This functional view stems from some of the papers that first stimulated the development of this field, those by Cobb (1976), Kaplan, Cassel, and Gore (1974), and particularly Weiss (1974). The functional approach to social support measurement is linked to the buffering hypothesis, the idea that social support as a protective factor becomes important when an individual is experiencing a stressor. The basis for the functional approach is that if support is to be effective, it must match the need created by the stressor being experienced (Weiss, 1974; Cohen & Wills, 1985). Many social support instruments, measures of both perceived and received support, are constructed along functional lines (see Cutrona & Russell, Chapter 13 in this volume, for examples). Two perceived social support measures that use the functional approach are the Interpersonal Support Evaluation List (ISEL; Cohen, Mermelstein, Karmack, & Hoberman, 1985) and the Social Provisions Scale (SPS; Cutrona & Russell, 1987). Cutrona and Russell (1987) presented the results of a series of research studies that they believe demonstrate how developmental status and life situation lead to the need for different types of social support. This means that at different periods in life social support must have different functions to be effective.

Although the factor structure of some functional measures has been verified across independent samples, the problem with the existing instruments measuring the functions of social support is that the scales representing the different functions tend to be highly correlated. For this reason, a number of researchers have expressed dissatisfaction with the functional approach, as it is currently operationalized (House & Kahn, 1985; Orth-Gomer & Unden, 1987; B. Sarason et al., 1987; Stokes, 1983). The scales measuring the different functions often have intercorrelations as high as the subscale reliabilities, a finding that suggests that the subscales are not measuring distinct constructs.

As we have tried to make clear, the measures in the general category of perceived support are, at best, only moderately related, and these moderate relationships can be attributed mainly to the differing measurement approaches within the perceived support perspective. However, despite this range of association among measures of perceived social support, in general they relate more closely to one another than to social support measures based on other definitions such as network or received support measures (B. Sarason et al., 1987). This difference in magnitude of relationships makes clear the influence of the different definitions of social support on research outcome.

THE NEED FOR REDEFINITION AND RECONCEPTUALIZATION

We have reviewed several different conceptualizations of social support. Each comes from an established body of knowledge, and all raise questions. The main problem has been that although measures have multiplied like rabbits, relatively little work has been done to establish their comparability or lack of it. In this chapter we examined the various conceptions of social support as a source of the conflicting findings in this research area. We should note another source of these conflicting findings, the psychometric characteristics of the different instruments. Relatively few of the social support measures that are available have pertinent published validity and reliability information. Even among those that do, the types of information provided about validity differ widely. Furthermore, the reliability information that is provided suggests a wide range of reliabilities, many of them relatively low. Thus, the widespread use of assessment instruments of even moderately low reliability may be responsible for many of the discrepant findings about relationships between social support and differing variables. These aspects of social support measurement were not discussed in this chapter but have been reviewed elsewhere (see, for example, Heitzmann & Kaplan, 1988; O'Reilly, 1988; B. Sarason & Sarason, in press).

More important, however, than these psychometric issues to understanding the concept of social support is an appreciation that assessment instruments based on different aspects of social support measure different things, show different relationships with predictor variables, and have different problems in regard to confounded measurement. This situation calls for a new and comprehensive look at the theory—or, better, theories—of social support. All types of social support measures can give us relevant information, and so what we need now is an examination of how the measures are related and why. The cry for theory-driven research in the area of social support is frequently and increasingly heard. To help create a climate in which theory can develop, this chapter considered the different aspects of persons and situations that are measured and that are called social support, the historical settings that led to an interest in measuring them, and the advantages and disadvantages to each approach. Not only can history help us avoid the mistakes of the past, but an awareness of the various issues that have shaped social support research can help us appreciate the breadth and depth of the theoretical approach needed before we can understand the ways that the individually based and environmentally supplied aspects of social support interact with and affect the outcome.

REFERENCES

Aneshensel, C. S., & Frerichs, R. R. (1982). Stress, support, and depression: A longitudinal causal model. *Journal of Community Psychology, 10*, 363–376.

Antonucci, T. C., & Israel, B. A. (1986). Veridicality of social support: A comparison of principal and network members' responses. *Journal of Consulting and Clinical Psychology, 54*, 432–437.

Auerbach, S. M., & Kilmann, P. R. (1977). Crisis intervention: A review of outcome research. *Psychological Bulletin, 84*, 1189–1217.

Barrera, M., Jr. (1981). Social support in the adjustment of pregnant adolescents: Assessment issues. In B. H. Gottlieb (Ed.), *Social networks and social support* (pp. 69–96). Beverly Hills, CA: Sage.

Barrera, M., Jr., Sandler, I. N., & Ramsey, T. B. (1981). Preliminary development of a scale of social support: Studies on college students. *American Journal of Community Psychology, 9*, 435–447.

Belle, D. (1982). Social ties and social support. In D. Belle (Ed.), *Lives in stress: Women and depression*. Beverly Hills, CA: Sage.

Berkman, L. F., & Syme, S. L. (1979). Social networks, host resistance, and mortality: A nine-year followup study of Alameda County residents. *American Journal of Epidemiology, 109*, 186–204.

Blazer, D. (1982). Social support and mortality in an elderly community population. *American Journal of Epidemiology, 115*, 684–694.

Bowlby, J. (1969). *Attachment and Loss: Vol. 1. Attachment*. New York: Basic Books.

Bowlby, J. (1979). The making and breaking of affectional bonds. *British Journal of Psychiatry, 130*, 201–210.

Bowlby, J. (1980). *Attachment and loss: Vol. 3. Loss: sadness and depression*. New York: Basic Books.

Cassel, J. (1976). The contribution of the social environment to host resistance. *American Journal of Epidemiology, 104*, 107–123.

Cobb, S. (1976). Social support as a moderator of life stress. *Psychosomatic Medicine, 38*, 300–314.

Cohen S., & Hoberman, H. M. (1983). Positive events and social supports as buffers of life change stress. *Journal of Applied Social Psychology, 13*, 99–125.

Cohen, S., Mermelstein, R., Kamarck, T., & Hoberman, H. N. (1985). Measuring the functional components of social support. In I. G. Sarason & B. R. Sarason (Eds.), *Social support: Theory, research and applications* (pp. 73–94). Dordrecht, Netherlands: Martinus Nijhoff.

Cohen, S., & Wills, T. A. (1985). Stress, social support, and the buffering hypothesis. *Psychological Bulletin, 98*, 310–357.

Coyne, J. C., Aldwin, C., & Lazarus, R. S. (1981). Depression and coping in stressful episodes. *Journal of Abnormal Psychology, 90*, 439–447.

Coyne, J. C., & DeLongis, A. (1986). Going beyond social support: The role of social relationships in adaptation. *Journal of Consulting and Clinical Psychology, 54*, 454–460.

Cutrona, C. E., & Russell, D. W. (1987). The provisions of social relationships and adaptation to stress. In W. H. Jones and D. Perlman (Eds.), *Advances in personal relationships* (Vol. 1, pp. 37–67). Greenwich, CT: JAI Press.

Darwin, C. (1872/1965). *Expression of the emotions in man and animals*. Chicago: University of Chicago Press.

Dean, A., & Ensel, W. M. (1982). Modelling social support, life events, competence, and depression in the context of age and sex. *Journal of Community Psychology, 10*, 392–408.

deJong-Gierveld, J. (1989). Personal relationships, social support, and loneliness. *Journal of Social and Personal Relationships, 6*, 197–221.

Durkheim, E. (1897/1951). *Suicide*. New York: Free Press.

Fiore, J., Becker, J., & Coppel, D. (1983). Social network interactions: A buffer or a stress? *American Journal of Community Psychology, 11*, 423–439.

Fleming, L., Baum, A., Gisriel, M. M., & Gatchel, R. J. (1982). Mediating influences of social support at Three Mile Island. *Journal of Human Stress, 8*, 14–22.

Folkman, S., Schaefer, C., & Lazarus, R. S. (1979). Cognitive processes as mediators of stress and coping. In V. Hamilton & D. M. Warburton (Eds.), *Human stress and cognition: An information-processing approach*. London: Wiley.

Gallo, F. (1982). The effects of social support networks on the health of the elderly. *Social Work in Health Care, 8*(2), 65–74.

Gore, S. (1984). Stress-buffering functions of social supports: An appraisal and clarification of research models. In B. S. Dohrenwend & B. P. Dohrenwend (Eds.), *Stressful life events and their contexts* (pp. 202–222). New Brunswick, NJ: Rutgers University Press.

Gottlieb, B. (1985). Theory into practice: Issues that surface in planning interventions which mobilize support. In I. G. Sarason & B. R. Sarason (Eds.), *Social support: Theory, research, and applications* (pp. 417–437). Dordrecht, Netherlands: Martinus Nijhoff.

Gove, W. R., Hughes, M., & Style, C. B. (1983). Does marriage have positive effects on the psychological well-being of the individual? *Journal of Health and Social Behavior, 24,* 122–131.

Hammer, M. (1980). Some comments on the validity of network data. *Connections, 3,* 13.

Heitzmann, C. A., & Kaplan, R. M. (1988). Assessment of methods for measuring social support. *Health Psychology, 7,* 75–109.

Henderson, S. (1981). Social relationships, adversity and neurosis: An analysis of prospective observations. *British Journal of Psychiatry, 138,* 391–398.

Henderson, S., Byrne, D. G., & Duncan-Jones, P. (1981). *Neurosis and the social environment.* New York: Academic Press.

Henderson, S., Byrne, D. G., Duncan-Jones, P., Adcock, S., Scott, R., & Steele, G. P. (1978). Social bonds in the epidemiology of neurosis: A preliminary communication. *British Journal of Psychiatry, 132,* 463–466.

Hirsch, B. (1980). Natural support systems and coping with major life changes. *American Journal of Community Psychology, 8,* 159–172.

House, J. S., & Kahn, R. L. (1985). Measures and concepts of social support. In S. Cohen and S. L. Syme (Eds.), *Social support and health* (pp. 83–108). Orlando, FL: Academic Press.

House, J. S., Landis, K. R., & Umberson, D. (1988). Social relationships and health. *Science, 241,* 540–545.

House, J. S., Robbins, C., & Metzner, H. M. (1982). The association of social relationships and activities with mortality: Prospective evidence from the Tecumseh Community Health Study. *American Journal of Epidemiology, 116,* 123–40.

Ingersoll-Dayton, B., & Antonucci, T. C. (1983). *Non-reciprocal social support: Another side of intimate relationships.* Paper presented at the 36th annual meeting of the Gerontological Society, San Francisco.

Kaplan, B. H., Cassel, J. C., & Gore, S. (1977). Social support and health. *Medical Care, 15,* 47–58.

Kaplan, G. A., & DeLongis, A. (1983). *Psychosocial factors influencing the course of arthritis: A prospective study.* Paper presented at the annual meeting of the American Psychological Association, Anaheim, CA.

Kaplan, R. M. & Hartwell, S. L. (1987). Differential effects of social support and social networks on physiological and social outcomes in men and women with Type II diabetes mellitus. *Health Psychology, 6,* 387–398.

Kilworth, P., & Bernard, H. (1976). Informant accuracy in social network data. *Human Organization, 35,* 269–286.

Lakey, B., & Heller, K. (1988). Social support from a friend, perceived support, and social problem solving. *American Journal of Community Psychology, 16,* 811–824.

Lazarus, R. S., & Launier, R. (1978). Stress-related transactions between person and environment. In L. A. Pervin & M. Lewis (Eds.), *Perspectives in interactional psychology* (pp. 287–327). New York: Plenum.

Levitt, M. J. (in press). Attachment and close relationships: A life span perspective. In J. L. Gewirtz & W. F. Kurtines (Eds.), *Intersections with attachment.* Hillsdale, NJ: Erlbaum.

Lin, N., & Ensel, W. M. (1984). Depression-mobility and its social etiology: The role of life events and social support. *Journal of Health and Social Behavior, 25,* 176–188.

McCormick, I. A., Siegert, R. J., & Walkey, F. H. (1987). Dimensions of social support: A factorial confirmation. *American Journal of Community Psychology, 15,* 73–77.

O'Reilly, P. (1988). Methodological issues in social support and social network research. *Social Science and Medicine, 26,* 863–873.

Orth-Gomer, K., & Unden, A. L., (1987). The measurement of social support in population surveys. *Social Science and Medicine, 24,* 83–94.

Pierce, G. R., Sarason, B. R., & Sarason, I. G. (1989). *Quality of relationships and social support: Empirical and conceptual distinctions.* Paper presented at the annual meeting of the American Psychological Association, New Orleans.

Pierce, G. R., Sarason, I. G., & Sarason, B. R. (1988). *Quality of relationships and social support as personality characteristics.* Paper presented at the annual meeting of the American Psychological Association, Atlanta.

Sandler, I. N., & Barrera, M., Jr. (1984). Toward a multimethod approach to assessing the effects of social support. *American Journal of Community Psychology, 12,* 37–52.

Santayana, G. (1905–1906). *The life of reason.* New York: Scribner's.

Sarason, B. R., & Sarason, I. G. (in press). The assessment of social support. In S. Shumaker & S. M. Czajkowski (Eds.), *Social support and cardiovascular disease.* New York: Plenum.

Sarason, B. R., Sarason, I. G., Hacker, T. A., & Basham, R. B. (1985). Concomitants of social support: Social skills, physical attractiveness, and gender. *Journal of Personality and Social Psychology, 49,* 469–480.

Sarason, B. R, Shearin, E. N., Pierce, G. R., & Sarason, I. G. (1987). Interrelationships among social support measures: Theoretical and practical implications. *Journal of Personality and Social Psychology, 52,* 813–832.

Sarason, I. G., Johnson, J. H., & Siegel, J. M. (1978). Assessing the impact of life changes: Development of the Life Experiences Survey. *Journal of Consulting and Clinical Psychology, 46,* 932–946.

Sarason, I. G., Levine, H. M., Basham, R. B., & Sarason, B. R. (1983). Assessing social support: The Social Support Questionnaire. *Journal of Personality and Social Psychology, 44,* 127–139.

Sarason, I. G., Sarason, B. R., & Shearin, E. N. (1986). Social support as an individual difference variable: Its stability, origins, and relational aspects. *Journal of Personality and Social Psychology, 50,* 845–855.

Sarason, I. G., Sarason, B. R., Shearin, E. N., & Pierce, G. R. (1987). A brief measure of social support: Practical and theoretical implications. *Journal of Social and Personal Relationships, 4,* 497–510.

Schoenbach, V. J., Kaplan, B. H., Fredman, L., & Kleinbaum, P. G. (1986). Social ties and mortality in Evans County, Georgia. *American Journal of Epidemiology, 123,* 577–591.

Seeman, T. E., & Berkman, L. F. (1988). Structural characteristics of social networks and their relationship with social support in the elderly: Who provides support. *Social Science and Medicine, 26,* 737–749.

Shulman, N. (1976). Network analysis: A new addition to an old bag of tricks. *Acta Sociologica, 23,* 307–323.

Stokes, J. P. (1983). Predicting satisfaction with social support from social network structure. *American Journal of Community Psychology, 11,* 141–152.

Stokes, J. P., & Wilson, D. G. (1984). The inventory of socially supportive behaviors: Dimensionality, prediction, and gender differences. *American Journal of Community Psychology, 12,* 53–69.

Tardy, C. H. (1985). Social support measurement. *American Journal of Community Psychology, 13,* 187–202.

Taylor, C. B., Bandura, A., Ewart, C. K., Miller, N. H., & DeBusk, R. R. (1985). Exercise testing to enhance wives' confidence in their husbands' cardiac capability soon after clinically uncomplicated acute myocardial infarction. *American Journal of Cardiology, 55,* 635–638.

Thoits, P. A. (1982). Conceptual, methodological and theoretical problems in studying social support as a buffer against life stress. *Journal of Health and Social Behavior, 23,* 145–159.

VanTilburg, T. G. (1986). *A comparison of two methods of support measurement: Global assessment and relation-specific summation.* Paper presented at the third ICPR Congress, Herzlia, Israel.

VanTilburg, T. G. (1989). The size of the supportive network in association with the degree of loneliness. In T. C. Antonucci & C. P. M. Knipscheer (Eds.), *Social network research: Methodological questions and substantive issues.* Lisse, Netherlands: Swets & Zeitlinger.

Vaux, A., & Harrison, D. (1985). Support network characteristics associated with support satisfaction and perceived support. *American Journal of Community Psychology, 13,* 245–267.

Weiss, R. S. (1974). The provisions of social relationships. In Z. Rubin (Ed.), *Doing unto others* (pp. 17–26). Englewood Cliffs, NJ: Prentice-Hall.

Wethington, E., & Kessler, R. C. (1986). Perceived support, received support, and adjustment to stressful life events. *Journal of Health and Social Behavior, 27,* 78–89.

Whitcher, S. J., & Fisher, J. D. (1979). Multidimensional reaction to therapeutic touch in a hospital setting. *Journal of Personality and Social Psychology, 36,* 87–96.

Wood, Y. R. (1984). Social support and social networks: Nature and measurement. In P. Reynolds & G. J. Chelune (Eds.), *Advances in psychological assessment* (Vol. 4, pp. 312–353). San Francisco: Jossey-Bass.

CHAPTER 2

What Structural Equation Modeling Can Tell Us About Social Support

MICHAEL D. NEWCOMB

University of California at Los Angeles and University of Southern California

Linear structural equation modeling, particularly with but also without latent variables, has become a popular and powerful method for testing theories and hypotheses in the social sciences. Although some researchers shy away from using this approach, in part because of the less than user-friendly aspects of the most popular computer program for conducting such analyses (LISREL: Jöreskog & Sörbom, 1984), it may be one of the most elegant and parsimonious methods currently available for empirically researching psychological and health issues such as social support. In particular, it is useful for analyzing data that are plagued by measurement error (such as self-report measures, survey research, and rater judgments) and/or that are correlational (nonexperimental, even though they may be longitudinal), in which controls and effects must be introduced and tested statistically rather than manipulated and controlled experimentally in the design. In addition, structural equation modeling can be used to analyze experimental data. These features of structural equation modeling seem ideally suited to the study of social support, from both a measurement and a prediction/consequence standpoint. In particular, because social support research has grown beyond exploratory studies into testing theories and hypotheses (e.g., Sarason & Sarason, 1985), structural equation modeling offers an important approach to test these complex, interactive, and multidimensional theories that have emerged from this rich area of investigation.

In this chapter, I present a nontechnical introduction to structural modeling as it has been applied to understanding and studying social support. My goals for this chapter are twofold. First, I want to provide sufficient detail for researchers to understand and perhaps appreciate the use of these methods in the literature. In other words, one of my goals is to make readers informed and knowledgeable recipients and consumers of such research. My second goal is to tantalize some of you into using this method in your own research. This chapter is not the place,

This research was supported by grant DA01070 from the National Institute on Drug Abuse. The production assistance of Julie Speckart is warmly appreciated.

however, for details about exactly how to run the various programs, although I include sources for more practical aspects of the applications.

This chapter is arranged into three sections. The first is a general description of structural modeling, including the measurement and structural portions of a model, graphic depictions, latent factors, distributional assumptions, sample size, fit indices, model and parameter evaluations, model modifications, multiple groups, and cross validation. In the second section, I introduce specific applications of structural modeling to social support and offer examples from the social support literature as well as some reanalyses of published social support data. The topics included are measurement models (for first-order models, second-order models, and multitrait–multimethod approaches), structural models (for the main effect of social support and for testing the buffering hypothesis), multiple-group models, structured means, and uses with experimental data. The final section addresses how structural equation modeling can benefit future research on social support. Here I shall review some of the limitations and drawbacks of structural modeling in conjunction with its potential benefits and discuss the criteria for causal inferences.

COMPONENTS OF STRUCTURAL EQUATION MODELS

What Is Structural Equation Modeling?

Structural equation modeling (SEM) is a method of simultaneously analyzing multiple variables in a confirmatory and hypothesis-testing manner that may include latent or unmeasured constructs. This method is simultaneous in that it solves at one time a specific group of linear equations and the results reflect a system of dependent relationships. These relationships reflect the associations predicted among many variables. Most importantly, what sets this method apart from the multivariate analyses of the past, is that all of the associations among variables must be hypothesized beforehand, if possible on theoretical grounds. This is not an exploratory procedure in the typical sense, although it can have exploratory aspects. The results of the analysis will confirm or disconfirm the hypothesized associations among the system of variables.

Notice that in my definition of SEM I avoided the term *causal*, even though SEM has frequently been called *causal modeling* (e.g., Bentler, 1980). I believe, however, that this term has created a great deal of confusion about and misunderstanding of this method. This relates to the fact that the word *causal* refers to several aspects of the SEM procedure. It is possible, given the appropriate longitudinal data, to make some causal inferences about the effect of one variable on another (the conditions for this inference are discussed in the final section of this chapter). This is never possible, however, when cross-sectional data are used, even if directional relationships are imposed on and tested in cross-sectional data. At most, these within-time associations (even if they are depicted as unidirectional pathways), represent a test of one plausible causal sequence. But other configurations or paths between variables may represent the data equally well (e.g., Stelzl, 1986). Thus, even though a causal model is used to test for the impact of one variable on the other in cross-sectional data, it cannot be concluded that in fact one variable caused the other.

Another use of the term *causal* in SEM refers to identifying a latent factor or construct. In this usage, a hypothesis is tested that an unmeasured or latent tendency or construct generated or "caused" the variation (level of correlation) among carefully selected observed or measured variables.

The basic components and features of a SEM are not difficult to understand. Most are based on earlier methods, such as factor analysis and multiple regression, that we all have used in our research. However, I must concede that there is something perhaps intimidating about a statistical hopper that eats up hundreds of subjects and many variables and spits out various matrices (denoted with Greek letters), a variety of fit indices, and some thinly veiled calculus (i.e., first-order derivatives), which when assembled into a figure resembles something more akin to chicken wire than a test of theory. Nevertheless, I repeat that the conceptual grounding for the SEM approach is primarily an extension, elaboration, and combination of standard exploratory procedures into a confirmatory method.

To begin, a SEM model can be understood as having two components: a measurement aspect and a structural or path aspect. These can be combined into a full structural equation model with latent variables (which includes a measurement and path model), or they can be used separately, depending on the focus of the research. A measurement model alone is a confirmatory factor analysis (CFA), often used for scale construction and the conceptual clarification of constructs. A path model alone (without a measurement portion) is a path analysis, which tests directional relationships between variables and partitions variance among predictors, mediators, and outcomes.

Measurement Models

A measurement model operationalizes how a researcher expects latent factors or constructs to be reflected in measured variables. In a standard exploratory factor analysis, a researcher assumes that variables that load above a certain criterion (e.g., .35) are the essential identifiers of that factor. The exact nature of this factor is not directly known or not measured and so is considered latent. The variables with the highest loadings are assumed to reflect whatever trait or construct underlies them. On the other hand, variables with low loadings are not assumed to be strong indicators of the construct.

In a latent variable measurement model, these low loadings are fixed at zero, and the high loadings are allowed to be estimated. Thus, the measurement model is a test to confirm whether the variables selected to represent specific constructs in fact reflect them adequately. In a standard confirmatory factor analysis or measurement model, the latent factors or constructs are allowed to correlate freely (as in an obliquely rotated exploratory factor analysis), and so it is sometimes called a saturated measurement model. It is also possible to test whether the latent factors are uncorrelated or orthogonal, by fixing the factor intercorrelations at zero.

Such a model should be compared with one with correlated factors to determine whether an orthogonal solution is justified.

Measurement or confirmatory factor analyses (CFA) models can also be hierarchical, with several orders of magnitude. A first-order CFA includes latent factors that only reflect the measurement variables in a hypothesized manner. Higher-order CFA models incorporate latent constructs at a higher order to reflect latent factors at a lower order, which in turn reflect the measured variables.

Structural or Path Models

A SEM's path or structural portion tests hypothesized relationships among the variables or factors. When the variables (i.e., not the latent factors) are measured, this is a standard simultaneous path analysis that can include multiple predictors, mediators, and consequences (e.g., Wolfle, 1980). Path analysis is an extension of multiple regression, in which more than one dependent variable can be included. Path analysis can test whether a series of hypothesized directional effects between variables (regression paths) can reflect the sample correlation matrix among the variables.

When the model contains latent constructs, the pathways between them can be tested. Here the researcher must, on an a priori basis (theory), impose one of four types of relationships between every pair of variables. Two variables can be correlated (related but with no hypothesized directional effect); one can predict the other (unidirectional effect); each can predict the other (bidirectional effect); or they can be unrelated (no direct effect). This type of model can test for plausible causal effects but can make causal inferences no stronger than the data can support.

This portion of a SEM is based on standard multiple regression analysis. Note that the advantages of the SEM approach over multiple regression are that more than one dependent variable can be studied simultaneously and that various types of associations can be tested among the predictor variables. For example, if I wanted to study, with multiple regression analysis, the impact of coping skills and social support on both physical health and emotional health, I would need two separate analyses, one for physical health as a dependent variable and one for emotional health as a dependent variable. Aside from being awkward and redundant, these two analyses cannot divide up the prediction variance between the two dependent variables, and we know that physical and emotional health are related. This association between dependent variables can lead to misleading results if separate analyses are used; but the effect of this problem can be reduced when both dependent measures are included simultaneously in the same model, as they can with a SEM approach.

Graphic Depictions

Figures are often used to depict SEMs, because they can convey at a glance many important features of a model and do not require detailed knowledge of the operating structure of particular computer programs. There is no reason that the results of a SEM should be presented to the reader in the exact matrices that the LISREL program produces or in the equations that EQS produces. Rather, I believe that researchers can offer their findings to the reader in a straightforward manner, although this has not always been done. An appropriate figure greatly facilitates this process.

Several conventions have been developed and are generally (but not universally) used to depict SEMs. Typically, large circles or ovals denote latent constructs; rectangles represent measured variables; and small circles reflect residuals (e.g., Bentler, 1980). Figure 2.1 presents an example of these denotations as applied to a model of Environmental Stress, Coping Skills, Social Support, and Satisfaction in Life. This is a simplified version of the hypothetical model offered by Thoits (1986). I use it as an illustration and not as an example of state-of-the-art conceptualization and theory in this area of research. However, the model does contain certain hypothesized relationships that can be tested empirically with appropriate data. Furthermore, this general model is used to demonstrate several aspects of structural modeling throughout this chapter. The large circles with Fs indicate latent constructs; the rectangles with Vs are measured variables or scales; the small circles with Es reflect measured-variable residuals; and the small circles with Ds are the factor residuals remaining after prediction.

The paths from the latent constructs (Fs) to the measured variables (Vs) are factor loadings. In this instance, the factor structure is considered to be "pure," as each variable loads on only one factor. For instance, the factor loading from Environmental Stress (F1) to problem-focused coping (V4) is not included in the figure and is constrained at zero. It certainly is possible to have a "complex" factor structure, in which one measured variable is allowed to load on more than one factor, although when this occurs, the latent factors may be more difficult to interpret (i.e., to know what they really represent). The Es represent the residual variances that remain from the measured variables after the variance shared with the latent factor is removed through a freed factor loading.

This figure also shows several standard types of structural paths. The two-headed arrow between F3 and F4 is a correlation, and the one-headed arrows from F1 to F2, F2 to F3, and F4 to F5 are direct regression effects. Finally, the small circles with arrows pointing at F2, F3, and F5 represent the residual variance of these dependent (predicted) latent factors (denoted as Ds) remaining after prediction from independent variables, in this case F1, F2, and F4. These are sometimes called *disturbance terms*. My use of Vs, Es, Fs, and Ds is based on the program structure of EQS, which requires no matrix notation to use (e.g., Bentler, 1986b).

Latent Factors

Its ability to study latent or unmeasured constructs is an important feature of SEM. Virtually all research that requires measuring something is influenced by measurement error, for nothing can be measured exactly and there is always a

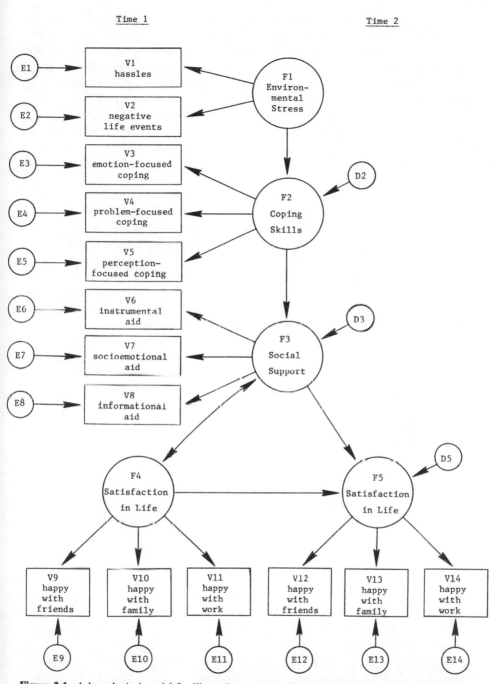

Figure 2.1. A hypothetical model for illustration purposes. Rectangles (Vs) are measured variables; large circles (Fs) are latent constructs; small circles with Es represent residual or uniqueness terms remaining from the Vs after accounting for the Fs; and small circles with Ds are residual disturbance terms of Fs remaining after prediction from other variables.

degree of distortion or bias. SEM provides a method for separating the common, true, or error-free qualities or aspects of measured variables that reflect latent constructs from measurement error. A latent factor is represented only by the commonality of the association among its observed-variable indicators (the measured variables or Vs in Figure 2.1) as reflected in the intercorrelations among the measured variables.

Latent constructs are useful in three conditions. The first is the traditional perspective of SEM and factor analysis that each of a group of measured variables is actually assessing the same latent construct and that the uncorrelated variance among each of the measured variables reflects measurement error. For instance, if I ask a subject to indicate the number of friends to whom he or she can turn in times of stress, the subject will give me a number. If I ask the subject how many people he or she can ask for help when feeling bad, I will get another number. If I ask the subject again how many individuals to whom he or she can turn when feeling upset, I will get yet another number. Even though these three questions ask essentially the same thing, the responses may vary owing to uncontrollable or random influences (measurement error). These random influences add noise or distortion to the data and reduce the chances of finding significant relationships because of increased error variance. This is because the degree of association between variables is attenuated by measurement error. If the three items are added together, the measurement error will still be included in the scale (three times over, in fact). However, if I hypothesize that a single latent factor or construct underlies the response to each of these questions, I can evaluate this by studying the correlations among the three items. In this case, the unmeasured or latent construct could be "the number of people available when experiencing distress." Greater conceptual similarity among a factor's measured indicators will contribute to a more reliably assessed latent factor.

At least two variables are necessary to identify a latent factor. Three or more variables are preferable, as they create a more stable latent factor than do those factors reflected by two variables. Multiple-item, unidimensional instruments can be divided into three or more subscales to reflect a latent construct of that scale. The correlations among these three subscales (which should be quite high) would reveal the latent factor that is hypothesized to underlie the responses to the subscales' items. The remaining variance of the subscales that is not part of the latent factor is measurement error and is separated into the residuals of the subscales. One example of this approach is the use of the UCLA Loneliness Scale (Russell, Peplau, & Cutrona, 1980) in SEMs. Both Newcomb and Bentler (1986) and Weeks, Michela, Peplau, and Bragg (1980) created random subscales of the 20 items in the scale and then used these subscales to display a single latent construct of Loneliness.

Another instance in which latent factors are useful is when several moderately similar variables are included in a design. For instance, as in Figure 2.1, if I have three scales of coping, such as emotion-focused coping, problem-focused coping, and perception-focused coping, it is quite likely that they will be moderately correlated (e.g., Dunkel-Schetter, Folkman, & Lazarus, 1987). Each of these scales has a common component, a unique component, and an error component. The common component, which might be general Coping Skills, could be captured as a latent construct, as depicted in Figure 2.1 as F2. The residuals would then contain both the unique aspect of each scale (i.e., the specific type of coping) and the measurement error. Using the EQS program (Bentler, 1986b), it is possible to study both the effects of the latent construct and the effects of or the associations with the residual component that incorporates the unique features of each scale independent of the common factor.

Associations with this residual or unique portion of the variance we call *non-standard effects* (Newcomb & Bentler, 1988a), to denote the deviation from the standard LISREL-type models, in which associations are typically restricted to those between latent factors. These nonstandard effects can be either correlations or directional paths. This is an important advantage of SEM that is not easily tested in the LISREL program. For instance, in this example, general Coping Skills may affect certain types of outcomes, whereas only problem-focused coping may affect other outcomes. Although the technical details of this distinction are beyond the scope of this chapter (see Bentler, 1987a; Bentler & Newcomb, in preparation; Newcomb & Bentler, 1988a), the conceptual and practical advantages of this approach are numerous and can be directly applied to social support research, as I discuss later in this chapter.

A final instance in which a latent factor is useful is when two or more predictors are modestly correlated (some conceptual similarity) and about equally correlated with a dependent variable. In a standard multiple regression analysis, the predictor with the highest correlation with the outcome may be significant and capture the common variance of the other predictors. The other predictors may then be unrelated to the outcome and perhaps even demonstrate suppressor effects with the dependent variable. Or the variance of the dependent variable may be split among the predictors, with none of the effects reaching significance. The true situation may be that the common variance among the predictors is actually related to the outcome. This common variance can be captured as a latent factor, and this factor can then be used as the predictor. This would indicate that the commonality among the predictors is the important influence and not simply the predictor with the slightly higher correlation with the dependent variable. This would minimize the ambiguity often associated with multiple regression, resulting from colinearities among predictors and the dependent variable. In this situation, the residuals of the variables would also be crucial to study, as they contain variances uniquely related to the specific predictor variable.

Distributional Assumptions

The parameters and fit indices of SEM are estimated by minimizing a mathematical function through an optimization procedure. Several estimators can be used, including maximum likelihood (ML) and least squares. The most common estimator of SEM is ML.

The advantage of ML is that it provides standard errors for the parameter estimates, which the least squares estimator cannot. ML generally requires multivariately normal data in order to provide accurate results. Fortunately, both recent theory and empirical tests have demonstrated that ML is fairly robust over normality violations (e.g., Harlow, 1985; Huba & Harlow, 1986, 1987; Newcomb, 1986; Satorra & Bentler, 1987). In other words, the parameter estimates of ML are fairly accurate even with normality violations. However, if the variables are extremely nonnormal, other methods should be considered. For instance, the distribution-free estimator developed by Browne (1982, 1984) makes no distributional assumptions. Unfortunately, this method requires many subjects in order to yield stable results and so cannot be used practically with a large number of variables (say over 20). For dichotomous data, LISCOMP should be used (Muthén, 1984, 1987). Other estimators exist with different assumptions but are rarely used (e.g., Bentler, 1983).

Fortunately, many of the variables typically used in social research have fairly normal distributions (e.g., available support, support satisfaction, level of coping skills), although some of the variables related to social support may not be normally distributed. For instance, catastrophic life events are not common, and most young adults are healthy and asymptomatic. It thus is incumbent on researchers to know their data and to use the most appropriate method, given realistic constraints and limitations.

Sample Sizes

All SEM methods are sample-intensive procedures and so require many subjects. The minimum number of subjects varies with the estimation method and the number of variables included in a particular model. Tanaka (1987) examined this issue and concluded that in moderately sized models (i.e., 20 or so variables) at least 200 subjects are necessary to provide stable ML results. Two to three times as many subjects are needed for stable results using the distribution-free method. As a rule of thumb, it is not advisable to use these methods (even ML) with many fewer than 100 subjects. When large models (i.e., many variables) must be tested with only a moderate-sized sample, a practical compromise is to develop and test conceptually meaningful submodels of the full model.

Fit Indices

A SEM is said to "fit" if the relationships in a hypothesized model generate an estimated covariance matrix that closely matches the covariance matrix obtained from the sample data. A hypothesized model that "fits" may not be the only model that adequately reflects the data. As a result, a model that fits is said to be a plausible representation of the data. There is no way in current practice to guarantee that it is the only model that fits the data. Further, simply because a model fits does not necessarily mean that the original hypotheses are confirmed; rather, the magnitude of the hypothesized paths and relationships must also be examined. For instance, a model that includes a direct path from Coping to Good Health could fit the data, but the path coefficient may not be significant. Thus, even though a model fits, certain parts of the hypothesis may not be confirmed.

Several indices gauge the degree to which a model fits the data. The most common index is the p-value associated with a chi-square test (relative to the degrees of freedom). The chi-square is generated by comparing the elements of the model covariance matrix with those of the sample covariance matrix. The more closely the two covariance matrices match, the lower the resulting chi-square and the larger the p-value will be. Conversely, the greater the discrepancy is between the two covariance matrices, the larger the chi-square and the smaller the p-value will be. Thus, for a model to fit, a high p-value is desirable (i.e., greater than .05 or whatever criterion is chosen). The chi-square, however, is sensitive to the number of variables in the model and the sample size (e.g., Bentler & Bonett, 1980). It is extremely unlikely that a large model with many subjects will ever fit initially according to the p-value. In other words, the power to reject a model increases with the number of variables and subjects. As a general rule, if the chi-square is less than two times the degrees of freedom, the model is a pretty good representation of the data.

As a result of this problem with the p-value, several other fit indices have been introduced. The most typical alternative indices include the normed (NFI) and nonnormed (NNFI) fit indices (Bentler & Bonett, 1980), the root mean squared residual (RMSR), and the adjusted goodness of fit index (AGFI: Jöreskog & Sörbom, 1984). Values for the NFI and AGFI range from zero to one, with the higher values (i.e., above .90) indicating a better fit. The NNFI behaves similarly but can exceed 1.00. On the other hand, smaller values of the RMSR indicate a better fit. The NNFI and AGFI are corrected for degrees of freedom, whereas the NFI and RMSR are not. As a result, the NFI and RMSR may misleadingly indicate that models with fewer degrees of freedom (with more paths being estimated) fit the data better.

Model and Parameter Evaluations

In many instances, the most important question is not whether a model fits but which of two models is the better representation of the data. If one model is a proper subset of the other, then a difference chi-square test can determine whether one model is a significant improvement over the other. A proper subset is defined by the fact that all of the parameters in one model are also included in the other, the only difference being that one model has additional parameters. In this case, one model is said to be nested within the other model.

The importance of a single parameter can be evaluated in two ways. Using a difference chi-square test between two models that differ by the inclusion of a single additional parameter determines whether that parameter is a significant addition to the model. The second method is to examine the critical ratio associated with each parameter (the parameter estimate divided by its standard error). This critical ratio is distributed approximately as the t statistic, in which values greater than 2.00 are significant with a two-tailed test.

Unfortunately, there currently is no accepted way for directly comparing dissimilar (nonnested) models and deciding which is the best. This emphasizes, therefore, the critical role of theories and hypotheses in using SEMs. The ideal situation is one in which competing models can be operationalized so that they are nested, because this enables the alternatives to be tested directly.

Model Modifications

If as gauged by the fit indices a model does not reflect the data (which is often, if not always the case, as our theories may not be totally accurate or complete), the model can be modified, by either adding paths to the model (i.e., important relationships that were not initally included) or removing paths from the model (whose estimates are not significant). For a model to fit, paths usually must be added. Deleting nonsignificant paths generally cleans up a model by removing unnecessary hypothesized effects, but it only marginally improves the fit (by gaining degrees of freedom). Paths are added to a model by using selected modification indices available in LISREL (Jöreskog & Sörbom, 1984) or the Lagrangian Multiplier Test in EQS (Bentler, 1986b; Bentler & Chou, 1986).

MacCallum (1986) examined the effects of adding or deleting parameters to a model on how closely these procedures lead to identifying the "true" or underlying model by using a series of Monte Carlo studies. He found that the best way of modifying a model was first to overfit it by adding parameters and then removing nonsignificant paths. He found that modifying a model only to where the p-value related to the x^2/df fit was just at the .05 level often omitted important effects. In other words, if a model "fits" according to the fit index p-value (i.e., $p > .05$), it will not guarantee that the model contains all important or significant paths.

One fairly common method of modifying a model is to add correlations between residuals of measured variables. These associations typically represent small associations between variables that are not accounted for by the latent constructs. When adding effects to a model, researchers are advised to continue when possible to allow their theory and conceptualization to guide this process and not to add indiscriminantly whatever parameters the program suggests.

Multiple Groups

One interesting and rather useful feature of SEMs that can be found in LISREL, EQS, and LISCOMP is their ability to examine more than one sample simultaneously. If the same variables have been assessed in one or more different populations of interest, this procedure can determine whether a specific model fits both samples equally well. Either the entire model or specific parameters can be compared. For instance, a latent factor structure can be tested to determine whether it is invariant across subjects (males and females, for example). Both the structure or pattern of a model as well as the magnitude of the parameter estimates can be tested. For instance, even though a factor structure may hold in two groups, the magnitude of the loadings may differ. Further, correlations and structural or path coefficients can also be contrasted across two or more groups. Finally, means of the latent factors can be compared across two or more groups or over multiple assessments.

Cross Validation

Because SEM models are often modified and may have changed dramatically from their starting point, it is necessary to determine whether these shifts were based on idiosyncrasies of the sample or whether they represent important substantive results that may require modifying the theory. Cross validation of the final model in an independent sample can test for this. Unfortunately, this is rarely done, for obvious practical reasons. Most of us do not have the luxury of having large sample sizes (or multiple samples) to split and so must await the research of other investigators to confirm our findings. However, if one or more independent samples are available, there are two methods of cross validating the SEM results. The first is a procedure developed by Cudek and Browne (1983) that assesses the decrement in fit by imposing a model developed in one sample on another sample. The second method is to use the multiple-group features of LISREL, EQS, or LISCOMP. In this procedure, all or groups of parameters are contrasted to determine their degree of similarity.

SOCIAL SUPPORT APPLICATIONS OF STRUCTURAL EQUATION MODELING

In this section, I give some general and specific examples of how SEM has been and can be used for studying social support and related issues. The section is organized into several general topic areas, including measurement models, structural or path models, multiple-group models, structured means, and experimental designs.

Measurement Models

Basic to any science is the accurate conceptualization and assessment of central constructs. In the social support area, they include such broad constructs as support, coping, loneliness, stress, health, and psychological functioning. In order for research on social support to progress, the reliability and validity of the measurement instruments designed to assess these constructs must be verified. The measurement aspects of SEM provide an ideal method for establishing the reliability, discriminant validity, and convergent validity of these constructs. Three types of measurement models are relevant to testing these qualities of social support measures: first-order latent factor models, higher-order latent factor models, and multitrait–multimethod latent factor models. We will offer several examples of how these approaches are used to examine social support constructs.

First-Order Latent Factor Models

The Social Support Questionnaire (SSQ: I. G. Sarason, Levine, Basham, & Sarason, 1983) was designed to assess perceived available support. In general, two scales emerge from the measure: SSQN represents the number of perceived available supports on which a person can rely in times of need, as measured across a range of conditions, and SSQS reflects the anticipated or perceived satisfaction with the perceived available support. Correlations between these two scales have been moderate, ranging from .34 to .51 (B. R. Sarason, Shearin, Pierce, & Sarason, 1987). Although only moderately associated, there is sufficient overlap between the scales to suggest that a latent construct may represent them. This latent factor might be called Perceived Available Support. The Inventory of Socially Supportive Behaviors (ISSB: Barrera, Sandler, & Ramsey, 1981) determines the number of times in the past month that the subjects received comfort, support, and information from their social support network. Forty items are used that have been found to reflect four moderately correlated subscales (Stokes & Wilson, 1984): emotional support, tangible assistance, cognitive information, and directive guidance. B. R. Sarason et al. (1987) found that these four scales were correlated between .44 and .74, indicating that a latent factor of Received Social Support may underly them.

B. R. Sarason et al. (1987) reported the intercorrelations for these six scales (the two SSQ scales and the four ISSB scales) from a sample of 194 undergraduates. I used these correlations to test a two-factor confirmatory latent factor analysis model. The first model I tested is given in Figure 2.2. I allowed the two SSQ scales to be indicators of the Perceived Available Support latent factor and the four ISSB scales to be indicators of the Received Social Support latent factor. As evident in the figure, the factor loadings were moderate to large in magnitude, supporting the hypothesized factor structure. In addition, the two latent factors were correlated .35, indicating a moderate degree of overlap between perceiving and receiving social support.

As is often the case when initally attempting to fit a latent variable model to a set of data, this model did not initially fit the data well, $x^2 = (8, n = 194) = 47.06$, $p < .001$, NFI $= .89$. Using selected modification indices for adding correlations to a model, available in the EQS program (Bentler & Chou, 1986), I added three correlations between residuals and one nonstandard correlation to the initial model. This resulted in a final model that fit the data quite well, $x^2 (4, n = 194) = 2.49$, $p = .65$, NFI $= .99$. This model is presented in Figure 2.3.

As evident in Figure 2.3, the addition of these four correlations did not substantially alter the magnitude of the factor loadings or the correlation between factors. Their magnitude fluctuated somewhat, but the general conclusions remained the same. But this is not always the case when modifications are made, and it is always important to compare models before and after adding empirical changes, to ascertain whether the additions or deletions may have changed the model's basic structure. The correlations among residuals are typically small and are not routinely interpreted. The one nonstandard correlation between Perceived

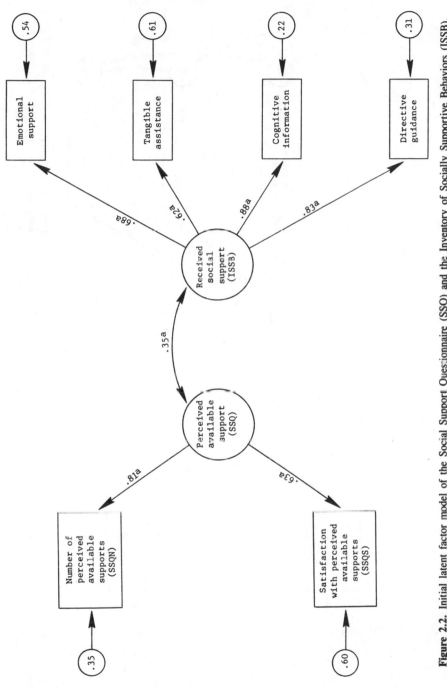

Figure 2.2. Initial latent factor model of the Social Support Questionnaire (SSQ) and the Inventory of Socially Supportive Behaviors (ISSB). Parameter estimates are standardized; residual variables are variances; and significance levels were determined by critical ratios (a = $p < .001$).

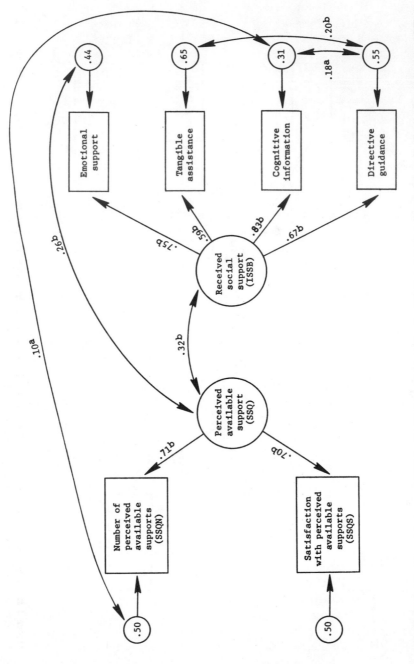

Figure 2.3. Final latent factor model of the Social Support Questionnaire (SSQ) and the Inventory of Socially Supportive Behaviors (ISSB). Correlations between residuals and one nonstandard correlation are included. Parameter estimates are standardized; residual variables are variances; and significance levels were determined by critical ratios (a = $p < .01$; b = $p < .001$).

Available Support and the residual of emotional support, however, is interesting: It indicates that in addition to the common portion of emotional support related to Perceived Available Support via the latent factor of Received Social Support, there remained a unique portion of emotional support that was also directly related to Perceived Available Support. This suggests that the SSQ taps a more emotional or affective form of support, compared with more instrumental support.

This example illustrates reliability when assessing latent factors and convergent and discriminant validity when comparing the two latent constructs (including the nonstandard effect). The general conclusion reached from this latent variable model, that there is only a moderate degree of similarity between perceived and received support, was the same as that drawn by B. R. Sarason et al. (1987) using a different approach. The added benefits of the present analyses are that (1) a single correlation was found to represent the association between these constructs (rather than many bivariate correlations), (2) this correlation was disattenuated for measurement error, (3) a nonstandard effect was found that would not have been detected using only subscales or total scores, and (4) it confirms the reliability of two latent constructs that can now be built into larger models examining the correlates, predictors, and consequences of these two aspects of social support.

Brookings and Bolton (1988) offer a confirmatory factor analysis model with latent variables of the Interpersonal Support Evaluation List (ISEL: Cohen & Hoberman, 1983; Cohen, Mermelstein, Kamarck, & Hoberman, 1985). This measure was designed to assess four types of perceived support: tangible support in the form of material aid, appraisal support in the form of advice and discussion, self-esteem support in the form of favorable comparisons with others, and belonging support in the form of identification with a social network. Even though Cohen and Hoberman (1983) claimed that the four subscales of the ISEL "evidence reasonable independence from one another" (p. 104), Brookings and Bolton (1988) suspected that the subscales might be substantially correlated. Within each of the subscales, Brookings and Bolton divided the summed items into three random parcels and used them to reflect latent constructs for each of the subscales. A summary of their first-order latent variable confirmatory factor analysis model is given in Figure 2.4.

As this figure shows, all factor loadings were moderate in size, supporting the hypothesized factor structure. Of particular interest, however, are the high correlations among the latent constructs. These correlations ranged from .38 to .84, indicating that the four constructs assessed by the ISEL were moderately to highly correlated and thus were not independent.

Table 2.1 presents the latent factor intercorrelations derived from the confirmatory factor analysis of the ISEL that I just described (in the lower triangle) and the zero-order product–moment correlations between the subscales derived from simple sums (in the upper triangle: also from Brookings & Bolton, 1988). The magnitude of the latent factor correlations is substantially greater than that of the measured variable correlations, ranging from .38 to .88. This is a clear demonstration of SEM's ability to remove measurement error (noise), which can substantially attenuate the true correlations (or paths) between constructs. When carefully and properly identified, latent constructs are much more powerful variables than are measured scales, and they are able to locate subtle effects that might be masked or obliterated by random measurement error.

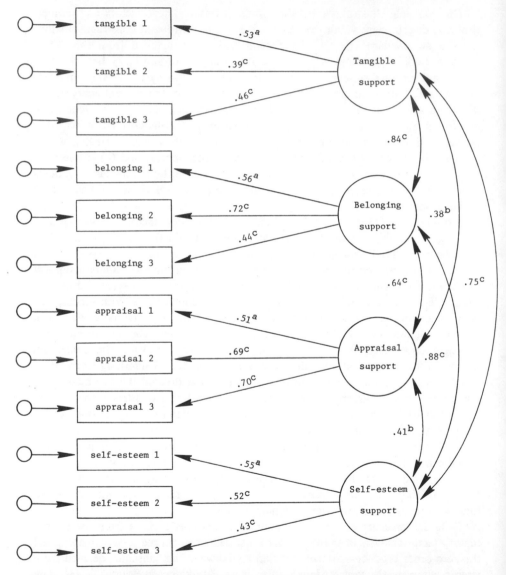

Figure 2.4. Latent variable confirmatory factor analysis model of the Interpersonal Support Evaluation List. Parameter estimates are standardized, and significance levels were determined by critical ratios (a = parameter fixed to identify the model; b = $p < .01$; c = $p < .001$).

TABLE 2.1.   Correlations Among the Measured Scales and Latent Factors of the Interpersonal Support Evaluation List

	I Tangible Support	II Belonging Support	III Appraisal Support	IV Self-esteem Support
I Tangible Support	—	.50[b]	.32[b]	.40[b]
II Belonging Support	.84[b]	—	.50[b]	.54[b]
III Appraisal Support	.38[a]	.64[b]	—	.29[b]
IV Self-esteem Support	.75[b]	.88[b]	.41[a]	—

[a] $p < .01$
[b] $p < .001$
Note: Measured-variable correlations are above the diagonal, and latent variable correlations are below the diagonal.

Higher-Order Latent Factor Models

Another useful feature of SEM's measurement aspects is its ability to test whether higher order constructs can account for lower-order constructs. For instance, even though strong latent factors can be identified that are not the same construct (i.e., are correlated significantly less than 1.00), they may be associated highly enough to suggest that a construct at the next higher level of abstraction may be accounting for the first-order factors. This is what Brookings and Bolton (1988) hypothesized when they examined their first-order factor analysis of the ISEL.

As a result, they tested whether a second-order construct of Global Support could account for the high intercorrelations among the four first-order latent factors. This model is depicted in Figure 2.5 without the measured variables, although the model of course did include them. Their analyses confirmed that this second-order factor could capture the associations among the first-order factors. In essence, this indicates that Global Support generated the four specific types of support, which in turn generated the variation in the measured variables.

In summarizing their conclusions, Brookings and Bolton (1988) suggested that "both individual subscale scores *and* the total support score" be used in subsequent analyses of the ISEL. Because the total score and the four subscales could not be included in a single analysis, because of linearity problems, I would like to offer a more comprehensive way of using this measure (or any measure with moderate intercorrelations among subscales). This involves examining the correlations or effects of the second-order factor, representing the commonality of the first-order constructs, and also the residuals or disturbances of the first-order constructs, which represent the unique aspects of each factor. Because building a second-order factor model into a larger structural equation model is rather cumbersome and might include too many variables, I advise moving down one level of abstraction. This can be done by creating sum scores of the observed indicators corresponding to each first-order latent factor. Thus, the first-order factors become measured variables, and the second-order factor becomes a first-order factor, as depicted in Figure 2.6. (I present another example of this shift from one

level of abstraction to another with latent constructs in a paper on nuclear attitudes: Newcomb, 1986.)

This one factor model was generated from the correlations given in Table 2.1
and accurately reflects the data, x^2 (2, $n = 133$) $= 1.62$, $p = .45$, NFI $= .99$.
The one latent factor represents the common construct of Global Support underlying the ISEL. The residual variances reflect the unique aspects of each scale, in
addition to measurement error. Nonstandard correlations and paths can be associated with the latent construct, any of the residual variables, or both (Bentler,

First–Order Factors   Second–Order Factor

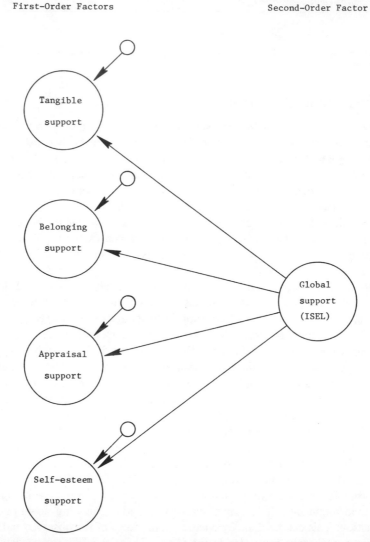

Figure 2.5. Second-order latent factor model of the Interpersonal Support Evaluation List. Small
circles with arrows represent residual or disturbance terms of the first-order latent factors after prediction from the second-order latent factor.

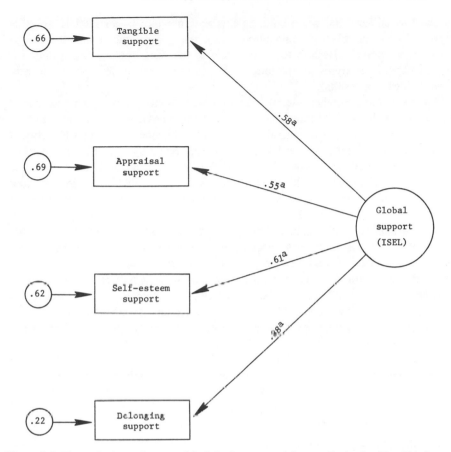

Figure 2.6. First-order latent factor model of the Interpersonal Support Evaluation List. This is one level lower in abstraction from Figure 2.5. First-order latent factors in Figure 2.5 are measured variables (summed) in this model. Parameter estimates are standardized; residual variables are variances; and significance levels were determined by critical ratios (a = $p < .001$).

1987a; Bentler & Newcomb, in preparation; Newcomb & Bentler, 1988a). This type of modeling cannot be accomplished easily in LISREL but is quite straightforward in EQS.

A similar approach to that of Brookings and Bolten (in press) was used to examine the hypothesized latent factor structure of the Social Provisions Scale by Cutrona and Russell (1987). They found that six first-order latent factors represented the hypothesized types of social provisions as assessed by the items in this social support instrument. These latent constructs were correlated sufficiently highly to support a second-order construct of Global Social Support. Thus, both Brookings and Bolten (in press) and Cutrona and Russell (1987) took a similar approach in regard to different social support inventories, and both arrived at similar conclusions. Thus, my suggestion about using the common factor portion (latent construct) and unique variances (residuals) applies equally as well to the

Social Provisions Scale when building this measure into larger models. In other words, latent variable modeling allows both the general factor and the unique portions of individual scales to be included in the same model, and it does not require separate analyses for the total score and individual scales (which can generate misleading results).

I demonstrated another use of a second-order factor in my own research. I hypothesized that despite their conceptual distinctiveness, both loneliness and social support may reflect a general construct of Attachment to Social Network. I formed a latent factor from the UCLA Loneliness Scale by creating three random subscales of the 20 items (Russell et al., 1980). Another latent factor represented the Differential Loneliness Scale (Schmidt & Sermat, 1983) by using the four subscales as measured variable indicators. A construct of Socially Supportive Relationships (Newcomb & Bentler, 1986, 1988a, 1988b) had four indicators of good relationships with parents, family, peers, and adults. A fourth latent construct of Social Resources was reflected in three measured scales of the number of family members, friends, and organizations to which one could turn in times of need. Two method factors were hypothesized to reflect Family-specific Support and Peer-specific Support. The two loneliness factors and two social support factors were confirmed and, although highly correlated, were not identical constructs (i.e., the correlations between factors were significantly less than 1.00). However, a second-order factor of Attachment to Social Network was able to account for the high associations between the first-order constructs. The final model is depicted in Figure 2.7. These analyses were able to demonstrate that although both loneliness and social support were conceptually and empirically distinct, they were similar enough to be accounted for by a higher-order factor of Attachment to Social Network.

Multitrait–Multimethod Models

Measurement conceptualizations in social support research offer an ideal basis for using multitrait–multimethod models. These are latent variable measurement models that are hypothesized not to include a pure factor structure, and in fact each measured variable may have loadings on several latent constructs. For example, social support researchers have made conceptual distinctions regarding perceived support, solicited support, received support, amount of support, satisfaction with support, source of support (i.e., family or friends), nature of support (i.e., emotional or informational), and area of life given support (e.g., House, 1981). Many of these facets of support can be crossed or combined in specific variables. For instance, a researcher may assess the satisfaction with informational support received from a friend regarding a financial problem. Similarly, an item may measure the number of family members to whom one could turn for emotional support if one had a relationship problem with one's spouse. On the other hand, multiple informants may be used to assess the amount of support that a target subject received. For instance, measures can be taken from friends, family, spouse, and co-workers regarding how much support they gave a particular target person and how satisfied they felt that this person was with their support.

Thus, amount and satisfaction of support are crossed with several information sources, an ideal design for multitrait–multimethod analyses. Schmidt and Stults (1986) argued convincingly that latent variable confirmatory factor analysis models are the most appropriate method for analyzing multitrait–multimethod data.

In the previous example of the distinctiveness of loneliness and social support (Figure 2.7), we included two method factors representing support and loneliness experienced from friends and from family. Loadings for these factors spanned the loneliness and social support variables, so that several variables had loadings on two latent constructs. Thus, this model can be considered a multitrait–multimethod design.

Figure 2.8 depicts a hypothesized latent factor structure representing 36 measured social support items (Newcomb & Chou, 1987). Each item assessed three components of social support: one of six substantive areas (e.g., drug problems, health problems), three sources of support (from family, friends, and organizations), and two types or methods of support (number of perceived available supports and satisfaction with perceived support). Each item loaded on three different latent constructs. In this model, though for clarity not depicted in the figure, the six substantive factors were allowed to correlate; the three source-of-support factors were allowed to correlate; and the two type-of-support factors were allowed to correlate. Correlations between groups of factors of particular types (i.e., substantive areas versus sources) must be constrained at zero in order to identify the model.

In this model, the substantive factors were correlated high enough to support a second-order factor of Social Support. On the other hand, the three source-of-support and the two type-of-support constructs were only moderately correlated. This approach provides an interesting heuristic for identifying and isolating various components or facets of social support, which is not feasible when only measured variables are considered.

Structural or Path Models

The structural or path portion of a SEM tests for the effects of one variable on the other. Thus, rather than simply allowing the latent factors to correlate, directional relationships can be hypothesized and tested (with causal inferences only as strong as the data, not the method, can support). Paths can be made between measured variables, groups of measured variables, latent constructs, or residual variables. For instance, de Jong-Gierveld (1987) tested a model of loneliness that simultaneously regressed blocks of variables on one another, creating a general path model between clusters of variables. She hypothesized and tested a model that included measures of background variables, living arrangements, and personality characteristics as independent variables, loneliness as the dependent variable, and characteristics and subjective evaluations of social support network as mediating variables. Unfortunately, the data were cross-sectional, and thus no causal inferences could be drawn. It might have been useful to create latent constructs of some of the variables in order to reduce measurement error. However,

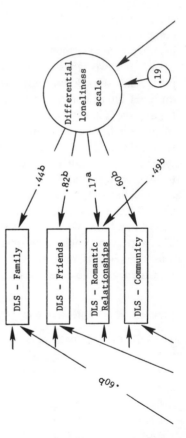

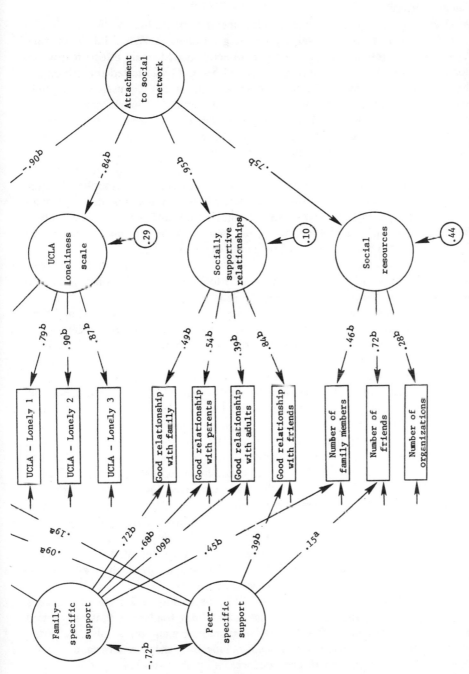

Figure 2.7. Second-order latent factor model of loneliness and social support (Newcomb & Bentler, 1986), with two method factors. Parameter estimates are standardized; factor disturbance variables are variances; and significance levels were determined by critical ratios (a = p < .01; b = p < .001).

this study does provide an interesting example of block path analysis without latent constructs.

Path or structural models are an ideal method for testing the hypothesis of a direct or main effect of social support (e.g., Cohen & Wills, 1985). In other words, is the presence of social support directly related (main effect) to psychological or physiological health? Billings and Moos (1982) tested this hypothesis by examining the relationship between social support and depression. Longitudinal data were used, but without creating latent factors. Although they found differential effects for work and family support, they did not consider that these two constructs may be correlated and so may indicate a general support factor. A latent construct could have addressed this issue, particularly when some of the differential effects appeared to be only slight changes in significance levels and may not truly have reflected differences in the beta weights. In other words, even though certain paths may be significant and others may not, this does not guarantee that the parameters themselves are significantly different from one another. This is particularly a problem when the predictors or outcome measures are highly correlated and probably reflect latent factors or constructs.

Figure 2.1 depicts a hypothetical model for testing the main effects of social support. The path from Social Support (F3) to Time 2 Satisfaction in Life (F5) tests whether Social Support can increase Satisfaction in Life after accounting for the baseline association between Social Support and Satisfaction in Life. Non-panel studies can examine only the cross-sectional association between Social Support and Satisfaction in Life (the correlation between F3 and F4). Even though a direct path (one-headed arrow), instead of the correlation, can be inserted and found significant, this does not prove any causality.

Nonstandard effects also can be tested in this general model. For instance, the latent construct of Social Support may not have a significant effect on Time 2 Satisfaction in Life. Perhaps only certain types of support are important. This can be tested by including paths from the residual variables at Time 1 to Time 2 Satisfaction in Life. For example, perhaps only socioemotional aid contributes to changes in Life Satisfaction. This can be tested by including a path from E7 to F5 and evaluating the significance of this parameter (see Figure 2.9). Or perhaps Social Support influences happiness in only one area of life, for instance, happiness with friends. This can be tested by including a path from F3 to V12 and evaluating the significance of this parameter (see Figure 2.9). Many other nonstandard paths can be tested in this model. Ideally, inclusion of these other paths should be theory driven, but when theory is inadequate for such fine-tuned hypotheses, modification searches can be performed.

Figure 2.9 depicts the same general SEM as in Figure 2.1, but it includes various types of nonstandard effects as dotted lines (including those suggested earlier). These are only a few illustrative examples; many others also are possible. As shown, nonstandard effects can include both measured variables and/or their residuals as predictors or consequences in an analysis. The basic distinction is that nonstandard effects do not occur strictly between two latent factors (as in the paths designated by the solid lines).

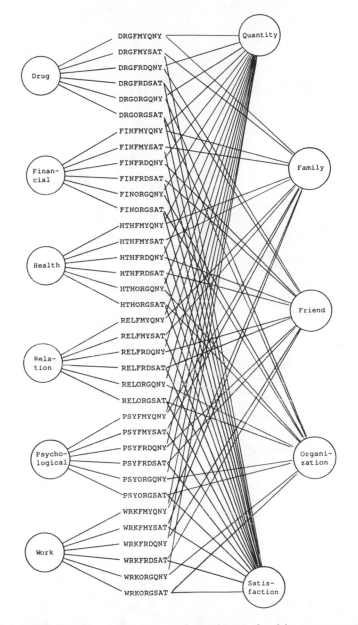

Figure 2.8. A multitrait–multimethod assessment of several types of social support constructs. Each measured variable contains three components: Area of Life (DRG = drug problem, FIN = financial problem, HTH = health problem, REL = relationship problem, PSY = psychological problem, WRK = work problem, source of support, FMY = family, FRD = friends, ORG = organization), and type of support (QNY = quantity of perceived support, SAT = satisfaction with perceived support). Not depicted in the figure are the two-headed arrows (correlations) between all latent factors within each type of support: area, source, and type. All lines should have arrowheads pointing at the measured variables indicating factor loadings.

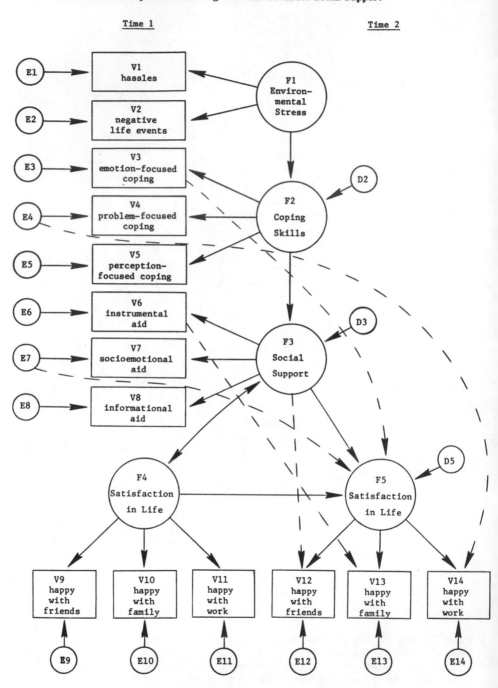

Figure 2.9. A hypothetical model built on Figure 2.1 but showing nonstandard regression effects as dotted lines. These represent only a few of the many possible nonstandard paths that could be tested in this model.

Patterson and Capaldi (in press) hypothesized that a latent factor of good peer relationships mediates the relationship between family environment and child depression. In their analyses, they found that Normal (good) Peer Relations had a direct relationship with less depression, even after accounting for Academic Skill and Child Self-esteem. Interestingly, the Peer Relations construct was based not on self-reports but on information provided by parents, teachers, and peers. Although it did use latent constructs, this model did not use longitudinal data, and so it was impossible to determine whether Peer Relations generated any actual change in Depression. For such conclusions, panel data must be used.

Using panel data from late adolescence to young adulthood, we found that Social Support reduced problems in seven areas of life (Newcomb & Bentler, 1988b). For example, social support in adolescence reduced Drug Problems, Emotional Distress, Relationship Problems, Work Problems, Health Problems, Psychosomatic Complaints, and Family Problems. An interesting feature of this model was that the controls for baseline (adolescent) levels of these problems were not directly included into the model, owing to the sheer number of variables. Instead, we multivariately partialed these earlier variables from the model. Thus, when we found a direct effect from adolescent Social Support on a young adult problem, the effect was a partialed effect representing a change in the outcome measure.

The stress-buffering effect of social support can also be tested using structural paths in SEMs. There are two methods for doing this. One incorporates an interaction latent construct, and the other uses multiple groups.

Testing the stress-buffering effect of social support typically means searching for an interaction (Cohen & Wills, 1985; Rook, 1987). Different levels of association are hypothesized between stress and illness (or another outcome construct), depending on how much social support is experienced. Kenny and Judd (1984) detailed the ways to create latent constructs that represent interaction factors. This requires having multiple indicators of stress (e.g., at home and work) linked to multiple indicators of social support (e.g., at home and work). Each pair of variables is combined to create an interaction variable in the standard manner (e.g., cross-product term: Cohen & Wills, 1985). These interaction variables should be highly correlated to reveal an interaction latent construct. This construct is then included with the Social Support and Stress latent constructs to predict the criterion or outcome factor (e.g., Health, Depression). I cannot give a concrete example of this approach, as it has not yet been applied to the stress-buffering function of social support. Further, interaction factors have not been used widely by SEM researchers in general, because of various complexities engendered by interaction factors, not the least of which is arriving at clear and unambiguous interpretations.

Multiple-Group Models

The multiple-group model provides an alternative and perhaps more easily interpreted way of testing the stress-buffering hypothesis. In this approach, the sample is divided into various levels of social support—say high and low for this example (Cohen & Wills, 1985). These two subsamples would be the two groups in a multiple-group model. Following from the abstract example of Figure 2.1, the association (or path) between Environmental Stress and Satisfaction in Life is examined for those high and low on social support. This is depicted in abbreviated form in Figure 2.10. One hypothesis is that the association between these two constructs would be significantly higher for the low–social support group (correlation a') when compared with the high–social support group (correlation a). This can be tested directly in the model. The added advantages of SEM with multiple groups are that the associations are between error-free latent constructs (bringing more power to the analysis) and that the similarity in factor structure between the groups can be examined simultaneously. In addition, nonstandard paths can be included and tested as well.

Multiple-group analysis can also be used to stratify or subdivide the sample on variables other than social support (e.g., degree of coping, help-seeking behavior, levels of stress) and then these subsamples can be used to examine associations among variables that may be different by group, as well as to test the variability of measurement models or factor structures among different groups. For instance, it is possible to compare directly the latent factor structures (both factor loadings and correlations between constructs) for men and women. Further, different processes may be operating for different groups, and so this method provides an ideal technique for directly contrasting them. This method should also be useful for studying the more process-oriented interactional theories of social support discussed in other chapters in this book.

Structured Means

Another interesting and useful feature of SEM that has received little attention is the comparison of latent variable mean structures. Aside from being able to identify and manipulate latent factors, SEM can also study the means (and variances, if one chooses) of these latent constructs. These means represent true scores, as the measurement error has been removed. Thus, these latent factor means are more sensitive to differences than are those formed directly from measured variables (i.e., more powerful because of no random error).

For instance, in addition to comparing the factor associations between high- and low-support groups in Figure 2.10, it is possible to compare mean levels of Environmental Stress (E to E') or Satisfaction in Life (S to S') for these two groups. The groups can be selected on any mutually exclusive basis that one chooses.

Another use of structured means is for studying developmental processes in a particular sample over time. For instance, by using repeated assessments of the same people over critical phases of life, it is possible to identify changes in the amount of social support they perceive or receive. In other words, in addition to studying the stability or consistency of social support over time, one can also trace changes in the amount of support by using latent means.

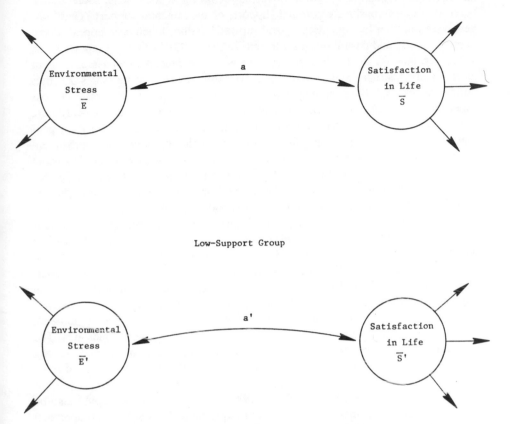

Figure 2.10. A two-group design for comparing structural paths and correlations, as well as latent factor means in high- and low-support groups a = correlation between latent factors in the high-support group; a' = the analogous correlation in the low-support group; $\overline{E}$ and $\overline{S}$ = means on the latent factors in the high-support group; $\overline{E}'$ and $\overline{S}'$ = the analogous means in the high-support group.

Experimental Designs

Although one advantage of SEM is its application to nonexperimental, correlational survey data, it also has advantages for experimental designs. The primary advantage concerns the issue of measurement. Even though conditions can be carefully manipulated in experimental studies, dependent measures are always plagued by measurement error, which may obscure treatment or experimental effects.

Two approaches are used to test experimental data in SEMs. The first is the multiple-group models just discussed. Each treatment condition or control group represents a unique group, and both the magnitude of association between constructs (paths or correlations) and the mean levels of latent factors are directly contrasted across groups. For instance, Rook (1987) reported an experiment that had male and female target subjects varied across three conditions: social deficit based on companionship, emotional support, or instrumental support. These targets were rated on five qualities: friendship satisfaction, loneliness, appeal, effort to meet others, and desirability as a friend. In the ANOVAs that she reported, she did not account for the likely correlation between the dependent measures. One or more latent constructs could be used to reflect these dependent measures and thus utilize the overlap. Then the means of these constructs could be contrasted across experimental conditions. The advantages of this approach would be to incorporate the association between dependent variables in order to prevent them from generating misleading results and gaining power by including latent factors disattenuated for measurement error. Ideally, multiple indicators of each of the dependent variables of concern would be included in order to form latent factors for each.

Sarason, Sarason, and Shearin (1986) could have used a similar procedure to study perceptions of high– and low–social support individuals. The advantage in this study would be the use of a latent construct to reflect the high associations found among the three subscales (leadership, consideration, and attractiveness) of the Dyadic Effectiveness Scale (DES). There appears to be a general latent construct underlying the DES that can be contrasted across the experimental conditions. In addition, the residual of the three subscales, remaining after the common portion is controlled with the latent factor, can also be compared across groups.

The second method for analyzing experimental data in SEMs is to combine all subjects and to create dummy variables to represent experimental conditions. The disadvantage of this approach is that it assumes homogeneity of variance among the experimental conditions, which may not always hold true. For general discussions of using SEMs with experimental designs, see Blalock (1985).

Returning to the I. G. Sarason et al. (1986) example, these data could also be tested in a one-group method for analyzing experimental data. Such an approach is depicted in Figure 2.11. The main effects of sex of target and social support level of target are captured as dummy predictor variables, as is the interaction term. The dependent measures form one latent construct. The paths represent effects that the original researchers located in the step-down MANOVA, as reported in their article. This method of using a single-group SEM to analyze experimental data is both a parsimonious and an elegant way of testing the hypotheses. Separate analyses are not necessary to look at total scores and subscales as performed in the original paper; both of these are captured in the latent construct and the measured variables (or their residuals) in the simultaneous SEM.

This approach can be extended to a repeated measures intervention design by considering it a type of longitudinal study. Premeasures and postmeasures can be selected to reflect relevant latent constructs. The pretest constructs are used to predict the posttest constructs (capturing stability effects); dummy-coded treatment condition variables are allowed to correlate with pretest constructs (to control for baseline differences in group assignment); and then treatment variables are allowed to predict the posttest constructs (testing for treatment effects).

Kaplan and Hartwell (1987) presented interesting data on social support and diabetes that could be analyzed in this manner. They reported on an intervention to help manage Type II diabetes mellitus. They gathered pre- and postphysiological dependent measures (weight, cholesterol, triglycerides, glycosylated hemoglobin, blood glucose, and symptoms) and related these scores to the two subscales of the SSQ for men and women separately.

A SEM analysis of these data could use the pre- and posttest scores to show one or more latent factors (because physiological measures may be highly correlated) and the two SSQ scales to form a Perceived Available Support latent factor (as demonstrated). The pretest factors would be used to predict the posttest factors, and the Perceived Available Support factor would be allowed to correlate with the pretest factor and then to predict the posttest factors (to determine whether support generated any change in the targeted measures and symptoms). Men and women could be compared directly in a multiple-group analysis, and both standard and nonstandard correlations between factors and residuals could be carried out simultaneously.

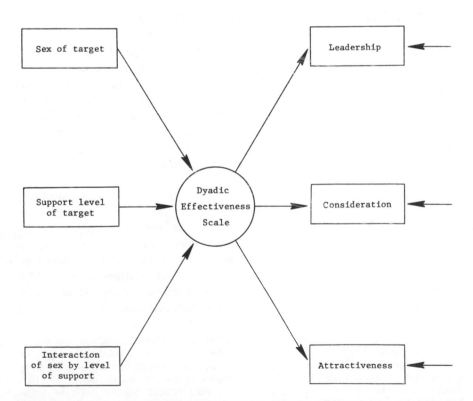

Figure 2.11. An experimental design incorporating the treatment conditions as dummy variables and the dependent measures as a latent construct.

A final way to analyze experimental data is to use differences or change scores, comparing pretest and posttest on related dependent measures, to form a latent change factor or construct. In this case, treatment conditions can again be included as dummy variables to predict the dependent variable or constructs. Alternatively, treatment or experimental conditions can be included as separate groups in a multiple-group model, and contrasts can be tested between latent change factor means in each group. There are problems in using change scores, and in general, it is preferable to use the pre- and postscores in a small longitudinal design, as I discussed.

There are several advantages to using SEMs to analyze such data. The overlap or common variance among the dependent variables is captured as a latent factor; the sexes are contrasted directly (on both correlations and factor means); the association among variables is captured as a simultaneous system (rather than performing separate analyses when the overlap between variables is not considered and misleading results can emerge); and the unique aspects of the dependent measures are captured in nonstandard effects, representing the specific components of these criterion measures.

ADVANTAGES, LIMITATIONS, AND FUTURE RESEARCH

Despite my obvious enthusiasm for applying structural equation modeling to social support research, the method has some legitimate drawbacks, and it is certainly not the panacea for all of our analytic woes. For instance, these methods are both data and subject intensive. Each construct must be assessed carefully with more than one indicator, and many subjects are necessary to produce stable results. So it is not a feasible approach for data sets with only a few subjects or for data sets that do not include a range of relevant variables. Ideally, the design and instrumentation of a study should be approached with the requirements of SEM in mind.[1]

This leads to one of the principal and critical differences between SEM and standard multivariate techniques. SEM must have a good deal of sound theoretical backing to yield meaningful results. It is not an exploratory procedure, although as discussed, there certainly are exploratory aspects to fitting a model. However, the fundamental nature of the model, the identification of latent constructs with appropriate indicators, and the hypothesized relationships among the constructs must be specified before a model can be tested. This is both an advantage to and a limitation of the method. Researchers must know their data quite

[1]I have not given any details about the nuts and bolts of setting up and testing a SEM, as this was not my goal for this chapter. Instead, I have focused on the conceptual issues and the advantages that SEM offers to social support research. Other publications provide more detailed instruction for using various SEM programs. These more technical summaries include the program manuals for EQS (Bentler, 1986b), LISREL (Jöreskog & Sörbom, 1984), and LISCOMP (Muthén, 1987), as well as Anderson (1987), Bentler and Chou (1987), Bentler & Newcomb (1986), Hertzog and Nesselroade (1987), Loehlin (1987), Long (1983), and Wolfle (1980).

well and have good hypotheses before using a structural equation model. Not all types of data are appropriate (i.e., variables should be continuous and normally distributed) and not all research hypotheses can be tested.

Opponents of SEM (Baumrind, 1983; Freedman, 1987; Martin, 1982, 1987), though appearing to criticize the method, in fact attack its misapplications. They point out both violations of assumptions, drawing conclusions beyond the data's capabilities, and general critiques of all statistical procedures (e.g., omission of variables, exclusion of stability effects; see Gollob & Reichardt, 1987). However, none of these criticisms has demonstrated that the principles underlying SEM are invalid (Bentler, 1987b). As a result, we wind up with the old saw of statistical lore: "Garbage in, garbage out."

However, there is one point to be drawn from these criticisms. SEM has rightfully been touted as a minor revolution in statistical methods and, as such, holds promise (Bentler, 1986a). And so when it is not applied properly, it is particularly discouraging and disheartening, as bigger hopes have been dashed.

This leads to perhaps another limitation of SEM. It is new and so its implementation requires careful thought. In this chapter, I have presented the concepts of SEM in basic and recognizable terms. Nevertheless, I must admit that it is probably not as simple or straightforward as are t tests, correlations, or ANOVAs. However, I do not believe that it is really any more difficult (though certainly different) than are MANOVAs, hierarchical multiple regression, or factorial repeated measures designs. Any additional complexity is amply rewarded by SEM's richness, comprehensiveness, and utility. For instance, I do not believe that there is a better method currently available for analyzing multitrait–multimethod data. Nor do I believe that there is a rival approach for analyzing longitudinal data.

This leads me to one of my major recommendations for social support research. Prospective studies must be conducted to understand the processes and interactions of social support in many areas of life. Too few panel studies are currently available to answer many of the pressing questions regarding the development, etiology, and consequences of social support. Most of the studies published on social support are cross-sectional, although they are often couched (misleadingly) in causal terms. Theory is sufficiently advanced in the social support area to yield powerful, important and specific hypotheses about how social support functions for an individual. To test such hypotheses and make causal inferences, either panel data or experimental studies are necessary.

When panel data are used, causal inferences can be advanced if certain criteria are met. Three criteria were offered by Clayton and Tuchfeld (1982) and Hirschi and Selvin (1973). (1) There must be a statistically reliable association between cause and effect; (2) the cause must precede the effect in time; and (3) the association between cause and effect must not be the result of a third or confounding variable. A fourth criterion that I have felt necessary to include in these stipulations (Newcomb, 1987) is that two measures of the consequences or outcome must be available: One must be assessed concurrently with the predictor, and the other must be assessed at some point in the future. First, this fourth criterion controls for the within-time association between cause and effect, by including a correlation between these at the baseline assessment (e.g., the correlation between F3 and F4 in Figure 2.1). And second, it guarantees that if a significant effect or influence is found across time, it will actually represent a change in the outcome or consequence construct. This is operationalized by including a stability path between the same construct assessed at two times (e.g., the path from F4 to F5 in Figure 2.1: see Gollob & Reichardt, 1987).

The second approach to testing causal hypotheses is to use an experimental design. Of course, not all hypotheses are amenable to experimental manipulation, owing to ethical and practical issues, and so must be examined in prospective studies or naturally occurring experiments. Nevertheless, when an experimental design can be used, it can provide an extremely powerful method for testing hypotheses. However, as mentioned, even experimental designs suffer from measurement error. When possible, it would seem an ideal combination to use latent variables in an experimental study. In this way, strict control can be exercised on the treatment manipulations and latent constructs can control for the random vagaries of measurement error.

REFERENCES

Anderson, J. G. (1987). Structural equation models in the social and behavioral sciences: Model building. *Child Development, 58,* 49–64.

Barrera, M. J., Sandler, I. M., & Ramsey, T. B. (1981). Preliminary development of a scale of social support: Studies of college students. *American Journal of Community Psychology, 9,* 435–447.

Baumrind, D. (1983). Specious causal attributions in the social sciences: The reformulated stepping-stone theory as exemplar. *Journal of Personality and Social Psychology, 45,* 1289–1298.

Bentler, P. M. (1980). Multivariate analysis with latent variables: Causal modeling. *Annual Review of Psychology, 31,* 419–456.

Bentler, P. M. (1983). Some contributions to efficient statistics in structural models: Specification and estimation of moment structures. *Psychometrika, 48,* 493–517.

Bentler, P. M. (1986a). Structural modeling and *Psychometrika:* An historical perspective on growth and achievements. *Psychometrika, 51,* 35–51.

Bentler, P. M. (1986b). *Theory and Implementation of EQS: A Structural Equations Program.* Los Angeles: BMDP Statistical Software.

Bentler, P. M. (1987a). *Latent variable structural models for separating specific from general effects.* Paper presented at the meetings of the Health Services Research Conference on Strengthening Causal Interpretations of Non-experimental Data, Tucson, AZ.

Bentler, P. M. (1987b). Structural modeling and the scientific method: Comments on Freedman's critique. *Journal of Educational Statistics, 12,* 151–157.

Bentler, P. M., & Bonett, D. G. (1980). Significance tests and goodness of fit in the analysis of covariance structures. *Psychological Bulletin, 88,* 588–606.

Bentler, P. M., & Chou, C. P. (1986, April). *Statistics for parameter expansion and construction in structural models.* Paper presented at the American Educational Research Association meeting, San Francisco.

Bentler, P. M., & Chou, C. P. (1987). Practical issues in structural modeling. *Sociological Methods and Research, 16*, 78–117.

Bentler, P. M., & Newcomb, M. D. (in preparation). Some nonstandard approaches to structural modeling: Conditional covariance matrices and separation of general from specific effects.

Bentler, P. M., & Newcomb, M. D. (1986). Personality, sexual behavior, and drug use revealed through latent variable methods. *Clinical Psychology Review, 6*, 363–385.

Billings, A. G., & Moos, R. H. (1982). Social support and functioning among community and clinical groups: A panel model. *Journal of Behavioral Medicine, 5*, 295–311.

Blalock, H. M. (1985). *Causal models in panel and experimental designs.* New York: Aldine.

Brookings, J. B., & Bolton, B. (1988). Confirmatory factor analysis of the Interpersonal Support Evaluation List. *American Journal of Community Psychology, 16*, 137–147.

Browne, M. W. (1982). Covariance structures. In D. W. Hawkins (Ed.), *Topics in applied multivariate analysis* (pp. 72–141). Cambridge, England: Cambridge University Press.

Browne, M. W. (1984). Asymptotically distribution-free methods for the analysis of co-variance structures. *British Journal of Mathematical and Statistical Psychology, 37*, 62–83.

Clayton, R. R., & Tuchfeld, B. S. (1982). The drug-crime debate: Obstacles in understanding the relationship. *Journal of Drug Issues, 12*, 153–165.

Cohen, S., & Hoberman, H. M. (1983). Positive events and social supports as buffers of life change stress. *Journal of Applied Social Psychology, 13*, 99–125.

Cohen, S., Mermelstein, R., Kamarck, T., & Hoberman, H. N. (1985). Measuring the functional components of social support. In I. G. Sarason & B. R. Sarason (Eds.), *Social support: Theory, research, and applications* (pp. 73–94). Dordrecht, Netherlands: Martinus Nijhoff.

Cohen, S., & Wills, T. A. (1985). Stress, social support, and the buffering hypothesis. *Psychological Bulletin, 98*, 310–357.

Cudeck, R., & Browne, M. W. (1983). Cross-validation of covariance matrices. *Multivariate Behavioral Research, 18*, 147–167.

Cutrona, C. E., & Russell, D. W. (1987). The provisions of social relationships and adaptation to stress. In W. H. Jones & D. Perlman (Eds.), *Perspectives on interpersonal behavior and relationships* (pp. 37–67). Greenwich, CT: JAI Press.

de Jong-Gierveld, J. (1987). Developing and testing a model of loneliness. *Journal of Personality and Social Psychology, 53*, 119–128.

Dunkel-Schetter, C., Folkman, S., & Lazarus, R. S. (1987). Correlates of social support receipt. *Journal of Personality and Social Psychology, 53*, 71–80.

Freedman, D. A. (1987). As others see us: A case study in path analysis. *Journal of Education Statistics, 12*, 101–128.

Gollob, H. F. & Reichardt, C. S. (1987). Allowing for time lags in causal models. *Child Development, 58*, 80–92.

Harlow, L. L. (1985). *Behavior of some elliptical theory estimators with nonnormal data in a covariance structures framework: A Monte Carlo study.* Unpublished doctoral dissertation, University of California at Los Angeles.

Hertzog, C., & Nesselroade, J. B. (1987). Beyond autoregressive models: Some implications of the trait–state distinction for the structural modeling of developmental change. *Child Development, 58,* 93–109.

Hirschi, T., & Selvin, H. (1973). *Principles of survey analysis.* New York: Free Press.

House, J. S. (1981). *Work, stress, and social support.* Reading, MA: Addison-Wesley.

Huba, G. J., & Harlow, L. L. (1986). Robust estimation for causal models: A comparison of methods in some developmental datasets. In P. B. Baltes, D. L. Featherman and R. M. Lerner (Eds.), *Life-span development and behavior* (Vol. 6, pp. 69–111). New York: Academic Press.

Huba, G. J., & Harlow, L. L. (1987). Robust structural equation models: Implications for developmental psychology. *Child Development, 58,* 147–166.

Jöreskog, K. G., & Sörbom, D. (1984). *LISREL VI: User's guide.* Mooresville, IN: Scientific Software.

Kaplan, R. M., & Hartwell, S. L. (1987). Differential effects of social support and social network on physiological and social outcomes in men and women with Type II diabetes mellitus. *Health Psychology, 6,* 387–398.

Kenny, D. A., & Judd, C. M. (1984). Estimating the nonlinear and interactive effects of latent variables. *Psychological Bulletin, 96,* 195–200.

Loehlin, J. C. (1987). *Latent variable models: An introduction to factor, path, and structural analysis.* Hillsdale, NJ: Erlbaum.

Long, J. S. (1983). *Covariance structure models: An introduction to LISREL.* Newbury Park, CA: Sage.

MacCallum, R. (1986). Specification searches in covariance structure analyses. *Psychological Bulletin, 100,* 107–120.

Martin, J. A. (1982). Application of structural modeling with latent variables to adolescent drug use: A reply to Huba, Wingard, and Bentler. *Journal of Personality and Social Psychology, 43,* 598–603.

Martin, J. A. (1987). Causes, causal theories, and structural equation modeling. *Child Development, 58,* 33–37.

Muthén, B. (1984). A general structural equation model with dichotomous, ordered categorical, and continuous latent variable indicators. *Psychometrika, 49,* 115–130.

Muthén, B. (1987). *LISCOMP: Analysis of linear structural relations using a comprehensive measurement model.* Mooresville, IN: Scientific Software.

Newcomb, M. D. (1986). Nuclear attitudes and reactions: Associations with depression, drug use, and quality of life. *Journal of Personality and Social Psychology, 50,* 906–920.

Newcomb, M. D. (1987). Consequences of teenage drug use: The transition from adolescence to young adulthood. *Drugs and Society, 1* (4), 25–60.

Newcomb, M. D., & Bentler, P. M. (1986). Loneliness and social support: A confirmatory hierarchical analysis. *Personality and Social Psychology Bulletin, 12,* 520–535.

Newcomb, M. D., & Bentler, P. M. (1988a). *Consequences of adolescent drug use: Impact on the lives of young adults.* Beverly Hills, CA: Sage.

Newcomb, M. D., & Bentler, P. M. (1988b). Impact of adolescent drug use and social support on problems of young adults: A longitudinal study. *Journal of Abnormal Psychology, 97,* 64–75.

Newcomb, M. D., & Chou, C. P. (1987). *Social support among young adults: A multi-trait–multimethod assessment of quantity and satisfaction in six areas of life.* Manuscript under editorial review.

Patterson, G. R., & Capaldi, D. (in press). A comparison of models for boys' depressed mood. In J. E. Rolf, A. Masten, D. Cicchetti, K. Neuchterlein, & S. Weintraub (Eds.), *Risk and protective factors in the development of psychopathology.* Boston: Syndicate of the Press, Cambridge University.

Rook, K. S. (1987). Social support versus companionship: Effects on life stress, loneliness, and evaluation by others. *Journal of Personality and Social Psychology, 52,* 1132–1147.

Russell, D., Peplau, L. A., & Cutrona, C. E. (1980). The revised UCLA Loneliness Scale: Concurrent and discriminant validity evidence. *Journal of Personality and Social Psychology, 39,* 472–480.

Sarason, B. R., Shearin, E. N., Pierce, G. R., & Sarason, I. G. (1987). Interrelations among social support measures. *Journal of Personality and Social Psychology, 52,* 813–832.

Sarason, I. G., Levine, H. M., Basham, R. B., & Sarason, B. R. (1983). Assessing social support: The Social Support Questionnaire. *Journal of Personality and Social Psychology, 44,* 127–139.

Sarason, I. G., & Sarason, B. R. (1985). *Social support: Theory, research, and applications.* Dordrecht, Netherlands: Martinus Nijhoff.

Sarason, I. G., Sarason, B. R., & Shearin, E. N. (1986). Social support as an individual difference variable: Its stability, origins, and relational aspects. *Journal of Personality and Social Psychology, 50,* 845–855.

Satorra, A., & Bentler, P. M. (1987). *Robustness properties of ML statistics in covariance structure analysis.* Manuscript under editorial review.

Schmidt, N., & Sermat, V. (1983). Measuring loneliness in different relationships. *Journal of Personality and Social Psychology, 44,* 1038–1047.

Schmidt, N., & Stults, D. M. (1986). Methodology review: Analysis of multitrait–multimethod matrices. *Applied Psychological Measurement, 10,* 1–22.

Stelzl, L. (1986). Changing a causal hypothesis without changing the fit: Some rules for generating equivalent path models. *Multivariate Behavioral Research, 21,* 309–331.

Stokes, J. P., & Wilson, D. G. (1984). The Inventory of Socially-Supportive Behaviors: Dimensionality, prediction, and gender differences. *American Journal of Community Psychology, 12,* 53–69.

Tanaka, J. (1987). How big is big enough: The sample size issue in structural equation models with latent variables. *Child Development, 58,* 134–146.

Thoits, P. A. (1986). Social support as coping assistance. *Journal of Consulting and Clinical Psychology, 54,* 416–423.

Weeks, D. G., Michela, J. L., Peplau, L. A., & Bragg, M. E. (1980). Relation between loneliness and depression: A structural equation analysis. *Journal of Personality and Social Psychology, 39,* 1238–1244.

Wolfle, L. E. (1980). Strategies of path analysis. *American Educational Research Journal, 17,* 183–209.

CHAPTER 3

Social Support in Young Children: Measurement, Structure, and Behavioral Impact

ANA MARI CAUCE, MOLLY REID, SHARON LANDESMAN, and NANCY GONZALES

University of Washington

University of Washington

University of North Carolina at Chapel Hill

University of Washington

Our capacity to create and maintain social relationships, as well as our need for such relationships, has been considered a hallmark of the human condition. Most people experience their greatest joys and sorrows as a result of their social ties. Life would surely seem easier without the frustration of misunderstood communications with friends, unrequited love, and stormy battles with family members. Yet it would seem rather dry, if not totally meaningless, were it not for those moments in which one feels understood, loved, and cared for by another. Indeed, this need to be a part of a social circle is so strong that children, battered and abused by their parent(s), often protest being separated from them.

One reason for the urgency and strength of this need for interrelatedness is our long period of dependence before we are able to survive physically on our own. Despite the literature that stressed the many skills and competencies of the human newborn, compared with those of other species, we enter the world in a relatively vulnerable state. The increasingly complex structure of our technologically oriented, and urbanized Western society, moreover, has further lengthened this period of dependence. Young children thus must learn to cultivate relationships with others. And those relationships must serve a protective function. The recognition of this fact is at the heart of attachment theories (Bowlby, 1969, 1980).

Cauce's research was supported by the University of Washington Graduate Research Fund, the W. T. Grant Foundation (86-1093-86) and the National Institute of Child Health and Human Development (HD-24056-01). Reid's and Landesman's research was supported by the National Institute of Child Health and Human Development and the MacArthur Foundation Network on Childhood Transitions. Reid was also supported by HD-19348 and HD-24116, and Landesman was also supported by HD-1938.

Such theories, in short, posit that a secure bonding experience (usually with the mother) provides the foundation on which children build when exploring their environment. The nature of this first bond has also been viewed as a template for other interpersonal relationships.

Nonetheless, it is a long road from this first attachment to the development of the complex array of friends, friends of friends, colleagues and acquaintances, family of origin, created family, in-laws, and lovers and/or spouses that comprise the social networks of typical adults. In this chapter we will present our views on young children's social networks and the support they derive from them, with an emphasis on issues of measurement, descriptions of children's networks from both a structural and developmental perspective, and the behavioral impact of perceived social support. We will then conclude with recommendations for selecting social support instruments and directions for future research.

Research on children's social support networks began to appear in the literature almost a decade ago, but it is only now that a coherent body of work is emerging (e.g., Belle, 1989). Underlying this recent surge of interest has been the convergence of two bodies of literature, one on the antecedents or precursors of perceived social support among adults and the other on the rising prominence of social ecological models of child and family adaptation.

Antecedents of Social Support

Although the last decade produced relatively little work on children's social support networks, research on the social networks of adults and college students has become almost ubiquitous. Hundreds of studies have now been carried out and reports published that suggest that support from others improves individuals' ability to cope with general life stress and also enhances their psychological well-being (see Cohen & Wills, 1985, for a comprehensive review). In addition, social support has been found to ease life transitions (Hirsch, 1980), occupational stress (Gore, 1978), and employment disruption (Gore, 1978; Pearlin, Menaghan, Lieberman, & Mullen, 1981; Schaefer, Coyne, & Lazarus, 1981). The prototypical study in this area examined the role of social support as a buffer of life stress (as measured by life events scales) or as a direct contributor to well-being. The psychological outcome most commonly studied is depression. Although such studies did not consistently and strongly demonstrate these effects (Rook & Dooley, 1985), the sheer weight of evidence is sufficient for public (see Heller & Swindle, 1983) and private calls to be issued for a moratorium of sorts on further research illustrating the classic stress-buffering or enhancement effects of social support using the prototypical cross-sectional designs with adult populations.

Although some researchers responded to this message by trying to identify more clearly the conditions under which specific effects are most likely to occur (Cohen & McKay, 1984), others began to dig deeper into the social support construct itself, rather than focusing solely on its impact. A watershed article in this respect was that by Sarason, Sarason, and Shearin (1986), which presented the results of three studies examining the stability, origins, and relational aspects of social support in a college student sample. The results suggested that at least by late adolescence or early adulthood, social support seemed to be as much an individual difference variable as an environmental provision. More specifically, social support indices showed a great deal of stability over a three-year period, and individuals who reported high levels of support during their college years also reported having received more parental care than did those who reported low levels of social support. Sarason et al. concluded from this work that "the ability to perceive a supportive network and feel satisfied with what is perceived may be related to a specific type of early experience" (p. 850). In addition, they stated that "if perceived social support and the individual's satisfaction with it are stable over time and across situations, it becomes important to search for their developmental precursors" (p. 853). And so a call was issued for examining social support from an explicitly developmental perspective.

Ecological Models of Child and Family Development

The increasing prominence of social ecological models of child and family development paralleled the rise of social network/support research (Bronfenbrenner, 1979; Cochran & Brassard, 1979; Garbarino, 1982). As Zigler and Weiss (1985) aptly expressed it: "The conventional wisdom about how to promote child and family development is shifting from a child-centered to a more ecological approach, one that emphasizes the importance of interrelationships between the child, the family, and the social support available to them."

Ecological models stress the social contexts in which the family, and hence the child, is embedded. According to Garbarino, "Contexts of development are those regularly-occurring environmental settings that can affect development by presenting risks or opportunities" (p. 3). Although these contexts can be as broad as the nation or state in which one resides (i.e., the macrosystem), they can also be the more intimate settings of family, friendship groups, and school (i.e., the microsystem).

Much of the research undertaken from an ecological perspective examined second-order or indirect environmental effects. For example, various studies assessed how a mother's social network affects her parenting skills and her child's development (Cochran & Brassard, 1979; Crittendon, 1985; Crnic, Greenberg, Ragozin, Robinson, & Basham, 1983; Crnic, Greenberg, Robinson, & Ragozin, 1984). Such studies suggest that children's adjustment is, in fact, influenced by their mothers' relationships in which the children do not participate.

Nonetheless, ecological theory predicts that it is those relationships that form a direct part of the child's life (i.e., the child's *own* social network), which create his or her daily experience and influence him or her most profoundly. In this respect, Garbarino (1982) stated that "as the child develops, complexity normally increases: the child does more, with more people, in more places." That is, as children grow, their social networks and sources of support become more varied. A test of this hypothesis would require a developmental examination of children's social support networks over time. As such, research on both the social networks of adults and the ecological models of child development provide compelling reasons to investigate social support.

MEASUREMENT ISSUES IN ASSESSING CHILDREN'S SOCIAL SUPPORT

Approaches to Measurement

Exploring and quantifying the multidimensional nature of children's social support is a challenging undertaking. Methods for assessing children's relationships with others include behavioral observation, parent report, and self-report. Behavioral observations have the advantage of offering an objective perspective on children's interactions with others, including parents, siblings, and peers. Observations typically provide a direct sampling of the child's behaviors with one or two network members at a time (e.g., mother, sibling), in one and sometimes several situations (e.g., see Brody, Stoneman, & MacKinnon, 1982; Clarke-Stewart, 1978; Dunn, 1983; Parke, Power, & Gottman, 1979). A disadvantage of using behavioral observations is that they usually represent a brief time period and are restricted to the specific people and situations that are observed. Behavioral observations have not been used to measure the broad parameters of children's networks, and indeed, they would be cumbersome and intrusive to use for this purpose.

Parental reports (usually maternal reports) are also commonly used as a means of obtaining objective information about children's relationships (e.g., Cochran & Riley, 1985; Lewis, Feiring, & Brooks-Gunn, 1987; Lewis, Feiring, & Kotsonis, 1984). Parental reports have the advantage of providing a broad view of the child's social relationships. However, despite their wide usage, they have been criticized as providing unreliable and systematically distorted data (Kagan, 1984). As a means of gathering information about children's social relations, the accuracy and extent of parental reports depend heavily on parental perception of events that occur within the home and on how actively the parents monitor their child's everyday activities.

In contrast with behavioral observations and parent reports, self-report has the advantage of tapping into a large number of remembered experiences (e.g., those occurring over time in a variety of situations) as well as into those experiences "weighted" by the child as most salient. In addition, self-reports contain information about the child's life from his or her own perspective, which is difficult to obtain in any other way. That is, self-report is the only method that provides information about the subjective, phenomenological aspect of the child's relationships.

The child's subjective appraisal of his or her social support may theoretically be the critical mediator of the effect that support from others has on development. In fact, the adult social support literature indicates that the individual's subjective evaluation or perception of having access to social support is more predictive of mental health status than is size of social network or frequency of contacts (Sarason & Sarason, 1985).

Recent work supports the use of children as informants. Berndt and Perry (1986), Bryant (1985), Tietjen (1982), and Wolchick, Beals, and Sandler (in press) interviewed 7-, 10-, and 12-year-old children, and Furman and Buhrmester (1985) designed questionnaires to be given to groups of preadolescents. Inquiries into children's social support typically examine support unidimensionally and often concentrate on the support received from a single member in the child's network (e.g., emotional support from a friend). A notable exception is the work by Furman and Buhrmester (1985) that considers both multiple providers or sources of support (e.g., mother, father, sibling) and multiple support functions (e.g., reliable alliance, instrumental help, companionship, affection).

The findings from research using children's perceptions of social support offer interesting glimpses into their social worlds. However, the reports generally cannot be readily compared with the adult social support research (Berndt, in press). The reliability and validity of the children's data also have not been well delineated; often only their internal consistency is verified (Wolchick et al., in press). Similarly, the effects of children's characteristics that could interact with their task performance have not been studied. Such characteristics include the child's age, attentional skills, communications abilities (e.g., reading comprehension and expressive verbal skills) and willingness to participate.

Guidelines for Developing Instruments

A major obstacle in studying children's subjective appraisals is that children are notoriously difficult to interview in a manner that yields reliable and comparable data across subjects. Attempts to interview children using techniques designed for adults are usually unsuccessful. For example, in comparison with adults, when children are asked open-ended questions, their attention is more apt to wander, and/or they are more likely to give an unrelated or incomplete answer that is difficult to compare in any uniform way across children (Bigelow, 1977; Hayes, 1978). When standard questionnaire techniques are used, young children are likely to guess in order to avoid revealing that they are unable to read or to understand a question. In addition, children tend to lapse into random responding or to answer in ways that may change their intentions and/or oversimplify their thoughts or feelings (cf. Bierman, 1983).

The difficulties in trying to obtain reliable reports from children underscore the need to use techniques that are guided by cognitive-developmental theories about children's abilities to attend, comprehend, and respond (cf. Borkowski, Reid, & Kurtz, 1984; Brown, Bransford, Ferrara, & Campione, 1983; Vygotsky, 1978; Wellman, 1978). Reid, Landesman, Treder, and Jaccard (1989) offer some guidelines for maximizing young children's abilities to provide subjective appraisals of their social relationships. They recommend that instruments (1) be interesting to and enjoyable for children, regardless of differences in their temperament (e.g., shyness, attention span); (2) use a format that is developmentally sensitive to children's cognitive and emotional understanding; (3) include visual and manipulative materials to help hold the children's attention and to make abstract concepts concrete and visible; (4) use an interactive format that contains opportunities to evaluate and, if necessary, increase the children's understanding of the task (e.g., by encouraging them to ask questions of clarification); (5) build on existing knowledge about children's social support; and (6) provide a comprehensive view of children's social support, by including all family members at home and key individuals outside the home (e.g., friends, teachers, other relatives, and care providers).

In addition, a self-report tool will have wider application if it is suitable for a large age span of children and parallels in content the social support instruments for adults. Such a tool permits studying social support across people of different ages (e.g., members in the same family) as well as looking longitudinally at the childhood precursors of individual differences in adult social support (cf. B. R. Sarason, Shearin, Pierce, & Sarason, 1987).

A conceptualization of social support that is commonly used and has received some theoretical and empirical endorsement in research with adults divides social support into four areas: esteem or emotional support, informational support or advice, social companionship, and instrumental help or material aid (Cohen & Wills, 1985). Berndt (in press) gave a sound theoretical rationale for using this schema to assess social support in child populations. Although some research with adults shows that a unidimensional and global definition of support is sufficient, this has not been well investigated with younger populations. From a developmental perspective, a specific type of support from a specific provider (e.g., a grandparent who provides good instrumental help, a friend who is great to have fun with) may be an important resource during both normative (e.g., entry into school) and nonnormative (e.g., death of a parent, chronic illness) childhood transitions.

Using Child Dialogue Tools with 4- to 15-Year-Olds

"My Family and Friends" is a dialogue format instrument that was created to elicit children's perceptions in a multidimensional and age-appropriate manner (Reid & Landesman, 1986). It was based on many of the recommendations just outlined. Two studies tested and standardized the dialogue, using a total of 314 children (65 children were in the Test Development Phase, and 249 were in the final evaluation and Standardization Study). The children were 5 to 14 years old and from a population-based sample of black and white families (50% single-parent and 50% two-parent, equally distributed among families with an only child, two children, and three or more children). A subsample of the children in the Test Development Phase were described by their parents as not yet able to read standard directions. These children were included, however, because of recommendations that the linguistic and attentional abilities of young children who are not yet reading should be an area of concern when designing new instruments (Kagan, Hans, Markowitz, Lopez, & Sigal, 1982). Families were selected as part of the larger University of Washington Family Behavior Study designed to evaluate a model of family functioning (Landesman, Jaccard, & Gunderson, in press).

"My Family and Friends" consists of 12 dialogues designed to yield information about a child's social network, the perceived availability of individuals to provide different types of support, and the child's appraisal of the quality of support received. The interactive dialogue format was based on the work by Vygotsky (1978) that suggests that successful interviews with children (1) use a dialogue rather than a monologue and (2) engage the child as an active collaborator. The stems in the dialogue script incorporated words and phrases familiar to children in this age group that were obtained through the open-ended questioning in the Test Development Phase.

Two each of the 12 dialogues deal with informational, instrumental, and companionship support; 5 focus on emotional support, owing to the special significance that most people attach to it; and 1 is a conflict question. Conflict was evaluated based on the finding that even close, supportive relationships may contain anger and negative interactions (Berndt & Perry, 1986; Braiker & Kelly, 1979; Furman & Buhrmester, 1985). Other features of the dialogue scripts are an opportunity at the beginning and end to make sure that the child understands the task, and attractive and personalized props to make aspects of the dialogue more concrete and less abstract. These props, illustrated in Figure 3.1, include name cards for members in the social network, a ranking board, and a colorful barometer with a moving level indicator for showing amount of satisfaction.

The actual procedures, which are detailed elsewhere (Reid & Landesman, 1986; Reid et al., in press), begin by introducing the child to the task and identifying the members of the child's active social network. The names or pictures of these people are put on a set of cards. Then for each of the dialogue questions, the child (1) uses the cards to rank the order in which he or she would go to each of the people—for example, "If you did something that you felt really bad about, that no one knew about, who would you talk to?"—and (2) uses the barometer with the moving level indicator to rate how satisfied he or she is with the support received from each individual—for example, "When you talk to your brother when you feel bad, how much better do you feel afterward?" The dialogue ends with a brief inventory of the other people who are important to the child, including their age, frequency seen, and shared activities. The instrument is administered in two sessions of 10 to 12 minutes each, with a break between sessions. Part 1 consists of dialogues 1 through 6, and Part 2 contains dialogues 7 through 12.

The evaluation of "My Family and Friends" as an instrument for studying social support in young to preadolescent children was based on the Standardization Study noted earlier and contains separate test–retest and validity studies. The principal areas studied were the degree to which young children were interested in the activity and could reliably differentiate the four types of social support and the individuals who provided them; the stability of the children's reported perceptions over a short time, as well as variables accounting for the children's "unreliability"; and the children's ability to provide good examples, from their own lives, of the different types of social support.

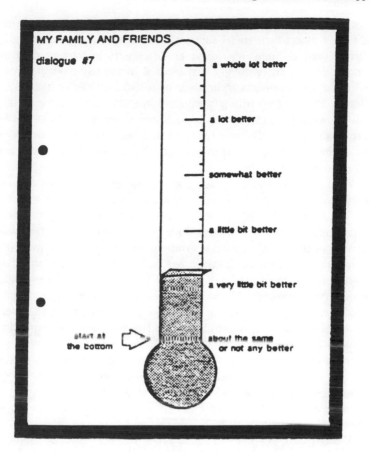

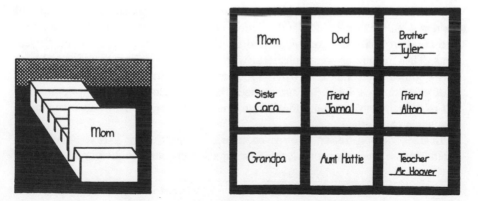

Figure 3.1. Props used in "My Family and Friends."

The Standardization Study is a systematic investigation of young children's abilities to self-report their social support, and it yielded the following findings:

1. Virtually all children, regardless of differences in temperament, language skills, or family context, willingly participated in the study when given the opportunity to act as informants about their own lives. Of the originally scheduled 250 children, 249 (99.6%) willingly engaged in and completed the social support dialogues. In addition, independent ratings of the children obtained while they were participating in the dialogue revealed that over 90% were rated as showing moderate to high interest, cooperation, comprehension of questions and activities, and enjoyment of the task.

2. Children provide reliable (stable) reports. Test–retest correlations were within the acceptable high–moderate range for social and personality inventories for children. The medians for the children's rankings of their network members was .68 and the medians for the children's ratings of support satisfaction was .69.[1]

Sensitivity of the social support instrument was supported by the finding that children report more variation in their perceptions when undergoing family upheaval. An examination of the small group of "unreliable" children revealed that they did not differ from the "reliable" group in terms of child characteristics (e.g., intelligence, age, gender) or participatory behaviors (e.g., rated enjoyment, cooperation, interest, comprehension). However, 85% of the children who gave widely different reports at Time 1 and Time 2 were from families who were in a state of stress and upheaval. One of these children summed up the impact of family stress on her social network: "Life at home is so difficult right now that I don't know who to turn to and it's just easier to go to my own diary."

3. Children differentiate the four types of support found in the adult literature (i.e., emotional, informational, instrumental, and companionship) and can provide good behavioral examples of those types of social support appropriate to their developmental stage. Internal consistencies for the scales had a mean Cronbach Alpha of .72, with a range of .58 to .92. The only exception was the instrumental support scale, which later was reworded.

In a manner recommended by Harter and Pike (1984), convergent validity was assessed by asking the children (after the dialogue was over) the reasons for their responses. Content analyses indicated that the children's spoken understanding of the test items was related to the theoretical construct the test purports to measure. The children had good comprehension of over 90% of the social support questions. Their responses were consistent with the general definitions of social support outlined by Cohen and Wills (1985) and yet contained examples typical of middle childhood. Table 3.1 summarizes the descriptions that the children gave the most frequently for emotional, instrumental, informational, and companionship social support.

Besides demonstrating the psychometric properties of "My Family and Friends" as a child report tool, this investigation encourages the pursuit of social

---

[1] These are intraclass correlations ranging from -1 to 1 and represent chance-adjusted agreement scores.

TABLE 3.1.   Categorization of the Social Support Needs Described Most Frequently by Children

I. Emotional Support
  A. Support for negative events and experiences (e.g., bad news and negative feelings a child shares)
    • getting braces, doing poorly in a subject at school
    • taking drugs, hitting someone
    • parents filing for divorce
  B. Support for positive experiences (e.g., good news and positive feelings a child shares)
    • doing well in a spelling bee, doing the job "right"
    • having a new baby in the family
    • chance events, such as being dismissed early from school because of a heating failure or winning a raffle
  C. Support for understanding self (e.g., letting a child know he or she is understood)
    • knows the child well enough to give good personal advice
    • answers questions the child does not know how to word well
    • looks approvingly at the child rather than having a puzzled facial expression
    • child reports "just knowing" when an individual understands him or her
  D. Enhancement of self-worth (i.e., making the child feel good about who he or she is)
    • tells the child they like him or her, commends the child on doing a good job
    • child reports, "I know people think I am neat when they envy me and want to imitate me"
II. Information Support
    • understanding the news on TV, finding out how wars start, learning that chemicals will ruin the earth
    • learning how to be safe and say "no" to strangers
    • learning about school subjects or how to build and make things
III. Instrumental Support
    • help with science projects, help move heavy loads, help clean the fish tank
    • help make a model, help nailing together a clubhouse
    • help find lost clothes, school supplies, or a lost pet
IV. Companionship: Ways children have fun with or enjoying being with others
    • going together to the shopping center, working together on projects such as operating a lemonade stand or making a Lego village
    • listening to music together or watching videos
    • committing minor social infractions together, such as annoying sibs or making prank phone calls

Note: Adapted from Reid, Landesman, Jaccard, & Rabkin (1987).

support research with young children. Collectively, these data indicate that children's subjective appraisals of social support can be gathered reliably and validly from early childhood through early adolescence.

YOUNG CHILDREN'S SOCIAL SUPPORT NETWORKS

Structural Features

Most measures used to evaluate adults' social support networks ask the respondents to list providers for specific types of supportive interactions. As we pointed out, for younger populations, it is better to give more specific cues for certain categories of providers, such as family members or those living in the same home. (We recommend this approach for young adolescents as well.)

Although this strategy does not allow us to obtain some of the traditional indicators of social network structure (e.g., network density), it does give us a more complete portrait of the types of support that children receive from key providers. When we refer to structural aspects of children's social networks, we mean the types of support that children obtain from various types of providers.

Because it is easier to construct measures for older populations and because such measures can often be administered to groups, most of the existing research on children's support networks has been conducted with adolescents and early adolescents. This research generally suggests that family, same-age friends, and school personnel are the key sources of support to which most young persons have some access (Cauce, Felner, & Primavera, 1982; Cauce, Hannan, & Sargeant, 1987; Furman & Buhrmester, 1985). Indeed, whereas in the adult literature much of the research concentrated on the functional characteristics of social support (Barrera, 1981; Cohen & Wills, 1985), in the child literature more energy has been spent examining the role of the source or provider of social support (Cauce & Srebnik, in press).

In a functional model of social support, the type or content of the supportive interaction is considered most salient. Social support is broken down into various functions such as emotional support or instrumental help, as described earlier. Other support functions assessed include reliable alliance, affection, and intimacy (Furman & Buhrmester, 1985). A structural or relationship model of social support (which we will refer to as a *provider model*) proposes that it is the sources or providers of support (i.e., adults vs. peers, family vs. nonfamily) that differ most in young people's social networks.

The work of Cauce and her colleagues has suggested that a provider model should be used to evaluate adolescents' social networks (Cauce et al., 1982, 1987; Cauce & Srebnik, in press). However, because they examined only emotional support, it was not possible to use a functional model. But a paper by Wolchick et al. (in press) specifically addressed this issue. Does the organizing structure of children's social support networks more closely approximate a functional model or a provider model?

Wolchick et al.'s study was based on research on 285 families with children between the ages of 8 and 16. Structural equation modeling provided a sophisticated assessment of these two models, as well as a third, single-factor or "null" model. (The null model essentially predicted that no such organizing structures exist.) Their results indicate that the provider model followed by the functional model best fit the data. The null model fit poorly by comparison. More specifically, although the provider model accounted for the lion's share of the variance, a substantial amount of the leftover residual covariance was explained by functional indices. These results were invariant across gender and age.

Wolchick et al. concluded from this that "children's social support networks appear to be organized in terms of the type of tie rather than the content of supportive exchanges that occur within these ties" (p. 30). But "concluding that relationship variables are the only organizing structure is an oversimplification of children's social networks" (p. 31).

In the Standardization Study, Reid, Landesman, Treder, and Jaccard (in press) likewise found support for both a provider and a functional model. Even at young ages, children rated parents, sibling, friends, teachers, and other adults differently in terms of their social support contributions. Significant main effects were obtained for support function F (2.75, 440.48) = 86.07, $p < .001$, provider, F (3.28, 525.02) = 69.29, $p < .001$, and their interaction F (8.30, 1328.44) = 135.76, $p < .001$. The same pattern of results emerged from the data on preschool children (Cauce & Gonzales, in progress).

We believe that a simple "eyeball" inspection of these combined data best shows how these two models are interrelated. The data set that examines preschool children's social support is based on a larger study of children's adjustment to first grade (Cauce & Gonzales, in progress). The data presented here were collected from 60 children just before (i.e., in August) their entry into first grade. The children ranged in age from 5 to 7, with a median age of 6. The sample was middle class and well educated, and almost all the children lived in two-parent homes (87%). Seventy-two percent of the children were white, and 23% were black (3% were from other ethnic backgrounds). All of the children were interviewed in their homes by trained graduate students or advanced under graduate students.

The data that examine elementary school–aged and middle school–aged children's social networks were derived from a subsample of children who participated in the Standardization Study. The findings presented here were based on analyses of the data collected from 120 children in two-parent homes. This sample of children was considerably more heterogenous than was that of the preschool children and varied substantially by education and income. Eighty percent of the children were white, and 20% were black.

Figure 3.2 shows the mean ratings across all children in both studies for each support function nested within the key provider: mother, father, sibling, friend, and teacher. (Although some sex and race differences were obtained, they are not presented for the sake of clarity; these data can be obtained by writing to the authors.) The data presented here, and in the subsequent sections, are based on ratings (using the barometer) of questions about the children's satisfaction with their support. These ratings represent the perceived quality of the support from specific persons.

When examining these composite ratings, one notes first the different profiles of support provisions within each key provider. For example, the profiles of support from the mothers and fathers are generally flat. In fact, the ratings for the different support functions obtained from the mother or father, respectively, do not significantly differ from each other. Yet, when we compare the ratings of mothers and fathers with those of the other providers, it becomes evident that the children rated both their parents as giving them relatively high degrees of support across all categories. In such comparisons, the children generally rated support from their mother, in particular, as significantly higher than support from other sources.

On the other hand, the profiles for sibling, friend, and teacher appear quite "jagged." That is, companionship is quite high for siblings, followed by emo-

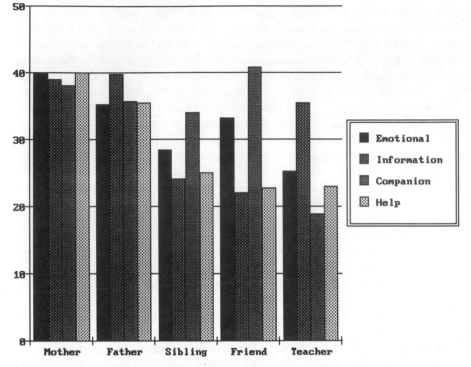

Figure 3.2. Mean ratings for children (ages 5 to 12) on social support functions obtained from key providers.

tional support. Instrumental and informational support are significantly lower. For friends, like siblings, companionship is the highest, followed by emotional support. And like siblings, friends are not viewed as particularly good sources of informational or instrumental support, either when compared with the other types of support that they do provide or with the other providers of these types of support.

Not surprisingly, teachers are viewed as providing mostly informational support. Other types of support from teachers are relatively rare.

The published study most similar to ours was conducted by Furman and Buhrmester (1985), who examined fifth- and sixth-grade children's relationships with their mother, father, grandparent, teacher, friend, and sibling. In general, their results were strikingly similar to ours. Friends were seen as the greatest sources of companionship, with both parents and siblings also relatively high in this category. Teachers were viewed as relatively uncommon sources of companionship. In addition, similar to our results, parents were viewed as the best sources of instrumental help, with friends and siblings rated significantly lower in this respect.

As such, our findings are quite consistent with those of earlier research with older children and indicate that the pattern of social support functions served by specific social relationships is established relatively early in life. Returning to our discussion of the organizing structure for these supportive relationships, we believe that such findings are best interpreted within the framework of support generalists and specialists. This framework for conceptualizing social networks was first introduced by Bogat, Caldwell, Rogosch, and Kriegler (1985) in order to address "the *interaction* between source and type of support" (p. 24, emphasis in original). A support generalist is a "core" network member who gives an individual many types of support, and a support specialist gives an individual a more limited type of support.

According to Figure 3.2, those individuals with "flat" profiles (i.e., the mother and father) function as support generalists; those with "jagged" profiles (i.e., siblings, friends, and teachers) function as support specialists. (Of course, it is possible to have a flat profile indicating no support of any type at all. Such persons are commonly referred to as "dead weight." They certainly should not be considered support generalists.) Establishing relationships with both support generalists and specialists is probably desirable, as they serve complementary functions. In an ecological model, this dual layering of relationships would be viewed as expanding not only the child's opportunities but also his or her "safety net" against developmental risks.

Our finding that parents act as support generalists is consistent with earlier research that family members were most apt to serve as support generalists for elementary school–aged children (Williams, Kriegler, & Bogat, 1988) and even for college students (Bogat et al., 1985). However, we should note that siblings, at least for our age groups, were clearly support specialists rather than generalists. This latter finding is consistent with the work by Cauce et al. (1987), which found that siblings were more similar to friends than to family in providing early adolescents with support.

Developmental Changes

Figure 3.3 illustrates the developmental changes in social support and conflict ratings for each provider. We included ratings for conflict here because the research on adults' social networks (Fiore, Becker, & Coppel, 1983) and adolescents (Barrera, 1981) suggests that the amount of conflict experienced in key relationships may be an important predictor of psychological adjustment, especially for individuals who are already experiencing high degrees of life stress. The youngest group we examined was drawn from the Cauce and Gonzales study (in progress). These children ranged in age from 5 to 7 and had not yet entered the first grade. The elementary and middle school–aged groups were drawn from the Standardization Study by Reid, Landesman, Treder, and Jaccard (in press). The elementary school–aged group were children 6 to 9, all of whom were already enrolled in at least the first grade. The middle school–aged group were preadolescent children aged 10 to 12. Although there is some overlap in age between our two youngest groups, all the children in the elementary school group were already attending the first grade.

An examination of Figure 3.3 reveals some intriguing developmental trends. The ratings of support from the mother are uniformly high and relatively consistent across ages. However, the older children tended to rate their mothers as a better source of information and help. The ratings of support from the father appear to increase with age across all categories. As was the case with mothers, such ratings are relatively high for all ages.

For siblings, support in all categories appears to decrease slightly for elementary school–aged children and then to increase for middle school–aged children. Nonetheless, these fluctuations in support appear to be relatively minor. More noteworthy is the high degree of reported conflict with siblings by children of all ages, which suggests that "sibling rivalry" is quite normal. The apparent increase in this conflict, which emerges after preschool, may be related to the beginning of formal school, an arena in which comparisons among children (including siblings) are common.

The ratings for informational support from teachers increase dramatically with age. This makes sense, especially because the youngest sample has yet to begin formal schooling. It is interesting, however, that the ratings for companionship from teachers decrease with age and that the ratings for conflict increase. This is in line with parents' observations that during the elementary school years, children are often quite close to their teachers and at times idealize them. However, by the time children are in middle school and/or junior high school, peer norms

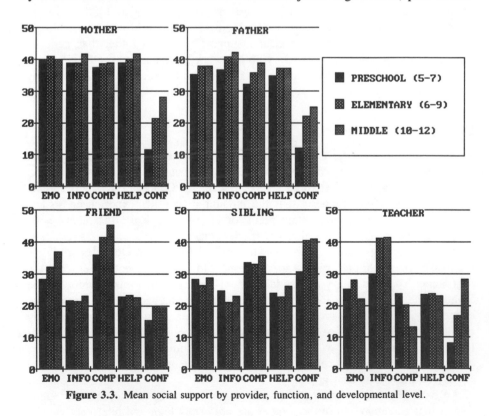

Figure 3.3. Mean social support by provider, function, and developmental level.

discourage strong attachments between children and their teachers. In fact, children who continue to have intense relationships with their teachers may come to be branded as "teacher's pets" or "traitors."

The ratings for support from friends demonstrate the most striking developmental changes. Although informational support and instrumental support change little throughout this age range, there is a dramatic increase, with age, in the degree to which friends are viewed as good sources of companionship and emotional support.

This finding is consistent with previous literature in this area. For example, Belle's and Longfellow's (1984) research with 5- to 12-year-old children indicates that with increasing age, children confide more in siblings and friends. Confiding may be seen as similar to our measures of companionship and/or emotional support. Hunter and Youniss (1982) studied children in the 4th, 7th, and 10th grades and found that intimacy (similar to our measure of emotional support) with mothers and fathers was relatively high and consistent across ages, whereas intimacy with friends increased with age. Berndt and Perry (1986) specifically examined children's perceptions of social support derived from friends and also found that the ratings for intimacy in friendships increased with age. Their study was conducted with 2nd-grade through 8th-grade students and also showed that older children more frequently mentioned emotional support as something they obtained from friendships.

Although for the younger children, friends functioned primarily as support specialists for companionship, for the older preadolescent children, friends also served as increasingly important sources of emotional support. It may even be that with increasing age, friends become support generalists. Indeed, it is our hunch that distinctions among support providers may become less relevant (if not irrelevant) during adulthood. At this time support specialists and generalists may be so well differentiated that specialists are rare in one's informal social network. For adults, the same persons with whom one feels most intimate and closest (i.e., high on emotional support and companionship) may also be those on whom they depend to provide instrumental and informational support. If adults need help moving, advice about how to deal with a troublesome colleague, or even a small loan, they will most likely turn to siblings, parents, or friends to whom they feel close.

The need for highly specialized types of information and aid surely does not cease in adulthood. But such help or support may be more likely to come from more remote (and remunerated) sources. Such sources may be lawyers, bankers, accountants, auto mechanics, and salesclerks, or even books and magazines—someone must be buying all those "self-help" and "how-to" manuals!

Yet such sources are not likely to be named as part of one's informal social network. This may, in part, explain why B. R. Sarason et al. (1987), in research with a college student sample, found that instruments that divided social support into distinct functions (e.g., instrumental support, informational support) did not produce sufficiently discrete subscales to be meaningful. Rather, their study identified a common core of support based on the "extent to which an individual is accepted, loved, and involved in relationships in which communication is open" (p. 813). This is consistent with our research with children.

For most children living in two-parent homes, our data indicate that this common core of support best explains the nature of their relationships with their parents. However, children also form important relationships with other children (siblings and peer friends) and "built-into their environment" professionals (school personnel), which are better understood within a framework of more detailed differentiations among support functions.

Teachers, for example, play an important role in most children's lives. Yet this role is structured in such a way that information is the support function that the teachers are expected to provide. Furthermore, those children to whom other children feel close as companions are apt to be too developmentally immature and lacking in resources to serve as appropriate sources of informational or instrumental support. It may even be counterproductive for children to use such persons as key providers of such support: We all probably can remember the disastrous effects of obtaining help from a slightly older sibling in fixing a broken vase or the friend who told us that beer had as much Vitamin C as orange juice did. If our hunches are correct, we should find confirmatory evidence in the relationship between social support and children's behavioral adjustment.

The Behavioral Impact of Children's Social Support

As we mentioned earlier, the research on social networks first flourished because the social support that social networks gave to persons was expected to enhance their adjustment and to protect them from the damaging effects of cumulative life stress. However, the research on children's social support networks has less often focused on such behavioral impacts. Early attempts to establish a relationship between the quality or amount of social support perceived by children or adolescents and their adjustment were inconclusive and at times quite discouraging.

In one of the earliest studies of this type, Burke and Weir (1978) examined the relationship between two sources of support, parents and peers, and their effect on the emotional and physical well-being of adolescents. They noted that girls, although perceiving more peer support, also reported more life stress and less well-being. An early study by Gad and Johnson (1980) also found no evidence that social support had a significant stress-buffering function for adolescents.

On the other side of the coin, Sandler's (1980) study of the relationship between the presence or absence of three possible support resources (i.e., one vs. two parents, the presence of an older sibling, and ethnic congruence with the neighborhood) on the adjustment of primary-grade inner-city children was more encouraging. He found that both parental and sibling support were associated with lower levels of maladjustment in these children. Cauce, Felner, and Primavera (1982), in a study of inner-city adolescents, likewise found that parental support (in this case gauged in more detail than simple presence or absence) was also associated with beneficial effects on adjustment. However, peer support was found to have both beneficial (in terms of self-esteem) and deleterious (on school achievement) impacts.

Most of these early studies were marred by the methodological shortcomings typical of that time, such as the use of measures without previously established reliability and, in some cases, relatively crude and global uses of the support construct. More recent and methodologically stringent studies have been conducted since then, but many of these deal exclusively with the role of peer friends (see Berndt, in press; Cauce, 1987). And no studies to date have focused on the behavioral impact of young children's own ratings of social support.

Yet the relatively sophisticated descriptions of children's networks that are now appearing in the literature are relevant to public policymakers and professionals working with children only if we can anchor children's social support to behavioral adjustment. If not, we are talking only to other researchers. Although this is certainly a useful activity, it cannot be the sole interest for those wanting to offer intervention programs for improving children's well-being.

Although the analyses still are preliminary, the initial findings of a study on children's adjustment to first grade (Cauce & Gonzales, in progress) allow us to examine such effects. This study used ratings of social support from the "My Family and Friends" scale, obtained from children in the late summer, before their entry into first grade. At that same time, their mothers completed a series of questionnaires, which yielded indices of their children's adjustment. The measures included:

1. The Achenbach Child Behavior Checklist (CBC), a widely used measure of children's adjustment. This measure yields two broad-band scores for Internalizing (INT) disorders and for Externalizing (EXT) disorders.

2. The Peabody Picture Vocabulary Test (PPVT), a widely used measure of children's receptive language vocabulary that yields an IQ score.

3. The Child Health and Behavior Inventory (CHB), developed by Landesman, Jaccard, and Reid (1988) for their study of grade-school children's families. The subscales used in this study were derived from factor analysis and are Cognitive Competence and Curiosity (COGN), Social Adjustment (SOCIAL), and Self-confidence (SELF).

4. The Adjustment to First Day and First Month of First Grade scales (DAY and MONTH, respectively) are unique to this study. Ratings for adjustment were provided by mothers on a simple Likert-type scale.

Table 3.2 reports the simple correlations between the children's ratings of the quality of social support they received—and the degree of conflict they experienced—in their relationships with key providers and the indices of adjustment. The relationships between support and adjustment are shown at the top of the table, and those between conflict and adjustment are at the bottom. The table is organized according to the provider, functional, and interactional models of support. In examining the provider model, we summed across all functional indices

TABLE 3.2.   Correlations Between Child's Social Support and Behavioral Adjustment

	INT	EXT	PPVT	COGN	SOCIAL	SELF	DAY	MONTH
Social Support								
PROVIDER MODEL								
Parents	−.01	−.15	−.16	.04	.24ᵃ	.22ᵃ	.13	.10
Peers	.13	.02	.01	−.23ᵃ	.03	−.11	.28ᵃ	.13
Teachers	−.01	−.08	.08	−.06	.03	.16	.09	.04
FUNCTIONAL MODEL								
Emotional	.07	−.09	.03	−.11	.20	.12	.20	.07
Informational	.08	−.02	.11	−.14	.04	.08	.21	.03
Companionship	.06	−.06	.05	.04	.10	.05	.12	.08
Instrumental	.07	−.01	.15	−.07	.02	.09	.13	.04
INTERACTIONAL MODEL								
Parents								
Emotional					.24ᵃ	.16		
Informational					.14	.22ᵃ		
Companionship					.01ᵃ	.18		
Instrumental					.25ᵃ	.22ᵃ		
Peers								
Emotional				−.20			.30ᵃ	
Informational				−.26ᵃ			.26ᵃ	
Companionship				.02			.21	
Instrumental				−.17			.16	
Conflict								
FUNCTIONAL MODEL	.19	.14	.16	−.05	.18	.09	−.22	−.31ᵃ
PROVIDER/INTERACTIONAL MODEL								
Parents	.27ᵃ	.02	.18	−.03	.18	−.06	−.35ᵇ	−.39ᵇ
Peers	.01	.02	.24ᵃ	−.03	.26ᵃ	.18	.31ᵃ	.17
Teachers	.05	.22ᵃ	−.12	−.03	−.09	.07	−.28ᵃ	−.26ᵃ

INT=CBC Internalizing; EXT=CBC Externalizing; PPVT=Peabody Picture Vocabulary Test; COGN=CHB Cognitive Competence and Curiosity; SOCIAL=CHB Social Adjustment; SELF=CHB Self-worth; DAY=Adjustment to First Day of First Grade; MONTH=Adjustment to First Month of First Grade.
[a] $p < 0.05$
[b] $p < 0.01$
$n = 59$ for parental and peer support; $n = 54$ for peer support except for analyses with school adjustment, in which $n = 45$ and 43, respectively.

of support to obtain a measure of total support for each provider. We then constructed indices of parental support by summing across mothers and fathers. We constructed the indices of peer support by summing across friends and siblings, and we studied teacher support by itself. These demarcations among support systems were suggested by previous research (Cauce et al., 1982, 1987) as well as by more detailed analyses of the data presented here.

For the functional model, we summed across all providers of each support function to obtain a measure of total support within each function across support providers. The interactional model delineates specific functional indices of support for specific categories of support providers. Because there is only one measure of conflict, in this case the provider and interactional model are identical.

Because of the large number of correlations that could otherwise be obtained, we examined relationships in the interactional model only if significant effects had been obtained from the other models. For example, we did not look into whether emotional support from parents was related to CBC Internalizing because neither total support from parents nor total emotional support was related to this measure. Although this approach might mask some effects, we felt that it was a minimal safeguard against Type I errors.

According to Table 3.2, an examination of the provider model suggests that the children's reports of total support from their parents was related to their mothers' reports of both social adjustment and self-esteem, whereas total peer support was related to cognitive competence and curiosity and to adjustment on the first day of school. Support from teachers was not related to any measures of adjustment. (Support from teachers, at this time, was gauged for the children's preschool or day care "teachers," not their first-grade teacher.)

By comparison, we discovered no significant relationships based on the functional model. As such, the provider model appears to be a more sensitive barometer of adjustment. Nonetheless, the interactional model provides information that further elucidates the relationships previously obtained. More specifically, it is emotional support and instrumental support from the parents that most strongly influence the children's social adjustment. Simple companionship (a measure that looks at enjoyment of shared activities) was not important in this respect. This finding makes sense, as it is probably within loving but relatively structured interactions such as those involved in helping a child with specific projects at home or school (the questions that were asked in this category) that children learn about norms for appropriate behavior. On the other hand, the relationship between parental support and self-esteem seems to be less predicated on any specific support function.

It is interesting that peer support was negatively related to cognitive competence and curiosity. Although research with adolescents produced similar results (Cauce et al., 1982, 1988), we were rather surprised to find them replicated for such young children. However, as an examination of the interactional model suggests, it is the use of peers as providers of information that is strongest in this respect. Companionship, the type of support most common (and possibly most appropriate) for peers at this age, does not demonstrate such negative effects. As we earlier noted, it may be counterproductive for young children to rely on peers for many types of information or instrumental help. Likewise, the positive relationship between informational support from peers and adjustment to the first day at school remains somewhat anomalous. Perhaps children are not good sources of general information, but they are better at giving one another information relevant to specific contexts, like school, with which they are intimately acquainted.

Similar to the relationship between parental support and self-esteem, that between peer support and adjustment to the first day of school seemed less specific to support function, although emotional support and informational support do seem most important. It is noteworthy that the bulk of our sample had either a sibling or a friend attending the same school. Therefore the simple presence of a close peer in the same setting may serve to ease the "first-day jitters," as one parent described the transition. However, this did not seem to extend beyond this very initial adjustment period.

In regard to the role of conflict in adjustment, the functional model reveals a significant relationship between total conflict and poorer adjustment at the end of the first month of school. However, once again the provider/interactional model appeared to be a more sensitive predictor. In terms of adjustment to both the first day and the first month of school, it seems that conflict with parents has deleterious effects. Conflict, especially when experienced during a stressful transition, may exacerbate this stress and overwhelm the child's capacity to cope effectively. Likewise, studies with adults and adolescents that find the greatest relationship between conflict and adjustment were conducted with high-stress samples, such as caregivers for victims of Alzheimer's disease (Fiore et al., 1983; Pagel & Becker, 1988) or pregnant teenagers (Barrera, 1981).

In our sample, conflict with parents also seemed related to higher scores on Internalizing. This measure largely refers to social withdrawal, depression, and somaticizing. It makes sense that children who are angry at their parents may express it through such indirect means, given the degree to which parents, at least for such young children, essentially control most parameters of the relationship. It is interesting that conflict with teachers is, instead, related to Externalizing disorders, which consist largely of "acting out" and aggressive behaviors. Perhaps children feel safer acting out their anger toward their teachers. Or, more likely, children with an externalizing style elicit more conflict with teachers. The fact that those children who report more anger in interactions with their preschool teachers are also apt to have more difficulty adjusting to the first day and month of school agrees with the notion that knowledge acquired in one setting generalizes to similar settings.

It was surprising that conflict with peers was positively related to higher scores on the PPVT, better social adjustment, and better adjustment to the first day of school. At first we suspected that children who reported more conflict with peers were more cognitively advanced and that this was responsible for the other effects. However, partial (second-order) correlations, controlling for this relationship, did not suggest that this was the case. In addition, we should note that conflict and support from peers were not highly related. Perhaps conflict with peers (as opposed to conflict with adults) indicates a healthy manifestation of assertiveness. Given the hierarchical, individualistic, and competitive nature of Western societies, engaging in "combat" with peers, but not authorities, may well be adaptive. Further investigation of this phenomenon is needed.

As such, it appears that the children's ratings of their social support do relate to their behavioral adjustment. Although relatively small in magnitude, the correlations obtained in our analyses were highly interpretable. The generally positive effects of adult support and the mixed effects of peer support are similar to patterns obtained with adolescents. Such results are also strengthened by the fact that social support (and conflict) ratings were obtained from the children them-selves, whereas ratings of behavioral adjustment were obtained from a separate source, the mother. In most of the adult and adolescent research, the individual is the source of both support and adjustment ratings. We noted that relationships obtained in this fashion may be "artificially inflated" (Gore, 1978). That is, persons may, in effect, explain their current levels of distress (or well-being) through their ratings of relationships with others. The results we present, how-ever, are free of this possible confound.

These results are preliminary and should be interpreted cautiously. The sample size was small and quite homogenous. Currently we are analyzing the results for these same indices obtained during our second and third waves of data collection. Replications of these results both within time two and time three panels as well as in longitudinal analyses would lend further credence to our initial findings.

SUMMARY AND OVERVIEW

Compelling reasons to investigate social support came from (1) research with adult populations indicating that individual differences in perceived support may originate in early childhood (I.G. Sarason et al., 1986) and (2) ecological models of child development that emphasize the importance of children's own developing social networks in influencing daily experiences and adjustment (Bronfenbrenner, 1979; Garbarino, 1982).

Methods for assessing social support during childhood include behavioral ob-servations, parent reports, and self-reports. Although there are advantages and disadvantages to each of the methods, self-report has the distinct advantage of providing information from the child's own perspective about his or her social world.

An overview of children's descriptions of the types of support obtained from key providers reveals profiles for parents, siblings, peers, and teachers that differ from one another in a highly interpretable manner. For example, children perceive their parents as multipurpose social support providers or support generalists, in contrast with friends and teachers whom they perceive as support specialists, more limited in their social value. That is, friends are perceived as being good sources of companionship but less able to provide direct help or informational support. Conversely, teachers receive high ratings for informational support.

Developmental trends were found in the perceptions of social support reported by children during middle childhood (ages 5 to 12). Although children of all ages rated support from mothers as relatively high, they rated support from fathers higher with age. Young children (ages 5 to 9) tended to perceive their teachers as better sources of companionship support than did the preadolescents (ages 10 to 12), who also perceived their relationships with their teachers as more conflic-tual. In addition, friends appear to serve as an increasingly important source of support as children grow older. Preadolescents reported perceiving their friends as significantly better sources of emotional and companionship support than did the younger children. Siblings, like friends, appeared to be an important source of companionship. Unlike friends, however, the relationship appears to be normatively fraught with conflict. This conflict appears to increase with the onset of formal schooling.

There has been some controversy over whether the organizing structure of a person's social support networks more closely approximates a functional or a provider model. Collectively, our data, which pertain to both preschool and elementary school–aged children, support both the Provider and the Provider x Functional (i.e., interactional) models. That is, although our data clearly show that a provider model is superior to a functional model, the combination of both enhances our understanding of the behavioral impact of children's social support.

Although we view as preliminary those analyses relevant to the behavioral impact of support, they do indicate that support from parents is related to higher self-esteem and better social adjustment in children. Support from peers appears to ease the transition into first grade (albeit only on the first day), but it is also negatively related to cognitive competence. This negative relationship appears to be mainly a function of using peers for informational support, a function for which peers may not be well suited. Support from teachers did not appear to be related to adjustment, at least in preschool.

In interpreting these results, it is important to remember that it is not appropriate to infer causality from correlational analyses. Less socially adept and self-confident children may elicit less support from their parents, friends, and/or teachers, or they may simply view such persons as less supportive. Social relationships go both ways, and so in stressing the importance of social support we should not forget that sometimes you get only what you ask for or work toward. The most definitive statement we can make at this time is that more research is needed.

TIPS FOR SELECTING MEASURES OF CHILDREN'S SOCIAL SUPPORT

Tip 1

We urge researchers in the field to select measures of social support for children that already have been developed. Part of the problem in wading through the extensive research with adults is that so many investigations used measures unique to their study. It thus is difficult to build up a coherent body of knowledge in the field because the results obtained from different studies are not comparable. Although this tip may seem self-serving, Wolchik et al. (in press) provide a good summary of tools available from other researchers.

Tip 2

We recommend using a scale with good psychometric properties and clear conceptual rationales. Because of children's developmental "limitations" and their relative lack of control over their environment, psychometric properties considered "good" for adults and children's measures will vary. In particular, internal and test–retest reliabilities for most children's measures run lower than do comparable measures for adults. Nonetheless, we believe that alpha coefficients of about .50 should be considered a lower boundary for adequacy. Lower limits for test–retest reliability are harder to speculate about. First, they depend on the time interval between assessments. Second, Reid et al. (in press) found that low test–retest reliability, in children, may reflect an unstable environment and a very sensitive tool. Beyond internal consistency, we believe that it is most important to look for sound conceptual rationales for measures. Sound convergent validity is still not available for most measures at this time. However, as research progresses, this consideration should become an increasingly important guide.

Tip 3

When working with children it is essential to keep in mind their developmental level. For younger children, we recommend your choosing tools that allow the child to make ratings in as concrete a way as possible. Such tools should allow the child to express himself or herself through more than one modality: verbal, visual, and manual, for example. Our own experience revealed that sometimes children initially give rather global and seemingly facile verbal responses to questions, such as "Oh, my brother, we fight all the time." Yet when asked to make ratings on a barometer, the same child might wrinkle his brow and then conclude, "Well, it's really not all the way up at the top," and while moving the barometer down some, "It's less than that for sure; sometimes we like to play."

We believe that it is possible for older children to use tools similar to those used with adults. But, here, too, the child's developmental level needs to be considered. Cauce and her colleagues gathered meaningful data from early adolescents as young as 12 years of age, using a simple measure that gives children specific categories of support provider(s) (such as mother or friends). In one study, however, Cauce asked seventh graders to fill out a social network scale (like the one used by Hirsch, 1980, with adults) and found that they were unable to grasp the necessary procedures, even though there were four experimenters helping each group of 20 to 30 children.

This attempt was made with an inner-city, mostly ethnic minority sample of youths who, on average, were two grades behind the norm on academic achievement tests. It is possible that such tasks can be completed by middle- to upper-class children, although the results obtained still could not be compared with those from less-advantaged children. In general, we believe that it is better to use tools that can be completed even by children in the lowest 20% of their age's academic-functioning level. (Of course, there will always be some children in the extreme lower ranges of functioning for whom more specialized procedures are required.)

Tip 4

For young populations you should choose measures that at least allow you to gauge support from different categories of providers. Evidence from various studies now shows that a provider model of social support is most suitable for children. But the evidence for a purely functional model is, at best, shaky, and so we think that such measures are probably not a good bet to use with children. We believe that measures that take into account both provider and function are best, at least at this time. Such measures will permit you to examine the effects of support using the interactional model. In the research we presented, this model appeared to enhance our understanding of relationships obtained using the simple provider model.

Tip 5

When theoretically justifiable, adjust the social support scales to be relevant to your sample. In many respects, most of the social support scales for children primarily provide a format for gathering data. When examining the social networks of children with chronic health problems, for example, it seems perfectly reasonable to include "doctor" or "nurse" among the other potential sources of support to be examined.

FUTURE DIRECTIONS IN SOCIAL SUPPORT RESEARCH WITH YOUNG CHILDREN

When mapping directions for future social support research on children, we still are in unexplored territory, and so the possibilities are endless. We urge only that you do not let the model provided by the adult literature hamper your creativity. Such research has in the past often concentrated on the relationship between support and pathology, but instead, we would like the child literature to retain a focus on the development of competence and health. In addition, we recommend that research strategies with young children adopt a more idiographic approach than was typical of early research in the adult literature.

We also would like to see some research on those children who report low levels of support. Reid et al. (in press) discovered that not all children reported the "average" social support profile discussed earlier, in which parents were considered the best multipurpose social provider. That is, some children reported being very dissatisfied or "let down" by the lack of support from parents. A small portion of children reported that they did not have friends or siblings in whom they could confide satisfactorily. Children with atypical support profiles represent a potentially "at-risk" group warranting further investigation and follow-up.

When examining the factors relating to the low levels of social support reported by some children, it is important to consider both child and situation variables. That is, some of the children may be in socially deprived environments in which support is simply not available. However, some children may also have developed behavioral patterns that in effect "scare away" support or hinder the child's receptivity to support when it is offered. Very different interventions would be suitable for these different groups of children.

We also would like further research to find out whether there is a "minimal" level of social support that children need in order to thrive. For example, one adult figure who serves as a support generalist may be sufficient for most children for healthy functioning. Conversely, the absence of such a figure may be a strong indicator of potential risk. Research on children's friendships, for example, shows that it is the presence of one or a few close friendships that is important to adequate adjustment, rather than a child's general popularity with the larger peer group (Berndt, in press). Studies of adults likewise indicate that the presence of one intimate confidant may be more important than a wider social network without such a person.

Research addressing this question would best be conducted with varied populations of children considered to be at high risk. For example, we still know little, if anything, about the social networks of children who live in poverty, those who are homeless, or those who live with parents who may be psychologically or physically unavailable because of alcoholism, drug abuse, or physical and/or mental health problems. (An exception is the work by Hirsch and Reischl [1985] with children of depressed and arthritic parents.) We also know little about the social networks of children in multiple-problem homes, and we know more about the networks of children in the underclass from journalism than from research.

We also believe that there is a need for more research on environmental and cultural differences in patterns of social support networks. Tietjen (in press) offered an interesting account of the differences in the typical social networks of children living in urban and suburban Sweden, as compared with those growing up on a village beach between the sea and jungle in Papua, New Guinea. Although we would expect such differences to be less striking among children who currently live in the United States, ethnicity, social class, and religion[2]—as well as residence in urban and suburban as opposed to rural regions—may, in effect, lead to different expectations, norms, and possibilities for social relationships.

In regard to research strategies, we believe that it is important to conduct longitudinal studies. Although cross-sectional research, like that reported in this chapter, is helpful in elucidating developmental changes, longitudinal studies more adequately address this issue. A better understanding of naturally occurring changes in children's networks would, in turn, help us construct interventions that are age appropriate and more likely to be accepted by the children they serve. For example, peer-based interventions seem particularly suitable for pre-adolescents.

Longitudinal research is also needed to address the relationship between social support/conflict and behavioral adjustment. In the study we presented, conflict with adults, both parents and teacher, appeared to have an impact that extended to the first month of school. Although support from peers made adjustment easier

---

[2]By differences in religion, we are referring not only to identification with a specific religious group (e.g., Catholic, Jewish) but, rather, to variations in the degree to which religious concerns are central to family life. Indeed, it could be argued that in some fundamentalist denominations, religion is culture.

on the first day of school, its effects had faded away by the end of the first month. A better understanding of which types of support from which providers have more lasting impacts at what ages would also help us develop more effective strategies for intervention.

Finally, we recommend that whenever possible, research designed to inform public policy include children's own reports. A review of the literature reveals that children's own appraisals are not frequently used, even in family research for which children's social and emotional adjustment is the principal outcome measure. Our data indicate that even young children understand their social world and can tell us about it. Because the welfare of children is so often the avowed goal of our social policy and prevention/intervention programs, we should pay attention to what the children themselves can tell us.

Likewise, we would like to see more collaboration and exchange among those conducting research on children's social support (i.e., academic researchers), using what Rook and Dooley (1985) called "analytic" strategies, and those whose knowledge comes from applied efforts with programs and interventions aimed at increasing children's social support. A recent initiative by the Carnegie Council on Adolescence (1988), which brought together analytic researchers and program developers, is a good first step in this direction.

Evaluations of programs that purport to have social support as a key ingredient would be more useful if they included measures of social support, similar to those used by analytic researchers, in their assessments. As such, they could determine whether increases in social support were a result of the intervention and how children's ratings of support (before and after the intervention) compared with normative data.

The study of children's social support networks is still in its infancy. But the child is most certainly born, and rapid growth is the norm in these early years. We hope that continued research will result in firm and confident first steps.

REFERENCES

Achenbach, T. M., & Edelbrook, C. S. (1982). *Manual for the Child Behavior Checklist and Child Behavior Profile*. Burlington, VT: Child Psychiatry, University of Vermont.

Barrera, M. (1981). Social support in the adjustment of pregnant adolescents: Assessment issues. In B. Gottlieb (Ed.), *Social networks and social support* (pp. 69–96). Beverly Hills, CA: Sage.

Belle, D. (1989). *Children's social networks and social supports.* New York: Wiley.

Belle, D., & Longfellow, C. (August, 1984). *Turning to others: Children's use of confidants.* Paper presented at the meeting of the American Psychological Association, Toronto.

Berndt, T. J. (in press). Obtaining support from friends during childhood and adolescence. In D. Belle (Ed.), *Children's social networks and social supports.* New York: Wiley.

Berndt, T. J., & Perry, T. B. (1986). Children's perceptions of friendships as supportive relationships. *Developmental Psychology, 22,* 640–648.

Bierman, K. L. (1983). Cognitive development and clinical interviews with children. In B. Lahey & A. Kazdin (Eds.), *Advances in clinical child psychology* (Vol. 6, pp. 217–250). New York: Plenum.

Bigelow, B. J. (1977). Children's friendship expectations: A cognitive–developmental study. *Child Development, 48,* 246–253.

Bogat, G. A., Caldwell, R. A., Rogosch, F., & Kriegler, J. A. (1985). Differentiating specialists and generalists within college students' social support networks. *Journal of Youth and Adolescence, 14,* 23–35.

Borkowski, J. G., Reid, M. K., & Kurtz, B. E. (1984). Metacognition and retardation: Paradigmatic, theoretical, and applied perspectives. In P. H. Brooks, R. Sperber, & C. McCauley (Eds.), *Learning and cognition in the mentally retarded* (pp. 55–75). Hillsdale, NJ: Erlbaum.

Bowlby, J. (1969). *Attachment and loss: Vol. 1. Attachment.* New York: Basic Books.

Bowlby, J. (1980). *Attachment and loss: Vol. 3. Loss: Sadness and depression.* New York: Basic Books.

Braiker, H. B., & Kelly, H. H. (1979). Conflict in the development of close relationships. In R. L. Burgess & T. L. Huston (Eds.), *Social exchange in developing relationships* (pp. 135–168). New York: Academic Press.

Brody, G. H., Stoneman, Z., & MacKinnon, C. (1982). Role asymmetries in interactions between school-aged children, their younger siblings, and their friends. *Child Development, 53,* 1364–1370.

Bronfenbrenner, U. (1979). *The ecology of human development.* Cambridge, MA: Harvard University Press.

Brown, A. L., Bransford, J. D., Ferrara, R. A., & Campione, J. D. (1983). Learning, remembering, and understanding. In P. H. Mussen (Ed.), *Handbook of child psychology* (4th ed., vol. 3, pp 77–166). New York: Wiley.

Bryant, B. K. (1985). The neighborhood walk: Sources of support in middle childhood. *Monographs of the Society for Research in Child Development, 50*(3, Serial No. 210).

Burke, R. J., & Weir, T. (1978). Benefits to adolescents of informal helping relationships with their parents and peers. *Psychological Reports, 42,* 1175–1184.

Cauce, A. M. (1986). Social networks and social competence: Exploring the effects of early adolescent friendships. *American Journal of Community Psychology, 14,* 607–628.

Cauce, A. M. (1987). School and peer competence: A test of domain-specific self-concept. *Developmental Psychology, 23,* 287–291.

Cauce, A. M., Felner, R. D., & Primavera, J. (1982). Social support in high-risk adolescents: Structural components and adaptive impact. *American Journal of Community Psychology, 10,* 417–428.

Cauce, A. M., & Gonzales, N. (in progress). *Children's social support and their adjustment to first grade.* Manuscript, University of Washington.

Cauce, A. M., Hannan, K., & Sargeant, M. S. (August, 1987). *Negative events, social support, and locus of control in early adolescence: Contributions to well-being.* Paper presented at the meeting of the American Psychological Association, New York.

Cauce, A. M. & Srebnik, D. (in press). Peer social networks and social support: A focus for preventive efforts. In L. A. Bond & B. Compas (Eds.), *Primary prevention in the schools.* Newbury Park, CA: Sage.

Clarke-Stewart, K. A. (1978). And Daddy makes three: The father's impact on mother and young child. *Child Development, 49,* 466–478.

Cochran, M. M., & Brassard, J. A. (1979). Child development and personal social networks. *Child Development, 50,* 601–616.

Cochran, M. M., & Riley, D. (1985). *Mother reports of children's personal networks: Antecedents, concomitants, and consequences.* Paper presented at the meeting of the Society for Research in Child Development, Toronto.

Cohen, S., & McKay, G. (1984). Social support, stress, and the buffering hypothesis: A theoretical analysis. In A. Baum, J. E. Singer, & S. E. Taylor (Eds.), *Handbook of psychology and health* (Vol. 4, pp. 253–267). Hillsdale, NJ: Erlbaum.

Cohen, S., & Wills, T. (1985). Stress, social support, and the buffering hypothesis. *Psychological Bulletin, 98,* 310–357.

Crittenden, P. M. (1985). Social networks, quality of child rearing and child development. *Child Development, 65,* 1299–1313.

Crnic, K. A., Greenberg, M. T., Ragozin, A. S., Robinson, N. M., & Basham, R. B. (1983). Effects of stress and social support on mothers and premature and full-term infants. *Child Development, 54,* 209–217.

Crnic, K. A., Greenberg, M. T., Robinson, N. M., & Ragozin, A. S. (1984). Maternal stress and social support: Effects on the mother–infant relationship from birth to eighteen months. *American Journal of Orthopsychiatry, 54* (2), 365–379.

Dunn, J. (1983). Sibling relationships in early childhood. *Child Development, 54,* 787–811.

Fiore, J., Becker, J., & Coppel, D. (1983). Social network interactions: A buffer or a stress. *American Journal of Community Psychology, 11,* 423–439.

Flavell, J. H. (1982). On cognitive development. *Child Development, 53,* 1–10.

Furman, W., & Buhrmester, D. (1985). Children's perceptions of the personal relationships in their social networks. *Developmental Psychology, 21,* 1016–1024.

Gad, M. T., & Johnson, J. H. (1980). Correlates of adolescent life stress as related to race, SES, and levels of perceived social support. *Journal of Clinical Child Psychology, 9,* 13–16.

Garbarino, J. (1982). *Children and Families in the Social Environment.* New York: Aldine.

Gore, S. (1978). Effects of social support in moderating health consequences of unemployment. *Journal of Health and Social Behavior, 19,* 157–165.

Harter, S., & Pike. R. (1984). The pictorial scale of perceived competence and social acceptance for young children. *Child Development, 55,* 1969–1982.

Hayes, D. S. (1978). Cognitive bases for liking and disliking among preschool children. *Child Development, 49,* 906–909.

Heller, K., & Swindle, R. (1983). Social networks, perceived social support, and coping with stress. In R. Felner, L. Jason, J. Moritsugu, & S. Farber (Eds.), *Preventive psychology* (pp. 87–103). NY: Pergamon.

Hirsch, B. J. (1980). Natural support systems and coping with major life changes. *American Journal of Community Psychology, 8,* 159–172.

Hirsch, B. J., & Reischl, T. (1985). Social networks and developmental psychopathology: A comparison of adolescent children of a depressed, arthritic, or normal parent. *Journal of Abnormal Psychology, 94,* 272–281.

Hunter, F. T., & Youniss, J. (1982). Changes in functions of three relationships during adolescence. *Developmental Psychology, 18,* 806–811.

Kagan, J. (1984). *The nature of the child.* New York: Basic Books.

Kagan, J., Hans, S., Markowitz, A., Lopez, D., & Sigal, H. (1982). In B. A. Maher & W. B. Maher (Eds.), *Progress in experimental personality research* (Vol. 11, pp. 120–141). New York: Academic Press.

Landesman, S., Jaccard, J., & Gunderson, V. (in press). The family environment: The combined influence of family behavior, goals, strategies, resources, and individual experiences. In M. Lewis and S. Fienman (Eds.), *Social influences and development.* New York: Plenum.

Landesman, S., Jaccard, J., & Reid, M. (1988). *Child Health and Behavior.* Unpublished instrument, University of Washington.

Lewis, M., Feiring, C., & Brooks-Gunn, J. (1987). The social networks of children with and without handicaps: A developmental perspective. In S. Landesman, P. M. Vietze, & M. J. Begab (Eds.), *Living environments and mental retardation* (pp. 377–400). Washington, DC: American Association of Mental Deficiency.

Lewis, M., Feiring, C., & Kotsonis, M. (1984). The social networks of 3-year-old children. In M. Lewis (Ed.), *Beyond the dyad* (pp. 351–378). New York: Plenum.

Pagel, M., & Becker, J. (1988). Depressive thinking and depression: Relations with personality and social resources. *Journal of Personality and Social Psychology, 52,* 1043–1052.

Parke, R. D., Power, T. G., & Gottman, J. M. (1979). Conceptualizing and quantifying influence patterns in the family triad. In M. E. Lamb, S. J. Suomi, & G. R. Stephenson (Eds.), *Social interaction analysis: Methodological issues.* Madison: University of Wisconsin Press.

Pearlin, L. I., Menaghan, E. G., Lieberman, M. A., & Mullen, J. T. (1981). The stress process. *Journal of Health and Social Behavior, 22,* 337–356.

Reid, M., & Landesman, S. (1986). *My family and friends: A social support dialogue instrument for children.* Seattle: University of Washington Press.

Reid, M., Landesman, S., Jaccard, J., & Rabkin, J. (1987). *Dialogues with children: The child as reporter for family and self.* Paper presented at the Society for Research in Child Development, Washington, DC.

Reid, M., Landesman, S., Treder, R., & Jaccard, J. (1989). "My family and friends." 6 to 12 year old children's perceptions of social support. *Child Development, 60,* 896–910.

Rook, K. S., & Dooley, D. (1985). Applying social support research: Theoretical problems and future directions. *Journal of Social Issues, 41,* 5–28.

Sandler, I. N. (1980). Social support resources, stress, and maladjustment of poor children. *American Journal of Community Psychology, 7,* 425–440.

Sarason, I. G., & Sarason, B. R. (Eds.). (1985) *Social support: Theory, research, application.* Dordrecht, Netherlands: Martinus Nijhoff.

Sarason, I. G., Sarason, B. R., & Shearin, E. N. (1986). Social support as an individual difference variable: Its stability, origins, and relational aspects. *Journal of Personality and Social Psychology, 50,* 845–855.

Sarason, B. R., Shearin, E. N., Pierce, G. R., & Sarason, I. G. (1987). Interrelations of social support measures: Theoretical and practical implications. *Journal of Personality and Social Psychology, 52,* 813–832.

Schaefer, C., Coyne, J., & Lazarus, R. (1981). The health-related functions of social support. *Journal of Behavioral Medicine, 4*, 381–406.

Tietjen, A. M. (1982). The social networks of preadolescent children in Sweden. *International Journal of Behavioral Development, 5*, 111–130.

Tietjen, A. (in press). The ecology of children's social support networks. In D. Belle (Ed.), *Children's social networks and social supports*. New York: Wiley.

Vygotsky, L. S. (1978). *Mind in society: The development of higher psychological processes* (M. Cole, V. John-Steiner, S. Scribner, & E. Souberman, Eds. and Trans.). Cambridge, MA: Harvard University Press.

Wellman, H. M. (1978) Knowledge of the interaction of memory variables: A developmental study of metamemory. *Developmental Psychology, 14*, 24–29.

Williams, K. M., Kriegler, J. A., & Bogat, G. A. (1988). *Age, gender, and racial differences in children's social support*. Unpublished manuscript, Michigan State University.

Wolchik, S. A., Beals, J., & Sandler, I. N. (in press). Mapping children's support networks: Conceptual and methodological contributions. In D. Belle (Ed.). *Children's social networks and social supports*. New York: Wiley.

Zigler, E., & Weiss, H. (1985). Family support systems: An ecological approach to child development. In N. Rapoport (Ed.), *Children, youth and families: The action–research relationship*. Cambridge, England: Cambridge University Press.

PART TWO

Social Support in Personal Relationships

A major emphasis in the current research on social support is the change from measuring aggregated support to understanding the roles, both positive and negative, of specific relationships in the perception of social support and the effects of being supported.

Chapter 4 discusses a theoretical structure that might be used to integrate the various historically held conceptions of social support. To illustrate how the interacting facets of this theoretical view might be explored, the authors concentrate on one, the sense of acceptance, which they define and relate to other parts of the model through a discussion of research findings. They show how research on particular relationships—past, present, and continuing—can improve our understanding of social support.

Chapter 5 argues that social support may be most usefully viewed as an interdependence between the recipient and the provider that includes both the needs and goals of each and the problems of coordinating them. The authors discuss these issues in the context of a study of couples in which one spouse had had an uncomplicated myocardial infarction. The adjustment of each member of the couple was part of a dyadic process in which each partner struggled to preserve his or her own well-being as well as that of the other person and at the same time tried to carry out the specific tasks related to adapting to changed circumstances and recovery.

Stable self-conceptions are important to helping people organize their experiences, guide their behavior, and predict the future. For this reason, individuals may work to maintain even negative self-conceptions. Chapter 6 suggests that one aspect of relationships that may promote health is their provision of identity support in times of stress. Social support offered in relationships, however, may sometimes undermine health because it may also undermine the recipient's self-conception and perception of control of his or her environment.

One aspect of the interactional approach to social support is the degree of reciprocity of supportive interactions. Chapter 7 offers ideas and questions that can be used to clarify the contradictions in what little is known about the effects of balanced and imbalanced support patterns. The authors provide information on racial differences and on the effect of age and disability status on perceptions of reciprocity and on happiness and satisfaction.

A person's cultural context shapes his or her interpretation of objects, events, and relationships as supportive or not supportive and influences his or her perception of what constitutes support, who should provide it, to whom, and under what circumstances. Chapter 8 discusses these differences in examples of culturally related conceptions of the self and social relationships. The stress commonly experienced by members of newly constituted stepfamilies is used to illustrate the effects of these cultural factors. Such stress is intensified by the absence of terminology and rules in the American culture that could help structure stepfamily life.

According to Chapter 9, if social support is defined as interpersonal transactions in which problem-focused aid and encouragement are exchanged, rather than as the feeling of being cared for by others, social support and companionship are not identical. Companionship has a continuing importance and describes a source of intrinsic pleasure of shared leisure rather than a feeling of embeddedness. Each of the two constructs may be relevant to somewhat different dimensions of psychological well-being: Support helps restore equilibrium, and companionship helps elevate current contentment.

CHAPTER 4

Social Support: The Sense of Acceptance and the Role of Relationships

BARBARA R. SARASON, GREGORY R. PIERCE, AND IRWIN G. SARASON

University of Washington

For better, for worse, for richer, for poorer, in sickness and in health, to love and to cherish till death us do part.

THE BOOK OF COMMON PRAYER

It may seem unusual to start a chapter on social support with a passage from the Episcopal marriage vows. Yet its message refers to the two most important points to be discussed in this chapter: (1) the concept of perceived support as a sense of unconditional acceptance no matter what happens and (2) the role of social relationships in creating this perception and in validating it over time. This chapter will make a case for the need to integrate information about specific relationships and categories of relationships, both past and present, to understand perceived social support. First we will examine what is known about the role of early experience in shaping people's perceptions of themselves and of what they can expect from relationships. In addition to exploring the role of relationships in the development of these stable personal characteristics, we will show how the effects of both perceived support and supportive behavior can be better understood by studying them in the context of the ongoing relationships in which they occur.

The term *social support* is an umbrella term that covers a variety of diverse phenomena. This chapter describes some of what we think is hiding under that umbrella. Social support, like a root-bound potted plant, can profit not only from being divided but also from the fertilization of its theoretical underpinnings. There are a number of reasons that a division would be beneficial. Despite the growing consensus that social support research findings have been muddied by constructs based on various definitions, researchers, paying lip service to this view, continue to use different conceptions of social support for their investigations (B. Sarason, Shearin, Pierce, & Sarason, 1987). Further, social support as a predictor variable has not performed as well as most researchers would like. This too suggests that we need to think about how to refine our measuring instru-

97

ments and also our definitions. In this chapter we will present our ideas about how this division might take place and suggest how the resulting constructs might be defined, studied, and interrelated.

Perhaps one of the most important developments in the social support literature is the agreement that the only aspect of social support that is related to health outcomes is *perceived support,* or the belief that help would be available if needed, as contrasted with help that is actually received (Blazer, 1982; Kessler & McLeod, 1984). These data raise questions about what processes are involved and about how people who perceive this availability differ from others who do not. Although this second question has some commonsense answers, most of them can be refuted, at least in part. For instance, it can be argued that perceived support is simply an expectation based on the past receipt of socially supportive behaviors. A number of studies (Abdel-Halim, 1982: Ganster, Fusilier, & Mayes, 1986; Kaufman & Beehr, 1986), however, make a convincing case for a negative relationship between the receipt of socially supportive behaviors and health. Much of what we often call socially supportive behavior usually is offered only when a person is clearly experiencing stress, rather than when he or she is in less difficult circumstances (Cutrona, 1986). Because not all the stressful situations in which people find themselves are independent of personal behaviors, at least some stressful situations and the resulting support may occur as a result of personal characteristics and coping styles. Another explanation for the differences in perception of support is that some people are fortunate enough to be a part of a network of others who will provide support should the need arise. But this explanation, too, is not completely satisfactory because many ways of assessing social network characteristics do not show a close relationship between them and measures of perceived social support (B. Sarason et al., 1987). What, then, are perceived social support instruments measuring, and how can we best evaluate this construct?

SOCIAL SUPPORT AS A PERSONALITY CHARACTERISTIC

We earlier stated that perceived social support might be considered as a personality variable, as it remains quite stable over time, even during periods of developmental transition when environmental change may peak (I. Sarason, Sarason, & Shearin, 1986).

If we consider social support as a personality variable, we must then ask how it develops. One of the simplest explanations is that it develops as a consequence of a person's physical attractiveness. Research by developmental psychologists has shown that people respond differently to attractive young children than to children not so appealing in appearance. Not only do people pay more attention to attractive children, but their judgments regarding the child's behavior and personality characteristics also differ (Berkowitz & Frodi, 1979; Dion, 1974; Ritter & Langlois, 1988). A simplified explanation of how perceived social support develops is that children who receive this increased interest and attention may develop more positive self-concepts and may also come to have different and more positive expectations of the reactions of others with whom they have contact. These expectations may then lead these children to be more outgoing and, consequently, to be more sociable, thereby reinforcing and enhancing their social skills, with the result that in adulthood they have an extensive supportive network.

Most people would agree that such an explanation is too simple, but is there any truth in it? Although the literature on social psychology has demonstrated that attractiveness is important in at least the initial stages of attraction and relationship formation, few data pertain directly to the issues of either physical attractiveness or social skills as they may affect social support. However, in one study of college students' interactions, raters judged photographs of students differing in social support (B. Sarason, Sarason, Hacker, & Basham, 1985). This study did not find significant differences in physical attractiveness between those at the high and low ends of the perceived social support distribution. But this same study, as well as subsequent research, discovered that people high in perceived social support do have social skills superior to those of people low in social support (I. Sarason, Sarason, & Shearin, 1986) but the causal factors in this relationship have yet to be established.

Researchers with a social psychological perspective deal with issues of attraction between individuals on a quite different level of explanation. In studies of attraction they recognize the effects of familiarity on attitudes of liking and the positive view of others. Such information can also help explain the development of relationships. This work can be extended from the acquisition and maintenance of current relationships to thinking about early relationships as well. For example, most young children see their mothers as beautiful and enjoy stroking their familiar facial contours. Later, even into adult life, familiarity often leads to positive affect. For example, reminders of favorite dishes from childhood create nostalgia in most people and often make them think of their mother as a wonderful cook, even if she was not.

Another explanation of individual differences in social support takes a more psychodynamic view. That is, it uses attachment theory, as developed in the writings of John Bowlby (1969, 1973, 1980, 1988) who originally emphasized the ethological tendency of people, especially of the young, to approach the familiar and to avoid the unfamiliar as a part of their self-preservation strategy.

In Bowlby's view (1988), these early experiences shape the development and quality of intimate adult relationships. Some of the work on familiarity may be relevant here. According to researchers interested in the long-term results of attachment, one result of the appeal of familiarity may be reflected in individuals' selection of partners who fit their mental model of previous attachment figures, even if these were not optimal relationships as judged by outside viewers or personal criteria.

The development of a stable characteristic related to perceptions of support availability and a propensity to interpret behaviors as supportive we will call a *sense of social support*. This sense is a consequence of the personality development ensuing from such experiences. In the next section we will discuss how the attachment literature can help in understanding how such a deeply embedded and consistent characteristic might arise.

THE ATTACHMENT EXPERIENCE AS A SOURCE OF PERCEIVED SOCIAL SUPPORT

Some researchers hypothesized that the early experience with an attachment figure contributes to a person's schema for future relationships and feelings of self-worth, self-efficacy, and a capacity to enjoy intimacy (Hazan & Shaver, 1987; Reis & Shaver, 1987, B. Sarason et al., 1987; I. Sarason, Sarason, Shearin, & Pierce, 1987).

The attachment experience itself may help form the child's personality rather than simply manifest his or her genetically determined characteristics. This is a reasonable conjecture, as attachment, operationally defined as parent–child behavior in Ainsworth's Strange Situation (Ainsworth & Wittig, 1969; Ainsworth, Blehar, Waters, & Wall, 1978), seems to be a true interaction between mother and child rather than a measure of infant temperament (Paterson & Moran, 1988; Sroufe, 1985).

Bowlby explicitly stated that the attachment experience is the source of cognitive structures or working models related to the self and the relationship partner. One of the problems in evaluating this appealing view is that there are no longitudinal data beyond middle childhood, and even within that period, the results do not always support this theoretical position (Paterson & Moran, 1988). Further, in most of the cases that have been studied, because the child remains in close contact with the attachment figure in the ensuing years, the confounding of the specific early experience and the continued stability of the child's environment and personal relationships means that their contributions cannot be readily evaluated.

Similar to the effects of social support, some of the questions about attachment pertain to whether the effects of secure attachment pervade the person's behavior at all times or whether they serve as a kind of buffer that has little effect except in times of stress. Although Ainsworth concentrated on the role of the attachment behavior system, she also emphasized the importance to the infant of the exploratory behavior system by which he or she develops skills for later use. Ainsworth pointed out that when the child "is rested, healthy, and not hungry, his attachment system is likely to be inactive" (Ainsworth, 1982, p. 4). This inactivity means that the child is free to move away from the mother in order to examine and manipulate aspects of the environment. Only when the distance from the mother increases too much, a considerable time has passed, or the child perceives some threat in the environment, is this attachment system reactivated, and the child then seeks the mother's reassuring presence. Ainsworth saw these two systems for attachment and exploratory behavior as complementary or mutually inhibitory (Ainsworth, 1982). The first is activated by a perceived threat and the second by a desire for novelty. Whichever is more strongly activated at any particular time gains expression. The importance of this view is its conceptualization of the development of autonomy and the needs for dependence as mutually facilitative rather than antagonistic. If children feel secure in the mother–child relationship, they need not worry about the mother's availability or the kind of reception the mother will give when they need to renew their contact with her.

Bowlby (1977) stressed the idea of a secure base as a parent's primary function. He focused on the importance to the child of the parent's ready availability, the responsiveness to the child's needs, and the willingness to accept the child as a person. If these conditions are not met, the child may become anxiously attached and preoccupied with the fear of losing the attachment figure. In this situation the attachment system is activated too easily and frequently, with the result that the child clings to the parent and becomes jealous of the parent's other relationships. This may result in the child's feeling distress or anxiety and may give rise to manipulative behavior designed to verify the existence of the relationship. In contrast, children whose attachment experience is categorized as avoidant/ambivalent "give up" on the relationship and withdraw into a compulsively self-reliant mode. In this case, Bowlby and others believe that the apparent independence is illusory and indicates a fear of the consequences of a close relationship. When this type of behavior is carried into adulthood, the person may pay a penalty in truncated personal development because of a fear of initiating relationships and responding to the overtures of others.

A secure attachment, in contrast, enhances not only the children's exploratory behavior but also their coping skills and hence their feelings of personal effectiveness or self-efficacy. These skills and self-perceptions reduce the children's anxiety and enable them to develop the kind of positive risk-taking behaviors that lead to the formation of relationships, because their anxiety about potential rejection is not as salient. In addition, because the attachment relationship is secure over time, it encourages the children to tolerate and also to value emotional intimacy. If we can equate the concept of attachment in childhood with perceived social support in adulthood, this view of the function and effect of secure attachment will have important implications for the concept of perceived social support. It suggests that someone who is high in perceived social support believes that specific people will be available if needed and will be accepting under all or most conditions.

Epstein's (1980) personality theory similarly emphasizes early relationships and their effect on later perceptions and characteristics. He considered the self-concept as a theory of self, inductively derived from an emotionally significant experience (1973, 1976). Epstein argued that the major postulates of self-theory are formed early in life and that later experiences are assimilated and subsumed under them. According to this set of rules, even an unpleasant but predictable world is preferable to a chaotic one. Although some postulates, such as "I am not worthy of love," may appear maladaptive to outsiders, they have the advantage of organizing experience. The person adhering to such a postulate will interpret the behavior of others according to this postulate, will adamantly resist evidence to the contrary, and may even provoke others into behaving in this way. This view has characteristics similar to the effects of familiarity on attraction and relationship formation mentioned earlier.

Bowlby (1988) expressed a similar idea when he stated that over time the patterns of attachment become increasingly the property of the child himself or herself. The child does this by building working models that contain separate models of the mother and father, their ways of communicating with and behaving toward the child, and models of the child interacting with each parent. These models have important implications for the child's self-concept and working models of relationships. Some of the implications of these internalized aspects of the attachment experience will be discussed later in the section dealing with the testable propositions that arise from viewing social support as the adult consequence of the attachment experience.

When attachment researchers try to study the adult equivalents of attachment behavior in adulthood, they encounter serious definitional issues. For instance, what aspects of adult behavior represent the same phenomenon as measured by the Strange Situation is unclear. But despite these problems, a number of researchers have made a compelling case for the potency of attachment over time. Several researchers, using a cross-sectional approach, demonstrated that those features of personality characteristic of each of the attachment patterns can be observed in adulthood (Cassidy & Kobak, 1988; Hazan & Shaver, 1987; Kobak & Sceery, 1988). They argue that except when the family relationships have drastically altered over time, in changes in behavior or substitutions or deletions in the family constellation, these characteristic attachment patterns probably have not changed throughout the developmental stages leading to young adulthood.

Other researchers believe that even if the cast of characters changes, the patterns of behavior created by early attachment experiences remain, because the individual seeks continuity and familiarity. Rutter (1984) reviewed empirical studies suggesting that parenting experiences in childhood affect the choice of a spouse. For example, Sroufe and Fleeson (1986) contended that abusive relationships tend to be perpetuated by individuals who were abused as children, because they bring the same type of abusive behavior into relationships when they are adults. Sroufe and Fleeson saw this continuity as a function of mental representations that tend to repeat themselves. Such a person has learned the roles of both the abused and the abuser and tends to become involved in situations in which these familiar roles continue to play themselves out. This suggests the search for familiar relationship patterns discussed earlier, although it adds a considerable psychodynamic overlay, and it also is compatible with Epstein's construct of self-theory (1980).

Longitudinal data currently do not extend beyond the middle childhood years for subjects who were assessed in the Strange Situation as young children. This deficit creates a problem in empirically determining the effect of early attachment status on adult behavior and adjustment. Some researchers interested in the effects of attachment in adulthood have dealt with this difficulty by relating adult behavior to recollections of early experiences with parents. It is generally agreed, however, that the question of accurately reconstructing the past is a troubling one, as recall of the past may be affected by current experiences and cognitive structures (Piaget & Inhelder, 1973) and by mood (Bower, 1981). For instance, Schaffer and Bayley (1967) did not find significant relationships in the Berkeley Growth Study data concerning adults' recollection of parental behavior toward them when they were younger than three and the actual observations made by researchers at that time. However, the parents' description of their own parental behavior when the children were teenagers was significantly related to the children's retrospective accounts as adults.

Main and her co-workers (Main & Goldwyn, in press; Main, Kaplan, & Cassidy, 1985) took another approach to studying the continuity of attachment experiences across generations, by looking at individual differences in the mental representation of the self in relation to attachment. Although she believes that working models show a high degree of stability across time, Main does not consider them as templates but, rather, as structured processes that obtain or limit access to information. She maintains that in childhood it is not possible to alter these working models of relationships except as a consequence of concrete experiences. Later in the developmental process, as a person acquires the ability to use formal operations (Piaget, 1967), these models, though still resistant to change, can be altered if the person can step outside a particular relationship system and see them operating.

Main's definition focuses on individual differences in patterns of representation, language, and nonverbal behavior as keys to understanding individual working models. Her view is far more complex than assessing a history of rejection, trauma, or loss. She believes that if adults recognize the information about their childhood experiences as part of a coherent whole, then they can produce a securely attached child. The consequence of this view is that it is not the experiences themselves but the cognitive representation of them that determines whether a mother will rear a child with the same attachment status as that the mother experienced herself. Through the use of a structured interview, the Adult Attachment Interview, Main categorized the adult's attachment experience and related it to the attachment category assigned to her child as assessed in the Strange Situation. She considers that such a systematic approach can be used to show continuities in attachment patterns across generations, despite the lack of traditional longitudinal data.

One of the most difficult problems for researchers interested in connecting attachment in childhood to adult personality characteristics is describing the kinds of behaviors that might indicate secure attachment in adulthood. Main assessed retrospective views of parent–child relationships and then looked at attachment behavior in the next generation, the children of her subjects. Hazan and Shaver (1987; Shaver & Hazan, 1987) tackled the problem somewhat differently. Their interest was based in part on the observation that adults frequently appear to make poor partner selections that hasten the termination of love relationships and that many individuals tend to keep choosing problematic partners over time. Hazan and Shaver wondered whether and how adult attachment styles affected the course of romantic relationships.

Hazan and Shaver translated Bowlby's conception of attachment into terms applicable to an adult relationship with a significant other and then constructed a questionnaire of romantic attachment styles. The results suggest that compared with adults who are securely attached, adults who are insecurely attached typically have more conflicted and fewer long-lasting love relationships. Hazan and Shaver argued that there should be individual differences in the threshold at which this adult attachment system is activated and also differences in the perception of whether the romantic partner (attachment figure) is sufficiently available and responsive when the system is activated. According to this view, people who have a low threshold for activating their attachment system should move quickly from an ended relationship into a new one and should be expected to be less discriminating in choosing a new partner. At the other extreme, those who fit Ainsworth's category of anxious avoidant attachment (who defend against the attachment experience) should be expected to engage in what might appear to be excessive discrimination when selecting an appropriate partner, to the detriment of their ability to find and enter a relationship.

In summary then, the early attachment experience is thought to have long-term effects on how people view themselves and others in relationships. This effect is hypothesized to be mediated by working models or cognitive schemata of the self and of appropriate relationship behavior. It also affects a person's ability to enter into relationships and what he or she perceives to take place in them. The attachment experience may have long-term effects throughout adulthood, and the same patterns, whether adaptive or maladaptive, may even be transmitted to another generation through the environment created in the new parent–child dyad. If the degree of perceived social support is seen as the result of the quality of the attachment experience, a study of the findings of attachment research should yield various predictions about other characteristics that should be differentially present in adults with varying degrees of social support.

RESEARCH ON PREDICTED CORRELATES OF PERCEIVED SOCIAL SUPPORT AS DERIVED FROM ATTACHMENT THEORY

For a number of years we have been conducting a series of studies on the individual difference variables associated with social support. This work has explored the behavioral, cognitive, and affective differences among those who differ in perceived social support. Recently we have also begun to look systematically at differences in relationship schemata associated with social support differences.

The use of attachment theory leads to predictions in all these areas. We would expect differences in effective interpersonal behaviors, ability to cope, and anxiety in interpersonal situations. In addition, there should be differences in self-concept, different expectations of what other people are like, and different ideas about the characteristics of relationships. In short, social support should be linked to differences in skills and behavior, especially in interpersonal situations, and even more to expectations about relationships and the perception or interpretations of what actually transpires in these interactions.

Personal Efficacy and Social Support

Behavioral predictions based on attachment theory focus on the freedom of the securely attached child to explore the environment with the confidence that a secure base will always exist in case of trouble, fatigue, or loneliness and, even more important, that acceptance will be available no matter what the outcome of the exploration. The consequence of this freedom resulting from secure attachment should be the increased tendency to explore the environment, with the consequent acquisition of skills, both cognitive and social, that come from dealing successfully with challenges and broadening one's experiental base.

Social Skills

Earlier in the chapter we cited research demonstrating that people differing in perceived social support also differed in social skills, at least in the case of a dyadic interaction (B. Sarason et al., 1985). The study we discussed indicated clear agreement from several perspectives that people who differed in social support also differed in likability. This difference was noted by persons both inside and outside the situation (the subject himself or herself, the other person in the interaction, and trained raters viewing the interaction). However, the particular behaviors that caused this differential perception could not be reliably discriminated when studied in terms of the specific actions identified in the social skill literature as component social skill behaviors (e.g., amount of eye contact, amount of time speaking, and various body-language indicators). Rather, it seemed to be the general affective response to those individuals (pleasure in their company, a feeling of ease) and the impression of competence they created that distinguished people who differed in self-described perceived social support. This impression of what differentiated them was confirmed by another set of ratings of these data, when raters were asked to assess both the likability and the competency of each subject, by answering questions such as "How much would you like to work under the direction of this person?" (I. Sarason et al., 1987).

Coping Style

An important part of competence is coping style. Attachment theory suggests that securely attached individuals will develop a more effective coping style than others will, for several reasons. First, the securely attached individual spends more time in exploratory activity, as mentioned earlier, and so can be expected to gain more information about how the world works and thus also has more opportunities to make interpersonal contacts, to observe models, and to learn skills in interacting with others. In addition, these skills should enhance a child's feelings of self-efficacy as someone who is able to do all kinds of things. Further, the securely attached child does not have to worry that failure will lead to parental rejection because the parent can be expected to deal with failures without diminishing the amount of positive regard and unconditional acceptance offered to the child. This lack of anxiety about parental response should give the child the confidence to try to cope with at least mildly problematic situations rather than to avoid them.

Based on these considerations, a view of perceived social support as the adult equivalent of attachment would predict that people high in social support would have a more task-focused coping style rather than using what are ordinarily less effective approaches such as denial or some type of emotional response such as upset or anger. We obtained some confirmation of this prediction in a study of university women. In a series of two studies (Kerr, Albertson, Mathes, & Sarason, 1987; B. Sarason, Mathes, & Albertson, 1989), we examined the self-described coping styles of three groups of women: freshmen who had come directly to the university from high school, upper division women whose school careers had been continuous with no time off, and reentry women who had been out of school for at least five years before beginning or resuming a university education. In all of these groups, a higher social support level was related to more self-reported problem-focused coping and less of the other types. These results support the prediction of more effective coping styles based on the attachment paradigm.

Another finding that supports the idea that individuals high in perceived social support are effective copers comes from several studies that considered the relationship between perceived social support and support that is reported as being received (Barrera, 1981; Sandler & Barrera, 1984; B. Sarason et al., 1987; Stokes, 1985; Wethington & Kessler, 1986). These studies all found that people high in perceived support are not likely to report actually receiving a high level of support. That is, people seem to receive social support if others see them as having a difficult time, experiencing negative life events, and being generally unable to deal with the problems in their environment. But if the person is perceived by others as performing well in the face of adversity or is not currently threatened by negative or stressful life events, then that person does not appear to elicit socially supportive behavior (Cutrona, 1986).

Cognitive Performance and Cognitive Interference

An investigation of cognitive performance also confirmed the enhanced effectiveness of those high in social support and further provided some clues to the reasons for that effectiveness. In a study of ability to solve difficult anagrams, subjects high in perceived social support performed significantly better than did subjects low in such social support (I. Sarason et al., 1987). Even more interesting were the results of an assessment of cognitive interference during the task. Subjects high in social support reported far less cognitive interference than did the other subjects. This means that they concentrated more on performing the task than did the other subjects and reported many fewer interfering thoughts and worries. Cognitive interference has been shown to be significantly associated with performance anxiety and a primary factor in causing test-anxious people to perform poorly in testing situations (I. Sarason, 1984; I. Sarason, Sarason, Keefe, Hayes, & Shearin, 1986). This finding is consonant with the prediction from the attachment literature that securely attached children experience less anxiety because they are more convinced that the parent will offer unconditional acceptance.

The Self-concept

Attachment theories also lead to predictions about the effect of secure attachment on the child's self-concept. Bowlby (1988) emphasized that the working models that children build of themselves as a result of the early parental relationship reflect the parents' images of their children and what the parents say to their children and how they treat them. These models then determine not only how children feel about their parents but also how they feel about themselves. Eventually the models lead to patterns of interaction that become habitual and internalized. In most cases these persist into adult life and result in the perception of interactional situations as similar to those in childhood, even when the now-adult child is dealing with people who behave entirely differently than the parents did.

The prediction based on social support as an extension of the attachment situation is that people who differ in social support will also differ in self-image and, further, will differ in how they believe others perceive them. Both general and specific evidence support each of these predictions. In the early stages of work with the Social Support Questionnaire, we found that the scores for support availability and satisfaction were related in a predictable way to measures of neuroticism, introversion-extroversion, and loneliness (I. Sarason et al., 1983) and self-described social skills (B. Sarason et al., 1985). These findings show that people who differ in social support scores also describe themselves differently in other ways. These self-descriptions of personality and behavioral characteristics suggest that people high and low in social support may also have quite different self-images.

We discovered more direct evidence of differences in self-concept in several of our recent studies. In one, the subjects completed self-descriptions on several scales of the Adjective Checklist: Favorable Adjectives, Unfavorable Adjectives, Self-confidence, and Personal Adjustment. On all of these scales except Self-confidence, the subjects high in social support described themselves more favorably than did the subjects low in social support (Rosser, 1986). In another study the subjects who differed in social support also differed in their responses to a measure of self-esteem (Pierce, Sarason, & Sarason, 1989). In a third study, the subjects were asked to indicate which items on a list of 102 self-descriptive words and phrases described them accurately and which did not (B. Sarason et al., 1989c). Again, as in the results from the Adjective Checklist, those higher in social support listed more positive and fewer negative qualities as describing themselves than did those subjects lower in social support. In this study the subjects were also asked to complete the self-descriptive list three more times, as they believed their mothers, fathers, and close same-sex friend would describe them. Consistent with findings in other research on the self, the subjects' ratings of themselves as they believed important others saw them correlated highly with their own self-ratings. The subjects high in social support believed those with whom they had close relationships saw them more positively and less negatively, than did the subjects lower in social support.

In this study we also found some objective substantiation for the subjects' view of the way others saw them. We asked the subjects to allow us to contact the people whose opinions they had predicted, and so we were able to ask these close network members to describe the subjects using the same adjective list. Not only were the subjects quite good at predicting the ways in which these people would describe them, but the descriptions of the others also were related to how the subjects described themselves. Although the subjects and their parents and friend could have been in accord because they all were acute empirical observers, these data also agree with the hypothesis that the subject's self-concept is at least partly related to the way that intimate others conceptualize him or her. Despite the relationship between self-concept and perceived social support, the results of this study also made clear that the two constructs were not measures of the same phenomenon. Although there was a significant relationship, the amount of common variance was moderately low.

Perceptions of Others

As Bowlby (1988) pointed out, attachment theory should also lead to the prediction that a person's perceptions of how others are expected to behave and the meaning of their behavior will be affected by the working models developed in early life. We just illustrated how self-concepts are related to social support level. The next question is how perceived social support as a representation of the early attachment experience may affect people's expectations about others' self-views. In one study that provides some evidence on this point, we asked students to complete a number of personality measures, and then in another session, either before or after this one, the subjects saw a slide show of various campus scenes depicting students in typical activities (B. Sarason et al., 1989c). The subjects were then asked to complete many of the same measures as they thought a typical student of their own sex and age would answer them. The results were consistent with the model we are developing based on attachment theory. That is, the students differed in their assessment of personality characteristics of the typical student as a function of their own social support level. Those students who were higher in perceived support rated the typical student as higher in social support than the actual group mean, and those students low in social support saw their typical peers as lower than the overall group mean in social support. The findings suggest that students' perceptions of their own social support served as a reference for assessing the perceived support of the typical student.

The divergence between the ratings for oneself and a typical student increased as social support level increased. Thus those high in self-described social support saw themselves as more different from the typical student in social support than did those students lower in social support. The student's own social support level also influenced his or her ratings of the typical student's loneliness and shyness.

The lower the subject's social support level was, the more lonely and shy the typical student was thought to be. Thus, a difference in perceived social support is related both to what the person thinks might be available to him or her from specific others and also to a working model of the availability of social support and of other personality characteristics of a generalized peer.

The results of this study cannot be explained in terms of implicit personality theories or halo effects, because the actual relationship among the variables of social support, loneliness, and shyness for the students based on their self-descriptions was greater than the relationship among the variables based on the responses for the typical student.

The results of this series of studies that connect a differential perception of self and others to different levels of social support can be seen as consistent with predictions based on the attachment literature that working models of the self and others develop differentially on the basis of early experience.

PERCEIVED SOCIAL SUPPORT AS THE SENSE OF ACCEPTANCE

The studies described in the preceding section illustrate the value of a coherent program of laboratory research in explaining the theoretical underpinnings of the social support construct. Many researchers—those represented in this volume and others as well—have called for a more theoretical approach to the study of social support. Based on the support for the hypotheses generated from attachment theory and redefined in terms of perceived social support, the outcomes of this experimental work have been consistent with and supported the notion that perceived social support, at least as defined by the Social Support Questionnaire (I. Sarason et al., 1983), might be a consequence and continuation of the working models of self and others generated by important relationships in early life.

In accordance with our research findings, we think it would be appropriate to define this type of perceived social support as the *sense of acceptance*. This change in nomenclature emphasizes what seem to be the defining aspects of perceived social support: heightened interpersonal skills, a sense of self-efficacy leading to adaptive behavior under stress, low levels of anxiety, positive self-image, positive expectations of interactions with others, and a positive view of others' adjustment.

The choice of this new term stems not only from the experimental findings we described but also from the work on the measurement issues in the social support literature. In the series of studies comparing social support measures (B. Sarason et al., 1987), which were discussed in Chapter 1 of this volume, we reported that in the comparisons of several measures of social support, the Social Support Questionnaire shared more variance with the other social support measures, no matter what their definitional base, than did any of the other social support measures we studied. An inspection of the items on each of these measures suggested that what is common among the measures, but possessed by them in different degrees, is the measurement of the extent to which the individual is accepted, loved, and involved in relationships with open communication. How closely the instruments looked at the availability of emotional support, as opposed to any of the other possible supportive functions, seemed to be important to determining their degree of relationship.

Our work on the development of a short form of the Social Support Questionnaire led to the same conclusion. We found that the items that were most predictive of the total score on the original measure also reflected the subjects' feelings that they were loved, valued, and unconditionally accepted (I. Sarason, Sarason, Shearin, & Pierce, 1987). This result, together with the results from comparing social support instruments, and the consistency of support for predictions based on attachment theory convinced us that perceived social support is a measure of a person's belief that he or she is valued not for superficial characteristics or performance, but as someone independently worthy of this status without contingency. This then is best defined as the sense of acceptance, an inherent, stable personality characteristic that contributes to the perception of social support separately from what the environment actually offers at any particular time.

THE ROLE OF RELATIONSHIPS IN SOCIAL SUPPORT

Although individual difference variables, as defined by a sense of acceptance, may be important to protecting an individual from stressors, we should remember that according to this view, not only did social support arise from early relationships but later relationships served to perpetuate the pattern of these early associations. Researchers' interest in the phenomenon of perceived social support and in received support has begun to focus not only on the behaviors involved but on their meaning to the participants in the interaction. The research examined cultural expectations (Jacobson, 1987) and the contextual effects of specific close relationships to determine how particular supportive behaviors are evaluated.

A QUICK SURVEY OF RELATIONSHIP RESEARCH

The research on relationships includes areas of interest in social psychology, for example, the development of relationships, the factors that predict whether they will endure, and studies of intimacy. Another body of research on relationships that is relevant to this discussion is the literature on marital relationships and marital therapy. We will not attempt to survey all the literature but, rather, to consider how some of the findings may be combined with research on social support to construct a more effective theoretical framework.

A close relationship may be defined as one of strong, frequent, and diverse interdependence that lasts over a considerable period of time (Kelley et al., 1983). Most of the research was on the development (and also the dissolution) of love relationships. These four factors—strength, frequency, diversity, and duration—apply, however, to several other types of relationships, such as friendships, serious love affairs, marriages, and parent–child relationships. What is striking about this list is its similarity to ideas about social support. Socially supportive relationships are thought to be characterized by feelings of attachment (Henderson, Byrne, & Duncan-Jones, 1981; Parker, 1983), frequency of contact (Brown & Harris, 1978), a diversity of functions (Cobb, 1976; Weiss, 1974), and a dependable relationship that endures over time. However, as relationship researchers have found, operationally defining some of these terms is not so simple. An example is using affective strength to define the closeness of a relationship.

Affective Strength as a Measure of Relationships

Close relationships are characterized by various emotions, ranging from love to jealousy to rage, and also by various levels of emotional experience (Berscheid, 1983). Both the range of emotions and their intensity need to be considered. Neither the type of emotion nor its intensity is an infallible predictor of the enduring quality or meaningfulness of the relationship to the participants. Although those who exhibit high levels of positive affect can probably be reliably classified as experiencing a close relationship, the other three quadrants composed of the remaining combinations of intensity and positivity are less easy to categorize as close or not close.

People who experience a great deal of intense negative affect in a relationship pose particular problems when describing the degree of closeness. Many relationships that would be classified as close using nonaffective criteria—for example, family membership—may sometimes be characterized by intense negative emotion. For instance, not only has the family been called the most physically violent group or institution the typical person is likely to encounter (Straus & Hotaling, 1980), but most of the anger that adults experience in their daily lives is also in a relationship with a blood relative or, to a slightly lesser degree, with a heterosexual partner (Fitz & Gerstenzang, 1978). In addition, the level of anger experienced in this sort of relationship tends to be higher than the level of anger resulting from interactions in other, less "close" relationships (Argyle & Furnham, 1983). The literature on close relationships makes it clear that some close relationships are characterized by high levels of negative emotion and that for close relationships as a whole, negative emotion is common.

The predominance of less intense emotion in a relationship does not necessarily exclude it from the close category. One reason is that emotional highs are always transitory (Klinger, 1977). According to Freud (1930/1961), "When any situation that is desired by the pleasure principle is prolonged, it only produces a feeling of mild contentment" (p. 23). Over time, the degree of emotional intensity in relationships tends to moderate, although this does not always mean that the relationship becomes less satisfying. Indeed, many long-term relationships could be described in such terms, and yet this description in no way implies that they lack closeness or positivity.

The magnitude of the emotional reaction to separation might seem to be a good measure of a relationship's closeness. Despite the appealing face validity of this approach and its usefulness in research on child–parent relationships using the attachment concept (Berscheid, 1983), research findings with adults indicate that neither the strength nor the positivity of affect reported in a relationship is an infallible guide to the kind of response that will be seen if the relationship ends by either separation or death. Weiss (1975) documented that the intensity of emotion, both euphoric and distressed, that is felt as a result of a partner's temporary or permanent absence is not necessarily matched to either the frequency or the intensity of emotion experienced in that person's presence.

Measurement Issues Relating to Affect and Closeness

Two measurement problems are relevant to equating degree of positive affect with closeness. One is the measurement of affect strength. Most measures pertain to a global summary statement such as "How happy are you in this relationship?" The subjects are forced to complete some unknown but probably complex cognitive calculations to come up with a response that most likely requires averaging simple or weighted positive and negative components of the relationship. The way in which different people do this is probably highly individual and may also fail to discriminate between relationships with small highs and lows and those with extreme variances in positive and negative components. A second problem is that the variance among individuals in such assessed happiness may be slight. Studies of happiness consistently report that most people report happiness not only in marriage but also in their jobs and in other aspects of their lives (Gurin, Veroff, & Feld, 1960). Such problems suggest that although satisfaction with support actually experienced or believed to be available, though acknowledged to be an important predictor of outcome, needs not only to be looked at relationship by relationship but also to be broken down by either an event-related approach or by its positive and negative components.

Whether Attachment Equates with a Need for Closeness

The equation of the concepts of attachment and a desire for affective and physical closeness in adult relationships is appealing, but it seems to be somewhat problematic. Even as a measure in young child–parent relationships, operationalization of the concept has some problems (Cohen, 1974). In adulthood, attachment behavior becomes even more difficult to measure because the experience of proximity becomes increasingly internalized and therefore also more difficult to measure. As a consequence of their better-developed cognitive abilities, adults are less likely than children are to perceive a separation as irrevocable, unless the separation is brought about by death. Further, in adulthood, many voluntary separations are instigated or maintained, even though the person has strong emotional reactions to the separation (Hunt & Hunt, 1977).

The Ability to Achieve and Enjoy Intimacy

Probably that part of the social psychology literature most applicable to understanding social support is the work on intimacy. Proponents of attachment theory believe that a secure attachment experience lays the foundation for a person's ability to establish, tolerate, and maintain intimacy in relationships. Intimacy can be defined as "a *subjective relational experience* in which the core components are *trusting self-disclosure* to which the response is *communicated empathy*" (Wynne & Wynne, 1986, italics in original). This definition includes many, though not all, of the constituents of the sense of acceptance we discussed earlier.

Intimacy is a concept seen similarly by researchers and those who encounter it in daily life. In a study to determine what nonspecialists thought intimacy meant, Waring and his co-workers (Waring, Tillman, Frelick, Russell, & Weiss, 1980) asked members of the general public, "What does intimacy mean to you?" A content analysis of the responses showed that the most salient concepts were sharing private thoughts, beliefs and fantasies, interests, goals, and backgrounds. Neither an expression of anger nor sexuality was seen as a primary determinant in the public's conception of intimacy. Of special interest were the subjects' reports and beliefs that for themselves, their early experiences and observation of intimate relationships and the growth of their own personal identities were important to the development of their capacity for intimacy. Helgeson, Shaver, and Dyer (1987) also studied the public's emphasis on the affection, validation, and support that derive from intimacy rather than their simply seeing it as an increased disclosure of personal thoughts and feelings to another. The data from these studies of conceptions of intimacy are similar to conclusions from the attachment literature and from the research on social support that we report in this chapter. Both sets of findings stress the importance of early experience because of its effect on working models of the characteristics of both others and the self and expectations of what relationships are like.

One area of work on intimacy that seems relevant is the study of metacommunication in intimate, as opposed to nonintimate, relationships. Satir (1967, p. 76) defined metacommunication as "a message about a message." Much of this metacommunication is conveyed through nonverbal channels such as facial expression, posture, and tone of voice. In most interactions all will go well if the communication and the metacommunication coincide. But if the two are giving different messages, trouble may ensue. In this case, although the respondent may reply to what is said, if he or she does not also deal with what is meant, a problem may be created. That is, both aspects of the communication must be included in the response in order for the speaker to feel understood.

Perlmutter and Hatfield (1980) referred to this ability to treat both aspects of the process as "intentional metacommunication," which they described as the hallmark of intimate relationships. Such metacommunications cannot be achieved by disclosure alone: To become intimate, one must also make clear to the other person the subjective meaning of one's messages. Yet this is not without risk, for it forces people to transcend the usual rules of social interaction and thus to be unable to predict the effect of this behavior. It seems likely that people who have developed the sense of acceptance that we discussed earlier are more likely to take such risks because they not only are drawing on their working models of others as accepting and nonjudgmental in a close relationship but they also have had frequent experiences in which both aspects of their communication were acknowledged and understood. Such a finding suggests that people with a sense of acceptance would be more likely to desire affiliative experiences and also would be better able to read others' metacommunications.

The ability to enter into intimate relationships is important to psychological development, marital adjustment, and functioning within a family. Likewise, the failure to establish an intimate relation is important from a mental health standpoint and was identified in one study as patients' most common reason for seeking outpatient psychotherapy (Horowitz, 1979). In another longitudinal study of men who were first tested when they were Harvard undergraduates, those who had been rated high in intimacy motivation, on the basis of their stories for Thematic Apperception Test pictures, were found to be significantly better adjusted psychosocially 17 years later (McAdams & Vaillant, 1982). The measures included career success, constructive use of free time, alcohol and drug misuse, psychiatric visits, and marital enjoyment. The relationship was particularly strong between intimacy motivation and marital stability and happiness at midlife. Power and achievement motives were not related to marital happiness or adjustment.

The presence of intimacy does not, however, mean the absence of conflict. For example, even when marital partners described their relationship to be above average in marital satisfaction, they reported conflict to occur reasonably often (Rands, Levenger, & Mellinger, 1981). Intimacy's contribution seems to be to allow confrontation without escalating the problem.

Couples who are high in intimacy are able to handle their conflicts constructively by dealing with instances of unfairness directly but without confrontation. Levenger (1983, p. 346) gave the following example: Two wives each described an experience early in marriage when her husband had forgotten her birthday.

> One wife said nothing about it all day but made sure that evening her husband would notice she had received birthday cards from her family. After he noticed it contritely, she teased him unmercifully, but with laughter; since that occasion, she says he has never again forgotten her birthday. The second wife perceived her husband's forgetfulness as no joking matter, but as a sign of his lack of care; she felt too hurt to say or do anything about it. Years later, long after their divorce, she reports that this incident first "proved" that he was insensitive and unconcerned about her.

Looking at these examples from the point of view of a sense of acceptance and what we know about attachment theory, we might conclude that the meanings of the forgotten birthday were very different to the two wives. That is, one interpreted it as a rejection of the relationship; the other, like a participant in a securely attached relationship, saw it as a behavior that reflected not her worth but other factors such as a busy schedule and worry over business affairs. Her sense of acceptance allowed her to deal directly with the behavior. In intimate relationships, partners feel committed to association over and above momentary variations in positive or negative feelings.

The issues of intimacy and the metacognitive closeness associated with it have been discussed extensively not only in the social psychological literature but also by those with a clinical perspective in their research on marital relationships and appropriate therapeutic interventions for difficulties in these relationships. The findings are complementary. For instance, Gottman and his co-workers (Gottman et al., 1976) found a significant discrepancy between the intent of the sender and the perception of the receiver of messages exchanged by distressed—but not by nondistressed—couples. They also found well-adjusted couples to be better at nonverbally communicating emotion than were not-well-adjusted couples. Not only do perceptions of the meaning of communicative behavior in the relationship vary between distressed and nondistressed couples, but also the types of behaviors noticed and reported differ if each member of the pair is asked to monitor their interactions. For instance, distressed couples were discovered to agree less than did nondistressed couples in reporting both their own and their partner's behavior (Christensen, Sullaway, & King, 1983).

Intimate relationships contribute to a person's self-worth by providing the support, understanding, and the positive regard of others. Achieving intimacy depends on the ability to understand how another person is feeling. But it also depends on one's willingness to disclose one's feelings and one's vulnerability to being hurt. This willingness helps create an intimate relationship, but it can also result in rejection or exploitation (Derlega, 1984).

Clinicians and theorists with both psychodynamic and existential perspectives have examined the importance of intimacy. Sullivan (1953) saw dyadic intimacy as necessary for the validation of personal worth. In his view, intimacy becomes salient as early as preadolescence, and thus before adult intimacy can occur, each adult must have a stable personal identity. Like Sullivan, Rogers (1951) saw the validation of one's worth as a basic consequence of intimacy.

Intimacy and Social Support

High levels of intimacy have been linked with social support (Brown & Harris, 1978; Hobfoll, Nadler, & Lieberman, 1986). Research by Gove and others (Gove, Hughes, & Style, 1983) found that only high-quality marriages that include intimacy also produced social support. In fact, intimacy may be central to certain types of social support. Reis (1984) suggested that social support derives more from intimacy than does any other aspect of social interaction. For instance, Reis (1987) found that interaction intimacy was the best predictor of appraisal support (the feeling that useful advice and guidance are available) and group-belonging support (feeling part of a community of friends). Both of these kinds of social support have been related to health benefits. Indeed, it may be the role of intimacy as a stress buffer (Miller & Lefcourt, 1983) that is responsible for the health-protective effect of social support.

The findings in research on intimacy indicate not only that it is important to social support but also that it would be beneficial to study social support in those close relationships that provide it. Close relationships high in intimacy give the participants a feeling of being understood, validated, and cared for (Reis & Shaver, 1987).

SOCIAL SUPPORT IN RELATIONSHIPS

Earlier in this chapter we talked about the individual's perceptions, without regard for his or her views of how a sense of acceptance might be related to the various close relationships in which the person is involved. A number of researchers have considered characteristics of particular relationships as well as cultural expectations that dictate the appropriateness of different types of support from different types of relationships. Work in our laboratory also helps confirm the idea that perceived support has different meanings depending on the relationship involved.

When we speak of the role of relationships in social support, we refer not simply to other people en masse but, rather, to the role of either specific relationships or specific classes of relationships. Although it is no doubt true that a person's own characteristics may be an important determinant of relationship events and the general character of the relationships into which he or she enters, the interaction within the relationship adds unique variance above that determined by the characteristics of either participant. Bradbury and Fincham (1988) demonstrated how both the participants' stable characteristics (e.g., beliefs about relationships, self-views) and more proximal characteristics of the interaction (such as the memory of what the partner did or said before the current exchange) can be shown to affect the outcome. Endler (1984) also focused on the dynamic characteristics and mutual influences of the dyad in determining the outcome of any interaction. Another way of expressing the relative contribution of both personal and relationship characteristics to an outcome is in terms of the Social Relations Model (Kenny & LaVoie, 1984). Using this model, Ingraham and Wright (1987) demonstrated with several different groups that relationship-specific variance accounted for a significant amount of the systematic variance in the experience of anxiety in dyadic interactions in a group setting. These findings echo the theory set forth by Sullivan (1953) in his provocative theory of the role of interpersonal relations as a source of both personality and variability in an individual's behavior. These empirical findings and theoretical arguments point to the importance of specific relationships in determining the behavior, affective response, and personal validation referred to earlier.

Specific relationships also bring with them different degrees and types of satisfaction and conflict. Argyle and Furnham (1982, 1983) showed this in a study of various relationship types ranging from spouse to neighbor and co-worker, in which they found distinctive patterns of satisfaction and conflict for each relationship category. The spouse was by far the highest source of both satisfaction and conflict. The relative amount of conflict, as opposed to the absolute amount, was greater in less voluntary relationships and those in which the person has less power (e.g., with relatives and work supervisors). The nature of satisfaction also varied with the relationship. Satisfaction with parents, spouses, and bosses was related to the financial and material help and advice provided, whereas satisfaction with friends was related more to shared interests.

CONFLICT AND SOCIAL SUPPORT IN RELATIONSHIPS

Not only do patterns of satisfaction and conflict vary across relationships, but Braiker and Kelley (1979) discovered that there also appears to be no association between the amount of interdependence and love in a relationship and the amount of negative affect and open conflict found in the same relationship.

A number of researchers have investigated how the conflict in a relationship affects a person's perception of the socially supportive behavior that may also occur in the relationship. The help or emotional support that comes from a conflict-filled relationship may exact a price high enough to vitiate its positive qualities (Coyne & DeLongis, 1986), and sometimes the recipient may feel the emotional price is not worth paying. Sandler and Barrera (1984) found a positive association between the proportion of conflicted relationships in the social network and the level of self-reported psychological symptoms, but they found no relationship between psychological symptoms and either total network size or the proportion of unconflicted relationships. The crucial impact of relationship conflict is also suggested by findings indicating that persons whose marital relationships involve high levels of conflict may experience poorer adjustment than do persons who are not married (Gove et al., 1983; Kaplan & DeLongis, 1983). Fiore, Becker, and Coppel (1983) discovered that the degree of upset with network members—but not their assessed helpfulness—was significantly and positively related to depression scores. Similar results were obtained by several other investigators (Barrera, 1981; Stephens, Kinney, Norris, & Ritchie, 1987).

The support provided in a close relationship may undermine the recipient's esteem because it may carry with it the implicit message that the recipient is incapable of solving his or her own problems (Brickman et al., 1982). If the situation does not improve, that is, if the recipient's problems do not diminish, the support givers may feel angry, frustrated, and ineffective, and the recipient may feel guilty (Coyne, Wortman, & Lehman, 1988).

UNDERSTANDING THE ROLE OF SPECIFIC TYPES OF RELATIONSHIPS IN SOCIAL SUPPORT

Heller and his co-workers argued that perceived social support from two relationship sources, family and friends, have different implications and so should be measured separately (Heller & Lakey, 1985; Procidano & Heller, 1983). The findings by Argyle and Furnham (1983) mentioned earlier and the work on conflict and social support in close relationships point up the usefulness of this view. Another type of data resulting from the comparison of various measures of social support (B. Sarason et al., 1987) also helps confirm this view. This research found that the friends scale of Procidano's and Heller's social support instrument (Perceived Social Support from Family and Friends) measured something different from that assessed by measures of generalized perceived social support. Other researchers (Rook, 1984, 1987; Seeman & Berkman, 1988) showed that at least for older Americans, different relationships are expected to provide different types of support. Children were seen as primary sources of instrumental support but not as the only or even major source of emotional support. Instead, that role is filled by a confidant who might be a spouse or friend. However, having a spouse is not automatically equivalent to having a confidant. Both Rook (1987) and Jacobson (1987) pointed out that the sources of different types of support are important for their cultural appropriateness. In particular, instrumental or tangible support from friends is not seen as appropriate if family members are available. However, not only is emotional support more often obtained from friends, but they also are seen as a suitable source of this kind of support.

We began a program of research to help elucidate the role of relationships in social support. Two studies (Pierce, Sarason, & Sarason, 1988; Pierce, Sarason, & Sarason, 1989) reported the development of the Quality of Relationships Inventory (QRI), which assesses three aspects of close relationships. These include Depth, the perceived importance, positivity, and security of a relationship; interpersonal Conflict; and the availability of Social Support. Multivariate analyses of several data sets support the three QRI scales' construct validity as measures of important characteristics of specific categories of interpersonal relationships. They also demonstrated that quality of relationships and social support are empirically distinct constructs and that the prediction of personal adjustment by social support is increased by considering the interpersonal context in which it occurs. These findings suggest that the quality of the relationship between support providers and recipients strongly influences the impact of social support on personal adjustment.

We also carried out an observational study in which students were stressed in the presence of a friend or a stranger (B. Sarason, Pierce, Sarason, Shearin, & Rosenkranz, 1989b). Raters judged the friend and stranger to behave differently in terms of the number and type of their supportive behaviors. The students who were stressed also perceived proportionally more supportive behaviors if they were paired with friends rather than strangers. Of even greater interest was the finding that many behaviors perceived by the raters as definitely nonsupportive were seen as supportive by the students, but only if they were performed by friends. This study makes clear the importance of assessing both relationship and recipient perception of a behavior when evaluating how people attempt to be supportive.

A THEORETICAL MODEL

The all-encompassing term of social support would be more useful if it were divided into its associated parts and these parts were organized into a testable theoretical framework. Based on our research findings over the last several years, we began to evaluate the hypothetical model shown in Figure 4.1. This model divides the concept of social support into several parts: (1) those trait or personality aspects that we call a sense of acceptance, (2) the support that is believed to be available or what is usually called perceived available support, (3) the support that is received from others, and (4) the recipients' perceptions of that support and their satisfaction with it. Also included in this model are the primary relationships, both early and current, that we believe to be important to understanding the effects of supportive behavior. The model presents our best guess as to the ways in which the sense of acceptance and both past and present relationships may contribute to support perceived to be available, to perceptions of the supportive behavior of others, and to the outcome. The use of a model such as this enables the application of structural equation modeling, the technique discussed in Chapter 2 of this volume, as a powerful tool in a programmatic investigation of these relationships.

The model relates the variables we have discussed in this chapter, particularly the role of relationships in the development of a person's sense of acceptance and how that sense of acceptance influences a person's response to stress. The model shows that a positive sense of acceptance influences (1) the development of current primary relationships, (2) the acquisition of self-efficacy feelings that are both generalized and related to specific tasks, and (3) the perceived availability of social support. A positive sense of acceptance also affects coping, by facilitating task orientation. This coping style reduces self-preoccupation and cognitive interference about the negative consequences of failure. A person's sense of acceptance also influences his or her perceptions of the nature of received social support. Those with a high sense of acceptance are more likely to perceive the actions of others as intentions of support and to be satisfied with the results of those behaviors than are other individuals. Such people are also less likely to experience negative emotions such as guilt, anger, or shame at receiving assistance than are others.

The model deals first with the antecedents of the sense of acceptance which include early primary or attachment relationships. It indicates that early primary relationships lead an individual to develop a sense of acceptance that reflects the extent to which the individual believes that he or she is loved, valued, and accepted by significant others. This idea is consistent with research findings from our laboratory (B. Sarason et al., 1987; I. Sarason et al., 1987). These early experiences also influence a person's ability to develop and maintain satisfying adult relationships. Early primary relationships influence the development of adult relationships by influencing personality development in childhood. It is likely that the sense of acceptance influences the development of adult relationships by enhancing the development of social skills, feelings of self-efficacy, and comfort in social relationships. It may also provide a working model of relationships as rewarding and enable a person to engage in emotionally satisfying relationships. The model also indicates that a person's early childhood relationships may continue into adulthood to become part of the person's group of

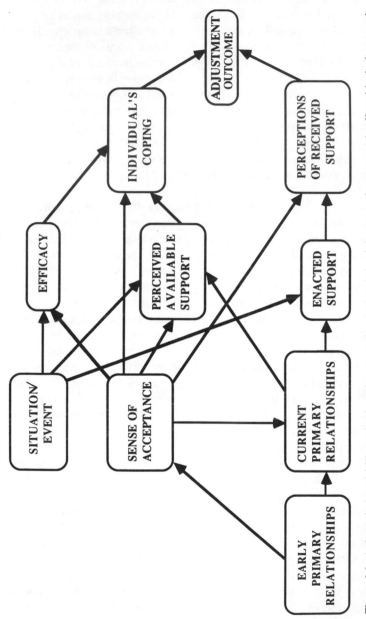

Figure 4.1. A theoretical model illustrating how the personality characteristic of the sense of acceptance is affected by both past and present relationships and the role that both relationships and the sense of acceptance play in the perception of available support, received support, evaluation of received support, and, ultimately, outcome or adjustment.

current primary adult relationships, which if terminated would cause considerable distress.

Investigations of the impact of stressful life events on a person's adjustment indicate that it depends on a complex interaction of many factors. For example, people differ in their specific task-related skills (efficacy) to deal with specific stressful situations. The nature of the stressful situations also affects the availability of support received from primary relationships. For example, challenging situations that occur far from home are likely to narrow the range of people who are available to assist in coping. The severity and social acceptability of the stressful event also determine the availability and the suitability of help available (see Chapter 15 in this volume). But people with a positive sense of acceptance should be more likely to develop the type of relationships that produce individuals willing to assist, regardless of the personal costs to themselves.

A high sense of acceptance is also likely to contribute to a high level of perceived available social support, another factor that should enhance coping effectiveness. Such a person, confident that others will come to his or her aid should circumstances require it, does not need to worry as much about potential negative outcomes as does an individual who does not believe that others will assist him or her. This greater ability to attend to solving a situation rather than worrying about solving it should also increase coping effectiveness.

It is probably impossible to distinguish between when coping ends and when an outcome has been reached. Thus it may be better to conceptualize outcome in terms of a person's adjustment at specific times. In this way we can talk about outcome at several stages of coping, while still acknowledging that a final outcome may be difficult or impossible to identify because of the ongoing process that may extend over the remainder of the subject's lifetime. Research on bereavement provides an example of this point of view (Lehman, Wortman, & Williams, 1987).

Although this model clearly applies to many relationships that need further investigation, it offers a more theoretical approach to understanding the various findings regarding social support. Testing this model and using a design that allows for structural modeling would allow the evaluation of many predictions based not only on the developmental view of the sense of acceptance we proposed but also on the role of specific relationships, each with its own characteristics. Looking at the relationship patterns characteristic of each individual should help us bring together these two aspects of social support.

A NEW APPROACH TO SOCIAL SUPPORT

As we have suggested throughout this chapter, it is time to rethink the concept of social support and to use theory and research on closely allied topics to help provide the data for this reconceptualization. Hinde called for the development of an interactive science of interpersonal relations that allows us to account for the fact that "relationships influence the nature of individuals and individuals influence the nature of the relationships they enter" (Hinde, 1981, p. 5). In addition, relationships "occur across a kaleidoscope of social–situational contexts which also influence and are influenced by the relationships occurring in them" (Chelune, Robbison, & Kommor, 1984, p. 11).

It is important to keep this interactive view at the forefront of our thinking. But we should also define social support more precisely and view it in a more theoretical context that includes hypotheses about its origins and uses relevant data from other areas. Then the interactive view will lose some of its vagueness, which even its proponents have readily conceded, and the stage will be set for testing the hypotheses.

The current conceptualizations of social support need to be changed. First, we believe that what has been called perceived social support should be redefined as a personality variable called a sense of acceptance. Second, we should disaggregate our view of social support to consider both what is provided and what is available in the specific relationships or classes of relationships from which social support comes. Third, we need to know much more about what people do when they try to be supportive and how personality factors and the character of the relationship involved affect the impact of their behavior.

REFERENCES

Abdel-Halim, A. A. (1982). Social support and managerial affective responses to job stress. *Journal of Occupational Behavior, 3,* 281–295.

Ainsworth, M. D. S. (1982). Attachment: Retrospect and prospect. In C. M. Parkes & J. Stevenson-Hinde (Eds.), *The place of attachments in human behavior* (pp. 3–30). New York: Basic Books.

Ainsworth, M. D. S., Blehar, M. C., Waters, E., & Wall, S. (1978). *Patterns of attachment: A psychological study of the Strange Situation.* Hillsdale, NJ: Erlbaum.

Ainsworth, M. D. S., & Wittig, B. A. (1969). Attachment and exploratory behavior of one year olds in a strange situation. In B. M. Foss (Ed.), *Determinants of infant behavior* (Vol. 4, pp. 111–136). London: Methuen.

Argyle, M., & Furnham, A. (1982). The ecology of relationships: Choice of situation as a function of relationship. *British Journal of Social Psychology, 21,* 259–262.

Argyle, M., & Furnham, A. (1983). Sources of satisfaction and conflict in long-term relationships. *Journal of Marriage and the Family, 45,* 481–493.

Barrera, M. (1981). Social support in the adjustment of pregnant adolescents: Assessment issues. In B. H. Gottlieb (Ed.), *Social networks and social support* (pp. 161–196). Beverly Hills, CA: Sage.

Berkowitz, L., & Frodi, A. (1979). Reactions to a child's mistakes as affected by her/his looks and speech. *Social Psychological Quarterly, 42,* 420–425.

Berscheid, E. (1983). Emotion. In H. H. Kelley, E. Berscheid, A. Christensen, J. H. Harvey, T. L. Huston, G. Levinger, E. McClintock, L. A. Peplau, & D. R. Peterson (Eds.), *Close relationships.* San Francisco: Freeman.

Blazer, D. (1982). Social support and mortality in an elderly community population. *American Journal of Epidemiology, 115,* 684–694.

Bower, G. (1981). Mood and memory. *American Psychologist, 36,* 129–148.

Bowlby, J. (1969). *Attachment and loss: Vol. 1. Attachment.* New York: Basic Books.

Bowlby, J. (1973). *Attachment and loss: Vol. 2. Separation: Anxiety and anger.* New York: Basic Books.

Bowlby, J. (1977). The making and breaking of affectional bonds. I. Aetiology and psychopathology in the light of attachment theory. *British Journal of Psychiatry, 130,* 201–210

Bowlby, J. (1980). *Attachment and loss: Vol. 3. Loss: Sadness and depression.* New York: Basic Books.

Bowlby, J. (1988). Developmental psychiatry comes of age. *American Journal of Psychiatry, 145,* 1–10.

Bradbury, T. N., & Fincham, F. O. (1988). Individual difference variables in close relationships: A contextual model of marriage as an integrative framework. *Journal of Personality and Social Psychology, 54,* 713–721.

Braiker, H. B., & Kelly, H. A. (1979). Conflict in the development of close relationships. In R. L. Burgess & T. L. Huston (Eds.), *Social exchange in developing relationships* (pp. 135–168). New York: Academic Press.

Brickman, P., Rabinowitz, V. C., Karuza, J., Jr., Coates, D., Cohn, E., & Kidder, L. (1982). Models of helping and coping. *American Psychologist, 37,* 368–384.

Brown, G. W., & Harris, T. (1978). *Social origins of depression.* New York: Free Press.

Cassidy, J., & Kobak, R. (1988). Avoidance and its relation to other defensive processes. In J. Belsky & T. Nezworski (Eds.), *Clinical implications of attachment.* Hillsdale, NJ: Erlbaum.

Chelune, G. J., Robbison, J. T., & Kommor, M. J. (1984). A cognitive interactional model of intimate relationships. In V. J. Derlega (Ed.), *Communication, intimacy, and close relationships* (pp. 11–40). New York: Academic Press.

Christensen, A., Sullaway, M., & King, C. (1983). Systematic error in behavioral reports of dyadic interaction: Egocentric bias and content effects. *Behavioral Assessment, 5,* 131–142.

Cobb, S. (1976). Social support as a moderator of life stress. *Psychosomatic Medicine, 38,* 300–314.

Cohen, L. J. (1974). The operational definition of human attachment. *Psychological Bulletin, 81,* 207–217.

Coyne, J. C., & DeLongis, A. (1986). Going beyond social support: The role of social relationships in adaptation. *Journal of Consulting and Clinical Psychology, 54,* 454–460.

Coyne, J. C., Wortman, C. B., & Lehman, D. R. (1988). The other side of support: Emotional overinvolvement and miscarried helping. In B. Gottlieb (Ed.), *Social support: Formats, processes, effects* (pp. 305–330). Beverly Hills, CA: Sage.

Cutrona, C. E. (1986). Behavioral manifestations of social support: A microanalytic investigation. *Journal of Personality and Social Psychology, 51,* 201–208.

Derlega, V. J. (1984). Self-disclosure and intimate relationships. In V. Derlega (Ed.), *Communication, intimacy, and close relationships* (pp. 1–9). Orlando, FL.: Academic Press.

Dion, K. K. (1974). Physical attractiveness and evaluation of children's transgressions. *Journal of Personality and Social Psychology, 24,* 207–213.

Endler, N. S. (1984). Interactionism. In N. S. Engler & J. M. Hunt (Eds.), *Personality and the behavior disorders* (Vol. 1, pp. 183–217). New York: Wiley.

Epstein, S. (1973). The self-concept revisited or a theory of a theory. *American Psychologist, 28,* 404–416.

Epstein, S. (1976). Anxiety, arousal, and the self-concept. In I. G. Sarason & C. D. Spielberger (Eds.), *Stress and anxiety* (pp. 185–229). Washington, DC: Hemisphere.

Epstein, S. (1980). The self-concept: A review and the proposal of an integrated theory of personality. In E. Staub (Ed.), *Personality: Basic aspects and current research.* Englewood Cliffs, NJ: Prentice-Hall.

Fiore, J., Becker, J., & Coppel, D. (1983). Social network interactions: A buffer or a stress? *American Journal of Community Psychology, 11,* 423–439.

Fitz, D., & Gerstenzang, S. (1978). *Anger in everyday life: When, where and with whom?* St. Louis: University of Missouri (ERIC Document Reproduction Service No. ED 160966).

Freud, S. (1930/1961). *Civilization and its discontents.* (J. Strachey, Ed. and Trans.). New York: Norton.

Ganster, D., Fusilier, M., & Mayes, B. (1986). Role of social support in the experience of stress at work. *Journal of Applied Psychology, 71,* 102–110.

Gottman, J. M., Notarius, C., Markman, H., Bank, S., Yoppi, B., & Rubin, M. E. (1976). Behavior exchange theory and marital decision making. *Journal of Personality and Social Psychology, 34,* 14–23.

Gove, W., Hughes, M., & Style, C. B. (1983). Does marriage have positive effects on the psychological well-being of the individual? *Journal of Health and Social Behavior, 24,* 122–131.

Gurin, G., Veroff, J., & Feld, S. (1960). *Americans view their mental health: A nationwide interview survey.* New York: Basic Books.

Hazan, C., & Shaver, P. (1987). Romantic love conceptualized as an attachment process. *Journal of Personality and Social Psychology, 52,* 511–524.

Helgeson, V. S., Shaver, P., & Dyer, M. (1987). Prototypes of intimacy and distance in same-sex and opposite-sex relationships. *Journal of Social and Personal Relationships, 4,* 195–233.

Heller, K., & Lakey, B. (1985). Perceived support and social interaction among friends and confidants. In I. G. Sarason & B. R. Sarason (Eds.), *Social support: Theory, research, and applications* (pp. 287–300). The Hague: Martinus Nijhoff.

Henderson, S., Byrne, D. G., & Duncan-Jones, P. (1981). *Neurosis and the social environment.* New York: Academic Press.

Hinde, R. A. (1981). The bases of a science of interpersonal relationships. In S. Duck & R. Gilmour (Eds.), *Personal relationships* (Vol. 1). New York: Academic Press.

Hobfoll, S. E., Nadler, A., & Leiberman, J. (1986). Satisfaction with social support during crisis: Intimacy and self-esteem as critical determinants. *Journal of Personality and Social Psychology, 51,* 296–304.

Horowitz, L. M. (1979). Cognitive structure of interpersonal problems treated in psychotherapy. *Journal of Consulting and Clinical Psychology, 47,* 5–15.

Hunt, M., & Hunt, B. (1977). *The divorce experience.* New York: McGraw-Hill.

Ingraham, L. J., & Wright, T. L. (1987). A social relations model test of Sullivan's anxiety hypothesis. *Journal of Personality and Social Psychology, 52,* 1212–1218.

Jacobson, D. (1987). The cultural context of social support and support networks. *Medical Anthropology Quarterly, 1,* 42–67.

Kaplan, G. A., & DeLongis, A. (1983). *Psychosocial factors influencing the course of arthritis: A prospective study.* Paper presented at the annual meeting of the American Psychological Association, Anaheim, CA.

Kaufman, G. M., & Beehr, T. A. (1986). Interactions between job stressors and social support. *Journal of Applied Psychology, 71,* 522–526.

Kelley, H. H., Berscheid, E., Christensen, A., Harvey, J. H., Huston, T. L., Levinger, G., McClintock, E., Peplau, L. A., & Peterson, D. R. (1983). Analyzing close relationships. In H. H. Kelley, E. Berscheid, A. Christensen et al. (Eds.), *Close relationships.* San Francisco: Freeman.

Kenny, D. A., & LaVoie, L. (1984). The social relations model. In L. Berkowitz (Ed.), *Advances in experimental social psychology* (Vol. 19, pp. 141–182). New York: Academic Press.

Kerr, K., Albertson, L., Mathes, P., & Sarason, B. R. (1987). *Psychological characteristics of reentry and traditional university women.* Paper presented at the meeting of the Western Psychological Association, Long Beach, CA.

Kessler, R. C., & McLeod, J. D. (1984). Sex differences in vulnerability to undesirable life events. *American Sociological Review, 49,* 620–631.

Klinger, E. (1977). *Meaning and void: Inner experience and the incentives in people's lives.* Minneapolis: University of Minnesota Press.

Kobak, R. R., & Sceery, A. (1988). Attachment in late adolescence: Working models, affect regulation, and representations of self and others. *Child Development, 59,* 135–146.

Lehman, D. R., Wortman, C. B., & Williams, A. F. (1987). Long-term effects of losing a spouse or child in a motor vehicle crash. *Journal of Personality and Social Psychology, 52,* 218 231.

Levenger, G. (1983). Development and change. In H. Kelley, E. Berscheid, A. Christensen et al. (Eds.), *Close relationships.* San Francisco: Freeman.

Main, M., & Goldwyn, R. (in press). Predicting rejection of her infant from a mother's representation of her own experiences: A preliminary report. *International Journal of Child Abuse and Neglect.*

Main, M., Kaplan, N., & Cassidy, J. (1985). Security in infancy, childhood, and adulthood: A move to the level of representation (pp. 66–106). In I. Bretherton & E. Waters (Eds.), *Growing points of attachment theory and research. Monographs of the Society for Research in Child Development, 50* (1–2, Serial No. 209).

McAdams, D. P., & Vaillant, G. E. (1982). Intimacy motivation and psychosocial adjustment: A longitudinal study. *Journal of Personality Assessment, 46,* 586–593.

Miller, L. C., & Lefcourt, H. M. (1983). The stress buffering function of social intimacy. *American Journal of Community Psychology, 11,* 127–139.

Parker, G. (1983). *Parental overprotection: A risk factor in psychosocial development.* New York: Grune & Stratton.

Paterson, R. J., & Moran, G. (1988). Attachment theory, personality development, and psychotherapy. *Clinical Psychology Review, 8,* 611–636.

Perlmutter, M. S., & Hatfield, E. (1980). Intimacy, intentional metacommunication and second order change. *American Journal of Family Therapy, 8,* 17–23.

Piaget, J. (1967). *Six psychological studies.* New York: Random House.

Piaget, J., & Inhelder, B. (1973). *Memory and intelligence.* New York: Basic Books.

Pierce, G. R., Sarason, I. G., & Sarason, B. R. (1988). *Quality of relationships and social support as personality characteristics.* Paper presented at the annual meeting of the American Psychological Association, Atlanta.

Pierce, G. R., Sarason, B. R., & Sarason, I. G. (1989). *Quality of relationships and social support: Empirical and conceptual distinctions.* Paper presented at the annual meeting of the American Psychological Association, New Orleans.

Procidano, M. E., & Heller, K. (1983). Measures of perceived social support from friends and from family: Three validation studies. *American Journal of Community Psychology, 11,* 1–24.

Rands, M., Levenger, G., & Mellinger, G. (1981). Patterns of conflict resolution and marital satisfaction. *Journal of Family Issues, 2,* 297–321.

Reis, H. T. (1984). Social interaction and well-being. In S. Duck (Ed.), *Personal Relationships: Vol. 5. Repairing personal relationships.* London: Academic Press.

Reis, H. T. (1987). *Where does social support come from?* Manuscript in preparation. University of Rochester, Rochester, NY.

Reis, H. T., & Shaver, P. (1987). Intimacy as an interpersonal process. In S. Duck (Ed.), *Handbook of personal relationships: Theory, relationships, and interventions.* New York: Wiley.

Ritter, J. M., & Langlois, J. H. (1988). The role of physical attractiveness in the observation of adult–child interactions: Eye of the beholder or behavioral reality? *Developmental Psychology, 24,* 254–263.

Rogers, C. R. (1951). *Client centered therapy: Its current practice, implications, and theory.* Boston: Houghton Mifflin.

Rook, K. S. (1984). The negative side of social interaction: Impact on psychological well-being. *Journal of Personality and Social Psychology, 46,* 1097–1108.

Rook, K. S. (1987). Social support versus companionship: Effects on life stress, loneliness, and evaluations by others. *Journal of Personality and Social Psychology, 52,* 1132–1147.

Rosser, C. (1986). [Self-concept, personal disclosure, and social support]. Unpublished data, University of Washington.

Rutter, M. (1984). Psychopathology and development, II: Childhood experiences and personality development. *Australia–New Zealand Journal of Psychiatry, 18,* 314–327.

Sandler, I. N., & Barrera, M., Jr. (1984). Toward a multimethod approach to assessing the effects of social support. *American Journal of Community Psychology, 12,* 37–52.

Sarason, B. R., Mathes, P., & Albertson, L. (1989). *Social support, coping, and achievement in reentry and traditional university women.* Manuscript in preparation. University of Washington, Seattle.

Sarason, B. R., Pierce, G. R., Sarason, I. G., & Rosenkranz, S. (1989a). *Parent–child relationships: Correlates of parents' responses to children's stress.* Manuscript in preparation. University of Washington, Seattle.

Sarason, B. R., Pierce, G. R., Sarason, I. G., Shearin, E. N., & Rosenkranz, S. (1989b). *Supportive behavior under stress: Observations by the provider, recipient and observer.* Manuscript in preparation. University of Washington, Seattle.

Sarason, B. R., Pierce, G. R., Shearin, E. N., Sarason, I. G., Waltz, J. A., & Poppe, L. (1989c). *Perceived social support and working models of self and actual others.* Manuscript submitted for publication.

Sarason, B. R., Sarason, I. G., Hacker, T. A., & Basham, R. B. (1985). Concomitants of social support: Social skills, physical attractiveness, and gender. *Journal of Personality and Social Psychology, 49,* 469–480.

Sarason, B. R., Shearin, E. N., Pierce, G. R., & Sarason, I. G. (1987). Interrelations of social support measures: Theoretical and practical implications. *Journal of Personality and Social Psychology, 52,* 813–832.

Sarason, I. G. (1984). Stress, anxiety, and cognitive interference: Reactions to tests. *Journal of Personality and Social Psychology, 46,* 929–938.

Sarason, I. G., Levine, H. M., Basham, R. B., & Sarason, B. R. (1983). Assessing social support: The Social Support Questionnaire. *Journal of Personality and Social Psychology, 44,* 127–139.

Sarason, I. G., Sarason, B. R., Keefe, D. E., Hayes, B. E., & Shearin, E. N. (1986). Cognitive interference: Situational determinants and traitlike characteristics. *Journal of Personality and Social Psychology, 51,* 215–226.

Sarason, I. G., Sarason, B. R., & Shearin, E. N. (1986). Social support as an individual difference variable: Its stability, origins, and relational aspects. *Journal of Personality and Social Psychology, 50,* 845–855.

Sarason, I. G., Sarason, B. R., Shearin, E. N., & Pierce, G. R. (1987). A brief measure of social support: Practical and theoretical implications. *Journal of Social and Personal Relationships, 4,* 497–510.

Satir, V. (1967). *Conjoint family therapy* (rev. ed.). Palo Alto, CA: Science and Behavior Books.

Schaffer, E., & Bayley, N. (1967). *Validity and consistency of mother–infant observations, adolescent maternal interviews, and adult retrospective accounts of maternal behavior.* Proceedings of the 75th Annual Convention of the American Psychological Association, Washington, DC.

Seeman, T. E., & Berkman, L. F. (1988). Structural characteristics of social networks and their relationship with social support in the elderly: Who provides support. *Social Science and Medicine, 26,* 737–749.

Shaver, P., & Hazan, C. (1987). Being lonely, falling in love: Perspectives from attachment theory. *Journal of Social Behavior and Personality, 2,* 105–124.

Sroufe, L. A. (1985). Attachment classification from the perspective of infant–caregiver relationships and infant temperament. *Child Development, 56,* 1–14.

Sroufe, L. A., & Fleeson, J. (1986). Attachment and the construction of relationships. In W. W. Hartup & Z. Rubin (Eds.), *Relationships and development* (pp. 51–71). Hillsdale, NJ: Erlbaum.

Stephens, M. A. P., Kinney, J. M., Norris, V. K., & Ritchie, S. W. (1987). Social networks as assets and liabilities in recovery from stroke by geriatric patients. *Psychology and Aging, 2,* 125–129.

Stokes, J. P. (1985). The relation of social network and individual difference variables to loneliness. *Journal of Personality and Social Psychology, 48*, 981–990.

Stokes, J. P., & Wilson, D. G. (1984). The Inventory of Socially Supportive Behaviors: Dimensionality, prediction, and gender differences. *American Journal of Community Psychology, 12*, 53–69.

Straus, M. A., & Hotaling, G. T. (Eds.). (1980). *The social causes of husband–wife violence*. Minneapolis: University of Minnesota Press.

Sullivan, H. S. (1953). *The interpersonal theory of psychiatry*. New York: Norton.

Tesch, S. A., & Whitbourne, S. K. (1982). Intimacy and identity status in young adults. *Journal of Personality and Social Psychology, 43*, 1041–1051.

Waring, E. M., Tillman, G. W., Frelick, L., Russell, L., & Weisz, G. (1980). Concepts of intimacy in the general population. *Journal of Nervous and Mental Disease, 168*, 471–474.

Watson, D., & Tellegen, A. (1985). Toward a consensual structure of mood. *Psychological Bulletin, 98*, 219–235.

Weiss, R. S. (1974). The provisions of social relationships. In Z. Rubin (Ed.), *Doing unto others*. Englewood Cliffs, NJ: Prentice-Hall.

Weiss, R. S. (1975). *Marital separation*. New York: Basic Books.

Wethington, E., & Kessler, R. C. (1986). Perceived support, received support, and adjustment to stressful life events. *Journal of Health and Social Behavior, 27*, 78–89.

Wynne, L. C., & Wynne, A. R. (1986). The quest for intimacy. *Journal of Marital and Family Therapy, 12*, 383–394.

CHAPTER 5

Social Support, Interdependence, and the Dilemmas of Helping

JAMES C. COYNE, JOHN H. ELLARD, AND DAVID A. F. SMITH

University of Michigan Medical School

University of Calgary

University of Michigan Medical School

The social support literature has called attention to the role of social relationships in coping with stress. This represents an important first step away from the reductionism inherent in viewing stress and coping processes solely as characteristics of stressor events and the coping of the individual. Yet, the literature holds some assumptions that may seriously limit its usefulness as a guide to how social relationships determine adaptation and how these relationships may be influenced to allow more favorable outcomes. Now that it has been well established that the quality of one's social relationships is a good predictor of how a person will deal with stress, the notion of social support is in danger of becoming an obstacle to rather than a vehicle for exploring this influence. It therefore is time for some open-minded skepticism about what measures of social support actually assess and what they miss, as well as for a more basic reevaluation of the direction that theory and research have been taking.

In this chapter, we will begin by identifying and questioning assumptions that have been accepted as fundamental to the social support literature as it has been developing until now. We will then turn to a study of couples coping with myocardial infarction to illustrate some of our concerns. The study highlights some features of close relationships under stress that have largely been ignored in current theory and research. One of their most distinctive features is the interdependence of the persons involved. An overriding theme throughout this chapter is that social support is best viewed as a general rubric for some of the effects of involvement in social relationships rather than as a working theoretical concept (Coyne & DeLongis, 1986). As such, the term *social support* has some utility, but it is abstract and by no means comprehensive. Yet as it is currently being

Preparation of this chapter was supported in part by a grant from the Family Health Foundation. Special thanks to Niall Bolger and Geraldine Downey for extensive comments on earlier drafts.

used, the concept of social support is being granted greater explanatory power and precision than it rightfully possesses, and it is taking the place of a more elaborated understanding of the complexities of social life.

UNSUPPORTED ASSUMPTIONS IN THE STUDY OF SOCIAL SUPPORT

Perhaps one of the most basic and uncontroversial ideas in the current literature is that social support is explicitly provided or communicated in specific, observable transactions (Albrecht & Adelman, 1987). It thus is assumed that the labels we give our measures and the boxes in our flowcharts represent more than methodological and theoretical convention and, instead, are direct reflections of crucial features of the lives of the respondents in our studies, that is, people receiving something: social support. Similarly, discussions of research routinely shift back and forth, from a finding of a "buffering" effect in the form of a statistical interaction to allusions to transactions that ostensibly can be observed between people, without the discussions' either noting that such shifts are being made or identifying the kinds of assumptions that are involved in such an extrapolation.

Only occasionally did such studies actually assess such transactions, in terms of the respondents' reporting having explicitly sought or received support. Furthermore, these studies' findings were different from what might have been anticipated. Studies of both seeking (Coyne, Aldwin, & Lazarus, 1981; Lieberman & Mullin, 1978) and receiving (Barrera, 1981) support found that support was related negatively to adaptational outcomes and was accompanied by "reverse buffer effects" (Husiani, Neff, Newborough, & Moore, 1982). In general, measures of perceived support were more consistently related to adaptational outcomes than were measures of supportive transactions (Wethington & Kessler, 1986). One plausible explanation of these results is that the latter measures confuse support with stress and neediness: Persons who face the greatest stress— particularly those who appear to be floundering—seek and elicit more support. A broader hypothesis is that such transactions represent the breakdown or inadequacy of the shared meanings and routines of relationships under stress. Explicitly supportive transactions occur when remedial work is needed—for instance, when persons in stress seek or receive indications of emotional support when their view of themselves or their standing in a relationship is in question.

If such a focus on social support as an explicitly supportive transaction is inadequate, what is the alternative? Sarason, Shearin, Pierce, and Sarason (1987) suggested the usefulness of viewing support as an individual's ongoing involvement in relationships of varying degrees of quality and caring. The most crucial sources of support are intimate or close relationships, and there is evidence that support from other sources cannot compensate for deficiencies in them (Coyne & DeLongis, 1986; Lieberman, 1982). Clark and Mills (1979) argued that what distinguishes such relationships is that they are "communal" rather than exchange based, that they tend to be a matter of ongoing mutual commitment and responsiveness and are not dependent on specific exchanges for their definition. Ideally, at least, persons in such relationships can assume that the other is concerned about them, that they share goals and responsibilities, and that assistance will be forthcoming when needed. Perhaps, then, social support questionnaires elicit judgments about the quality of mutual commitment and responsiveness, based on the history of a relationship, and not about recent, explicitly supportive transactions. They are thus broader judgments about the circumstances in which stress and coping processes will occur and what will shape and determine these processes, rather than about any specific exchanges.

Another seemingly uncontroversial set of assumptions in the literature is that social support is fundamentally a unipolar construct and that "low support" represents having less of something and "high support" more of it. Empirical demonstrations of the deleterious effects of a lack of social support have thus routinely been interpreted as the presence of some features in the lives of persons who report having support and their absence from the lives of people who report that they do not. This in turn has led to the conclusion that what is most needed by persons who are doing badly in stressful circumstances is more social support. Just as old toothpaste advertisements proclaimed that the addition of fluoride provided an "invisible protective shield against tooth decay," so too there has been the recurring promise that an increase in social support is a straightforward way of providing a buffer against adversity. Simple correlations among measures of stress, support, and adaptational outcomes, however, tell us little about the circumstances producing these associations or what is needed by persons who are faring badly.

We now know that the problems and burdens posed by social relationships may be more closely related to adaptational outcomes than to the support that is provided (Rook, 1984) and, similarly, that the degree of upset that relationships cause can be more important than their helpfulness (Sandler & Barrera, 1984; Pagel, Erdly, & Becker, 1987). On this basis, Fiore, Becker, and Coppel (1983) speculated that responses to social support questionnaires are "summary assessments composed of not only positive, but negative stressful perceptions as well" (p. 424). Expanding on this, Pagel et al. (1987) suggested that

> what people are really saying when they report satisfaction with their networks is that they have relatively few complaints or problems, rather than they find their networks very helpful or supportive. Or, perhaps less cynically, both features lead to their overall impression, but it is primarily the problematic features that cause, maintain, or fail to reduce psychological symptoms. (p. 794)

If this is the case, then what persons low in perceived support need is relief from relationships that are conflictive, demanding, or otherwise problematic. They might be able to find this relief by resolving some of the difficulties posed by these relationships or insulating themselves from them, rather than instigating more involvement. The research agenda that is relevant to such goals would cover not just what is represented by having support or how support is communicated but, rather, what conditions are reflected in an endorsement of low support. That is, low support needs a sharper definition. Indeed, the argument has been made that support has a threshold effect (Coyne & DeLongis, 1986) that therefore limits the benefits of having social resources beyond a minimum (Lieberman, 1986). Many of the apparent effects of social support on adaptation to stress may thus be due to the handicaps faced by persons in particularly negative relationships.

Readily obtainable correlations with measures of psychological distress have obscured unresolved issues about the construct validity of measures of social support. Indeed, the very ease of conducting studies of social support with such measures can prove to be a drawback, in that it reduces the burden on investigators to find out more about the phenomena of interest (Lofland, 1976). The necessity of theorists and researchers having some understanding of the experience of people grappling with stress in their close relationships may seem to be diminished by the availability of such measures as substitutes. Yet, if we temporarily suspend our confidence that our measures and theoretical concepts are mirror images of the most crucial features of their daily lives, and if we allow our respondents to talk about themselves without being constrained by our theoretical frameworks or categories, we may begin to learn about how much we have been missing.

The pilot work for a study of couples in which one partner had suffered an uncomplicated myocardial infarction underscored this conclusion (Coyne, 1988; Smith & Coyne, 1988). The study had two phases, starting with the pilot phase that allowed post–myocardial infarction couples—who were similar to those who would later take part in the survey phase—to help design the study. In effect, these couples were hired as consultants to help write the research questions and measures. They met in focus groups, and the investigators identified key research questions that emerged from these discussions, as well as the variables influencing the couples' adjustment and how they might best be measured in a survey instrument. The consultants then reviewed these provisional variables and survey questions in more focus group meetings. They thus provided at least a partial check on the investigators' tendency to force unwittingly the phenomena being studied into their preconceived theoretical framework and categories. The findings of the resulting survey are relevant to the study of stress processes in close relationships, but together, the focus groups and survey study raised more conceptual issues concerning social support in close relationships than they settled.

STRESS, COPING, AND SUPPORT IN CLOSE RELATIONSHIPS: THE MICHIGAN FAMILY HEART STUDY

For a number of reasons, the occurrence of an uncomplicated myocardial infarction would seem to be an ideal opportunity to study stress, coping, and support processes. The stressor can be well defined medically, and so at least in these terms, the subjects offer some uniformity to the nature of the event. Unlike many other stressors, a myocardial infarction is a discrete event and is not intrinsically a change in available support, as would be the case in marital separation or the death of a loved one. The usual questions of the possible confounding of measures of stress and support (Schaefer, Coyne, & Lazarus, 1982; Thoits, 1982) are thus avoided. There also are meaningful psychological outcomes that one would expect social support to influence. For example, persons who have suffered a heart attack are at risk for psychological distress, and the degree to which they maintain a sense of self-efficacy is a crucial predictor of their functional recovery, even more so than is the comprehensive cardiological examination when they are discharged from the hospital (Ewart, 1988).

Studies of the spouse's role in the patient's recovery from a heart attack are limited, but there are hints that there may be problems with simple dichotomous designations of the spouse as the support provider and the patient as its recipient. The reason is that the wives of men who have had a heart attack are themselves vulnerable to psychological distress and also experience considerable anxiety and depression (Skelton & Dominian, 1973; Stern & Pascale, 1979). Further, anecdotal and case studies suggest that the spouse's support is important to the patient but that her overprotectiveness and pessimism and marital conflict frequently impede the patient's recovery (Bellak & Haselkorn, 1956; Davidson, 1979; Wishnie, Hackett, & Cassem, 1971).

Focus Groups

The focus groups' discussions confirmed this finding, and they more generally challenged the adequacy of the conventional stress and coping paradigm, with its main allowance for a role for close relationships being through one person's perception of support. That is, the spouses were more than sources of perceived support; they were active participants in the process of coping and brought to it their own vulnerabilities, goals, and demands. Moreover, the groups' discussions revealed the extent to which the heart attack was a stressor for both partners in the couple: It was a direct blow to the spouse as well as the patient. The spouses were threatened by the near loss of a loved one, and they were uncertain about their own future, as well as about the more immediate problems of adjusting to their spouse's not being able to participate as fully as previously in the tasks of maintaining a family and a household. There were also financial hardships, and for some couples one or both partners needed to reduce the demands of work or even to retire. Coping with a heart attack was indeed a dyadic affair. Both the patients and their spouses were faced with having to make changes in their lifestyle, perform certain instrumental tasks, manage their own distress, and, in complex ways, come to terms with the presence of the other. These agendas could prove to be a source of conflict for the individual and for the two members of the couple: Their coping efforts could be independent, carefully coordinated, simply concatenated, or even at cross purposes. It was clear that different styles worked for different couples. What needed to be done and what worked—that is, what was effective coping for each person—depended on what the partner was doing.

To a large degree, these middle-aged and elderly couples relied on long-established understandings and routines to tackle the new challenges they faced.

This reliance had both advantages and disadvantages. There were too few women patients in the groups to make broad generalizations about postinfarction women, but it appeared that even when the women in the groups had just been discharged from the hospital, they became locked into their preexisting caretaker roles vis-à-vis their husbands. When male patients went home, their wives took care of them; but when female patients went home, they fell back into the routine of caring for their husbands.

Many changes were made without formal discussion, and many patients were unaware of the specific accommodations that their spouses had made. Consistent with Clark and Mills's (1979) notion of a marriage as a communal relationship, the patients could generally count on these efforts, and in many instances they were probably unaware of the extent to which adjustments were being made. As the wife in a seemingly otherwise well-functioning couple remarked, "We don't talk much about what we need to do. Luckily we don't need to, because we would probably disagree and wouldn't get anything done." This is consistent with past research that suggests that the advantage of married couples over pairs of strangers in resolving differences is not that the married couples work better together, but that they have acquired shared understandings (Winter, Ferreira, & Bowers, 1973).

Most of these patients and spouses felt that the crisis posed by the heart attack had brought them closer together, but they tended to lack highly differentiated conceptions of how they worked together or what they did that was helpful. Struggling individually and together in the aftermath of the heart attack, it is unlikely that they would have spontaneously labeled what they did for each other as *support*. Undoubtedly, on a questionnaire, most would have rated their partners as supportive, but their patterns of interaction were often such that they did not reach the point that they had to solicit or provide support explicitly. For such couples, "being supported" was probably better construed as being freed from particular worries, concerns, and conflicts that might otherwise burden coping efforts, rather than as a cognition that guided their coping. Like formal discussions, explicitly supportive exchanges tended to represent the breakdown of existing routines, such as when a patient became demoralized by the fatigue following what had previously been a relatively effortless activity.

Despite generally functioning well together in the first few months after the heart attack, many couples experienced conflict regarding the patients' and spouses' efforts to manage each other's distress, as well as disagreeing over how much the spouses were responsible for the patients' well-being and recovery (see Christ, 1983, for similar observations). It was clear that tending to the spouses' emotional needs was as crucial a coping task for the patients as taking care of the patients was for the spouses. Probably the couples that fared the worst were those in which both partners allowed the management of each other's distress to take precedence over other tasks, demands, and concerns.

The patients and spouses expressed frustration with themselves and each other over the way that they dealt with issues of spouse responsibility versus patient autonomy. Spouses reported getting caught up in situations in which they knew what needed to be done but still failed to do it (Coyne, Wortman, & Lehman, 1988). A strong sense of responsibility for the patient's fate could override considerations of their own well-being and the partner's need for autonomy and self-respect, and they could become locked into what could be obviously futile confrontations over what the patient should or should not do. The patients conceded that in the face of pressures from their spouses, relationship issues could take precedence over their doing what was needed in terms of life-style changes and other accommodations to having had a heart attack and that they became stubborn and occasionally even defiant.

The spouses were obviously caring, but not unconditionally or purely altruistically. It was in their interest that the patients protect their health and proceed with the recovery process while avoiding unnecessary risks. Thus although the spouses were generally loving, they also had a sense of responsibility for the situation, so that they did not view being helpful and supportive as a choice but, rather, as an automatic and necessary response. As a spouse, they owed this to the patient. Further, the spouses seemed to feel that in conflicts they could invoke the patient's responsibility to the spouse: They recognized that there were certain things that only the patient could do and that the welfare of both people depended on the patient's doing them. Arguments about the patient's taking what the spouse considered an unnecessary risk or not making needed life-style changes could become intense moral struggles. The spouse might take the position that the patient owed her certain behavior, and even if he might disagree, he should do it for his wife's sake. In such situations, the spouse might become insistent, pressuring and cajoling the patient—sometimes effectively and sometimes to the detriment of the patient's well-being and sense of efficacy. It is likely that some of the "supportive" spouses' effectiveness resulted from seemingly unsupportive exchanges and that much of the overprotectiveness, counterproductive exchanges, and sheer upset sprang from an intention to be helpful and not harmful.

As the patients knew well, being in a couple creates obligations to protect the emotional and practical investment of the spouse and look after the spouse's needs. The heart attack did not diminish these obligations; if anything, it increased them. At critical points, being in the marriage can be a mixed blessing and even a burden. On the other hand, one's responsibility to one's spouse can be an impetus for appropriate behavior such as life-style changes, even when one's own sense of self-responsibility fails. In that way, some of the benefits of close relationships come from the constraint or social control that they provide, rather than their supportiveness per se.

The Survey

Our survey covered 56 couples in which the husband had had an uncomplicated myocardial infarction an average of six months earlier. The questionnaires looked at a full range of variables, including the quality of the preexisting relationship, the extent and quality of the couple's contact with the medical system, the psychological distress and functional health of both the patient and the spouse, and the patient's self-efficacy as judged by both the patient and the spouse. The efficacy questions concerned the extent to which the patient could confidently meet a number of challenges, such as dealing with medical personnel, making changes in life-style, and resuming normal activities. The coping measures tapped the extent to which each partner adopted each of two strategies. *Active engagement* was involving the partner in discussions, asking how the partner felt, and other constructive problem-solving methods. *Protective buffering* was hiding concerns, denying worries, and yielding to the partner in order to avoid disagreements. Besides the coping measure, there were questions concerning spousal *overprotectiveness,* or the extent to which the spouse saw herself as being intrusive or interfering too much in her husband's life or doing things that he could do for himself. Thus, whereas protective buffering entailed hiding and suppressing affect, overprotectiveness involved intrusion. A parallel measure of overprotectiveness assessed the patient's perception of his spouse on this dimension.

Overall, the quantitative data from the survey substantiated many of the focus groups' suggestions, but they also went beyond them. In particular, the data revealed how crucial the spouse and the marital relationship were to the patient's postinfarction adjustment. For instance, at a bivariate level, the adequacy of the spouse's initial contact with medical personnel (before the patient's discharge from the hospital), the quality of the marriage before the heart attack, and the spouse's assessment of the patient as efficacious all were strongly related to the patient's efficacy (Smith & Coyne, 1988). Relevant to the latter finding, past research showed that the spouse's perception of the patient's efficacy adds to what can be predicted about the patient's performance on a stress test (treadmill) from the patient's own self-ratings (Taylor, Bandura, Ewart, Miller, & Debusk, 1985). This suggests that the spouse's perceptions are more than a mere reflection of the patient's perceptions and that they may independently affect the patient's behavior. Interestingly, despite being strongly correlated with the patients' own ratings of their self-efficacy, their spouses' ratings of them were significantly lower in both our results and those of Taylor and his colleagues. Among the patient variables related to their own self-efficacy, their adoption of a protective-buffering coping style toward their spouse was one of the strongest, and it was negatively related to efficacy. Thus, the patient's pursuit of the goal of managing the spouse's distress could compete with and even take precedence over the tasks of recovery.

Multiple regression models of the contributions of the patients' and the spouses' variables relative to the patients' self-efficacy indicated that the patients' actively engaging their spouses was positively related to their self-efficacy, but as in the bivariate analyses, the patients' adopting a buffering role with their spouse was negatively related (Smith & Coyne, 1988). The spouses' own sense of efficacy and their adoption of a buffering style contributed to the patients' self-efficacy, but their being overprotective was negatively related, as were the spouses' health limitations and sense of being burdened.

Our survey also revealed that the spouses were at as much risk for psychological distress as the patients were (Coyne, 1988). Approximately a third of the spouses met or exceeded a standardized cutoff score suggesting a need for psychological referral. These spouses tended to have husbands who were also distressed. Like the patients, the spouses benefited from having had a satisfactory relationship before the heart attack, but the adequacy of the spouses' initial contact with medical personnel was also crucial to determining their level of distress. Apparently, what transpired between the spouse and the medical personnel before the patient's discharge continued to have a profound impact on the spouse and patient even six months later, and an inadequate early contact was not compensated by a better later contact. Interestingly, discussions about coping with the heart attack were useful only if the spouses were adequately informed, and this was true for the effects on both the spouses' and the patients' well-being.

Other variables predicting the spouses' distress were the specific burdens they experienced from the heart attack, their overprotectiveness, and the extent to which they or their spouse adopted a buffering coping style. The latter association is noteworthy. Spouses adopting a buffering style contributed to the patients' well-being and self-efficacy but damaged their own well-being. There was thus a trade off. In regression analyses, the adoption of a buffering coping style, the burden posed by the heart attack, and the adequacy of the spouses' contact with medical personnel at the patients' discharge (six months earlier) accounted for 61% of the variance in the spouses' distress (Coyne, 1988).

The survey also examined the phenomenon of overprotectiveness. The patients and spouses agreed on their perceptions of the degree of overprotectiveness occurring in a couple. Overprotectiveness was not related to the preexisting quality of the marriage. Apparently, even in couples that had previously functioned well, spouses could become intrusive and restrictive and do things for the patients that the spouses indicated they knew the patients could do for themselves. Rather, overprotectiveness was related to adopting a protective, buffering coping style, but it was related in an opposite fashion to the patients' self-efficacy. Overprotectiveness undermined the patients' self-efficacy, but its correlates suggested that it was primarily a matter of the spouses' feeling burdened and perceiving the patients as lacking efficacy, rather than of the spouses' feeling hostile. The strongest correlates of the spouses' overprotectiveness were their being psychologically distressed and burdened, their initially lacking adequate contact with medical personnel, and (negatively) the patients' own assessment of their self-efficacy. Overprotectiveness was also more strongly related to spouses seeking therapy after the infarction than was their level of psychological distress. Thus, the context of the spouse's overprotectiveness seemed to be one in which the patient's coping efforts and morale may have been flagging and the spouse was distressed and yet had inadequate information about what to do.

Overview

If the study of the role of social relationships in stress and coping processes had started with what close relationships are like under stress, it is likely that different concepts and paradigms would have evolved. In the couples we studied, the very nature of the heart attack and the challenges, threats, and demands it entailed were defined by the marital context. What we observed in these couples was fundamentally a dyadic process in which each partner struggled to preserve his or her own well-being as well as the other's, while attempting to master the specific tasks of adaptation and recovery. Notions of the spouses as either sources of support or additional stress do not adequately capture the richness of their involvement with their husbands, their impact on the unfolding events, or their own vulnerability to these events.

Elsewhere, it has been noted how thoroughly "cognitized" the study of social support has become (Coyne & DeLongis, 1986). One of the many drawbacks of this is that there has been so little attention to persons who are the sources of support, their motives and vulnerabilities, and, in turn, how these affect the motives and vulnerabilities of the recipient of the support and the outcome of the stress process. Studies such as this one only begin to address these issues. However, the study did highlight the need to expand the considerations of "outcome"; that is, what was most beneficial for the patients did not always coincide with what was most beneficial for their relationship or spouse. Deliberately or inadvertently, spouses might sacrifice their own well-being to that of the patient or, in their zeal, undermine the spouse when they were most concerned about being helpful. The patients in turn might choose protecting their spouse over meeting the demands of postinfarction life. Struggles could ensue in which the well-being of neither was served, even though each was seemingly ready to put the other's well-being first. Overall, the study invites a closer look at the implications of one person's being involved with another person in the face of stress that affects both of them. This would include examining the significance of the one person's assuming or—by virtue of their relationship—having responsibility for helping the other, the demands on the situation that it legitimizes, and the dilemma this poses for the recipient of these efforts.

INTERDEPENDENCE AND THE DILEMMAS OF HELPING

Our discussion points to the need for a more encompassing framework for understanding both the successes and failures of social support. A key feature of such a framework, in our view, is the recognition that social support is best viewed from the perspective of the interdependence between recipient and provider. Interdependence refers to the extent to which the needs and goals of both the recipient and the provider are apparent in the relationship and the problems of coordination that both parties face in meeting each other's needs. Such a view acknowledges explicitly that social support represents, if nothing else, efforts at helping with the various needs and objectives of both parties. From an interdependency point of view, the details of how support is provided should always be viewed against a backdrop of how individual needs are generally being met in the relationship. Our understanding of the complexity of people's coordinating their outcomes in relationships makes us aware that any support effort may have various implications for the larger problems of interdependence in the relationship. In many instances it will not be surprising to find that a supportive person's actions—which seem to be helpful when viewed in isolation (e.g., reminding the recipient to take medication)—prove to be counterproductive, owing to their negative implications for other needs the recipient might have (autonomy, self-efficacy).

Countless instances of problems of interdependence were apparent in the couples' efforts to cope with the needs and demands generated by a myocardial infarction. By allowing for the perspectives of the patients and their spouses to take precedence, we were able to go beyond summary ratings of supportiveness and see more fully the context of each partner's coping efforts in the ongoing coordination of needs and demands in these relationships.

Another important observation that comes with viewing social support as an aspect of interdependence is that even the most intimate and successful relationships are not always able to achieve a successful outcome for the individuals involved (Kelley, 1979; Kelley & Thibaut, 1978). That is, most relationships entail some degree of conflict between the parties in meeting their needs. Thus, in emphasizing the interdependence between provider and recipient and the inevitable conflicts that arise concerning the mutual coordination of their needs, it is possible to normalize the problems associated with achieving effective support. Indeed, from an interdependence perspective, that support efforts may miscarry or fail is hardly surprising. Such lapses represent only a few instances of the many ways in which we fail one another in our relationships.

In searching for ways to avoid miscarrying support efforts, we should shift from analyzing individuals' limitations and vulnerabilities to the ways in which they are able to coordinate their mutual needs in a relationship, notwithstanding the conflicts they face. Consistent with some past work (Coyne et al., 1988), we seek a situational perspective on miscarried support or helping, rather than one that blames the helper, recipient, or both. For a beginning, we need a more elaborate consideration of the needs and concerns of both provider and recipient in situations in which we might expect social support to make a difference. Only then will it be possible to see how effective support can emerge from the mutual coordination of needs.

Problems of Interdependence

Although there are countless needs that individuals must coordinate in their relationships, some are common to life crises. Furthermore, when considering likely issues for both the provider and the recipient of help or support, we can identify predictable patterns of conflict between each person's needs. We will refer to these recurrent conflicts as the *dilemmas of helping*. The search for better answers to when and why support is either effective or fails will depend on how well we come to understand these dilemmas. We will examine the dilemmas of helping in terms of some of the needs and demands that the situation produces. Our list of needs should not be viewed as exhaustive, and we should not expect that each of them will always be distinguishable in or even salient to a particular situation. In addition, to understand how these differing concerns can contribute to conflict, it is important to keep in mind that the participants in any relationship are seldom aware of all of their own or others' needs or of the demands that they may be implicitly making. Indeed, it is precisely because these needs and demands are in the "psychological background" and inform people's perceptions and behavior out of awareness that they make the experience of the dilemmas so intractable from the actors' point of view.

Managing One's Own Distress

Like the Michigan Family Heart Study (Coyne, 1988), other research has shown that spouses and family members of persons facing chronic and catastrophic illness may be at as great or greater risk for psychological distress as may be the patients themselves (Gillis, 1984; Kline & Warren, 1983). This distress has several sources. Obviously, a major one is an empathic concern about what has happened to the patient and what this bodes for the future. In addition, there is the direct personal threat or loss posed to family members by the illness, as well as the changes and demands that the illness imposes on them. The illness may place restrictions on their lives and thrust them into new situations for which they feel poorly prepared, despite their sense that the outcome for both them and the patient depends on what they do. There may even be a contagion effect associated with repeated exposure to a patient who is in distress or demoralized (cf. Coyne, 1976; Howes, Hokanson, & Lowenstein, 1986; Strack & Coyne, 1983). Whatever its sources, this distress can lead to supportive behavior, but the connection is not certain, and efforts to reduce or manage distress may actually interfere with the quality or appropriateness of the efforts that one does undertake.

Cialdini et al. (1987) produced evidence that even in situations of heightened empathy, the motivation of a helper may be to reduce the personal distress that is engendered by the empathy, rather than any selfless desire to relieve the sufferer. Within such a Negative State Relief Model, help or support may be seen as an egotistic response designed to dispel the distress of the person who provides it. In two studies, Cialdini and his colleagues showed that distress, not empathy, predicted helping efforts. In many situations, there may be no conflict between what would reduce this distress and what would be most beneficial to the person who is its object. Yet, particularly in situations in which what would be most helpful is unclear or a positive outcome is unlikely or simply uncertain, efforts to reduce one's distress may result in behavior that is contrary to what would be most efficacious for the partner's well-being. Distancing oneself from the situation by derogating the partner is one example of this.

Further, even when strengthening one's commitment to be helpful, efforts to manage one's personal distress can interfere with effective problem solving and instrumental action. Efforts to manage one's own distress may result in self-absorption and make it more difficult to attend to social cues and another's expression of need (Ziomek, Coyne, & Heist, 1983). They may disrupt the performance of concrete tasks. Thus, on the basis of this assumption, physicians believe that a more detached neighbor may be more effective than a spouse in providing cardiopulmonary resuscitation (St. Louis, Carter, & Eisenberg, 1982).

The phenomenon of overprotectiveness observed in the Michigan Family Heart Study may be in part understood as the spouses' efforts to manage their own distress. Recall that the measure of overprotectiveness was strongly correlated with the spouses' distress and that it involved their indicating that according to their own judgment they were being intrusive, interfering in their partner's life and doing things that he could do for himself. The study data were cross sectional, but given the negative correlation between the spouse's overprotectiveness and the patient's efficacy, we may infer that this behavior is self-defeating. The correlation with spouses who sought personal psychotherapy suggests that they may have realized this. But although it is ineffective as an influence on the patient, being overprotective nonetheless may relieve the spouses' distress over their predicament. Ostensibly, instrumental actions or problem-focused coping may have thus actually been emotion-focused coping confused by the spouses' identification of alleviating their own distress with what would be helpful for the patient. Put differently, the spouses' own distress may have mediated their helping efforts, but what would relieve this distress was a fallible guide to what would help resolve the source of this distress. In many instances, more effective action would have entailed the spouses overriding their own empathic concern for the patient and letting him do things that were alarming. Paradoxically, the spouses would have been more effective if they had cared less and did not tie the resolution of their own distress to what the patient did or did not do.

Our survey distinguished between wives who were overprotective and who adopted a protective, buffering coping strategy, that is, who suppressed and hid their affect from their husband. In contrast with overprotectiveness, the spouse's protective buffering promoted the patient's self-efficacy. Yet it also was associated with increased distress for the spouse. In a sense, the spouse's task of supporting her husband's efficacy might be seen as her having to subordinate or hide her own need for support and thereby remaining distressed. Yet aside from whether this is a fair or reasonable expectation, the wisdom of the wives' doing this depends on what their husbands were attempting to accomplish. Presumably the patients were already aware that the wife was distressed and felt some responsibility to her—empathic concern, even—and her attempt to deny her feelings might have further complicated the coping task for both and made matters more difficult.

Self-efficacy

As we noted, a sense of self-efficacy in tackling the specific tasks of postinfarction life may be a better predictor of patient outcome than are physiological measures of damage to the myocardium (Taylor et al., 1985). For patients to develop a sense of efficacy, they must reduce their anxieties about being able to resume their normal activities, particularly those requiring exertion. Furthermore, this may conflict with their need to avoid further distressing their spouse. Taylor and his colleagues (1985) found that the men's experience on a treadmill heightened their sense of self-efficacy, whereas the wives witnessing this lowered their sense of their husband's efficacy. Informational counseling for the wives did not remedy this discrepancy, but having the wives try the treadmill themselves did. Apparently, without their directly experiencing it, the wives focused on the signs of their husband's physical strain, whereas the husbands were focusing on their accomplishment. We may presume that this was alarming for the wives. In everyday activities in which they are not able to adopt their husband's perspective so easily, such discrepancies are not readily resolved, and this could become a recurring issue in the patient's adaptation and recovery.

Taylor and his colleagues did not pursue the larger implications of these findings, but one implication may be a more pervasive conflict for the patients between what would promote their self-efficacy and what would avoid increasing their spouse's distress. Indeed, in the Michigan Family Heart Study there seemed to be a trade-off for the patients between promoting their own self-efficacy in adapting and their protective buffering of their wife. To the extent to which the patients attempted to buffer their spouses, their own self-efficacy was reduced.

We know less about the issues associated with the wives' self-efficacy as both helpers or support to their husband as well as with mastering their own coping tasks. Presumably, their self-efficacy in specific tasks is similarly important to them, and very likely there could be conflict between what would benefit the wives' efficacy and what would benefit their husband's self-efficacy. The focus groups certainly revealed instances in which the spouse's dogged efforts to get the patient to do particular things were separate from her initial commitment to help the patient feel more confident and efficacious—getting the patient to do what was asked became an end in itself, even if both felt worse as a result. Obviously, one feels more positive if one's efforts to be helpful succeed than if they fail, but here something more seemed to be at stake. Not to succeed could be an intolerably distressing state, perhaps even more so than merely witnessing the patient floundering without having invested in an effort to help.

Although there is little mention of the helper's needs for self-efficacy in the experimental literature on helping, the issue of the helper's self-esteem and its investment in a helping effort has been raised. Whereas self-efficacy refers to highly specific perceptions of one's ability to perform requisite behaviors, self-esteem refers to more general self-evaluations. The issues may be similar, however.

Self-esteem

Discussions of the helper's self-esteem have built on an understanding of the recipient's self-esteem needs of help. To understand the recipient's sometimes complex reactions to receiving support from another, Fisher and Nadler developed a general model of reactions to aid that emphasizes the recipient's self-esteem needs and the extent to which certain kinds of help can threaten the recipient's self-esteem (Fisher, Nadler, & Whitcher-Alagna, 1982; Nadler & Fisher, 1986). According to the model, help is self-threatening "to the extent that it transmits a negative self-relevant message to the recipient, conflicts with important socialized values (e.g., independence and self-reliance; fairness in social relations), and fails to contain instrumental benefits" (Nadler & Fisher, 1986, p. 90). When help is self-threatening to the recipient, his or her response can include refraining from seeking further help and taking steps to be self-supportive so as to reduce his or her dependence on the support provider. According to this model, self-threatening help can be effective if it encourages the recipient to become more independent and motivated to engage in self-help.

Although the Fisher and Nadler model was initially inspired by a desire to shift the research focus from helping behaviors to helping relations, the model does not fully address the interdependence between provider and recipient and the problems created for their relationship by such recipient reactions, however adaptive they might seem. Work by Rosen and colleagues speaks to this issue in examining the reactions of providers to having their help spurned (Rosen, Mickler, & Collins, 1987; Rosen, Mickler, & Spiers, 1986). This work produced evidence that spurned help produces negative affect in the would-be provider and unfavorable evaluations of the recipient. Rosen et al. (1987) suggested that these reactions arise from the threat to the helper's self-image posed by the spurned help created by raising doubts about his or her self-efficacy, control, and image of the self as humanitarian.

The focus groups' discussions of the Michigan Heart Project suggest the usefulness of looking more closely at situations that the wives constructed as involving their help being spurned. On the one hand, there were the obvious situations in which the patients simply disregarded their wife's advice or efforts and in that sense spurned them. However, there were other instances in which the wives' efforts were simply ineffective—a common one being their attempt to give pep talks to their demoralized husband—and they then construed this ineffectiveness as a rejection by their husband. Involvement in such helping efforts became an investment of the wives' self-esteem, and a failure to recover this in successful influence could become an issue for the couple, aggravating the patient's initial sense of demoralization and failure. To paraphrase the previously cited comments by Nadler and Fisher about the self-threat of help to recipients, to the extent that help fails, it transmits a "negative self-relevant message" to the helper in terms of important socialized values—in this case, their adequacy in their role as a spouse.

Together the two literatures provide additional ways to view support efforts in the context of interdependence. Support efforts that have negative implications for a recipient's self-esteem can set in motion reactions that on the one hand may be helpful to the recipient (an impetus to self-help) but on the other hand may create further problems in the relationship by causing the helper to react negatively to the recipient. The latter point is important with respect to the Fisher et al. (1982) self-esteem model, which draws attention to the helpfulness of help that motivates the recipient to become more independent. However, from an interdependence perspective, the work of Rosen et al. (1987) highlighted the limitations of trying to assess the adaptiveness of reactions without referring to the relationship between the support provider and the recipient. Whatever gains one can see for the individual as a result of becoming more independent and self-sufficient may be more than offset by the consequent negative reactions from the helper. Further, the helper's struggles to recover a sense of self-esteem when it is threatened by a failure to be effective in a distressing situation may override considerations of the recipient's independence and well-being and even the spouse's own well-being.

Dispositional Interdependence

An emerging theme in our discussion of issues of personal distress, self-efficacy, and self-esteem is that for couples facing a stressful event such as a heart attack, much of what transpires is shaped by each partner's having assumed responsibility for the other—not just the spouse for the patient but also the patient for the spouse. In crucial ways each partner can depend on the other's concern and involvement. This is not an expectation of future reciprocity but the very nature of such a communal relationship. Although this is a distinctive strength of such relationships, it is also a source of vulnerability: We cited ways in which both patients and spouses could take responsibility for the other in a manner that was to the detriment of one or both. Ostensibly helpful efforts can become miscarried and unduly costly or destructive.

Kelley and Thibaut (1978) contended that in close relationships, people depend on each other not just at the level of given outcomes (what will be the immediate consequences for both partners if one offers help to the other?) but also at a more abstract dispositional level (what implications will the help have for the love, respect and commitment they feel for each other?). According to Kelley (1979), *dispositional interdependence* refers to the interdependence that partners in a close relationship feel with respect to the dispositions on which the relationship depends: "Each individual gains rewards and incurs costs as a function of the kinds of interpersonal propensities that he/she and the partner display in their transactions" (p. 95). Thus, the payoffs of transactions are not just the concrete costs and gains but also what they establish about the persons involved and the kind of relationship that they have (cf. Watzlawick, Jackson, & Beavin, 1967).

The levels of interdependence analysis that Kelley (1979) offered has important implications for understanding how issues of "burden" and "need" are handled in close relationships. To the extent that individuals in a close relationship attempt to help each other, the relationship may be sustained and even strengthened over time. Note too that it is precisely the kinds of help that someone else would view as "costly" and "burdensome" to the provider that provide the clearest opportunities for the provider to contribute to dispositional interdependence. One feature of persons in close relationships, then, is their willingness to sustain such burdens. However, as we noted, one complication of this is that both spouses and patients have distress and needs that are apparent to the other, and a struggle may develop over who is going to be allowed to assume responsibility for whom.

One feature of this model is that it allows for some disjunction between the satisfaction that individuals may be experiencing at the concrete "given" level of outcomes and the satisfaction that they are experiencing at the level of interpersonal dispositions, such as when dispositional outcomes are adequate but concrete outcomes are poor. Kelley characterized such a relationship as "impractical" (a label that was undoubtedly invented without thought of the kinds of issues to which it is being applied here). His observations about how people adapt to such relationships are useful for understanding some support relationships. That is, people may adapt to poor outcomes by devaluing their importance and exaggerate instead the importance of rewards at the dispositional level: "The rewards at the dispositional level are exaggerated in significance, and life is lived for the satisfactions to be gained there, divorced from practical considerations of the given level. In the extreme case poor given outcomes are taken as proof that dispositional ideals are being fulfilled" (Kelley, 1979, p. 135). Thus, when concrete positive outcomes cannot be attained, persons persist anyway because of what is being established about them and their relationship.

SUMMARY: THE DILEMMAS OF HELPING AND THE PARADOX OF INTERDEPENDENCE

We suggested a number of dilemmas of helping arising from persons in an interdependent relationship. By virtue of being in such a relationship, their own well-being is directly and indirectly affected when something distressing happens to their partner. Their own distress may be an important part of the basis for their efforts to help their partner, but it can also lead to inappropriate and self-defeating action. Managing their own distress can become confused with what is effective in remedying the situation, even when one is counter to the other. Further, distress can become a burden on the partner and disrupt that person's focus on what needs to be done. Getting help, attempting to give help, and letting a partner get by without help pose complex issues for each person's self-esteem, and what is beneficial to one partner may be detrimental to the other. Finally, people's actions in these circumstances must be understood not only according to what is being accomplished concretely, but also according to how these actions define or reveal the nature of the relationship or the persons involved.

These considerations suggest how efforts to be supportive can be miscarried or otherwise prove inadequate, precisely because the parties involved have so much at stake. These considerations are complex. That close relationships can nevertheless prove so beneficial to persons facing stress is probably less a matter of the persons' deliberating about these issues and resolving them than of their being able to rely on well-established routines and shared understandings that are relevant to the tasks at hand.

We may speculate about other factors in successfully coping with stress in close relationships (see also Coyne et al., 1988). It appears crucial that both spouses and patients be adequately informed and have realistic expectations and well-defined tasks that allow them to manage their needs and to contribute to a positive outcome. Indeed, the results of the survey from the Michigan Family

Heart Study show that initial inadequacies in how well spouses are informed can have long-term consequences for the adjustment of both spouses and patients. Also, many of the issues that are likely to arise concern each person's efforts to take responsibility for the other's well-being. As Kaplan-DeNour and Czackes (1970) discovered, the persons who deal best with such issues are probably not excessively prone to guilt and are able to get upset with each other and then get on with the tasks at hand.

The strength of close relationships under stress is the extent to which they entail mutual responsiveness, shared goals, and simple caring as a result of the basic interdependence of the persons involved. Yet, these relationships may fail to live up to their potential as the most crucial sources of support to someone facing stressful circumstances. When they do fail, it may often be a matter of the persons' too intensely and single-mindedly attempting to be supportive. What may be needed most is not "more social support" but a disengagement from efforts that are not working, based on an appreciation of the limits of social relationships and of one person's taking responsibility for the other. It is possible to care too much to make a positive difference.

We know very little about how close relationships respond to stress. Much of the social support literature considers those persons who are crucial to someone's efforts to cope with stress as solely sources of perceived support. This literature says little about these supporters' vulnerabilities or stakes in the coping process. Laboratory studies of helping would seem to be relevant, but most of them examine fleeting encounters between strangers who otherwise have no relationship to each other. We need a fuller understanding of the implications of persons being interdependent when stressful events happen to one of them.

REFERENCES

Albrecht, T. L., & Adelman, M. B. (1987). *Communicating social support.* Beverly Hills, CA: Sage.

Barrera, M., Jr. (1981). Social support in the adjustment of pregnant adolescents: Assessment issues. In B. H. Gottlieb (Ed.), *Social networks and social support* (pp. 69–96). Beverly Hills, CA: Sage.

Bellak, L., & Haselkorn, F. (1956). Psychological aspects of cardiac illness and rehabilitation. *Social Casework, 37,* 483–489.

Christ, G. H. (1983). Loss of self: A fundamental form of suffering in the chronically ill. *Sociology of Health and Illness, 5,* 168–195.

Cialdini, R. B., Schaller, M., Houlihan, D., Arps, K., Fultz, J., & Beaman, A. L. (1987). Empathy-based helping: Is it selflessly or selfishly based? *Journal of Personality and Social Psychology, 52,* 749–758.

Clark, M. S., & Mills, J. (1979). Interpersonal attraction in exchange and communal relationships. *Journal of Personality and Social Psychology, 37,* 12–24.

Coyne, J. C. (1976). Depression and the response of others. *Journal of Abnormal Psychology, 85,* 186–193.

Coyne, J. C. (1988, August). *The role of the spouse in coping with a myocardial infarction: Psychological distress, coping, and overprotectiveness.* Symposium presentation to the annual meeting of the American Psychological Association, Atlanta.

Coyne, J. C., Aldwin, C., & Lazarus, R. S. (1981). Depression and coping in stressful episodes. *Journal of Abnormal Psychology, 90,* 439–447.

Coyne, J. C., & DeLongis, A. M. (1986). Going beyond social support: The role of social relationships in adaptation. *Journal of Consulting and Clinical Psychology, 54,* 454–460.

Coyne, J. C., Wortman, C., & Lehman, D. (1988). The other side of support: Emotional overinvolvement and miscarried helping. In B. Gottlieb (Ed.), *Social support: Formats, processes, and effects* (pp. 305–330). Beverly Hills, CA: Sage.

Davidson, D. M. (1979). The family and cardiac rehabilitation. *Journal of Family Practice, 8,* 253–261.

Ellard, J. H., Wortman, C. B., & Silver, R. L. (1986, August). *Coping with tragedy: Coming to terms with shattered assumptions about the world.* Paper presented to the annual meeting of the American Psychological Association, Washington, DC.

Ewart, C. K. (1988, August). *Effects of couples' interaction on the outcome of myocardial infarction.* Symposium presentation to the annual meeting of the American Psychological Association, Atlanta.

Fiore, J., Becker, J., & Coppel, D. A. B. (1983). Social network interactions: A buffer or a stress. *American Journal of Community Psychology, 11,* 423–440.

Fisher, J. D., Nadler, A., & Whitcher-Alagna, S. (1982). Recipient reactions to aid. *Psychological Bulletin, 91,* 27–54.

Gillis, C. L. (1984). Reducing family stress during and after coronary artery bypass surgery. *Nursing Clinics of North America, 19,* 1103–1111.

Howes, M. J., Hokanson, J. E., & Lowenstein, D. A. (1985). The induction of depressive affect after prolonged exposure to a mildly depressed individual. *Journal of Abnormal Psychology, 49,* 1110–1113.

Husaini, B. A., Neff, J. A., Newborough, J. R., & Moore, M. C. (1982). The stress-buffering role of social support and personal confidence among the rural married. *American Journal of Community Psychology, 10,* 409–426.

Kaplan-Denour, A., & Czackes, J. C. (1970). Resistance to home dialysis. *Psychiatry in Medicine, 1,* 20–221.

Kelley, H. H. (1979). *Personal relationships: Their structures and processes.* Hillsdale, NJ: Erlbaum.

Kelley, H. H., & Thibaut, J. W. (1978). *Interpersonal relations: A theory of interdependence.* New York: Wiley-Interscience.

Kline, N. W., & Warren, B. A. (1983). The relationship between husband and wife perceptions of the prescribed health regimen and level of function in the marital couple post-myocardial infarction. *Family Practice Research Journal, 2,* 21–280.

Lieberman, M. A. (1982). The effects of social supports on response to stress. In L. Golberger & S. Breznitz (Eds.), *Handbook of stress: Theoretical and clinical aspects* (pp. 764–784). New York: Academic Press.

Lieberman, M. A. (1986). Social support—The consequences of psychologizing: A commentary. *Journal of Consulting and Clinical Psychology, 54,* 461–465.

Lieberman, M. A., & Mullin, T. J. (1978). Does help help? The adaptive consequences of obtaining help from professionals and social networks. *American Journal of Community Psychology, 6,* 499–517.

Lofland, J. (1976). *Doing social life.* New York: Wiley.

Nadler, A., & Fisher, J. D. (1986). The role of self-esteem and perceived control in recipient reaction to help: Theory development and empirical validation. In L. Berkowitz (Ed.), *Advances in experimental social psychology* (Vol. 19, pp. 81–122). Orlando, FL: Academic Press.

Pagel, M. D., Erdly, W. W., & Becker, J. (1987). Social networks: We get by with (and in spite of) a little help from our friends. *Journal of Personality and Social Psychology, 53,* 793–804.

Rook, K. (1984). The negative side of social interaction: Impact on psychological well-being. *Journal of Personality and Social Psychology, 46,* 1097–1108.

Rosen, S., Mickler, S. E., & Collins, J. E., II. (1987). Reactions of would-be helpers whose offer of help is spurned. *Journal of Personality and Social Psychology, 53,* 288–297.

Rosen, S., Mickler, S. E., & Spiers, C. (1986). The spurned philanthropist. *Humboldt Journal of Social Relations, 13,* 145–158.

St. Louis, P., Carter, W. B., & Eisenberg, M. S. (1982). Prescribing CPR: A survey of physicians. *American Journal of Public Health, 2,* 1158–1160.

Sandler, I. M., & Barrera, M., Jr. (1984). Toward a multimethod approach to assessing the effects of social support. *American Journal of Community Psychology, 12,* 3–52.

Sarason, B. R., Shearin, E. N., Pierce, G., & Sarason, I. G. (1987). Interrelations among social support measures: Theoretical and practical implications. *Journal of Personality and Social Psychology, 52,* 813–832.

Schaefer, C., Coyne, J. C., & Lazarus, R. S. (1982). The health-related aspects of social support. *Journal of Behavioral Medicine, 4,* 381–406.

Skelton, M., & Dominian, J. (1973). Psychological stress in wives of patients with myocardial infarction. *British Medical Journal, 2,* 101.

Smith, D. A. F., & Coyne, J. C. (1988, August). *Coping with a myocardial infarction: Determinants of patient self-efficacy.* Symposium presentation to the annual meeting of the American Psychological Association, Atlanta.

Stern, M. J., & Pascale, L. (1979). Psychosocial adaption post-myocardial infarction: The spouse's dilemma. *Journal of Psychosomatic Research, 23,* 101–103.

Strack, S., & Coyne, J. C. (1983). Social confirmation of dysphoria: Shared and private reactions to depression. *Journal of Personality and Social Psychology, 44,* 798–806.

Taylor, C. B., Bandura, A., Ewart, C. K., Miller, N. H., & Debusk, R. R. (1985). Exercise testing to enhance wives' confidence in their husband's cardiac capacity soon after clinically uncomplicated acute myocardial infarction. *American Journal of Cardiology, 55,* 635–638.

Thoits, P. A. (1982). Conceptual, methodological, and theoretical problems in studying social support as a buffer against life stress. *Journal of Health and Social Behavior, 23,* 145–159.

Watzlawick, P., Jackson, D. D., & Beavin, J. (1967). *Pragmatics of human communication.* New York: Norton.

Wethington, E., & Kessler, R. C. (1986). Perceived support, received support, and adjustment to stressful life events. *Journal of Health and Social Behavior, 27,* 78–89.

Winter, W. D., Ferreira, A. J., & Bowers, N. (1973). Decision making in married and unrelated couples. *Family Process, 12,* 83–94.

Wishnie, H. A., Hackett, T. P., & Cassem, N. H. (1971). Psychological hazards of convalescence following myocardial infarction. *Journal of the American Medical Association, 215,* 1291–1296.

Ziomek, M., Coyne, J. C., & Heist, P. (1983, August). *Interactions involving depressed persons.* Paper presented to the annual meeting of the American Psychological Association, Anaheim, CA.

CHAPTER 6

From Self to Health:
Self-verification and Identity Disruption

WILLIAM B. SWANN, JR. AND JONATHON D. BROWN

University of Texas at Austin

University of Washington

In the not too distant past, physicians treated illnesses with a host of remarkable and inventive procedures; cholera, for example, called for a red-hot poker to be applied to the patient's heel. Such treatments had the distinct advantage of discouraging malingering. On the down side, though, the poker treatment and its compatriots inspired ambivalence among would-be patients, ambivalence that can still be found today.

Small wonder, then, that excitement ran high when researchers suggested that people could use a simple and painless strategy to keep their doctors at bay. In particular, in the 1960s several behavioral scientists suggested that receiving "social support" from others might help people remain healthier in the face of stress (for reviews, see Berkman, 1985; Cobb, 1976; Cohen & Wills, 1985; Kessler & McLeod, 1985; Kessler, Price, & Wortman, 1985).

After nearly two decades of intensive research, it is now fairly clear that social support does indeed have salutary effects on health. Unfortunately, the *mechanisms* that underlie such effects are poorly understood. This theoretical deficit has an important consequence. Without understanding how social support works, practitioners cannot begin to exploit the beneficial effects of social support in designing treatment programs.

To date, the most widely accepted hypothesis is that social support effects are mediated by a tendency for people to provide their relationship partners with positive feedback or "emotional support." This hypothesis presumes that all people are motivated to get favorable feedback from others and that getting such feedback improves their emotional well-being, level of motivation, and ability to resist disease.

Although we acknowledge that people sometimes desire and benefit from positive feedback, we believe that it is too early to conclude that emotional support is the only or even the major benefit that people gain from their relationships. In this chapter we contend that an important yet largely overlooked feature of relationships is the tendency for the people in them to give each other *identity support*,[1] that is, feedback that confirms their identities and self-conceptions. Although identity support amounts to much the same thing as emotional support for individuals who possess positive self-views (i.e., it consists of favorable feedback), the two forms of support are quite distinct for people who possess negative self-views. Indeed, our analysis suggests that although people with negative self-views desire and benefit from identity support, they may avoid and suffer from emotional support.

Our focus here, then, is on the nature and consequences of people's struggle to acquire identity support. We emphasize two formulations that deal with complementary aspects of this struggle: self-verification and identity disruption. We begin by making the case that people are highly motivated to verify their self-conceptions because such conceptions play an important role in their efforts to predict and control their social worlds. We then consider how self-verification strivings influence how people organize their social relationships and how their relationships, in turn, stabilize their self-conceptions.

The next section of the chapter deals with the identity disruption formulation, which serves as a conceptual bridge between self-verification processes and physical health. We argue that the identity support that people receive from their relationship partners stabilizes their self-conceptions and increases their perceptions of control. These perceptions, in turn, promote health. An overview of the process we are proposing here, from the desire to self-verify to the impact of identity support on health, is outlined in Figure 6.1.

THE NATURE AND FUNCTION OF SELF-CONCEPTIONS

When children are born, they have a powerful need to predict and control their environments. To do this, they form conceptions of themselves, primarily by observing their own behavior, the reactions of others to them, and the relation of their own performances to those of others (e.g., Cooley, 1902; Mead, 1934).

Once people form self-conceptions and become relatively sure of them, they become concerned with seeing that these conceptions do not radically change (cf. Backman, 1988; Lecky, 1945; Secord & Backman, 1965). There are several reasons for this. One is that in a world in which there are rapid changes in one's surroundings, interaction partners, and rules governing survival, stable self-conceptions may be important to organizing one's experience (Derry & Kuiper, 1981) and to predicting future events (cf. Epstein, 1973; Lecky, 1945; Mead, 1934; Secord & Backman, 1965). In fact, self-conceptions may be construed as

---

[1]In this chapter, we use the terms *self-conception* and *identity* almost interchangeably. They are distinct, however, in that an identity is usually tied to a specific role and a self-conception is typically associated with several roles or self-attributes. For example, three identities (e.g., being a parent, an academic adviser, and the owner of a puppy) may support a single self-conception (e.g., being a nurturant person). It is also important to distinguish self-conceptions and self-esteem. Self-conceptions refer to specific beliefs about the self. Self-esteem refers to global sense of self-worth, a sense that is only partially determined by self-conceptions (e.g., Pelham & Swann, 1989).

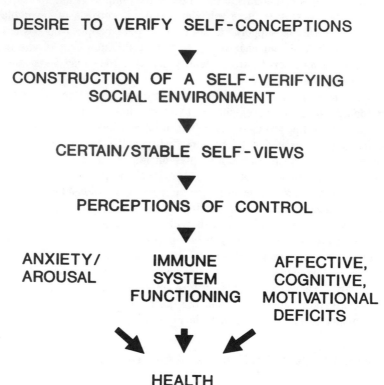

Figure 6.1. Self-verification and health.

the lenses through which people view the world, *the* means through which they define their existence and maintain a sense of control over their world. Thus, substantial changes in self-conceptions may require a massive reorganization of people's conceptual systems and undermine their sense of existential security (e.g., Thoits, 1983a).

People may also rely on their self-conceptions to guide behavior. Consider that before social interactions can proceed smoothly and efficiently, people must secure a "working consensus" that specifies the identity that each party is to assume. In establishing such a working consensus, people should want to assume only those identities that they believe they can honor. Those who see themselves as unsociable or unintelligent, for example, should want others to see them as such, lest their interaction partners place demands on them that they are unwilling or unable to meet (cf. Baumeister, Hamilton, & Tice, 1985). From this vantage point, bringing others to see one as one sees oneself is a prerequisite to successful social interaction (Athay & Darley, 1981; Goffman, 1959; Swann, 1987).

For these and other reasons, people are likely to think and behave in ways that promote the survival of their self-conceptions, even if the self-conception happens to be negative. Although there surely are painful consequences associated with verifying negative self-conceptions, the foregoing analysis suggests that failing to verify such conceptions may at least sometimes have even more painful consequences.

Research has supported the notion that people strive to verify their self-conceptions by acquiring self-confirmatory feedback. For example, Swann and Read (1981b) found clear evidence of a preference for self-confirmatory feedback, whether they studied the extent to which participants paid attention to such feedback, remembered it, or actively sought it. Three additional investigations by Swann & Read (1981a) showed that both males and females solicited self-confirmatory feedback about both valenced and unvalenced self-conceptions. Furthermore, people were undaunted in their quest for self-confirmatory feedback, even when they had reason to believe that it would depress them (Swann, Krull, & Pelham, 1988) and even when they had to spend their personal funds to get it (Swann & Read, 1981a).

The specific strategies that people use to verify their self-conceptions fall into two distinct classes (e.g., Swann, 1983, 1987). In the first class are behavioral activities through which targets strive to influence the reactions of perceivers. Specifically, targets work to create around themselves self-confirmatory social environments, that is, social environments that give them identity support.

In the second class of self-verification strategies are cognitive processes through which targets systematically distort their perceptions of social reality. In particular, the targets process feedback from perceivers in ways that make the perceivers' responses seem much more supportive of their self-views than they actually are. Because we are especially interested in the interpersonal activities through which people actively recruit identity support, the following discussion will focus exclusively on the behavioral activities through which people strive to verify themselves.

DEVELOPING A SELF-CONFIRMATORY SOCIAL ENVIRONMENT

Many biologists and ecologists have noticed that every living organism inhabits a "niche" that routinely satisfies its needs and desires (cf. Clarke, 1954; Odum, 1963; Wilson, 1974). People are no exception to this rule. In fact, people seem to be particularly adept at constructing social environments that satisfy their desire for self-confirmatory feedback.

In their efforts to construct self-verifying social environments, people may employ several strategies, two of which are of particular interest here. First, they may strategically choose interaction partners and social settings in which they are apt to receive support for their identities. Second, they may adopt interaction strategies that evoke self-confirmatory responses. We will consider each of these strategies.

Selective Interaction

For years, researchers have entertained the notion that people seek social contexts that will give them self-confirmatory feedback (e.g., Secord & Backman, 1965). Although it is inherently difficult to obtain definitive support for this hypothesis, several researchers have collected correlational evidence that is consistent with it. Pervin and Rubin (1967), for example, found that if students enroll in colleges that are compatible with their self-views, they are less likely to drop out and are happier (see also Backman & Secord, 1962; Broxton, 1963; Newcomb, 1956).

Two field investigations by Swann and Pelham (1988a, 1988b) offer somewhat more direct evidence for the selective interaction hypothesis. In an initial study of college roommates, these investigators discovered that individuals were inclined to keep roommates whose appraisals of them were congruent with their self-views and to drop roommates whose appraisals were not congruent with their self-views. The means plotted in Figure 6.2 show that this tendency was symmetrical with respect to self-esteem. That is, just as people with positive self-conceptions were poised to flee from overly unfavorable roommates, so too were people with negative self-views inclined to flee from overly favorable roommates. Subsidiary analyses helped rule out several alternative explanations of this finding: The effects were not due to a tendency for subjects in congruent relationships to be more similar to one another, to engage in more self-disclosure, or to spend more time with their roommates. Nor was it true that people with negative self-conceptions preferred roommates who were favorably disposed toward them in general but happened to have low assessments of their specific attributes. That is, those roommates whom people with negative self-views preferred perceived them negatively, not merely in a specific sense, but in a global sense as well, as indicated by the tendency of such preferred roommates to endorse items like "My roommate is worthless."

A complementary investigation (Swann & Pelham, 1988b) revealed a similar preference for congruence among individuals in friendship relationships. This investigation also revealed that the preference for congruent partners was most apparent when participants were relatively certain of their self-views; congruency mattered very little for people who were uncertain of their self-views. Apparently, as people become more certain of their self-conceptions, they become more inclined to rely on these conceptions to organize their experiences, predict future events, and guide behavior. For this reason, high certainty is associated with intensified efforts to verify oneself through selective interaction.

These data therefore offer fairly clear evidence that people gravitate toward social relationships in which they think they will receive self-confirmatory feedback. An important characteristic of this selective interaction strategy is that once people enter a particular social relationship or institution, forces such as legal contracts and social pressures tend to keep them there. Although such contractual arrangements are particularly salient in the case of marriage, even dating couples often find that breaking up with each other also means severing ties with the circle of friends who have come to regard them as a couple. From this per-

Selective interaction

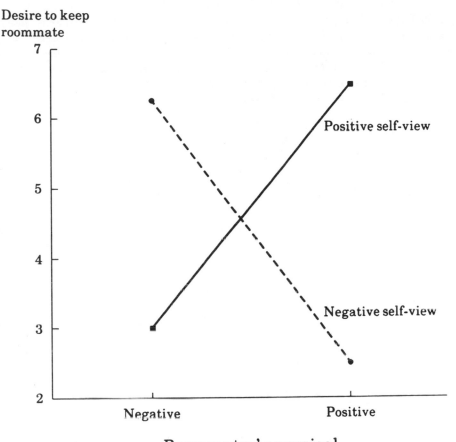

Figure 6.2. Selective interaction.

spective, the selective interaction strategy of self-verification often locks people into interpersonal feedback systems that are self-sustaining as well as self-verifying.

Interaction Strategies

Even if people fail to gain self-confirmatory feedback through selective interaction, they may still acquire such feedback by adopting appropriate interaction strategies. Swann and Read (1981a, Study 2), for example, had targets who perceived themselves as either likable or dislikable interact with perceivers. Some targets were led to suspect that the perceiver might have positive regard for them;

others learned that the perceiver might have negative regard for them; and still others learned nothing of the perceivers' evaluation of them.

Targets who perceived themselves as likable tended to elicit more favorable reactions than did targets who perceived themselves as dislikable. Moreover, the means in Figure 6.3 show that this tendency was especially pronounced when the targets suspected that the perceivers' appraisals might disconfirm their self-conceptions. That is, just as targets who thought of themselves as likable elicited the most favorable reactions when they thought that the perceivers disliked them, targets who thought of themselves as dislikable elicited the most negative reac-

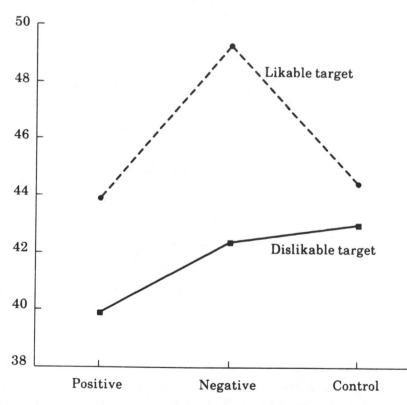

Figure 6.3. Self-verification through interaction.

tions when they suspected that the perceivers liked them. Therefore, targets were particularly inclined to elicit self-confirmatory feedback from perceivers when they suspected that the perceivers' appraisals were incompatible with their self-views (cf. Hilton & Darley, 1985).

Swann and Hill (1982) obtained a similar pattern of results using a different dimension of the self-concept (dominance) and a different procedural paradigm. Targets began by playing a game with a confederate in which each player alternately assumed the dominant "leader" role or the submissive "assistant" role. There was a break in the game, and the experimenter asked the players to decide who would like to be the leader for the next set of games. This was the confederate's cue to deliver feedback to the participant. In some conditions, the confederate said that the participant seemed dominant; in other conditions the confederate asserted that the participant seemed submissive.

If the feedback confirmed the targets' self-conceptions, they more or less passively accepted the confederate's appraisal. If the feedback disconfirmed their self-conceptions, however, the targets reacted quite vehemently, resisting the feedback and striving to demonstrate that they were not the person the confederate made them out to be. Thus, the self-conceived dominants labeled as submissive became all the more dominant, and the self-conceived submissives labeled as dominant became especially submissive.

An interesting feature of the Swann and Hill study was that some people behaviorally resisted the discrepant feedback more than others did. Swann and Ely (1984) speculated that such differences in resistance might reflect variability in the extent to which people were certain of their self-conceptions. To test this hypothesis, Swann and Ely (1984) had perceivers interview targets who were either certain or uncertain of their self-conceived extroversion. They led the perceivers to develop an expectancy of the targets that was discrepant with the targets' self-conceptions. This created the potential for a "battle of wills," with the perceivers' experimentally manipulated beliefs vying against the targets' chronic self-views.

Consistent with earlier research by Snyder and Swann (1978b; see also Swann & Giuliano, 1987), the perceivers acted on their expectancies by soliciting responses that would confirm their own expectancies but *dis*confirm the targets' self-conceptions. For example, perceivers who believed that the target was an extrovert often asked questions such as "Do you like to go to lively parties?" Targets who were low in self-certainty generally answered in ways that confirmed the perceivers' expectancies (but disconfirmed their own self-conceptions) when the perceivers were highly certain of their expectancies. In contrast, targets who were high in self-certainty actively resisted the questions, regardless of the perceivers' level of certainty (see also Swann, Pelham, & Chidester, 1988c). In this way, highly certain targets brought the perceivers' expectancies into line with their self-views. Thus, as long as targets were high in self-certainty, self-verification "won" over behavioral confirmation in the battle of wills (for a further discussion of factors that influence the outcome of such battles, see Swann, 1984).

This research, then, suggests that by carefully choosing self-congruent interaction partners and by evoking self-confirmatory reactions from others, people may bring others to see them as they see themselves. In so doing, people should theoretically create interpersonal environments that help stabilize their self-conceptions. In the next section we ask whether self-verification processes do indeed stabilize people's self-conceptions.

THE PSYCHOLOGICAL CONSEQUENCES OF SELF-CONFIRMATORY FEEDBACK

Although the foregoing research indicates that people strive to bring the appraisals of others into line with their self-views, it does not show that such activities actually do stabilize their self-conceptions. Swann and Hill (1982) thus asked whether self-verification activities do indeed help stabilize people's self-views. As we mentioned, some targets in the Swann and Hill study first received feedback from a confederate that disconfirmed their self-perceived dominance. Half of these targets then had an opportunity to interact with the confederate; the others received no such opportunity. Afterwards, all targets completed a measure of self-perceived dominance.

Targets in the interaction-opportunity conditions actively sought to undermine the discrepant feedback by behaving in a manner that exemplified their self-conceptions: The self-conceived dominants showed just how overbearing they could be, and the self-conceived submissives grew especially wimpy and passive. Furthermore, this opportunity to refute the feedback had important cognitive consequences. As can be seen in Figure 6.4, just as participants who had the opportunity to repudiate the feedback displayed very little self-rating change, those who were deprived of this opportunity displayed substantial change. Therefore, if they could do so, targets actively sought to undermine self-discrepant feedback and so displayed little self-rating change.

Believers in the malleability of self-concepts will be quick to point out that Swann and Hill's (1982) findings suggest that people will be vulnerable to self-concept change when they receive self-discrepant feedback in highly structured situations in which they are unable to resist the feedback they receive. Nevertheless, even when people receive discrepant feedback in highly structured situations, afterwards they often will return to environments that offset the effects of the self-discrepant feedback. Imagine, for example, a highly talented woman who for some reason (e.g., an abusive parent) has developed a negative view of her capabilities. Her therapist may try to deal with this problem by encouraging her to focus on her many talents. Although this technique may produce momentary improvements in her self-view, such improvements may be completely undone when she returns home to a husband who showers her with abuse. Hence, once people negotiate identities with their relationship partners, these partners may tend to reinforce these identities even if such identities are negative.

Of course, although people typically succeed in locating relationship partners who have congruent appraisals of them (i.e., appraisals that confirm their self-

Self-verification and change

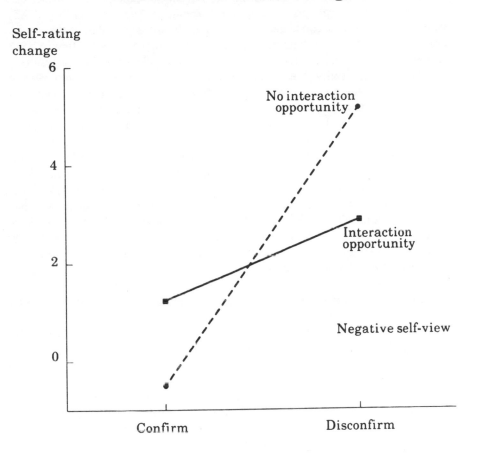

Figure 6.4. Self-verification and change.

views), they do not always do so. Relationship partners should help stabilize the self-conceptions of their mates only if they see them in a congruent manner; partners who see their mates in a *non*congruent manner may actually promote changes in their self-concepts.

To test this reasoning, Swann and Predmore (1985) recruited pairs of individuals ("targets" and "intimates") who had been in intimate relationships for an average of 18 months. Some targets had positive self-views, and others had negative self-views. The experimenter separated the targets and the intimates upon their arrival and asked the intimates to report their perceptions of the targets. Although most of the intimates saw the targets as the targets saw themselves, $r = .41$, in some couples the amount of congruency was relatively high (congruent), and in others it was relatively low (incongruent).

While the intimates were evaluating the targets, an experimenter posing as a clinician had the targets complete a bogus Thematic Apperception Test (TAT). When the targets had completed the test, the "clinician" ushered them into a room where either their intimate or a complete stranger was waiting. Shortly thereafter, the "clinician" returned with what were alleged to be the results of the TAT test. In reality, these "results" had been prepared in advance; in all cases, the feedback disconfirmed targets' self-views. The experimenter then withdrew, leaving the targets to interact for five minutes with either their intimate or a stranger. At the end of this period the experimenter returned to measure the targets' final self-views.

The results showed that interacting with congruent intimates insulated the targets against the self-discrepant feedback but that interacting with strangers did not. Incongruent intimates had some insulating influence on the targets, although not as much as the congruent ones did, presumably because incongruent intimates had appraisals of the targets that were only modestly associated with the targets' self-views. One particularly interesting finding, however, was that the congruent intimates of low self-esteem targets were as effective in insulating them against positive feedback as the congruent intimates of the high self-esteem targets were in insulating them against negative feedback!

Why should relationship partners offer their intimates support for their *negative* identities? Perhaps the most obvious reason is that they believe that their partners want such unfavorable feedback. Thus, for example, a woman who believes that her husband is submissive and wishes to be patronized may treat him as such because she recognizes that he will be anxious and upset if she fails to do so. In addition, spouses may themselves want their mates to maintain negative identities. Family therapists, for example, note that changes in the "dependent" marriage partner often disturb the "dominant" member of the relationship more than they do the dependent member (e.g., Fry, 1962). In fact, a major obstacle to therapy in such instances is that the "dominant" person sometimes fights like a tiger to maintain the status quo, presumably because dominant persons need dependent individuals to verify their self-conceived dominance. In such instances, people may work to maintain their partner's self-view in the service of verifying their own self-views.

Of course, people's efforts to maintain their relationship partners' self-views can be understood from other perspectives as well. For example, people may encourage their relationship partners to believe the worst about themselves as a means of maintaining power over them, the logic being that convincing someone that they are worthless will put that person in a relatively weak bargaining position (cf. Kelley, 1979).

Whatever their reason for doing so, people may clearly play an integral role in stabilizing the self-views of their relationship partners. From this perspective, people's intimates may serve as "accomplices" who assist them in their self-verification attempts by offering feedback that verifies and sustains their self-conceptions.

One reason that such identity support may be important is that it may help people deal with stress. Consider, for example, parents who suddenly lose their jobs. Although such individuals are apt to question their adequacy as bread-winners and providers (Pearlin, Menaghan, Lieberman, & Mullan, 1981), they may feel better if their friends and intimates reinforce their positive self-views. (Swann, Pelham, and Krull, 1989, showed that even people with very low global self-esteem have some positive self-conceptions.) Indirect support for this idea comes from a study by Gore (1978), who found that individuals who enjoyed high levels of social support were less likely to become ill as a function of unexpected job loss.

Although Gore's findings buttress the idea that social relationships protect in-dividuals from ill health under periods of high stress (see Cohen & Wills, 1985, for a review), the mechanism underlying his results is unclear. Given that most people possess positive self-views (e.g., Swann, 1987), it may be that the so-cially supportive actions of relationship partners were beneficial because they of-fered identity support. Alternatively, the actions of their relationship partners may have served as a source of emotional support. In the next section, we will consider research that provides somewhat clearer evidence that identity support promotes health.

THE MIND–BODY LINK: STRESS, IDENTITY DISRUPTION, AND HEALTH

The foregoing analysis suggests that (1) people want to verify their self-conceptions, (2) they engage in a variety of activities designed to do so, and (3) receiving self-verifying feedback stabilizes people's self-views. We now turn to the final link in the chain of events under consideration here: that between self-conceptions and health. Brown's (1987) identity-disruption formulation fo-cuses explicitly on this link.

The identity-disruption formulation rests on two assumptions. The first is that major life events produce uncertainty and change in people's identities and asso-ciated self-conceptions. For example, graduating from college means leaving the undergraduate identity behind; getting married means taking on the spouse iden-tity; and having children requires that people incorporate the parent identity into their self-conceptions. Major life events, such as the death of a spouse, taking a new job, or moving to a new city, may therefore require individuals to relinquish cherished identities, adopt new identities, or restructure existing identities. All of these activities may produce uncertainty and change in people's self-conceptions.

The identity-disruption formulation assumes further that uncertainty or change in self-conceptions may undermine health. At least two distinct mechanisms may cause this effect. First, self-concept change may undermine the perceptions of control theoretically enjoyed by people with stable, coherent self-conceptions. Diminished perceptions of control may produce anxiety and rumination (e.g.,

Pennebaker, 1985) and have been linked to a wide array of cognitive, motivational, and affective deficits (e.g., Seligman, 1975). Brown and Siegel (1988), for example, indicated that negative life events that are perceived as controllable are less stressful and less likely to produce the cognitive and motivational deficits ordinarily linked to lack of control. Avoiding these deficits should help ensure that people retain the resources necessary to forestall illness and disease (cf. Selye, 1956).

In addition, the perceptions of control emanating from stable self-conceptions may help people cope with stressful life changes by improving immune system functioning (e.g., Taylor, 1986). Research on stress in animals has demonstrated a link between controllability and immune system functioning: Acute stress is less immunosuppressive when it is controllable than when it is uncontrollable (Laudenslager, Ryan, Drugan, Hyson, & Maier, 1983; Sklar & Anisman, 1979). Similarly, studies with human subjects suggest that controllability diminishes physiological reactivity to stress. That is, individuals who believe they can control aversive events, such as crowding or noise, display relatively low catecholamine levels (Lundberg & Frankenhaeuser, 1978; Singer, Lundberg, & Frankenhaeuser, 1978).

Whatever the specific mechanism may be, the identity-disruption formulation suggests that stable, relatively certain self-views foster perceptions of control, which, in turn, promote health. Although there is no direct evidence that this is the case, several investigations of the relationship among self-certainty, stress, and health support it indirectly. We now turn to these investigations.

Certainty of Self-concept as a Moderator of Stress

As mentioned earlier, people who are relatively certain of their self-views are not only more inclined to enter into relationships with individuals whose appraisals confirm their self-views (Swann & Pelham, 1988b), they are also more inclined to resist self-discrepant feedback. Such activity should help stabilize people's self-conceptions. In support of this, Pelham (1989) found that the more certain people were of their self-views, the more stable their self-views were. That is, after asking people to rate themselves on various dimensions (e.g., sociable, athletic, intelligent, attractive, artistic), he had them indicate how certain they were of each of their ratings. When he collected self-rating scores again several weeks later, he found that individuals displayed more stability in those self-views of which they were relatively certain (average $r = .88$) than in the self-views of which they were relatively uncertain (average $r = .53$).

Recent evidence also suggests that as self-certainty increases, so too do people's perceptions of control. To wit, Brown (1987) found that self-concept certainty was reliably associated with measures of control and mastery. Of course, the fact that self-certainty is related to perceptions of control and to the stability of self-views does not clarify the causal relation between these variables. Nevertheless, these findings are at least consistent with the notion that relatively certain self-views foster greater stability, which in turn heightens perceptions of control.

If self-concept certainty influences perceptions of control, individuals who are relatively certain of their self-conceptions should be less susceptible to stress-induced deteriorations in health than should individuals who are relatively uncertain of their self-conceptions. Brown and Smart (1989) tested this hypothesis in an investigation of stress and illness among college students. The participants began by completing Rosenberg's (1965) measure of self-concept certainty (e.g., "I feel that nothing, or almost nothing, can change the opinion I currently hold of myself"). Later, they completed a measure of stress (Dohrenwend, Krasnoff, Askenasy, & Dohrenwend, 1978) as well as a measure of health (Siegel & Brown, 1988; this measure inquired about the occurrence of 36 illnesses, ranging in severity from a cold or sore throat to diabetes and cancer).

As expected, self-certainty moderated the relation between stress and illness. The means in Table 6.1 show that stressful life events had much more adverse effects on the health of those who were low compared with high in self-certainty. These findings were subsequently replicated in a second, more conservative study that used a more objective measure of illness (i.e., visits to a health facility). Together, these studies provide converging evidence that people who are relatively uncertain of their self-conceptions are much more vulnerable to stress than are those who are relatively certain of their self-conceptions (see Linville, 1987, for a related investigation of the moderating influence of self-complexity on health).

At the very least, Brown and Smart's (1989) findings suggest that high levels of self-certainty are associated with greater resistance to stress-induced deteriorations in health than are low levels of certainty. In addition, however, there is reason to believe that self-certainty might have this effect because it engenders perceptions of control. After all, certainty is associated with perceptions of control (Brown, 1987), and perceptions of control appear to play an important role in reducing the negative consequences of stressful circumstances (cf. Rodin, 1986). From this perspective, firmly established, highly certain self-conceptions may protect individuals from stress-induced degenerations in health via their capacity to promote enhanced perceptions of control over the environment.

The Cost of Success

The identity-disruption formulation implies that the health of people with negative self-views should be impaired by favorable events because their self-

TABLE 6.1. Illness Reports as a Function of Life Stress and Certainty of Self-concept

		Life Stress	
		Low	High
Certainty of Self-concept	Low	4.22	6.06
	High	4.68	4.08

Note: Adapted from Brown and Smart (1989), Study 1.

conceptions do not lead them to expect such events. That is, because the self-conceptions of people with negative self-views lead them to expect undesirable events, favorable life events will challenge and disrupt their self-conceptions, and such disruptions may, in turn, promote illness. Favorable events should not, however, undermine the health of people with positive self-conceptions, as the self-views of such individuals lead them to expect such events.

Consider, for example, a female attorney who is promoted to partner in her law firm. If she thinks of herself as incompetent, the promotion may challenge her self-view and place her at risk for developing illness. Of course, if she has high esteem for her own abilities, the promotion should not threaten her self-concept or health. The identity formulation, then, predicts that positive events should undermine the health only of people with low self-esteem.

To test this hypothesis, Brown & McGill (1989) first had university students complete the Life Experiences Survey (LES; Sarason, Johnson, & Siegel, 1978). A widely used measure of life events, this instrument allows individuals to state whether any events they have experienced in the preceding six-month period had a positive or negative impact on their lives. The number of events that people rated as desirable served as a measure of positive life events. In addition to completing the LES, the participants also completed a measure of self-esteem (Rosenberg, 1965). Subjects' visits to the university health center for illness were then monitored throughout the academic year.

Brown and McGill (1989) expected that positive life events would undermine the health of people who thought poorly of themselves but would have little negative impact on the health of those who thought well of themselves. The pattern of means displayed in Table 6.2 supports this prediction. That is, the greater the number of positive events experienced by participants with low self-esteem, the worse their health was. In contrast, the greater the number of positive events experienced by participants with high self-esteem, the better their health.

These results may help resolve the long-standing debate in the life events literature concerning the impact of positive life events on physical health (for reviews, see Sarason & Sarason, 1984; Suls, 1983; and Thoits, 1983a). Past researchers were frustrated in their efforts to show that desirable life events contribute to the onset of illness; in fact, some have found that desirable life events have reduced the adverse impact of negative life events on health (Cohen & Hoberman, 1983; Siegel & Brown, in press). The results of Brown and McGill's (1989) research showed that if researchers had compared the effects of desirable

TABLE 6.2.   Illness Reports as a Function of Positive Life Events and Self-esteem

		Positive Life Events	
		Low	High
Self-esteem	Low	5.35	7.63
	High	5.64	3.57

Note: Adapted from Brown & McGill (1989), Study 1.

events on people with high, versus low, self-esteem, they would have found that such events improved the health of people with high esteem but undermined the health of their counterparts with low self-esteem.

THE COGNITIVE–AFFECTIVE CROSSFIRE AND HEALTH

The major message of this chapter is that people seek and benefit from feedback that confirms their self-views—even if their self-views happen to be negative. Skeptics, however, invariably point out that although people with negative self-views may prefer unfavorable feedback on a cognitive level, they do not feel very good when they receive it. Thus the paradox: Why do people with negative self-views seek unfavorable feedback if receiving it makes them miserable?

The answer is that there seems to be a fair amount of independence between the psychological mechanism that controls what people *think* about social feedback and the mechanism that controls how they *feel* about it (for more complete discussions of this argument, see Swann, 1987; Swann, Griffin, Predmore, & Gaines, 1987; and Zajonc, 1980, 1984). Swann, Krull, and Pelham (1988), for example, gave individuals who had either positive or negative self-concepts a choice of either favorable or unfavorable social feedback. As the self-verification formulation would suggest, participants with positive self-concepts (e.g., nonde-pressed or high-esteem individuals) were especially inclined to solicit favorable feedback, and participants with negative self-views (e.g., depressed or low-esteem individuals) were especially inclined to solicit unfavorable feedback. Nevertheless, a follow-up study showed that people with positive and negative self-concepts alike were considerably more depressed when they received unfavorable, as compared with favorable, feedback (for a review of related evidence, see Shrauger, 1975).

The obvious implication of such findings is that people who have negative self-views are of two minds when it comes to social feedback: Although they desire self-confirmatory feedback because it bolsters their perceptions of control, on an emotional level they want positive, self-enhancing feedback. The existence of this independent motive to self-enhance poses no problem for people who have positive self-views because the motives to self-verify and self-enhance simultaneously encourage them to seek positive feedback and steer clear of negative feedback. In contrast, the two motives trap people with negative self-conceptions in a crossfire between a desire for self-confirmatory (i.e., negative) feedback and a desire for positive feedback. On the one hand, if such individuals seek and receive favorable feedback, their perceptions of control will be diminished, and they will probably become anxious. On the other hand, if they seek and receive unfavorable feedback, their desire for self-enhancement will be frustrated, and they will feel unhappy.

How do people with negative self-views deal with the conflict created by competing desires to self-verify and self-enhance? Research by Swann, Pelham, and Krull (1989) suggests that they try to avoid it altogether by seeking feedback that is both self-verifying and self-enhancing. These investigators first showed that people's self-concepts are sufficiently differentiated that even those with very low global self-esteem (lowest 10%) believe that they possess a "ray of hope," that is, a positive attribute that might serve as a source of pride and inspiration (cf. Higgins, 1987; James, 1890; Linville, 1987). They then asked whether even people with globally negative self-views would seek to verify their (relatively rare) positive attributes. Consistent with earlier research, they found that when people sampled feedback about their negative attributes, they solicited feedback that verified these negative attributes (i.e., unfavorable feedback). In contrast, however, when people's feedback-seeking activities were relatively *un*constrained, they tended to seek feedback from their roommates that would verify their positive attributes. This tendency was equally apparent among people with high and low global self-esteem.

One implication of the Swann, Pelham, and Krull (1989) findings is that when they can, people try to avoid getting into cognitive-affective crossfires by seeking support for their positive attributes. This means that when they select relationship partners—although people may prefer individuals who recognize their vices over those who are oblivious to them—they would ideally like to have persons who recognize and focus on their virtues rather than their vices. A follow-up investigation confirmed this hypothesis.

It is important to remember, of course, that, try as they might, people cannot always avoid getting in crossfires between their desire for self-verifying and positive feedback. When choosing a friend or intimate, for example, people with one or more negative self-conceptions may discover that it is impossible to locate someone who will verify both their positive and their negative attributes, because halo biases or illusory correlations (e.g., Chapman & Chapman, 1967; Hamilton & Gifford, 1976) tend to homogenize people's appraisals of one another. This means that individuals must sometimes choose between partners who are generally positive or generally negative toward them, a choice that places them squarely in the middle of the crossfire they wish to avoid.

What happens when people find themselves in such inescapable crossfires? The research reviewed in this chapter shows that if people are certain of their self-views and if they are aware of epistemic and pragmatic consequences of failing to self-verify, they will choose relationship partners on the basis of self-verification rather than self-enhancement. Thus, for example, Swann and Pelham (1988a) found that people who were relatively certain of their negative self-conceptions planned to abandon relationships in which they were perceived favorably and to remain in relationships in which they were perceived unfavorably. Apparently, if people cannot avoid a crossfire between self-verification and self-enhancement, they will self-enhance only if they feel that they can avoid the aversive epistemic and pragmatic consequences associated with failing to self-verify (see also Schlenker, 1985).

A central concern in this chapter, of course, is how conflicting tendencies to self-enhance and self-verify influence physical health. On the one hand, even negative self-verifying feedback may engender perceptions of control that make people less anxious and better able to resist stress. On the other hand, self-enhancing feedback may help people remain happy, motivated, and healthier (e.g., Taylor & Brown, 1988). Although it is not yet clear how the two motives combine to influence physical health, the notion of latitude of acceptance may be useful here. That is, Sherif, Sherif, and Nebergall (1965) indicated that people's beliefs are structured in such a way that they can tolerate a certain range of information as self-descriptive—a *latitude of acceptance*. This means that although a particular instance of feedback may not be exactly consistent with one's self-view, as long as it falls within a person's latitude of acceptance it will not threaten people's perceptions of control and undermine their health. Furthermore, as long as feedback falls within one's latitude of acceptance, the more positive it is, and the better it will be for health.

SUMMARY AND CONCLUSIONS

Social support researchers have generally assumed that the desire for positive feedback is a major organizing force in interpersonal relationships. It is generally believed, for example, that people seek relationship partners who are apt to enhance their self-views. Further, receiving positive feedback is presumed to yield significant dividends; it is assumed that such feedback not only makes people feel good but that it also promotes the recipients' physical health.

The research reviewed in this chapter challenges the notion that positive feedback is the sine qua non of people's social relationships. Although individuals clearly enjoy receiving positive feedback, we suggest that when such feedback is inconsistent with their self-views, their enjoyment is marred by bewilderment and anxiety. For this reason, people strive to enter relationships with individuals who see them as they see themselves, even if this means seeking relationship partners who think poorly of them. In addition, entering such relationships and receiving support for identities may bolster perceptions of control, thereby improving health.

We drew support for our belief in the importance of identity support from two independent lines of research. Research on self-verification processes shows that people strive to enter and maintain relationships with people who see them as they see themselves. Thus, for example, people who have negative self-conceptions gravitate toward relationships with partners who have unfavorable appraisals of them and flee from relationships with partners who have favorable appraisals of them. Research on identity disruption suggests that the fit between people's self-views and the feedback they receive influences their health. Whereas people with positive self-views stay healthier when they experience favorable outcomes, people with negative self-views do not seem to benefit from favorable outcomes.

Yet if people are so apt to seek and benefit from identity support, why have past researchers focused almost exclusively on emotional support? In part, the reason may be that most people have relatively positive conceptions of themselves (for a discussion of this phenomenon, see Swann, 1987). This means that for most people, positive feedback simultaneously satisfies their desire for emotional and identity support. In addition, many researchers have assessed the impact of feedback and events on people by relying on measures of depression. The problem with this is that depression is an index of emotional well-being only; a given piece of feedback may make a person feel happy but diminish perceptions of control and thereby introduce health-threatening anxiety.

Perhaps the most straightforward implication of our analysis is that emotional support and positive events are good only if they are generally consistent with people's self-views. This may explain why life-events researchers have obtained such mixed results in their efforts to test the idea that positive events have deleterious effects on health (e.g., Brown & McGill, 1989).

More generally, our findings suggest that it may be time for researchers interested in social support to develop more sophisticated views of the needs of the human organism and how social contacts help satisfy those needs. Our work, for example, suggests that people are not wholly emotional creatures who hunger for nothing more than a warm smile and a pat on the head. Rather, people also are active information processors who carefully formulate their identities and work to ensure that their relationship partners offer support for these identities. Although identity support may not always make people feel happy, it may nevertheless help them live longer and healthier lives.

REFERENCES

Athay, M., & Darley, J. M. (1981). Toward an interaction centered theory of personality. In N. Cantor & J. F. Kihlstrom (Eds.), *Personality, cognition, and social interaction* (pp. 281–308). Hillsdale, NJ: Erlbaum.

Backman, C. W. (1988). The self: A dialectical approach. In L. Berkowitz (Ed.), *Advances in experimental social psychology.* (Vol. 21, pp. 229–260). New York: Academic Press.

Backman, C. W., & Secord, P. F. (1962). Liking, selective interaction, and misperception in congruent interpersonal relations. *Sociometry, 25,* 321–335.

Baumeister, R. F., Hamilton, J. C., & Tice, D. M. (1985). Public versus private expectancy of success: Confidence booster or performance pressure? *Journal of Personality and Social Psychology, 48,* 1447–1457.

Berkman, L. F. (1985). The relationship of social networks and social support to morbidity and mortality. In S. Cohen & S. L. Syme (Eds.), *Social support and health* (pp. 241–262). Orlando, FL: Academic Press.

Brown, J. D. (1987). *An identity disruption model of stress.* Unpublished manuscript, Southern Methodist University, Dallas.

Brown, J. D., & Smart, S. A. (1989). *Role of self-concept certainty in buffering the adverse impact of stressful life events.* Manuscript submitted for publication.

Brown, J. D., & McGill, K. L. (1989). *The cost of good fortune: When positive life events produce negative health consequences. Journal of Personality and Social Psychology,* 57.

Brown, J. D., & Siegel, J. M. (1988). Attributions for negative life events and depression: The role of perceived control. *Journal of Personality and Social Psychology, 54,* 316–322.

Broxton, J. A. (1963). A test of interpersonal attraction predictions derived from balance theory. *Journal of Abnormal and Social Psychology, 66,* 394–397.

Chapman, L., & Chapman, J. (1967). The genesis of popular but erroneous psychodiagnostic observations. *Journal of Abnormal Psychology, 72,* 193–204.

Clarke, G. L. (1954). *Elements of ecology.* New York: Wiley.

Cobb, S. (1976). Social support as a moderator of life stress. *Psychosomatic Medicine, 38,* 300–314.

Cohen, S., & Hoberman, H. (1983). Positive events and social support as buffers of life change stress. *Journal of Applied Social Psychology, 13,* 99–125.

Cohen, S., & Wills, T. A. (1985). Stress, social support, and the buffering hypothesis. *Psychological Bulletin, 98,* 310–357.

Cooley, C. S. (1902). *Human nature and the social order.* New York: Scribner's.

Derry, P. A., & Kuiper, N. A. (1981). Schematic processing and self-reference in clinical depression. *Journal of Abnormal Psychology, 90,* 286–297.

Dohrenwend, B. S., Krasnoff, L., Askenasy, A. R., & Dohrenwend, B. P. (1978). Exemplifications of a method for scaling life events: The PERI life events scale. *Journal of Health and Social Behavior, 19,* 205–229.

Epstein, S. (1973). The self-concept revisited: Or a theory of a theory. *American Psychologist, 28,* 404–416.

Epstein, S. (1985). The implications of cognitive–experiential self-theory for research in social psychology and personality. *Journal for the Theory of Social Behavior, 15,* 283–310.

Fry, W. F., Jr. (1962). The marital context of the anxiety syndrome. *Family Process, 1,* 245–252.

Goffman, E. (1959). *The presentation of self in everyday life.* New York: Anchor Books.

Gore, S. (1978). The effect of social support in moderating the health consequences of unemployment. *Journal of Health and Social Behavior, 19,* 157–165.

Hamilton, D. L., & Gifford, R. K. (1976). Illusory correlation in interpersonal perception: A cognitive basis of stereotypic judgments. *Journal of Experimental Social Psychology, 12,* 392–407.

Higgins, E. T. (1987). Self-discrepancy: A theory relating self and affect. *Psychological Review, 94,* 319–340.

Hilton, J. L., & Darley, J. M. (1985). Constructing other persons: A limit on the effect. *Journal of Experimental Social Psychology, 21,* 1–18.

Holmes, T. H., & Rahe, R. H. (1967). The social readjustment rating scale. *Journal of Psychosomatic Research, 11,* 213–218.

James, W. (1890). *The principles of psychology* (Vols. 1, 2). New York: Henry Holt.

Kelley, H. H. (1979). *Personal relationships: Their structures and processes.* Hillsdale, NJ: Erlbaum.

Kessler, R. C., & McLeod, J. (1985). Social support and mental health in community samples. In S. Cohen & L. Syme (Eds.), *Social support and health* (pp. 219–240). New York: Academic Press.

Kessler, R. C., Price, R. H., & Wortman, C. B. (1985). Social and cultural influences on psychopathology. *Annual Review of Psychology, 36,* 531–572.

Laudenslager, M. L., Ryan, S. M., Drugan, R. C., Hyson, R. L., & Maier, S. F. (1983). Coping and immunosuppression: Inescapable but not escapable shock suppresses lymphocyte proliferation. *Science, 221,* 568–570.

Lecky, P. (1945). *Self-consistency: A theory of personality.* New York: Island Press.

Linville, P. W. (1987). Self-complexity as a cognitive buffer against stress-related illness and depression. *Journal of Personality and Social Psychology, 52,* 663–676.

Lundberg, U., & Frankenhaeuser, M. (1978). *Adjustment to noise stress.* Unpublished manuscript, University of Stockholm.

Mead, G. H. (1934). *Mind, self and society.* Chicago: University of Chicago Press.

Newcomb, T. M. (1956). The prediction of interpersonal attraction. *American Psychologist, 11,* 575–586.

Odum, E. P. (1963). *Ecology.* New York: Holt, Rinehart and Winston.

Pearlin, L. I., Menaghan, E. G., Lieberman, M. A., & Mullan, J. T. (1981). The stress process. *Journal of Health and Social Behavior, 22,* 337–356.

Pelham, B. (1989). On confidence and consequence: The certainty and importance of self-knowledge. Unpublished doctoral dissertation, University of Texas, Austin.

Pelham, B., & Swann, W. B., Jr. (1989). From self-conceptions to self-worth: On the sources and structure of self-esteem. *Journal of Personality and Social Psychology, 57,* 672–680.

Pennebaker, J. W. (1985). Traumatic experience and psychosomatic disease: Exploring the roles of behavioral inhibition, obsession, and confiding. *Canadian Psychology, 26,* 82–95.

Pervin, L. A., & Rubin, D. B. (1967). Student dissatisfaction with college and the college dropout: A transactional approach. *Journal of Social Psychology, 72,* 285–295.

Rodin, J. (1986). Aging and health: Effects of the sense of control. *Science, 233,* 1271–1276.

Rosenberg, M. (1965). *Self-esteem scale.* Princeton, NJ: Princeton University Press.

Sarason, I. G., Johnson, J. H., & Siegel, J. M. (1978). Assessing the impact of life changes: Development of the Life Experiences Survey. *Journal of Consulting and Clinical Psychology, 46,* 932–946.

Sarason, I. G., & Sarason, B. R. (1984). Life changes, moderators of stress, and health. In A. Baum, J. E. Singer, & S. E. Taylor, (Eds.), *Handbook of psychology and health: Social psychological aspects of health* (Vol. 4, pp. 279–299). Hillsdale, NJ: Erlbaum.

Schlenker, B. R. (1985). Identity and self-identification. In B. R. Schlenker (Ed.), *The self and social life* (pp. 65–99). New York: McGraw-Hill.

Secord, P. F., & Backman, C. W. (1965). An interpersonal approach to personality. In B. Maher (Ed.), *Progress in experimental personality research* (Vol. 2, pp. 91–125). New York: Academic Press.

Seligman, M. E. P. (1975). *Helplessness: On depression, development, and death.* San Francisco: Freeman.

Selye, H. (1956). *The stress of life.* New York: McGraw-Hill.

Sherif, C. W., Sherif, M., & Nebergall, R. E. (1965). *Attitudes and attitude change.* Philadelphia: Saunders.

Shrauger, J. S. (1975). Responses to evaluation as a function of initial self-perceptions. *Psychological Bulletin, 82,* 581–596.

Siegel, J. M., & Brown, J. D. (1988). A prospective study of life strain, illness symptoms, and depressed mood among adolescents. *Developmental Psychology, 24,* 715–721.

Singer, J. E., Lundberg, U., & Frankenhaeuser, M. (1978). Stress on the train: A study of urban commuting. In A. Baum, J. E. Singer, & S. Valins (Eds.), *Advances in environmental psychology* (Vol. 1, pp. 41–56). Hillsdale, NJ: Erlbaum.

Sklar, L. S., & Anisman, H. (1979). Stress and coping factors influence tumor growth. *Science, 205,* 513–515.

Snyder, M., & Swann, W. B., Jr. (1978). Hypothesis testing processes in social interaction. *Journal of Personality and Social Psychology, 36,* 1202–1212.

Suls, J. (1983). Social support, interpersonal relations, and health: Benefits and liabilities. In G. S. Sanders and J. Suls (Eds.), *Social psychology of health and illness.* Hillsdale, NJ: Erlbaum.

Swann, W. B., Jr. (1983). Self-verification: Bringing social reality into harmony with the self. In J. Suls & A. G. Greenwald (Eds.), *Social psychological perspectives on the self* (Vol. 2, pp. 33–66). Hillsdale, NJ: Erlbaum.

Swann, W. B., Jr. (1984). The quest for accuracy in person perception: A matter of pragmatics. *Psychological Review, 91,* 457–477.

Swann, W. B., Jr. (1987). Identity negotiation: Where two roads meet. *Journal of Personality and Social Psychology, 53,* 1038–1051.

Swann, W. B., Jr., & Ely, R. J. (1984). A battle of wills: Self-verification versus behavioral confirmation. *Journal of Personality and Social Psychology, 46,* 1287–1302.

Swann, W. B., Jr., & Giuliano, T. (1987). Confirmatory search strategies in social interaction. When, how, why, and with what consequences. *Journal of Clinical and Social Psychology, 5,* 511–524.

Swann, W. B., Jr., Griffin, J. J., Predmore, S. C., & Gaines, B. (1987). Cognitive–affective crossfire: When self-consistency meets self-enhancement. *Journal of Personality and Social Psychology, 52,* 881–889.

Swann, W. B., Jr., & Hill, C. A. (1982). When our identities are mistaken: Reaffirming self-conceptions through social interaction. *Journal of Personality and Social Psychology, 43,* 59–66.

Swann, W. B., Jr., Krull, D. S., & Pelham, S. C. (1988). *Seeking truth, reaping despair: Self-verification among people with negative self-views.* Manuscript submitted for publication.

Swann, W. B., Jr., Pelham, B., & Krull, D. S. (1989). Agreeable fancy or disagreeable truth? Reconciling self-enhancement and self-verification. *Journal of Personality and Social Psychology, 57,* 782–791.

Swann, W. B., Jr., & Pelham, B. W. (1988a). *To be known or to be adored? Selection of relationship partners and the self.* Unpublished manuscript.

Swann, W. B., Jr., & Pelham, B. W. (1988b). Unpublished data.

Swann, W. B., Jr., Pelham, B. W., & Chidester, T. R. (1988c). Change through paradox: Using self-verification to alter beliefs. *Journal of Personality and Social Psychology, 54,* 268–273.

Swann, W. B., Jr., & Predmore, S. C. (1985). Intimates as agents of social support: Sources of consolation or despair? *Journal of Personality and Social Psychology, 49,* 1609–1617.

Swann, W. B., Jr., & Read, S. J. (1981a). Acquiring self-knowledge: The search for feed-back that fits. *Journal of Personality and Social Psychology, 41*, 1119–1128.

Swann, W. B., Jr., & Read, S. J. (1981b). Self-verification processes: How we sustain our self-conceptions. *Journal of Experimental Social Psychology, 17*, 351–372.

Taylor, S. E. (1986). *Health psychology.* New York: Random House.

Taylor, S. E., & Brown, J. D. (1988). Illusion and well being: A social psychological perspective on mental health. *Psychological Bulletin, 103*, 193–210.

Thoits, P. A. (1983a). Dimensions of life events that influence psychological distress: An evaluation and synthesis of the literature. In H. B. Kaplan (Ed.), *Psychosocial stress: Trends in theory and research.* New York: Academic Press.

Thoits, P. A. (1983b). Multiple identities and psychological well-being: A reformulation and test of the social isolation hypothesis. *American Sociological Review, 48*, 174–187.

Wilson, E. O. (1974). *Sociobiology: The new synthesis.* Cambridge, MA: Harvard University Press.

Zajonc, R. B. (1980). Feeling and thinking: Preferences need no inferences. *American Psychologist, 35*, 151–175.

Zajonc, R. B. (1984). On the primacy of affect. *American Psychologist, 39*, 117–123.

CHAPTER 7

The Role of Reciprocity in Social Support

TONI C. ANTONUCCI AND JAMES S. JACKSON

Institute for Social Research,
University of Michigan

Over the last fifteen years enormous progress has been made in the area of social support. We have moved from what might best be described as an astute clinical observation, made first by Cassel (1976) and Cobb (1976), to large-scale epidemiological studies documenting the relationship between health and social support (such as Berkman & Syme, 1979; Blazer, 1982; Cohen & Syme, 1985; House, Robbins, & Metzner, 1982; Schoenbach, Kaplan, Fredman, & Kleinbaum, 1986) and to extensive descriptive studies of social support and social networks in large representative samples (Antonucci & Akiyama, 1987; Cantor, 1979; Fischer, 1982; Litwak, 1985). In addition, there have been numerous studies demonstrating the relationships between social support (variously defined) and an array of important physical and psychological outcomes, for example, cardio vascular disease, emergency room usage, use of postoperative anesthetics, and labor and delivery complications (Haynes, Feinleib, & Kannel, 1980; Joseph, 1980; Medalie & Goldbourt, 1976; Norbeck & Tilden, 1981; Nuckolls, Cassel, & Kaplan, 1972; Wan, 1982; Wan & Weissert, 1981).

More recent work took another step forward and called for a new direction in social support research (Antonucci, 1985; Antonucci & Jackson, 1987; Berkman, 1984; Brehm, 1984; Cohen, 1988; Pearlin, 1985). These researchers argued that we now can begin to explore the processes and mechanisms by which social support affects health and well-being. This book focuses on the interactional nature of social support and is a major step in that direction.

This chapter was written while Antonucci held a Research Career Development Award from the National Institute on Aging and a *bourse* from the Fondation de la Recherche Medicale to be a visiting scholar at the Institut National de la Santé et de la Researche Medicale. Both authors would like to acknowledge the assistance provided by research grants from the National Institute on Aging, the National Institute of Mental Health, and the Carnegie Corporation and to thank Halimah Hassan, Linda Shepard and Rebecca Fuhrer for their help in the preparation of this manuscript.

The data computation on which this paper is based used the OSIRIS IV computer software package developed by the Institute for Social Research, the University of Michigan, using funds from the Survey Research Center, Inter-University Consortium for Political Research, National Science Foundation, and other sources.

This chapter highlights the inter- and intraindividual life-span developmental aspects of social support. We begin with a theoretical discussion of these issues and follow with a limited empirical investigation of them using three diverse data sources: two national American data sets (one of white Americans over 50, the other of black Americans over 18) and preliminary data from a study still in progress of people over 65 in the Bordeaux region of France.

THEORETICAL ISSUES

Support as an Inter- and Intraindividual Variable

The research on social support has been cyclical. It began with an essentially clinical observation and moved to epidemiological and descriptive study techniques. Both approaches have been extremely useful but have, in some ways, distracted researchers from the central question of how social support has the positive (or negative) effects that it has been shown to have. In some of our other writings, as well as the writings of several others, this question is being explored (see, for example, Antonucci & Jackson, 1987; Berkman, 1984; Brehm, 1984; Pearlin, 1985). In this chapter we examine one aspect of the concept, the inter- and intraindividual development of social support, particularly as it influences and is influenced by the individual's concept of reciprocity in social relationships. It is perhaps worth mentioning at the outset that we view this as only one aspect of a complex developmental pattern of social relationships, each of which needs to be explored further (e.g., Clark & Reis, 1988).

Although the empirical research on social support has largely lacked a theoretical foundation, one approach that has proved useful is that of attachment (Antonucci, 1976). Borrowed from ethologists (Bowlby, 1969) and child developmental psychologists (Ainsworth, Blehar, Waters, & Wall, 1979), this concept originally referred to the relationship of an infant with his or her mother and, by extension, with other important early caregivers. Attachment, however, is a term that has usually been confined to one or two close relationships. Thus, although the extension of this concept to adult relationships has been extremely useful, the concept of social support as generally presented in the literature might best be seen as extending to a wider range of individual relationships. The adult analogue to the mother–child relationship might be the adult child and his or her older parent, or it might be the relationship between husband and wife. Also relevant are important adult social relationships such as those with close friends, siblings, other relatives, in-laws, and co-workers. In order to incorporate this larger sphere of adult social relationships, Kahn and Antonucci (1980) described a convoy of social support and social relationships.

The convoy concept was designed to include more social relationships than those described in the attachment literature and to incorporate the dynamic and continuous nature of social relationships over the life course. This dynamic and continuous nature is relevant to our notion of inter- and intraindividual differences in social relationships and consequently to the individual's conception of reciprocal social relationships over time.

Social support has been defined as interpersonal transactions that include one or more of the following: affect (expressions of liking, loving, admiration, respect), affirmation (expressions of agreement or acknowledgment of the appropriateness or rightness of some act, statement, or point of view), and aid (transactions in which direct aid or assistance is given, including things, money, information, advice, time, or entitlement) (Kahn & Antonucci, 1980). The point to be made when focusing on the inter- and intraindividual nature of social support and social relationships is that each exchange of aid, affect, or affirmation involves two (or more) people at one time. This exchange is at least partly determined by each person's specific development, that is, his or her intraindividual development, and by the particular point of development in the relationship between the two individuals, or its interindividual development. An example is the exchange of affection between two people. Affection exchanged at one period can be considered and understood from both the perspective of a developing relationship between the two people and the state of each individual's development at the time of the exchange.

The exchange of affection between an adult parent and his or her young child is the exchange between two individuals at different developmental stages. The parent, who is at a more advanced developmental stage, has had a history of other social relationships, indeed, probably has specific expectations of the relationship that will develop with the child. The child, on the other hand, is at the other end of the developmental continuum, with no prior experiences, and except for what one might grant in the way of genetic or species predispositions, no expectations about the relationship. Thus, intraindividually they enter the relationship at different points. At the same time, because the relationship is new for both of them, it can be seen on one level as being similar interindividually. The reason for noting these intra- and interindividual differences with respect to social relationships is to offer some idea of how a person comes to have expectations about what appropriate exchanges in social relationships are. Indeed, to stretch this point a bit further, one could imagine these notions as influencing what an individual comes to view as supportive behaviors. We see these concepts of long-term individual development and the development of various relationships over time as important to the notion of reciprocity in social relationships.

Reciprocity in Social Support

We believe that the concept of reciprocity may be important to understanding how social support operates both contemporaneously and longitudinally. The concept of reciprocity is not new to the social sciences. In 1960 Gouldner wrote a seminal article on the norm of reciprocity, contending that it has far-reaching implications for how individuals interpret and understand human interactions. Anthropologists have long known this. Indeed, some of the first work incorporating the notion of reciprocity into an understanding of social relationships among the elderly was introduced by the anthropologist Wentowski (1981). It thus may be useful to review both her work and that of the social psychologist Clark (1984) outlining differences in the norms and characteristics of social exchanges. Also of interest is the work of equity or exchange theorists who have examined the rules by which exchanges are evaluated by social interactors (Walster, Walster, & Berschied, 1978). Finally, we shall consider when relationships are seen as reciprocal, when they are not, the potential negative (and positive) effects of nonreciprocity, and the relevance of cultural context to the evaluation of social exchanges (Akiyama, Antonucci, & Campbell, 1990; Austin & Walster, 1974; Brehm & Brehm, 1981; Coyne & Delongis, 1986; DePaulo & Fisher, 1980; Rook, 1984).

Both Clark and Wentowski argued that the rules of exchange vary according to the nature of the relationship. Wentowski's (1981) research focused on the role of exchanges among older people. She found that the characteristic which distinguished relationships was not age but the nature of the relationship itself. She concluded that both types of relationships seemed to use unwritten codes or rules of exchange. Wentowski reported that relationships between people who were not close or intimate, that is, relationships that were relatively superficial, appeared to use rather strict rules of exchange. Thus, if something were provided, the receiver tended to reciprocate immediately, either in kind, for example, returning exactly what was received, or in equivalent value, such as money. Besides the equivalence of exchange, also noteworthy is the immediacy of the exchange; that is, some time pressure is noted in the need to return equivalent benefit to the provider. On the other hand, relationships that were more intimate and longitudinal tended to require less immediate exchange and less immediate equivalence of value. It appears that a long-term relationship allows both members of the dyad to assume that equivalence or reciprocity will eventually be achieved.

Clark's (1984) work on types of social relationships is similar but not identical. Her interests are less in social support per se and more in the nature of social relationships and exchange. She distinguished two types of relationships: communal and exchange. Communal exchanges are those in which both parties feel obligated to be responsive to each other's needs in a general rather than in a specific way. They assume a certain level of relationship, such as that between kin, romantic partners, and friends. On the other hand, exchange relationships are considerably more pragmatic, as the dyadic partners are responsible for, in Clark's terms, "benefiting" the other in response to specific benefits received from that other. Business relationships or the exchanges among acquaintances are examples. In regard to the current reciprocity discussion, people who have close, intimate relationships tend not to conceptualize them in terms of immediate or specific exchanges but, rather, as part of an ongoing series of exchanges that are ultimately equally "beneficial." On the other hand, exchange relationships are common among people who have no expectation of mutually beneficial, long-term interactions.

Exchange theory is often used to explain ostensibly reciprocal relationships (Clark & Reis, 1988; Fisher, Nadler, & Whitcher-Alagna, 1982). This theory focuses on the extent to which characteristics or entities are given and received. It argues that equal exchange or reciprocity is optimal and that if one receives more than one provides, the result may be a feeling of indebtedness that is experienced as aversive (Greenberg, 1980; Greenberg & Shapiro, 1971). It has been assumed, and documented experimentally, that if an exchange is unequal, it is better to receive more than to provide more. The reason is that the costs of providing are seen as the inconvenience of being interrupted or imposed on as well as being the burden of another's dependency (Brehm & Brehm, 1981; DePaulo & Fisher, 1980). Additional work has attempted to specify further those circumstances when receiving is experienced more negatively; for example, people who are unable to reciprocate are more likely to feel indebted or guilty about receiving unreciprocated help (Shumaker & Jackson, 1979), are less likely to ask for help when they need it (Greenberg & Shapiro, 1971), and are likely to react unfavorably to the support provider (Brehm & Brehm, 1981). The bulk of this work has been done in laboratory settings among relative strangers rather than lifetime associates (Clark & Reis, 1988).

Several theorists used equity or exchange theory as a basis for understanding the social aging process. For example, Dowd (1975, 1980, 1984) used exchange theory to explain the changing nature of social relationships among the elderly. He found that exchanges are based on power and resources and that as individuals grow older they have less power and fewer resources. Therefore, they are at a disadvantage in the exchange market, because they are most frequently in the position of receiving "valued goods" from people who are in more powerful or prestigious positions while, because of their increased age, they are in a position of less power and prestige. Lee (1985) incorporated Dowd's (1975) work into a social exchange theory that he proposed as an explanatory framework within which to consider the supportive interactions and social networks of older people.

Although we agree fundamentally that reciprocity, equity, and exchange are important concepts in the understanding of social interactions, we propose creating a more dynamic, complex view of social relationships (e.g., Graziano, 1984). To this end we note that there is now evidence to suggest that not all social exchanges that may be viewed by an external observer as equitable are experienced as such by the participants in the exchange (Clarke & Reis, 1988; Fisher et al., 1982). Similarly, providing more than one receives may be perceived as the burden of another's dependency, whereas the experience of receiving may be experienced as indebtedness. Notwithstanding the characteristics of specific social exchanges that have been experimentally investigated in the United States, the importance of cultural differences in exchange and equity rules must also be considered. Akiyama (1984) and Akiyama, Antonucci, and Campbell (1990) have showed, in a comparison of three generations of American and Japanese women, that evaluations of when one might or should feel indebted varies significantly by culture as well as generation. Individuals in the two cultures had different expectations of social exchanges and varied considerably in terms of what they considered appropriate across-age exchanges. Akiyama's (1984) research strongly confirmed the notion of a longitudinal, culturally specific view of social exchanges and can be seen as suggesting a long-term accounting system, what we labeled a *Support Bank,* for assessing social interactions.

The Support Bank

We offered in other writings some preliminary thoughts concerning the concept of a Social Support Bank (Akiyama et al., 1990; Antonucci, 1985; Antonucci & Jackson, 1987; Ingersoll-Dayton & Antonucci, 1988), but we will review the concept here and extend it in light of the above-mentioned research in social and developmental psychology. Basically, the idea of a Support Bank is that individuals take a long-term developmental view of their social exchanges, interactions, and relationships with other people. The concept is not meant to have a pejorative connotation; rather, we propose that people maintain an ongoing account of the amount of support or various benefits they have given to and received from others. This account may be kept at different levels of consciousness; that is, people may say in specific circumstances, "I am doing this for someone because he or she previously did that for me or so that he or she will do such and such for me in the future." Or people may have a more global conception of their relationships with specific others (or a generalized other such as family) and be willing to provide for others in time of need, assuming that they will also receive assistance if and when they are in need (Clark, 1984; Fisher et al., 1982).

Much of the work we discuss here can be incorporated into this notion of a Support Bank. To begin with the attachment literature, we assume that an individual's notions of what an appropriate exchange is and what the rules of exchange are, are first learned in the early attachment exchanges (Clark, 1984). As the child gets older, the parents change their expectations of the child, assuming and expecting certain behaviors in response to others, for example, beginning with affection in response to affection and extending to increasingly more complicated exchanges.

Levitt and her colleagues (Levitt, in press; Levitt, Weber, & Clark, 1986) provided evidence in their work on the relationship between social networks of mothers and attachment in their infants, and among three-generation matrilineal family units. In her extension of the Kahn and Antonucci (1980) convoy model, Levitt detailed the developmental progression of evolving expectations, arguing that the individual—based on past relationships, current level of social–cognitive development, and social norms—develops specific expectations regarding the behavior of specific others. When these expectations are tested through naturally occurring events, the individual's expectations are met, exceeded, or unmet. The relationship is affected accordingly, remaining stable or changing in a positive or a negative direction. This individually oriented model, which takes into account both intra- and interindividual development and change, can easily be generalized to other social relationships. We can also assume that the development of these expectations about exchanges are influenced by the same factors that influence socialization more generally, that is, sociodemographic and cultural factors.

Both Wentowski (1981) and Clark (1984) noted that individuals tend to categorize their social relationships. These two approaches are similar in many ways, despite their coming from different theoretical and disciplinary backgrounds. For example, both highlight the relationship's duration and intimacy as important characteristics that influence the individual's assessment and expectations concerning the exchanges. These characteristics may likewise influence the individual's notion of deposits into and withdrawals from the Support Bank. The idea of the Support Bank is that individuals continually calculate the amount of support they give to and receive from others. Wentowski's and Clark's work may be interpreted as revealing those characteristics of the exchange that people use to organize, assess, and evaluate these exchanges. Thus, support given to people with whom one has a limited or superficial relationship may be best seen as deposits into a very short term interindividual account, whereas support given to more intimate, longitudinal relationships can be considered longer-term deposits. These deposits can be drawn on in future times of need.

The problem with applying equity and exchange theories to social relationships is that both tend to be temporally static. They assume that people prefer relationships that are currently reciprocal and that if this is not to be the case, people prefer relationships in which they receive more than they give. This view makes sense if there is no expectation of future exchanges. In that case, one would want to make sure, according to the Support Bank concept, that no investment is made without at least an equal return. If, however, one assumes that the relationship will continue over the long term, then one may view unreturned investments in the relationship, that is, the support one provides, as rainy day investments. Support provided thus creates a support debt or resource that can be called on during an unknown, unspecified future time of need.

Dowd's (1975, 1984) notion that exchanges are based on resources, power, and prestige is also temporally limited. When outlining the application of exchange theory to social relationships among the elderly, he discovered that with age, older people often face a situation of declining resources, power, and prestige. This is true only if one takes a temporally limited point of view. But in a life-span developmental view of relationships—if people have made sufficient deposits into their Support Bank—"deposits" made when their resources, power, and prestige were at a maximum—they will have deposits on which to draw. Both equity and exchange theories work relatively well when applied to short-term, limited relationships; both theories can be seen as at least hypothetically congruent with Wentowski's and Clark's account of less intimate relationships. It is only when the longer-term, more intimate relationships are considered that their application to understanding these exchanges breaks down.

The influence of sociodemographic and cultural factors also is important to consider if one is to understand specific exchanges. Young parents expect to provide for their young children, whereas older parents might expect to be provided for by their adult children. This example demonstrates the potential effect of the demographic characteristic of age. But the degree and extent of this effect are influenced by other sociodemographic and cultural factors. For example, socioeconomic status directly affects aid provided to a child and aid needed (and provided) by the aging parents. To take an extreme example, poor people might have as an instrumental goal providing for their children's basic physical needs (i.e., food and shelter). As they grow older, they may be less in a position to help their own aging parents monetarily but may be more likely to provide physical help when the aging parents become frail. More socioeconomically advantaged parents might set a goal of providing excellent schooling or diverse cultural experiences for their young children. They may be more likely to receive financial aid from their own parents than to provide it, or to meet their older parents' physical needs by hiring someone to provide any physical assistance required, thus helping their older parents maintain their independence.

The effects of cultural differences are similar. The work by Akiyama (Akiyama, 1984; Akiyama et al., 1990) offers some interesting examples of cultural differences between Japanese and American women, especially in regard to the notion of independence. In the United States, most older people wish to maintain independent housing arrangements. If they are not able to do so, they may move into a child's home. But in Japan, it is commonly accepted that older parents will live with their adult children, beginning with the marriage of the adult child. That child, in a culturally determined order (that is, son before daughter, older before younger) moves into the house of his parents upon marriage and lives with them until their death. This is an interesting difference in the pattern of exchange, because it is the adult child living with his parents rather than the reverse. It may be that these sociodemographic and cultural factors influence the expectations and the contents of the exchanges. Next we offer an additional consideration: that the hypothesized Support Bank may offer a clue to a psychological process that brightens the prospects for successful aging (Rowe & Kahn, 1987).

Life-span Reciprocity for Successful Aging

We accept the basic tenet of exchange theories—that individuals prefer reciprocal relationships (Clark & Reis, 1988; Fisher et al., 1982). But we propose qualifications and extensions. For short-term or nonintimate relationships, such as those described by Wentowski (1981) as superficial and by Clark (1984) as acquaintance relationships, the straight exchange or equity paradigms are perhaps the most acceptable (see Fisher et al., 1982 for an alternative view). Indeed, these relationships are most similar to the types examined in the traditional, laboratory-based, experimental social psychological research (Carnevale, Pruit, & Carrington, 1982). For longer-term relationships, that is, relationships that have continued for years and are between people who are close and important to each other, other variations have been proposed (Clark & Reis, 1988).

Based on our notion of a Support Bank, we hypothesize that people envision relationships with intimate others as long-term, cumulative interaction sequences. Thus, one can make an investment in a relationship by giving to another and, in return, expect that one would be provided for in the future if necessary. We assume that this deposit–withdrawal concept is a psychological rather than an objective evaluation and, therefore, is relatively complex. People are influenced, of course, by objective factors such as sociodemographics, but they also are influenced by their own psychological state, which is the product of their intra- and interindividual development.

Although this notion is complicated, we suggest its utility for successful aging (Rowe & Kahn, 1987). As Dowd (1975) and others (e.g., Lee, 1985) noted, with age often comes a reduction of resources, power, and prestige. This is not a direct effect of age, as all people do not so suffer—witness President Ronald Reagan who despite advanced age enjoyed almost unlimited resources, power, and prestige. However, it cannot be denied that a reduction of resources is often a concomitant of age. In any case, although not all old people are frail or functionally disabled, with age the probability of both certainly increases.

The Support Bank concept can be seen as a mechanism that provides the individual with resource deposits. If it is true, as exchange theories predict, that individuals do not like to be in nonreciprocal relationships, then having support reserves will enable older people who are facing a reduction of resources but a probability of increased need, to maintain psychological reciprocity. For example, an individual who is unable to do her daily shopping because of advanced arthritis maintains an equitable relationship with her neighbor who does her shopping for her, by minding the neighbor's infant while she shops. This could be called an example of contemporaneous reciprocity. However, an individual with similar functional disabilities and unable to provide a service for her neighbor may feel more comfortable asking her daughter to shop for her, as she provided many supports to her in the past. This would satisfy the older person's specific physical need and would also allow her to avoid a feeling of indebtedness. That is, even though she cannot provide a similar service to her daughter right now, she does feel that she did provide services in the past that are either similar or of equivalent value. Thus, the Support Bank process can help an individual cope with the declining resources often associated with aging, by maintaining a longer-term view of reciprocity and social exchanges.

In sum, we propose that the concept of reciprocity is important to understanding how an individual assesses his or her social exchanges. However, both a contemporaneous and a lifetime/long-term view of relationships must be considered in order to understand the complex psychological processes of assessing reciprocity. Although contemporaneous reciprocity is useful, in terms of a lifetime view of exchanges, it may be better to give more than one receives, at least in relationships that are viewed as long term and intimate, in order to build up resources for future need. Then when one can no longer continue this contemporaneous reciprocity, the possibility of drawing on these resources may be critical to maintaining one's well-being. Rather than feeling indebted, as one might if all previous relationships had been reciprocal, one might assume that previous investments or provisions of support can now be drawn upon, thus avoiding feeling indebted for supports currently being provided but not being reciprocated. We also believe that sociodemographic and cultural factors may influence the concrete and psychological characteristics of these exchanges.

EMPIRICAL DATA ON RECIPROCAL RELATIONSHIPS IN OLDER AGE

The two major data sets considered in this chapter that provide cross-sectional data on the concept of reciprocity are the Supports of the Elderly (SSE) (Antonucci & Akiyama, 1987) and the National Survey of Black Americans (NSBA) (Jackson, Tucker, & Gurin, 1987). Each offers relevant and suggestive data. Also available are the preliminary comparative data from a continuing prospective study of people 65 years of age and over living in the southwest Bordeaux region of France.

Supports of the Elderly (SSE)

The SSE was conducted in 1980 and was based on a national representative sample of 718 men and women over 50 years of age. The major focus of the face-to-face hour-long interview was social networks and social supports, but it also included questions concerning well-being, health, work, and retirement. The data presented in this chapter are based on the subsample of 561 respondents with children and used specially constructed variables. Of interest are the respondents' perceptions of the amount of support given and received. The respondents were asked to whom they gave and from whom they received each of six types of supports. The types of support were confiding, reassurance, respect, sick care, talk when upset, and talk about health.

Only those supports given to and received from children are included in our analyses here. The perceived reciprocity for the respondents was calculated as the arithmetic difference between the total number of supports received from children and the total number of supports provided to children. The resulting variable can thus be considered a composite reciprocity measure for supports exchanged between parents and their children, coded as receiving more help than is given, equality of supports given and received, and giving more help than receiving help. This variable is not identical to, but is conceptually similar to, the variable created in the NSBA study and the variable used in the French survey.

National Survey of Black Americans: Reinterview (NSBA)

The NSBA is based on a national probability sample of 2,107 noninstitutionalized black American citizens over 18 years of age residing in households in the continental United States in 1979–1980 (Jackson et al., 1987). The study focused on a wide variety of topics, including, but not limited to, social support, mental and physical health, work, and unemployment. The data used in our analyses were drawn from a subsample of 866 respondents from the cross-sectional study who were reinterviewed as part of the National Three-Generation Family Study (Jackson & Hatchett, 1986). Analyses of this subsample did not reveal any particular sampling or selection biases (Jackson & Hatchett, 1986), and for analyses of exchange and reciprocity among parents and children it is particularly suitable.

The NSBA reciprocity variable used in this chapter was constructed from two questions that determine the general frequency of supports given to ("How often do you help your children?") and provided by children and immediate family ("How often does your family help you?"). Thus, the measure is not as clean as it is in the SSE, as help given to and received from both children and immediate family are included. The reciprocity measure is simply the arithmetic difference between the respondents' perceived frequency of help given and help received coded as receiving more help than help given, equality of frequency of support given and received, and receiving less help than giving help. For our analyses and discussion, the equality of frequency of help given and received is considered to be reciprocal.

In this chapter, data from the full adult NSBA sample were used. In certain cases a subgroup of 239 respondents, age matched with the SSE, was used. Because the sample was designed as an adult cross section, analyses of the NSBA, aged matched for the SSE (50 years of age and above), resulted in a significant drop in the number of respondents. Differences in comparisons between the SSE and the full adult and age-matched NSBA samples are noted in the text. The use of the full adult age range in the NSBA also permitted some observations of a broader span of age differences than were possible in the SSE and provided the basis for some speculations about age-related changes. It also may help in interpreting age differences in the 50-and-above SSE sample, by offering a longer age series to observe differences in the reciprocity of social supportive exchanges.

The French Study

The French study is a cooperative effort based at the University of Bordeaux and conducted by the PAQUID Research Group. It is a prospective longitudinal study of aging currently in progress in the Bordeaux region of France. Planned as a five-year study, only preliminary data from the first data collection were available at the time of our writing. Antonucci was involved in the study's early stages and helped the PAQUID Research Group select several questions for the study concerning social support and social networks. The data reported in this chapter are based on responses to the question "En reflechissant aux echanges que vous avez eu avec les personnes de votre entourage ces derniers temps, diriez-vous que . . . ?" (Thinking about the exchanges you have with the people in your network right now, would you say that . . .) you give more than you receive, it's about equal, or you give less than you receive.

A note of caution concerning these preliminary data: They represent fewer than 600 responses currently available from the study, which is meant ultimately to include 4,000 people from southwestern France.

In general, these three studies provide a wide variety of data concerning exchanges among family and intimates over the life span and in old age. The study variables differ somewhat because none of them, particularly the SSE and NSBA, was designed specifically for the current question. Exactly comparable measures would be preferable. But although the lack of exact replicates causes some difficulty in interpretation, it is also a source of some strength for generalizability.

Analysis Approach

We view the analyses in this chapter as preliminary. We are grappling with complex conceptual notions that these data sets were not necessarily designed to address. The first analysis focuses on a descriptive account of reciprocal relationships as perceived by the respondents to exist between themselves and other family members. Age was used as the principal independent measure, and percentages are presented by age and averaged across age. The next analysis examines in a multivariate framework the potential demographic and social predictors of reported relational exchanges. Logistic regression was used to examine the efficacy of a resource-based model, which assumed that good health, education, income, availability of spousal support, geographical context, and gender all may play independent predictive roles in the currently reported support exchanges. The major question addressed was the source and nature of factors related to different support relationships.

The next analysis investigates the role of different support exchanges in reports of psychological well-being. Three self-report well-being items were used separately: happiness, life satisfaction and family satisfaction. A univariate analysis of variance was used to look at the relationship of type of support exchanges on the well-being items. These analyses are followed by ordinary least square regression analyses that examined the effect of type of support exchanges on well-being, controlling for the social and demographic resource variables used in the previous analyses of the sources of support exchanges. The major question addressed was the nature and role of support exchanges in perceptions of well-being among respondents, independent of their social and demographic resources.

Because all the data sets were derived from different sampling frames, we did not attempt to combine them. Significance tests were confined to differences among variables within the data sets. Thus, comparisons among the data sets could be made only by observation. Strict statistical comparisons, particularly between the major race groups represented by the SSE and NSBA, will have to await future data. In some cases the differences were striking and statistical analyses were not needed. We were, of course, cautious in our interpretations because of differences between data sets and variables and the inappropriateness of applying statistical tests to observed differences across data sets and, by default, across race groups.

CORRELATES OF SUPPORT RELATIONSHIPS

Percentages of Current Support Exchanges by Age

Table 7.1 shows the percentages of respondents in each of the two American data sets who indicated that they receive more than they provide, receive the same as they provide, and receive less than they provide. These questions, as we noted, focus on family support. The most startling and consistent difference between the SSE, a predominantly white data set of older Americans, and the NSBA, a data set of black Americans, either by matched age or across all ages, is that the respondents in the SSE data set were much less likely to say that their exchanges among people in their family were reciprocal. Across all ages, blacks were twice as likely as whites were to indicate being in reciprocal exchange relationships. Across all the matched ages (50 and above) this differential increased at ages 75

TABLE 7.1.   Age and Perceived Reciprocity of Current Support:[a] Social Supports of the Elderly (SSE) and National Survey of Black Americans (NSBA)

Age	18–29		30–39		40–49		50–64	
Survey	NSBA	SSE	NSBA	SSE	NSBA	SSE	NSBA	SSE
Received More	5.9%	—	0.7%	—	6.1%	—	15.6%	17.2%
Received Same	34.9	—	29.4	—	37.1	—	46.7	18.7
Received Less	59.2	—	69.9	—	56.8	—	37.7	64.0
	100.0%		100.0%		100.0%		100.0%	100.0%
n	152		153		132		122	267

Age	65–74		75 and over		Totals		
Survey	NSBA	SSE	NSBA	SSE	NSBA[b]	SSE	NSBA[c]
Received More	23.2%	25.7%	42.4%	45.5%	10.1%	26.0%	21.9%
Received Same	46.4	19.3	42.2	12.2	37.8	17.5	46.0
Received Less	30.4	55.0	15.2	42.3	52.0	56.5	32.1
	100.0%	100.0%	100.0%	100.0%	100.0%	100.0%	100.0%
n	69	171	33	123	661	561	224

[a]Current exchanges of social support among respondents and family were assessed. The extent of reciprocity was measured by the arithmetic differences between two questions that ask about the respondents' perception of current supports given to and received from children and family.
[b]Total percent for 18 years of age and older.
[c]Total percent for 50 years of age and older.

and above to nearly 30 percentage points. White respondents showed a slightly steeper decline over age groups (18.7, 19.3, and 12.2) than did black respondents (46.7, 46.4, and 42.2) in the percentage of those reporting being in reciprocal relationships. For blacks, as shown in Table 7.1, this fairly stable percentage of respondents reporting reciprocal relationships was actually an increment over ages 18 to 49 (34.9, 29.4, and 37.1).

As we mentioned, the data from the PAQUID French study are preliminary and should thus be viewed with considerable caution. However, the descriptive statistics are interesting and suggest still another pattern of responses, perhaps hinting at cultural differences in how this concept is construed. Data for current support relationships measured by a single question and for people over 65 are available.

The French respondents' probability of reporting that their network relationships are reciprocal for the same age groups, that is, 65 to 74 and over 75 was considerably greater than that of the SSE and NSBA respondents. A total of 63.4% of the French respondents aged 65 to 74 (compared with 46.4% of the NSBA and 19.3% of the SSE) and 58.5% of the French respondents over 75 years of age (compared with 42.2% and 12.2% of the NSBA and SSE respondents, respectively) reported that their support exchanges are reciprocal. When comparing the nonreciprocal responses, however, the pattern was not quite as consistent. French people aged 65 to 74 were more likely than either American group to indicate that they received more support (32.7%) than they provided (compared with 23.2%, NSBA, and 25.7%, SSE, respectively) and were much less likely than Americans were to say that they received less (3.8%) than they provided (30.4%, NSBA; 55.0%, SSE). On the other hand, among the oldest age group, those 75 and over, the French respondents (6.7%) were less likely than were the oldest NSBA respondents (15.2%) and much less likely than the SSE respondents were (42.3%) to say that they received less than they provided. They were slightly less likely than were the NSBA elders (42.4%) and the SSE elders (45.5%) to say that they received more than they provided (French, 34.7%).

Overall, the older French respondents seemed to report consistently either reciprocal relationships or receiving more than they provided at all age groups. Both are equitably satisfying positions. When nonreciprocal, the French respondents—unlike the majority of nonreciprocal responses from the two American samples—reported that they received more support from their network than they provided. A similar situation was found only among the oldest black Americans and not at all for whites. Another way of considering these data is to note that if the relationship were nonreciprocal, the French were less likely than the Americans were to give more support to their children than they received. This may reflect the limited resources available to them, although the testing of this hypothesis must await additional data.

In summary, whites in the SSE showed a decided lack of reciprocal relationships when compared with blacks in the older age groups, and if anything, these reciprocal relationships were lower in the advanced age groups. For blacks these relationships were fairly stable across older groups. The totals are instructive. Generally whites above 50, in comparison with blacks of similar ages, were less likely to report reciprocal relationships, much more likely to report receiving less than they gave, and slightly more likely to report receiving more than they gave. For both groups there was a decrease in reports of receiving less than giving and an increase in receiving more, in older age groups. This is consistent with Dowd's (1975) observations of declining resources in older ages. People have less to give and yet need more. This decline in receiving less than one gives can be shown to be precipitous among blacks, moving from a high of 70% at ages 30 to 39 to a low of 15.2% at ages 70 and above.

These descriptive data are consistent with notions of resource availability. It may be true that whites, because of superior resources in the older ages, can "afford" to give more than blacks can, though with advanced ages even these resources may give out and whites, like blacks, may become more dependent on the supports provided by others. In the next section the viability of this proposition is examined by conducting parallel logistic regression analyses on dummy variables constructed to represent supportive relationships.

Multivariate Correlates of Support Relationships

Table 7.2 contains separate summaries of the logistic regression analyses for the National Survey of Black Americans (NSBA) and the Supports of the Elderly (SSE) data sets. These regressions explore the independent effects of social and demographic variables on reported reciprocal support relationships. The analyses were conducted on two dichotomous variables: receives more than is given versus reciprocity, and receives less support than is given versus reciprocity. The combination of the two logistic regressions for each data set revealed the relative contribution of each social or demographic variable to reported reciprocity.

As shown, these analyses were conducted separately for black and white respondents and among black respondents for all ages combined (18+) as well as for only the older black respondents (i.e., 50 years and over to match the SSE white sample). For blacks (NSBA), significant effects were found for age, disability, and sex. Similar analyses of a subsample of blacks 50 years of age and older showed a slightly different pattern of results, with education emerging as a marginally significant effect and age and sex no longer significant. For whites (SSE) age, education, marital status and sex were significant predictors of exchange relationships.

In the black sample, the age effect suggests that in comparison with equal giving and receiving, being older is associated with an increase in the likelihood of receiving more and a decrease in the likelihood of receiving less support. This

TABLE 7.2. Logistic Regression Summary Table of Current Reciprocity for Social and Demographic Variables: National Survey of Black Americans and Social Supports of the Elderly

Data sets	National Survey of Black Americans				Social Supports of the Elderly	
Model	Receives More		Receives Less		Receives More	Receives Less
Coefficients	B^a	B^b	B^c	B^d	B^e	B^f
Variable						
Constant	−4.07	−3.64	1.12	−.62	−3.53	.86
Age	$.06^i$	$.05^h$	$-.03^i$	−.02	$.05^i$	$-.03^i$
Education	−.03	−.03	.01	.11+	$-.10^i$	$.12^i$
Family Income	−.05	−.05	.03	.01	.04	−.01
Disability	$-.18^h$	$-.18^h$	$-.07^g$	−.08	−.01	−.02
Region (Non-South)	−.09	−.19	−.14+	−.01	−.06	.10
Marital Status						
Married	−.12	−.07	.09	−.20	$-.18^h$	.11
Sex						
Female	−.02	.19	$.13^h$	−.17	$.31^h$	$-.27^i$

Note: Three of the variables in the models—marital status, region and gender—are represented by dummy variables. For marital status, not married is the excluded category. For region the excluded category is South, and for sex the excluded category is male. Models 1 and 4 were estimated on the full 18-years-and-above NSBA sample, and Models 2 and 3, on the 50-years-and-above NSBA subsample.
[a]Model: X^2 (7) = 54.36^i N = 595
[b]Model: X^2 (7) = 15.58^h N = 198
[c]Model: X^2 (7) = 66.26^i N = 595
[d]Model: X^2 (7) = 14.47^h N = 198
[e]Model: X^2 (7) = 64.51^i N = 527
[f]Model: X^2 (7) = 57.63^i N = 527
[g]$p < .10$, [h]$p < .05$, [i]$p < .01$

effect was also clear in Table 7.1, but this analysis indicates that it is independent of other social and demographic variables. Exactly the same effect was found in the SSE sample.

The analyses also indicate that functional disability is associated in a complex manner with social support exchange relationships. The coefficients in the NSBA analyses indicate that increased disability is associated with a greater likelihood of reciprocal social support relationships with family. It should be noted that though not significant, the coefficients for disability in the white sample show the same pattern of effects as does the subsample of NSBA respondents 50 years of age and older. We originally speculated that being disabled may initially lead to increased perceptions of a lack of reciprocity, because of the greater need for the receipt of support from others. Control of the length of disability could further elucidate this point. With increased disability the individual may be forced to reduce the number of individuals with whom he or she has exchange relationships, resulting in higher levels of either actual or perceived reciprocal exchanges. Or as we speculated earlier, with increased disability, regardless of age, the individual may bring into play a lifetime accounting system, thereby maintaining a sense of reciprocity despite a greater need for help. This could be the case in the reciprocal relationships considered in this chapter, as they focus on parent–child exchanges.

The effect of education in the SSE data set and the NSBA subsample indicates that increased education is associated with both a greater likelihood of having more reciprocal relationships, in comparison with receiving more than one gives and with greater reports of receiving less, in comparison with reciprocal relationships. Although not significant, the coefficients for income, another important socioeconomic variable, show exactly the same pattern in both data sets. It suggests that the possession of economic resources permits one to maintain nonequitable relationships of receiving less, that is, giving to others more than one receives, or reciprocal relationships. Overall, this relationship is stronger for whites than blacks, possibly indicating the greater range of valued resources possessed by whites or their greater importance to the type of support exchanged among family members.

For whites, being married leads to a greater likelihood of being in a reciprocal relationship or receiving less than one provides. Having a spouse may allow one to maintain reciprocal relationships with one's children or even to give more to them, as the spouse provides an equivalent amount of support. In this manner, marital status, at least for whites, may serve the same resource role as do education and income.

In addition to the disability effect, one of the most noteworthy things about Table 7.2 is what appears to be a reversed effect for sex between blacks and whites. That is, for blacks across all ages, being female is positively related to an increased likelihood of receiving less, that is, providing more to one's children, in comparison with reciprocity. However, this relationship does not hold for black women aged 50 and over; in fact, it reverses (though not significantly). For older whites, being female is significantly related to a greater likelihood of receiving more than is given and a greater likelihood of reciprocal relationships in comparison with receiving less than is given. Because marital status was controlled, these effects were not just due to whites' having greater relationship resources in comparison with blacks. These patterns of effects suggest that for black females across the life span, relationships with children are marked by negative inequality, that is, a tendency to provide more than they receive, in support exchanges. Among older whites and possibly (though in these analyses, not significantly so) among older blacks, this unequal negative exchange was true for males.

In sum, the analyses in Table 7.2 indicate modest similarities between blacks and whites in the predictors of reciprocity of support relationships. The existence of social, economic, and physical resources increased either reciprocal relationships or altruistic (giving more than one receives) relationships with family. These relationships tended to be stronger for whites than blacks. For blacks, increased functional disability or need seemed to lead to a greater likelihood of reciprocal relationships. This same pattern, though not statistically significant, was also found for whites and for the subsample of blacks 50 years of age and older. Although a number of interpretations are possible, we speculate that individuals with disability, regardless of age, resources, or gender, may reduce their social exchange networks and call on their lifetime patterns of relationships in order to maintain perceptions of reciprocal exchange relationships, even in the presence of greater physical need (Smerglia, Deimling, & Barresi, 1988).

The sex effect is the most curious, suggesting a distinctly different pattern of relationships for black and white males and females. Unlike their white counterparts, black females reported receiving less than they gave, in comparison with reciprocal relationships with family, whereas white females reported just the opposite; that is, they were more likely to report receiving more than they gave in comparison with reciprocal support relationships. Although it is impossible to interpret this finding definitely, we note that rather than a race/gender difference, this may be an age/gender difference. The reversed effect was present when black women of all ages were compared with white women over 50. However, analyses focusing on black women over 50 did not yield the same significant effect. The means for older black and white women were in the same direction, although analyses of the older black women (which involved a much smaller cell size) were not significant. Other possible explanations may be the different marital experiences of black and white women, for example, the number of years married, age at birth of the first child, and timing of and total number of children.

Perceived Reciprocity and Well-being

For the remainder of the chapter, we will explore the relationship of reciprocity to reports of psychological well-being. Thus, our concern will shift from the nature of support to the consequences of that support for psychological health. In this section, we will discuss differences in the means for self-reported happiness, life satisfaction, and family satisfaction, by reciprocity and age, respectively, for the NSBA and SSE data sets.[1]

Among blacks 18 years of age and older, increased happiness was related significantly to reports of reciprocity. Individuals reporting either receiving more than they gave or reciprocity in support exchanges were significantly happier than those who reported having received less than they gave. Consistent with other findings that positive deviations from equality and equity are associated with positive outcomes (Clark & Reis, 1988; Fisher et al., 1982), those who reported receiving more than they gave were significantly happier than were either those who reported reciprocal relationships or receiving less than they gave. This same relationship, though not statistically significant, was also present in the overall means for the subsample of blacks 50 years of age and older.

The effect of reciprocity on happiness for blacks was confined to the oldest and youngest age groups. Somewhat surprisingly, because it confirms some general notions of equity that have gone largely unconfirmed, blacks between ages 18 and 49 reported significantly greater happiness in the reciprocity condition than did those either receiving less than they gave or more than they gave. The latter two conditions were also significantly different from each other, suggesting that the lowest levels of happiness for 18- to 49-year-old blacks were for those who reported receiving more than they gave, in comparison with giving more than they received or a reciprocity of exchange relationships. A somewhat similar effect was also found in the group aged 75 years and older. The highest level of happiness was found in the reciprocity group and the lowest in the group receiving less than they gave. Both the reciprocity group and the group receiving more than they gave were significantly happier than was the group receiving less. Unlike the group of blacks aged 18 to 49 years old, the two nonreciprocity exchange groups did not differ significantly from each other. Although the mean differences in happiness supported the role of reciprocity in promoting feelings of happiness among blacks, particularly in the oldest and youngest age groups, neither significant effects nor trends were found for whites.

For blacks, the means for life satisfaction indicated a slightly different pattern than that observed for happiness. No significant differences were found for the different age groups, and the only significant effects were for the totals averaged across age. The small number of individuals in some of the age groups may have contributed to the lack of observed effects. For the whole age range, reciprocity was related significantly to life satisfaction. Unlike happiness, however, the greatest reported life satisfaction was found for receiving more than one gives, which was significantly greater than the means for the reciprocity group or the group receiving less than they gave. No significant differences were discovered between the reciprocity group and those receiving less than they gave. Although not statistically significant, the analyses of the black respondents over 50 years old indicated the same pattern of means. Unlike happiness, feelings of life satisfaction

---

[1]The mean tables on which the following discussion is based are available on request from the authors.

among blacks appear linked to increased receipt of supports from others, over and beyond those obtained in reciprocal support exchanges. The analyses of the white respondents in the SSE revealed no significant effects or trends for reciprocity on life satisfaction.

The same relationships were examined for reports of family satisfaction. For blacks, averaged over all ages, as with life satisfaction, both receiving more than one gives and reciprocity were associated with reports of greater family satisfaction, compared with those who reported receiving less than they gave, but the former two groups were not statistically different. This same trend, though not statistically significant, was also found for the subsample of blacks over 50 years of age. Like the analyses of the previous well-being items, whites did not show any consistent pattern of results on the satisfaction with family item.

Because disability showed a significant relationship to reciprocity for blacks and, as argued earlier, was thought to help moderate the effects of reciprocity, the relationship of reciprocity to well-being was examined for different levels of functional disability (none, moderate, and high). For blacks 18 years of age and older, with no functional disability, both receiving more than one gives and reciprocity were significantly associated with greater reports of happiness than was the group who reported receiving less than they gave. For those with moderate disabilities, reciprocity was not related to happiness. For those with great disabilities, a pattern similar to that found in the no-disability group was recorded, except that the group who reported receiving less had an even lower mean happiness than did those with no disability. Although not statistically significant, the pattern for blacks 50 years of age and older was similar to that for the whole sample.

For whites, only one interesting relationship emerged. Although not statistically significant, persons with great disabilities in equal support exchanges reported lower levels of happiness, in comparison with either of the unequal exchange groups. This is in marked contrast with the black respondents, who consistently showed greater happiness with more favorable support exchanges. The same relationship for life satisfaction showed a pattern similar to that found for happiness. Among blacks with both moderate and great functional disabilities, increased support, based on either reciprocity or receiving more than is given, was related to higher satisfaction than it was for those who reported receiving less than they gave. This relationship was not as clear in the sample of blacks over 50, although a similar pattern was seen for those with great disabilities. For whites, the pattern was similar (though not statistically significant) to that observed with the happiness and satisfaction analyses for blacks with moderate disabilities. Higher reports of satisfaction were associated with receiving more than was given and reciprocity of supports over those of individuals in the group that received less than it gave. On the other hand, for those with great disabilities, like the happiness analysis, reciprocity was associated with lower levels of satisfaction in comparison with both unequal exchange conditions.

Finally, for blacks, reciprocity showed no particularly important relationship to satisfaction with family. The only exception was that for those with no disabilities, receiving more than is given was associated with reports of greater family satisfaction than for those who reported receiving less than was given. For whites, on the other hand, a complex picture of satisfaction with family was revealed. For those with moderate disabilities, whites looked much as blacks did for happiness and life satisfaction; higher receipt of support resources was associated with higher reports of satisfaction with family. However, for those with great disabilities, as in happiness and life satisfaction previously reported for whites, reciprocity was associated with lower levels of family satisfaction than in either unequal exchange condition.

In sum, the trends in the SSE data set suggest that for whites with great functional disabilities, maintaining reciprocal support exchanges may incur a personal cost manifested in lower feelings of happiness, life satisfaction, and satisfaction with family. For blacks, disability appears to operate in a more need-based fashion, and greater happiness and life satisfaction are related to an increased receipt of support, based on both reciprocity and receiving more than is given.

In order to investigate the independent effects of reciprocity on well-being, regression analyses were conducted separately on the NSBA and SSE respondents. The summaries of these analyses are given in Tables 7.3 and 7.4. Table 7.3 shows the presence of significant effects of reciprocity on all the well-being items for blacks, independent of resources and social status variables. For happiness, receiving less than one gives, in comparison with reciprocity relationships, is associated significantly with decreased happiness. On the other hand, receiving more than one gives, in comparison with reciprocal relationships, is associated with increased life satisfaction. The same, but marginal, effect was also found for satisfaction with family. As shown in the second, fourth, and sixth columns of Table 7.3, similar but not as strong effects were found for the black subsample over 50 years of age.

Not surprisingly, given the univariate results, Table 7.4 indicates that among older whites (SSE), reciprocity had no independent effects on any of the well-being items over and beyond that contributed by the social and economic resources and social status variables.

The pattern of results for reciprocity as a predictor of well-being is fairly clear. Unlike the similarity of effects found for blacks and whites for predictors of reciprocity, blacks and whites differed greatly in the importance of reciprocal support relationships as sources of personal well-being. A distinct trend was found in the data for blacks, on all three well-being indices, for equality of social supportive exchange relationships to be associated with increased well-being. This was particularly true in the youngest (18 to 49) and oldest age groups (over 75 years old). The remaining age groups showed nonsignificant results.

For whites, no significant univariate effects of reciprocity on well-being were found. Unlike that for blacks, no overall discernible pattern was evident. When the relationship of reciprocity to well-being was examined under different conditions of disability, blacks and whites exhibited a different pattern. For whites with great disabilities, the reciprocity of support exchanges were related to lower levels of well-being than they were for the two unequal exchange groups. For blacks, the existence of need in the form of functional disability resulted in increased

TABLE 7.3.   Summary of Regressions of Psychological Well-being on Reciprocity with Social and Demographic Controls: National Survey of Black Americans

Model	Happiness		Life Satisfaction		Family Satisfaction	
Regression Coefficients	B^a	B^b	B^c	B^d	B^e	B^f
Variable						
Constant	1.71	1.95	2.71	2.49	3.58	3.98
Reciprocity						
Received More	.03	.14	.19[h]	.27[h]	.01	.03
Received Less	−.15[i]	.01	−.03	.07	−.09[g]	−.05
Age	.01[i]	.01[g]	.01[i]	.01+	.01[i]	.00
Education	−.01	−.01	−.01[i]	−.02	−.04[h]	−.01
Family Income	.00	−.01	.02[h]	.01	−.01	−.04[i]
Disability	−.05[i]	−.04[h]	−.04[h]	−.02	−.04[i]	−.02[h]
Region						
(Non-South)	.10[h]	.12	.23[i]	.25[h]	.01	−.09
Marital Status						
Married	.20[i]	.26[i]	.17[i]	.14	.13[i]	.18[i]
Sex						
Female	.02	.03	−.02	−.17	.01	.04

Note: Four of the variables in the models—reciprocity, marital status, region, and gender—are represented by dummy variables. Reciprocity is represented by two dummy variables. In each case the excluded category is reciprocal exchange. For marital status, not married is the excluded category. For region the excluded category is South, and for sex the excluded category is male. Models 1, 3, and 5 are estimated on the full 18-years-and-above NSBA sample. Models 2, 4, and 6 are estimated on the 50 years-and-older NSBA subsample.
[a]Model: R^2 (ADJ) − .12[i] N = 864
[b]Model: R^2 (ADJ) = .06[i] N = 262
[c]Model: R^2 (ADJ) = .08[i] N = 864
[d]Model: R^2 (ADJ) = .10[i] N = 262
[e]Model: R^2 (ADJ) = .09[i] N = 864
[f]Model: R^2 (ADJ) = .09[i] N = 262
[g]$p < .10$, [h]$p < .05$, [i]$p < .01$

support resources, both based on reciprocity and receiving more than is given, leading to greater well-being than for those blacks who reported receiving less than they gave.

For blacks, the multivariate analyses revealed that the univariate statistical relationships were fairly independent of the resource, social, and relational variables used as controls. For whites, no significant multivariate results were found.

SUMMARY AND CONCLUSIONS: IMPLICATIONS FOR A THEORY OF LIFE-SPAN RECIPROCITY AND WELL-BEING

The findings of these analyses provide limited but preliminary support for the theoretical propositions presented at the beginning of this chapter. For both blacks and whites, meaningful predictors of reciprocal supportive family relationships

TABLE 7.4. Summary of Regressions of Psychological Well-being Variables on Reciprocity with Social and Demographic Controls: Social Supports of the Elderly

Model	Happiness	Life Satisfaction	Family Satisfaction
Regression Coefficients	B^a	B^b	B^c
Variable			
Constant	2.11	4.10	5.36
Reciprocity			
Received More	−.11	.05	.02
Received Less	.03	.02	−.08
Age	$.02^f$	$.03^f$	$−.01^e$
Education	.00	−.03	$−.06^f$
Family Income	.01	.01	−.02
Disability	$−.14^f$	$−.19^f$	−.01
Region			
(Non-South)	$.22^e$	$.30^f$	$.55^f$
Marital Status			
Married	$.23^e$	$.32^f$	$.32^f$
Sex			
Female	.10	$.22^d$	.10

Note: Four of the variables in the models—reciprocity, marital status, region, and gender—are represented by dummy variables. Reciprocity is represented by two dummy variables. In each case the excluded category is reciprocal exchange. For marital status, not married is the excluded category. For region the excluded category is South, and for sex the excluded category is male.
[a]Model: R^2 (ADJ) = $.02^f$ N = 718
[b]Model: R^2 (ADJ) = $.04^f$ N = 718
[c]Model: R^2 (ADJ) = $.07^f$ N = 718
[d]$p < .10$ [e]$p < .05$ [f]$p < .01$

were found. For whites, negative deviations from reciprocity seemed to be clearly related to the possession of valued social and economic resources; that is, they could afford to have negative support exchanges because they possessed other tangible resources. Need, when conceptualized as functional disability, did not play a significant role in the nature of reciprocal relationships among whites.

On the other hand, for blacks, these resources were less important in the younger years. In the age ranges comparable to those of the SSE, the NSBA respondents also showed significant education effects on receiving less from family than they gave, in comparison with reciprocity. For blacks, the most important predictor of reciprocity was disability. In this case, increased physical limitations were clearly linked to increased reciprocity of supportive relationships. Although the same sign for the coefficients indicated a similar relationship for whites, it was not a significant effect.

This latter finding probably offers the best support for our notions of reciprocity, indicating that individuals with disabilities, regardless of age, social and economic resources, marital status, and sex, will attempt to maintain reciprocal supportive relationships. We speculate that this attempt may take various forms, including reducing the numbers of family network members combined with selecting those members that enable a perception of reciprocity to be maintained.

The age relationships also support this notion among blacks, particularly the greater reciprocity shown in Table 7.1 with increased age.

We judge these results as indicating that the concept of reciprocity, both contemporaneously and over life, may influence an individual's ability to cope with life and age (Rowe & Kahn, 1987). Clearly, the parent–child relationship is special, and so other relationships may operate differently. In addition, the descriptive differences among blacks and whites, and as evidenced in the preliminary French data, suggest that there are cultural, ethnic, and lifetime experiential differences that influence, and are influenced by, roles, resources, and expectations regarding reciprocity of support exchanges.

REFERENCES

Ainsworth, M. D. S., Blehar, M. C., Waters, E., & Wall, S. (1978). *Patterns of attachment.* Hillsdale, NJ: Erlbaum.

Akiyama, H. (1984). *Resource exchanges in dyadic family relationships in the United States and Japan: Dependence of the elderly.* Unpublished doctoral dissertation, University of Illinois at Champaign-Urbana.

Akiyama, H., Antonucci, T. C., & Campbell, R. (1990). Rules of support exchange among two generations of Japanese and American women. In J. Sokolovsky (Ed.), *Growing old in different societies.* Belmont, CA: Wadsworth.

Antonucci, T. C. (1976). Attachment: A life-span concept. *Human Development, 19* (3), 135–142.

Antonucci, T. C. (1985). Personal characteristics, social networks and social behavior. In R. H. Binstock & E. Shanas (Eds.), *Handbook of aging and the social sciences* (2nd ed., pp. 94–128). New York: Van Nostrand Reinhold.

Antonucci, T. C., & Akiyama, H. (1987). Social networks in adult life and a preliminary examination of the convoy model. *Journal of Gerontology, 42* (5), 519–527.

Antonucci, T. C., & Jackson, J. S. (1987). Social support, interpersonal efficacy, and health. In L. Carstensen & B. A. Edelstein (Eds.), *Handbook of clinical gerontology* (pp. 291–311). Elmsford, NY: Pergamon.

Antonucci, T. C., & Jackson, J. S. (1989). Successful ageing and life course reciprocity. In A. Warnes (Ed.), *Human ageing and later life: Multidisciplinary perspectives.* London: Hodder & Soughton Educational.

Austin, W., & Walster, E. (1974). Reactions to confirmations and disconfirmations of expectancies of equity and inequity. *Journal of Personality and Social Psychology, 30,* 208–216.

Berkman, L. S. (1984). Assessing the physical health effects of social networks and social support. *Annual Review of Public Health, 5,* 413–432.

Berkman, L. S., & Syme, S. L. (1979). Social networks, host resistance, and mortality: A nine-year follow-up study of Alameda County residents. *American Journal of Epidemiology, 109* (2), 186–204.

Blazer, D. G. (1982). Social support and mortality in an elderly population. *American Journal of Epidemiology, 115,* 684–694.

Bowlby, J. (1969). *Attachment and loss: Vol. 1. Attachment.* New York: Basic Books.

Brehm, S. (1984). The social support process. In J. C. Masters and K. Yarkin-Levin (Eds.), *Boundary areas in social and developmental psychology* (pp. 107–129). Orlando, FL: Academic Press.

Brehm, S. S., & Brehm, J. W. (1981). *Psychological reactance: A theory of freedom and control.* New York: Academic Press.

Cantor, M. H. 1979. Neighbors and friends: An overlooked resource in the informal support system. *Research on Aging, 1,* 434–463.

Carnevale, P. J. D., Pruit, D. G., & Carrington, P. (1982). Effects of future dependence, liking, and repeated requests for help on helping behavior. *Social Psychology Quarterly, 45,* 9–14.

Cassel, J. (1976). The contribution of the social environment to host resistance. *American Journal of Epidemiology, 104 (Vol. 3),* 253–286.

Clark, M. S. 1984. A distinction between two types of relationships and its implications for development. In J. C. Masters & K. Yarkin-Levin (Eds.), *Boundary areas in social and developmental psychology* (pp. 241–270). New York: Academic Press.

Clark, M. S., & Reis, H. T. (1988). Interpersonal processes in close relationships. In M. R. Rosenzweig & L. W. Porter (Eds.), *Annual Review of Psychology, 39,* 609–672.

Cobb, S. (1976). Social support as a moderator of life stress. *Psychosomatic Medicine, 38* (5), 300–314.

Cohen, S. (1988). Psychosocial models of the role of social support in the etiology of physical disease. *Health Psychology, 7* (3), 269–297.

Cohen, S., & Syme, S. L. (Eds.). (1985). *Social support and health.* New York: Springer.

Coyne, J. C., & DeLongis, A. (1986). Going beyond social support: The role of social relationships in adaptation. *Journal of Consulting and Clinical Psychology, 54,* 454–460.

DePaulo, B. M., & Fisher, J. D. (1980). The costs of asking for help. *Basic and Applied Social Psychology, 1,* 23–35.

Dowd, J. J. (1975). Aging as exchange: A preface to theory. *Journal of Gerontology, 30,* 584–594.

Dowd, J. J. (1980). *Stratification among the aged.* Monterey, CA: Brooks/Cole.

Dowd, J. J. (1984). Beneficence and the aged. *Journal of Gerontology, 39,* 102–108.

Fischer, C. S. (1982). *To dwell among friends: Personal networks in town and city.* Chicago: University of Chicago Press.

Fisher, J. D., Nadler, A., & Whitcher-Alagna, S. (1982). Recipient reactions to aid. *Psychological Bulletin, 91,* 27–54.

Gouldner, A. W. (1960). The norm of reciprocity: A preliminary statement. *American Sociological Review, 25,* 161–178.

Graziano, W. G. (1984). A developmental approach to social exchange processes. In J. C. Masters & K. Yarkin-Levin (Eds.), *Boundary areas in social and developmental psychology* (pp. 161–194). New York: Academic Press.

Greenberg, M. S. (1980). A theory of indebtedness. In K. Gergen, M. S. Greenberg, & R. Willis (Eds.), *Social exchange: Advances in theory and research.* New York: Plenum.

Greenberg, M. S., & Shapiro, S. P. (1971). Indebtedness: An adversive aspect of asking for and receiving help. *Sociometry, 34* (2), 290–301.

Haynes, S., Feinleib, M., & Kannel, W. (1980). The relationship of psychosocial factors to coronary heart disease in the Framingham Study. III. Eight year incidence of coronary heart disease. *American Journal of Epidemiology, 111,* 37–58.

House, J. S., Robbins, C., & Metzner, H. C. (1982). The association of social relationships and activities with mortality: Prospective evidence from the Tecumseh community health study. *American Journal of Epidemiology, 116,* 123–140.

Ingersoll-Dayton, B., & Antonucci, T. C. (1988). Reciprocal and non-reciprocal social support: Contrasting sides of intimate relationships. *Journal of Gerontology, 43,* 565–573.

Jackson, J. S., & Hatchett, S. J. (1986). Intergenerational research: Methodological considerations. In N. Datan, A. L. Green, & H. W. Reese (Eds.), *Intergenerational networks: Families in context.* Hillsdale, NJ: Erlbaum.

Jackson, J. S., Tucker, M. B., & Gurin, G. (1987). *National survey of black Americans 1979–1980.* Ann Arbor, MI: Inter-University Consortium for Political and Social Research, Institute for Social Research.

Joseph, J. (1980). *Social affiliation, risk factor status, and coronary heart disease: A cross-sectional study of Japanese-American men.* Unpublished doctoral dissertation, University of California at Berkeley.

Kahn, R. L., & Antonucci, T. C. (1980). Convoys over the life course: Attachment, roles and social support. In P. B. Baltes & O. G. Brim (Eds.), *Life-span development and behavior* (pp. 253–286). New York: Academic Press.

Lee, G. R. (1985). Kinship & social support of the elderly: The case of the United States. *Aging & Society, 5* (1), 19–38.

Levitt, M. J. (in press). Attachment and close relationships: A life span perspective. In J. L. Gewirtz & W. F. Kurtines (Eds.), *Intersections with attachment.* Hillsdale, NJ: Erlbaum.

Levitt, M., Weber, R., & Clark, S. (1986). Social network relationships as sources of maternal support and well-being. *Developmental Psychology, 22,* 310–316.

Litwak, E. (1985). *Helping the elderly: The complementary roles of informal networks and formal systems.* New York: Guilford.

Medalie, J. H., & Goldbourt, U. (1976). Angina pectoris among 10,000 men. Psychosocial and other factors as evidenced by a multivariate analysis of a 5 year incidence study. *American Journal of Medicine, 60,* 910–921.

Norbeck, J. S., & Tilden, V. (1981). Life stress, social support and emotional equilibrium in complications of pregnancy: A prospective multivariate study. *Journal of Health and Social Behavior, 24,* 30–46.

Nuckolls, K. B., Cassel, J., & Kaplan, B. H. (1972). Psychosocial assets, life crisis and the prognosis of pregnancy. *American Journal of Epidemiology, 95,* 431–441.

Pearlin, L. I. (1985). Social structure and processes of social support. In S. Cohen & S. L. Syme (Eds.), *Social support and health* (pp. 43–60). New York: Academic Press.

Rook, K. (1984). The negative side of social interaction: Impact on psychological well-being. *Journal of Personality and Social Psychology, 46,* 1097–1108.

Rowe, J., & Kahn, R. L. (1987). Human aging: Usual and successful. *Science, 237,* 143–149.

Schoenbach, V. J., Kaplan, B. H., Fredman, L., & Kleinbaum, D. G. (1986). Social ties and mortality in Evans County, Georgia. *American Journal of Epidemiology, 123*, 577–591.

Shumaker, S. A., & Jackson, J. S. (1979). The aversive effects of nonreciprocated benefits. *Social Psychology Quarterly, 42*, 148–158.

Smerglia, V. L., Deimling, G. T., & Barresi, C. M. (1988). Black/white family comparisons in helping and decision-making networks of impaired elderly. *Family Relations, 37*, 305–309.

Walster, E. G., Walster, W., & Berscheid, E. (Eds.) (1978). *Equity: Theory and research.* Boston: Allyn & Bacon.

Wan, T. T. H. (1982). *Stressful life events, social-support networks and gerontological health.* Lexington, MA: Heath.

Wan, T. T. H., & Weissert, W. G. (1981). Social support networks, patient status and institutionalization. *Research on Aging, 3*, 240–256.

Wentowski, G. J. (1981). Reciprocity and the coping strategies of older people: Cultural dimensions of network building. *The Gerontologist, 21*, 600–609.

CHAPTER 8

Stress and Support in Stepfamily Formation: The Cultural Context of Social Support

DAVID JACOBSON

Brandeis University

In this chapter, I examine, in the case of stepfamily formation, the cultural context in which the meaning of support is determined. The current research on social support suggests that the perceived aspects of social relationships, rather than what is actually given or received in them, is related to the ways in which individuals cope with stressful situations. Other contributors to this volume discuss psychological variables that might influence the perception of social support; this chapter deals with cultural factors that shape the interpretation of objects, events, and relationships as instances of social support.

A PARADIGMATIC SHIFT IN THE STUDY OF SOCIAL SUPPORT

A "cognitive revolution" is now taking place in the research on social support. Its development resembles a similar movement that occurred in stress research, brought about by the work of Lazarus (Lazarus & Folkman, 1984) and Brown (1974, 1983), among others. Their emphasis on the variable meaning of stressful events led to studies of "beliefs" or "perceptual lenses" that mediate the ways in which people see the world and attribute significance to it. Likewise, researchers have begun to focus on the meaning of social support, rather than on the structure and/or content of supportive relationships. This shift was stimulated by findings in several studies that individuals in supportive transactions, whether as the intended provider or the prospective recipient, differed in their assessments of the existence, quantity, and/or quality of support given and/or received (Albrecht & Adelman, 1987b; Jacobson, 1986, 1987).

Supportive transactions can be interpreted differently because of the varying conceptual foundations and research methods used in studies of social support. Most studies, concentrating on its types or sources (Payne & Jones, 1987), assume social support to be some sort of entity and so do not examine the meaning of statements made regarding its provision or receipt. For example, the Inventory of Socially Supportive Behaviors (ISSB), devised by Barrera (1981), asks about types of support received by an individual (e.g., emotional, cognitive, and material support). Although this scale refers to specific behaviors that are presumably objectively defined, it is evident that its items require interpretation. For example, emotional support is tapped by responses to the statement "Listened to you talk about your private feelings" (Barrera, 1981, p. 88). Yet listening is not simply a description of an auditory event; the term connotes caring and sympathetic attentiveness. Therefore, this measure of social support is based on the perception of other people—their motivations and capacities for warmth, kindness, and responsiveness—and of the relationship in question—the expectation that a good friend or relative should act in that way. However, the standards by which such perceptions are made are neither studied nor assessed. This situation is not peculiar to this research instrument.

Other measures of social support also require interpretations of actions and relationships. The Perceived Social Support from Family and Friends (PSSFA-FR), devised by Procidano and Heller (1983), consists of self-report measures, including positive and negative assessments of items such as "I rely on my family for emotional support" and "My family is sensitive to my personal needs." These items incorporate classification and interpretation regarding what constitutes "emotional support" and being "sensitive" (as well as understandings of the terms *family* and *personal needs*). Moreover, the Social Relationship Scale (SRS) developed by McFarlane and his associates (McFarlane, Neale, Norman, Roy, & Streiner, 1981) asks individuals to identify others with whom they have discussed life stress and to rate the helpfulness (i.e., supportiveness) of these discussions on a scale ranging from "makes things a lot worse" to "makes things a lot better." Again, such ratings are not simply descriptive statements but, rather, are judgments implying some standard or norm according to which respondents evaluate not only the activity but also the expected fit between the activity and the relationship in which it occurred.

Furthermore, the interpretation of an event or a relationship as an instance of support is different from that of its amount or its adequacy. The former is concerned with the constitutive elements of social support, the latter with the magnitude of its properties. Some studies do attempt to measure the differential evaluation of support, as Payne and Jones indicated (1987), by asking about how a respondent "feels" about it, measured by degree of satisfaction or level of perceived adequacy. However, few studies consider the more fundamental question of the social definition of the category itself.

In sum, disagreements between support givers and support receivers have led analysts to view social support as an act of interpretation rather than as an attribute of an objectively defined entity. Albrecht and Adelman (1987), for example, suggested that it is useful to regard social support as a "symbolic activity" requiring a common semantic or referential framework to produce a shared view of supportive exchanges. They argued that to the extent that people have different referents, they will disagree about the supportiveness of their interaction. When support is viewed as a symbolic activity, understanding its interpretive framework—the set of assumptions, beliefs, and values that constitute its *cultural context*—is critical, as it shapes the perception of what constitutes support, as well as who should provide it, to whom, and under what circumstances.

PSYCHOSOCIAL TRANSITIONS AND THE STUDY OF MEANING

A meaning-centered approach to conceptualizing social support is consistent with certain analytical traditions in stress research. For example, studies of "psychosocial transitions" (Parkes, 1971) examine questions of meaning. In the study of transitions, stress is viewed as stemming from a relatively abrupt change in a person or in the environment, including "other persons, material possessions, the familiar world of home and place of work," that affects the individual's beliefs about the world and his or her place in it (Parkes, 1971, p. 103). These beliefs constitute an "assumptive world," which "includes everything we know or think we know . . . our interpretation of the past and our expectations for the future, our plans and our prejudices" (Parkes, 1971, p. 103). According to this model of stress, these beliefs or assumptions shape behavior, and events that challenge or change them—which in turn undermine the individual's sense of meaning—are experienced as stressful.

This "transitional" conceptualization of stressful events complements other models that deal with questions of meaning. For example, in a transactional model of stress (Lazarus & Folkman, 1984), the meaning of an event is defined according to its impact on the balance between an individual's demands and his or her resources. Studies based on such a model look primarily at the immediate consequences of an event and typically at its significance within a framework of ideas, beliefs, and values. In a transitional model of stress, however, the meaning of an event is related to the changes that it precipitates in the very framework of ideas, beliefs, and values in which individuals evaluate themselves and their relation to their world. It examines the long-term implications of an event and typically its role in helping individuals restructure themselves cognitively.

The different senses of meaning associated with these models can be illustrated in the example of divorce. On the one hand, an individual who is divorced and who is responsible for maintaining a household and providing for children may be stressed by a discrepancy between such demands and a decrease in the resources available to meet them. This would reflect adjustments that occur within a set of ideas, beliefs, and values that remains intact despite existential changes affecting the individual. On the other hand, stresses associated with developments in the individual's thinking about himself or herself as a single person and how he or she relates to others reflect transformations of a cognitive framework.

Likewise, in the event of a psychosocial transition, support is what helps reorganize an individual's "assumptive world," according to which he comprehends himself and his relation to his world. Note that this process of reorganization or cognitive restructuring refers to changes that occur in the individual's assumptive world rather than in his or her perception or definition of the situation's reality. In other words, support in circumstances that require a cognitive transformation is what helps the individual reconstruct his or her assumptive world so that it better fits a changed reality.

CULTURE AND MEANING

A meaning-centered approach to the study of social support is also consistent with the analytical models used in ethnographic research. Anthropologists define culture as a set of standards according to which meaning is assigned to objects, events, actions, and relationships. Although this is a common tenet of cultural anthropology, one of the best-known formulations of it is found in Geertz's (1973) distinction between "thin" description and "thick" description. Thin description depicts behavior in the sense of physical motions, as seen, for example, by the eye of a camera. In contrast, thick description reveals its significance, as illustrated by "twitches" and "winks." Both entail the same physical movement—the contraction of the muscles of the eyelid. A wink, however, conveys meaning: It may be a conspiratorial signal or some other message possible within the framework of a socially established code. To grasp the meaning of an action requires understanding the frames of interpretation within which behavior is classified and meaning is attributed to it. This means apprehending and depicting the structures of meaning in terms of which people behave and in terms of which that behavior is intelligible to them.

These structures of meaning consist of a group's classifications of their world and their ideas of the ways in which people should act, ought to act, or are expected to act. Anthropologists describe such classifications as "cultural categories" or "conceptions" (Geertz, 1973), "representations" (Holy & Stuchlik, 1983; Schneider, 1976), and "cultural units" (Schneider, 1976), which reflect a "body of definitions, premises, statements, postulates, presumptions, propositions, and perceptions about the nature of the universe and man's place in it" (Schneider, 1976, pp. 203, 206). And anthropologists label behavioral expectations as "normative rules" or "norms" (Holy & Stuchlik, 1983; Schneider, 1976). Schneider (1976, p. 203) contrasted "culture," the term he uses to encompass cultural categories and units, with "norms":

> Where norms tell the actor how to play the scene, culture tells the actor how the scene is set and what it all means. Where norms tell the actor how to behave in the presence of ghosts, gods, and human beings, culture tells the actor what ghosts, gods, and human beings are and what they are all about.

Cultural analysis and the study of psychosocial transitions are not unrelated. A cultural category, like an assumption, is an idea or an expectation that people typically take for granted; it also implies a norm or a guideline that people use to evaluate objects, events, and relationships and that tells them how they and others should behave. Meaning, then, is not inherent in resources or relationships but, rather, is established by comparing them with expectations embodied in culturally based categories and norms.

The cultural basis of meaning is illustrated in different conceptions of the self and social relationships. For example, in Confucian thought, according to DeVos and his colleagues (1985, p. 19), the notion that human nature is characterized by frailty and fallibility is associated with the belief that the "individual seeking development alone, without the experiential support of a community, is inconceivable; hence, one must seek out supportive relationships in the human endeavor." This, they pointed out, contrasts with the assumption in Buddhist thought that the development of the individual is based on his or her "retreat" from the world and from relationships with others. That is, Buddhist beliefs lead to a devaluation of attachments and a different assessment of social relationships that a believer in Confucian precepts would view as supportive. Obeyesekere expressed a similar argument in his commentary (1985, p. 134) on the way that the Western concept of depression would be viewed in a Buddhist culture:

> Brown and Harris in their exploration of depression as essentially caused by social and psychological conditions make the following statement: "The immediate response to loss of an important source of positive value is likely to be a sense of hopelessness, accompanied by a gamut of feelings, ranging from distress, depression, and shame to anger. Feelings of hopelessness will not always be restricted to the provoking incident—large or small. It may lead to thoughts about the hopelessness of one's life in general. It is such *generalization* of hopelessness that we believe forms the central core of depressive disorder."

> This statement sounds strange to me, a Buddhist, for if it was placed in the context of Sri Lanka, I would say that we are not dealing with a depressive but a good Buddhist. The Buddhist would take one further step in generalization: it is not simply the general hopelessness of one's own lot; that hopelessness lies in the nature of the world, and salvation lies in understanding and overcoming that hopelessness.

Thus, our expectations about the world influence our judgments of it. In order to understand the meaning of such evaluations, we must understand the underlying or implicit standards of comparison. We will now examine this view of the cultural context of meaning in the case of stress and support in American stepfamilies.

STEPFAMILIES AND STRESS

Stepfamilies are created when a couple marries and either or both husband and wife has a child or children from a previous marriage. Some analysts include in their definition of a stepfamily a domestic group consisting of a couple (married or not) and the children from a previous union of either or both adults (Espinoza & Newman, 1979; Sager et al., 1983; Visher & Visher, 1979). Both marriage and coresidence are used to define stepfamilies, although as analytical criteria they are not consistently applied within or across different studies. A stepfamily and a stepfamily household or domestic group are differentiated by reference to coresidence. The focus of this chapter is the stepfamily household, a residential group consisting of a couple and stepchildren (who are the biological or adoptive children of at least one spouse), although it may also include the children of this union. It is the membership of a stepfamily household that has to face and resolve the problems of living together.

Stepfamilies are at risk for stress, as shown in measures of marital quality, of family cohesiveness, of child abuse, and of the mental and physical health and well-being of individual stepfamily members (Ahrons & Rodgers, 1987; Cherlin, 1978; Espinoza & Newman, 1979; Messinger, 1976; Mikesell & Garbarino, 1986; Visher & Visher, 1979). It is also apparent in divorce rates, a demographic feature that has been described as the "best objective indicator of differences in family unity between remarriages and first marriages" (Cherlin, 1978, p. 639). For example, the rate of marital dissolution is higher for remarriages than it is for first marriages. In the United States, approximately half of first marriages end in divorce (Spanier & Furstenberg, 1987). On the other hand, about 55% of remarried couples divorce (Spanier & Furstenberg, 1987). Although remarriage divorces include couples with and without children, stepfamily households seem particularly vulnerable to dissolution (Becker, Landes, & Michael, 1977; Benson van der Ohe, 1987; Cherlin, 1978; Clingempeel & Brand, 1985; White & Booth, 1985). White and Booth (1985), for example, found that couples with stepchildren were twice as likely to divorce as were those without stepchildren.

PSYCHOLOGICAL AND STRUCTURAL EXPLANATIONS OF STEPFAMILY STRESS

Explanations of stepfamily stress vary in their emphases on one or another causal factor and, likewise, in their implications with respect to the nature and role of social support. They can be classified as psychological, structural, and cultural models or interpretations.

There are several subtypes of psychological explanation. For example, some analysts contend that the divorce rate among remarrieds is due primarily to "personality disorders," which also led to the dissolution of the previous marriages (Cherlin, 1978). Others suggest that the experience of divorce leads to subsequent marital instability (Cherlin, 1978; Clingempeel, 1981; Spanier & Furstenberg, 1987). That is, remarriages may be unstable because those who enter them accept divorce as a solution to an unhappy marriage and are thus predisposed to divorce.

Other psychological explanations emphasize questions of mourning and displacement. Some theorists feel that stepfamilies are founded on the loss of a primary relationship or set of relationships and that adjustment (in the stepfamily) is related to successfully mourning that loss (Bohannan, 1984, 1985; Kleinman, Rosenberg, & Whiteside, 1979; Moss, 1984; Visher & Visher, 1979, 1982). If the resolution of grief requires two to four years in the case of marital separation (Weiss, 1975) and three to four years in the case of bereavement (Parkes & Weiss, 1983), and if 50% of remarriages take place within three years of the ending of a previous marriage, then it would follow that remarriage could be undermined by unresolved grief.

Still other psychologists (Bettelheim, 1976; Flugel, 1921) emphasize that the conflict between stepchildren and stepparents is a displacement of the children's hostility toward their biological parents. Bettelheim, for example, stated that a stepchild's conflict with a stepmother reflects the child's ambivalence toward his or her own mother and a "splitting" of positive and negative feelings, thereby displacing this hostility onto the stepparent. In short, conflict between a stepchild and a stepparent does not depend on the dissolution of a biological family and the formation of a stepfamily; rather, it is inherent in the process of child development.

Structural explanations stress the complexity of stepfamilies, a complexity produced by the expansion of the number of persons and relationships within a family system. It is argued that this change compounds interaction and communication, leading to the possibility of conflict. For example, Wald (1981) cited a study by Bossard and Boll that indicated that the number of possible dyads in a system increases the potential for distress within it. However, family or household size is not a distinguishing feature of stepfamily instability, as it does not differentiate between "biological" or nuclear families and stepfamilies, both of which can add members without necessarily adding types of relationships. For example, a biological or nuclear family household has eight basic kinship roles (husband, wife, father, mother, son, daughter, brother, sister), regardless of the number of individuals occupying them (cf. Bohannan, 1963, 1970, 1984, 1985). A stepfamily household, by contrast, adds roles (e.g., stepparent, stepchild, stepsibling, and perhaps half-siblings); it also loses at least one (i.e., mother or father, from a child's perspective). Its structural complexity is thus better measured by role differentiation than by role replication.

Expanding the family system, or loosening its boundaries, also complicates stepfamily life by increasing demands, often from people outside the household. Extrahousehold relationships, including the children's parents (ex-spouses), spouses of ex-spouses, and the children of ex-spouses' spouses, constitute stepfamily networks, described variously as "divorce chains" (Bohannan, 1970, 1985), "rem[arried] suprasystems" (Sager et al., 1983), "divorced–remarried families" (Keshet, 1987), and "binuclear families" (Ahrons & Rodgers, 1987). For example, Keshet (1987) described the case of a man who had to change his plans because his ex-wife's second husband's ex-wife's mother became ill and he took over caring for his children, who were living with his ex-wife, so that she and her husband could take over caring for his children, who were living with his ex-wife, so that she could take over caring for her mother.

The problem with this sort of explanation, as with all network analyses, is that relationships entail potential or possible obligations that are not necessarily recognized or, if they are recognized, are not necessarily honored (Jacobson, 1985).

In an analysis, it is necessary to consider how relationships are perceived and obligations are evaluated, matters that are shaped by cultural beliefs and normative guidelines.

CULTURAL EXPLANATIONS OF STEPFAMILY STRESS

Cultural explanations of stepfamily stress emphasize the role of expectations, embodied in cultural categories and social norms, in shaping patterns of behavior. Such explanations hold that concepts of stepfamily and stepfamily household structure and functioning influence the formation, operation, and dissolution of stepfamilies. Cross-cultural and subcultural differences in ideas (assumptions, beliefs, norms) about who is included and excluded from a family and about how family members ought to behave correlate with variations in the perception of stress and support in stepfamily interactions. That is, cultural models of family organization influence the expectations and experiences of stepfamily formation, including its stressfulness and the interpretation, provision, and receipt of social support. Cultural explanations may be subdivided into three groups with different emphases.

The first type of cultural explanation focuses on the *absence* of terms and rules in American culture for structuring stepfamily life. Many observers of the American stepfamily conclude that its instability is related to a lack of cultural guidelines for it. For example, there is little agreement on what to call a family created by a remarriage: Indeed, there are at least seventeen different terms for this group (Wald, 1981), including blended family, reconstituted family, reconstructed family, and stepfamily. Similarly, there is uncertainty about who are steprelatives. Stepparents, stepchildren, and stepsiblings are acknowledged as steprelatives, kin categories modeled on the membership of a nuclear family, but people are unsure about giving the same status to the relatives of steprelatives, such as stepuncles and stepnephews or stepgrandparents and stepgrandchildren. People accept as steprelatives a parent's spouse and a spouse's child but hesitate about the relatives of these stepparents and stepchildren.

Furthermore, there is linguistic and normative confusion. There are no terms in English for the divorced and remarried or for the mother's husband or the father's wife (Mead, 1970). The prefix *step* derives from Old English, meaning "bereaved," and was originally applied to a child who had lost a parent, and only later was it extended to the replacement parent (Wald, 1981). Nor are there terms for a child's parent who is no longer a spouse. And as with other relatives through marriage, (i.e., in-laws), people are often uncertain about how to address steprelatives (for example, a mother's spouse), resorting to the practice of "no naming" (cf. Firth, Hubert, & Forge, 1970; Schneider, 1968), by which the steprelatives are called on and communicated with through the device of "hmm" or other gutteral sounds. Most significantly, there are no clear and agreed-upon cultural standards or rules for steprelationships; there are no common understandings about how a person should behave toward a spouse's child or how that child should behave toward his or her parent's spouse. In short, for Americans, the stepfamily is an "incomplete institution" (Cherlin, 1978) involving relationships that are "culturally uncharted" (Spanier & Furstenberg, 1987).

A different sort of cultural interpretation emphasizes the *presence* of concepts, beliefs, and norms that imply the nuclear family as the ideal, thereby devaluing and undermining the stepfamily. For example, in our system of kinship terminology, the nuclear family is differentiated from and contrasted with all other kin types. Our terms for members of the nuclear family (i.e., husband, wife, father, mother, son, daughter, brother, sister), as Fox noted (1967, p. 250; see also Bohannan, 1963, 1970, 1971, 1984, 1985; Firth et al., 1970) are "not used for anyone outside the family," an emphasis very different from that of most other kinship systems in which the nuclear family has no special terminological status. Even sociological textbooks on the American family distinguish between the nuclear family and "secondary kin . . . that is, all blood kin and the affines outside the nuclear family" (Adams, 1980, p. 328).

Our ideas about marriage and household composition also detract from stepfamily relationships. We expect, for example, marriage to be "neolocal" (i.e., we expect a couple to form its own household independent of the households of their parents) and households to contain normally no more than two generations (Bohannan, 1984; Mead, 1970; Schneider, 1968; Schneider & Smith, 1978). We also assume that if a household contains a family, it will consist of a parental couple and their (preadult) children. These assumptions are consistent with the suggestion (Visher & Visher, 1979) that stepfamily stress is related in part to the presence of a biological parent outside the household and a same-sex nonparent adult inside the household. This arrangement is contrary to our expectations that a nuclear family be contained within a household.

Furthermore, Americans believe not only that a household should contain a nuclear family but also that it should not be shared with others. To the extent that Americans see the nuclear family and a household as synonymous, other family forms may not be considered "real" families. These alternative forms include the single-parent household, the "binuclear" family (Ahrons & Rodgers, 1987), which, from the perspective of a child whose parents are divorced, includes his or her mother and father, although each of them lives in a different household, and the stepfamily, which includes people who are not kin. In short, our assumptions about domestic group boundaries and composition do not facilitate stepfamily integration.

Beliefs about relationships created through marriage may further weaken the stepfamily. For example, in American thought, kin are relatives because they share a substance (e.g., "blood") and in-laws are relatives because they are connected by a legal relationship (Schneider, 1968; Schneider & Smith, 1978). Likewise, steprelatives are in-laws: If there had not been a marriage, there would not have been a relationship (Bohannan, 1984). Although the term *in-law* is usually applied to a spouse's parent or a child's spouse, steprelatives (e.g., a parent's spouse or a spouse's child) are in structurally equivalent positions (Bohannan, 1985). The identification of steprelatives with in-laws is consistent with disharmony in stepfamilies, as we believe that the coresidence of in-laws creates tension (Adams, 1980; Bohannan, 1963, 1971, 1984, 1985; Komarovsky, 1962).

Culturally, a household containing steprelatives and/or other in-laws is a situation ripe for conflict.

Moreover, our beliefs about family and household relationships appear to undermine stepfamily functioning. First is the issue of relational priorities (Bohannan, 1963, 1971). That is, one relationship in a household is typically considered dominant or fundamental, in that if two or more relationships conflict, one will be favored over the other. For example, in American culture, the husband–wife relationship is considered the basic relationship, taking priority over parent–child relationships (Bohannan, 1963, 1971, 1985; Schneider & Smith, 1978). Indeed, it has been suggested (Schneider & Smith, 1978, p. 43) that in American culture, and especially in middle-class culture, not only is the husband–wife relationship seen as the primary relationship but it is "felt wrong to sacrifice this relationship to the demands of children." These assumptions are embedded in the thinking of therapists who work with stepfamilies and who contend that if a stepfamily is to achieve "harmony" and "integration," the couple relationship (husband–wife) must take precedence over other relationships and must be made strong, even at the expense of other relationships (Boss & Greenberg, 1984; Keshet, 1987; Kleinman, Rosenberg, & Whiteside, 1979; Moss, 1984; Ransom, Schlesinger, & Derdeyn, 1979).

People in other cultures have different ideas. For example, among the patrilineal Tiv of Africa (Bohannan, 1963, 1971, 1985), the household is built on the father–son relationship. A Tiv marriage is expected to be "virilocal" and "patrilocal" (in which a wife goes to live with her husband in the household of his father), in contrast with the norm of "neolocal" residence for American couples. That is, although an American couple expects (and is expected) to establish a home of their own (and one that ideally will house only two generations), a Tiv woman goes to live with her husband, who, in turn, continues to reside in the household occupied by his father, his own siblings, his "uncles" (fathers' siblings), his "cousins" (father's siblings' children), and perhaps even his grandfather (and their respective spouses), as the Tiv value households that contain three to four generations.

Neither marriage nor divorce seriously alters the structure of a Tiv household, as neither significantly changes the father–son relationship. But for Americans, for whom a household is based on a married couple, divorce leads to the breakup of households. For the Tiv, marital dissolution does not lead to a rupture in household organization; rather, a household is dissolved when a father and son become estranged. In most "divorces" among the Tiv, children remain with the father. In this case, other women in the household (e.g., father's co-wives, father's mother) are addressed by the term for mother and will take care of them. If the children go with their mother, they will reside in the household of her father (and/or brother) or in the household of her new husband. In either case, no new roles or relationships are created or established. As Bohannan noted (1971, p. 54), "Step relationships are not as complex and certainly not as difficult as they are with Americans," adding that "Tiv have no special kinship terms for steprelatives, not even anything analogous to the modifier 'step' of English."

A third explanation for stepfamily stress centers on the cultural differences within a family. For example, remarriages create stepfamily households in which members may have different conceptions, expectations, and standards of behavior, including ideas about family boundaries, family relationships, domestic routines, and the allocation of resources. This model of the culture *of* a stepfamily (rather than the stepfamily *in* culture) is shared across disciplinary boundaries: Various researchers agree that the difficulties of stepfamily formation are related to intrafamilial cultural conflicts (Ahrons & Rodgers, 1987; Bernard, 1956; Bohannan, 1984; Espinoza & Newman, 1979; Keshet, 1987; Moss, 1984; Spanier & Furstenberg, 1987; Visher & Visher, 1979; Wald, 1981).

The "minicultures" of the two families brought together in a stepfamily may be so alien to each other that the differences between them may generate a form of culture shock. This experience was described as follows:

> When a number of people come together from a variety of previous family and household backgrounds, each one already has ideas about how the television set should be used, where the dog sleeps, who prepares the breakfast, how the laundry is folded, and how the hamburgers are cooked. The problem, of course, is that there is no agreement. Everyone brings different traditions from their former family experiences—most of them givens below conscious awareness until the startling experience of trying to mind a parent who allows watching television before dinner or finding the dog sleeping at the foot of the bed. (Visher & Visher, 1982, pp. 107–108)

STEPFAMILY SUPPORT

The model of psychosocial transitions and the cultural explanations of stepfamily stress show what would be supportive for individuals coping with changes in family and household composition and relationships. From both analytical perspectives, adjustment requires the review and reorganization of one's assumptions and the structure of meaning they entail. This was identified as a central task of stepfamily formation. Furstenberg and Spanier (1984, p. 54) observed that in "the process of remarriage, individuals must both revise and disassemble the micro-culture of their first marriage and create a new belief system." Thus, support probably consists of information that enables individuals to undertake a process of cognitive restructuring. Such support offers feedback that alters the way in which a person views and experiences the world as meaningful, enabling him or her to achieve a better "fit" between the assumptive world and the self or environment (Marris, 1982; Parkes, 1971).

STEPFAMILY SUPPORT GROUPS

This cognitive restructuring process occurs in different contexts, including psychotherapy and support groups Parkes (1971, p. 105) proposed that psychotherapy exists "to facilitate change in the assumptive world and it makes use of the relationship between patient and therapist as a 'test bed' in which old assumptions can be questioned and new ones [can] be rehearsed." Arntson and Droge (1987) argue that support groups in general function by providing a rationale for their members' problems, thereby demystifying the stress they experience, and by creating "an alternate or substitute culture . . . within which members can develop new definitions for their personal identities and new norms" (p. 152). Stepfamily support groups (Brady & Ambler, 1982; Messinger, 1976; Visher & Visher, 1979, 1982), like parent education support groups (Wandersmann, 1987), attempt to facilitate stepfamily adjustment by communicating knowledge about stepfamily development and stepfamily relationships that increases understanding of stepfamily life and by offering alternative solutions to the problems of living in stepfamilies that broaden their members' choices. That is, support groups, like psychotherapy, are contexts in which individuals are enabled to reflect on the ideas that shape their behavior and thereby to begin developing another perspective from which to evaluate and establish the meaning of the circumstances in which they find themselves.

This is illustrated in meetings of the Stepfamily Association of America. (My comments on this particular stepfamily support group are based on observations of various sessions of a chapter of this organization over a period of three years; they are consistent with those reported in the *Stepfamily Bulletin*, the association's official publication). The monthly meetings of this support group are typically organized around a presentation and discussion. A speaker, usually a professional who works with stepfamilies or with people who are dealing with issues central to stepfamily functioning, gives a talk on a topic such as "stages of stepfamily adjustment," "adolescent development and adolescents in stepfamilies," or "grandparents and stepfamilies," which is followed by a discussion between the speaker and the group members. Here, accounts of stepfamily life are shared and compared, revealing the assumptions and normative standards by which people structure and interpret their experiences. Such discussions constitute cognitive support and provide a basis for members to articulate and reformulate their concepts of stepfamily life.

A recurrent theme in the speakers' presentations and the members' comments is the frequency and intensity of arguments in stepfamilies over apparently trivial matters, especially in the early years of living together. That is, household members fight over such issues as standards of neatness (e.g., dirty dishes in the kitchen sink, wet towels on the bathroom floor), household schedules (e.g., bed times, shower times, meal times), and culinary customs (e.g., kinds of food to eat, table manners), among other things, all of which are points of contention commonly reported in the stepfamily literature (cf. Keshet, 1987; Visher & Visher, 1982). For example, one person recounted an argument between a stepparent and stepchild over the ingredients of a sandwich: The former believed that it should contain whole wheat bread, lettuce, tomato, and "real" meat (roast beef, chicken, turkey), and the latter thought it should be white bread, mayonnaise, and a slice of "processed" meat. Another participant described a conflict over leftovers, in which one household member complained that the bits of food wrapped in plastic and stored in the refrigerator made it look like a pile of junk, whereas another rebutted that if the complainant cooked and served less food in the first place, then it would not be necessary to save the uneaten portions.

Through discussions of such matters, group members come to appreciate a pattern of behavior common to the initial phases of adjustment to stepfamily life. Thus what appears to be a meaningless fight is seen in a different light, a point made repeatedly in the members' affirmations that this or that group discussion helped them "put things in a new perspective." Cultural values (and the categories and norms through which they are expressed) define the meaning of objects, events, and relationships, and conversely, objects, events, and relationships imply cultural values. Thus, conflicts over mere trivialities are in fact conflicts about structures of meaning. The details of everyday living, including which names go on the household mailbox or in the telephone directory, or what, when, where, how, and with whom to eat, reflect not simply behavioral choices but also assumptions about how the world is and how it should be. In fights over such petty issues, stepfamily members are struggling to determine what makes sense, that is, to establish rules that provide meaning and a basis for a coherent social world. With the members' recognition of this process, puzzling and painful interactions become more intelligible and less problematic to them.

The process is also illustrated in discussions of money matters. Ideas about inheritance often underlie conflicting conceptions within stepfamilies. Consider this example of a remarried couple. Each is a stepparent: he has two children from a previous marriage, and she has one child from a previous marriage. They have one child together. They agree on a principle of inheritance but disagree on how it should be applied (cf. Firth et al., 1970). That is, each says that the children should inherit "equally," but they disagree about what the actual distribution should be, a disagreement that reflects different assumptions about the unit of inheritance.

His proposal reflects a child-oriented perspective. He thinks that all of the children should share equally, and because there are four children, each would get one quarter of the inheritance. This means that the two children from his first marriage would get 50% of the inheritance, whereas the child of their current marriage would receive 25% of the pool, an amount equal to what would go to the child of her first marriage.

Her proposal suggests a parent-oriented viewpoint. She counts their children according to the number produced by each parent. From this perspective, she has two children (one from each of her marriages) and her husband has three children (one from his current marriage and two from his previous marriage). Thus, she concludes that in this sense they have five children between them and that, by the principle of equality, each should receive one fifth of the inheritance. By this method of calculation, their common child would receive 40%, because that child would be entitled to a one-fifth share from each parent; the two children of his first marriage would also receive 40% (each getting 20%); and the child from her first marriage would receive 20%.

There is another way to figure the distribution of resources that would produce roughly the same amount for the child they have in common. First, they would have to divide their resources equally between themselves, so that each parent would have 50% of their common resources to "spend." Then the parents would divide their shares among their respective offspring. Consequently, each of her two children would receive half of her half, or 25% of the whole. Each of this three children would receive one third of his half, or 17% of the whole. Their mutual child would receive shares from both parents, and thus that child would get 42% (25% and 17%) of the family's estate.

There also are other possibilities. For example, one could use marital units as a basis for dividing the inheritance pool. In this case, offspring from each of the three marriages that produced their children would get equal shares. The units would be (1) her child, (2) his children, and (3) their child, each receiving one third of the inheritance. This would change the share distributed to their mutual child, splitting the difference between their respective proposals (i.e., 33% in contrast with 25% or 40%).

The differences in their proposals appear to have two bases. First, they do not agree on ways of categorizing and counting those who will receive bequests from them or on the proportion of their joint estate that each child should inherit. However, the problem is further complicated because they differ with respect to the significance they attach to resources that will be available to the different children from sources outside their household. For example, his and her children from their previous marriages will inherit in different measures from the parent with whom they do not live (the ex-spouses of the stepfamily household couple) and from their extended families. Thus, the lack of agreement about providing for their children stems also from their beliefs and expectations about the unit from which children will inherit—on the one hand, their marital relationship and the resources they have in common and, on the other, the different kinship networks of which husband and wife (and grandchildren and stepgrandchildren) are a part.

Questions about household maintenance in stepfamilies also reveal confusion around the assumptions underlying this area of behavior. Group members speak of variations in and uncertainties about the ways in which daily expenses should be met and who should meet them. Few people think that one person, husband or wife, should bear the primary financial obligations for running the household. Yet, there is no easy agreement about the principle(s) by which this responsibility ought to be divided. Should the costs be divided evenly between husband and wife? Should household expenses be divided according to their respective incomes? Should costs be divided with or without regard to extrahousehold obligations or resources—as exemplified in incoming and outgoing alimony or child-support payments? Should the division of expenses be proportional to household occupancy and patterns of consumption (e.g., he has two children who live in the household half the time, and she has two children who live with them all of the time, thus making his contribution, according to this principle, 40% and hers, 60%)?

Different solutions to these questions follow from different presuppositions, which, in turn, may be part of different and complex systems of beliefs. It is not simply what either husband or wife thinks about "marriage," "family," or "household." As Espinoza and Newman (1979) suggested, in stepfamilies, ideas about money and evaluations of financial arrangements may reflect underlying concepts regarding (1) the role of men in assuming financial responsibility for running a household, (2) continuing relations between ex-spouses regarding child support, and (3) different children (his, hers, theirs) having access to different resources, present and future. The allocation of resources among children of step-families could also be interpreted as a communication about being loved and valued: that a spouse is loved and valued more than a (biological) child or that one child (biological or step) is loved and valued more or less than another. And Bohannan (1985, p. 3) pointed out that "the term 'family' is a code word for deeper values of the place of women and of men and of children in the social world." Thus, it seems that to understand any one concept or attitude regarding how people in a stepfamily should behave would involve viewing it in a wider ideational context. Support group members attempt this task in their discussions of these issues. It seems that support researchers would also better understand what support is and how it works by similarly analyzing people's assumptions and clarifying the cultural bases of their conflicts.

DIRECTIONS FOR FURTHER RESEARCH

Stress and social support are reciprocally related. Stress occurs when assumptions, beliefs, and values are challenged; support is what enables individuals to review and revise expectations. Both stress and support are shaped by the cultural context in which they appear. Comparative studies of stressful situations, such as step-family formation, should shed light on the meanings of both stress and support. Thus, analyzing stepfamily formation raises several questions for research on so-cial support and on the stresses that provide the occasion for its mobilization.

First is the question of how stepfamilies fare in cultures, including American subcultures, that have different ideas about family and household composition and relationships. For example, some studies (Liebow, 1967; Schneider & Smith, 1978; Stack, 1974) indicate that there may be less stress associated with step-family formation among lower-class Americans than among those of middle-class status, insofar as the former believe that it is not unusual to have elastic family boundaries and a diverse household composition and accept the primacy of the mother–child bond, relative to the spousal relationship. If this is the case, then it is evidence for the role of challenged assumptions as a source of stress.

There is also the task of describing and analyzing "successful" stepfamilies, including those that remain intact after several years and that show other signs of stability and integration. Understanding the belief systems and other circum-stances of such stepfamilies is important, although as researchers have noted, little is known about the successful adjustment to stepfamily life (Cherlin, 1978; Esses & Campbell, 1984; Furstenberg, 1979; Walker, Rogers, & Messinger, 1977). Therefore, it seems reasonable to study successful stepfamilies in order to compare the experiences of their members during the early years of living with those of individuals currently coping with the problems of stepfamily formation.

Examining successful stepfamilies suggests another area of inquiry, one calling for longitudinal analyses. Assuming that having a common culture facilitates stepfamily integration, it seems reasonable to suppose that stability would prevail in households in which members of a stepfamily household share beliefs. This hypothesis could be tested by identifying and interviewing stepfamilies with similar and dissimilar expectations at the beginning of coresidence and then reinterviewing them periodically over several years, looking at various measures of unity and disunity. To the extent that stepfamily members do not begin life together with common concepts and norms, attention should be paid to the types of common understandings that emerge among successful stepfamilies and to the ways in which they develop.

A concern with the process by which stepfamily members develop shared beliefs is related to the question of the timing of stepfamily transitions. Goldner (1982, p. 197) suggests that it takes a stepfamily about two years to "stabilize," by which she means "developing a coherent sense of itself via internal rules, traditions, and subsystems." Moreover, Lutz (1983) found that teenagers who had lived in stepfamilies for less than two years reported more stress than those did who had lived in them for more than two years, and Keshet (1987), on the basis of clinical experience, suggested that it takes approximately one to three years for a stepfamily to negotiate the first stage of "unification," in which members have the task of "accepting" their cultural "differences." Thus, it seems that the first two years of coresidence would be the critical period in which to study the ways in which cognitive restructuring is accomplished. It is in this period that one would expect to observe the most dramatic changes among stepfamily members regarding their assessment of what is and what is not perceived as an example of social support.

Finally, more work needs to be done on the role of support groups in facilitating cognitive restructuring. It is clear that adjustment to a transition entails changing one's beliefs and values. Especially in the case of stepfamily formation, several individuals are involved in learning a new culture (or worldview, family tradition, or household rules). Support groups appear to contribute to this effort by providing a forum in which people realize that the problems of stepfamily formation are not unique to them and in which they have the opportunity to reflect on the assumptions, beliefs, and expectations that underlie their actions and reactions. However, many questions remain unanswered about such groups. For example, to what extent does participation in a stepfamily support group contribute to adjustment within a stepfamily? This could be assessed by studying individuals' beliefs and values before and after such participation. (It would also be necessary to analyze simultaneously other situations or relationships in which support group members are involved and that may facilitate or obstruct the adjustment process). Moreover, it would be important to identify the conditions under which participation in a support group does *not* help bring about change in an assumptive world, individual and/or collective, and the behavioral changes associated with it. Such conditions would, in effect, block or undermine the process of cognitive restructuring and perhaps lead to a negative evaluation of actions intended to be supportive. These questions are of concern not only to those undergoing a transition to stepfamilyhood but also to those who want to understand better the meaning and measurement of social support.

REFERENCES

Adams, B. N. (1980). *The family: A sociological interpretation* (3rd ed.). Chicago: Rand McNally.

Ahrons, C. R., & Rogers, R. H. (1987). *Divorced families: A multidisciplinary developmental view.* New York: Norton.

Albrecht, T. L., & Adelman, M. B. (1987a). Communicating social support: A theoretical perspective. In T. L. Albrecht & M. B. Adelman (Eds.), *Communicating social support* (pp. 18–38). Beverly Hills, CA: Sage.

Albrecht, T. L., & Adelman, M. B. (1987b). Dilemmas of supportive communication. In T. L. Albrecht & M. B. Adelman (Eds.), *Communicating social support* (pp. 240–254). Beverly Hills, CA: Sage.

Arnston, P., & Droge, D. (1987). Social support in self-help groups: The role of communication in enabling perceptions of control. In T. L. Albrecht & M. B. Adelman (Eds.), *Communicating social support* (pp. 148–171). Beverly Hills, CA: Sage.

Barrera, M. (1981). Social support in the adjustment of pregnant adolescents: Assessment issues. In B. H. Gottlieb (Ed.), *Social networks and social support* (pp. 69–96). Beverly Hills, CA: Sage.

Becker, G. S., Landes, E. M. & Michael, R. T. (1977). An economic analysis of marital instability. *Journal of Political Economy, 85,* 1141–1187.

Benson van der Ohe, E. (1987). *First and second marriages.* New York: Praeger.

Bernard, J. S. (1956). *Remarriage: A study of marriage.* New York: Russell & Russell.

Bettelheim, B. (1976). *The uses of enchantment: The meaning and importance of fairy tales.* New York: Random House.

Bohannan, P. (1963). *Social anthropology.* New York: Holt, Rinehart and Winston.

Bohannan, P. (1970). Divorce chains, households of remarriage, and multiple divorcers. In P. Bohannan (Ed.), *Divorce and after* (pp. 113–123). New York: Doubleday.

Bohannan, P. (1971). Dyad dominance and household maintenance. In F. L. K. Hsu (Ed.), *Kinship and culture* (pp. 42–65). Chicago: Aldine.

Bohannan, P. (1984). Stepparenthood: A new and old experience. In R. S. Cohen, B. J. Cohler, & S. H. Weissman (Eds.), *Parenthood: A psychodynamic perspective* (pp. 204–219). New York: Guilford.

Bohannan, P. (1985). *All the happy families: Exploring the varieties of family life.* New York: McGraw-Hill.

Boss, P., & Greenberg, J. (1984). Family boundary ambiguity: A new variable in family stress theory. *Family Process, 23,* 535–546.

Brady, C. A., & Ambler, J. (1982). Use of group educational techniques with remarried couples. In L. Messinger & J. C. Hansen (Eds.), *Therapy with remarriage families* (pp. 145–158). Rockville, MD: Aspen Systems.

Brown, G. W. (1974). Meaning, measurement, and stress of life events. In B. S. Dohrenwend & B. P. Dohrenwend (Eds.), *Stressful life events: Their nature and effects* (pp. 217–243). New York: Wiley.

Brown, G. W. (1983). Accounts, meaning, and causality. In G. N. Gilbert & P. Abell (Eds.), *Accounts and actions* (pp. 35–68). Hampshire, England: Gower.

Cherlin, A. J. (1978). Remarriage as an incomplete institution. *American Journal of Sociology, 84*, 634–650.

Cherlin, A. J. (1981). *Marriage, divorce, and remarriage*. Cambridge, MA: Harvard University Press.

Clingempeel, W. G. (1981). Quasi-kin relationships and marital quality in step-father families. *Journal of Personality and Social Psychology, 41*, 890–901.

Clingempeel, W. G., & Brand, E. (1985). Quasi-kin relationships, structural complex, and marital quality in stepfamilies: A replication, extension, and clinical implications. *Family Relations, 34*, 401–409.

DeVos, G., Marsella, A. J., & Hsu, F. L. K. (1985). Introduction: Approaches to culture and self. In A. J. Marsella, G. Devos, & F. L. K. Hsu (Eds.), *Culture and self: Asian and Western perspectives* (pp. 2–23). New York: Tavistock.

Espinoza, R., & Newman, Y. (1979). *Stepparenting*. Rockville, MD: DHEW Publication No. (ADM) 78-579.

Esses, L. M., & Campbell, R. (1984). Challenges in researching the remarried. *Family Relations, 33*, 415–424.

Firth, R., Hubert, J., & Forge, A. (1970). *Families and their relatives: Kinship in a middle-class sector of London: An anthropological study*. London: Routledge & Kegan Paul.

Flugel, J. C. (1921). *The Psycho-analytical study of the family*. London: Hogarth.

Fox, R. (1967). *Kinship and marriage*. Baltimore: Penguin.

Furstenberg, F. F., Jr. (1979). Recycling the family: Perspectives for a neglected family form. *Marriage and Family Review, 2* (3), 12–21.

Furstenberg, F. F., Jr., & Spanier, G. B. (1984). *Recycling the family: Remarriage after divorce*. Beverly Hills, CA: Sage.

Geertz, C. (1973). *The interpretation of cultures*. New York: Basic Books.

Goldner, V. (1982). Remarriage family: Structure, system, future. In J. C. Hansen & L. Messinger (Eds.), *Therapy with remarriage families* (pp. 189–206). Rockville, MD: Aspen Systems.

Holy, L., & Stuchlik, M. (1983). *Actions, norms, and representations*. Cambridge, England: Cambridge University Press.

Jacobson, D. (1985). Boundary maintenance in support networks. *Social Networks, 7*, 341–351.

Jacobson, D. (1986). Types and timing of social support. *Journal of Health and Social Behavior, 27*, 250–264.

Jacobson, D. (1987). The cultural context of social support and support networks. *Medical Anthropology Quarterly, 1* (1), 42–67.

Keshet, J. K. (1987). *Love and power in the stepfamily*. New York: McGraw-Hill.

Kleinman, J., Rosenberg, E., & Whiteside, M. (1979). Common developmental tasks in forming reconstituted families. *Journal of Marital and Family Therapy, 5* (2), 79–86.

Komarovsky, M. (1962). *Blue-collar marriage*. New York: Random House.

Lazarus, R. S., & Folkman, S. (1984). *Stress, appraisal, and coping*. New York: Springer.

Liebow, E. (1967). *Tally's corner*. Boston: Little Brown.

Lutz, P. (1983). The stepfamily: An adolescent perspective. *Family Relations, 32*, 367–375.

Marris, P. (1982). Attachment and society. In C. M. Parkes & J. Stevenson-Hinde (Eds.), *The place of attachment in human behavior* (pp. 185–201). New York: Basic Books.

McFarlane, A. H., Neale, K. A., Norman, G. R., Roy, R. G., & Streiner, D. L. (1981). Methodological issues in developing a scale to measure social support. *Schizophrenia Bulletin, 7*, 90–100.

Mead, M. (1970). Anomalies in American postdivorce relationships. In P. Bohannan (Ed.), *Divorce and after* (pp. 97–112). New York: Doubleday.

Messinger, L. (1976). Remarriage between divorced people with children from previous marriages: A proposal for preparation for remarriage. *Journal of Marriage and Family Counseling, 2*, 193–200.

Mikesell, J. W., & Garbarino, J. (1986). Adolescents in stepfamilies. In J. Garbarino, C. J. Schellenbach, & J. M. Sebes (Eds.), *Troubled youth, troubled families* (pp. 235–251). Chicago: Aldine.

Moss, N. I. (1984). The stepfamily: Its psychological structure and its psychotherapeutic challenge. In C. C. Nadelson & D. C. Polonsky (Eds.), *Marriage and divorce: A contemporary perspective* (pp. 240–257). New York: Guilford.

Obeyesekere, G. (1985). Depression, Buddhism, and the work of culture in Sri Lanka. In A. Kleinman & B. Good (Eds.), *Culture and depression* (pp. 134–152). Berkeley and Los Angeles: University of California Press.

Parkes, C. M. (1971). Psycho-social transitions: A field for study. *Social Science and Medicine, 5*, 101–115.

Parkes, C. M., & Weiss, R. S. (1983). *Recovery from bereavement*. New York: Basic Books.

Payne, R. L., & Jones, J. G. (1987). Measurement and methodological issues in social support. In S. V. Kasl & C. L. Cooper (Eds.), *Stress and health: Issues in research methodology* (pp. 167–205). New York: Wiley.

Procidano, M. E., & Heller, K. (1983). Measures of perceived social support from friends and from family: Three validation studies. *American Journal of Community Psychology, 11*, 1–24.

Ransom, J. W., Schlesinger, S., & Derdeyn, A. P. (1979). A stepfamily in formation. *American Journal of Orthopsychiatry, 49* (1), 36–43.

Sager, C. J., Brown, H. S., Crohm, H., Engel, T., Rodstein, E., & Walker, L. (1983). *Treating the remarried family*. New York: Brunner/Mazel.

Schneider, D. M. (1968). *American kinship: A cultural account*. Englewood Cliffs, NJ: Prentice-Hall.

Schneider, D. M. (1976). Notes toward a theory of culture. In K. H. Basso & H. A. Selby (Eds.), *Meaning in anthropology* (pp. 197–220). Albuquerque: University of New Mexico Press.

Schneider, D. M., & Smith, R. T. (1978). *Class differences in American kinship*. Ann Arbor: University of Michigan Press.

Spanier, G. B., & Furstenberg, F. F., Jr., (1987). Remarriage and reconstituted families. In M. B. Sussman & S. K. Steinmetz (Eds.), *Handbook of marriage and the family* (pp. 419–434). New York: Plenum.

Stack, C. B. (1974). *All our kin.* New York: Harper & Row.

Visher, E. B., & Visher, J. S. (1979). *Stepfamilies: A guide to working with stepparents and stepchildren.* Secaucus, NJ: Citadel.

Visher, E. B., & Visher, J. S. (1982). Stepfamilies in the 1980s. In J. C. Hansen & L. Messinger (Eds.), *Therapy with remarriage families* (pp. 107–119). Rockville, MD: Aspen Systems.

Wald, E. (1981). *The remarried family: Challenge and promise.* New York: Family Service Association of America.

Walker, K. N., Rogers, J., & Messinger, L. (1977). Remarriage after divorce: A review. *Social Casework, 58,* 276–285.

Wandersmann, L. P. (1987). New directions for parent education. In S. L. Kagan, D. R. Powell, B. Weissbourd, & E. F. Zigler (Eds.), *Family support programs: Perspectives and prospects* (pp. 207–227). New Haven, CT: Yale University Press.

Weiss, R. S. (1975). *Marital separation.* New York: Basic Books.

White, L. K., & Booth, A. (1985). The quality and stability of remarriages: The role of stepchildren. *American Sociological Review, 50,* 689–698.

CHAPTER 9

Social Relationships as a Source of Companionship: Implications for Older Adults' Psychological Well-being

KAREN S. ROOK

University of California at Irvine

Gerontologists have had an enduring interest in the question of how social relationships affect the emotional and physical health of older adults. This interest emerged nearly four decades ago when researchers and policy makers first began to recognize the magnitude of the demographic changes that the nation was experiencing and when concerns began to be voiced about how growing numbers of older adults could be integrated successfully into society once they had relinquished the role of worker (see Maddox & Wiley, 1976, for a historical review). Concerns about the impact of mandatory retirement and other age-related events, such as widowhood, led researchers to wonder whether informal social involvement could compensate for the formal role losses to which the elderly are particularly vulnerable.[1] Two theories, disengagement theory (Cumming & Henry, 1961) and activity theory (Maddox, 1963, 1964), offered competing predictions about the significance to older adults of informal social ties. These two theories stimulated dozens of studies in the 1960s and 1970s that examined the mental health correlates of older adults' involvement with friends, family members, and community organizations (see review by Larson, 1978). Many of these early studies, as well as the theories themselves, were subsequently criticized (Hochschild, 1975), but they clearly document gerontologists' intense interest in older adults' social relationships. This interest has continued into the present, with more recent work addressing such issues as the role of social support in facilitating older adults' adjustment to stressful events (Cutrona, Russell, & Rose, 1986; Krause, 1986, 1987; Lopata, 1979) and the difficulties that support providers face in attempting to provide long-term aid to disabled older adults (e.g., Haley, Levine, Brown, & Bartolucci, 1987).

---

[1] These concerns are less significant today because analyses indicate that retirement is voluntary rather than mandatory for most people (Atchley, 1987). Indeed, workers are electing at increasing rates to retire before age 65 (Atchley, 1987).

Some researchers believe that knowledge about social support processes and effects among the elderly is sorely lacking (e.g., Minkler, 1985), but this pessimistic view may stem from a tendency to overlook relevant research that is not couched in the terminology familiar to social support researchers. A respectable knowledge base does exist if one looks beyond studies cast in the conventional stress-buffering framework, and this body of work has much to contribute to social support researchers. For example, gerontological studies of caregiving to the elderly (e.g., Cantor, 1979; Rundall & Evashwick, 1982) offer many insights about an issue of considerable interest to social support researchers—which potential support providers tend to be preferred or solicited for specific kinds of support. Whereas work by social support researchers on the sources of support has been largely descriptive, gerontologists have offered specific theoretical predictions regarding the factors that lead older adults to prefer certain support providers over others and seek help from others in an orderly sequence when the most preferred support providers are unwilling or unable to render support (see Cantor's 1979 hierarchical-compensatory model of help seeking and Litwak's 1985 task-specific model of help seeking; see also Peters, Hoyt, Babchuk, Kaiser, & Iijima, 1987).

In a related vein, gerontologists have examined the balance of informal and formal care given to older adults (Litwak, 1985; Seltzer, Irvy, & Litchfield, 1987) and also have studied how members of older adults' social networks, particularly family members, function as liaisons with formal service bureaucracies (Shanas & Sussman, 1977). Studies have investigated older adults' expectations for support and the implications of discrepancies in the expectations of recipients and providers (Brody, Johnsen, & Fulcomer, 1984; Brody, Johnsen, Fulcomer, & Lang, 1983; Cicirelli, 1981; Townsend & Poulshock, 1986). Studies of the elderly offer insights into the mobilization and delivery of social support in the face of chronic stressors, such as a stroke or visual impairment (Schulz & Decker, 1985; Stephens, Kinney, Norris, & Ritchie, 1987). Researchers have also extensively examined how efforts to provide long-term care affect caregivers (Brody, 1985; Cantor, 1983; George & Gwyther, 1986; Haley et al., 1987; Poulshock & Deimling, 1984; Zarit, Reever, & Bach-Peterson, 1980) and have begun to study interventions to reduce the strain on caregivers (Haley, Brown, & Levine, 1987; Zarit & Zarit, 1983). Gerontological studies offer information about factors that affect adaptation to potentially stressful but normative life-course transitions, such as retirement (e.g., Lowenthal & Haven, 1968; Wan, 1982). Research has also examined the extent to which older adults' exchanges of support are characterized by reciprocity and the manner in which nonreciprocity may influence psychological well-being (Beckman, 1981; Roberto & Scott, 1986; Rook, 1987a).

Thus, a considerable amount of research has been conducted on social support in late life, and several excellent reviews of this work have been published (e.g., Antonucci, 1985; Schulz & Rau, 1985). My goal in this chapter is not to discuss work that has been so ably reviewed elsewhere but, instead, to consider an aspect of older adults' social relationships that has received less attention: social relationships as a source of companionship rather than of support per se. Specifically, I will consider the contributions of companionship to psychological well-being in the context of older adults' everyday activities and plans rather than in the more specialized context of efforts to cope with stressful life events.

COMPANIONSHIP AND SOCIAL SUPPORT

Companionship and Support as Theoretically Distinct Functions

Both companionship and support represent important functions of close relationships; yet little effort has been made to identify their complementary contributions to emotional health.[2] Most social support researchers have been interested in how social relationships facilitate adaptation to stressful life events and, accordingly, have emphasized the various types of aid that people give to distressed friends and family members, such as emotional support, appraisal support, and instrumental support (e.g., Cobb, 1976; Cohen & McKay, 1984; House, 1981; Kahn & Antonucci, 1980). For example, Thoits (1985, p. 55) suggested that social support "most commonly refers to helpful functions performed for an individual by significant others."

This emphasis on the utilitarian functions of social interaction is appropriate, given the interest in factors that cushion the impact of life stress, but it has led to a neglect of more expressive aspects of social interaction. Although social relationships are often desired for the aid and security they afford (Bowlby, 1977), they also are sought because they provide opportunities for purely pleasurable interaction. Companionship does not serve an extrinsic purpose but, instead, offers intrinsic satisfactions, such as shared leisure activities, private jokes and rituals, and playful and uncensored spontaneity. Unlike interaction oriented toward solving problems, these companionate activities are pursued for their own sake (cf. Gordon & Gaitz, 1976). Simmel (1949, p. 254) observed that such "pure sociability" is "the art or play form of association, related to the content and purposes of association . . . as art is related to reality." According to Sullivan (1953), the need for companionship first emerges in childhood in the form of a desire for adult interest and participation in the child's play. The need continues throughout life, presumably into old age, as a desire to be involved with others in mutually interesting and enjoyable activities.[3]

This discussion suggests that companionship and support differ in several respects. First, the basic motivations for seeking companionship and support may differ. Companionship appears to be motivated by the intrinsic pleasures it affords, whereas support appears to be motivated more often by the goal of obtaining assistance with personal problems, including relief from distressing emotions (cf. Thoits, 1984). In addition, companionship and support may be important in

---

[2]See Lawton and Moss (1987) for a discussion of the different meanings of the term *function*.
[3]Hansson (1986) noted that this need may be less salient to the very oldest members of the elderly population.

different contexts (Rook, 1987b). Companionship is likely to be important as part of the fabric of daily life, whereas help provided by others is apt to be singularly important in times of stress. This hypothesized differentiation by context parallels social support researchers' distinction between the "main effects" and "buffering effects" of support (see Lin, 1986, for a critical analysis of the various meanings of these terms). Some argue that social interaction is beneficial regardless of an individual's level of life stress (main effect); others contend that social interaction is beneficial only under conditions of high stress (buffering effect). Distinguishing between support and companionship provides a basis for predicting both kinds of effects. Main effects of social contact would be expected when the contact involves primarily companionship, whereas buffering effects would be expected when the social contact involves problem-focused help (cf. Rook, 1987b).

Companionship and support may also be relevant to different dimensions of psychological well-being. If social support is indeed most important when an individual's equilibrium has been disrupted by some adverse life event, then support may contribute to well-being principally by restoring equilibrium (or returning the individual to a previous baseline of functioning). That is, social support may help alleviate anxiety, anger, self-doubt, or other negative affect states and thereby reduce the likelihood that emotional disorders will develop (Thoits, 1984), but it may do little to elevate one's psychological state beyond an ordinary baseline.

Companionship, in contrast, may contribute to well-being through recreation, humor, and affection. As such, companionship should help elevate a person's current level of contentment. Weiss (1974, p. 23) pointed out in this regard that friendships "offer a base for social events and happenings" and "in the absence of such ties life becomes dull, perhaps painfully so." Others have similarly argued that positive mental health involves more than the absence of pathology, that it requires stimulation, challenge, and levity as well (e.g., Diener, 1984; Lawton, 1982, 1983; Solano, 1986). Thus, support may be especially important in preventing threats to mental health, whereas companionship may be especially important in fostering positive mental health.

Constructs related to companionship appear in some taxonomies of social support functions, but their meaning generally differs from that intended here. Cohen and McKay (1984), for example, included belonging support, or feelings of solidarity with others, in their taxonomy of basic support functions. Others similarly have emphasized the value of embeddedness, or integration in a network of cohesive social ties (see reviews by Barrera, 1986; Leavy, 1983). These researchers believe that important psychological benefits stem from the mere existence of such social connections, apart from benefits derived from specific interpersonal transactions. This echoes the distinction made by Levinger and Huesmann (1980) between relational rewards (which are based on the mere existence of the relationship) and behavioral rewards (which are based on specific behavioral exchanges among participants).

Although embeddedness or a sense of belonging may clearly contribute to well-being (Cobb, 1976; Thoits, 1985), the term *companionship* in this chapter refers not to such global social connections or sentiments but, rather, to shared leisure and other social activities that are initiated primarily for the intrinsic goal of enjoyment. As used in this chapter, the term *social support* refers not to the general feeling of being adequately supported or cared for by others but, rather, to interpersonal transactions in which problem-focused aid and encouragement are exchanged.[4] Thus social support and companionship are conceptualized on a commensurate level as referring to specific behavioral exchanges or interaction processes.

Companionship and Support as Empirically Distinct Functions

In addition to their theoretical differences, companionship and support can be distinguished empirically. For example, measures of companionship and support have been found to correlate but not so highly as to suggest that the constructs are completely redundant. For example, in a large community sample, I found a correlation of .39 between the number of companionate functions and the number of supportive functions that social network members performed in respondents' lives and a correlation of .40 between the number of network members who functioned as support providers and the number of network members who functioned as social companions (Rook, 1987b, Study 1). In a sample of college students, Cohen and Hoberman (1983) found correlations that ranged from .26 to .56 between a measure of belonging support (defined as knowing people "to do things with") and measures of other kinds of support. Buunk (1988) factor analyzed daily interaction records that 40 police officers in the Netherlands had kept for a five-day period and found three distinct dimensions of social interaction: intimate support (which includes emotional, informational, and appraisal support), instrumental support, and companionship. In factor analyses of data sets from several different age groups, Cutrona and Russell (1987) similarly found that items assessing "social integration" (being part of a group of people who share similar interests, concerns, and recreational activities) clustered as a factor distinct from other factors that reflected the receipt and provision of social support.

Studies also have demonstrated that companionship and support make somewhat different contributions to feelings of friendship. Fischer (1981) found, for example, that people applied the term *friend* to associates who were sources of emotional support as well as to associates who were companions for various social activities, but companionship was a somewhat stronger predictor of who was regarded as a friend. In a longitudinal study of the development of friendships among college freshmen, Hays (1985) found that companionship was more consistently related to the intensity of the subjects' friendships than were affection, consideration, and communication. This led Hays to conclude that "companionship may lie at the base of the friendship bond" (p. 921). The same study also indicated, however, that emotional support was a more sensitive indicator than was companionship of who was considered to be an intimate friend.

---

[4]See Sarason et al. (1987) for an analysis of this general feeling as the common core of various conceptions of social support.

Further evidence that social support and companionship can be usefully distinguished comes from gerontological research on the contributions to older adults' emotional health of contact with friends versus family members. A surprising but nonetheless robust finding in this literature is that contact with family members is negligibly, or even negatively, related to morale, whereas contact with friends is positively related to morale (see reviews by Lee, 1979; Lee & Ishii-Kuntz, 1987). Research also indicates that family members serve as the primary source of support for older adults but are less important as companions for leisure activities. Friends, in contrast, less often give support to older adults but do figure prominently as companions for leisure activities (Allan, 1986; B. Adams, 1967; Hill, Foote, Aldous, Carlson, & MacDonald, 1970; Stoller & Earl, 1983; Troll, Miller, & Atchley, 1979). Findings such as these indicate that there usually is at least some specialization by function in older adults' social networks.

Evidence demonstrates, moreover, that similar specialization can occur in younger age groups (e.g., Rook, 1987b; Weiss, 1974), either because of personal preference or external constraints. Thus, merely knowing that a person's social network contains individuals who are willing and able to provide social support does not tell us whether the network contains potential companions for desired leisure activities. That is, relationships that are supportive in a generic sense do not guarantee opportunities for satisfying companionship. The fact that social relationships are not always characterized by high levels of multiplexity (cf. Hall & Wellman, 1985) further underscores the importance of distinguishing among the various functions that specific individuals may perform.

Additional evidence of the usefulness of distinguishing between companionship and support comes from studies that has examined how these two different kinds of interaction are related to psychological well-being. In a representative community sample, I found that companionship had a main effect on psychological well-being and a buffering effect on minor life stress, whereas social support had only a buffering effect on major life stress (Rook, 1987b, Study 1). Although the buffering effect of companionship on minor life stress was not entirely expected, the pattern of results otherwise was consistent with theory. In three other studies (Rook, 1987b, Studies 2, 3, and 4), one that used a different community sample and two that used college students, companionship and support exhibited different associations with friendship satisfaction and loneliness. In general, companionship was more consistently associated with greater friendship satisfaction and lower loneliness than were emotional support or instrumental support.

In the study of 40 police officers mentioned earlier, Buunk (1988) found that companionship more effectively buffered job-related stress than did social support. The fact that data regarding social interaction, stress, and psychological adjustment were collected over a five-day period allowed Buunk (1988) to conduct both between-subjects and within-subjects analyses of stress buffering. Both kinds of analyses documented singularly important benefits of companionship. Thus, more positive moods and fewer negative moods were reported by those who enjoyed a generally higher level of companionship and by all officers on days when they experienced companionship. A high level of social support, in contrast, was associated with worse psychological adjustment and more health complaints.

Summary

In sum, although not all studies have successfully distinguished between companionship and social support (see critiques by House & Kahn, 1985; Sarason, Shearin, Pierce, & Sarason, 1987), the emerging empirical evidence seems sufficiently strong to suggest that efforts to investigate these conceptually distinct interpersonal functions should not be abandoned prematurely. Because other researchers have devoted much attention to the processes by which social support may influence psychological well-being, I will emphasize below the processes by which companionship may affect well-being.

PROCESSES THAT LINK COMPANIONSHIP TO PSYCHOLOGICAL WELL-BEING

In comparison with the effort devoted to identifying the specific processes by which social support contributes to psychological well-being (e.g., Cohen & McKay, 1984; Pearlin, 1985; Thoits, 1984, 1985; Wills, 1985), considerably less effort has been devoted to understanding the processes that may underlie beneficial effects of companionship (Hays & Oxley, 1986; Rook, 1985). Hays and Oxley (1986, p. 312) argued in this regard that researchers should devote more attention to "social processes that are not directly 'supportive' in purpose," such as "positive socializing." Wills (1985, p. 75) similarly suggested that it would be helpful if researchers distinguished activities that provide enjoyment or diversity ("social companionship") from those that provide an opportunity to seek assistance with one's personal problems.

Researchers who have discussed the contributions of companionship usually have done so with reference to the statistical main effects of social interaction, and at least some of these researchers appear to have regarded such main effects as either obvious or uninteresting (see Wills, 1985, for an exception). For example, House (1981) mentioned that social integration meets basic needs for security, social contact, approval, belonging, and affection but did not discuss this idea further. Moreover, some researchers who found main effects in their studies did not explain the effects they observed (e.g., Williams, Ware, & Donald, 1981). Those explanations that were offered tended to be quite general. Turner (1981), for example, argued that "the experience of being supported by others" is a core human requirement, and Thoits (1982) suggested similarly that companionship fulfills basic human needs.

These explanations may be sufficient to understand generally why people who have opportunities for satisfying companionship experience less emotional distress than do relatively isolated people, but such general accounts do not identify the specific feelings and processes that emerge in companionate interaction and that constitute potentially important links to emotional health. References in these general accounts to the fulfillment of basic needs represent essentially a kind of shorthand for the more specific gratifications and psychological benefits that companionate interaction affords.

This section considers some of these specific benefits, emphasizing neither the mere existence of social companions nor the symbolic rewards that such bonds provide but, rather, the positive emotions and cognitive processes that companionate interaction promotes. This section also considers ways in which companionate interaction avoids some of the psychological costs or difficulties associated with receiving social support. The explanations offered are by no means exhaustive, but they hopefully illustrate that companionship plays a more varied and more interesting role in sustaining emotional health than social support researchers typically have acknowledged.

Stimulation of Arousal and Positive Affect

Companionship provides a context in which people can share adventures (even if modest ones), spontaneous and permissive interaction (Blau, 1973; Hess, 1972), and humor (Mannell & McMahon, 1982). The elements of surprise and spontaneity recur in theoretical discussions of companionship, and theories of emotion assert that surprise is important in generating arousal and positive affect (e.g., Mandler, 1975). Moreover, companionship tends to be structured around interactions with friends that are intermittent and time-limited in nature (Larson, Mannell, & Zuzanek, 1986). These qualities, coupled with the fact that shared leisure activities are responsive only "to the requirements of pleasure" (Larson et al., 1986, p. 116), lend a quality of freshness and novelty to friendship interactions (Larson et al., 1986). In this sense, companionate interaction facilitates the genuine renewal that the term *recreation* connotes.

A study of older adults by Larson et al. (1986) provided empirical evidence consistent with these ideas. The researchers used an innovative time-sampling methodology to investigate the immediate subjective experiences of 92 elderly individuals engaged in interaction with friends or family members. Participants carried electronic pagers for one week and were signaled at randomly chosen times to describe in a brief questionnaire what they were doing at that moment, who (if anyone) they were with, what they were thinking about, and what their subjective state was (assessed in terms of arousal and emotion).

The results indicated that the older adults experienced substantially more positive affect and higher arousal when they were with friends than when they were with family members. This pattern held regardless of whether the family members were adult children or spouses. Further analyses traced the benefits of contact with friends partly to differences in the content of the interactions with friends versus family members. Participants spent the greatest amount of time with friends socializing and engaging in active forms of leisure (such as hobbies, sports, and religious and cultural activities). They spent the greatest amount of time with family members, in contrast, engaged in maintenance activities (such as eating and doing housework) and passive forms of leisure (such as watching television or reading).

In addition, even when the elderly participants engaged in equivalent activities with their friends and family members, the very process of engaging in the activities with friends still appeared to contribute to elevated mood. Analyses indicated that engaging in a particular activity with a friend was associated with greater arousal and more positive mood than engaging in the same activity with a family member. Larson et al. (1986) attributed this to differences in the quality of older adults' interactions with their friends versus their family members. Older adults' interactions with friends are believed to be characterized by novelty and spontaneity, whereas their interactions with family members are often viewed as sterile, stiff, and ritualized (e.g., Lowenthal & Robinson, 1976; Wood & Robertson, 1978).

Thus, at least in old age, friends are most likely to serve as companions for meaningful leisure activities. Moreover, the kinds of activities that elderly friends engage in and the quality of interaction during such activities appear to stimulate arousal and thereby enhance mood.

Transcendence of Mundane Concerns

Companionship may also contribute to psychological well-being by helping people transcend mundane concerns and problems. When people get together to socialize, it is often with the goal of leaving behind worries about work, family members, or other problems. Shared leisure represents a vehicle by which people attempt to escape their routine preoccupations, even if only briefly. Leisure activities appear to encourage a fluid, open state of mind that people experience as enjoyable and that promotes creativity (Csikszentmihalyi, 1975; Larson et al., 1986). This fluid, creative state of mind helps people shift their attentions from mundane preoccupations to other, more enjoyable matters (Larson et al., 1986).

Consistent with this, Larson et al. (1986) found that when older adults were with family members, they most frequently reported thinking about television, household chores, transportation, finances, and other matters related to daily routines. But when they were with friends, older adults reported thinking more often about games, exercise, entertainment, and religious activities. Thus, the companionship of their friends more often allowed the elderly participants in the study to transcend everyday concerns.

As noted earlier, I found in a community sample that companionship appeared to be a more effective antidote to minor life stresses (such as transportation difficulties, inadequate household space, residential noise, and job pressures) than did social support (Rook, 1987b, Study 1). By providing enjoyment and stimulation, companionship may have given the study participants periodic opportunities to escape these persistent daily stresses (cf. Lazarus & Folkman, 1984). As compared with companionship, providing social support for such stresses may turn the recipient's attention to potentially intractable problems and thus may fail to enhance the recipient's subjective state (even if the recipient nonetheless appreciates the supportive gesture). For major life stresses, of course, victims clearly need to evaluate their problems and alternative courses of action, and in this context, social support may be essential.

Behavioral Affirmation of Self-worth

Although emotional support is often viewed as making the greatest contribution to self-esteem (e.g., House, 1981; Wills, 1985), companionship may be equally important in this regard. When people choose each other as companions for their leisure time, a commodity that is usually limited and therefore precious, they signal behaviorally that they view each other with high regard. They do not need to verbalize their feelings of respect and appreciation; their actions convey these sentiments. Such behaviorally expressed affirmation of worth may be at least as powerful as the verbal assurances of respect and esteem that social support theorists typically have emphasized in discussions of emotional support. Consistent with this, Hirsch (1980) found that companionship was significantly related to higher self-esteem in a sample of women who were coping with major mid-life transitions, whereas emotional support, instrumental support, cognitive guidance, and social reinforcement (praise or criticism of specific actions) were not related to the women's self-esteem.

It might be tempting to assume that after retirement older adults have unlimited time to interact with others—that because leisure time has become more abundant, invitations to socialize would have less significance for older adults' feelings of self-worth. Empirical evidence refutes this view. The time that adults invest in social interaction does not appear to balloon after age 65 to fill the void left by retirement (Larson, Zuzanek, & Mannell, 1985). Rather, older adults continue to be selective about the people with whom they socialize (e.g., R. Adams, 1987; Carstensen, 1987). Thus, social invitations are likely to have the same affirming significance to older adults as they do to other age groups.

Deflection of Attention from Self-scrutiny

Companionship may also contribute to psychological well-being by helping deflect attention from self-scrutiny. Self-conscious preoccupation with oneself arouses negative affect (Duval & Wicklund, 1972; Wicklund, 1975). Focusing attention on oneself, particularly from an evaluative perspective, encourages one to dwell on one's inadequacies (Wicklund, 1975) and thereby contributes to depressed mood (Pyszczynski & Greenberg, 1985). The stimulation and pleasure afforded by companionship, however, may serve to counter these tendencies. That is, companionship not only may help people transcend worries about mundane problems, but it also may help people transcend detrimental preoccupation with their own imagined or real inadequacies.

The idea that companionship discourages self-focused attention may appear to contradict the idea that companionship conveys esteem and thereby confirms self-worth. Yet these ideas are not actually incompatible. Unambiguous confirmation of one's self-worth eliminates the need to scrutinize oneself and to dwell on issues of one's stature in the eyes of others. Research has shown that people with low self-esteem are the most prone to self-consciousness (Ickes, Wicklund, & Ferris, 1973). Experimental studies similarly have demonstrated that preoccupation with the self as an object can be induced by failure or other events that trigger self-doubt (Wicklund, 1975). Thus, to the extent that companionship bolsters feelings of self-worth (e.g., Hirsch, 1980), it should similarly discourage the kind of self-preoccupation that has been found to be associated with negative affect (Pyszcynski & Greenberg, 1985). Lawton and Moss (1987) stated in this regard that a favorable self-evaluation leaves one's affective system at rest and, in a sense, frees one to engage in cognitive activities and adaptive behaviors that are appropriate to the tasks at hand.

Avoidance of Costs Associated with Receipt of Social Support

Companionship may enhance emotional health not only by fostering positive psychological processes but also by avoiding some of the costs that may be associated with social support. Researchers have noted that receiving social support can make one feel indebted to or less competent than the support provider (DiMatteo & Hays, 1981; Eckenrode, 1983). Companionship does not involve the asymmetries that a helper–helpee relationship entails and accordingly may be less vulnerable to these ambivalent reactions. Simmel (1949) noted that companionship has a democratic structure because it occurs among equals, thereby reducing the risk of friction.

Uncertainty about a support provider's motivations may further complicate reactions to the receipt of support. A support provider's actions may be attributed either to genuine caring and liking or to feelings of obligation. Social norms dictate that people should help friends or family members in distress. Attributional ambiguity thus surrounds the social support that is elicited by revealing a problem to another person (cf. Suls, 1982). Companionship, in contrast, is more likely to be seen as motivated by mutual appreciation of one another's company and may therefore invite more appealing attributions. As a result, there is less risk that the pleasure of companionship will be diminished by the kind of attributional ambiguity that sometimes surrounds social support (cf. Suls, 1982).

Issues for Further Research

This effort to identify the specific processes that link companionship to psychological well-being raises many questions. Given the scarcity of relevant empirical evidence, perhaps the most basic question is how these hypothesized processes should be studied. Those just discussed emphasize the immediate subjective perceptions and affective reactions of the individuals involved in a companionate interaction. Therefore, methodologies that focus on immediate experiences seem most promising.

The time-sampling methodology devised by Larson and Csikszentmihalyi (1983) appears able to capture such experiences with relatively few problems of reactivity. Because the time-sampling approach permits researchers to assess the participants' subjective experiences in many different natural settings at randomly designated times, it yields enormously rich contextual data. Such data would allow researchers not only to explore whether companionate interaction is associated with the processes discussed earlier but also to study the specific circumstances in which these processes are most likely to emerge. For example, perhaps companionship more readily helps older adults escape preoccupations with mundane concerns when it involves interaction with certain categories of partners, such as friends or grandchildren rather than adult children or siblings. The influence of gender, age, and other attributes of social companions could also be easily investigated using this methodology, as could the influence of the time of day or week when companionship occurs. Larson et al. (1985) reported, for example, that unmarried older adults become most depressed when they are alone in the evening; yet this may be precisely when companionship is least available to them. Most community-based social programs for the elderly are scheduled during the day rather than at night, but at least occasional opportunities to socialize in the evening might benefit the emotional health of older adults who live alone (Larson et al., 1985).

Daily diary methods, such as those developed by Cutrona (1986), Hirsch (1980), and Wheeler and Reis (Wheeler, Reis, & Nezlek, 1983; Reis, Wheeler, Kernis, Spiegel, & Nezlek, 1985) to study social support, represent a cost-effective alternative to the more expensive time-sampling approach to learn about the subjective states that older adults experience in companionate interaction. Such diary data may be somewhat vulnerable to memory distortion, however, because they are not gathered when the social interaction is actually occurring. Retrospective reports of subjective states experienced earlier in the day in conjunction with various social activities may similarly be influenced by the person's mood when completing the diary forms. Despite such limitations, however, diary methods have been used successfully in research on older adults' time budgets (e.g., Moss & Lawton, 1982) and could be adapted to investigate the effects of companionship (see Carp & Carp, 1981a, for a more general discussion of the issues in using diaries to study the elderly).

Social support researchers have urged greater use of experimental methods as a means of studying the processes by which support ameliorates the effects of stress (Heller, 1979; Sarason & Sarason, 1985), and experimental studies have appeared in response to this call (Costanza, Derlega, & Winstead, 1988; Sarason, 1981; Sarason & Sarason, 1986). Although the processes by which companionship contributes to emotional well-being may be more difficult to investigate experimentally, such methods should not be ruled out.

An important substantive issue that invites further research is the extent to which the benefits of companionship are contingent on the proactive initiation of companionate contact. People seek companionship for the specific gratifications it affords. Presumably they regard companionship as an effective means of enhancing their emotional states. Social support similarly has been conceptualized in terms of its contributions to emotion management, or emotion self-regulation (e.g., Thoits, 1984), but such models are generally *reactive* in nature. That is, social support is viewed as being mobilized in response to stressful events and is important primarily as a means of restoring emotional equilibrium. A *proactive* model of the association between companionship and psychological well-being, in contrast, would assume that people actively seek companionship because it provides specific pleasurable experiences that enhance mood and life satisfaction (cf. Lawton's 1988 analysis of proactive self-regulation of emotion). Acknowledging the possibility that older adults proactively manage their social lives helps to counter the common image of older adults as passive recipients of others' good will. Of course, it remains an empirical question whether the elderly derive equivalent benefits from companionship that others initiate and from companionship that they themselves initiate.

This discussion also raises questions about the extent to which older adults' needs or preferences for companionship influence the amount of pleasure they derive from companionate interaction or the energy they are willing to invest in pursuit of such interaction. The next section discusses several issues related to the construct of need in analyses of companionship.

THE CONSTRUCT OF NEED IN ANALYSES OF COMPANIONSHIP

Researchers often invoke the idea of a need for companionship when they discuss links between social interaction and emotional health (McClelland, 1985; Murray, 1938), but there are important differences in how researchers construe this need. For example, some researchers view the need for companionship as universal, as a basic human striving (e.g., Weiss, 1974). Given this view, it would not be necessary to measure the need for companionship in studies of social interaction and well-being because it is essentially invariant. Most people would be expected to ascribe great importance to the need for companionship; thus low ratings of importance would be attributed to a defensive denial of the need for companionship (Fromm-Reichmann, 1959; Rook & Thuras, 1988).

Other researchers view the need for companionship as varying widely across people. This is explicit, for example, in research on extraversion (Geen, 1986; Morris, 1979), sociability (Buss & Plomin, 1984; Farley & Farley, 1970), the need for affiliation (McAdams & Constantian, 1983; McClelland, 1985), and related topics. This view underlies work on loneliness as well. The adage that being alone should not be equated with being lonely stems from the conviction that people have widely varying needs for social contact and that some people are content with relatively little contact (e.g., Peplau & Perlman, 1979). From this perspective, the need for companionship should not be viewed as a given but, instead, should be measured in empirical studies. Ward (1985) pointed out with reference to work on the elderly, however, that researchers seldom have measured older adults' needs or preferences for social contact (see Mancini, Quinn, Gavigan, & Franklin, 1980; Rundall & Evashwick, 1982, for exceptions).

This section explores the meaning of a low expressed need for companionship. As suggested, the disavowal of a need for companionship could have several alternative interpretations, an issue that has special relevance to the elderly because they often are characterized as having a lower need for companionship than do members of other age groups (e.g., Larson et al., 1985). Examining the meaning of a low expressed need for companionship may also help shed light on the sometimes-puzzling empirical associations reported between older adults' objective levels of social involvement and their subjective evaluations of the adequacy of their social relationships. For example, as compared with other age groups, older adults generally report higher satisfaction with their social relationships, even though they have somewhat smaller social networks and less frequent contact with others (Antonucci, 1985). Moreover, among the elderly themselves, some studies have found large social networks and frequent social interaction to be associated with higher levels of network satisfaction or overall morale, whereas other studies have not found such associations (see reviews by Peplau, Bikson, Rook, & Goodchilds, 1982; Ward, Sherman, & LaGory, 1984). Preferences or needs for companionship thus may color older adults' evaluations of their social networks.

In focusing on the meaning of low need, I do not wish to suggest that older adults ascribe little personal importance to companionship. Indeed, existing evidence challenges such a view (Antonucci, 1985; Ward, 1985), even though there may be age differences in the overall importance of companionship (Larson et al., 1985). I have chosen to focus on low expressed need for companionship because its interpretation seems to be ambiguous. Clarifying these various interpretations may have methodological and substantive implications for further research.

Alternative Interpretations of a Low Expressed Need for Companionship

Contentment with Limited Companionship

Perhaps the simplest interpretation of a low expressed need for companionship is that some older people simply prefer not to socialize extensively with others or manage to satisfy their interest in social interaction with infrequent contacts (Peplau & Perlman, 1979; Peplau et al., 1982). Such individuals are apt to have small social networks. If asked to evaluate the adequacy of their social lives, they would be expected to offer positive evaluations that reflect genuine feelings of satisfaction or contentment.

Resigned Acceptance of Limited Companionship

A related interpretation is that some older adults may report a low need for companionship not because this reflects a strongly felt and perhaps long-standing personal preference but, rather, because the exigencies of old age have forced them to lower their social expectations (Peplau et al., 1982). That is, some older adults may adjust their personal need for companionship to accommodate what they perceive to be fewer opportunities for companionship. This would allow them to express satisfaction with rather restricted social lives, but their satisfaction would differ qualitatively from that expressed by the older adults just discussed. Specifically, whereas satisfaction in the above scenario would be likely to reflect genuine gratitude that one's social life corresponds closely to one's preferences, satisfaction in this scenario would be more likely to reflect the resigned acceptance that one's current social life may represent all that one can reasonably expect.

Campbell, Converse, and Rodgers (1976) distinguished between the "satisfaction of contentment" and the "satisfaction of resignation" in attempting to explain why some older adults give positive evaluations of housing that is clearly deficient by objective standards. Campbell et al. (1976) noted in this regard that identical levels of reported satisfaction (for example, as assessed by standard Likert-type ratings), may reflect quite different patterns of personal aspirations and experiences.

One methodological implication of this distinction is that older adults who express only a modest need for companionship and those who report feeling satisfied with limited social contacts may actually represent two different populations (the genuinely content and the resigned). For some research purposes it may be important to distinguish these two different groups, and this in turn may require researchers to supplement conventional measures of social network satisfaction with questions that more extensively probe participants' interpersonal preferences, expectations, and evaluations.

Defensive Denial of the Need for Companionship

Older adults may also report a low need for companionship if they are bitter or disappointed with their social lives but do not wish to view themselves (or to be viewed by others) as social failures. As a result, they may defensively deny a need for companionship (Fromm-Reichmann, 1959; Rook & Thuras, 1988). This group differs from the resigned group just described in a subtle but important respect. The resigned individuals would report only modest needs for companionship because they would consider it realistic to expect only limited contact; that is, they would have reconciled themselves to lowered expectations for companionship. The current group, in contrast, would continue to harbor high expectations for social contact and a strong interest in contact but would deny such an interest as a means of self-protection (see Lazarus & Folkman, 1984, for a discussion of defensive denial). That is, these individuals would minimize the importance of companionship in an effort to avoid or reduce their emotional distress.

An interesting question in this regard is whether such denial does indeed protect against emotional pain. Some theorists have argued that people who defensively deny a need for companionship may nonetheless suffer the same psychological distress that typically accompanies loneliness (e.g., see H. E. Peplau's discussion of unconscious loneliness; Rook & Peplau, 1982). Other theorists have suggested that denying social needs reduces vulnerability to the anguish and lowered self-esteem that would otherwise arise from having one's needs remain unmet (see review by Lazarus & Folkman, 1984). Older adults report less loneliness than do other age groups (e.g., Peplau et al., 1982), are less likely to report that they wish they had more friends (Antonucci, 1985), and, more generally, have been shown to exhibit a "positivity bias" in evaluating various aspects of their lives, including their interpersonal relationships (Campbell et al., 1976; Carp & Carp, 1981b). These findings may reflect older adults' success in surrounding themselves with largely satisfying relationships. Alternatively, they may reflect a protective denial of social needs.

This potentially protective function of disavowal of social needs was examined in an ongoing study of older adults at the University of California at Irvine (Rook & Thuras, 1988). Specifically, we examined how denial of social needs was related to older adults' social network satisfaction and psychological health. The study participants were 147 older community residents who volunteered to take part in a five-year longitudinal study of aging. Their average age was 70.6 years; roughly two-thirds were women; and most (92%) were white. The majority (64%) were currently widowed, divorced, or single.

We interviewed each participant for approximately 90 minutes, asking about their background, social networks, health status, and psychological functioning. Sixteen questions that were adapted from McCallister and Fischer (1978) asked the participants to name the people to whom they could turn for various kinds of support or companionship (e.g., to have a companion for social outings or someone to chat with on the telephone, to receive advice or financial assistance). Most of the participants readily named at least one person, but some indicated that they did not need or desire the kind of interaction that the question specified. We then constructed a measure of denial of social needs by tallying the number of times that respondents stated that the kind of social exchange specified was not important to them. Consistent with their expressed lack of interest in social contact, respondents who scored higher on the denial measure interacted less frequently with members of their social networks. Thus, although our measure of denial was crude, it was related in the expected direction to the participants' social involvement.

To allow us to examine the association between denial and social network satisfaction, the participants rated their satisfaction with their friendships and their family relationships on two 7-point scales, and also completed a 12-item measure of loneliness. Measures of depression and self-esteem were included to assess the association between denial and psychological health.

The analyses conducted thus far (which included controls for the participants' gender, marital status, age, education, and number of chronic health problems) indicate that the denial of social needs generally was not related to satisfaction with family members and friends, but was associated with substantially greater loneliness. Thus, denial of social needs did not appear to protect these older adults from the emotional distress of loneliness. Surprisingly, however, denial was associated with greater self-esteem and with slightly less depression. These differential associations suggest that denial may cushion self-esteem and help ward off global feelings of despair but, ironically, may afford little protection from more narrowly defined social longing and disappointment.

Researchers need to be prepared to accommodate the responses of older adults who do not simply answer yes or no to questions about the availability of specific social network resources and who, instead, volunteer additional and potentially enlightening information about the personal significance of such resources. It may be useful to distinguish between older adults who defensively deny that social contact is personally important and older adults whose apparent disinterest in social contact has a different motivational basis. Substantively, these results suggest that the denial of social needs, although associated with strong feelings of self-worth, does not fully protect older adults from feelings of loneliness. The protective function of denial invites further research using more sophisticated methods of operationalizing denial.

Low Need in the Context of High Social Involvement

Thus far the various meanings of low expressed need for companionship have been considered only for low levels of social involvement. Yet some older adults who express relatively little need for social interaction may find themselves experiencing more interaction than they desire. For example, unwanted visits or social invitations that are difficult to decline may lead some older adults to feel that their privacy has been violated. Hochschild (1973) expressed concern in this regard about age-homogeneous residences, suggesting that older adults who are basically "loners" by preference might feel pressured to participate in group activities in such residences.

In a sample of 553 elderly public housing residents, Rundall and Evashwick (1982) constructed a theoretical typology of social network involvement that included a "trapped" category—older adults who have a high level of social involvement but who would prefer less involvement. They classified participants on the basis of responses to questions about the frequency of visits and telephone conversations with social network members and about the desired level of interaction with social network members. Parallel questions about family members and friends allowed the researchers to develop separate typologies of kin and friend involvement. Interestingly, very few participants (less than 1% of those who could be classified reliably) fell into a trapped category defined in terms of friend or family involvement. Many more of the participants who could be classified fell into a category that Rundall and Evashwick labeled "abandoned"—older adults who had a low level of social contact and who desired more contact. The abandoned category was greater when defined in terms of family involvement (22%) than in terms of friend involvement (3%). Although these results need to be replicated in further studies, they suggest that having too much social interaction with others may be a relatively rare problem among the elderly.

Issues for Further Research

Very little is known about the origins of the need for companionship—why some people are content with relatively little social contact, whereas others prefer a great deal of contact. The Sarasons and their colleagues (e.g., Sarason, Sarason, & Shearin, 1986; Sarason, Shearin, Pierce & Sarason, 1987) have urged greater attention to personality factors that influence a person's propensity to seek or elicit social support. Indeed, they argued that it may be reasonable to construe social support as a personality variable in itself, and they offered evidence that social support in adulthood may be influenced by early experiences of parental bonding. Similar efforts to trace variations in the need for companionship to personality factors and developmental experiences would be helpful.

Larson et al. (1982) stated that cultural norms also influence the perceived need for companionship. Although cultural imperatives for companionship may be felt more strongly in adolescence and young adulthood than in old age, researchers nonetheless might usefully investigate the extent to which sociocultural factors create a subjectively experienced "press" for companionship (cf. Gordon, 1976) or serve to dishearten or stigmatize those whose companionate interactions fall below culturally accepted thresholds (cf. Rook & Peplau, 1982; Rook, 1987b).

A related issue for research is the extent to which a person's need for companionship changes or remains stable across the life course. Some research has suggested that this need is relatively stable (e.g., Costa, Zonderman, & McCrae, 1985; Lowenthal, Berkman, & Associates, 1967), just as core personality attributes such as extroversion and neuroticism have been shown to be relatively stable (McCrae & Costa, 1984). Other research suggests that common age-related role losses and health changes may alter older adults' motivation to engage in companionate interaction (Antonucci, 1985), although the direction in which motivation changes remains unclear. Further research is needed that examines the extent to which changes occur in the personal significance that people ascribe to companionship, the circumstances that may lead to such changes, and the implications of such changes for psychological health.

We also know relatively little about how socially active older adults balance the need for companionship with the complementary need for privacy. Finding an acceptable equilibrium is a challenge that confronts older adults daily (Larson et al., 1985). The next section examines this issue of balance and, more generally, the manner in which access to companionship may shape older adults' feelings about the time they spend alone.

SOLITUDE AND COMPANIONSHIP

Efforts to understand the significance of companionship to the elderly would benefit from complementary efforts to understand the significance of solitude. Older adults' attitudes toward companionship may at least partly reflect their attitudes toward its alternative, solitude. Similarly, their ability to enjoy time spent alone may be influenced by the degree to which they perceive companionship to be readily available. Lowenthal and Robinson (1976) pointed out some time ago that social interaction and solitude should be considered in tandem, that older adults' social lives are apt to be characterized by oscillation between periods of social involvement and periods of retreat from involvement. Despite Lowenthal and Robinson's (1976) call for greater work on such rhythms, researchers are only beginning to investigate how older adults allocate their time to solitary versus social activities and how each kind of activity affects their psychological well-being (e.g., Larson et al., 1985).

Loneliness theorists have devoted the most attention to solitude and its implications for psychological well-being (Larson et al., 1982; Rook & Peplau, 1982; Shaul, 1982; Suedfeld, 1982; Young, 1982), although their work rarely has focused explicitly on older adults. Nonetheless, this section reviews some of the major conceptual distinctions that loneliness theorists have offered and suggests how these distinctions may apply to the elderly. This section also considers the scant empirical evidence that has examined older adults' subjective experiences when they are alone versus when they are with others.

Problematic Attitudes Toward Solitude as a Cause of Loneliness

Although loneliness typically is traced to difficulties in relating to others, it also has been traced to difficulties in spending time alone. Arguments that link loneliness to attitudes toward solitude generally take two forms: one that emphasizes avoiding solitude and one that emphasizes retreating into solitude.

Avoiding Solitude

Some theorists feel that lonely people have little tolerance for aloneness (Greene & Kaplan, 1978; Winnicott, 1958), that they actually fear being alone (Young, 1982). Thus, being alone is a more undesirable condition for the lonely than it is for others (Young, 1982), and the intense distress caused by being alone is assumed to have "driving power" (Sullivan, 1953), in that it motivates lonely people to seek social contact. Sullivan (1953) regarded this driving power as desirable because it ensures that lonely people eventually will try to break out of their isolation. But other theorists (e.g., Young, 1982; Weiss, 1973) consider such driving power to be dangerous if desperation about being alone leads people to launch relationships too hastily or with ill-matched partners; loneliness is merely aggravated when these relationships fail. From this perspective, lonely people would benefit from learning how to engage in satisfying solitary activities (from increasing their "solitude skill"). This presumably would make them less dependent on others for enjoyment, thereby reducing the urgency with which they seek relationships (Rook, 1984; Rook & Peplau, 1982; Shaul, 1982; Young, 1982).

Retreating into Solitude

A second and quite different version of the link between loneliness and solitude suggests that solitude offers protection from interpersonal threats and demands and therefore may be particularly appealing to lonely people (e.g., Larson et al., 1982; Satran, 1978). Clinical observations (Fromm-Reichmann, 1959; Weiss, 1974) and empirical data (Cheek & Busch, 1981; Jones, Freemon, & Goswick, 1981; Perlman, Gerson, & Spinner, 1978) portray the lonely as highly self-conscious and sensitive to imagined or real rejections. Moreover, limited assertion skills make it difficult for some lonely individuals, including lonely older adults (Hansson, Jones, Carpenter, & Remondet, 1986–1987; Perlman et al., 1978), to resist others' demands and expectations (Satran, 1978). Withdrawal into solitude, therefore, offers protection from a variety of interpersonal stresses (Jones, 1985) and potential threats to self-esteem (Horowitz, 1983; Rook, 1984), although it also serves to perpetuate loneliness. From this perspective, lonely people need assistance in bolstering their self-esteem and in finding ways to make interactions with others less threatening.

Empirical Evidence

These two versions clearly make different predictions about how attitudes toward solitude may affect vulnerability to loneliness. Little evidence exists for evaluating these different predictions. Evidence consistent with the "retreat" version emerged in a study of relational stress and loneliness among college students by Jones, Cavert, Snider, and Bruce (1985). They found that students who had experienced numerous interpersonal stresses exhibited both an increased desire to affiliate with others and, paradoxically, an increased tendency to avoid others. Shaver, Furman, and Buhrmester (1985) found that chronically lonely students (those for whom loneliness resembled an enduring personality trait) had intense social needs but nonetheless engaged in coping strategies that did not include other people (such as watching television alone). In a study of the subjective states associated with being alone versus being with others, Larson et al. (1982) found that those people who reported the most positive moods when they were alone also tended to report discomfort being with others, and, not surprisingly, tended to be the most lonely.

In preliminary analyses of data collected from college students at the University of California at Irvine, we have found evidence of distinctly ambivalent feelings about solitude (Rook & Thuras, 1987). On the one hand, responses to scales that were designed to measure attitudes toward solitude indicated that lonely students dislike engaging in activities by themselves and are critical of others who do so. On the other hand, their responses also indicated that they wished they could more easily protect their privacy and that they derived some comforts from being alone, such as feeling "freer to be myself."

The findings from these different studies suggest that lonely individuals' attitudes toward solitude are neither unidimensional nor static. Indeed, such attitudes are likely to shift over time as lonely people struggle to balance their needs for intimacy and privacy. Moreover, the meaning of solitude and the motivation to use solitude productively may vary with one's age and life circumstances (Larson et al., 1982).

Research by Larson and his colleagues (Larson et al., 1982, 1985) documented the influence of such developmental and situational factors on patterns of solitude. Using the time-sampling methodology described earlier, they found that older adults spend roughly 48% of their waking time alone (Larson et al., 1985), whereas adolescents and adults under age 65 spend only 25% to 30% of their waking time alone (Larson et al., 1982). Among the elderly, marital status and living arrangements also influenced the amount of time spent alone. Unmarried individuals who lived by themselves spent nearly 73% of their time alone. Yet even married individuals who were living with their spouses reported a considerable amount of time alone (40%).

The greater proportion of solitary time among the elderly can be attributed to retirement and reduced family demands. Nevertheless, friendship does not appear to expand to fill "the lacuna left by these role losses" (Larson et al., 1985, p. 379). Older adults reported spending 9% of their time in interactions with friends and neighbors, which was virtually identical to the amount of time (7%) that adults under age 65 spent in such interactions and far less than the time spent by adolescents (29%). Moreover, because the older adults that Larson et al. (1985) studied were relatively affluent and generally healthy, it is unlikely that they experienced major impediments to social interaction. Their considerable solitary time, coupled with only a modest commitment of time to contacts with friends and neighbors, may indicate that the elderly desire companionship less intensely or regard solitude more favorably than do other age groups.

Data from this research on participants' subjective states when they were alone and with others provide more direct evidence of the personal meaning of solitude. Participants of all ages in these studies reported more negative moods when they were alone than when they were with others, although the younger groups experienced the greatest mood decrements (Larson et al., 1985). For example, participants (particularly the younger groups) felt less happy, less cheerful, less friendly, less sociable, and more bored when they were alone. The younger groups, however, also reported an improved ability to concentrate on hobbies, studies, reading, and other activities when they were alone (Larson et al., 1982). Older adults did not share this benefit of solitude (Larson et al., 1985), although married older adults appeared to reap some benefits in terms of increased arousal. The married elderly reported substantially higher arousal (excitement, concentration, and challenge) when they were alone than when they were with others; the opposite pattern was true for the unmarried elderly. The married elderly also were significantly less likely than the unmarried elderly to wish that they were doing something else when they were alone. Larson et al. (1985) concluded that the opportunity to be alone appears to be energizing for the married but enervating for the unmarried.

These findings suggest that at least for older middle-class adults, solitude is not a strongly aversive experience. At the same time, solitude appeared to offer distinctive benefits only to married older adults. For married individuals, solitude appeared to provide an occasion for greater stimulation and deeper engagement in their activities than would otherwise have been possible (Larson et al., 1985). Thus, in old age, solitude may provide a context for renewal (Larson et al., 1982; Suedfeld, 1982) only when it is voluntary and can be balanced by readily available opportunities for intimacy and companionship. This conclusion should be viewed as tentative, of course, in light of the scant empirical evidence that exists.

Issues for Further Research

The interdependent meanings and rhythms of solitude and companionship in late life clearly merit much greater attention. The above discussion suggests, for example, that older adults' attitudes toward solitude and their ability to derive any benefits from solitude may be influenced by the extent to which they suffer from loneliness. Moreover, reactions to solitude may vary even among the lonely as a function of the degree of discomfort they experience interacting with others. For some lonely individuals, solitude may represent a haven from the stress of social interaction; for others it may represent a dreaded experience of emptiness that must be avoided. Future studies might usefully explore how older adults' attitudes toward solitude and their subjective experience of solitude are affected by their access to social partners and their level of comfort interacting with others.

A related issue that warrants further research concerns the extent to which "solitude skill" (cf., Rook & Peplau, 1982; Shaul, 1982; Young, 1982) influences older adults' attitudes about being alone or their ability to derive pleasure from time spent alone. That is, older adults' attitudes toward solitude may be shaped not only by their access to companionship but also by their ability to identify and carry out by themselves activities that give them pleasure. Research on younger age groups suggests that people vary greatly in their ability to make constructive use of time spent alone (e.g., Rubenstein & Shaver, 1982), and researchers have argued that this variation may reflect differences in the actual skill or competence with which people approach solitary leisure time (e.g., Shaul, 1982). Some gerontologists have expressed concern that the current cohort of older adults may lack the educational experiences needed to equip them with adequate skills for constructively using their leisure time following retirement (Atchley, 1987). Although these gerontologists did not study solitary leisure per se, their concept of "leisure competence" seems relevant to the concept of solitude skill.

These concepts could be investigated usefully in analyses that compare different age groups and that examine variations within the current cohort of older adults. Such analyses must distinguish time spent alone that is devoted to maintenance tasks (such as housework and self-care) from time spent alone that is devoted to genuine leisure (such as working on a hobby or going to a movie). Failing to distinguish these two different kinds of solitary time could make people appear to have less leisure competence than they actually do and could also make solitary time seem unnecessarily negative.

Another issue that should be considered is the possible aftereffects of solitude, as compared with its actual experience. In analyses of their adolescent and middle-aged samples, Larson et al. (1982) found evidence of positive aftereffects of solitude. Even though being alone was associated with more negative mood states, people appeared to experience a substantial rebound of affect once they rejoined the company of others. Specifically, not only did some moods return to their normal levels, but other moods rose to higher than normal levels. Larson et al. (1982) inferred from these data that solitude had a renewing effect on the study participants' mood, that it contributed to a kind of increased social buoyancy. Researchers have not yet determined whether older adults exhibit comparable buoyancy following periods of solitude, but if such a mood rebound were documented, it would underscore further the complex interdependence of solitude and companionship in older adults' lives.

CONCLUSION

Companionship and social support represent two important and complementary functions of social relationships that help sustain emotional health at all ages, including old age. Social support appears to be particularly important in protecting people from threats to well-being, whereas companionship appears to be singularly important in enhancing mood and the perceived quality of life. Because most research has focused on understanding the ways in which social support contributes to psychological well-being, in this chapter I emphasized several ways in which companionship may contribute to well-being. I also discussed the significance of individual variations in the need for companionship and the perceived availability of companionship. Finally, I urged greater attention to the ways in which the personal meaning and psychological impact of companionship may be influenced by older adults' attitudes toward solitude and the amount of time they spend alone.

Some researchers will disagree that the effort to distinguish companionship from social support is worthwhile, just as some researchers question the usefulness of efforts to distinguish among different kinds of support (e.g., House & Kahn, 1985; Sarason et al., 1987). For some, these reservations will stem from the fact that previous attempts to operationalize conceptually distinct interpersonal functions have not always succeeded. For example, some researchers have reported high intercorrelations among indicators of specific kinds of support (House & Kahn, 1985; Sarason et al., 1987). Yet such high intercorrelations must be interpreted in light of the manner in which support is assessed (cf. Sarason et al., 1987). Measures of the *perceived availability* of social support (or companionship) may exhibit high correlations (cf. high intercorrelations among measures of perceived support reported in Study 2, Sarason et al., 1987) because many social network members provide both support and companionship. Yet the fact that the same individuals are perceived as being available to perform multiple interpersonal functions does not mean that those functions are redundant or indistinguishable.[5] Measures of actual interactions involving companionship and support seem likely to be less highly correlated and, more important to the issue of discriminant validity, seem likely to exhibit nonredundant associations with outcome measures of interest.

Thus, empirical efforts to distinguish social support and companionship (or other interpersonal functions) should be guided by a theoretical framework and an awareness that even subtle differences in the manner of assessing the functions (e.g., whether in terms of behavioral occurrence, perceived availability, personal preferences, or needs) may greatly affect the associations observed and the extent to which the associations legitimately constitute evidence of distinguishability. Our current understanding of the links between social relationships and psychological well-being seems too limited to justify abandoning efforts to identify distinct functions of social bonds that differentially protect or enhance emotional health.

Other reservations about the usefulness of attempting to differentiate companionship and social support may stem from the conviction that the hypothesized benefits of social relationships can be subsumed by a single core element of feeling loved and valued by others (e.g., Sarason et al., 1987). From this perspec-

---

[5]By analogy, high correlations are routinely reported between demographic characteristics such as education and income; yet few would argue that these resources are indistinguishable.

tive, measures of specific kinds of positive social exchanges represent mere proxies for or antecedents of this core sentiment (Sarason et al., 1987). Measures that emphasize an individual's experience of being loved and accepted may indeed yield powerful associations from a *predictive* standpoint. That is, if one's goal is to identify individuals who are at greatest risk for various emotional disorders, then assessing the extent to which people feel loved and cared for may prove to have considerable value. Limiting assessment to this core element, however, does not answer the question of what gives rise to such health-protective feelings (Sarason et al., 1987). Presumably, these feelings emerge (at least partly) from a history of specific positive exchanges with others (cf., Gottlieb, 1985), undoubtedly including the companionate interaction discussed in this chapter. If one's goal is to learn how feelings of being loved and accepted develop or how such feelings can be engendered through interventions, then it may be necessary to adopt a microanalytic perspective that tracks the occurrence of specific kinds of social exchanges (cf., Cutrona, 1986). Research guided by such a microanalytic perspective seems likely to yield evidence that supportive interactions focused on alleviating distressing problems and companionate interactions focused on recreation and pleasure each make important contributions to the quality of one's attachments to others and to one's emotional health.

REFERENCES

Adams, B. (1967). Interaction theory and the social network. *Sociometry, 30,* 64–78.

Adams, R. G. (1987). Patterns of network change: A longitudinal study of friendships of elderly women. *The Gerontologist, 27,* 222–227.

Allan, G. (1986). Friendship and care for elderly people. *Ageing and Society, 6,* 1–12.

Antonucci, T. C. (1985). Personal characteristics, social support, and social behavior. In R. H. Binstock & E. Shanas (Eds.), *Handbook of aging and the social sciences* (2nd ed., pp. 94–128). New York: Van Nostrand Reinhold.

Atchley, R. C. (1987). *Aging: Continuity and change* (2nd ed.). Belmont, CA: Wadsworth.

Barrera, M. (1986). Distinctions between social support concepts, measures, and models. *American Journal of Community Psychology, 14,* 413–445.

Beckman, L. J. (1981). Effects of social interaction and children's relative inputs on older women's psychological well-being. *Journal of Personality and Social Psychology, 41,* 1075–1086.

Blau, Z. (1973). *Old age in a changing society.* New York: Viewpoints.

Bowlby, J. (1977). The making and breaking of affectional bonds. I. Aetiology and psychopathology in the light of attachment theory. *British Journal of Psychiatry, 130,* 201–210.

Brody, E. M. (1985). Parent care as a normative family stress. *The Gerontologist, 25,* 19–29.

Brody, E. M., Johnsen, P. T., & Fulcomer, M. C. (1984). What should adult children do for elderly parents? Opinions and preferences of three generations of women. *The Gerontologist, 39,* 736–746.

Brody, E. M., Johnsen, P. T., Fulcomer, M. C., & Lang, A. M. (1983). Women's changing roles and help to the elderly: Attitudes of three generations of women. *Journal of Gerontology, 38,* 597–607.

Buss, A. H., & Plomin, R. (1984). *Temperament: Early developing personality traits.* San Francisco: Freeman.

Buunk, B. (1988, July). *Companionship and support in organizations: A microanalysis of the stress-reducing features of social interaction.* Paper presented at the 4th International Conference on Personal Relationships, Vancouver, Canada.

Campbell, A., Converse, P. E., & Rodgers, W. L. (1976). *The quality of American life.* New York: Sage.

Cantor, M. H. (1979). Neighbors and friends: An overlooked resource in the informal support system. *Research on Aging, 1,* 434–463.

Cantor, M. H. (1983). Strain among caregivers: A study of experience in the United States. *Gerontologist, 23,* 597–604.

Carp, F. M., & Carp, A. (1981a). The validity, reliability, and generalizability of daily data. *Experimental Aging Research, 7,* 281–292.

Carp, F. M., & Carp, A. (1981b). It may not be the answer, It may be the question. *Research on Aging, 3,* 85–101.

Carstensen, L. L. (1987). Age-related changes in social activity. In L. L. Carstensen & B. A. Edelstein (Eds.). *Handbook of clinical gerontology* (pp. 222–237). New York: Pergamon Press.

Cheek, J. M., & Busch, C. K. (1981). The influence of shyness and loneliness in a new situation. *Personality and Social Psychology Bulletin, 7,* 572–577.

Cicirelli, V. G. (1981). *Helping elderly parents: The role of adult children.* Boston: Auburn House.

Cobb, S. (1976). Social support as a moderator of life stress. *Psychosomatic Medicine, 38,* 300–314.

Cohen, S., & Hoberman, H. M. (1983). Positive events and social supports as buffers of life change stress. *Journal of Applied Social Psychology, 13,* 99–125.

Cohen, S., & McKay, G. (1984). Social support, stress and the buffering hypothesis: A theoretical analysis. In A. Baum, J. E. Singer, & S. E. Taylor (Eds.), *Handbook of psychology and health* (Vol. 4, pp. 253–267). Hillsdale, NJ: Erlbaum.

Costa, P. T., Jr., Zonderman, A. B., & McCrae, R. (1985). Longitudinal course of social support among men in the Baltimore Longitudinal Study of Aging. In I. G. Sarason & B. R. Sarason (Eds.), *Social support: Theory, research and applications* (pp. 137–154). The Hague: Martinus Nijhoff.

Costanza, R. S., Derlega, V. J., & Winstead, B. A. (1988). Positive and negative forms of social support: Effects of conversational topics on coping with stress among same-sex friends. *Journal of Experimental Social Psychology, 24,* 183–193.

Csikszentmihalyi, M. (1975). *Beyond boredom and anxiety.* San Francisco: Jossey-Bass.

Cumming, E., & Henry, W. (1961). *Growing old: The process of disengagement.* New York: Basic Books.

Cutrona, C. E. (1986). Behavioral manifestations of social support: A microanalytic investigation. *Journal of Personality and Social Psychology, 51,* 201–208.

Cutrona, C. E., & Russell, D. W. (1987). The provisions of social relationships and adaptation to stress. In W. H. Jones & D. Perlman (Eds.), *Advances in personal relationships* (Vol. 1, pp. 37–67). Greenwich, CT: JAI Press.

Cutrona, C. E., Russell, D., & Rose, J. (1986). Social support and adaptation to stress by the elderly. *Psychology and Aging, 1,* 47–54.

Diener, E. (1984). Subjective well-being. *Psychological Bulletin, 95,* 542–575.

DiMatteo, M. R., & Hays, R. (1981). Social support and serious illness. In B. H. Gottlieb (Ed.), *Social networks and social support* (pp. 117–148). Beverly Hills, CA: Sage.

Duval, S., & Wicklund, R. A. (1972). *A theory of objective self-awareness.* New York: Academic Press.

Eckenrode, J. (1983). The mobilization of social supports: Some individual constraints. *American Journal of Community Psychology, 11,* 509–528.

Farley, F. H., & Farley, S. V. (1970). Impulsiveness, sociability, and the preference for varied experience. *Perceptual and Motor Skills, 31,* 47–50.

Fischer, C. S. (1981, August). *What do we mean by "friendly"?* Paper presented at the annual meeting of the American Psychological Association, Los Angeles.

Fromm-Reichmann, F. (1959). Loneliness. *Psychiatry, 22,* 1–15.

Geen, R. G. (1986). Physiological, affective, and behavioral implications of extraversion-introversion. In W. H. Jones, J. M. Cheek, & S. R. Briggs (Eds.), *Shyness: Perspectives on research and treatment* (pp. 265–278). New York: Plenum.

George, L. K., & Gwyther, L. P. (1986). Caregiver well-being: A multidimensional examination of family caregivers of demented adults. *The Gerontologist, 26,* 253–259.

Gordon, C., & Gaitz, C. M. (1976). Leisure and lives: Personal expressivity across the life span. In R. H. Binstock & E. Shanas (Eds.), *Handbook of aging and the social sciences* (pp. 310–341). New York: Van Nostrand Reinhold.

Gordon, S. (1976). *Lonely in America.* New York: Simon & Schuster.

Gottlieb, B. H. (1985). Social support and the study of personal relationships. *Journal of Social and Personal Relationships, 2,* 351–375.

Greene, M., & Kaplan, B. L. (1978). Aspects of loneliness in the therapeutic situation. *International Review of Psychoanalysis, 5,* 3321–3330.

Hall, A., & Wellman, B. (1985). Social networks and social support. In S. Cohen & S. L. Syme (Eds।), *Social support and health* (pp. 23–41). New York: Academic Press.

Haley, W. E., Brown, S. L., & Levine, E. G. (1987). Experimental evaluation of the effectiveness of group intervention for dementia caregivers. *The Gerontologist, 27,* 377–383.

Haley, W. E., Levine, E. G., Brown, S. L., & Bartolucci, A. A. (1987). Stress, appraisal, coping, and social support as predictors of adaptational outcomes among dementia caregivers. *Psychology and Aging, 2,* 323–330.

Hansson, R. O. (1986). Relational competence, relationships, and adjustment in old age. *Journal of Personality and Social Psychology, 50,* 1050–1058.

Hansson, R. O., Jones, W. H., Carpenter, B. N., & Remondet, J. H. (1986–1987). Loneliness and adjustment to old age. *International Journal of Aging and Human Development, 24,* 41–53.

Hays, R. B. (1985). A longitudinal study of friendship development. *Journal of Personality and Social Psychology, 48,* 909–924.

Hays, R. B., & Oxley, D. (1986). Social network development and functioning during a life transition. *Journal of Personality and Social Psychology, 50,* 305–313.

Heller, K. (1979). The effects of social support: Prevention and treatment implications. In

A. P. Goldstein & F. H. Kanfer (Eds.), *Maximizing treatment gains: Transfer enhancement in psychotherapy* (pp. 353–382). New York: Academic Press.

Hess, B. (1972). Friendship. In M. Riley, M. Johnson, & A. Foner (Eds.), *Aging and society: Vol. 3. A sociology of age stratification* (pp. 357–393). New York: Russell Sage.

Hill, R. N., Foote, J., Aldous, R., Carlson, R., & MacDonald, R. (1970). *Family development in three generations.* Cambridge, MA: Schenkman.

Hirsch, B. (1980). Natural support systems and coping with major life changes. *American Journal of Community Psychology, 8,* 159–172.

Hochschild, A. R. (1973). *The unexpected community.* Berkeley and Los Angeles: University of California Press.

Hochschild, A. R. (1975). Disengagement theory: A critique and proposal. *American Sociological Review, 40,* 553–569.

Horowitz, L. M. (1983). *The toll of loneliness: Manifestations, mechanisms and means of prevention.* Monograph prepared for the National Institute of Mental Health, Office of Prevention.

House, J. S. (1981). *Work stress and social support.* Reading, MA: Addison-Wesley.

House, J. S., & Kahn, R. L. (1985). Measures and concepts of social support. In S. Cohen & S. L. Syme (Eds.), *Social support and health* (pp. 83–108). New York: Academic Press.

Ickes, J., Wicklund, R., & Ferris, C. (1973). Objective self-awareness and self-esteem. *Journal of Experimental Social Psychology, 9,* 202–219.

Jones, W. H. (1985). The psychology of loneliness: Some personality issues in the study of social support. In I. G. Sarason & B. R. Sarason (Eds.), *Social support: Theory, research and application* (pp. 225–241). The Hague: Martinus Nijhoff.

Jones, W. H., Cavert, C. W., Snider, R. C., & Bruce, T. (1985). Relational stress: An analysis of situations and events associated with loneliness. In S. W. Duck & D. Perlman (Eds.), *Understanding personal relationships: An interdisciplinary approach* (pp. 221–242). London: Sage.

Jones, W. H., Freemon, J. R., & Goswick, R. A. (1981). The persistence of loneliness: Self and other determinants. *Journal of Personality, 49,* 27–48.

Kahn, R. L., & Antonucci, T. (1980). Convoys over the life-course: Attachment, roles and social support. In P. B. Baltes & O. Brim (Eds.), *Life-span development and behavior* (Vol. 3, pp. 252–286). Lexington, MA: Lexington.

Krause, N. (1986). Social support, stress, and well-being among older adults. *Journal of Gerontology, 41,* 512–519.

Krause, N. (1987). Life stress, social support, and self-esteem in an elderly population. *Psychology and Aging, 2,* 349–356.

Larson, R. (1978). Thirty years of research on the subjective well-being of older Americans. *Journal of Gerontology, 33,* 109–125.

Larson, R., & Csikszentmihalyi, M. (1983). The Experience Sampling Method. In H. Reis (Ed.), *New directions for naturalistic methods in the behavioral sciences* (pp. 41–56). San Francisco: Jossey-Bass.

Larson, R., Csikszentmihalyi, M., & Graef, R. (1982). Time alone in daily experience: Loneliness or renewal? In L.A. Peplau & D. Perlman (Eds.), *Loneliness: A sourcebook of current theory, research and therapy* (pp. 41–53). New York: Wiley-Interscience.

Larson, R., Mannell, R., & Zuzanek, J. (1986). Daily well-being of older adults with friends and family. *Psychology and Aging, 1,* 117–126.

Larson, R., Zuzanek, J., & Mannell, R. (1985). Being alone versus being with people: Disengagement in the daily experience of older adults. *Journal of Gerontology, 40,* 375–381.

Lawton, M. P. (1982). The well-being and mental health of the aged. In T. M. Field, A. Huston, H. C. Quay, L. Troll, & G. E. Finley (Eds.), *Review of human development* (pp. 614–628). New York: Wiley-Interscience.

Lawton, M. P. (1983). Environment and other determinants of well-being in older people. *The Gerontologist, 23,* 349–357.

Lawton, M. P. (1988, February). *Environmental proactivity and affect in older people.* Paper presented at the 5th Annual Claremont Symposium on Applied Social Psychology, Claremont, CA.

Lawton, M. P., & Moss, M. (1987). The social relationships of older adults. In E. F. Borgatta & R. J. V. Montgomery (Eds.), *Critical issues in aging policy: Linking research and values* (pp. 92–126). Newbury Park, CA: Sage.

Lazarus, R. S., & Folkman, S. (1984). *Stress, appraisal, and coping.* New York: Springer.

Leavy, R. L. (1983). Social support and psychological disorder. *Journal of Community Psychology, 26,* 3–21.

Lee, G. R. (1979). Children and the elderly: Interaction and morale. *Research on Aging, 1,* 335–360.

Lee, G. R., & Ishii-Kuntz, M. (1987). Social interaction, loneliness, and emotional well-being among the elderly. *Research on Aging, 9,* 459–482.

Levinger, G., & Huesmann, L. R. (1980). An "incremental exchange" perspective on the pair relationship: Interpersonal reward and level of involvement. In K. J. Gergen, M. S. Greenberg, & R. H. Williams (Eds.), *Social exchange: Advances in theory and research* (pp. 165–188). New York: Plenum.

Lin, N. (1986). Modeling the effects of social support. In N. Lin, A. Dean, & W. M. Ensel (Eds.), *Social support, life events, and depression* (pp. 173–209). New York: Academic Press.

Litwak, E. (1985). *Helping the elderly: The complementary roles of informal networks and formal systems.* New York: Guilford.

Lopata, H. Z. (1979). *Women as widows: Support systems.* New York: Elsevier.

Lowenthal, M. F., Berkman, P., & Associates. (1967). *Aging and mental disorder in San Francisco.* San Francisco: Jossey-Bass.

Lowenthal, M. F., & Haven, C. (1968). Interaction and adaptation: Intimacy as a critical variable. *American Sociological Review, 33,* 20–30.

Lowenthal, M. F., & Robinson, B. (1976). Social networks and isolation. In R. H. Binstock & E. Shanas (Eds.), *Handbook of aging and the social sciences* (pp. 432–456). New York: Van Nostrand Reinhold.

Maddox, G. L. (1963). Activity and morale: A longitudinal study of selected elderly subjects. *Social Forces, 42,* 195–204.

Maddox, G. L. (1964). Disengagement theory: A critical evaluation. *The Gerontologist, 4,* 80–82.

Maddox, G. L., & Wiley, J. (1976). Scope, concepts and methods in the study of aging. In R. H. Binstock & E. Shanas (Eds.), *Handbook of aging and the social sciences* (pp. 3–34). New York: Van Nostrand Reinhold.

Mancini, J. A., Quinn, W., Gavigan, M. A., & Franklin, H. (1980). Social network interaction among older adults: Implications for life satisfaction. *Human Relations, 33,* 543–554.

Mandler, G. (1975). *Mind and emotion.* New York: Wiley.

Mannell, R., & McMahon, L. (1982). Humor as play: Its relationship to psychological well-being during the course of a day. *Leisure Sciences, 5,* 143–155.

McAdams, D. P., & Constantian, C. A. (1983). Intimacy and affiliation motives in daily living: An experience sampling analysis. *Journal of Personality and Social Psychology, 45,* 851–861.

McCallister, L., & Fischer, C. S. (1978). A procedure for surveying personal networks. *Sociological Methods and Research, 7,* 131–148.

McClelland, D. C. (1985). How motives, skills, and values determine what people do. *American Psychologist, 40,* 812–825.

McCrae, R. R., & Costa, P. T., Jr. (1984). *Emerging lives, enduring dispositions: Personality in adulthood.* Boston: Little Brown.

Minkler, M. (1985). Social support and health of the elderly. In S. Cohen & S. L. Syme (Eds.), *Social support and health* (pp. 199–216). New York: Academic Press.

Morris, L. W. (1979). *Extraversion and introversion.* Washington, DC: Hemisphere.

Moss, M., & Lawton, M. P. (1982). Time budgets of older people: A window on four lifestyles. *Journal of Gerontology, 27,* 115–123.

Murray, H. A. (1938). *Explorations in personality.* New York: Oxford University Press.

Pearlin, L. I. (1985). Social structure and processes of social support. In S. Cohen & S. L. Syme (Eds.), *Social support and health* (pp. 43–61). New York: Academic Press.

Peplau, H. E. (1955). Loneliness. *American Journal of Nursing, 55,* 1476–1481.

Peplau, L. A., & Perlman, D. (1979). Blueprint for a social psychological theory of loneliness. In M. Cook & G. Wilson (Eds.), *Love and attraction: An International Conference* (pp. 101–110). Elmsford, NY: Pergamon.

Peplau, L. A., Bikson, T. K., Rook, K. S., & Goodchilds, J. D. (1982). Being old and living alone. In L. A. Peplau & D. Perlman (Eds.), *Loneliness: A sourcebook of current theory, research and therapy* (pp. 135–151). New York: Wiley-Interscience.

Perlman, D., Gerson, A. C., & Spinner, B. (1978). Loneliness among senior citizens: An empirical report. *Essence, 2,* 239–248.

Peters, G. R., Hoyt, D. R., Babchuk, N., Kaiser, M., & Iijima, Y. (1987). Primary-group support systems of the aged. *Research on Aging, 9,* 392–416.

Poulshock, S. W., & Deimling, G. (1984). Families caring for elders in residence: Issues in the measurement of burden. *Journal of Gerontology, 39,* 230–239.

Pyszcynski, T. A., & Greenberg, J. (1985). Depression and preference for self-focusing stimuli after success and failure. *Journal of Personality and Social Psychology, 40,* 31–38.

Reis, H. T., Wheeler, L., Kernis, M. H., Spiegel, H., & Nezlek, J. (1985). On specificity in the impact of social participation on physical and psychological health. *Journal of Personality and Social Psychology, 48,* 456–471.

Roberto, K. A., & Scott, J. P. (1986). Friendships of older men and women: Exchange patterns and satisfaction. *Psychology and Aging, 1,* 103–109.

Rook, K. S. (1984). Promoting social bonding: Strategies for helping the lonely and socially isolated. *American Psychologist, 39,* 1389–1407.

Rook, K. S. (1985). The functions of social bonds: Perspectives from research on social support, loneliness, and social isolation. In I. G. Sarason & B. R. Sarason (Eds.), *Social support: Theory, research and application* (pp. 243–268). The Hague: Martinus Nijhoff.

Rook, K. S. (1987a). Reciprocity of social exchange and social satisfaction among older women. *Journal of Personality and Social Psychology, 46,* 1097–1108.

Rook, K. S. (1987b). Social support versus companionship: Effects on life stress, loneliness, and evaluations by others. *Journal of Personality and Social Psychology, 52,* 1132–1147.

Rook, K. S., & Peplau, L. A. (1982). Perspectives on helping the lonely. In L. A. Peplau & D. Perlman (Eds.), *Loneliness: A sourcebook of current theory, research and therapy* (pp. 357–378). New York: Wiley-Interscience.

Rook, K. S., & Thuras, P. (1987). *Attitudes toward solitude, "solitude skill," and loneliness.* Unpublished manuscript, University of California at Irvine, Program in Social Ecology.

Rook, K. S., & Thuras, P. (1988, November). *Denial of social needs: Implications for social network satisfaction and psychological health.* Paper presented at the annual meeting of the Gerontological Society of America, San Francisco.

Rubenstein, C. M., & Shaver, P. (1982). The experience of loneliness. In L. A. Peplau & D. Perlman (Eds.), *Loneliness: A sourcebook of current theory, research and therapy* (pp. 206–223). New York: Wiley-Interscience.

Rundall, T., & Evashwick, C. (1982). Social networks and help-seeking among the elderly. *Research on Aging, 4,* 205–226.

Sarason, I. G. (1981). Test anxiety, stress, and social support. *Journal of Personality, 49,* 101–114.

Sarason, I. G., & Sarason, B. R. (1985). Social support: Insights from assessment and experimentation. In I. G. Sarason & B. R. Sarason (Eds.), *Social support: Theory, research and application* (pp. 39–50). The Hague: Martinus Nijhoff.

Sarason, I. G., & Sarason, B. R. (1986). Experimentally provided social support. *Journal of Personality and Social Psychology, 50,* 1222–1225.

Sarason, I. G., Sarason, B. R., & Shearin, E. N. (1986). Social support as an individual difference variable: Its stability, origins, and relational aspects. *Journal of Personality and Social Psychology, 50,* 845–855.

Sarason, B. R., Shearin, E. N., Pierce, G. R., & Sarason, I. G. (1987). Interrelations of social support measures: Theoretical and practical implications. *Journal of Personality and Social Psychology, 52,* 813–832.

Satran, G. (1978). Notes on loneliness. *Journal of the Academy of Psychoanalysis, 6,* 281–300.

Schulz, R., & Decker, S. (1985). Long-term adjustment to physical disability: The role of social support, perceived control, and self-blame. *Journal of Personality and Social Psychology, 48,* 1162–1172.

Schulz, R.,& Rau, M. T. (1985). Social support through the life course. In S.Cohen & S. L. Syme (Eds.), *Social support and health* (pp. 129–149). New York: Academic Press.

Seltzer, M. M., Ivry, J., & Litchfield, L. C. (1987). Family members as case managers: Partnership between the formal and informal support networks. *The Gerontologist, 27,* 722–734.

Shanas, E., & Sussman, M. (Eds.) (1977). *Family, bureaucracy and the elderly.* Durham, NC: Duke University Press.

Shaul, S. (1982, August). *The effectiveness of two counseling strategies for reducing loneliness.* Paper presented at the annual meeting of the American Psychological Association, Washington, DC.

Shaver, P., Furman, W., & Buhrmester, D. (1985). Aspects of a life transition: Network changes, social skills and loneliness. In S. W. Duck & D. Perlman (Eds.), *Understanding personal relationships* (pp. 193–219). London: Sage.

Simmel, G. (1949). The sociology of sociability. *American Journal of Sociology, 55,* 254–261.

Solano, C. H. (1986). People without friends: Loneliness and its alternatives. In V. J. Derlega & B. A. Winstead (Ed.), *Friendship and social interaction* (pp. 227–246). New York: Springer-Verlag.

Stephens, M. A. P., Kinney, J. M., Norris, V. K., & Ritchie, S. W. (1987). Social networks as assets and liabilities in recovery from stroke by geriatric patients. *Psychology and Aging, 2,* 125–129.

Stoller, E. P., & Earl, L. L. (1983). Help with activities of everyday life: Sources of support of the noninstitutionalized elderly. *The Gerontologist, 22,* 526–631.

Suedfeld, P. (1982). Aloneness as a healing experience. In L. A. Peplau & D. Perlman (Eds.), *Loneliness: A sourcebook of current theory, research and therapy* (pp. 54–67). New York: Wiley-Interscience.

Sullivan, H. S. (1953) *The interpersonal theory of psychiatry.* New York: Norton.

Suls, J. (1982). Social support, interpersonal relations, and health: Benefits and liabilities. In G. S. Sanders & J. Suls (Eds.), *Social psychology of health and illness* (pp. 255–277). Hillsdale, NJ: Erlbaum.

Thoits, P. A. (1982) Conceptual, methodological, and theoretical problems in studying social support as a buffer against life stress *Journal of Health and Social Behavior, 23,* 145–159.

Thoits, P. A. (1984). Coping, social support, and psychological outcomes: The central role of emotion. In P. Shaver (Ed.), *Review of personality and social psychology* (Vol. 5, pp. 219–238). Beverly Hills, CA: Sage.

Thoits, P. A. (1985). Social support and psychological well-being: Theoretical possibilities. In I. G. Sarason & B. R. Sarason (Eds.), *Social support: Theory, research and applications* (pp. 51–72). The Hague: Martinus Nijhoff.

Townsend, A. L., & Poulshock, S. W. (1986). Intergenerational perspectives on impaired elders' support networks. *Journal of Gerontology, 41,* 101–109.

Troll, L. E., Miller, S., & Atchley, R. (1979). Social support networks and the crisis of bereavement. *Social Science and Medicine, 11,* 35–41.

Turner, R. J. (1981). Social support as a contingency in psychological well-being. *Journal of Health and Social Behavior, 22,* 357–367.

Wan, T. T. (1982). *Stressful life events, social support networks and gerontological health.* Lexington, MA: Lexington.

Ward, R. A. (1985). Informal networks and well-being in later life: A research agenda. *The Gerontologist, 25,* 55–61.

Ward, R. A., Sherman, S. R., & LaGory, M. (1984). Subjective network assessments and subjective well-being. *Journal of Gerontology, 39,* 93–101.

Weiss, R. S. (1974). The provisions of social relationships. In Z. Rubin (Ed.), *Doing unto others* (pp. 17–26). Englewood Cliffs, NJ: Prentice-Hall.

Wheeler, L., Reis, H. T., & Nezlek, J. (1983). Loneliness, social interaction and sex roles. *Journal of Personality and Social Psychology, 35,* 742–754.

Wicklund, R. A. (1975). Objective self-awareness. In L. Berkowitz (Ed.), *Advances in experimental social psychology* (Vol. 5, pp. 233–275). New York: Academic Press.

Williams, A. W., Ware, J. E., & Donald, C. A. (1981). A model of mental health, life events, and social supports applicable to general populations. *Journal of Health and Social Behavior, 22,* 324–336.

Wills, T. A. (1985). Supportive functions of interpersonal relationships. In S. Cohen & S. L. Syme (Eds.), *Social support and health* (pp. 61–82). New York: Academic Press.

Winnicott, M. T. (1958). The capacity to be alone. *International Journal of Psychoanalysis, 39,* 416–420.

Wood, V., & Robertson, J. F. (1978). Friendship and kinship interaction: Differential effect on the morale of the elderly. *Journal of Marriage and the Family, 40,* 367–375.

Young, J. E. (1982). Loneliness, depression and cognitive therapy. In L. A. Peplau & D. Perlman (Eds.), *Loneliness: A sourcebook of current theory, research and therapy* (pp. 379–405). New York: Wiley-Interscience.

Zarit, S., Reever, K. E., & Bach-Peterson, J. (1980). Relatives of the impaired elderly: Correlates of feelings of burden. *The Gerontologist, 20,* 649–655.

Zarit, S., & Zarit, J. M. (1983). Families under stress: Interventions for caregivers of senile dementia patients. *Psychotherapy: Theory, Research and Practice, 19,* 461–471.

PART THREE

Social Support and Coping with Stress

The buffering effects of social support in stressful situations is a continuing focus of research on social support. The chapters in this section analyze social support and interactions between a person and a stressful situation as they affect immune system responses, personality factors, the matching of supportive effort with situational need, and the breadth of the effective supportive environment.

Chapter 10 reviews several areas of research—loneliness, chronic stressors in the family, and the effect of disclosing traumatic events—that relate aspects of interpersonal relationships to immune function. The findings reviewed corroborate those of work in other areas concerning psychological adjustment and the quality of relationships. The simple presence of a partner is not necessarily an asset; what is helpful is a confidant who will not be judgmental about negative disclosures and will not withdraw love or support in such a situation. The authors also point out the need to determine the actual health consequences of immunological changes.

Measures of perceived support and received support often produce discrepant findings. Chapter 11 reviews such measures and the reasons for the discrepancies. It also points out the implications of the distinction between perceived available support and received support for understanding their health-protective effects. For instance, social support perceived to be available may not be forthcoming in certain kinds of crises. Characteristics of the person's network may also contribute to the dissimilarity of the two types of measures. That is, those with large networks may expect much help, but the network members may not help as readily because they assume that others are already helping. Discrepancies in findings related to the buffering effects of received support may be the result of failing to consider the context of the support and differences in the specificity of measures of stressors, received support, and well-being.

The authors of Chapter 12 view hardiness as a characteristic of the individual and social support as an aspect of the environment, although they acknowledge that most of the current methods of assessing support confound the two. The available data do not differentiate between the possibility that behavior associated with hardiness fosters a supportive environment and the possibility that hardy attitudes are fostered by a supportive context. Some studies of the interactions among stress, support, and certain aspects of hardiness suggest that under certain circumstances, support can have negative effects on well-being. The authors also provide guidelines for future research on stress resistance.

A key question in social support research is whether certain types of social support are beneficial in relation to certain types of stress. If such matches could be identified, supportive interventions could be better designed. Chapter 13 presents a theory of optimal stress–social support matching and tests the theory in a series of studies that assessed both specific components of support and specific stressful events. This review concludes that specific components of social support can improve the outcome of some events but that a broad range of components are required for other events. The chapter also describes the types of events in each category.

Chapter 14 discusses how social networks develop, how people cope with multiple role stressors during periods of life stress, and how these multiple role involvements can best be combined to achieve a satisfactory quality of life. In different developmental stages and in different kinds of settings, role satisfaction may be tied to either the microsystem (specific setting) or the mesosystem (the person's multiple role involvements across settings). For instance, social relationships and consequent role satisfaction appear to differ more according to work/nonwork settings for working women than according to school/nonschool settings for adolescents. In addition, the same type of network density is not equally adaptive in all types of situations. That is, a dense network is more effective for role stabilization and a less dense network is more effective for role change. In stressful situations in which little active coping is possible, a dense network may be a handicap, because it reinforces anxieties. This observation is similar to that in Chapter 17.

CHAPTER 10

Social Support, Stress, and the Immune System

SUSAN KENNEDY, JANICE K. KIECOLT-GLASER, AND RONALD GLASER

Ohio State University College of Medicine

Until recently, human studies that provided the physiological evidence linking psychological variables and susceptibility to infectious disease were extremely rare. However, the past several years have witnessed a sharp increase in research efforts to associate psychological variables with immunological changes. These studies, in the field of psychoimmunology, have begun to unravel and clarify the relationships among psychological, endocrinological, and immunological functions. To date, the literature suggests that distressing psychological responses may be a common denominator of the psychological events or other psychologically related variables that affect the body's ability to combat infection and disease through changes in the immune system.

BACKGROUND: IMMUNE FUNCTION

Measurements of immune function typically calculate the numbers and/or functional abilities of subgroups of lymphocytes (white blood cells). Lymphocyte subpopulations perform specialized functions, and so it is not possible to use a single immunological assay to determine global immunological competence. However, there is considerable interdependence among various immunological components, and adverse changes in one lymphocyte subpopulation can have multiple cascading consequences. Most of the immunological components discussed in this chapter take days or weeks to change significantly; whereas several days of heightened dysphoria can alter many immunological parameters, a bad afternoon is not a sufficient stimulus to produce important immunological changes.

The immune response has two arms: The cellular immune response is important to the defense against intracellular viruses such as the human immuno-

This work was supported in part by National Institute of Mental Health Grants MH–40787 and MH–18831.

deficiency virus (HIV) responsible for AIDS, and cellular immunity refers to immunological activities that do not produce antibodies, particularly those that involve T-lymphocytes. T-lymphocytes, or lymphocytes that are derived from the thymus, have various subgroups with important activities. For example, some T-lymphocytes synthesize lymphokines, proteins such as gamma interferon, and the interleukins that function as communication links between immune and non-immune cells and thus are potent immunological mediators. Helper T-lymphocytes are so named because they stimulate a number of other immunological activities, particularly the B-lymphocytes' production of antibodies. Suppressor T-lymphocytes act in a feedback loop and shut off the activities of helper T-lymphocytes when a sufficient number of antibodies have been produced.

Blastogenesis is one of the most commonly used immunological assays in the psychoneuroimmunology literature. In this assay, mitogens (chemicals that mimic infectious agents such as bacteria or viruses) are used to stimulate the proliferation (replication) of lymphocytes. That is, lymphocyte proliferation in response to mitogen stimulation is thought to model the immune system's proliferative response when challenged by naturally occurring infectious agents. Poorer proliferative responses following mitogen exposure suggest that lymphocytes may be less efficient in their ability to respond to foreign invaders.

Natural killer (NK) cells are thought to provide an important defense against virus-infected cells and cancer cells (Herberman, 1982). Interferon, one of the lymphokines or chemical mediators, is a potent enhancer of a number of different immunological activities, including NK cell activity.

BASIC RESEARCH: STRESS AND IMMUNE FUNCTION

Before addressing the literature that is directly related to interpersonal relationships and immunity, we will briefly review some of the more general behavioral immunology literature. It is a literature that is still quite small, and many of the studies have serious methodological flaws (Kiecolt-Glaser & Glaser, in press-a). In addition, research published before the mid-1970s should be viewed with considerable caution. The field of immunology has undergone major changes since that time, and many of the earlier immunological laboratory procedures are not considered credible by contemporary immunologists.

Before 1980 there were only a few human studies in the literature, and their focus was the immunological sequelae of novel and intense events such as bereavement (Bartrop, Luckhurst, Lazarus, Kiloh, & Penny, 1977), the space flight of astronauts (Kimzey, 1975) or the consequences of 48 or 77 hours of noise and sleep deprivation (Palmblad, Bjorn, Wasserman, & Akerstedt, 1979).

One of the early psychoimmunology studies, however, still sets a standard for research in the field today. Kasl, Evans, and Niederman (1979) examined the relationship between psychosocial data and seroepidemiological data collected from West Point cadets. The cadets were part of a prospective study of the development of infectious mononucleosis, a disease whose etiologic agent is Epstein–

Barr virus (EBV), one of the human herpesviruses. Those cadets who were EBV seronegative on arrival at West Point (i.e., had no prior exposure to the virus and thus were not latently infected) and who had a triad of psychological risk factors (high motivation for military career, poor academic performance, and a father who was an "overachiever") were more likely to become infected with EBV, and they spent longer periods in the campus infirmary. Moreover, antibody titers to the latent virus showed a similar relationship among those cadets who did not develop clinical symptoms. These data were the first to show concurrent and significant relationships among psychological stressors, immunological indices, and actual health outcomes.

Contemporary human psychoimmunology research during this decade has had several aims. Psychiatric investigators have examined the relationship between various immunological parameters and certain psychiatric syndromes, particularly major depression (Schleifer et al., 1984). A primary goal of many of these investigators has been the identification of biological markers for psychopathology. In general, research has shown that major depression is associated with poorer immune function when depressed patients are compared with well-matched nondepressed comparison subjects (e.g., Stein, Keller, & Schleifer, 1985). However, most of the immunological differences that have been demonstrated to date do not appear to be unique to psychiatric disorders.

A second line of research looked at the relationship among various psychosocial variables and secretory IgA, an immunoglobulin produced by B-lymphocytes. Most of these investigators did not control for flow rate and/or hydration, a process that requires more than simply timing saliva collection (Stone, Cox, Valdimarsdottir, & Neale, 1987). Thus, because of the virtual absence of reliable and valid immunological data using this method, we will not review these studies.

Another line of research has concentrated on immune function in nonhuman primates, particularly that related to attachment and separation. Typically, these studies look at responses in animals separated from members of the same species. For example, altered responses of lymphocytes to mitogens were reported in macaque monkeys when separated from their peers (Reite, Harbeck, & Hoffman, 1981). In addition, antibody production to a challenge by an antigen was found to be significantly depressed in infant squirrel monkeys separated from their mothers (Coe, Wiener, Rosenberg, & Levine, 1985), but this immunosuppression could be ameliorated by the presence of peers (Coe et al., 1985).

INTERPERSONAL RELATIONSHIPS AND HEALTH

The beneficial effects of social companionship on immune function are particularly relevant to the social support literature concerning humans.

In the extensive social support literature, there is growing evidence that interpersonal support may affect health. For example, Blazer (1982) reported that three indices of social support (impaired roles and available attachments, perceived social support, and impaired frequency of social interaction) predicted mortality in a sample of elderly persons. Another study with older adults suggested that social networks directly influenced subsequent self-reported physical symptoms, even after controlling for initial symptom levels (Cohen, Teresi, & Holmes, 1985). The physiological mechanisms underlying these health differences, however, are not well understood.

In the remainder of this chapter we will review recent studies that address the relationships among certain aspects of interpersonal relationships and immune function in several human populations. First we will examine the effects of acute stressors on the immune system and their relationship to loneliness. Then we will discuss studies that look at the adaptation to two longer-term stressors, marital disruption and caring for a relative afflicted with Alzheimer's disease. An intervention study, considered next, suggests that self-disclosure of traumatic events may have immunological consequences. In the final section of the chapter, we will address health implications.

LONELINESS AND IMMUNE FUNCTION

For the last several years, our laboratory has been examining the immunological correlates of psychological distress in first- and second-year medical students during academic examinations. The paradigm compares data from blood samples drawn during an examination period with similar "baseline" data obtained four weeks before examinations (Glaser, Kiecolt-Glaser, Speicher, & Holliday, 1985a; Glaser, Kiecolt-Glaser, Stout, Tarr, Speicher, & Holliday, 1985b).

In the first study, data from the examination blood samples showed lower activity by natural killer (NK) cells, compared with the lower-distress baseline samples. As noted earlier, NK cells are those cells that are thought to be involved in the surveillance and destruction of virus-infected cells and tumor cells (Herberman, 1982).

In addition, there were higher antibody titers (levels) to EBV relative to the levels found on the students' return from summer vacation (Glaser et al., 1985a). *Higher* antibody titers to EBV and other herpesviruses indicate that the cellular immune response is *less* competent in controlling EBV latency. Once a person is infected with the virus, he or she will carry for life the virus in latently infected cells. It may be reactivated from these cells under a variety of circumstances, particularly if an individual is immunosuppressed. Reactivation of latent herpesviruses is thought to reflect poorer control of these viruses by the cellular immune response.

Of particular interest was the finding that those students who described themselves as lonelier (i.e., above the median on Russell's UCLA Loneliness Scale, 1982) had lower NK activity and higher EBV antibody titers than did those students who described themselves as less lonely (Glaser et al., 1985a; Kiecolt-Glaser et al., 1984a). Loneliness is associated with unsatisfactory interpersonal relationships (Jones, Freemon, & Goswick, 1981) and is generally perceived by individuals as distressing (Peplau & Perlman, 1982).

In a related study, lonelier psychiatric inpatients had poorer NK cell function and higher urinary cortisol levels (a stress-responsive hormone) than did patients who reported less loneliness (Kiecolt-Glaser et al., 1984b). In addition, lonelier patients had a poorer lymphocyte proliferative response to the mitogen phytohemagglutinin (PHA). Collectively, these data suggest that loneliness is associated with poorer immune function.

MARITAL DISRUPTION AND IMMUNE FUNCTION

Marital disruption is associated with high rates of psychological and physical dysfunction. Two studies addressed the possibility that the heightened distress associated with marital disruption in epidemiological studies might also have immunological consequences. On the average, separated individuals are generally fairly distressed, especially immediately after separation (Bloom, Asher, & White, 1978); as a group, they show considerably higher rates of clinical and subclinical depression than do married persons (Blumenthal, 1967). Separated/ divorced (S/D) individuals represent a greater percentage of both inpatient and outpatient populations than do married individuals (Bloom et al., 1978), and these differences are thought to be related in part to the stressfulness of the experience for many individuals.

Health-related changes following marital disruption have also been documented extensively. S/D individuals suffer from more acute and chronic illnesses than do married or single individuals (Verbrugge, 1979), and they visit physicians significantly more often than married persons do (Somers, 1979).

Psychological adjustment following marital separation typically occurs over a period of several years (Wallerstein & Kelly, 1980; Weiss, 1975), and so possible distress-related immunological changes might make S/D individuals more susceptible to illness during the first several years following separation. Therefore, certain immunological data from the S/D individuals were contrasted with data from married comparison subjects who were matched for age, sex, and socioeconomic status. Because distress following marital disruption is more pronounced within the first year after separation (Bloom, Hodges, Kern, & McFaddin, 1985), psychological and immunological data from 16 women who had been separated for 12 months or less were compared with 16 married comparison women. Table 10.1 shows the immunological data for the S/D and married women. The S/D women had significantly higher levels of antibodies to EBV VCA (viral capsid antigen) relative to those for married women, suggesting poorer cellular immune system control over the latent virus in the former group. In addition, the S/D women had significantly lower percentages of NK cells than did the married comparison subjects. Lymphocytes from S/D women had a lower proliferative response to the mitogens concanavalin A (Con A) and PHA, indicating a potential deficit in the cells' ability to respond to antigens (Kiecolt-Glaser et al., 1987a).

In addition, all the women's plasma albumin levels were assessed, because nutritional deficits can negatively affect the immune system. In all of the studies reported by Kiecolt-Glaser et al. (1987a), plasma albumin levels were within normal ranges for all subjects.

Marital satisfaction is critical to psychological well-being (Glenn & Weaver, 1981), but the simple presence of a spouse is not synonymous with a supportive relationship. In fact, a troubled marital relationship may actually place an individual at greater risk than would the absence of a partner; that is, the marital relationship may simultaneously be a source of stress and limit a person's ability to seek support in other relationships (Coyne & DeLongis, 1986). The relationship between immunological data and marital quality was examined using the Dyadic Adjustment Scale (DAS; Spanier, 1976).

Those women in the study who were more satisfied with their marital relationships had lower antibody titers to EBV VCA, as well as better proliferative responses of lymphocytes to Con A and PHA. These data therefore suggest that better marital quality is associated with better immune function.

It was also predicted that two variables would be related to poorer immune function in the S/D group, shorter separation times and greater continued attachment to the ex-husband (i.e., greater preoccupation with the ex-husband). Consistent with these hypotheses, those S/D women who were still more attached had a poorer blastogenic response than did those S/D women who were less attached to their ex-husband. In addition, women who were more attached to their ex-husband reported significantly more distress and loneliness.

Males and females may react in different ways following the disruption of a marriage, owing to economic, social, or other reasons (Albrecht, 1980; Bloom et al., 1985). Thus, in another study, psychological and immunological data were obtained from 32 S/D males and 32 matched married comparison subjects

TABLE 10.1.   Means (+/− SDs) for the 16 Women Who Were Separated 1 Year or Less and for 16 Matched Married Women

	S/D Women	Married Women
EBV VCA[a]	520.50 (706.84)	147.12 (191.88)
Percentage of Helper T-lymphocytes[a]	26.43 (7.59)	32.91 (7.03)
Percentage of Suppressor T-lymphocytes	20.01 (6.70)	22.66 (7.76)
Helper–Suppressor Ratio	1.49 (0.66)	1.69 (1.47)
Percentage of NK Cells[a]	7.50 (5.05)	12.79 (8.05)

[a]$p < .05$

Note: Also significant at .05 level:
- Interaction between group and concentration of Con A, with S/D women having poorer responses to the higher doses of Con A
- Differences between groups in response to PHA, with S/D women having a poorer proliferative response to PHA

Reprinted by permission of Elsevier Science Publishing Co., Inc. from J. K. Kiecolt-Glaser, L. D. Fisher, P. Ogrocki, J. C. Stout, C. E. Speicher, & R. Glaser, "Marital quality, marital disruption, and immune function," *Psychosomatic Medicine* (Vol. 49, pp. 13–34). Copyright 1987 by The American Psychosomatic Society, Inc.

(Kiecolt-Glaser et al., 1988). The S/D men were more distressed than were the married comparison subjects. The S/D men also reported significantly more infectious illness in the two months before the study. The two groups also differed significantly on two qualitative indices of immune function: Antibody titers to EBV VCA were two and one-half times as great for S/D men, and antibody levels to herpes simplex virus, Type-1 (HSV-1) were ten times as great in the S/D group. HSV-1, like EBV, is a herpesvirus that remains latent in infected cells and may be reactivated under certain conditions; this herpesvirus is the one that produces cold sores. Together, these data suggest that the cellular immune system was less competent in controlling herpesvirus latency in the S/D group, compared with that in the married cohort.

The data on S/D individuals are consistent with earlier work on the immunological consequences of bereavement. For example, Bartrop and his colleagues (Bartrop et al., 1977) found impaired proliferative responses by lymphocytes to mitogens in men following the death of their wives. Similarly, Stein and his associates (Schleifer, Keller, Camerino, Thornton, & Stein, 1983) reported decreases in lymphocyte responsiveness to mitogens in men whose wives had died from an extended illness, even though they had anticipated the death. Thus, even in situations of long-term distress, there appear to be significant impairments in immune function, with no apparent adaptation over time.

The data from studies of divorce and bereavement suggest collectively that marital disruption may have negative consequences for the immune system. Although it is not yet clear whether the immunological changes associated with marital disruption are actually of a magnitude to make individuals more susceptible to certain illnesses or infectious diseases, it is possible.

Moreover, these data on marital disruption are important in another context. Some data indicate that the immune system in rodents may adapt following chronic stress (i.e., Monjan & Collector, 1977). However, the stressors used in these and similar studies usually were physical stressors (e.g., noise, shock, cold). The data from these studies and the research on caregiving that we will discuss next suggest that adaptation to the emotional stressors that are more characteristic of humans may not be the same as adaptation to physical stressors.

CAREGIVING AND IMMUNE FUNCTION

Another study examined the immunological correlates of chronic distress associated with caring for a relative afflicted with Alzheimer's disease (AD; Kiecolt-Glaser et al., 1987b). AD is a progressive degenerative disease of the nervous system, characterized by severe dementia, confusion, and the need for total care. The modal time of survival for AD patients is 8 to 15 years after onset (Heston, Mastri, Anderson, & White, 1981). Caring for an AD patient is a chronic stressor, because caregivers face a host of adjustments associated with the gradual cognitive and behavioral deterioration of the loved one. In addition to the direct stresses of caregiving, social interactions may be limited because of the time demands of caregiving (George & Gwyther, 1984). Moreover, there may be financial changes associated with caring for the impaired relative.

In this regard, earlier studies showed significant alterations in the mental health of AD caregivers. For instance, George and Gwyther (1984) found much higher levels of psychiatric symptoms and lower life satisfaction in caregivers than in their community age-mates. Moreover, a substantial percentage of AD caregivers meet the criteria for clinical depression (Drinka & Smith, 1983; Eisdorfer, Kennedy, Wisnieski, & Cohen, 1983). An important question raised by these studies is that in addition to mental health consequences, caregiving experiences might also be associated with chronic changes in immunological function (Kiecolt-Glaser et al., 1987b). To assess this hypothesis, psychological questionnaires were given to 34 AD caregivers and 34 sociodemographically matched comparison subjects. Blood samples for immunological and nutritional assays were also obtained.

AD caregivers had significantly poorer immune function than did their well-matched comparison subjects. Specifically, caregivers had lower percentages of helper T-lymphocytes, lower helper–suppressor ratios, and higher antibody titers to EBV VCA. In addition, caregivers were more distressed than were comparison subjects. There were no differences in nutrition.

The caregivers had been providing care for an average of two years. There were no significant relationships between the duration of caregiving and either the immunological or the psychological indices.

Together, the data on marital disruption and caregiving provide evidence that chronic psychological distress may have significant negative effects on both quantitative and qualitative aspects of immune function. There was no evidence of adaptation to distress in the AD caregivers, despite the long-term stress of caregiving.

SELF-DISCLOSURE, IMMUNE FUNCTION, AND HEALTH

The data from studies on loneliness, marital quality, and marital disruption are consistent with the growing evidence that interpersonal relationships may have health-related consequences. Data from recent studies suggest that one facet of interpersonal relationships, self-disclosure, may be particularly important to health. The self-disclosure literature indicates that there are psychological benefits associated with sharing personal secrets, including the increased affection that results between individuals, as well as reduced feelings of isolation and loneliness (Pennebaker, 1985).

In addition, health benefits may be associated with the disclosure of traumatic events. Pennebaker and O'Heeron (1984) made contact by mail with 19 spouses who had been bereaved within the last year because of suicide or accidents. The researchers found that an increase in the illness rate from before to after the death was negatively related to talking with friends about the death. Furthermore, the increase in health problems was positively associated with thinking about the spouse's death, and the more the subjects talked with friends, the less they ruminated about their spouse's death. These health correlations remained intact after controlling for the number of close friends before and after the spouse's death. However, although these data show a correlational relationship, they do not provide evidence of the direction of the relationship. Therefore, Pennebaker and Beall (1986) designed a study to evaluate the direction of causality.

In that study, they had 46 undergraduates write for four consecutive days about either personally traumatic or trivial topics. The subjects in the "traumatic" group were asked to write about the emotions, the facts, or both the emotions and the facts associated with the traumatic event. Significantly fewer members of the group that wrote about both emotions and facts, compared with the other groups in the study, visited the health center during the several months following the study.

Based on these data, a later study investigated possible immunological correlates associated with the process of self-disclosure (Pennebaker, Kiecolt-Glaser, & Glaser, 1988). The subjects were 50 healthy undergraduates who were asked to write about either personal and traumatic events or trivial topics for four consecutive days, for 20 minutes a day. The topics that the trauma group discussed were personal and emotionally troubling, such as problems with homesickness on coming to college; loneliness; conflicts with members of the opposite sex; parental problems, including divorce, family quarrels, and family violence; death of a relative, friend, or pet; and serious injury or illness.

The immunological data were collected at the baseline (before the study began), at the end of the intervention four days later, at a six-week follow-up, and at a three-month follow-up. The immunological measures assessed the proliferative response of lymphocytes to Con A and PHA. Autonomic measures (blood pressure, heart rate, and skin conductance) were collected at the same intervals as the immunological measures.

There were no differences between the two randomly assigned groups at baseline, before the intervention began. However, significant differences began to emerge by the end of the intervention. Those subjects who wrote about traumatic events had a significantly higher mitogen response to PHA following the baseline than did those subjects who wrote about trivial events. Data from Con A, though not significant, were in the same direction as PHA. There were no differences in autonomic activity between the trauma and the trivial writing groups, and there were no changes in health-related behaviors (alcohol intake, caffeine intake, or exercise) over the course of the study.

Of particular importance were the differences between the groups in health center visits. The information concerning the students' health center visits was the average number of their visits in the preceding five months, data that were obtained from the health center with the students' permission. Mental health visits, accidents, and routine checkups were excluded. The number of visits in the preceding five months were compared with the number of visits in the six weeks between the intervention and the six-week follow-up. The trauma subjects made fewer visits following the baseline than the control subjects did. These health data replicate the earlier data from Pennebaker and Beall (1986) and thus suggest improvements in health associated with disclosing traumatic events. These health data followed much the same pattern as the immunological data did.

The data on the trauma group were analyzed further. High disclosers—those who reported that they had written about topics they had previously held back— were compared with low disclosers—those who reported they had written about topics they had previously discussed with other individuals. High disclosers had a better mitogen response following the baseline than did low disclosers. In addition, from the beginning of the study to the follow-up, high disclosers showed a greater decline than did low disclosers in both systolic and diastolic blood pressure. Similar nonsignificant trends were noted for heart rate and skin conductance.

Thus, it appears that self-disclosure was associated with better immune function and health. Moreover, those individuals who reported that they had written about topics they had previously held back appeared to benefit the most.

HEALTH IMPLICATIONS

The studies that we described in this chapter suggest that close relationships have immunological correlates and that the quality of the relationship is important. For example, the data on marital quality demonstrate that the simple presence of a partner is not necessarily an asset. Similarly, Pennebaker's research on self-disclosure highlights the importance of a confidant who will listen without judging or withdrawing love and support.

Although many of the physiological pathways are unclear, a prospective study by Levenson and Gottman (1985) provided evidence of a mechanism through which chronically abrasive relationships like poor marriages might affect immunity. In their longitudinal study they showed that greater autonomic arousal in interacting married couples was a very strong predictor of subsequent declines in marital quality. In addition, poorer health ratings at a three-year follow-up were also strongly correlated with greater declines in marital satisfaction.

If a partner's mere presence in a disturbed relationship is conducive to persistent physiological arousal, as can be inferred from Levenson and Gottman's data, then there may be concurrent endocrinological alterations (Baum, Grunberg, & Singer, 1982) that could contribute to the relationships observed between marital quality and immunity. The endocrine system is quite responsive to a variety of emotional states (Baum et al., 1982), and there is convincing evidence of endocrinological and neuroendocrinological modulation of immune function (Ader, 1981).

Although we discussed a number of studies that relate distressing psychological responses and immunological changes, we should emphasize that the actual health consequences are not well established. Only a few studies showed a confluence among distressing psychological responses, immunological down-regulation, and actual health changes (Glaser et al., 1987; Kasl et al., 1979;

Kiecolt-Glaser et al., 1988; Pennebaker et al., 1988). It is likely that psychologically mediated immunological changes have a limited impact on healthy young individuals.

In theory, those individuals who are most likely to be at risk for organically based illness are already immunocompromised, such as AIDS patients, or are elderly, who have less efficient immune systems owing to the aging process (Kiecolt-Glaser & Glaser, in press-b).

One of the factors that has fueled interest in behavioral immunology in recent years is the AIDS epidemic (Kiecolt-Glaser & Glaser, in press-b). It is clear that there is very wide variability among individuals at all stages of HIV infection. Not all individuals who are exposed to HIV during high-risk activities will actually become infected with the virus; and of those who do become infected with HIV, many will remain latently infected with no clinical symptoms for years. It is known that poor nutrition, drug use, repeated HIV exposure, and other concurrent viral infections all can enhance HIV disease progression. There is still considerable variability, however, in addition to these factors. Several laboratories are currently addressing the possibility of psychological influence on HIV progression.

Clearly, longitudinal studies are needed that follow "at risk" populations over long periods of time. Such studies will provide a better understanding of the kinetics of distress-related immunological changes and the role of interpersonal relationships in mediating these changes.

REFERENCES

Ader, R. (1981). *Psychoneuroimmunology*. New York: Academic Press.

Albrecht, S. L. (1980). Reactions and adjustments to divorce: Differences in the experiences of males and females. *Family Relations, 29*, 59–68.

Bartrop, R. W., Luckhurst, E., Lazarus, L., Kiloh, L. G., & Penny, R. (1977). Depressed lymphocyte function after bereavement. *Lancet, 1*, 834–836.

Baum, A., Grunberg, N. E., & Singer, J. E. (1982). The use of psychological and neuroendocrinological measurements in the study of stress. *Health Psychology, 1*, 217–236.

Blazer, D. (1982). Social support and mortality in an elderly community population. *American Journal of Epidemiology, 115*, 684–694.

Bloom, B. L., Asher, S. J., & White, S. W. (1978). Marital disruption as a stressor: A review and analysis. *Psychological Bulletin, 85*, 867–894.

Bloom, B. L., Hodges, W. F., Kern, M. B., & McFaddin, S. C. (1985). A preventive intervention program for the newly separated: Final evaluations. *American Journal of Orthopsychiatry, 55*, 9–26.

Blumenthal, M. D. (1967). Mental health among the divorced: A field study of divorced and never divorced persons. *Archives of General Psychiatry, 16*, 603–608.

Coe, C. L., Wiener, S. G., Rosenberg, L. T., & Levine, S. (1985). Endocrine and immune responses to separation and maternal loss in nonhuman primates. In M. Reite &

T. Field (Eds.), *The psychobiology of attachment and separation.* (pp. 163–199). Orlando, FL: Academic Press.

Cohen, C. I., Teresi, J., & Holmes, D. (1985). Social networks, stress, and physical health: A longitudinal study of an inner-city elderly population. *Journal of Gerontology, 40,* 478–486.

Coyne, J. C., & DeLongis, A. (1986). Going beyond social support: The role of social relationships in adaptation. *Journal of Consulting and Clinical Psychology, 54,* 454–460.

Drinka, T., & Smith, J. (1983). Depression in caregivers of demented patients. *The Gerontologist, 23,* 116.

Eisdorfer, C., Kennedy, G., Wisnieski, W., & Cohen, C. (1983). Depression and attributional style in families coping with the stress of caring for a relative with Alzheimer's disease. *The Gerontologist, 23,* 115–116.

George, L. K., & Gwyther, L. P. (1984). *The dynamics of caregiver burden: Changes in caregiver well-being over time.* Paper presented at the annual meeting of the Gerontological Society of America, San Antonio.

Glaser, R., Kiecolt-Glaser, J. K., Speicher, C. E., & Holliday, J. E. (1985a). Stress, loneliness, and changes in herpesvirus latency. *Journal of Behavioral Medicine, 8,* 249–260.

Glaser, R., Kiecolt-Glaser, J. K., Stout, J. C., Tarr, K. L., Speicher, C. E., & Holliday, J. E. (1985b). Stress related impairments in cellular immunity. *Psychiatric Research, 16,* 233–239.

Glaser, R., Rice, J., Sheridan, J., Fertel, R., Stout, J., Speicher, C. E., Pinsky, D., Kotur, M., Post, A., Beck, H., & Kiecolt-Glaser, J. K. (1987). Stress-related immune suppression: Health implications. *Brain, Behavior, and Immunity, 1,* 7–20.

Glenn, N. D., & Weaver, C. N. (1981). The contribution of marital happiness to global happiness. *Journal of Marriage and Family, 43,* 161–168.

Herberman, R. B. (1982). Possible effects of central nervous system on natural killer (NK) cell activity. In S. M. Levy (Ed.), *Biological mediators of health and disease: Neoplasia* (pp. 235–248). New York: Elsevier.

Heston, L. L., Mastri, A. R., Anderson, V. E., & White, G. (1981). Dementia of the Alzheimer type. *Archives of General Psychiatry, 38,* 1085–1091.

Jones, W. H., Freemon, J. A., & Goswick, R. A. (1981). The persistence of loneliness: Self and other determinants. *Journal of Personality, 49,* 27–48.

Kasl, S. V., Evans, A. S., & Neiderman, J. C. (1979). Psychosocial risk factors in the development of infectious mononucleosis. *Psychosomatic Medicine, 41,* 445–466.

Kiecolt-Glaser, J. K., Fisher, L., Ogrocki, P., Stout, J. C., Speicher, C. E., & Glaser, R. (1987a). Marital quality, marital disruption, and immune function. *Psychosomatic Medicine, 49,* 13–34.

Kiecolt-Glaser, J. K., Garner, W., Speicher, C. E., Penn, G., & Glaser, R. (1984a). Psychosocial modifiers of immunocompetence in medical students. *Psychosomatic Medicine, 46,* 7–14.

Kiecolt-Glaser, J. K., & Glaser, R. (in press-a). Methodological issues in behavioral immunology research with humans. *Brain, Behavior and Immunity.*

Kiecolt-Glaser, J. K., & Glaser, R. (in press-b). Psychological influences on immunity: Implications for AIDS. *American Psychologist.*

Kiecolt-Glaser, J. K., Glaser, R., Shuttleworth, E. C., Dyer, C. S., Ogrocki, P., & Speicher, C. E. (1987b). Chronic stress and immunity in family caregivers of Alzheimer's disease victims. *Psychosomatic Medicine, 49,* 523–535.

Kiecolt-Glaser, J. K., Kennedy, S., Malkoff, S., Fisher, L., Speicher, C. E., & Glaser, R. (1988). Marital discord and immunity in males. *Psychosomatic Medicine, 50,* 213–229.

Kiecolt-Glaser, J. K., Ricker, D., Messick, G., Speicher, C. E., Garner, W., & Glaser, R. (1984b). Urinary cortisol, cellular immunocompetency and loneliness in psychiatric inpatients. *Psychosomatic Medicine, 46,* 15–24.

Kimzey, S. L. (1975). The effects of extended spaceflight on hematologic and immunologic systems. *Journal of the American Medical Women's Association, 30,* 218–232.

Levenson, R. W., & Gottman, J. M. (1985). Physiological and affective predictors of change in relationship satisfaction. *Journal of Personality and Social Psychology, 49,* 85–94.

Monjan, A. A., & Collector, M. I. (1977). Stress induced modulation of the immune response. *Science, 196,* 307–308.

Palmblad, J., Bjorn, P., Wasserman, J., & Akerstedt, T. (1979). Lymphocyte and granulocyte reactions during sleep deprivation. *Psychosomatic Medicine, 41,* 273–278.

Pennebaker, J. W. (1985). Traumatic experience and psychosomatic disease: Exploring the roles of behavioral inhibition, obsession, and confiding. *Canadian Psychology, 26,* 82–95.

Pennebaker, J. W., & Beall, S. (1986). Confronting a traumatic event: Toward an understanding of inhibition and disease. *Journal of Abnormal Psychology, 95,* 274–281.

Pennebaker, J. W., Kiecolt-Glaser, J. K., & Glaser, R. (1988). Disclosures of traumas and immune function: Health implications for psychotherapy. *Journal of Consulting and Clinical Psychology, 56,* 239–245.

Pennebaker, J. W., & O'Heeron, R. C. (1984). Confiding in others and illness rate among spouses of suicide and accidental death victims. *Journal of Abnormal Psychology, 93,* 473–476.

Peplau, L. A., & Perlman, D. (Eds.). (1982). *Loneliness: A source book of current theory, research, and therapy.* New York: Wiley.

Reite, M., Harbeck, R., & Hoffman, A. (1981). Altered cellular immune response following peer separation. *Life Science, 29,* 1133–1136.

Russell, D. (1982). The measurement of loneliness. In L. A. Peplau & D. Perlman (Eds.), *Loneliness: A source book of current theory, research, and therapy* (pp. 81–104). New York: Wiley.

Schleifer, S. J., Keller, S. E., Camerino, M., Thornton, J. C., & Stein, M. (1983). Suppression of lymphocyte stimulation following bereavement. *Journal of the American Medical Association, 250,* 374–377.

Schleifer, S. J., Keller, S. E., Meyerson, A. T., Raskin, M. J., Davis, K. L., & Stein, M. (1984). Lymphocyte function in major depressive disorder. *Archives of General Psychiatry, 41,* 484–486.

Somers, A. R. (1979). Marital status, health, and use of health services. *Journal of the American Medical Association, 241,* 1818–1822.

Spanier, G. B. (1976). Measuring dyadic adjustment: New scales for assessing the quality of marriage and similar dyads. *Journal of Marriage & Family, 38,* 15–28.

Stein, M., Keller, S. E., & Schleifer, S. J. (1985). Stress and immunomodulation: The role of depression and neuroendocrine function. *Journal of Immunology, 135* (2, supplement), 827s.

Stone, A. A., Cox, D. S., Valdimarsdottir, H., & Neale, J. M. (1987). Secretory IgA as a measure of immunocompetence. *Journal of Human Stress, 13,* 136–140.

Verbrugge, L. M. (1979). Marital status and health. *Journal of Marriage and Family, 41,* 267–285.

Wallerstein, J. S., & Kelly, J. B. (1980). *Surviving the breakup: How children and parents cope with divorce.* New York: Basic Books.

Weiss, R. S. (1975). *Marital separation.* New York: Basic Books.

CHAPTER 11

Differentiating the Cognitive and Behavioral Aspects of Social Support

CHRISTINE DUNKEL-SCHETTER AND TRACY L. BENNETT
University of California at Los Angeles

The measurement of social support has been characterized as being in a "fairly primitive" state (House & Kahn, 1985). In part, this may be due to the lack of conceptual clarity regarding what social support is, its components, and the process by which it benefits an individual's psychosocial and physical well-being. Turner (1983) provided some conceptual clarification when he separated *social integration* and *social network* properties from *social support*. House and Kahn (1985) also distinguished these aspects but referred to them as the *existence, structure,* and *functions* of social relationships. They suggested that the term *social support* be reserved for the functions of social interactions and relations.

A further distinction is made by many researchers with regard to the functional aspects of social relationships, namely, that between available support and received support (e.g., Barrera, 1986; Gottlieb, 1985; Sarason, Shearin, Pierce, & Sarason, 1987; Wethington & Kessler, 1986). Available support refers to the perception of support believed to be available if needed. It has been argued that it is this perception of availability of support that is health protective and that the accuracy of the perception may not necessarily be pertinent. Therefore, many past conceptions of the functional aspects of social relationships have emphasized available social support (cf. Barrera, 1981). We believe, however, that there are important implications of the distinction between support that is perceived to be available and support that is actually received and that the issues are worthy of further investigation.

This chapter will focus on the difference between available support and support that is received. We begin by illustrating the difference in three ways: (1) how various researchers refer to each concept, (2) measurement approaches to each, and (3) empirical relationships between measures of available and received support. Second, we discuss why the concepts of available support and received support are largely unrelated. That is, what accounts for the discrepancies between resources that one believes to be available and actual support exchanges? Why might people tend to estimate inaccurately the support available to them?

Next we examine the implications of this distinction for understanding the observed health-protective effects of social support. Is available support or received support more health protective? Or is each health protective under certain conditions? Finally, we suggest directions for future research on social support.

Figure 11.1 summarizes the framework in which we are working. It depicts the distinctions among social integration, social networks, and social support and shows how social support is further characterized by whether it is available or is activated in particular interpersonal transactions. Defining social support as interpersonal transactions is not new (Kahn & Antonucci, 1980), but this conceptualization has been of increasing interest as the area of research has evolved (Shinn, Lehmann, & Wong, 1984; Shumaker & Brownell, 1984). Figure 11.1 also shows that when considering supportive transactions (i.e., social support that is activated rather than merely available), differences emerge among people in their need or desire for social support in particular situations, the extent to which they seek support, and the actual receipt of specific types of support and from particular persons. In addition, the adequacy of both received support and available support can be evaluated. Either subjects indicate their degree of satisfaction with

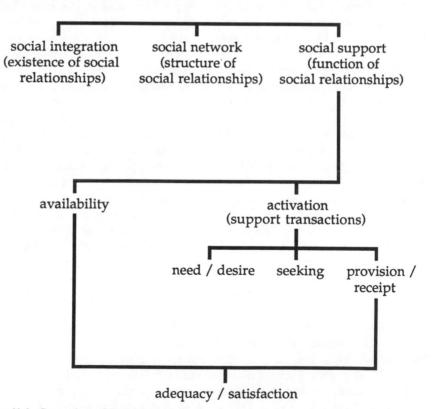

Figure 11.1. Conceptions of Social Support
Note: An orthogonal factor regarding those shown is whether the method of assessment is self-report or observer report.

what they receive (e.g., Dunkel-Schetter, Feinstein, & Call, 1987) or their satisfaction with what they perceive to be available (e.g., Sarason, Levine, Basham, & Sarason, 1983).

Thus, examining support activation leads to a more differentiated view of various aspects of interpersonal processes. This view is advantageous, as many authorities in this area have emphasized both the importance of exploring the processes underlying social support phenomena (Cohen & Syme, 1985; Heller, Swindle, & Dusenbury, 1986; Wortman, 1984) and integrating support research with research on interpersonal relations. The primary distinction of interest in this chapter, however, is that between the availability of support and support that is received.

THE DISTINCTION BETWEEN AVAILABLE
AND RECEIVED SUPPORT

Terminology

Although the terminology used differs, researchers working on social support have already highlighted the distinction between available and received support. Table 11.1 contains some of the different terms used to label the distinction between available and received social support. Available support is generally referred to as "perceived support" or "perceived available support." As can be seen in Table 11.1, however, received support has many names. In addition, the terms referring to received support carry slightly different connotations. For example, *administered support* reflects the provider's perspective, whereas *received support* concerns the recipient's view. But despite the differing terminology, all of the researchers are referring to support taking place in interpersonal transactions or exchanges. Such exchanges may include both nonverbal and verbal behaviors.

TABLE 11.1.   References to the Distinction Between Available and Received Support

	Available Support	Received Support
Barrera, 1986	perceived available support	enacted support
Cohen, Mermelstein, Kamarck, & Hoberman, 1985	perceived support	objective support
Gottlieb, 1985	psychological/perceived support	experienced/actual support
Heller, Swindle, & Dusenbury, 1986	perceived support	stress-related interpersonal transactions
Sarason, Shearin, Pierce, & Sarason, 1987	perceived available support	administered support
Tardy, 1985	available support	enacted support
Wethington & Kessler, 1986	perceived available support	received support

Measurement Approaches

Not surprisingly, different measures of support are generated depending on whether one attempts to operationalize available support or received support. Tables 11.2 and 11.3 give sample items from inventories designed to measure each. Only emotional support items are shown to simplify the comparison. In Table 11.2, the example items are from three of the most popular instruments used to measure available social support: the Interpersonal Support Evaluation List (ISEL; Cohen, Mermelstein, Kamarck, & Hoberman, 1985), the Perceived Support Scales for Family and Friends (PSS-Fa, PSS-Fr; Procidano & Heller, 1983), and the Social Support Questionnaire (SSQ; Sarason et al., 1983). These three instruments are similar in many respects, are highly correlated with one another, and appear to be measuring a common construct (Sarason et al., 1987).

The ISEL (general population version) is a 40-item scale with "probably true"/"probably false" response options. It yields four subscale scores (appraisal, belonging, tangible, and self-esteem) and a total score representing the perceived availability of potential social resources. Both the PSS-Fr and PSS-Fa are 20-item inventories with yes/no/don't know response options. These two instruments are intended to measure the extent to which family and friends fulfill an individual's need for support, information, and feedback. Each of the scales yields a total score that represents the amount of support perceived as available from one or two specific categories of network members (i.e., family or friends).

The SSQ, though highly correlated with the ISEL and PSS scales, has quite different response options. Each item requests the identification of the number of people that one "can count on" for a particular type of support, in addition to a global rating of satisfaction with the availability of each supportive behavior. Thus, the SSQ yields at least two scores: the average number of available support providers, and the average level of satisfaction with the amount of available sup-

TABLE 11.2. **Example Items for Available Emotional Support**

ISEL (Cohen, Mermelstein, Kamarck, & Hoberman, 1985)

1. There is no one that I feel comfortable talking to about intimate personal problems. (negatively keyed)
2. When I feel lonely, there are several people I can talk to.

PSS-FR & PSS-FA (Procidano & Heller, 1983)

1. There is a member of my family I could go to if I were just feeling down, without feeling funny about it later.
2. When I confide in friends, it makes me feel uncomfortable. (negatively keyed)

SSQ (Sarason, Levine, Basham, & Sarason, 1983)

1. Whom can you really count on to listen to you when you need to talk?
2. Whom can you count on to console you when you are very upset?

TABLE 11.3.   Example Items for Received Emotional Support

ISSB (Barrera, 1981)

During the past four weeks, how often did other people do these activities for you, to you, or with you?
1. Listened to you talk about your private feelings.
2. Told you that he/she feels very close to you.

ASSIS (Barrera, 1981)

Respondents are first asked:
"If you wanted to talk to someone about things that are very personal and private, who would you talk to?"
Then the following question is asked:
"During the last month, which of these people did you actually talk to about things that were personal and private?"

Stress Questionnaire (Dunkel-Schetter, Folkman, & Lazarus, 1987)

Respondents select a stressful episode in the past month.
Then they identify which of several possible persons provided assistance in the situation and are asked:
"In this situation, how much did each of these persons make you feel he or she cared about you?"

UCLA-SSI (Dunkel-Schetter, Feinstein, & Call, 1987)

1. At certain times, we want someone to listen to our concerns and feelings. How often did your (parent, friend, partner) listen to you within the past three months?
2. At certain times, we want someone to do more than listen to us. We want them to understand our situation and empathize with our feelings. How often did your (parent, friend, partner) understand and empathize with you within the past three months?

Chronic Childhood Illness Support Scale (Bennett, Gottlieb, & Cadman, 1987)

One or more people in my social circle:
1. gives me chances to open up about my most private feelings and concerns about my child.
2. shows understanding of what it's like for me to raise a child who has a medical condition.

port. Note that the number of available support providers is more akin to measures of social network size than to measures of functional support.

Table 11.3 presents various approaches to the measurement of received support. As can be seen, there is much more variation among these approaches than in the measures of available support. The most widely used instrument is the Inventory of Socially Supportive Behaviors (ISSB) developed by Barrera (Barrera, 1981; Barrera & Ainlay, 1983; Barrera, Sandler, & Ramsay, 1981; Sandler & Barrera, 1984) and validated with pregnant adolescents and college students. The ISSB consists of 40 specific supportive behaviors that represent four types of support: emotional, tangible, cognitive-informational, and directive guidance. Respondents are asked to indicate on a five-point scale (from "not at all" to "about every day") how often during the past four weeks each supportive behavior occurred. Therefore, an individual's scale score represents the average frequency of receipt of these particular supportive behaviors.

Another instrument developed by Barrera (1981), called the ASSIS (Arizona Social Support Interview Schedule), is also represented in Table 11.3. It begins by determining the numbers of people available for each of six types of social interactions (confiding, material aid, advice, positive feedback, physical assistance, and social participation). In this respect the ASSIS is similar to the SSQ index of the number of available support providers. However, to index the support received, subjects are also asked in the ASSIS how many of these people actually provided each function in the past month.

Another approach to measuring the receipt of emotional support is the Stress Questionnaire developed for research by Lazarus and colleagues (Dunkel-Schetter, Folkman, & Lazarus, 1987; Folkman, Lazarus, Dunkel-Schetter, De-Longis, & Gruen, 1986; Folkman, Lazarus, Gruen, & DeLongis, 1986). This questionnaire is unique in that it contains items on social support received in the context of specific stressful episodes (Dunkel-Schetter, Folkman, & Lazarus, 1987). Specifically, respondents are asked to identify a stressful episode occurring in the previous month. With respect to that episode, individuals then identify those persons who supplied each of three types of support (information, aid, and emotional support).

Another instrument that assesses received social support was developed by Dunkel-Schetter and her colleagues (UCLA–SSI; Dunkel-Schetter, Feinstein, & Call, 1987). The UCLA–SSI measures the receipt of three types of support (information/advice, aid/assistance, and emotional) from three particular persons. For undergraduate students, the sources of support have been specified as a parent, a friend, and a romantic partner (if one exists). However, the three sources about whom the subjects answer are a flexible aspect of this instrument. In the case of coping with cancer, for example, one may wish to inquire about support from a partner, a friend, and the primary physician.

Still another approach to measuring received support is that taken by Bennett, Gottlieb, and Cadman (CCISS; 1987). Unlike the other scales, this instrument was designed to measure social support received within a particular population— the primary caregivers of children with a chronic illness. The items are designed to determine the occurrence of four types of supportive behaviors (emotional, appraisal, instrumental, and informational; House, 1981) that might be provided either specifically to help caregivers cope with their chronically ill child or in the context of more general everyday concerns. Further, information regarding the most valued provider of each supportive behavior is solicited.

The ASSIS, UCLA–SSI, and the CCISS assess not only the support received but also the respondents' desire or need for support and their satisfaction with it (although each approach is somewhat different). The UCLA–SSI and the Stress Questionnaire also determine whether the support was sought by the subjects or volunteered by the providers.

Other self-report approaches to assessing received support besides those discussed have also been devised (Aneshensel & Frerichs, 1982; Antonucci & Israel,

1986; Carveth & Gottlieb, 1979; Eckenrode, 1983) but in the interest of brevity, we will not describe them here. In addition, descriptive work on social support receipt has accumulated that documents the types of interactions that various victim groups spontaneously report as helpful (Dakof & Taylor, 1988; Dunkel-Schetter, 1984; Gottlieb, 1978; Lehman, Ellard, & Wortman, 1986). Respondents' reports are then coded to indicate the specific types of support naturally occurring. For example, Dunkel-Schetter (1984) found instances of emotional support to be the most frequently reported type of effective support among cancer patients.

Validity of the Distinction Between Available and Received Support

Given both the conceptual distinction between available and received support and the differences in measures of these constructs, it seems reasonable to expect empirical support for the distinction. Table 11.4 shows some of the available evidence regarding the correlation between measures of available and received support. The studies vary in the particular approaches used to measure each of the two concepts and in the magnitude of the correlations they reported. For example, Cohen, McGowan, Fooskas, and Rose (1984), in a study using college students to investigate the role of positive life events and support as stress buffers, found a correlation of .46 between the ISSB and the ISEL (college student version), measures of received and available support, respectively. Another study (Wethington & Kessler, 1986) analyzed data from a 1976 national survey of adults aged 21 years or older (Veroff, Kulka, & Douvan, 1981). This study used nonstandardized measures of available and received support and found a correlation of .10 between the two.

The other studies in Table 11.4 used a variety of samples, including pregnant adolescents, parents whose child is chronically ill, and college students, and they employed a variety of measures of available support. Six of the eight studies, however, used the ISSB as their measure of received support. Overall, the correlations between available and received support ranged from no relationship to a moderate association ($r = .46$). None of the studies reported more than 21% shared variance between measures of these two aspects of support. In addition to

TABLE 11.4.   Correlations Between Available and Received Support in Past Research

	r	R squared
Barrera, 1981	−.13	.0170
Bennett, Gottlieb, & Cadman, 1987[a]	.27	.0730
L. Cohen, McGowan, Fooskas, & Rose, 1984	.46	.2120
S. Cohen & Hoberman, 1983	.46	.2120
Sandler & Barrera, 1984	.01	.0001
Sarason, Shearin, Pierce, & Sarason, 1987	.24	.0576
Valdenegro & Barrera, 1983	.02	.0004
Wethington & Kessler, 1986[a]	.10	.0100

[a]All but these studies used the ISSB (Barrera, 1981) to assess received support.

the correlations reported in Table 11.4, Newcomb (this volume) also examined the relationship between available and received support. He reanalyzed the data reported by B. Sarason et al. (1987) and tested a model that included two latent factors (i.e., available and received support), using structural equation modeling techniques. The results indicated strong support for the existence of two latent constructs representing available and received support, as well as evidence of a moderate degree of overlap between them.

In contrast with the studies that use self-report inventories of both available support and received support to examine their interrelationships, a few studies have looked at the relationship between inventories of available support and support provision in interpersonal transactions. For example, Cutrona (1986) considered the relationship between received support and available support among 41 undergraduates who completed daily diaries for 14 days regarding their social support interactions. The interactions were scored for the frequency of six specific helping behaviors, and each was predicted using multiple regression by scores on a measure of available social support (Social Provisions Scale; Cutrona & Russell, 1987; Russell & Cutrona, 1984). Using stringent statistical criteria, the results suggested that the students' perceptions of available support predicted one of the six helping behaviors, but only on days when at least one stressful event was reported. Nonsignificant trends in the data indicated that perceptions of available support were related to four of the other five helping behaviors. Thus, Cutrona's study (1986) suggested that perceptions of available support bear some relationship to reports of the actual behavioral support received in everyday contexts, but the relationship was not a very clear or strong one.

Lakey and Heller (1988) also examined the extent to which questionnaire measures of perceived available support were linked to actual support behaviors. Dyads were brought into the laboratory, completed several scales (including the PSS-Fr; Procidano & Heller, 1983), and then were observed for 10 minutes while they awaited a social problem–solving task. These 10-minute transactions were later content-analyzed for supportive as well as task-relevant exchanges. The results showed that the provision of supportive behaviors (e.g., offering advice, offering solutions) was not correlated with scores on an available support questionnaire (the PSS-Fr). No significant relationships between perceived support from friends and actual support provided in this laboratory context were found (see also Heller & Lakey, 1985, for further research of this type).

Summary

In sum, the distinction between available support and support that is received seems sound. A conceptual distinction between these constructs has been made by many researchers, operationalizations have differed, and correlations between self-report measures of available and received support suggest only a weak association between the two. Moreover, studies linking perceptions of available support to actual support behaviors have addressed the problem in a variety of ways, and again, find nonexistent (Lakey & Heller, 1988) or weak (Cutrona, 1986) relationships between the two. The next question we would like to address concerns the reason for the discrepancy between social support that is available and support that is received.

POSSIBLE EXPLANATIONS OF THE DISCREPANCY BETWEEN AVAILABLE AND RECEIVED SUPPORT

From a theoretical standpoint, perceptions of the availability of support would not be expected to be especially accurate. There are two likely sorts of inaccuracies. One sort is in judgments regarding the amounts of support expected. An individual may either believe that there is more support available than actually materializes in a time of stress, or more support may materialize than was perceived as available. In addition, though initial levels of support may meet expectations, there may be an unexpected decline over time in the extent of support received. Another sort of inaccuracy pertains to the quality of support. An individual may believe that close relations and friends are available to provide skillful support when in fact the support received is disappointingly inept and unhelpful. Past research suggests that these possibilities are worth exploring further. In the next section, we consider the conditions under which support may not be forthcoming as expected by people who are experiencing distress.

When Expectations of Support Are Too High: The Victimization Perspective

People who have a strong social network have reason to believe that support will be forthcoming if they need it, and in many circumstances their perceptions that support is available are probably correct. However, past research suggests that there are conditions where this does not occur, and these may be precisely the conditions under which support is most needed and desired. During major life crises or chronic stressful conditions, support is not always as abundant as people believed it would be, nor is it necessarily as highly skilled. Some of this may be due to a lack of available social network relationships. However, Wortman and her colleagues (Coates & Wortman, 1980; Coates, Wortman, & Abbey, 1979; Coyne, Wortman, & Lehman, 1988; Dunkel-Schetter & Wortman, 1982; Wortman & Lehman, 1985) theorized, in what has been called the "victimization perspective," that when major negative life events occur (such as the death of a loved one, a life-threatening illness, permanent paralysis, or a sexual assault), social networks may not always be responsive. Close relations and friends may have difficulty providing effective support under stressful conditions. Network members themselves may feel threatened by the event or uncertain about how best to help. In addition, stressful events often elicit emotional reactions in social network members, such as fear, discomfort, guilt, frustration, helplessness, and embarrassment. For potential support providers, these emotions can make it very difficult to extend effective support (Coates & Wortman, 1980; Dunkel-Schetter & Wortman, 1982; Wortman & Lehman, 1985).

In addition to the negative feelings engendered, support providers may be unable to extend effective or skillful support because they hold misconceptions about the coping process. A variety of beliefs about the effects of a life event will influence the support proffered. If such beliefs are incorrect, any support provided is not likely to be particularly effective (Silver & Wortman, 1980; Wortman & Lehman, 1985). For example, a commonly held belief is that it is better for victims to be cheerful and optimistic about their circumstances than to focus on and discuss negative aspects. Further, if victims do discuss their negative experiences and feelings, they are much more likely to encounter rejection from support providers (Coates et al., 1979). Therefore, misconceptions about victims' needs can lead to very unsupportive results (Dunkel-Schetter & Wortman, 1982; Peters-Golden, 1982; Silver & Wortman, 1980).

The victim may also be derogated or blamed. Lerner and colleagues (1970, 1971; Lerner, Miller, & Holmes, 1976) argued that people are motivated to believe in a "just world" in which people "get what they deserve and deserve what they get." If we can believe that people do not suffer unless something is wrong with them or their behavior, we will feel protected from undeserved suffering ourselves (Lerner, 1970, 1971; Lerner & Simmons, 1966; Walster, 1966). Although there is little documentation of the preconditions for this effect, derogation toward and blaming of victims may be most prevalent among strangers and acquaintances.

The combination of negative feelings and emotions, misconceptions about the coping process, and derogation can lead support providers to be negative or inconsistent in their behavioral reactions, which in turn may be unintentionally harmful to victims. Negative behavioral reactions may include nonverbal and verbal forms of rejection, physical avoidance, blocking of open communication, harmful attempts to influence coping or adjustment, inept support attempts, and blaming the victim (Dunkel-Schetter & Wortman, 1982; Silver & Wortman, 1980; Wortman & Lehman, 1985). Although effective support may also be offered, such negative responses may confuse or upset the distressed person. In response, some victims may devise strategies to increase the support or attention received from others, such as exaggerating their difficulties or, alternatively, presenting themselves as exceptionally good copers (Coyne et al., 1988; Dunkel-Schetter & Wortman, 1982). Unfortunately, when victims use these self-presentational strategies, it sends inaccurate messages to support providers, which may further compromise an already strained interpersonal situation.

Support for the victimization perspective comes from review articles that examine the evidence across many different types of life events or victimization (Silver & Wortman, 1980; Wortman & Lehman, 1985), as well as reviews of the literature regarding specific life events such as cancer (Dunkel-Schetter & Wortman, 1982; Wortman & Dunkel-Schetter, 1979), depression (Coates & Wortman, 1980; Coyne, 1976b), and major disasters (Solomon, 1986). Solomon (1986), for example, wrote that "social networks are not always supportive. . . . Behaviors intended to be supportive often fail. Furthermore, disaster may be disruptive of social networks and the loss of support may be a source of stress in itself" (p. 240).

In addition to these reviews, there are an increasing number of empirical investigations that are pertinent to this perspective (Coates et al., 1979; Coyne, 1976a; Dakof & Taylor, 1988; Dunkel-Schetter, 1984; Jung, 1988; Lehman et al., 1986; Lichtman, 1982; O'Brien, 1980; Peters-Golden, 1982; Silver, Wortman, & Crofton, this volume). Studies by Coyne (1976a) and Coates et al. (1979), for example, have demonstrated that the depressive symptomatology often exhibited by victims elicits avoidance and rejection. Thus, network members may have difficulty extending effective support to victims who are depressed.

Two empirical studies (Lehman et al., 1986; Peters-Golden, 1982) investigated support and social victimization from the perspective of both recipients and providers. Lehman et al. (1986) reported that the majority of the 94 bereaved individuals whom they interviewed had experienced a variety of unsupportive reactions. However, in a separate sample of nonvictims who were asked hypothetically what they would do for someone who was bereaved, little evidence was found of misconceptions about what is helpful to or supportive of bereaved persons. The authors speculated that support providers may be unsupportive because of negative feelings (especially anxiety) aroused during a face-to-face interaction with someone who has recently been bereaved.

Peters-Golden (1982) conducted a study that most clearly demonstrated the discrepancy between support believed to be available and support actually received. She investigated breast cancer patients' experiences and the perspectives of healthy adults about the social support they would expect if they were diagnosed with cancer. The healthy subjects believed that in general, a dense social network (composed of family, friends, and professionals) would supply an abundance of helpful support following the diagnosis of cancer. In addition, these subjects did not feel it likely that others would avoid them if they had cancer. The cancer patients, however, reported that the expected support never materialized and that much of the support they did receive was perceived as inappropriate. Further, a full third of the cancer patients reported receiving no support whatsoever. Thus, it appears that healthy individuals greatly overestimate the support they would receive if they experienced a negative life event such as a diagnosis of cancer.

Although there are an increasing number of studies pertinent to the victimization perspective, few studies focus on it directly. Therefore, the prevalence of negative feelings, derogation, and negative behavioral reactions among network members of different victimized or distressed populations remains to be documented. Further, very few studies have explored the factors that mediate the prevalence of negative reactions or lack of support. These studies are especially difficult to conduct well because of the many methodological pitfalls involved. For example, sampling bias is often introduced because those people with the most severe conditions cannot participate in interviews or complete questionnaires. Reporting biases are also likely because it is difficult for support providers to acknowledge their own socially undesirable and unsupportive behavior, and for victims to acknowledge dissatisfaction with people on whom they depend. Finally, measurement error is difficult to minimize because we do not have much expertise in the assessment of such factors as rejection, lack of validation, misconceptions about coping, etc. All of these problems tend to result in underestimating the prevalence of social victimization. Knowing the support providers' beliefs and intentions, their actual behaviors, and the recipients' perceptions of support attempts in various contexts (e.g., chronic illness, bereavement) would enhance our understanding of the victimization perspective.

When Initial Support Dissipates

It is also possible in the case of some stressful circumstances that the initial received support will be as expected but that it will either dissipate or decrease in quality over time. The victimization perspective, describing how undesirable events may engender negative feelings and reactions among potential support providers, tends to gloss over the fact that the network members' initial reaction may be to be attentive and helpful. Indeed, initial efforts are likely to be quite skillful and beneficial because support providers may try hard at first to help effectively. Their patience and energy have also not yet been depleted. However, several things may subsequently occur.

First, casual support providers may quickly tire of exerting effort and soon lapse into careless and less frequent support attempts. This is less likely for close relations and friends. But over time, even these close network members may come to feel burdened and overwhelmed by the distressed person's extensive, continuing needs for support, and this might result in their eventual withdrawal. This is most thoroughly documented in research on burnout among professional caregivers. Burnout is emotional exhaustion that occurs when professional support providers are overextended and overwhelmed by the magnitude and complexity of the problems confronting them (Maslach, 1976, 1978). Over time, burnout may lead to physical or psychological withdrawal (e.g., avoidance, detachment). Informal support providers who must extend support over time may feel similar effects.

A second possibility is that support providers may exhaust their full range of helping behaviors before the victim noticeably recovers (Dunkel-Schetter & Wortman, 1981, 1982; Wortman & Dunkel-Schetter, 1979). A few unsuccessful support attempts may illustrate to providers that they do not know what helps, which can lead to feelings of helplessness and frustration. Thus, support providers who are not rewarded by signs of appreciation and improvement may stop trying to help. There is evidence that people feel more positive about helping others when they believe that such help is leading to tangible improvements in the recipient's situation (see Brickman et al., 1982, for a review), but when there are no noticeable changes, efforts to help may be frustrating and upsetting.

In one study that investigated the social environment of chronically ill people over time, 63 hemodialysis patients were interviewed twice (separated by a three-year interval) concerning their social functioning and their expectations and experiences regarding social interactions (O'Brien, 1980). Although the patients reported that the amount of interaction with their family and friends increased over time, they also found that the quality of these social interactions decreased. While this study was not of social support per se, it provides evidence that undesirable changes in the social environment may occur over time among this group of chronically ill people. Furthermore, such changes are likely to influence the quantity and quality of support received.

Coyne (Coyne, 1976b; Coyne et al., 1988) discussed another sort of process in which the provision to depressed and chronically ill people of helpful support from close network members may diminish over time. Coyne et al. (1988) argued that when family members or close friends are emotionally involved with the victim, they may become overinvolved. Because they are highly invested in the victim's outcome, support providers can become intrusive and demanding, treating the event as a shared one rather than as the victim's own. Thus close network members may interpret continued displays of distress by the victim either as signs that their support is inadequate or as rejection. They may then become critical and hostile rather than supportive, and ultimately become psychologically distressed themselves. One aspect of this perspective that is appealing is that it blames neither the victim nor the support provider for ineffective support. Instead, the ongoing interpersonal dynamics between the two individuals are viewed as responsible for the erosion of initially helpful support.

In sum, although the initial support provided to individuals experiencing stressful events may be both skillful and beneficial, subsequent events may leave victims feeling relatively less supported. When support is extended over a period of time, providers may experience a reaction akin to burnout, eventually leading them to withdraw their support completely. They may also become frustrated or feel helpless if the support they extend does not seem to help alleviate the victims' distress. Finally, the providers' possible emotional overinvolvement in the recipients' outcome may lead to the erosion of initially helpful support.

When Expectations for Support Are Exceeded

Yet another way in which perceptions of available support may be inaccurate is that they may be too modest. One sometimes hears people say that they were overwhelmed by the amount of support and help they received during a time of unusual stress; yet we could find almost no studies that examined this phenomenon. What factors might be related to receiving more support than one is expecting? We believe that support may exceed expectations in situations in which it is relatively easy to help, situations that are not threatening to social network members, and situations in which support providers have had previous experience with the particular type of stressful event. Support may also be extensive in situations characterized by positive emotions or desirable life events (i.e., when providers find it pleasurable to become involved). Events such as having a baby, getting married, or making a major purchase (e.g., house, car) are examples of these kinds of events. Although there is little empirical evidence to support this hypothesis, some suggestive evidence may be found in the cases of pregnancy and childbirth (Brown, 1986; Cronenwett, 1985). Although neither study assessed the expectations of mothers or mothers-to-be regarding available support, both did document an increase in received support after a positive (although stressful) life event.

In the stress literature, positive life events are believed to involve major life changes, although these events also seem to have fewer effects on health and well-being than do negative events (Thoits, 1983). This could be due to the confounding of life events in general with amount of support received. If negative life events elicit less effective support and more negative social reactions, and positive life events elicit extremely strong support and no negative social reactions, then this could account for differences in their health effects. In any case, it might be useful to study positive stressful life experiences further to test whether they elicit more support than the recipients expected.

Summary

In sum, there is some empirical and anecdotal evidence to suggest that the support provided to people experiencing stress may not match previous perceptions of availability. Either more or less support may occur, and it may be more or less effective than expected. Further, there is reason to believe that effective support dissipates under some circumstances where people who need support expected sustained high quality support to be available. What possible factors, then, might determine the degree of discrepancy, or mediate the relationship between available support and support received? In the next section, we explore some plausible mediators of this discrepancy.

POSSIBLE MEDIATORS OF THE DISCREPANCY BETWEEN AVAILABLE AND RECEIVED SUPPORT

We alluded earlier to some possible mediators of the discrepancy between available and received support. From our discussion of the victimization perspective, for example, several conceptual mediating factors can be extracted. First, the network members' response is likely to be influenced by whether the stressful event is threatening to them. When potential support providers are threatened by an event (i.e., made to feel vulnerable), we would expect more support problems. In general, unfamiliar events are likely to be more threatening. Second, distress in the person experiencing the stressor may increase the divergence between support expected and that received. In particular, victims who are severely depressed seem to elicit unsupportive reactions. Third, the degree to which the stressor elicits strong emotional reactions in support providers is an important mediator. Providers who are themselves quite depressed, anxious, or angry about the victim's situation are unlikely to be effective interpersonally.

A central factor that may covary with both the victims' distress and the providers' feelings of vulnerability or emotional distress in providers is the severity of the stressor. There is some evidence that support is most compromised when the stressor is severe. Dunkel-Schetter (1984), for example, found that support problems were more frequent for cancer patients with a poor prognosis, compared with patients with a better prognosis. A proxy variable for the situational factors increasing the likelihood of support problems and negative social reactions, then, may be the degree of objective severity of the particular situation.

Another factor which could decrease beneficial support according to the victimization perspective is the prevalence of misconceptions about the coping process (e.g., Silver &Wortman, 1980). Although Lehman et al. (1986) found that people do not have misconceptions about what is helpful to a hypothetically bereaved person, they also suggested that support providers do not seem to behave accordingly when confronted with actual situations in which a loved one is distressed. There are several conceivable explanations for this. Network members may not always be strongly motivated to help, or they may lack sufficient skills to enact support effectively. Another possibility that Lehman et al. (1986) suggested is that particular features of face-to-face interaction may be responsible for social victimization phenomena. The best supportive interactions seem simple enough in the abstract but are often quite anxiety provoking to enact in reality, especially if the person to whom the help is directed is quite distressed. Anxiety is known to cause deficits in performance of a wide variety of behaviors and is likely to compromise support skills as well; yet it has received little research attention.

Thus, the victimization perspective and the research related to it contain a number of possible clues as to the mediators of support deficits. In the remainder of this section, we explore other possible categories of mediators of discrepancies between available support and support received.

Individual Differences

Certain individual difference variables should mediate the discrepancy between support believed to be available and what is actually received. Individual differences among support providers and among recipients may be important (Vinokur, Schul, & Caplan, 1987). Among support providers, the primary individual difference variables are probably interpersonal sensitivity or perceptiveness and interpersonal behavioral skills. Before behaving supportively, an individual must recognize that the other person needs support and then determine what type of behavior is needed. Indeed, matching support to the needs elicited by the situation has been hypothesized to be a major determinant of whether support is beneficial (Cohen & McKay, 1984; Cohen & Wills, 1985). An astute social observer would have an advantage in support transactions by virtue of having more accurate insight into the appropriate behaviors. For example, individuals who are high in self-monitoring (Snyder, 1974, 1979; Snyder & Cantor, 1980; Snyder & Gangestad, 1986; Snyder & Monson, 1975) appear to be more socially perceptive and therefore should be in a better position to provide effective support. In addition, interpersonal behavioral skills are useful in performing the appropriate behavior effectively (e.g., Riggio, 1986), for example, an ability to listen attentively while providing accepting nonverbal feedback.

Among support recipients, the individual difference variables that have been implicated as being important in social support exchanges are self-esteem, locus of control, generalized negative outlook, help-seeking tendencies, and attitudes toward seeking and accepting help (Eckenrode, 1983; Heller, 1979; Heller & Swindle, 1983; Lefcourt, Martin, & Saleh, 1984; Sandler & Lakey, 1982; Vinokur et al., 1987). For example, people low in self-esteem might expect less support than would individuals high in self-esteem, although in both cases these expectations may be distorted.

The propensity to seek help, that is, to communicate one's needs and request assistance, is another individual difference that is likely to influence the receipt of support (Heller, 1979; Heller & Swindle, 1983; Wortman & Dunkel-Schetter, 1987). Individuals tend to have varying beliefs about the appropriate times to seek help (Eckenrode & Gore, 1981). If it is necessary to seek help following an event in order to receive support, then those who are predisposed to wait for it to be offered may receive less support than they perceived would be available, in contrast with those who seek help when needed.

A study that provides some empirical support for this assertion was conducted by Eckenrode (1983), who investigated the relationship between beliefs about the efficacy of help seeking and support mobilization among 308 women users of a neighborhood health center. He used a six-item "efficacy of help-seeking scale" that assessed the "belief in the benefits versus costs of seeking and accepting help from others" (Eckenrode, 1983, p. 516), and he gathered information about supportive contacts following stressful events occurring within the previous year. Independent of the number of potential support providers, positive beliefs about help seeking and internal locus of control were found to be associated with greater support mobilization.

Coping Behavior

Particular coping styles and behaviors have also been found to be related to the amount of support people report receiving (Billings & Moos, 1981; Coates et al., 1979; Silver et al., this volume). Billings and Moos (1981), for example, found that people who use avoidance as a coping strategy tended to report few social resources. Coates et al. (1979) also found evidence to suggest that people's ability to cope well with an event influences the degree of avoidance and support by others. In addition, a longitudinal study of 150 middle-aged individuals in the community (Dunkel-Schetter, Folkman, & Lazarus, 1987) examined various psychological correlates of support receipt and discovered that individuals' coping strategies were strongly related to the social support they received. For example, problem solving, seeking support, and positive reappraisal coping all were associated with greater support received, whereas distancing was associated with less. The researchers speculated that coping may be viewed as a major determinant of received support because the coping strategies provided cues to social network members regarding needs or desires for support. On the basis of the available evidence, then, we suggest that the nature and skill of a person's coping strategies applied to particular stressful situations may mediate the extent to which available support materializes.

Social Network Characteristics

Other discrepancies between expected support and received support may be related to the characteristics of a person's social network. In some instances, receiving less support than expected may be explained by a diffusion of responsibility (Latane & Darley, 1970). That is, those persons who have a very large network may expect a great deal of support. However, if network members believe that everyone else is helping, few or none may actually initiate support efforts. Thus, social network size may be related in a curvilinear fashion to received support.

Another factor is the degree of intimacy of one's social relationships. Specifically, receiving more or less support than one believed was available from a particular person might reflect discrepant views of a relationship's intimacy. For example, one person may view a relationship as a close friendship, whereas the other may see it as a casual acquaintanceship. Such discrepancies may account for some of the differences between perceptions of available support and reports of received support. However, consistently inaccurate perceptions of the degree of intimacy of an entire social network are likely to reflect an underlying dispositional factor such as self-esteem.

It appears from past research that our current perceptions of available support are based on past experiences with received support (Cutrona, 1986; Vinokur et al., 1987). However, the changing nature of our social relationships implies that the past receipt of support may often be a poor indicator of future experiences. For example, exits from a social network due to geographical mobility, job changes, and death all decrease the number of support providers available. Conversely, the acquisition and formation of new relationships increase the number of support providers available. In addition, the amount of support available from or provided by a finite number of relationships is influenced by intrarelationship factors. Interpersonal factors such as conflict, competition, and indebtedness might produce fluctuations in expectations of support as well as actual support receipt. In sum, because our social networks and relationships are not static, the relationship between the past receipt of support and future available support should not be strong, especially over longer time periods. Further, some people who have never experienced major life problems will have had little opportunity to use available support. These people would therefore have no baseline of past received support on which to base expectations of future availability.

Summary

In sum, a large number of factors can be hypothesized to mediate the discrepancies between available support and support received. In addition to those factors suggested by the victimization perspective, it appears that individual differences such as the interpersonal skills of support providers and the self-esteem of recipients, the nature of a distressed person's coping behavior, and characteristics of their social network and social relationships, will play a role in mediating the discrepancy between support perceived as available and support received. Given the discrepancies previously discussed between available support and received support, and the variety of possible mediators of these discrepancies, the question arises as to what implications the distinction has for understanding the observed health-protective effects of social support.

THE EFFECTS OF SOCIAL SUPPORT

Social support has two sorts of health effects, main effects and buffer effects (Cohen & Wills, 1985; House, Landis, & Umberson, 1988). Studies of functions or types of support usually find evidence of the buffering effects of social support, and studies of social integration usually find that the main effects predominate (Cohen & Wills, 1985). Buffering implies that support protects people from the deleterious effects of stress on health and well-being. Specifically, individuals experiencing high stress will display lower levels of psychological and physical symptomatology if they have strong support than if they have weak support. Conversely, the effects of support on the stress–health relationship are weaker or absent for people experiencing little stress. Some researchers argue that there are different mechanisms or processes behind the main and buffer effects of social support (Heller et al., 1986; Thoits, 1985).

We pointed out earlier that severity of stress is an important moderator of the discrepancy between perceptions of available support and received support. We believe that these two support concepts are likely to be the least convergent under conditions of high stress, because this is when one's prior assumptions about available support are most likely to be challenged. The distinction between available support and received support thus seems especially pertinent to the buffering effect, to which the level of stress is important.

The results of the few studies that compared the health-protective effects of available and received support (e.g., Cohen et al., 1984; Cohen & Hoberman, 1983; Sandler & Lakey, 1982; Wethington & Kessler, 1986) have suggested that perceptions of available support moderate the relationship between stress and psychological outcomes and assessments of received support do not. Cohen et al. (1984), for example, conducted a prospective study with a sample of college students. They were interested in investigating the roles of available and received support in moderating the relationship between negative life events and psychological disorder. To assess available support they used the college-student version of the ISEL (Cohen & Hoberman, 1983), and to determine received support they used the ISSB (Barrera et al., 1981). Outcome measures included the Beck Depression Inventory (Beck, 1967) and the 22-item Langner Symptom Checklist (Langner, 1962). Stressful life events were assessed by means of the College Student Life Events Schedule (Sandler & Lakey, 1982). Data were gathered on life events and outcome measures at the first time point and again about two months later; data on social support were collected only at the second time point. Using regression analyses (both with and without initial symptomatology controlled), they found both main and buffering effects for available support but neither for received support.

A second study was conducted by Wethington and Kessler (1986), who analyzed cross-sectional data from a large-scale national survey (Veroff, Kulka, & Douvan, 1981). This study differed from the previous one in at least two respects. First, the sample was a community sample, and the respondents were married adults (aged 21 to 65 years). Second, it did not use standardized measures. Thus, life events were assessed by asking the respondents to describe "the last time something really bad happened to you" (p. 80). Psychological distress was measured by a 20-item scale consisting of statements about bodily feelings associated with depression and anxiety. Available support was assessed by a single item, "These days I really don't know who I can count on for help," which was rated on a 4-point scale (0 = very true; 3 = not at all true). Finally, for those individuals who reported an event, the researchers determined the received support for that event by asking them to describe who helped and how they were helped. These support data were combined into five measures of received support (e.g., whether one's spouse provided support, the total number of times emotional or instrumental support was reported). Using these measures, Wethington and Kessler (1986) found a stress-buffering effect for available but not for received support.

Although the two studies described differed on several dimensions, they both indicated that available support buffers the effect of stress, whereas received support does not. Yet, many researchers contend that received support will have a greater influence on health following a stressful event than will available support. For example, Gottlieb (1985) stated that the behavioral manifestation of support (or its materialization in interpersonal transactions) has the greatest significance for the course and outcome of stressful experiences and for understanding the coping process. Similarly, Gore (1985) observed that "the question of a stress-buffering effect of social support, strictly speaking, is contingent upon evidence that support is mobilized, not that it exists as a potential" (p. 269). Thoits (1985) also indicated that support "may consist of words and deeds intended to alter the self-perceptions of distressed individuals, and altered self-perceptions are the mechanisms through which support operates to buffer, or reduce, symptoms" (p. 61). Thus, all of these authors imply that received support will be more powerful in creating a buffering effect than will available support (see also Heller et al., 1986; Henderson, 1981).

It has also been argued that the perception of available support influences general health and well-being more than do specific supportive transactions; that is, perceptions that support is available should have a greater main effect on health (Gottlieb, 1988; Heller et al., 1986). One reason may be that the main effects of support on health may operate through a psychological or cognitive pathway rather than through a transactional process (Gottlieb, 1988).

We have struggled with how to reconcile the available empirical evidence with our belief, and the arguments of other researchers, that received support should have buffering effects and that available support should have main effects. A broader view of the conceptual issues offers at least two reasons that the past research regarding social support receipt may be inconclusive: (1) The context of received social support has been ignored, and (2) the measures of support, stress, and well-being used have not been comparable in their level of specificity.

The context in which social support is received is important to consider, for several reasons. A few years ago, Cohen and McKay (1984) proposed that received support must match the needs elicited by the stressor in order to be beneficial (see also Cohen & Wills, 1985). Cutrona and Russell (1987) documented this in a research program that compared a variety of stressors by using samples from several different populations. They found that the particular components of social support that were related to health and adjustment varied with the types of stressors. For example, reliable alliance and guidance were found to be beneficial to new mothers, whereas reassurance of worth was most helpful to nurses and teachers under stress.

Given a needs–fit model of support effects, one would have to use measures that are specific to the stressful situation of interest to test the buffer effects of received support. In studies in which researchers use the ISSB, buffer effects are not likely to be found because the ISSB is a context-free instrument that measures general support behaviors, but does not include all the specific behaviors that are likely to be uniquely important to a particular stressful situation. Buffer effects of received support are more likely to be found if the specific context in which the support was received is considered in its assessment (see Okun, Sandler, & Baumann, 1988). For example, some of the instruments in Table 11.3 measure support in either particular stressful situations or specific stressful episodes.

The timing of various types of support is another factor that is important to consider when testing the buffer effects of received support (Jacobson, 1986). That is, the recipient may judge the same supportive behavior as either helpful or unhelpful, depending on when it is provided. For example, a woman who had just given birth was visited in her hospital room by her doctor, who came in, announced that her child had spina bifida, and proceeded to provide information about the illness and treatment options. Although this kind of informational support was needed at some point, the mother's first need was for emotional support, and so she was unable to absorb any of the information provided. Another example is bereavement, in which the importance of the timing and type of social support is "common" knowledge to those who mount interventions (e.g., Parkes, 1982a, 1982b; Parkes & Weiss, 1983; Walker, MacBride, & Vachon, 1977). Thus, in addition to the stressful situation, the temporal context is important to consider in order to test the buffer effects sensitively. This may not be easy to do, but researchers should make at least some attempt to gauge the timing of social support relative to the onset of the stressor.

It has also been noted that the nature of the received support is more complex than simply knowing the frequency of support behaviors or amount of support received (Shinn, Lehmann, & Wong, 1984; Tardy, 1985; Wortman, 1984). As noted in Figure 11.1, support activation is a multifaceted process. Whether support is wanted, whether it is sought or passively received, and whether the recipient is satisfied with it are likely to be critical to determining the effects of the received support. For example, Bennett et al. (1987) found that neither whether support was received nor whether it was wanted were related to the subjective burden that the negative life event had imposed (both $rs = .02$). However, when this relationship was investigated utilizing the combination of these two variables, a significant relationship between support and subjective burden was found ($r = .31$). Because the ISSB (which Cohen et al., 1984, used to test for buffering) assesses only the frequency of support in the last four weeks (but not the desire for it or the satisfaction with it), a strong test of stress-buffering effects cannot be conducted using this instrument.

Assessing the multiple aspects of support receipt may be especially important when the samples used are heterogeneous with respect to the type of stressful event experienced. Both Cohen et al. (1984) and Wethington and Kessler (1986) used samples that had experienced a wide range of negative life events. Given the stressor's heterogeneity, it follows that widely varying amounts and types of support would be beneficial, depending on the context. In fact, Wethington and Kessler (1986) found that the interaction among the source of support, type of support, and type of event yielded an effect for received support, but because the number of respondents in each subgroup was very small, this finding was only suggestive. Wethington and Kessler (1986) stated that "received support effects would be more profitably pursued in case studies of particular types of life events rather than in general population surveys" (p. 83). In sum, the context of received support—by which we mean the specific stressful situation, the temporal context, and the process of support activation—cannot be ignored in logical and sensitive tests of buffer effects.

In addition to ignoring the context, past tests of the buffering effects of received support may not have been reliable because the researchers used measures of support, stress, and well-being that were not always comparable in their level of specificity. This problem is especially apparent in two cases. First, measures of received support must be comparable in specificity to measures of stress. For example, there is little reason to expect that support received in one context will buffer stress in general in people's lives. Similarly, a general support measure (e.g., the ISSB) is not the best choice for tests of buffering in a specific stressful situation (e.g., stress in college students; see Cohen et al., 1984). In a particular situation, many specific support behaviors may be relevant that are not common otherwise. For example, when investigating the support received by parents of children with a chronic illness, important areas to address include assistance in the child's daily care, planning for the child's future, and receipt of information regarding the illness. But these areas are not covered by a general measure of support such as the ISSB.

Second, in order to document the beneficial effects of received support, the measures of received support and of health outcomes should be comparable. For example, if general health and well-being are of interest, the measure of received support should be general too. Specifically, received support in this case would best be measured on multiple occasions spanning relatively short intervals, in order to provide information on the entire pattern of received support instead of just information on isolated instances (Dunkel-Schetter, Folkman, & Lazarus, 1987; Monroe & Steiner, 1986). If, as is often the case, one can assess received support only at one time, then an outcome measure that is highly specific to the problem for which the support is provided is desirable. For example, Bennett et al. (1987) were able to document the relationship between received support (in combination with other variables) by primary caregivers of children with a chronic illness and the subjective burden that the illness had imposed.

Summary

In sum, we would argue that the stress-buffering effects of received support have not been adequately tested as yet. The specific coping needs elicited by various stressors, the timing of receipt of support specific to those needs, and various facets of support activation, all need to be taken into account before the buffering effects of received support can be documented. Our argument rests on two assumptions: (1) that the context of support receipt is extremely important to consider, and (2) that the level of specificity of measurement of stressors, receipt of support, and well-being should be comparable. The latter argument is reminiscent of those employed in other areas of social psychology, where comparable levels of specificity regarding the measurement of independent and dependent variables greatly enhance predictive value (e.g., Ajzen, 1982; Ajzen & Fishbein, 1977). In addition, it is likely that the effects of received support will be more apparent in a sample that shares a common negative life event than in community and student samples experiencing diverse stresses. Before these problems can be properly addressed, the conceptualization and measurement of received support must be further developed.

FURTHER THEORETICAL IMPLICATIONS OF THE DISTINCTION

Up to this point we have been discussing the distinction between available support and support that is received, possible reasons for discrepancies between the two, and the relevance of each to the observed health-protective effects of social support. We now turn to other implications of the distinction that are worthy of future investigation.

First, like others (e.g., Barrerra, 1986; Heller et al., 1986), we believe that the global concept of social support should be abandoned in favor of more precise concepts and narrower models. Our reason is that it is possible to conceptualize available and received support as distinct constructs. Most precise definitions of general social support regard it as interpersonal transactions involving two or more individuals (House, 1981; Kahn & Antonucci, 1980; Shumaker & Brownell, 1984). If researchers were to use these current conceptions of support, then the construct of received support would be much more applicable than the construct of available support would be. The former involves an interactional approach consistent with these definitions. Yet the evidence so far of the health-protective effects of perceptions that support is available cannot be overlooked. Thus, our definitional frameworks must incorporate both aspects, which might be viewed as the *cognitive* and *behavioral* components of social support. We would expect these two components to be related but distinguishable empirically as well as conceptually. We should note that not all of the studies of received support have investigated actual behavioral support; nonetheless, we believe that the concept of support receipt implicitly (if not explicitly) takes a more behavioral perspective, one in which the phenomena consist of interpersonal exchanges and specific behaviors on the part of providers and recipients.

With respect to studying available support (i.e., the cognitive form), we need to distinguish between cognitions about the willingness or motivation of one's network to provide support, and cognitions about their level of capability or skill. That is, knowing that someone is willing to provide support is not the same as believing they could do so competently or skillfully. Sometimes we feel confident that our significant others would attempt to help us as best they can, but we are also aware that they would not be effective supporters because they are misguided or unskillful. For example, one college student mentioned to us that she knows that her parents are willing to come to her aid and that they mean well but that the support they have to offer would not be helpful. Assumptions or expectations about the *intent* behind socially supportive acts must be disentangled from expectations about the *skillfulness* of support. Concerning the effects of support, knowing a person's positive or altruistic intent alone may be beneficial, even if their behaviors are not. Alternatively, the detrimental effects of unhelpful support attempts may outweigh any positive effects of knowing that the person meant well.

Attempting to explicate the relationship between cognitive and behavioral components of support is a possible avenue for research. Studies that examine the relationships between perceptions of available support and actual behavioral support in interpersonal transactions (e.g., Cutrona, 1986; Lakey & Heller, 1988) are especially useful for this. Also, the two components of support (cognitive and behavioral) may be differentially related to other factors, such as personality or mood. We previously discussed ways in which individual differences and severity of the stress may influence the amount and kind of support received. Reports of perceptions of available support, however, also are related to such factors. For example, both the SSQ satisfaction index and the ISEL are correlated with developmental factors (care and protection from parents) and affective states (anxiety, depression), although the relationships are much stronger for women than for men (Sarason et al., 1987). Future investigation of whether available or received support is more or less related to other variables such as these could help explain how they are similar and different constructs.

We discussed our belief earlier that received support is more likely to have buffer effects, whereas available support is more likely to have main effects. Research that provides a good test of this hypothesis would be worthwhile, as would any research comparing the effects of the two forms of support. In addition, certain types of social support may have different effects (i.e., positive vs. negative) in their cognitive and behavioral forms. A case in point is financial support from parents for young adults. Knowing that it is available is often beneficial, but actually receiving it can be experienced as negative, because it increases feelings of dependency and obligation, which are often unwelcome at a time of life when autonomy and independence are especially important. Thus, cognitions that particular sorts of support are available may have effects different from those from received support.

Cognitive and behavioral forms of social support also appear to be differentially involved in the various processes discussed in the social support literature. For example, while the issue of reciprocity of support may seem obviously relevant to received support, it is also pertinent to available support. It may seem odd to consider reciprocity with respect to the feeling that you would be supported if you needed it, although sometimes it may be just this sense that we exchange with friends (e.g., "I'll be here for you in an emergency, if you'll be there for me").

Another set of questions concerns how perceptions of available support are formed. Is one's cognitive sense of support based more on recent past supportive transactions, as some research suggests, or on stable individual differences rooted in child development? Following individuals over time who are experiencing a chronic stressor may help shed light on this issue. Using a prospective design that begins collecting data before the occurrence of a life stress and then assesses both available and received support at multiple intervals would be ideal. It might be possible with such a design to determine the influence of received support on perceptions of available support, and vice versa.

These are just a few of the implications of our examination of the distinction between available and received social support. By presenting our thoughts, we hope to encourage others to look in this direction for research questions and issues.

REFERENCES

Ajzen, I. (1982). On behaving in accordance with one's attitudes. In M. P. Zanna, E. T. Higgins, & C. P. Herman (Eds.), *Consistency in social behavior: The Ontario symposium* (Vol. 2). Hillsdale, NJ: Erlbaum.

Ajzen, I., & Fishbein, M. (1977). Attitude–behavior relations: A theoretical analysis and review of empirical research. *Psychological Bulletin, 84,* 888–918.

Aneshensel, C. S., & Frerichs, R. R. (1982). Stress, support, and depression: A longitudinal casual model. *Journal of Community Psychology, 10,* 363–376.

Antonucci, T. C., & Israel, B. A. (1986). Veridicality of social support: A comparison of principal and network members' responses. *Journal of Consulting and Clinical Psychology, 54,* 432–437.

Barrera, M., Jr. (1981). Social support in the adjustment of pregnant adolescents: Assessment issues. In B. H. Gottlieb (Ed.), *Social networks and social support* (pp. 69–96). Beverly Hills, CA: Sage.

Barrera, M., Jr. (1986). Distinctions between social support concepts, measures, and models. *American Journal of Community Psychology, 14*, 413–445.

Barrera, M., Jr., & Ainlay, S. L. (1983). The structure of social support: A conceptual and empirical analysis. *Journal of Community Psychology, 11*, 133–143.

Barrera, M., Jr., Sandler, I. N., & Ramsay, T. B. (1981). Preliminary development of a scale of social support: Studies on college students. *American Journal of Community Psychology, 9*, 435–447.

Beck, A. (1967). *Depression: Clinical, experimental and theoretical aspects.* New York: Harper & Row.

Bennett, T. L., Gottlieb, B. H., & Cadman, D. (1987). *Social support for parents of children with chronic illness: Preliminary development of the CCISS.* Unpublished manuscript.

Billings, A. G., & Moos, R. H. (1981). The role of coping resources in attenuating the stress of life events. *Journal of Behavioral Medicine, 7*, 139–157.

Brickman, P., Rabinowitz, V. C., Karuza, J., Coates, D., Cohn, E., & Kidder, L. (1982). Models of helping and coping. *American Psychologist, 37*, 368–384.

Brown, M. A. (1986). Marital support during pregnancy. *Journal of Obstetric, Gynecologic, and Neonatal Nursing*, 475–483.

Carveth, W. B., & Gottlieb, B. H. (1979). The measurement of social support and its relation to stress. *Canadian Journal of Behavioral Science, 11*, 179–188.

Coates, D., & Wortman, C. B. (1980). Depressive maintenance and interpersonal control. In A. Baum & J. Singer (Eds.), *Advances in environmental psychology* (Vol. 2, pp. 149–182). Hillsdale, NJ: Erlbaum.

Coates, D., Wortman, C. B., & Abbey, A. (1979). Reactions to victims. In I. H. Frieze, D. Bartal, & J. S. Carrol (Eds.), *New approaches to social problems.* San Francisco: Jossey-Bass.

Cohen, L. H., McGowan, J., Fooskas, S., & Rose, S. (1984). Positive life events and social support and the relationship between life stress and psychological disorder. *American Journal of Community Psychology, 12*, 564–587.

Cohen, S., & Hoberman, H. M. (1983). Positive events and social supports as buffers of life change stress. *Journal of Applied Social Psychology, 13*(2), 99–125.

Cohen, S., & McKay, G. (1984). Social support, stress, and the buffering hypothesis: A theoretical analysis. In A. Baum, J. E. Singer, & S. E. Taylor (Eds.), *Handbook of psychology and health.* Hillsdale, NJ: Erlbaum.

Cohen, S., Mermelstein, R., Kamarck, T., & Hoberman, H. M. (1985). Measuring the functional components of social support. In I. G. Sarason & B. R. Sarason (Eds.), *Social support: Theory, research and applications* (pp. 73–94). Dordrecht, Netherlands: Martinus Nijhoff.

Cohen, S., & Syme, S. L. (1985). Issues in the study and application of social support. In S. Cohen & S. L. Syme (Eds.), *Social support and health* (pp. 3–22). Orlando, FL: Academic Press.

Cohen, S., & Wills, T. A. (1985). Stress, social support, and the buffering hypothesis. *Psychological Bulletin, 98*, 310–357.

Coyne, J. C. (1976a). Depression and the response of others. *Journal of Abnormal Psychology, 85,* 186–193.

Coyne, J. C. (1976b). Toward an interactional description of depression. *Psychiatry, 39,* 28–40.

Coyne, J. C., Wortman, C. B., & Lehman, D. R. (1988). The other side of support: Emotional overinvolvement and miscarried helping. In B. H. Gottlieb (Ed.), *Marshaling social support.* Newbury Park, CA: Sage.

Cronenwett, L. R. (1985). Parental network structure and perceived support after birth of first child. *Nursing Research, 34,* 347–352.

Cutrona, C. E. (1986). Behavioral manifestations of social support: A microanalytic investigation. *Journal of Personality and Social Psychology, 51,* 201–208.

Cutrona, C. E., & Russell, D. W. (1987). The provisions of social relationships and adaptation to stress. In W. H. Jones and D. Perlman (Eds.), *Perspectives on interpersonal behavior and relationships.* Greenwich, Conn.: JAI Press.

Dakof, G. A. & Taylor, S. E. (1988). *Recipient perceptions of social support: What is helpful from whom?* Manuscript submitted for publication.

Dunkel-Schetter, C. (1984). Social support and cancer: Findings based on patient interviews and their implications. *Journal of Social Issues, 40,* 77–98.

Dunkel-Schetter, C., Feinstein, L., & Call, J. (1987). *A self-report inventory for the measurement of social support.* Unpublished manuscript.

Dunkel-Schetter, C., Folkman, S., & Lazarus, R. (1987). Correlates of social support receipt. *Journal of Personality and Social Psychology, 53,* 71–80.

Dunkel-Schetter, C., & Wortman, C. B. (1981). Dilemmas of social support: Parallels between victimization and aging. In S. B. Kiesler, J. N. Morgan, & V. K. Oppenheimer (Eds.), *Aging: Social change* (pp. 349–381). New York: Academic Press.

Dunkel-Schetter, C., & Wortman, C. B. (1982). The interpersonal dynamics of cancer: Problems in social relationships and their impact on the patient. In H. S. Friedman & M. R. DiMatteo (Eds.), *Interpersonal issues in health care* (pp. 69–100). New York: Academic Press.

Eckenrode, J. (1983). The mobilization of social support: Some individual constraints. *American Journal of Community Psychology, 11,* 509–528.

Eckenrode, J., & Gore, S. (1981). Stressful events and social support: The significance of context. In B. H. Gottlieb (Ed.), *Social networks and social support* (pp. 43–68). Beverly Hills, CA: Sage.

Folkman, S., Lazarus, R. S., Dunkel-Schetter, C., DeLongis, A., & Gruen, R. (1986). Dynamics of a stressful encounter: Cognitive appraisal, coping, and encounter outcomes. *Journal of Personality and Social Psychology, 50,* 992–1003.

Folkman, S., Lazarus, R. S., Gruen, R., & DeLongis, A. (1986). Appraisal, coping, health status, and psychological symptoms. *Journal of Personality and Social Psychology, 50,* 571–579.

Gore, S. (1985). Social support and styles of coping. In S. Cohen & S. L. Syme (Eds.), *Social support and health* (pp. 263–278). Orlando, FL: Academic Press.

Gottlieb, B. H. (1978). The development and application of a classification scheme of informal helping behaviors. *Canadian Journal of Behavioral Science, 10,* 105–115.

Gottlieb, B. H. (1985). Social support and the study of personal relationships. *Journal of Social and Personal Relationships, 2,* 351–375.

Gottlieb, B. H. (1988). Marshaling social support: The state of the art in research and practice. In B. H. Gottlieb (Ed.), *Marshaling social support*. Newbury Park, CA: Sage.

Heller, K. (1979). The effects of social support: Prevention and treatment implications. In A. P. Goldstein & F. H. Kanfer (Eds.), *Maximizing treatment gains: Transfer enhancement in psychotherapy*. New York: Academic Press.

Heller, K., & Lakey, B. (1985). Perceived support and social interaction among friends and confidants. In I. G. Sarason & B. R. Sarason (Eds.), *Social support: Theory, research, and applications*. Dordrecht, Netherlands: Martinus Nijhoff.

Heller, K., & Swindle, R. W. (1983). Social networks, perceived social support and coping with stress. In R. D. Felner, L. A. Jason, J. Moritsugu, & S. S. Farber (Eds.), *Preventive psychology: Theory, research and practice in community intervention*. Elmsford, NY: Pergamon.

Heller, K., Swindle, R. W., Jr., & Dusenbury, L. (1986). Component social support processes: Comments and integration. *Journal of Consulting and Clinical Psychology, 54*(4), 466–470.

Henderson, S. (1981). Social relationships, adversity and neurosis: An analysis of prospective observations. *British Journal of Psychiatry, 138*, 391–398.

House, J. S. (1981). *Work, stress and social support*. Reading, MA: Addison-Wesley.

House, J. S., & Kahn, R. L. (1985). Measures and concepts of social support. In S. Cohen & S. L. Syme (Eds.), *Social support and health* (pp. 83–108). Orlando, FL: Academic Press.

House, J. S., Landis, K. R., & Umberson, D. (1988). Social relationships and health. *Science, 241*, 540–545.

Jacobson, D. E. (1986). Types and timing of social support. *Journal of Health and Social Behavior, 27*, 250–264.

Jung, J. (1988). Social support providers: Why do they help? *Basic and Applied Social Psychology, 9*, 231–240.

Kahn, T. L., & Antonucci, T. C. (1980). Convoys over the life course: Attachment, roles, and social support. *Life Span Development and Behavior, 3*, 253–286.

Lakey, B., & Heller, K. (1988). Social support from a friend, perceived support and social problem-solving. *American Journal of Community Psychology, 16*, 811–824.

Langner, T. (1962). A twenty-two item screening score of psychiatric symptoms indicating impairment. *Journal of Health and Social Behavior, 3*, 269–276.

Latane, B., & Darley, J. M. (1970). *The unresponsive bystander: Why doesn't he help?* New York: Appleton-Century-Crofts.

Lefcourt, H. M., Martin, R. A., & Saleh, W. E. (1984). Locus of control and social support: Interactive moderators of stress. *Journal of Personality and Social Psychology, 47*, 378–389.

Lehman, D. R., Ellard, J. H., & Wortman, C. B. (1986). Social support for the bereaved: Recipients' and providers' perspectives on what is helpful. *Journal of Consulting and Clinical Psychology, 54*, 438–446.

Lerner, M. J. (1970). The desire for justice and reactions to victims. In J. Macaulay & L. Berkowitz (Eds.), *Altruism and helping behavior*. New York: Academic Press.

Lerner, M. J. (1971). Observer's evaluation of a victim: Justice, guilt, and veridical perception. *Journal of Personality and Social Psychology, 20*, 127–135.

Lerner, M. J., Miller, D. T., & Holmes, J. (1976). Deserving and the emergence of forms of justice. In L. Berkowitz & E. Walster (Eds.), *Advances in experimental social psychology.* New York: Academic Press.

Lerner, M. J., & Simmons, C. H. (1966). Observer's reactions to the "innocent victim": Compassion or rejection? *Journal of Personality and Social Psychology, 4,* 203–210.

Lichtman, R. R. (1982). *Close relationships after breast cancer.* Unpublished doctoral dissertation, University of California at Los Angeles.

Maslach, C. (1976). Burnt out. *Human Behavior, 5,* 16–22.

Maslach, C. (1978). The client role in staff burn-out. *Journal of Social Issues, 34,* 111–124.

Monroe, S. M., & Steiner, S. C. (1986). Social support and psychopathology: Interrelations with preexisting disorder, stress, and personality. *Journal of Abnormal Psychology, 95,* 29–39.

Newcomb, M. D. (in press). What structural equation modeling can tell us about social support. In I. G. Sarason, B. R. Sarason, & G. R. Pierce (Eds.), *Social support: An interactional view.* New York: Wiley.

O'Brien, M. E. (1980). Effective social environment and hemodialysis adaptation: A panel analysis. *Journal of Health and Social Behavior, 21,* 360–370.

Okun, M. A., Sandler, I. N., & Baumann, D. J. (1988). Buffer and booster effects as event-support transactions. *American Journal of Community Psychology, 16,* 435–449.

Parkes, C. M. (1982a). Attachment and the prevention of mental disorders. In C. M. Parkes & J. Stevenson-Hinde (Eds.), *The place of attachment in human behavior.* New York: Basic Books.

Parkes, C. M. (1982b). Role of support systems in loss and psychosocial transitions. In H. C. Schulberg & M. Killilea (Eds.), *The modern practice of community mental health.* San Francisco: Jossey-Bass.

Parkes, C. M., & Weiss, R. S. (1983). *Recovery from bereavement.* New York: Basic Books.

Peters-Golden, H. (1982). Breast cancer: Varied perceptions of social support in the illness experience. *Social Science and Medicine, 16,* 483–491.

Procidano, M. E., & Heller, K. (1983). Measurements of perceived social support from friends and from family: Three validation studies. *American Journal of Community Psychology, 11*(1), 1–24.

Riggio, R. E. (1986). Assessment of basic social skills. *Journal of Personality and Social Psychology, 51,* 649–660.

Russell, D. W., & Cutrona, C. E. (1984, August). *The provisions of social relationships and adaptation to stress.* Paper presented at the annual meeting of the American Psychological Association, Toronto.

Sandler, I. N., & Barrera, M., Jr. (1984). Toward a multimethod approach to assessing the effects of social support. *American Journal of Community Psychology, 12,* 37–52.

Sandler, I. N., & Lakey, B. (1982). Locus of control as a stress moderator: The role of control perceptions and social support. *American Journal of Community Psychology, 10,* 65–78.

Sarason, B. R., Shearin, E. N., Pierce, G. R., & Sarason, I. G. (1987). Interrelations of social support measures: Theoretical and practical implications. *Journal of Personality and Social Psychology, 52,* 813–832.

Sarason, I. G., Levine, H. M., Basham, R. B., & Sarason, B. R. (1983). Assessing social support: The Social Support Questionnaire. *Journal of Personality and Social Psychology, 44,* 127–130.

Shinn, M., Lehmann, S., & Wong, N. W. (1984). Social interaction and social support. *Journal of Social Issues, 40,* 55–76.

Shumaker, S. A., & Brownell, A. (1984). Toward a theory of social support: Closing conceptual gaps. *Journal of Social Issues, 40,* 11–36.

Silver, R. C., Wortman, C. B., & Crofton C. (in press). The role of coping in support provision: The self-presentational dilemma of victims of life crises. In I. G. Sarason, B. R. Sarason, & G. R. Pierce (Eds.), *Social support: An interactional view.* New York: Wiley.

Silver, R. L., & Wortman, C. B. (1980). Coping with undesirable life events. In J. Garber & M. E. Seligman (Eds.), *Human helplessness* (pp. 279–375). New York: Academic Press.

Snyder, M. (1974). Self-monitoring of expressive behavior. *Journal of Personality and Social Psychology, 30,* 526–537.

Snyder, M. (1979). Self-monitoring processes. In L. Berkowitz (Ed.), *Advances in experimental social psychology* (Vol. 12, pp. 85–128). New York: Academic Press.

Snyder, M., & Cantor, N. (1980). Thinking about ourselves and others: Self-monitoring and social knowledge. *Journal of Personality and Social Psychology, 39,* 222–234.

Snyder, M., & Gangestad, S. (1986). On the nature of self-monitoring: Matters of assessment, matters of validity. *Journal of Personality and Social Psychology, 51,* 125–139.

Snyder, M., & Monson, T. C. (1975). Persons, situations, and the control of social behavior. *Journal of Personality and Social Psychology, 32,* 637–644.

Solomon, S. D. (1986). Mobilizing social support networks in times of disaster. In C. R. Fisley (Ed.), *Trauma and its wake: Vol. 2. Traumatic stress theory, research, and intervention.* New York: Brunner/Mazel.

Tardy, C. H. (1985). Social support measurement. *American Journal of Community Psychology, 13,* 187–202.

Thoits, P. A. (1983). Dimensions of life events that influence psychological distress: An evaluation and synthesis of the literature. In H. B. Kaplan (Ed.), *Psychosocial stress: Trends in theory and research* (pp. 33–103). New York: Academic Press.

Thoits, P. A. (1985). Social support and psychological well-being: Theoretical possibilities. In I. G. Sarason & B. R. Sarason (Eds.), *Social support: Theory, research, and applications.* Dordrecht, Netherlands: Martinus Nijhoff.

Turner, R. J. (1983). Direct, indirect and moderating effects of social support upon psychological distress and associated conditions. In H. B. Kaplan (Ed.), *Psychological stress* (pp. 105–155). New York: Academic Press.

Valdenegro, J., & Barrera, M. (1983, April). *Social support as a moderator of life stress: A longitudinal study using a multimethod analysis.* Paper presented at the meeting of the Western Psychological Association, San Francisco.

Veroff, J., Kulka, R., & Douvan, E. (1981). *Mental health in America: Patterns of help-seeking from 1957 to 1976.* New York: Basic Books.

Vinokur, A., Schul, Y., & Caplan, R. D. (1987). Determinants of perceived social support: Interpersonal transactions, personal outlook, and transient affective states. *Journal of Personality and Social Psychology, 53,* 1137–1145.

Walker, K. N., MacBride, A., & Vachon, M. L. (1977). Social support networks and the crisis of bereavement. *Social Science and Medicine, 11*, 35–41.

Walster, E. (1966). Assignment of responsibility for an accident. *Journal of Personality and Social Psychology, 3*, 73–79.

Wethington, E., & Kessler, R. C. (1986). Perceived support, received support, and adjustment to stressful life events. *Journal of Health and Social Behavior, 27*, 78–89.

Wortman, C. B. (1984). Social support and the cancer patient: Conceptual and methodologic issues. *Cancer, 53*, 2339–2360.

Wortman, C. B., & Dunkel-Schetter, C. (1979). Interpersonal relationships and cancer: A theoretical analysis. *Journal of Social Issues, 35*, 120–155.

Wortman, C. B., & Dunkel-Schetter, C. (1987). Conceptual and methodological issues in the study of social support. In A. Baum & J. E. Singer (Eds.), *Handbook of psychology and health* (Vol. 5, pp. 63–108). Hillsdale, NJ: Erlbaum.

Wortman, C. B., & Lehman, D. R. (1985). Reactions to victims of life crisis: Support attempts that fail. In I. G. Sarason & B. R. Sarason (Eds.), *Social support: Theory, research, and applications* (pp. 463–489). Dordrecht, Netherlands: Martinus Nijhoff.

CHAPTER 12

Hardiness and Social Support

PAUL H. BLANEY AND RONALD J. GANELLEN

University of Miami

Michael Reese Hospital and Medical Center

In the 1970s, as an awareness grew that the relation between stressors and stress responses was, though reliable, not strong, attention turned to the possibility that other variables might moderate the stressor–stress response relation—variables that might distinguish those persons on whom stressors have a strong deleterious effect from those on whom they do not. The search for resources that might moderate stress effects points in two general directions: the person's environment and the individual himself or herself. Indeed, it would appear obvious that a full account of resistance resources would deal with both domains.

This chapter deals with a major tradition in the "personal resources" domain, that encompassed by the construct of hardiness, especially as it relates to supportive social resources. We will first comment on the major constructs being considered and their measurement, noting their relation to similar constructs currently found in relevant literatures. Then we will discuss the relation between social support and hardiness and its components, focusing on conceptual and empirical relations among these constructs, on findings comparing their relative impact, and on the possibility that they may interact with one another in fostering well-being. Next we will briefly examine the evidence regarding the possibility that support and hardiness may moderate the stressor-stress response relation. Then we will explore ways in which these variables may interact with one another as part of the process of stress moderation, followed by a discussion of the relation between these variables and coping activities. Finally, we will comment briefly on future research directions.

Although we mainly will be reviewing and discussing published research, at various points we will be reporting heretofore-unpublished findings from our own research (Ganellen, Blaney, & Baggett, 1988). Briefly, this research consists of two cross-sectional, correlational studies, each including some variables of interest here. The Study 1 sample consisted of unselected undergraduates (51 male, 64 female) fulfilling a course requirement. We used the measure of social support used by Ganellen and Blaney (1984a), the Alienation Test (Maddi, Kobasa, & Hoover, 1979), and the Beck Depression Inventory. The Study 2 sample was composed of 40 male and 49 female undergraduates, screened to eliminate any depressed subjects, and examined relations among variables in a context in which depression could not be a confounding variable. Measures included the Alienation Test, the Social Support Questionnaire (Sarason, Levine, Basham, & Sarason, 1983), and the Ways of Coping scale (Folkman, Lazarus, Pimley, & Novacek, 1987).

THE CONSTRUCTS AND THEIR MEASUREMENT

In the domains relevant to this chapter, the ideal of consensus constructs, assessed by consensus instruments, remains elusive. In this section, we comment on the strengths and weaknesses of various conceptual and measurement approaches regarding our major variables and explain how we intend to deal with them in our review.

Hardiness

Among the personal resources relevant to stress resistance, the constellation of characteristics receiving the most attention has come to be known as *hardiness*. As defined by Kobasa (1979), this constellation consists of three components: a sense of having *control* over one's fate, the inclination to face adversity or novelty with a sense of *challenge* rather than defeat or intimidation, and a sense of *commitment,* as opposed to aimlessness, purposelessness, and meaninglessness.

Several cautions regarding Kobasa's (1979) formulation of hardiness must be quickly raised. First, insofar as hardiness implies invulnerability to stress, the use of this word to denote the control–challenge–commitment constellation tends to beg a crucial question. Whether this constellation in fact renders persons less vulnerable to stress is an empirical question, one on which a mere definitional decree sheds no light. But the field appears to have adopted the Kobasa (1979) usage, so that the current consensual meaning for hardiness is control, challenge, and commitment. Adopting this definition, however, does not reduce the need to be mindful that "hardy" persons might not be particularly hardy after all. Accordingly, although we use the now-conventional definition of hardiness, we reserve judgment on the question of what, if anything, this kind of hardiness has to do with well-being or with responses to stressful experiences.

The second problem has to do with the three-pronged nature of the hardiness constellation (cf. Blaney, 1985; Carver, 1989; Hull, Van Treuren & Virnelli, 1987). Kobasa and her associates summed scores from purported measures of control, challenge, and commitment with equal weights in a composite hardiness score. In the broader research literatures on which the hardiness construct draws, the three variables usually are treated as distinct; indeed, subdistinctions are often made within each (e.g., Anderson, Madonna, Bailey, & Wesley, 1987; Levenson, 1973). Perhaps Kobasa's (1979) handling of the three variables as one can be justified, but we do not think it has been. Moreover, no theoretical statement of the unitary hardiness model has made it clear whether the three components are to be viewed as independent or interactive and, if interactive, what form the interaction might take (Carver, 1989). Although, as we noted, we accept these characteristics as comprising hardiness, we do not accept the presumption that hardiness should be treated as a single variable. We will instead consider the empirical findings for each component separately when possible. Note, however, that the writings of Kobasa and colleagues leave some confusion regarding which component a given scale measures (cf. Hull et al., 1987). In addition, some researchers, while ostensibly accepting the standard conceptualization of hardiness, used measures whose relationship to it is unclear (e.g., Howard, Cunningham, & Rechnitzer, 1986; Kuo & Tsai, 1986).

Hardiness-relevant Constructs

Coherence

Antonovsky (1979) spoke of a "sense of coherence" as "a global orientation that expresses the extent to which one has a . . . feeling of confidence that one's internal and external environments are predictable and that there is a high probability that things will work out as well as can reasonably be expected" (p. 123). Because coherence includes the perception of "one as a participant in the processes shaping one's destiny as well as one's daily experience" (p. 128), it has some relevance to perceived control. However, the key aspect of coherence is not whether power lies with the self or externally but that it lies "where it is legitimately supposed to be" (p. 128). Even outcomes that are not contingent on one's voluntary responses can be "consistent with a strong sense of coherence" if they do "not confuse and bewilder one" (p. 154). Furthermore, Antonovsky treated coherence as, in part, a reflection of the quality of the societal environment, and he stated that coherence cannot be viewed simply as a trait. In short, the coherence model appears to minimize control and challenge as important personal characteristics, focusing instead on qualities akin to commitment, but in a way that is tied to whether the social environment is one in which the individual can find meaning and view as legitimate.

Potency

Ben-Sira (1985) proposed a construct with strong ties to both hardiness and coherence: potency. Like hardiness, he defined it in terms of both personal characteristics and the benefits that the personal characteristics are believed to bestow. The personal characteristics are (1) confidence in one's own capacities, (2) commitment to the social environment, and (3) perception of that environment as meaningful, predictable, and just. The benefit that potency is said to bestow is "to prevent tension, following occasional inadequate coping, from turning into lasting stress" (p. 399). Thus, whereas hardiness is commonly seen as fostering effective coping, Ben-Sira suggested that hardinesslike characteristics lessen the impact of ineffective coping.

Type A

One might surmise that the hardiness and Type A constellations have consider-able overlap, as the Type A stereotype is of an individual who constantly tries to take control, seeks out challenges, and is highly committed to his or her work. Type A is, of course, usually viewed as detrimental rather than helpful to health, and it is empirically associated with reduced levels of social support (Suls, Becker, & Mullen, 1981). The several studies that considered Type A and com-posite hardiness (Hull et al., 1987; Kobasa, Maddi, & Zola, 1983; Nowack, 1986; Rhodewalt & Agustsdottir, 1984; Schmied & Lawler, 1986) indicate that they have little or no correlation. Thus, if one assumes that Type A increases risk whereas hardiness reduces it, and if one assumes that both Type A and hardiness are related to notions of control, challenge, and commitment, one must then con-clude that they do so in markedly different ways.

Social Support

Just as calling a particular set of characteristics *hardiness* does not guarantee that having them makes a person stress resistant, calling particular social interactions *social support* can beg the question of whether they are supportive. Even a sub-ject's reports that interactions are supportive does not prove that the subject is better off with than without them. The key questions remain empirical.

In this chapter, we view hardiness and its components as person characteris-tics, and we view social support as addressing characteristics of the environment. We believe that the person-versus-environment distinction should, to the extent possible, be religiously maintained, as many of the terms used in this area have vague and varying uses. An example is the word *alienation*. About 10 years ago, two so-called alienation scales were published, the first (Maddi et al., 1979) ad-dressing personal beliefs and attitudes and the second (Millon, Green, & Mea-gher, 1976) exploring the supportiveness of the social environment. A field in which terms can be used in such different ways is a field in which special care is required if conceptual clarity is to be ensured.

The personal-versus-environmental resources distinction is, however, tenuous at best. When the assessment of support is through self-report, experiential as-pects of support are inevitably involved, and the resulting scores may reflect traitlike personal perceptions to a greater or lesser degree (depending on the ques-tions' wording). Insofar as a given measure pertains to perceived social support, it confuses personal with social resources, which in turn compromises the chance that research will generate an unclouded picture of the independent and interac-tive effects of these two classes of variables. On the other hand, just because ostensible social support measures are "objective" does not make them virtuous. Ideally, one would have objective measures that reflect how supportive the typi-cal person would experience a given social environment as being. We doubt that most support measures used in the studies that we review here would qualify. The measures employed appear to range from those dependent on idiosyncratic perceptions to those relying on the objective but trivial, and it often is not possible to discern the strengths and weaknesses of a given measure.

In addition, we doubt that social support should be construed in a way that ignores domain-to-domain differences (e.g., work support, family support) and distinctions related to the kind of support offered (e.g., tangible, emotional). Although some current studies consider various subaspects of support separately, many do not. We will gloss over, in this chapter, issues related to those subaspects, both because many of the studies we will report consider support in an undifferentiated fashion and because other chapters in this volume address support issues in more detail.

More generally, because the distinctive aspect of this chapter is its attention to hardiness, we will provide greater detail in our discussion of hardiness issues than in our discussion of equally important issues in the support domain.

Stress and Well-being

Most of the studies we will review in this chapter lie within a tradition in which stress is, for better or worse, quantified in terms of an individual's responses to a checklist of recent stressors. Because the strengths and limitations of this approach have been discussed at length elsewhere and because noting our misgivings about stressor measures would be disruptive, we will usually characterize stress levels in the terms used by the authors of the reports.

We will also give less attention to the dependent variable side of the equation than is ideal. Some studies used self-reported depression; others assessed physical health. We do not presume that those factors leading to one kind of distress also lead to all other kinds of distress. However, although some relevant empirical reports compare effects involving various outcomes (e.g., Brown & Gary, 1987; Krause, 1985), they are few and their differential findings have not been replicated. For this reason, and because ostensible measures of physical well-being commonly include psychological items and vice versa, our discussion will tend to treat various outcomes as interchangeable, and we will use nonspecific terms such as *well-being*, *distress*, and *stress responses* from time to time.

THE RELATION BETWEEN HARDINESS AND SOCIAL SUPPORT

Although we believe that a distinction should be maintained between personal and environmental factors, no reasonable model would presume that they are independent. In this section we look at findings on the relation between hardiness and support and talk about what those findings might mean.

Although the results are not entirely consistent (Kobasa, 1982a), there is considerable evidence suggesting that aspects of social support are strongly related to aspects of hardiness (Ganellen & Blaney, 1984a; Kobasa & Puccetti, 1983) and of potency (Ben-Sira, 1985). According to Ganellen et al. (1988), the correlations between hardiness and support were .42 ($p < .001$) in Study 1, and .32 (ns) between hardiness and the number of support resources and .47 ($p < .001$) between hardiness and satisfaction with received support in Study 2. The difference between these two correlations (.32 and .47), if replicable, might indicate that given similar objective social resources, the hardy individual would judge them as adequate and have a more positive outlook regarding them (cf. Vinokur, Schul, & Caplan, 1987). This possibility aside, there are two simple ways of accounting for such a relation (Ganellen & Blaney, 1984a): (1) Being hardy leads to behavior that fosters a supportive social environment, and (2) the experience of being in a supportive context encourages hardy attitudes. These two possibilities are not mutually exclusive, and both have been advocated in the literature.

For instance, Kobasa (1982b) suggested that the hardy individual, by valuing his or her acts, is likely to become involved "fully in many situations of life including work, family, interpersonal relations, and social institutions" (p. 6). In contrast, Wallston, Alagna, DeVellis, and DeVellis (1983) favored a support-fosters-control model, noting that "supportive others [may] help the individual to interpret events so as to reduce perceptions of personal noncontrol . . . and/ or . . . force or cajole adaptive responding that produces desirable outcomes and thus heightens the individual's sense of control" (p. 384; see also DeVellis & DeVellis, 1986); Cobb (1976) and Wilcox and Vernberg (1985) expressed similar viewpoints.

When two variables show concurrent variation, two possible empirical approaches can be taken to choose among the alternative causal pathways: experimental and longitudinal. In this case, an experimental approach might, for instance, consist of a treatment study in which change toward greater hardiness was the target of treatment, and the dependent variables of interest were pre- to posttreatment change in measures of the social environment's adequacy. Although some treatment studies do approach the design needed to address these causal questions (e.g., Nezu, 1986; Vachon, Lyall, Rogers, Freedman-Letofsky, & Freeman, 1980), we have found none that matches that design closely enough to be clearly relevant.

In regard to nonexperimental research, two longitudinal studies may be relevant. Holahan and Holahan (1987) presented data indicating that the belief in one's ability to manage social situations (a control-related variable) is, in fact, predictive of subsequent social support (and, inversely, distress); this is consistent with a hardiness-fosters-support account. Poresky and Atilano (1982), on the other hand, indicated that a measure of community involvement (a support-related variable) predicted subsequent alienation; this is consistent with a support-fosters-hardiness account.

We should note, however, that the hardiness-support relationship may vary from source to source of support (Kobasa & Puccetti, 1983). The picture is also complex when one considers hardiness components. The evidence regarding challenge is unclear (Clarke & Innes, 1983; Ganellen & Blaney, 1984a). Control and support are either unrelated (Caldwell, Pearson, & Chin, 1987; Ganellen & Blaney, 1984a; Lefcourt, Martin, & Saleh, 1984; Schultz & Saklofsky, 1983) or minimally related (Hibbard, 1985; Sandler & Lakey, 1982; Sarason et al., 1983; Turner & Noh, 1983). There is substantial reason to believe that commitment is related to support (Ganellen & Blaney, 1984a; Quisumbing, 1982; Sarason & Sarason, 1982) and inversely to loneliness (Goswick & Jones, 1982), although the findings are not entirely consistent (Kobasa, 1982a). Indeed, commitment in one life sphere may be negatively related to support in another. Ladewig and McGee (1986) reported that married women's levels of occupational commitment were negatively associated with levels of supportiveness of their family environment.

Krause (1987b) presented a finding that may indicate that some of the foregoing analyses provide a picture that is oversimplified at best. Specifically, in his data set, of four support aspects considered, two (emotional support and integration, but not informational or tangible support) showed clear nonmonotonic relationships with locus of control. For these two support variables, increased support is associated with increased control perceptions in the lower ranges, whereas in the higher ranges, increased support is associated with decreased control perceptions.

The nature of the hardiness-support association remains a question. Empirical clarification will probably require (1) an increased use of experimental and longitudinal designs, (2) consideration of hardiness components and even sphere-specific subcomponents (e.g., work commitment), (3) consideration of sphere-specific support, and (4) attention to the possibility that relationships between hardiness-relevant variables and support variables may be nonmonotonic.

HARDINESS AND SOCIAL SUPPORT AS SOURCES OF WELL-BEING

In this section we consider data indicating that hardiness and social support are related to physical and/or psychological well-being. Note that we are not yet addressing the stress-specific value of these resources. In an ANOVA or multiple regression idiom, we consider the main effects of support and hardiness and the interactions between them, but not the interaction of either of them with stress.

Note that a main-effect relation between a variable such as support or hardiness and well-being implies that the variable is ameliorative for both persons with high stressor exposure and persons with low stressor exposure. However, it does not necessarily mean that that variable is helpful when there is zero stress. Persons with zero stress may be so rare as to be empirically inconsequential, and support or hardiness may help in low-stressor contexts just because it helps in dealing with that low-level stress experience. (In fact, we lack a clear notion of zero stress, and if we did have one, it probably could not be reconciled with a total lack of social connectedness and personal resources.)

Social Support

The main-effect value of support is the subject of several reviews (e.g., Blaney, 1985; Cohen & Wills, 1985). The findings surveyed are quite consistent in suggesting an association between support and well-being. Most of the studies, but not all (e.g., Vachon et al., 1980), were nonexperimental and cross-sectional and thus ambiguous with regard to causation. The fact that loss experiences routinely appear among the most negative of stressors is also relevant. But because other chapters in this volume address these and related social support issues, we will not discuss them in depth here.

Hardiness

Hull et al. (1987) surveyed the existing studies and presented new data, and their findings are consistent in indicating that composite hardiness is related to well-being. Our reading of this literature (including studies more recent than those covered by Hull et al.) leads to the same summary, with one striking exception: Schmied and Lawler (1986) reported findings in which there is no relation between composite hardiness and a measure of recent physical illness. Note, however, that other studies found a relation between hardiness and physical health measures (e.g., Banks & Gannon, 1988; Kobasa, 1982a; Kobasa, Maddi, Puccetti, & Zola, 1985; Wiebe & McCallum, 1986). It is possible that the hardiness–health relation varies considerably from illness to illness (cf. Pollock, 1986).

Hull et al. (1987) also examined hardiness components, concluding that control and commitment are related to well-being but that challenge is not. Benassi, Sweeney, and Dufour (1988) reviewed the evidence regarding locus of control and depression, and they described the relation as moderately strong and consistent across studies. There also is evidence that control is associated with self-reported health and with objective measures of immune function (Okun, Zautra, & Robinson, 1988). The diverse literature on the relation between commitment-related variables (e.g., alienation; purpose in life) and well-being supports the conclusion that the two classes of variables are related (e.g., Phillips, 1980; Sexton, 1983; Thauberger & Cleland, 1981), although commitment-related measures commonly include items that overlap with aspects of depression. Sensation seeking and challenge are similar constructs, and so Hull and his colleagues' conclusion that challenge and distress are unrelated is supported by various findings in the sensation-seeking literature (e.g., Clarke & Innes, 1983; Kish, 1971; Zuckerman, Bone, Neary, Mangelsdorff, & Brustman, 1972; Zuckerman & Neeb, 1979). There is evidence indicating that neither commitment nor challenge is related to immune system variables (Okun et al., 1988).

As with social support, most of the available hardiness data are correlational and cross-sectional and thus ambiguous with respect to causality. The two longitudinal studies deserve special note. Banks and Gannon (1988) and Wiebe and McCallum (1986) found that composite hardiness appeared to have a direct, positive effect on self-reported health.

There remains the question of what coping styles might be associated with hardiness and its components that might make them ameliorative. We defer discussion of this issue to a later section, following a review of findings on hardiness as a stress moderator, because the literature on hardiness and coping is commonly cast in terms of stress-resistant behaviors. Note, however, that the level of stress is usually not a variable in studies of coping behavior as a function of hardiness. Accordingly, these studies may be appropriately regarded as reflecting coping aspects of hardiness that are not stress specific.

Support Versus Hardiness

There are a few reports of research that address both support and hardiness-related variables on the same data set, allowing for comparison between them vis-à-vis the strength of their relationships with well-being. Ben-Sira (1985) argued that personal resources are inherently superior to social ones, as the latter may render one dependent and inferior, and they are not omnipresent. Consistent with this, his data yielded larger correlations between potency and well-being than between social network and well-being, though perhaps nonsignificantly so. Our data (Ganellen et al., 1988, Study 1) show a hardiness–depression relation ($r = .42$, $p < .001$) that apparently is stronger than the support–depression relation ($r = .25$, $p < .005$).

Kobasa and Puccetti (1983) evaluated main effects for hardiness and support (from various sources) in the context of ANOVAs, with physical health as the dependent variable. In each case, the magnitude of effect was markedly stronger for hardiness. Using a sample that apparently overlaps with Kobasa and Puccetti's, Kobasa et al. (1985) entered both hardiness and support in a multiple regression analysis predicting physical health among a sample of high-stress males. Although hardiness accounted for much more of the variance than support did, it is not clear to what extent this reflects a stronger hardiness–health than support–health relation, as the two predictors were correlated and first-order correlations are not given. Kobasa (1982a) did offer first-order correlations, and they were clearly stronger for hardiness with symptoms than for support with symptoms.

In regard to studies of hardiness components, Hibbard (1985) examined the relations between control and social ties on the one hand and health variables on the other, controlling for demographic variables; if anything, control was more strongly related to health, though the differences were slight. Similar findings were reported by Levitt, Clark, Rotton, and Finley (1987); Husaini, Neff, Newbrough, and Moore (1982); and Lefcourt et al. (1984). However, Vernberg (1987) reported data in which the support–depression relation was considerably stronger than the control–depression relation. Finally, Quisumbing (1982) compared a measure of commitment with a measure of support (density) and found the former, and not the latter, to be related to well-being.

Of course, which variable wins in any such competition may reflect, in part, which variable is favored by (1) being measured more effectively or (2) being more contaminated with dependent-variable variance. Regarding this latter issue, there has long been concern (Lamont, 1972) that the standard measure of control may be inherently mood related, and as we noted, this concern may pertain to alienation measures as well. On the other hand, there also is considerable overlap between social support and some aspects of psychopathology (cf. Monroe &

Steiner, 1986), and mood level may influence self-reports of support (Procidano & Heller, 1983).

Interactions

Hardiness or its components may conceivably interact with support in promoting well-being. Two rationales for such an interaction can be sketched out. In the first, both hardiness and support are seen as providing marked ameliorative effects, such that the presence of either ensures the attainment of some well-being asymptote. The second rationale posits some kind of synergy between hardiness and support. For instance, if hardy persons are especially able to mobilize whatever supports are present in their life space (cf. Eckenrode, 1983), being hardy will be more helpful when there are many social resources to mobilize than when there are not. Whereas the first rationale would predict a special vulnerability of nonhardy, low-support individuals, the second rationale would predict a special invulnerability of hardy, high-support individuals. (Note that we still are not discussing effects that involve stress, though these lines of reasoning can be extrapolated to models that do.)

We found just one study (Kobasa & Puccetti, 1983) in which the Hardiness x Support interaction term was considered. The interaction was not significant when support from boss was considered, but it was significant when family support was considered. An examination of group means suggests that the interaction reflects a pattern predicted by neither rationale in the preceding paragraph. Instead, it suggests that although family support is somewhat ameliorative for hardy individuals, it is clearly associated with poorer health among nonhardy individuals. It is not clear what this means, although it may reflect, among persons lacking hardiness, (1) an association between family support and dependency and passivity and/or (2) increased family support in the face of ill health (as the direction of causation cannot be specified). It may also have something to do with the fact that families sometimes give advice that is irrelevant and counterproductive and that nonhardy individuals may be especially influenced by such advice.

Two studies considered the interaction between support and control. Seeman, Seeman, and Sayles (1985) presented findings relating health-oriented support and control perceptions to physical health. Two interesting findings deserve note from among the rather complex results. First, although there is little evidence of an effect for either control or instrumental support among women, among males an interaction emerges that shows long-term health levels to be lowest among the low-control, low-support males. Second, in regard to advice-oriented support, there was a clear interaction between control and support, but of an unexpected sort: With high control levels, high support predicted good health, but with low control levels, high support predicted poor health. Apparently, in the presence of low control, receiving advice has negative implications that it does not have in the presence of high control. This is somewhat similar to the pattern of results found by Kobasa and Puccetti (1983), and the same explanations may apply.

Hibbard (1985) considered a similar array of variables, albeit with a single index of support, and obtained evidence of a support–control interaction, such that a positive relation between support and health is seen primarily among externals; internals show little such relation, perhaps in part because their health levels are relatively good even in the absence of support.

HARDINESS AND SOCIAL SUPPORT AS BUFFERS

As we noted at the beginning of this chapter, behind much of the interest in hardiness, social support, and their relation with one another lies the hope that they may be able to distinguish persons who are more vulnerable to the effects of stress from those who are less so. In this section, we address the relevant empirical findings, for example, those that ascertain whether it is particularly in the face of stress that support and/or hardiness positively affects well-being. In ANOVA or multiple regression language, this would be expected to be a significant two-way interaction. In first-order correlation terms, it would be expected to show up in the form of an enhanced correlation between stressor and stress responses among low-support (or low-hardiness) persons, or in the form of an enhanced correlation between support (or hardiness) and well-being among high-stress individuals. The findings of main-effect associations of well-being with support and with hardiness by no means rule out the possibility of interaction effects in the case of these variables.

Support

As with the simple support effects, we will not cover here the research on support as a moderator of stressors' negative effects, as it has been reviewed elsewhere (e.g., Blaney, 1985). But briefly, the data are unclear. Although some studies appear to provide definitive evidence that stress effects are found primarily among low-support persons, other, large, well-designed studies showed no such interaction, and there are even instances of studies in which the presence of social support evidently amplified the negative effects of stressors (primarily family support, vis-à-vis job stressors).

Hardiness

In regard to evidence regarding hardiness as a moderator of the stressor–distress relationship, among the various reports by Kobasa and colleagues, significant Stress x Hardiness interactions appeared in two: Kobasa, Maddi, and Kahn (1982), and Kobasa, Maddi, and Puccetti (1982). But these should not be viewed as independent findings, as they were apparently on overlapping data sets. The first of the two is the more worthy of summary. In it, Kobasa, Maddi, and Kahn (1982) reported a longitudinal study in which, covarying for baseline health, baseline hardiness interacted with stressful events (assessed retrospectively at the outcome) in predicting physical health at the outcome. Unfortunately, the researchers did not provide the subgroup means and pairwise comparisons necessary to explicate the nature of the interaction (though the relevant data are presented elsewhere, for example, Table 3 of Kobasa, Maddi, & Courington, 1981), nor did they address whether the pattern of results might have been due to group differences in the covariate.

From the summaries in the published literature, one might assume that Kobasa and colleagues amassed a more varied array of data that support the hardiness as stress-moderator model. The reason is probably that they published more than one report on the same data set (cf. Hull et al., 1987) and that they tended to count the near-significant interactions (e.g., Kobasa et al., 1983; Kobasa & Puccetti, 1983) as supportive. In addition, some of the findings have been erroneously presented as supporting the model. For instance, Kobasa et al. (1985) portrayed a relation between hardiness and health among high-stress subjects as indicating a buffer effect. But because they provided no data on the low-stress controls, one cannot know to what extent the obtained effect is specific to stressful contexts, and the moderator idiom is unwarranted. In short, Kobasa and colleagues reported what appears to be a supportive pattern of results based on one data set, although a full explication of these data appears in none of the published papers, and some analyses of the same data set have yielded nonsupportive results.

Nowack (1986) presented data in which the Stress (i.e., hassles) x Hardiness interaction was significant when the dependent variable was job burnout, but not significant when it was psychological distress; the group means necessary to understand the significant interaction were not included. McCrainie, Lambert, and Lambert (1987) sought but did not obtain an interaction between hardiness and job stress, in which burnout was the dependent variable. Rhodewalt and Agustsdottir (1984) offered data that could be interpreted as indicating a stronger relation between undesirable events and depression in hardy than in nonhardy individuals, although this appeared to be due entirely to the tendency of hardy individuals to rate the events occurring to them as desirable. Banks and Gannon (1988), Wiebe and McCallum (1986) and Schmied and Lawler (1986) presented findings involving no Hardiness x Stress interaction, where dependent variables were illness levels, although Banks and Gannon did show one marginal finding.

In sum, the empirical literature on hardiness as a stress moderator is inconclusive. Although there are perhaps too many supportive findings to dismiss the possibility that hardiness may moderate the negative effects of stress, the effect is far from established.

Hardiness Components

In regard to studies that evaluated hardiness components as stress moderators, consider first the research on control. Ganellen and Blaney (1984b) reviewed the earlier literature and concluded that although the findings were mixed, they tended to support the control-as-stress-moderator position, a finding that subsequently received further support (Krause, 1985). Ganellen and Blaney's (1984b) data indicated that it is the aspect of control pertaining to the perception of outcomes as due to chance that functions as the stress moderator. High-chance, high-stress subjects were particularly depressed (see also Wheaton, 1983).

Other studies suggest that the picture is more complex. Specifically, Lefcourt et al. (1984, Study 1) indicated that when control is measured using scales specific to affiliation and achievement, affiliation externals show an especially strong stressor–distress relation (as expected), but achievement *internals* show an especially strong stressor–distress relation. Krause and Stryker (1984) presented data indicating that it is moderate internality that minimizes the stressor–distress relationship, whereas extreme internality (as well as externality) leaves one more vulnerable to stress effects. This may, of course, be related to Krause's (1987b) finding (on a different subject sample) of a nonmonotonic relation between locus of control and emotional support, in which maximal support levels are seen at moderate control levels.

Regarding commitment as a moderator, Ganellen and Blaney (1984a) reported a significant interaction between alienation from self and stress, in which high-alienation, high-stress subjects had particularly high depression scores. However, Quisumbing (1982) reported a similar analysis in which the interaction effect was not significant.

Several studies may be seen as addressing the stress-moderating role of challenge or sensation seeking. Although at least one study provided evidence indicating the presence of such a relation (Smith, Johnson, & Sarason, 1978), others did not (Cohen, 1982; Ganellen & Blaney, 1984a; Quisumbing, 1982), and one yielded an interaction in the unpredicted direction (Clarke & Innes, 1983).

Because our discussion addressed two different classes of two-way interactions (between support and stress and between hardiness and distress), we should note those studies that analyzed both interactions with the same subjects. Ganellen and Blaney (1984a) reported such a study, and a hardiness component (alienation from self) but not support showed the significant interaction with the stressor variable. In a similar study by Clarke and Innes (1983), support but not challenge (measured as sensation seeking) showed a significant interaction. Husaini et al. (1982) obtained significant interactions between stress and both support and a control-relevant variable, although the findings were considerably more consistent with control, especially among male subjects.

HARDINESS × SOCIAL SUPPORT × STRESS EFFECTS

The models covered in this section are those that considered the possibility that well-being is best seen in terms of a triple interaction among hardiness (or its components), support, and stress. Possible rationales for such a triple interaction would parallel those offered in an earlier section for Hardiness x Support interactions: that (1) either hardiness or support is ameliorative or (2) there is a synergism between them. In the case of the triple interaction, either rationale would be elaborated with the prediction that the effect in question is relevant only when stress levels are elevated.

We found only one study in which a Hardiness x Support x Stress interaction effect was considered. Kobasa and Puccetti (1983) obtained a near-significant triple interaction involving family support. An examination of the group means suggests that it reflects the fact that although low-stress subjects (hardy and nonhardy) and high-stress nonhardy subjects showed poorer health with high than with low support, high-stress hardy subjects showed better health with high than with low support. Although this is intriguing, its emergence is tied to an unusual finding (though not unique) in the research literature: Support was detrimental to health in several subgroups in this study. Stated otherwise, in showing a positive association between health and support, high-stress hardy subjects were unusual in this study but typical of unselected subjects in most studies. Given the failure of the interaction to reach significance (and the apparent failure of a parallel trend to emerge when boss support was considered), the finding should be viewed tentatively.

Several reports considered the possibility of a Control x Support x Stress interaction or its correlational equivalent. Sandler and Lakey (1982) were apparently the first to present data suggesting such a pattern. They obtained a stress-buffering effect of support for internals but not for externals, although they reported no test of the significance of the contrast. Similarly, in data reported by Lefcourt (1985), the positive stress-buffering effect of support was primarily evident among internal individuals. Analyses reported by Husaini et al. (1982) yielded triple interactions that were not, with rare exceptions, significant, despite the adequate sample size. Caldwell et al. (1987) assessed the effects of internality, support, stress, and gender. Although results were complex, mixed, and not easily summarized, a tendency for high-support internals to be especially protected from the effects of stress was evident, but only among males. Both Husaini and colleagues' (1982) and Lefcourt's (1985) findings, however, suggest that if the triple interaction effect exists, it probably is strongest among females, and Sandler and Lakey's (1982) sample was principally female. Kobasa and Puccetti's (1983) subjects were male. The role of gender in such effects clearly deserves further attention (see also Butler, Giordano, & Neren, 1985).

Although there thus is some consistency among studies, it is not striking enough to lead one to conclude that the Control x Support x Stress model provides the endpoint in our search for moderator effects, and the data do not make it clear what form a triple interaction will usually take if it does prove reliable. Moreover, one could, on theoretical and intuitive grounds, argue that there are other personal factors, not encompassed by the hardiness construct, that are at least as likely to interact with support. Strength of affiliative needs is such a factor, and there are research reports in which the effects predicted by such a line of reasoning do, in fact, emerge (Duckitt & Broll, 1983; Hill, 1987).

HARDINESS AND COPING

The kind of multiple interaction model implicit in the preceding section does not address some of the most interesting questions regarding processes inherent in stress resistance, particularly those having to do with what it is about the various personal and interpersonal resources that makes them beneficial. Such questions can be answered empirically in terms of those resources' response correlates. In this section we review data pertaining to the kinds of coping that are associated with hardiness and its components. As we noted, however, although the relevant research literature is commonly cast in terms of coping with stress, the study designs do not permit one to rule out the possibility that these coping mechanisms may be as important to low as they are to high stressor levels.

Kobasa (1982a) found that nonhardy individuals tend to use regressive coping, that is, to retreat from attempting to change a situation and to engage in pessimistic appraisals of it. Anderson (1977) and Parkes (1984) discovered similar results with respect to control, and Wiebe and McCallum (1986) reported the results of a longitudinal study indicating that composite hardiness was associated with good health care behaviors (which, in turn, influenced health). However, Grace and Schill (1986) saw no relation between control and problem-solving coping. Similarly, Ganellen et al. (1988) found no appreciable relation between hardiness (assessed with a commitment-oriented measure) and any coping style in Study 1, and hardiness was unrelated to problem-solving coping in Study 2. In Study 1 (but not Study 2), social support was associated ($r = .49$) with a measure of proactive stress-modifying coping.

Although Grace and Schill (1986) found that control was not associated with problem-solving coping, in their data, control was associated with seeking-support coping. It is possible that the relation between control and problem-solving (task-oriented, direct) coping shown in Anderson's (1977) and Parkes's (1984) studies reflects a similar effect, as these studies included seeking-support coping in their variables. Relevant to the control–support seeking relation, although the findings reviewed in an earlier section indicated that control is not closely related to most measures of social support per se, control was found to be associated with sociability (Hull et al., 1987) and social extroversion (Archer, 1980) and inversely with loneliness (Solano, 1987). Similarly, Eckenrode (1983) presented data indicating that although internality is not related to the amount of available support, it is related to the amount of support actually received while under stress. Eckenrode inferred from his data "that internals may not possess more social resources than externals, but that their resources are more effectively mobilized in times of stress" (p. 523). This inference appears to be consistent with the broader pattern of findings as well.

What hardiness was clearly related to in both of the Ganellen and colleagues' (1988) studies was a variable called *self-denigration* in Study 1 ($r = -.63$) and self-blame coping in Study 2 ($r = -.34$). More noteworthy still, in Study 2 hardiness was associated ($r = -.42$) with a measure of self-isolation (keeping to self) coping (a variable unique to Study 2). Support showed smaller but significant correlations with these variables. The relation between hardiness and self-isolation contrasted with the absence of a relation between hardiness and seeking-support coping. An examination of item content suggests that what is distinctive about self-isolation is that it reflects active efforts to keep others from knowing about one's negative experiences.

When one puts aside those findings that are contradicted by other studies, a striking picture emerges, one in which most of the remaining coping-style correlates of both control (cf. Grace & Schill, 1986) and hardiness (Ganellen et al., 1988) have to do with an individual's way of dealing with the social environment. In the case of control, an individual's ability to mobilize needed assistance (support seeking) appears to be crucial, whereas in the case of hardiness what appears important is whether or not one needs to hide one's negative experiences from others (self-isolation).

FUTURE DIRECTIONS

In reading various studies that show diverse levels of methodological and conceptual sophistication, reviewers form opinions about the kinds of features that future studies should incorporate if the research tradition is to be fruitful. We summarize ours here:

1.   Components and facets of the major variables (hardiness, social support, well-being) should be considered separately. Each stands for a complex array of possible subvariables, and clarity requires that this complexity not be ignored.

2.   Analyses should avoid relying on median splits and avoid assuming that relations between variables are monotonic (cf. Krause, 1987a; Krause & Stryker, 1984).

3.   Variables should be measured purely; that is, they should avoid possible variable-to-variable overlap in item content, which spuriously increases variable intercorrelations.

4.   Possible effects involving gender should be considered.

5.   Coping behaviors and styles should be entered as both predictor variables and dependent variables, to allow examination of the roles of both resistance resources in coping and coping as a resistance resource.

6.   The possibility that relevant control perceptions and support experiences may be somewhat stressor specific should be considered.

7.   In order to increase relevance to causal inferences, longitudinal designs should be used.

This need for longitudinal designs is crucial and deserves further comment. Consider the structure used in the most sophisticated of existing studies (e.g., Kobasa, Maddi, & Kahn, 1982). A relatively unselected sample was assessed with respect to personal (e.g., hardiness) and external (e.g., social support) variables at one time, and it was subsequently assessed with respect to a well-being outcome measure. When considering moderator effects, the focus was on the interaction between Time 1 resources and the level of stress between assessments. To increase the rigor of any causal inferences, some control over the initial (cross-sectional) well-being was imposed, typically by covarying for initial levels on the dependent variable.

However, this approach is not always as satisfactory a solution as is often assumed, in part because there often are interesting initial-assessment relations among these variables, relations that can make longitudinal effects difficult to interpret. Comparing change effects among subjects differing appreciably on initial levels is always a bit risky. It appears necessary to analyze subgroups that are homogeneous with respect to initial level of well-being, the simplest version of which is to use a preselection procedure that admits only persons who are not distressed. If this is done, so that all subjects initially are not distressed, those who report high levels of prior stress when initially assessed should probably be excluded (or segregated), as they are, by definition, persons who have already shown themselves resistant to the negative effects of stress.

It is possible, however, that implementing this kind of research is premature at this point, because we may not yet have a strong enough grasp of the issues surrounding sources of stress resistance. In particular, those resources that are crucial determinants of stress resistance may be latent and difficult to detect when a person is unstressed. For instance, some persons find that a crisis produces unexpected support resources, whereas others find that the friends one thought one could count on are unexpectedly absent (Peters-Golden, 1982). The situation may be similar with respect to resources within the individual. If exposure to stress can change the quantity or quality of one's social or personal resources, we should be giving some research attention to predicting such changes, and we should do it before embarking on large-scale studies that assume that stress moderators are static entities.

REFERENCES

Anderson, C. R. (1977). Locus of control, coping behaviors, and performance in a stress setting: A longitudinal study. *Journal of Applied Psychology, 62,* 446–451.

Anderson, H. N., Madonna, S., Bailey, G., & Wesley, A. (1987). Further considerations of the multidimensionality and factor structure of the Rotter locus of control scale. *Psychological Reports, 60,* 1059–1062.

Antonovsky, A. (1979). *Health, stress, and coping.* San Francisco: Jossey-Bass.

Archer, R. P. (1980). Generalized expectancies of control, trait anxiety, and psychopathology among psychiatric inpatients. *Journal of Consulting and Clinical Psychology, 48,* 736–742.

Banks, J. K., & Gannon, L. R. (1988). The influence of hardiness on the relationship between stressors and psychosomatic symptomatology. *American Journal of Community Psychology, 16,* 25–37.

Benassi, V. A., Sweeney, P. D., & Dufour, C. L. (1988). Is there a relationship between locus of control orientation and depression? *Journal of Abnormal Psychology, 97,* 357–367.

Ben-Sira, Z. (1985). Potency: A stress-buffering link in the coping–stress–disease relationship. *Social Science and Medicine, 21,* 397–406.

Blaney, P. H. (1985). Stress and depression in adults: A critical review. In T. M. Field, P. M. McCabe, & N. Schneiderman (Eds.), *Stress and coping* (pp. 263–283). Hillsdale, NJ: Erlbaum.

Brown, D. R., & Gary, L. E. (1987). Stressful life events, social support networks, and the physical and mental health of urban black adults. *Journal of Human Stress, 13,* 165–174.

Butler, T., Giordano, S., & Neren, S. (1985). Gender and sex-role attributes as predictors of utilization of natural support during personal stress events. *Sex Roles, 13,* 515–524.

Caldwell, R. A., Pearson, J. L., & Chen, R. J. (1987). Stress-moderating effects: Social support in the context of gender and locus of control. *Personality and Social Psychology Bulletin, 13,* 5–17.

Carver, C. (1989). How should multifaceted personality constructs be tested? Issues illustrated by self-monitoring, attributional style, and hardiness. *Journal of Personality and Social Psychology, 56,* 577–585.

Clarke, A., & Innes, J. M. (1983). Sensation-seeking motivation and social-support moderators of the life stress/illness relationship: Some contradictory and confirmatory evidence. *Personality and Individual Differences, 4,* 547–550.

Cobb, S. (1976). Social support as a moderator of life stress. *Psychosomatic Medicine, 38,* 300–314.

Cohen, L. H. (1982). Life change and the sensation seeking motive. *Personality and Individual Differences, 3,* 221–222.

Cohen, S., & Wills, T. A. (1985). Stress, social support, and the buffering hypothesis. *Psychological Bulletin, 98,* 310–357.

DeVellis, R. F., & DeVellis, B. M. (1986). An evolving psychosocial model of epilepsy. In S. Whitman & B. P. Hermann (Eds.), *Psychopathology in epilepsy: Social dimensions* (pp. 122–142). New York: Oxford University Press.

Duckitt, J., & Broll, T. (1983). Life stress, personality, and illness behavior: A prospective study. *Psychological Reports, 53,* 51–57.

Eckenrode, J. (1983). The mobilization of social supports: Some individual constraints. *American Journal of Community Psychology, 11,* 509–528.

Folkman, S., Lazarus, R. S., Pimley, S., & Novacek, J. (1987). Age differences in stress and coping processes. *Psychology and Aging, 2,* 171–184.

Ganellen, R. J., & Blaney, P. H. (1984a). Hardiness and social support as moderators of the effects of life stress. *Journal of Personality and Social Psychology, 47,* 156–161.

Ganellen, R. J., & Blaney, P. H. (1984b). Stress, externality and depression. *Journal of Personality, 52,* 326–337.

Ganellen, R. J., Blaney, P. H., & Baggett, L. (1988). *Hardiness, social support, and coping.* Unpublished manuscript.

Goswick, R. A., & Jones, W. H. (1982). Components of loneliness during adolescence. *Journal of Youth and Adolescence, 11,* 373–383.

Grace, G., & Schill, T. (1986). Expectancy of personal control and seeking social support in coping style. *Psychological Reports, 58,* 757–758.

Hibbard, J. H. (1985). Social ties and health status: An examination of moderating factors. *Health Education Quarterly, 12,* 23–34.

Hill, C. A. (1987). Social support and health: The role of affiliative need as a moderator. *Journal of Research in Personality, 21,* 127–147.

Holahan, C. K., & Holahan, C. J. (1987). Self-efficacy, social support and depression in aging: A longitudinal analysis. *Journal of Gerontology, 42,* 65–68.

Howard, J. H., Cunningham, D. A., & Rechnitzer, P. A. (1986). Personality (hardiness) as a moderator of job stress and coronary risk in Type A individuals: A longitudinal study. *Journal of Behavioral Medicine, 9,* 229–244.

Hull, J. G., Van Treuren, R. R., & Virnelli, S. (1987). Hardiness and health: A critique and alternative approach. *Journal of Personality and Social Psychology, 53,* 518–530.

Husaini, B. A., Neff, J. A., Newbrough, J. R., & Moore, M. C. (1982). The stress-buffering role of social support and personal competence among the rural married. *Journal of Community Psychology, 10,* 409–426.

Kish, G. B. (1971). CPI correlates of stimulus-seeking in male alcoholics. *Journal of Clinical Psychology, 27,* 251–253.

Kobasa, S. C. (1979). Stressful life events, personality, and health: An inquiry into hardiness. *Journal of Personality and Social Psychology, 37,* 1–11.

Kobasa, S. C. (1982a). Commitment and coping in stress resistance among lawyers. *Journal of Personality and Social Psychology, 42,* 707–717.

Kobasa, S. C. (1982b). The hardy personality: Toward a social psychology of stress and health. In G. Sanders & J. Suls (Eds.), *Social psychology of health and illness* (pp. 3–32). Hillsdale, NJ: Erlbaum.

Kobasa, S. C., Maddi, S. R., & Courington, S. (1981). Personality and constitution as mediators in the stress–illness relationship. *Journal of Health and Social Behavior, 22,* 368–378.

Kobasa, S. C., Maddi, S. R., & Kahn, S. (1982). Hardiness and health: A prospective study. *Journal of Personality and Social Psychology, 42,* 168–177.

Kobasa, S. C., Maddi, S. R., & Puccetti, M. C. (1982). Personality and exercise as buffers in the stress–illness relationship. *Journal of Behavioral Medicine, 5,* 391–404.

Kobasa, S. C., Maddi, S. R., Puccetti, M. C., & Zola, M. A. (1985). Effectiveness of hardiness, exercise and social support as resources against illness. *Journal of Psychosomatic Research, 29,* 525 533.

Kobasa, S. C., Maddi, S. R., & Zola, M. A. (1983). Type A and hardiness. *Journal of Behavioral Medicine, 6,* 41–51.

Kobasa, S. C., & Puccetti, M. C. (1983). Personality and social resources in stress-resistance. *Journal of Personality and Social Psychology, 45,* 839–856.

Krause, N. (1985). Stress, control beliefs, and psychological distress: The problem of response bias. *Journal of Human Stress, 11,* 11–19.

Krause, N. (1987a). Chronic financial strain, social support, and depressive symptoms among older adults. *Psychology and Aging, 2,* 185–192.

Krause, N. (1987b). Understanding the stress process: Linking social support with locus of control beliefs. *Journal of Gerontology, 42,* 589–593.

Krause, N., & Stryker, S. (1984). Stress and well-being: The buffering role of locus of control beliefs. *Social Science and Medicine, 18,* 783–790.

Kuo, W. H., & Tsai, Y. (1986). Social networking, hardiness and immigrants' mental health. *Journal of Health and Social Behavior, 27,* 133–149.

Ladewig, B. H., & McGee, G. W. (1986). Occupational commitment, a supportive family environment, and marital adjustment: Development and estimation of a model. *Journal of Marriage and the Family, 48,* 821–829.

Lamont, J. (1972). Item mood-level as a determinant of I–E test response. *Journal of Clinical Psychology, 28,* 190.

Lefcourt, H. M. (1985). Intimacy, social support, and locus of control as moderators of stress. In I. G. Sarason & B. R. Sarason (Eds.), *Social support: Theory, research, and applications* (pp. 155–171). Dordrecht, Netherlands: Martinus Nijhoff.

Lefcourt, H. M., Martin, R. A., & Saleh, W. E. (1984). Locus of control and social support: Interactive moderators of stress. *Journal of Personality and Social Psychology, 47,* 378–389.

Levenson, H. (1973). Multidimensional locus of control in psychiatric patients. *Journal of Consulting and Clinical Psychology, 41,* 397–404.

Levitt, M. J., Clark, M. C., Rotton, J., & Finley, G. E. (1987). Social support, perceived control and well-being: A study of an environmentally stressed population. *International Journal of Aging and Human Development, 25,* 247–258.

Maddi, S. R., Kobasa, S. C., & Hoover, M. (1979). An alienation test. *Journal of Humanistic Psychology, 19,* 73–76.

McCranie, E. W., Lambert, V. A., & Lambert, C. E. (1987). Work stress, hardiness, and burnout among hospital staff nurses. *Nursing Research, 36,* 374–378.

Millon, T., Green, C., & Meagher, R. (1976). *Millon Behavioral Health Inventory.* Minneapolis: National Computer Systems.

Monroe, S. M., & Steiner, S. C. (1986). Social support and psychopathology: Interrelations with preexisting disorder, stress, and personality. *Journal of Abnormal Psychology, 95,* 29–39.

Nezu, A. M. (1986). Efficacy of a social problem-solving therapy approach for unipolar depression. *Journal of Consulting and Clinical Psychology, 54,* 196–202.

Nowack, K. M. (1986). Type A hardiness and psychological distress. *Journal of Behavioral Medicine, 9,* 537–548.

Okun, M. A., Zautra, A. J., & Robinson, S. E. (1988). Hardiness and health among women with rheumatoid arthritis. *Personality and Individual Differences, 9,* 101–107.

Parkes, K. R. (1984). Locus of control, cognitive appraisal, and coping in stressful episodes. *Journal of Personality and Social Psychology, 46,* 655–668.

Peters-Golden, H. (1982). Breast cancer: Varied perceptions of social support in the illness experience. *Social Science and Medicine, 16,* 147–154.

Phillips, W. M. (1980). Purpose in life, depression and locus of control. *Journal of Clinical Psychology, 36,* 661–667.

Pollock, S. E. (1986). Human responses to chronic illness: Physiologic and psychosocial adaptation. *Nursing Research, 35,* 90–95.

Poresky, R. H., & Atilano, R. B. (1982). Alienation in rural women: A longitudinal cross-lagged analysis of its association with community and family involvement, socioeconomic status, and education. *Home Economics Research Journal, 11,* 183–188.

Procidano, M. E., & Heller, K. I. (1983). Measures of perceived social support from friends and family: Three validation studies. *American Journal of Community Psychology, 11,* 1–24.

Quisumbing, M. S. (1982). *Life events, social support and personality: Their impact on Filipino psychological adjustment.* Unpublished doctoral dissertation, University of Chicago.

Rhodewalt, F., & Agustsdottir, S. (1984). On the relationship of hardiness to a Type A behavior pattern: Perception of life events versus coping with life events. *Journal of Research in Personality, 18,* 212–223.

Sandler, I. N., & Lakcy, D. (1982). Locus of control as a stress moderator: The role of control perceptions and social support. *American Journal of Community Psychology, 10,* 65–80.

Sarason, I. G., Levine, H. M., Basham, R. B., & Sarason, B. R. (1983). Assessing social support: The Social Support Questionnaire. *Journal of Personality and Social Psychology, 44,* 127–139.

Sarason, I. G., & Sarason, B. R. (1982). Concomitants of social support: Attitudes, personality characteristics, and life experiences. *Journal of Personality, 50,* 331–344.

Schmied, L. W., & Lawler, K. A. (1986). Hardiness, Type A behavior and the stress–illness relation in working women. *Journal of Personality and Social Psychology, 51,* 1218–1223.

Schultz, B. J., & Saklofsky, D. H. (1983). Relationship between social support and selected measures of psychological well-being. *Psychological Reports, 53,* 847–850.

Seeman, M., Seeman, T., & Sayles, M. (1985). Social networks and health status. *Social Psychology Quarterly, 48,* 237–248.

Sexton, M. E. (1983). Alienation, dogmatism, and related personality characteristics. *Journal of Clinical Psychology, 39,* 80–86.

Smith, R. E., Johnson, J. H., & Sarason, I. G. (1978). Life change, the sensation seeking motive and psychological distress. *Journal of Consulting and Clinical Psychology, 46,* 348–349.

Solano, C. H. (1987). Loneliness and perceptions of control: General traits versus specific attributions. *Journal of Social Behavior and Personality, 2,* 201–214.

Suls, J., Becker, M. A. & Mullen, B. (1981). Coronary-prone behavior, social insecurity, and stress among college-aged adults. *Journal of Human Stress, 7* (3), 27–34.

Thauberger, P. C., & Cleland, J. F. (1981). Purpose in life and some correlates of social behavior and health. *Journal of Alcohol and Drug Education, 27,* 19–25.

Turner, R. J., & Noh, S. (1983). Class and psychological vulnerability among women: The significance of social support and personal control. *Journal of Health and Social Behavior, 24,* 2–15.

Vachon, M. L. S., Lyall, W. A. L., Rogers, J., Freedman-Letoesky, K., & Freeman, S. J. J. (1980). A controlled study of self-help intervention for widows. *American Journal of Psychiatry, 137,* 1380–1384.

Vernberg, E. M. (1987, April). *Friendship development, coping resources and psychological adjustment following relocation during early adolescence.* Paper presented at the meeting of the Society for Research in Child Development, Baltimore.

Vinokur, A., Schul, Y., & Caplan, R. D. (1987). Determinants of perceived social support: Interpersonal transactions, personal outlook, and transient affective states. *Journal of Personality and Social Psychology, 53,* 1137–1145.

Wallston, B. S., Alagna, S. W., DeVellis, B. M., & DeVellis, R. F. (1983). Social support and physical health. *Health Psychology, 2,* 367–391.

Wheaton, B. (1983). Stress, personal coping resources and psychiatric symptoms: An investigation of interactive models. *Journal of Health and Social Behavior, 24,* 208–229.

Wiebe, D. J., & McCallum, D. M. (1986). Health practices and hardiness as mediators in the stress–illness relationship. *Health Psychology, 5,* 425–438.

Wilcox, B. L., & Vernberg, E. M. (1985). Conceptual and theoretical dilemmas facing social support. In I. G. Sarason & B. R. Sarason (Eds.), *Social support: Theory, research, and applications* (pp. 3–20). Dordrecht, The Netherlands: Martinus Nijhoff.

Zuckerman, M., Bone, R. W., Neary, R., Mangelsdorff, D., & Brustman, B. (1972). What is the sensation seeker? Personality trait and experience correlates of the Sensation-Seeking scales. *Journal of Consulting and Clinical Psychology, 39*, 308–321.

Zuckerman, M., & Neeb, M. (1979). Sensation seeking and psychotherapy. *Psychiatry Research, 1*, 255–264.

CHAPTER 13

Type of Social Support and Specific Stress: Toward a Theory of Optimal Matching

CAROLYN E. CUTRONA AND DANIEL W. RUSSELL

University of Iowa

Although theorists differ on specifics, there is wide agreement that social support is a multidimensional phenomenon (Caplan, 1974; Cobb, 1976, 1979; Cohen & McKay, 1984; House, 1981; Kahn, 1979; Schaefer, Coyne, & Lazarus, 1981; Thoits, 1982; Weiss, 1974). A broad range of interpersonal behaviors by members of a person's social network may help him or her successfully cope with adverse life events and circumstances. Direct assistance, advice, encouragement, companionship, and expressions of affection all have been associated with positive outcomes for persons facing various life strains and dilemmas.

A key unanswered question is whether certain forms of social support are most beneficial following specific kinds of stress. If we could match support components to stress, we could design better social support–based interventions. We could design programs to promote the most beneficial kinds of supportive interactions, given the clientele's particular circumstances (e.g., recovery from surgery, bereavement, unemployment). Theoretically, the discovery of optimal stress–support combinations may help us understand better both how adverse life events threaten and how social support protects or enhances well-being.

Until recently, the empirical literature regarding the relative contributions of specific support components to adaptation to specific stressful events has revealed little. The early research tended to treat social support as a unidimensional construct or to analyze only aggregate support scores, thus obscuring the differential impact of specific components. A particularly cogent critique of that approach was offered by Heller, Swindle, and Dusenbury (1986, p. 467):

> One would never think of doing research on the relation of "personality" to health outcomes with the expectation that any personality variable would show the same

Preparation of this chapter was supported by grants R01–AG03846 and P01–AG07094 from the National Institute on Aging and grant R01–APR000931 from the Office of Population Affairs, Adolescent Pregnancy Programs.

pattern of relations with outcome variables as any other personality variable. Yet social support researchers have been engaged in similarly dubious endeavors.

Although a trend toward a multidimensional assessment and analysis of social support is now evident, another design feature of most research on social support has obscured the effects of specific components of support on adjustment to specific stressful events. Most researchers have tested the effects of social support in broad community samples, without regard for the specific types of stress that individuals encounter. Only the severity or number of events is coded, using cumulative life event measures (e.g., Holmes & Rahe, 1967). In 1985, Cohen and Wills estimated that 90% of the published social support studies used this approach. Although such methods are useful in establishing the *average* effects of support in protecting individuals who have experienced a wide range of stressful events, this epidemiological approach cannot advance our understanding of optimal matches between types of stress and types of support.

Because most studies have used either aggregate support measures or aggregate stress measures, earlier efforts to identify which kinds of support are most effective given different adverse circumstances have been largely theoretical (e.g., Cohen & McKay, 1984; Jacobson, 1986; Thoits, 1986; Weiss, 1976). Although studies that test the contribution to well-being of specific components of support in specific stressful circumstances are still relatively rare, their numbers are increasing and have reached sufficient mass to warrant review.

The purpose of this chapter is to review the evidence concerning the importance of matching the characteristics of a stressful event confronting an individual and the specific forms of social support that are most beneficial in that context. We will begin with a review of multidimensional models of social support, with a focus on commonalities among theoretical conceptualizations. Measures that have been developed to assess multiple components of social support will then be reviewed, with a focus on empirical tests of multidimensionality. The remainder of the chapter will address the issue of whether individual components of support are differentially associated with positive physical and mental health outcomes as a function of the kind of stress faced by the individual. Theoretical work on dimensions of stress will be discussed as a starting point to consider the different deficits or demands that confront individuals in various stressful contexts. Theory and research regarding the kinds of coping processes that are optimally effective for dealing with different kinds of stress will serve as another source of hypotheses concerning the forms of social support that are most helpful in the context of various stressors. After a summary of research on components of stress and the coping requirements associated with different kinds of stress, an optimal matching model will be presented. Empirical research that tests multiple components of social support as predictors of physical and mental health outcomes following specific stressful events will then be reviewed. Conclusions based on this review of the literature will be used to elaborate and refine the proposed model.

MULTIDIMENSIONAL MODELS OF SOCIAL SUPPORT

Researchers and theorists in the area of social support have proposed a number of different multidimensional models of social support (Caplan, 1974; Cobb, 1976, 1979; Cohen & McKay, 1984; Cohen & Wills, 1985; Hirsch, 1980; House, 1981; Kahn, 1979; Schaefer et al., 1981; Weiss, 1974). Their ideas about the different forms or components of social support appear to converge on a common set of dimensions. Table 13.1 presents the different forms of support described by five representative theoretical models. In this table, we attempted to draw parallels among forms of support that appear to be highly similar across models. So, for example, emotional support as described by Cobb (1979) and Schaefer and colleagues (1981) appears to be essentially identical to the concepts of attachment described by Weiss (1974) and affect described by Kahn (1979).

A study by Rose (1986) provided empirical support for the parallels across models in the support components shown in Table 13.1. She asked college students to divide the helping behaviors reported by a sample of elderly subjects into categories on the basis of the support classification schemes offered by Cobb (1979), Kahn (1979), and Weiss (1974). The parallels among the dimensions of support across these models shown in Table 13.1 were verified in her results. For example, a helping behavior that was classified as reflecting emotional support by Cobb tended also to be classified as reflecting affect as defined by Kahn and as attachment as defined by Weiss. Although further research exploring the com-

TABLE 13.1. Comparison of Component Models of Social Support

Weiss, 1974	Cobb, 1979	Kahn, 1979	Schaefer, Coyne, & Lazarus, 1981	Cohen, Mermelstein, Kamarck, & Hoberman, 1985
Attachment	Emotional support	Affect	Emotional support	
Social integration	Network support			Belonging support
Reassurance of worth	Esteem support	Affirmation		Self-esteem support
Reliable alliance	Material support	Aid	Tangible aid	Tangible support
Guidance	Instrumental support		Informational support	Appraisal support
Opportunity for nurturance	Active support[a]			

[a] Cobb (1979) defined active support as reflecting the receipt of care or "mothering" by the target person, whereas Weiss (1974) viewed the opportunity for nurturance as reflecting the provision of care to others by the target person.

monalities among these models of support is clearly warranted, the results here suggest that these theorists have found a common set of support dimensions.

From the dimensions of support presented in Table 13.1, we can derive a set of five basic support dimensions that appear in most of these models. First, *emotional support* appears to represent the ability to turn to others for comfort and security during times of stress, leading the person to feel that he or she is cared for by others. *Social integration* or *network support* refers to a person's feeling part of a group whose members have common interests and concerns. Such relationships reflect more casual friendships, which enable a person to engage in various forms of social and recreational activities. *Esteem support* represents the bolstering of a person's sense of competence or self-esteem by other people. Giving an individual positive feedback on his or her skills and abilities or expressing a belief that the person is capable of coping with a stressful event are examples of this type of support. *Tangible aid* refers to concrete instrumental assistance, in which a person in a stressful situation is given the necessary resources (e.g., financial assistance, physical help with tasks) to cope with the stressful event. Finally, *informational support* is providing the individual with advice or guidance concerning possible solutions to a problem.

A sixth form of support described by Weiss (1974) and also examined in some studies that we will review later is giving support to others. Defined by Weiss as the opportunity to provide nurturance, this aspect of interpersonal relationships reflects Weiss's belief that individuals need to feel that they are needed by others. Although there may be benefits to the individual of assisting others in coping with stress (e.g., a greater sense of personal competence), such benefits appear to accrue through mechanisms that are somewhat different from those associated with the receipt of social support.

Multidimensional Measures of Social Support

A number of different measures have been created to assess the dimensions of social support described in Table 13.1. The theoretical conceptualization of social support proposed by Weiss (1974) has inspired the greatest number of measurement efforts (Brandt & Weinert, 1981; Cutrona & Russell, 1987; Henderson, Duncan-Jones, Byrne, & Scott, 1980; Russell & Cutrona, 1984; Turner, Frankel, & Levin, 1983). Other scales have been based on the dimensions of support described by Cobb (Turner et al., 1983) and Kahn (Kahn & Antonucci, 1980; Kahn, Wethington, & Ingersoll-Dayton, 1987; Norbeck, Lindsey, & Carrieri, 1981, 1982). Still other multidimensional measures of support have been based on the dimensions of support derived by the authors of the inventories (Barrera, Sandler, & Ramsay, 1981; Cohen, Mermelstein, Kamarck, & Hoberman, 1985; Schaefer et al., 1981; Tetzloff & Barrera, 1987; Vaux, Riedel, & Stewart, 1987). Note that virtually all of these measures examine dimensions that correspond closely to those listed in Table 13.1.

It is beyond the scope of this chapter to address the psychometric properties of these instruments, but they have been considered in several reviews of social support measurement (e.g., Barrera, 1986; Bruhn & Philips, 1984; Heitzmann & Kaplan, 1988; House & Kahn, 1985; Tardy, 1985). However, we will discuss one psychometric issue, because it raises important conceptual questions regarding the dimensions of social support. For a number of these measures, very high correlations among the assessed dimensions were reported (see the discussion by Brown, 1986; House & Kahn, 1985). In some cases, the magnitudes of these correlations were as high as the respective reliabilities of the measures, thereby suggesting that one or more of the dimensions being assessed were redundant (Brandt & Weinert, 1981; Cohen et al., 1985; Norbeck et al., 1981; Schaefer et al., 1981; Tetzloff & Barrera, 1987). Some authors conducted factor analyses of items on instruments and, based on their results, combined two or more dimensions that were originally proposed as distinct (Barrera & Ainlay, 1983; Duncan-Jones, 1981a, 1981b; Stokes & Wilson, 1984; Tetzloff & Barrera, 1987; Turner et al., 1983).

These findings raise questions about the multidimensionality of social support. The results of these studies indicate that the support dimensions shown in Table 13.1 may need to be reduced to a smaller number (e.g., emotional support vs. tangible aid; see House & Kahn, 1985). One conclusion is that the investigators' inability to confirm the hypothesized dimensions of social support indicates that social support is a unidimensional construct, with no possible meaningful separation into distinct support functions.

Three more recent studies, however, provided empirical support for the dimensions of social support hypothesized to underly the measures being analyzed (Brookings & Bolton, 1988; Cutrona & Russell, 1987; Vaux et al., 1987). Of these studies, the most clear-cut findings were offered by Cutrona and Russell (1987) concerning the factor structure of the Social Provisions Scale, a measure we developed to assess the social provisions described by Weiss (1974; see Table 13.1). Using data from a sample of 1,792 individuals (which included college students, public school teachers, and nurses), we conducted a confirmatory factor analysis of responses to the scale to test for the existence of the six dimensions of support described by Weiss. This factor model was found to have a good fit with the data, with the factors clearly corresponding to the six social provisions. As expected, these factors were found to be significantly intercorrelated. Further analyses of these data indicated that a single second-order factor, reflecting the existence of a global support construct, accounted for the relations among the individual social provisions. Thus, just as in the case of intelligence, these results suggest the existence of a general support factor, which is further differentiated into the specific dimensions of support reflected by the individual social provisions.

In summary, the results of attempts to examine the dimensions of social support hypothesized in the conceptual models shown in Table 13.1 provide some justification for viewing social support as a multidimensional construct. The problems in differentiating the dimensions reported for many of these instruments clearly indicate the need for further developing these inventories, with particular attention to the measures' dimensional structure. We will give further empirical support for differentiating the specific support functions later in this chapter, when we discuss the effects of specific types of social support on adaptation to specific types of stressors.

DIMENSIONS OF STRESS

An understanding of stressful events is critical to an analysis of those interpersonal behaviors that may alleviate the effects of stress. Theorists have conceptualized stress quite differently and have addressed the question of dimensions or types of stress with different goals in mind. For example, Lazarus and his colleagues focused on individuals' cognitions regarding adverse situations, and they categorized stress in terms of the individuals' appraisals of the implications for valued resources (Lazarus, 1966; Lazarus & Folkman, 1984). Other investigators looked at dimensions of events that predict the onset of mental illness (Brown & Harris, 1978; Gersten, Langner, Eisenberg, & Orzek, 1974; Paykel, 1979). Categorizations of events were also based on their probabilities of co-occurrence or on perceived similarity (Miller, Bentz, Aponte, & Brogan, 1974; Rahe, Pugh, Erickson, Gunderson, & Rubin, 1971; Ruch, 1977; Skinner & Lei, 1980).

Cognitive Appraisal

A widely used definition of stress is that offered by Lazarus and his colleagues (Coyne & Lazarus, 1980; Folkman & Lazarus, 1984; Lazarus, 1966, 1981). In this model, stress is defined as a relationship between the person and the environment in which the individual perceives that something of personal value is at stake and judges that his or her resources are taxed or overwhelmed by the situation. Thus, if the individual determines that his or her personal or social resources are sufficient to forestall or overcome an impending threat, then the situation will not be defined as stressful. But even a seemingly minor loss may be highly stressful if it threatens a valued resource and the individual sees no way of resolving the situation. In this model, two kinds of cognitive appraisal are viewed as essential. Most relevant to our discussion is primary appraisal, in which the individual judges whether the situation poses a challenge (a potential for gain or growth), a threat (a potential for harm or loss), or actual harm or loss. The birth of one's first child is a good example of a challenging event that holds a potential for personal enrichment yet may tax personal resources. An example of a threat is a warning that unless one's work performance improves, one will lose one's job. In the case of threat, there has been no permanent harm or loss, and the damage can be averted or minimized. Finally, in the case of harm or loss, the damage has already been done, as by a death or divorce. Lazarus (1966, 1981) discussed three broad domains in which challenge, threat, or loss may be experienced. These domains include assets (e.g., material goods, health), relationships, and self-esteem.

This formulation is a simple but useful taxonomy of stressful events. Two dimensions are proposed: the individual's appraisal of the event as constituting a

challenge, a threat, or actual harm or loss; and the content domain—assets, relationships, or self-esteem—in which the stress occurs. These dimensions seem to
have implications for the type of social support that is most beneficial in a given
stressful situation. As we will show, closely related dimensions emerge repeatedly in attempts to categorize life events, and they will serve as the basis for our
matching framework.

Dimensions Predictive of Mental Illness

A number of researchers have attempted to discover dimensions of life events that
are associated with the onset of mental illness, especially depression. One controversy has centered on whether both positive and negative events are predictive
of mental illness. Reviews of the studies in this area have concluded that only
negative events predict subsequent psychological symptoms (e.g., Thoits, 1983).

Researchers have also investigated the controllability of events as a predictor
of psychopathology. Perceived controllability is a central aspect of cognitive theories of depression (Abramson, Seligman, & Teasdale, 1978; Seligman, 1975).
Thus, several studies tested the hypothesis that negative events perceived as uncontrollable are more depressogenic than are those perceived as controllable. The
results were generally consistent with this hypothesis (Fava, Munari, Pavan, &
Kellner, 1981; Grant, Sweetwood, Yager, & Gerst, 1981; Husaini & Neff, 1980,
1981; Paykel, 1974, 1979). A noteworthy exception is a study by Bulman and
Wortman (1977), in which patients recovering from spinal cord injuries adjusted
better if they attributed their accident to their own actions (e.g., participating in
competitive diving) than to those of someone or something outside themselves
(e.g., a drunken driver).

Duration of effect was examined as a dimension of life events that may predict
psychological aftereffects. Brown and Harris (1978) categorized events as "severe" if they posed a relatively long term threat to the individual and "non-
severe" if the threat was transient. They found that only severe events were associated with the onset of depression.

Finally, the content of events has received some attention in predicting mental
illness. In particular, it was hypothesized that events involving social loss ("exit
events") may be pathogenic for depression, and some support for this prediction
has been found (e.g., Paykel, 1979).

To summarize, four dimensions of stressful events were proposed on the basis of
their potential to precipitate psychopathology: desirability, controllability, duration of consequences, and experience of a social loss. Desirability, controllability,
and loss all were included or implied in the previous discussion of work by the
Lazarus group. Although Lazarus did not explicitly catalog events based on their
desirability or controllability, desirability is reflected in the distinction between
challenge versus threat, harm, or loss. Similarly, controllability was implied in
the distinction between challenge and threat versus harm or loss. Duration of
stress aftereffects was not included in the Lazarus scheme and provides another
dimension relevant to the kind of support that may be most beneficial.

Empirically Derived Dimensions of Events

Thoits (1983) reviewed research that used factor analysis and related statistical techniques to derive dimensions of life events. The resulting dimensions tend to differ from those just described in that their content was prominent. Rahe and colleagues (1971) reported four clusters of items from the Schedule of Recent Events, including personal and social changes, work changes, marital changes, and disciplinary changes (e.g., legal problems, arrest). Miller and associates (1974) also found four factors: life-space changes (recreational and work events), personal life-style changes, and relationship terminations (primarily deaths). Skinner and Lei (1980) found six factors, including changes in personal and social activities, work changes, marital problems, residence changes, family changes, and school changes. Redfield and Stone (1979) discovered three factors, including personal catastrophes (undesirable events), achievements (desirable events), and domestic changes (marriage, birth of a child, retirement). Finally, Ruch (1977) reported three dimensions: magnitude of change, desirability of change, and area of life change (personal and interpersonal events vs. financial and occupational events).

To summarize, although dimensions differ somewhat according to the specific sample and analysis technique, certain recurring content areas can be identified, such as personal activities, relocation, work, school, marriage, family, legal, and financial matters. In addition, desirability, magnitude, and interpersonal versus noninterpersonal dimensions emerge from empirical analyses of stress dimensions.

Integration of Dimensional Schemes

In the interest of parsimony, an integration and simplification of the various dimensions of stressful life events was attempted. Four dimensions were abstracted according to the literature just reviewed: desirability, controllability, duration of consequences, and life domain. Life domain was then subdivided into assets, relationships, achievement, and social roles (see Table 13.2). All four of these dimensions (desirability, controllability, duration of consequences, and life domain) emerged from both the theoretical (Lazarus, 1966, 1981) and the empirically based taxonomies of life events (Brown & Harris, 1978; Dohrenwend & Dohrenwend, 1978; Fava et al., 1981; Paykel, 1974, 1979; Redfield & Stone, 1979; Ruch, 1977).

In regard to desirability, events involving potential for gain or growth were viewed as desirable, and those involving potential or actual loss or harm were viewed as undesirable (Lazarus, 1966, 1981). Controllable events were seen as those in which an individual could achieve a desired goal, prevent an undesirable loss, or diminish the severity of the consequences of an experienced loss. Duration of consequences, which was used by Brown and Harris (1978) as the criterion for event severity, reflects a distinction between events whose stressful

TABLE 13.2. Dimensions of Stress

	Uncontrollable			
	Assets	Relationships	Achievement	Social Role
Negative	Financial strain[a] Unemployment[a] Medical illness[a] Crime victim[a] Military combat[a]	Bereavement[a]	Demotion	Mandatory retirement
Positive	Wins the lottery	Someone phones to ask you on a date	Undeserved promotion	Elected chair of committee

	Controllable			
	Assets	Relationships	Achievement	Social Role
Negative	Overeating	Divorce[a]	Job stress[a]	Caring for elderly in-laws[a]
Positive	Smoking cessation[a]	Marriage	Deserved promotion	Birth of first child[a]

[a] One or more studies on the topic are reviewed in this chapter.

aftereffects affect the individual for long periods of time and those events with shorter periods of effect.

Finally, we subdivided those life domains in which stressful events may occur into assets, relationships, achievement, and social roles. We chose a set of relatively broad groupings based on theoretical work by Lazarus (1966, 1981) and empirically derived categories of events (Miller et al., 1974; Rahe et al., 1971; Redfield and Stone, 1979; Ruch, 1977; Skinner & Lei, 1980). Assets include such resources as material goods, physical health, and access to desired recreational activities. Relationships include interpersonal challenges, threats, or losses across all relationship categories (e.g., family, friends, co-workers). Achievement includes events involving status, evaluation, or competition. The final category includes events that involve any kind of change in social role, such as role loss or the acquisition of a new role (Pearlin, 1983). Rather than classifying events on the basis of setting (e.g., work, home, school), we felt that the proposed taxonomy reflected more fundamental psychological distinctions.

It was our goal to build a theory of optimal stress–social support matching based on an understanding of the psychological processes stimulated by different classes of events. We considered desirability, controllability, duration of consequences, and life domain as meaningful markers of psychological consequences. Some evidence supporting the validity of these dimensions was described earlier.

As we described, research has shown that desirability, controllability, and duration of consequences differentiate between events that do and do not lead to depression (Thoits, 1983).

Additional evidence comes from the literature on coping processes. Coping was defined by Lazarus (1966, 1981) as cognitive and behavioral efforts to master, reduce, or tolerate the internal and/or external demands created by a stressful transaction. Presumably, events that differ in psychological demands require different coping strategies for adaptation. Some differences in psychological demands, as reflected by differential coping requirements, have been associated with the aforementioned dimensions. Little research has directly addressed the psychological needs associated with different kinds of events (cf. Cohen & Hoberman, 1983), and so we must rely on indirect evidence, such as the data on coping.

Coping may be regarded as serving two major functions: regulating emotions or distress (emotion-focused coping) and managing the problem that is causing the distress (problem-focused coping). The controllability of events consistently predicts whether an individual will use emotion-focused or problem-focused coping (Billings & Moos, 1981; Folkman & Lazarus, 1980; McRae, 1984; Pearlin & Schooler, 1978). Controllable events are followed by efforts to prevent or alter the distressing situation, whereas uncontrollable events are followed by efforts to diminish the intensity of aversive emotions caused by the situation. According to McRae (1984), the highest level of problem-focused coping is stimulated by events described as "challenges," with intermediate problem-focused coping for "threats," and the lowest levels for "harm/loss" events. The pattern for emotional coping was the opposite, with the highest levels for "harm/loss," the intermediate levels for "threats," and the lowest levels for "challenging" events.

Regarding the effects of life domain, interpersonal events have been associated with different coping activities than impersonal events (Billings & Moos, 1981; Pearlin & Schooler, 1978). Coping that requires continued interpersonal involvement has been found to be more effective in dealing with interpersonal than with impersonal events (Pearlin & Schooler, 1978).

As several writers note (Cohen & McKay, 1984; Pearlin & Schooler, 1978; Thoits, 1986), there are close parallels between the functions of coping and the functions of social support (i.e., both serve to minimize aversive emotional reactions to stress and/or the objective circumstances that cause distress). One assumption we made is that interpersonal interactions that maximize appropriate coping behaviors are most beneficial (Thoits, 1986). Although not all dimensions of stress have been studied with respect to their optimal coping responses, the model we develop below builds on our knowledge of coping demands and extends to make predictions for all four of the dimensions with respect to the kinds of socially supportive acts that will maximize an individual's ability to cope effectively with the stress that confronts him or her. After the model is presented, empirical literature that bears on optimal matches between social support components and specific stressful events will be summarized. In light of the empirical literature, a final section will offer an evaluation of the model's adequacy and offer possible modifications to the model.

A MODEL OF OPTIMAL MATCHING BETWEEN STRESS AND SOCIAL SUPPORT

Before summarizing the studies that have empirically examined specific components of support and categories of life events, we will propose a general model, based on both theory and empirical research in the area of coping. After the model has been described, results of all studies that we could locate which assessed both specific components of support and specific stressful events ($N = 42$) will be presented. These empirical studies will serve as a test of the theoretical model, and as a guide for further refinement of the model.

We will consider desirability first. The major difference between desirable and undesirable stressful events seems to be the nature and intensity of the negative emotions they engender. Desirable events in which stress derives from uncertainty over whether or not a desired goal can be achieved (e.g., promotion, success in the parenting role) are associated with feelings of anxiety (Beck & Emery, 1985), whereas undesirable events have been shown to produce depression (Thoits, 1983). Thus, social support that helps alleviate anxiety would be more beneficial in coping with positive events, whereas support that alleviates depression would be more beneficial in coping with negative events. Also, because undesirable events are more taxing than are desirable events (Holmes & Rahe, 1967), we hypothesize that more support would be needed to deal with an undesirable stressor than with a desirable stressor.

Perhaps the most influential dimension with regard to needed social support is controllability. Based on the coping literature cited above (Billings & Moos, 1981; Folkman & Lazarus, 1980; Pearlin & Schooler, 1978), we predict that uncontrollable events (harm or loss) will require social support components that foster emotion-focused coping and that controllable events (threat or challenge) will require social support components that foster problem-focused coping. At the most general level, we predict that emotional support should be relatively more effective for dealing with uncontrollable events and that instrumental support should be relatively more effective for dealing with controllable events. However, both emotional healing and instrumental action can be facilitated in a number of ways. For example, emotion-focused coping may be enhanced by opportunities to ventilate emotions, to reevaluate the severity of one's loss, or to experience positive emotions that derive from sources not lost because of the stress (e.g., reminders that one is loved). Problem-focused coping may be facilitated by advice, information, feedback on one's plans for actions, actual assistance, or by emotional support that communicates belief in one's competence.

Most studies do not examine components of social support closely enough to distinguish among different kinds of informational, emotional, or instrumental support. However, a few studies look separately at expressions of affection and esteem, and other studies divide informational and tangible support. Thus, it is possible to test the following specific hypotheses. First, we predict that expressions of caring will be relatively more effective following uncontrollable events and that expressions of esteem will be more effective following controllable events. In regard to instrumental support, we predict that tangible support will be more effective following uncontrollable events (to replace the resource that was lost or harmed) and that informational support will be more effective following controllable events (to help prevent or solve problems).

Duration of consequences is not entirely orthogonal to controllability, in that controllable events are more responsive to efforts aimed at preventing or fore-shortening effects. However, even some controllable events may require a long period of time to ease. The longer the effects last, the more emotional support will be required to bolster morale and the more tangible support will be required, because need persists over a longer period of time.

Turning finally to life domain, we based our hypotheses on Stroebe and Stroebe's (1983) deficit model, in which the nature of the loss affects the nature of the required replacement. Thus, the loss of or threat to assets would be asso-ciated with a need for tangible support. For example, an individual experiencing a financial crisis would need a loan. A loss of or threat to a relationship would leave a deficit in perceived attachment or social integration, depending on the nature of the threatened or lost relationship. This notion was drawn from Weiss's (1973, 1974) distinction between social and emotional loneliness (see also Rus-sell, Cutrona, Rose, & Yurko, 1984). If an intimate relationship were lost, then attachment would be most crucial. If network membership were lost (e.g., mov-ing with one's family to a new community), then social integration would be most crucial. When the loss or threat is primarily in the achievement domain (e.g., poor performance on a college examination), reassurance of capabilities and worth would most directly address the individual's deficit. Finally, when a valued social role is lost or threatened (e.g., retirement, empty nest), we hypoth-esize that social integration would be needed. Membership in role-related net-works was identified as an important source of identity and role-relevant affirmation (Cohen & Wills, 1985; Pearlin, 1983; Thoits, 1986).

According to our formulation, controllability and domain have the greatest im-pact on specific social support needs. Desirability affects the nature of the emo-tional support needed (i.e., whether depression or anxiety must be assuaged), but desirability also shares with duration of consequences an effect on the amount or duration of social support needed. When the influence of controllability, desir-ability, and domain are considered jointly (see Table 13.3), we predict that on the average, uncontrollable events will require relatively greater levels of emotional support, with an emphasis on emotional support that comforts, fosters accep-tance, and draws attention to the degree to which one is loved. Because uncon-trollable events often involve the loss of or harm to a valued asset, support in the specific domain in which the loss occurred should help replace what was lost. We hypothesize that the loss of assets would be associated with a need for tangible support. The loss of a relationship would be associated with a need for attach-ment or social integration, depending on the degree of intimacy of the lost rela-tionship. A loss in the achievement domain should result in a need for esteem support, and the loss of a social role should lead to a need for social integration that validates or confirms remaining roles. Controllable events should be accom-

TABLE 13.3.   Dimensions of Stress Predicting Components of Support

	Uncontrollable			
	Emotional Support (especially caring)			
	Assets	Relationships	Achievement	Social Role
Negative	Tangible support	Attachment or social integration	Reassurance of worth	Social integration
Positive	''	''	''	''
	Controllable			
	Instrumental Support (especially information) and Esteem Support			
	Assets	Relationships	Achievement	Social Role
Negative	Tangible support	Attachment or social integration	Reassurance of worth	Social integration
Positive	''	''	''	''

panied by a need for support that helps prevent or solve problems. This includes both instrumental support (especially information) and emotional support that encourages belief in one's abilities (esteem support). Controllable events should be associated with temporary replacements in the life domain affected by the stress, but the amounts and duration of needed replacements should be less than for uncontrollable events that create a permanent deficit.

Two general points should be emphasized. First, each event is characterized by several dimensions and, accordingly, is associated with needs for more than one component of social support. A second point is that some components of social support may be useful for all events. For example, Cohen and Wills (1985) have argued that informational and esteem support are useful in virtually all stressful circumstances. Individuals may always profit from relevant information and expressions of confidence in their capabilities. Jacobson (1986) and others contend that attachment is a universal need. We believe that some kinds of stressful events lead to an especially marked need for some kinds of support. Although virtually all components may play a role in well-being much of the time, we think that needs for specific components of support are relatively more intense as a function of the four dimensions of stress that we described.

We will test the predictions outlined in this section in light of research published or known to us at this time. Our criteria for deciding which studies we should review were as follows: (1) a multicomponent assessment of social support or the assessment of a single, clearly identifiable component; (2) a sample in which all participants had experienced the same stressful life event (e.g., the transition to parenthood, serious illness, unemployment) or, if a random community sample was used, appropriate analyses of subgroups that had experienced common stressors; and (3) tests of association between levels of specific components of social support and at least one psychological or physical health outcome for one or more specific life events or circumstances.

A REVIEW OF SOCIAL SUPPORT RESEARCH

We grouped these studies according to the stressful life event that was examined. Several studies considered some events (e.g., the transition to parenthood), whereas we found only a single study that looked at other events. We also tried to group the studies according to desirability, controllability, and domain. Because duration of consequences primarily influences the amount of support needed, rather than the type of support, we did not include it as a dimension. We were able to classify most studies with respect to event desirability and controllability, but even these dimensions were ambiguous in some cases. For example, the birth of one's first child is a positive event for most families, but for an unmarried adolescent, it may be strongly negative. Event domain also presented classification problems. Although we placed each event in a single domain category, some events clearly affect functioning in several domains. For example, unemployment entails a loss of income (assets), a setback in achievement, and the loss of a social role.

These studies operationalized the components of support in many different ways. In some cases, we treated as social support variables measures that differed from, but were closely related to, traditional social support components. For example, any measure of frequency of social contact or number of social contacts we viewed as an index of social integration (see House & Kahn, 1985). As another example, we regarded family cohesion as an index of emotional support, as we did the availability of a confidant.

These studies used statistical techniques ranging from t tests to multiple regression. One important difference among the studies is whether the components of support were tested individually or simultaneously. For example, in those studies using multiple regression techniques, some researchers tested each support component in a separate equation, whereas others entered all the components into the same equation. Both procedures can be justified, but it must be borne in mind that components of social support are typically intercorrelated and that when multiple components are tested in the same equation, multicollinearity may prevent some components from attaining statistical significance, even when their simple correlations with the outcome variable are significant. A formal meta-analysis of results, which would approach each data set using a standard analysis procedure, is planned for the future but is beyond the scope of this chapter.

Some studies examined several closely related mental health outcome variables. In the interest of brevity and in light of research showing the high intercorrelations among measures of different mental health symptoms (Gotlib, 1984), we did not report all outcomes for every study. Because most of the studies looked at some aspect of depression, we reported predictors of depression whenever possible, to maximize comparability across the investigations. Less often, physical health outcomes were investigated, and we always reported these results.

Uncontrollable Events

Loss of Assets

Studies of populations facing a loss or harm involving material, financial, and personal health assets were most numerous and will be considered first. We judged all of the events in this category to be negative and uncontrollable. We decided to view these events as uncontrollable because in most studies the subjects were either elderly (Krause, 1987) or of low socioeconomic status (Bolton & Oatley, 1987; Strogatz & James, 1986; Ullah, Banks, & Warr, 1985), and we determined that societal forces played a major role in their financial and employment difficulties. We will review studies of financial strain, unemployment, health problems, victimization by crime, and other threats to physical safety, in that order. Based on the model we described, these uncontrollable events should require high levels of emotional support to facilitate emotion-focused coping. In addition, in the context of scarce tangible assets, tangible support should help replace missing resources. Summaries of studies that assessed components of social support as predictors of adaptation to uncontrollable events may be found in Table 13.4.

FINANCIAL STRAIN.   Elderly community residents were assessed by Krause (1987) regarding chronic financial strain (i.e., whether the respondents had enough money for food, clothing, bills, and medical care), depressive symptoms, and four components of social support (emotional, tangible, informational, and support of others). A buffering effect was found for emotional support, informational support, and support to others, such that individuals who suffered from financial strain but had high levels of these components of support had more positive and/or less depressive affect than did individuals with low levels of support. A main effect was found for tangible support, such that all elderly individuals, regardless of financial strain, had higher levels of positive affect if they also reported high levels of tangible support. In a large-scale community survey of urban adults (Kessler & Essex, 1982; Pearlin & Johnson, 1977), the effects of inadequate financial resources on depressive symptoms were buffered by a sense of intimacy (emotional support) but not by social integration (network support). A large community survey of low income rural southern adults (Strogatz & James, 1986) examined the effects of tangible and emotional support on hypertension and found a buffering effect only for the lowest-income blacks, whose blood pressure was less elevated if instrumental support was available.

To summarize the findings concerning optimal support components in the context of financial strain, both studies that assessed tangible assistance found it to predict better outcomes. These results are consistent with the hypothesis that a deficit in assets, especially of long-term duration, would require some replace-

TABLE 13.4. Studies Assessing Components of Social Support as Predictors of Adaptation to Uncontrollable Events

Financial Strain

Authors	Sample	Support Components Assessed	Assessment Method	Outcome Variables	Support Components Predictive
1. Strogatz & James, 1986	Rural southern adults, $N = 2,030$	Tangible Emotional (someone to turn to with personal problems)	Dichotomous ratings of perceived availability	Hypertension	Instrumental for low SES blacks only
2. Krause, 1987	Elderly community residents, $N = 351$	Tangible Informational Support to others Emotional (empathy, love, trust)	Number of providers	Positive affect Depressive affect	Emotional Tangible Support to others Informational
3. Kessler & Essex, 1986	Urban adults, $N = 2,300$ (from Pearlin & Johnson, 1977)	Intimacy (oneness, openness) Social integration	Intensity ratings Composite of nine numbers and frequency of contact items	Depressive symptoms	Intimacy

Unemployment

Authors	Sample	Support Components Assessed	Assessment Method	Outcome Variables	Support Components Predictive
1. Mallinckrodt & Fertz, 1988	Older unemployed professionals, $N = 35$	Guidance Attachment Reassurance of worth Social integration Reliable alliance Opportunity to provide nurturance	Adequacy ratings	Psychological symptoms	Reassurance of worth Social integration
2. Bolton & Oatley, 1987	Unemployed blue-collar men, $N = 49$ Matched sample of employed men, $N = 49$	Quantity of social interaction Emotional support Material assistance Evenings out	Time with others outside working hours Presence or absence of four types Confidence in availability Number in preceding month	Depressive symptoms	Quantity of interaction (unemployed only)
3. Ullah, Banks, & Warr, 1985	British unemployed 17-year olds, $N = 1,150$	Monetary help Cheering up Information on: jobs, interesting things to do during day Someone to talk to about daily problems Peer group contact	Presence or absence of at least one source of each	Psychological distress	Monetary help Information on things to do during the day Peer group contact

TABLE 13.4. *Continued.*

Medical Illness

Authors	Sample	Support Components Assessed	Assessment Method	Outcome Variables	Support Components Predictive
1. Arling, 1987	Community-dwelling elderly, N = 2,146	Instrumental assistance Social contact	Number of supportive behaviors received Frequency of contact	Psychological distress Psychosomatic symptoms	Instrumental (more distress) Social context (less distress) Instrumental (buffers effects of low functional status)
2. Wethington & Kessler, 1986	National survey of adults (married subsample), N = 1,269	Emotional Instrumental from specific sources	Number of times support received	Emotional adjustment	Received instrumental support from spouse among subjects with serious medical illness
3. Dimond, 1979	Hemodialysis patients, N = 36	Family support Cohesiveness Expressiveness Spouse emotional support Confidant availability	Adequacy ratings (Rated by nursing staff) Presence or absence	Morale Negative change in social functioning Number of medical problems	Family expressiveness Family cohesiveness Confidant Family expressiveness Confidant
4. Frankel & Turner, 1983	Adult-acquired hearing impaired, N = 420	Reflected love Reflected esteem Family cohesiveness Confidant Companionship Social contact	Subjective ratings	Depressive symptoms	Reflected love Reflected esteem Family cohesiveness Social contact
5. Bloom, 1982	Breast cancer patients, N = 133		Subjective ratings Presence or absence Frequency	Adaptive coping	

Caregiving for a Medically Ill Family Member

Authors	Sample	Support Components Assessed	Assessment Method	Outcome Variables	Support Components Predictive
1. Lovett, Gallagher, Benedict, & Kwong, 1986	Caregivers of disabled elderly, N = 72	Material aid Advice Physical assistance Confidant Socializing Positive feedback	Number of providers	Self-efficacy	Number of confidants Number of advisers (negative)

Victimization by Crime

Authors	Sample	Support Components Assessed	Assessment Method	Outcome Variables	Support Components Predictive
1. Krause 1986	Elderly community residents, $N = 351$	Tangible Informational Support to others Emotional (empathy, love, trust)	Number of providers	Somatic depressive symptoms	Emotional (buffers effects of crime, legal problems)
2. Mitchell & Hodson, 1983	Battered women, $N = 60$	Empathic response Absence of avoidant response Social contact (with and without abusing partner) Number of supporters	Subjective ratings Frequency	Depressive symptoms	Social contact without partner Avoidant response (negative)
3. Popiel & Susskind, 1985	Rape victims, $N = 25$	Spends time Provides information Shows understanding Shows compassion Reassurance Tangible assistance General confidant Confidant for feelings about the rape Encourages independence	Number Subjective ratings	Psychological distress	None

TABLE 13.4. *Continued.*

Other Threats to Personal Safety

Exposure to Radiation Threat

Authors	Sample	Support Components Assessed	Assessment Method	Outcome Variables	Support Components Predictive
1. Solomon, 1985	Mothers of preschoolers residing near Three Mile Island nuclear reactor at time of 1979 accident, $N = 312$ Comparison group: mothers of preschoolers, $N = 124$ (Bromet, Parkinson, & Schulberg, 1980)	Expressive Instrumental	Adequacy ratings	Major depression Generalized anxiety	Expressive support predictive in both samples

Vietnam Combat

2. Keane, Scott, Chavoya, Lamparski, & Fairbank, 1985	Combat veterans in treatment for posttraumatic stress disorder, $N = 15$ Well-adjusted combat veterans, $N = 15$ Vietnam veteran medical inpatients with no combat experience and no PTSD, $N = 15$	Material aid Physical assistance Confidant Advice Positive social contact	Number of actual and potential sources	Posttraumatic stress syndrome	Confidant Advice Positive social contact

338

Bereavement

Authors	Sample	Support Components Assessed	Assessment Method	Outcome Variables	Support Components Predictive
1. Krause, 1986	Elderly community residents, $N = 351$	Tangible Informational Support to others Emotional (empathy, love, trust)	Number of providers	Somatic depressive symptoms Positive affect	Emotional Tangible Informational (all three buffer effects of bereavement) Support to others (reverse buffering)
2. Dimond, Lund, & Caserta, 1987	Recently bereaved adults over age 50, $N = 107$	Opportunity to express emotions Closeness Social integration	Yes/no Intensity rating Number of network members	Depressive symptoms	Perceived closeness Social integration
3. Maddison & Walker, 1967	Recently widowed women, $N = 132$	Expression of affect Review of the past Present and future focus Provision of concomitant needs (material and self-esteem)	Occurrence and helpfulness ratings	Mental and physical health	Expression of affect Review of the past Present and future focus Provision of concomitant needs

ment of the asset in low supply. All three studies looked at emotional support. In the two studies predicting mental health outcomes (Kessler & Essex, 1982; Krause, 1987), emotional support was associated with better outcomes. However, emotional support was not related to hypertension in the Strogatz and James (1986) study. It may be that emotional support is more strongly linked to mental health than to physical health.

UNEMPLOYMENT.   Unemployment involves a loss of material assets (income), status, and a valued social role. Thus, the components of support associated with all of these losses (tangible support, esteem support, and social integration) would be expected to contribute to positive outcomes. We found three studies that examined the functional components of support as predictors of health outcomes following unemployment. Other studies considered reactions to unemployment as a function of the source of support (e.g., Gore, 1978). There also may be associations between the source of support and the kind of support provided (Weiss, 1974), but we did not include these studies because they did not explicitly assess the functional components of support.

A longitudinal study of 49 unemployed blue-collar workers and 49 employed matched controls was conducted by Bolton and Oatley (1987). They studied emotional support, material assistance, and quantity of social interactions as predictors of depressive symptoms. Only quantity of interactions buffered the effects of unemployment on depressive symptoms. This effect was specific to the unemployed individuals. No association was found between any of the support components and depression for the employed controls. In a study of older unemployed professionals, of the six social provisions suggested by Weiss (guidance, reliable alliance, social integration, attachment, reassurance of worth, and opportunity to provide nurturance), only social integration and reassurance of worth were associated with lower levels of a variety of psychological symptoms (Mallinckrodt & Fertz, 1988). In a large sample of British unemployed 17-year-olds (Ullah et al., 1985), tangible (monetary) assistance, emotional support (cheering up when low), informational support (on jobs and interesting things to do during the day), availability of a confidant, and social integration (peer group contact) predicted psychological distress. Tangible assistance, social integration, and information on interesting things to do were associated with lower levels of psychological distress.

To summarize, some aspect of social integration was predictive of well-being in all three of the unemployment studies. It is noteworthy that this pattern emerged uniformly, despite the different methods of assessing social integration, including quantity of time spent with others outside working hours (Bolton & Oakley, 1987), whether or not the individual spends time with age peers (Ullah et al., 1985), and perceived availability of others with similar interests (Mallinckrodt & Fertz, 1988). The beneficial effect found for social integration is consistent with our view that unemployment entails the loss of a social role and that integration into a peer group is important to role-related morale. Surprisingly, tangible assistance predicted well-being in only one of the three studies in which it was assessed (Ullah et al., 1985). The sample that did benefit from tangible support was the most economically deprived of the three (unemployed school dropouts). Individuals in the other two studies had held full-time positions in the recent past and probably had greater financial resources on which to draw. Some aspect of emotional support was considered in all three studies, but only reassurance of worth was associated with better adjustment (Mallinckrodt & Fertz, 1988). Loss of employment clearly entails a loss of self-esteem for most people, and efforts to bolster one's self-worth were beneficial in the one study that assessed that specific component of support. These results highlight the fact that a single event can affect a number of life domains and that multiple components of social support may be required to address the multiple deficits that a stress like unemployment can create.

MEDICAL ILLNESS.   We categorized medical illness as a negative, uncontrollable event that involves the loss of or a threat to physical assets (and, potentially, to life). According to our model, emotional support should be essential, as the event cannot be prevented, and emotion-focused coping is of great importance in reducing the intensity of fear, depression, and anger that may result from serious illness. For some illnesses, physical limitations may lead to a need for instrumental assistance, in order to replace or compensate for abilities or assets (e.g., income) lost as a result of the illness. Five studies examined links between specific components of social support and mental or physical health outcomes among medically ill individuals. Four of the five studies looked at mental health outcomes only, and one looked at both mental and physical health consequences.

Frankel and Turner (1983) studied 420 hearing-impaired adults and found that both emotional support (reflected love) and esteem support (reflected esteem) were associated with lower levels of anxiety, depression, and paranoia. Bloom (1982), in a study of breast cancer patients without metastatic disease, assessed family cohesiveness, companionship during leisure activities, frequency of social contact, and availability of a confidant as predictors of adaptive coping and psychological symptoms. She found that adaptive coping was associated with both family cohesiveness and frequency of social contact. Both of these support variables were related to psychological symptoms only through the mediation of adaptive coping. A study of 36 hemodialysis patients (Dimond, 1979) evaluated the degree to which family cohesiveness, family expressiveness, spouse emotional support, and availability of a confidant predicted three different outcomes. She found that family expressiveness was associated with higher morale and fewer medical problems. Family cohesiveness predicted less decline in social functioning, and the availability of a confidant was associated with both fewer medical problems and less decline in social functioning. Surprisingly, emotional support from family (family expressiveness and cohesiveness) was more effective than was emotional support from spouse. However, emotional support from spouse was rated by the hospital staff, whereas support from family was rated by the patient, thereby raising questions of method variance affecting the results.

Two large community surveys conducted subgroup analyses to determine which components of support buffer the effects of medical illness on psychological adjustment. Wethington and Kessler (1986) found that received instrumental support from the spouse was associated with better emotional adjustment among seriously ill adults. Among community-dwelling elderly with impaired physical functioning, instrumental assistance was associated with fewer psychosomatic symptoms, but no association was found with emotional symptoms (Arling, 1987).

As predicted, some aspect of emotional support was associated with better psychological adjustment in all four of the studies in which it was assessed (Bloom, 1982; Dimond, 1979; Frankel & Turner, 1983; Wethington & Kessler, 1986). Instrumental support was also expected to be beneficial to individuals suffering from medical illness. This prediction was confirmed in both of the studies that looked at the effects of instrumental support (Arling, 1987; Wethington & Kessler, 1986). Social integration protected against the demoralization of medical illness in one of the two studies that assessed this variable (Bloom, 1982). Finally, esteem support was associated with better psychological health in the one study that included an esteem support measure (Frankel & Turner, 1983). The results were quite clear regarding the benefits of emotional support to medical illness, and there was evidence for the contribution to well-being of several other components of support. Debilitating illness can adversely affect all aspects of an individual's life, and a broad range of support needs are associated with medical problems. This set of studies in particular points to a need for the consistent assessment of multiple forms of support, so that their relative contributions to well-being can be systematically determined across studies.

CARING FOR THE DISABLED.   Disabling illness is stressful not only for the patient but also for his or her family members, who often care for the disabled individual. Caregivers of frail or disabled elderly relatives were studied by Lovett, Gallagher, Benedict, and Kwong (1986). They concentrated on six components of social support (confiding personal feelings, material aid, advice, physical assistance, socializing, and positive feedback) as predictors of the caregiver's feelings of self-efficacy in caring for the impaired person and in meeting his or her own personal needs. Number of confidants was associated with higher levels of self-efficacy, whereas number of advisers was associated with lower levels of self-efficacy. Again, emotional support appears to play a key role in coping with illness, for both the patients and their caregivers.

VICTIMIZATION.   Three studies examined the role of social support in the psychological recovery of crime victims. Because such victimization is usually perceived as totally uncontrollable, emotional support to facilitate coping with painful emotions of fear, anger, and depression should be essential to the recovery process. In a sample of elderly community residents, Krause (1986) found that only emotional support buffered the effects of crime or legal problems. Neither tangible nor informational support buffered the effects of crime on the level of depressive symptoms. Popiel and Susskind (1985) assessed a number of different components of social support as predictors of psychological distress among rape victims three months after the event. Emotional, tangible, informational, and network support all were unrelated to women's psychological adjustment following rape. In a study of battered women (Mitchell & Hodson, 1983), frequency

of social contact with friends and relatives without the partner in the month before leaving their partner was associated with lower levels of depression. Avoidance responses of friends to discussing the battering was associated with
significantly higher levels of depression. Contact with network members without
the partner present was associated with lower levels of avoidance coping, whereas
avoidance responses from friends were associated with lower levels of active cognitive and behavioral coping.

It is difficult to draw conclusions from these studies, because of their divergent
results. In the elderly sample of crime victims (Krause, 1986), emotional support
was connected to better outcomes. In the battered sample, social integration and
willingness of others to discuss the battering (emotional support) were beneficial
(Mitchell & Hodson, 1983). However, for the victims of rape, no aspect of social
support appeared to buffer the effects of this traumatic event (Popiel & Susskind,
1985). Further research into the social needs of the victims of various kinds of
crimes is clearly needed.

OTHER TRAUMATIC THREATS TO PERSONAL SAFETY.   We will discuss two
studies as examples of uncontrollable events involving threats to personal safety.
The first is a study of mothers of young children who lived in the vicinity of the
Three Mile Island nuclear reactor at the time of the 1979 nuclear accident
(Solomon, 1985, based on data collected by Bromet, Parkinson, & Schulberg,
1980). Expressive and instrumental support were assessed as predictors of depression and anxiety disorders. Only expressive support (availability of a confidant)
protected against depression and anxiety, both among those living near Three
Mile Island and in a comparable sample living near an intact nuclear reactor in
the same state.

A study of Vietnam veterans examined the perceived availability of five kinds
of social support (material aid, physical assistance, advice, availability of a confidant, and positive social contact) to determine whether levels of support were
associated with whether or not the veteran had developed posttraumatic stress
disorder (Keane, Scott, Chavoya, Lamparski, & Fairbank, 1985). Low reported
availability of a confidant, advice, and positive social contact all were associated
with the development of posttraumatic stress disorder following exposure to combat. Individuals who had undergone the prolonged stress of combat needed relatively broad social support, including all but material and physical assistance.
Individuals returning from combat faced strong negative emotions, a devalued
identity, and the problem of what to do next with their lives. Thus, it is not
difficult to understand their variety of support needs.

Loss of Relationships

According to our theoretical model, an uncontrollable loss, such as the death of a
loved one, should be followed by a need for high levels of emotional support to
promote emotion-focused coping (e.g., appropriate grieving). However, as
Stroebe and Stroebe (1983) pointed out, the death of a key support figure such as
the spouse creates deficits in all areas of support that were previously provided by

that individual (e.g., companionship, intimacy, guidance, tangible aid). Thus, the broadest range of support needs should be found when a multiplex relationship (one that provides multiple components of support) is lost.

Although a range of social support needs may follow the loss of a loved one, there is some evidence that different components are most crucial at different times. Based on his review of the bereavement literature, Jacobson (1986, p. 255) discussed phases of grief work and the kinds of support that are needed most during each phase:

> The struggle at first is to manage the feelings provoked by the loss and then to establish a new sense of the world without the presence of the other and/or to deal with the material changes which may follow the loss. The kinds of support appropriate to this process are emotional support, cognitive support, and material support, typically in that order.

Jacobson went on to say that cognitive support (e.g., advice on how to make a "new life" without the lost partner) is rarely appreciated or helpful until after the initial emotional intensity has subsided to some degree. Thus, the more general question of timing cannot be ignored when considering the best types of social support. Unfortunately, most studies do not offer enough information about the time that has elapsed since the traumatic life events, or their samples are heterogeneous with respect to time since the event occurred. Whenever findings are reported for different times, we will highlight them in our review.

BEREAVEMENT.   Three studies looked at specific components of support as predictors of adjustment to bereavement. In a study of 132 women who had been widowed one year before assessment, Madisson and Walker (1967) created a list of 59 specific interpersonal behaviors and divided them into four categories: expression of affect, review of the past, orientation toward the present and the future, and provision of concomitant needs (both material and self-esteem). Widows who reported poorer mental and physical health were dissatisfied with the quantity and/or quality of all four categories of support. An intensive longitudinal investigation of bereavement (Dimond, Lund, & Caserta, 1987) interviewed 107 widows and widowers 3 weeks, 8 weeks, and 6, 12, 18, and 24 months after the death of their spouse. The functional components of support that were assessed included an opportunity to express emotions, experienced closeness to network members, and integration into a social network (which included mutuality of assistance, mutuality of confiding, and frequency of contact). The social integration variable predicted lower levels of depression 2 months after bereavement, and an opportunity to express self predicted life satisfaction both 6 and 24 months after the loss of the spouse.

In a survey of elderly community residents, Krause (1986) tested whether the effects of bereavement would be buffered by tangible, informational, and emotional support and by providing support to others. His results showed significant buffering by tangible, informational, and emotional support, but individuals who gave support to others showed less positive affect than did those who did not (reverse buffering).

A broad spectrum of support types were associated with better psychological adjustment following bereavement. All of the studies reflected the importance of various aspects of emotional support, but instrumental and network support were also important, reflecting the variety of support functions that are lost when a key support figure (i.e., the spouse) is lost.

Controllable Events

Because controllable events can be prevented or their consequences minimized, we hypothesized that social support that maximizes problem-focused coping would be maximally beneficial in that context. In particular, various kinds of informational support (e.g., advice, input on norms, additional perspectives on problems, feedback on personal decisions) should be more salient for controllable events than for uncontrollable events, since preparation for effective action is most important. Emotional support that facilitates effective instrumental behavior would also be important in the context of controllable events. Some researchers have theorized that social support promotes effective instrumental behavior through its effects on self-esteem and self-efficacy beliefs (e.g., Cobb, 1979; Cutrona & Troutman, 1986). Thus, one would expect that various aspects of esteem support would be particularly beneficial in the context of events that can be modified by instrumental action.

As with uncontrollable events, it was predicted that the life domain in which the threat or challenge occurred would also affect the specific support components required, although for events that have only the potential to occur, no deficiency may have been created that would require replacement or compensation (e.g., the threat that one *may* be laid off from work). In this section we will consider both negative (loss or threat) and positive (challenge) events. According to our model, the need for problem-focused coping is paramount for both positive and negative controllable events.

Studies that met our inclusion criteria explored five controllable events: smoking cessation, abortion, network crisis, job stress, and transition to parenthood. Although any one of these events may be viewed as uncontrollable by the person involved, it was our judgment that they were relatively more controllable than were those we considered in the previous section (e.g., medical illness, bereavement, unemployment). As shown in Table 13.2, we viewed smoking cessation as a challenge in the domain of assets (i.e., an attempt to improve one's physical health resources). We saw network crises as threats in the domain of relationships, job stress as a threat in the achievement domain, and the transition to parenthood as a challenge in the domain of social roles. Abortion was very difficult to categorize because it is an event that can be controlled before the fact but is uncontrollable after it occurs. Although we decided to categorize abortion as controllable, the experience of loss is a major aspect of the event, and we predicted that support to facilitate emotion-focused coping would be crucial to recovery. A summary of studies that tested specific components of social support for controllable events is found in Table 13.5.

Threat or Challenge to Assets

SMOKING CESSATION.   Two studies examined components of social support as predictors of smoking cessation. In the first, by Coppotelli and Orleans (1985), 125 married women who had recently stopped smoking were asked to rate the degree to which their spouse expressed confidence in their ability to quit smoking, avoided dominating or "policing" behaviors, and facilitated their abstinence. The third variable, partner facilitation, was a mixture of instrumental and emotional support, including encouraging self-reward, minimizing stress by avoiding interpersonal conflict, taking over some of the quitter's usual responsibilities, offering general problem-solving assistance, helping with cravings or cigarette substitutes, empathizing, and tolerating moodiness. Only partner facilitation predicted continuous abstinence at a 6- to 8-week follow-up assessment. In another study, two separate samples of participants in a smoking cessation program were studied at the end of treatment and at 3 and 12 months after treatment (Mermelstein, Cohen, Lichtenstein, Baer, & Kamarck, 1986). Five components of social support were investigated as predictors of abstinence: appraisal, belonging, self-esteem, tangible aid, and partner support for quitting. Once again, partner support for quitting included a variety of instrumental and emotionally supportive acts intended to facilitate adherence to abstinence. The results were reported separately for the two samples. For the first sample, married or cohabiting adults, partner support was the only predictor of abstinence at the end of treatment, thus replicating the Coppotelli and Orleans (1985) study. However, only appraisal support predicted continued abstinence at 3 months, and no component of support predicted abstinence at 12 months. In the second sample, in which only about half of the participants were married, both appraisal support and self-esteem support predicted treatment success, but no aspect of support predicted abstinence at either follow-up assessment.

These results were generally consistent with our predictions of the kinds of social support resources that would be most helpful to meeting a challenge. Interpersonal behaviors that facilitate problem-focused coping emerged as the best predictors of smoking cessation. These included instrumental support (exchange of information, stress reduction) and emotional support to bolster self-efficacy cognitions. Of particular note was the significance of support *for the desired outcome* by the spouse in predicting abstinence. In both studies, it appeared that the spouse's efforts to engineer the quitter's environment so that it facilitated abstinence was highly effective, at least in the early stages of quitting.

Interpersonal Threat or Challenge

ABORTION.   Robbins and DeLamater (1985) conducted a study of 228 women who had recently had an abortion. Their dependent variable was feelings of loneliness, measured four weeks after the procedure. Three supportive acts were determined to be potential buffers against loneliness: attitudinal support for the decision to undergo the procedure, practical support by accompanying the woman to the clinic, and serving as a confidant after the procedure. These behaviors were examined with respect to four potential sources of support: the male partner, mother, father, and other friends and relatives. Only supportive acts by the male partner were associated with less loneliness following an abortion. All three kinds of support (attitudinal, practical, and serving as a confidant) were associated with less loneliness when they were provided by the male partner. Thus, for the particular stress of abortion, both emotional and instrumental support were important, but the most important dimension appeared to be the *source* of support.

NETWORK CRISES.   Three studies addressed the kinds of social support that may help individuals deal with network crises (e.g., divorce, interpersonal conflict, separation of family members, unemployment, or need for psychological treatment).

Tetzloff and Barrera (1987) tested the extent to which specific components of support buffered the effects of specific stressors on divorcing mothers. A sample of 73 women who had recently separated from their spouses and who had custody of at least one child were examined with respect to the number of divorce-related negative events they had experienced in each of three categories: tangible (changes in money and material resources), social (changes in relationships with other adults), and parenting (changes in child rearing demands). The researchers developed a social support scale to determine the availability of tangible, emotional, and parenting support. They predicted that tangible support would buffer the effects of tangible stressors, that emotional support would buffer the effects of social changes, and that parenting support would buffer the effects of parenting stressors. All three stress categories were positively associated with depressive symptoms. However, the expected buffering relations were not found. Instead, regardless of the type of stress experienced, both tangible and parenting support were discovered to predict lower levels of depression. All the subjects may have experienced significant levels of tangible and parenting stress, thereby accounting for the lack of specificity. Such results are consistent with our prediction that instrumental support (tangible and informational) would be most beneficial in the context of a potentially controllable event.

In a study of community-dwelling elderly, Krause (1986) examined the extent to which tangible, informational, and emotional support and support provided to others buffered the effects of network crises such as conflict and other misfortunes occurring in the lives of significant others. Only providing support to others protected elderly individuals against depressive affect for a misfortune befalling a network member. This appeared to reflect the psychological advantage of feeling that one can be of assistance to those who are actually facing a crisis.

In one of the few studies of adolescent social support and coping, Hirsch and Reischl (1985) studied the adolescent offspring of normal, depressed, and physically disabled parents. Participants were asked to report the number of individuals who had provided cognitive, emotional, and tangible assistance following a recent family stress. Hirsch and Reischl also looked at the degree of intimacy

TABLE 13.5. Studies Assessing Multiple Components of Support as Predictors of Outcomes for Controllable Life Events

Smoking Cessation

Authors	Sample	Support Components Assessed	Assessment Method	Outcome Variables	Support Components Predictive
1. Mermelstein, Cohen, Lichtenstein, Baer, & Kamarck, 1986	Smokers in cessation programs, Study 1, $N = 64$, Study 2, $N = 64$	Appraisal, Belonging, Self-esteem support, Tangible, Partner support for quitting	Availability ratings	Treatment success; Abstinence at 3-month follow-up; Abstinence at 12-month follow-up	Appraisal (Study 2), Self-esteem (Study 2), Partner support for quitting; Appraisal (Study 1); None
2. Coppotelli & Orleans, 1985	Married women who recently stopped smoking, $N = 125$	Partner facilitation, Expressed confidence, Nondomination	Subjective ratings	Continuous abstinence at 6- to 8-week follow-up	Partner facilitation

Abortion

Authors	Sample	Support Components Assessed	Assessment Method	Outcome Variables	Support Components Predictive
1. Robbins & DeLamater, 1985	Abortion recipients, $N = 228$	Supports decision, Accompanies to clinic, Confided before abortion, Expects to confide after abortion	Yes/no to each of four sources (male partner, mother, father, other)	Postabortion loneliness	Male partner only: supports decision, accompanies to clinic, expects to confide

Network Crisis

Authors	Sample	Support Components Assessed	Assessment Method	Outcome Variables	Support Components Predictive
1. Tetzloff & Barrera, 1987	Recently separated women, $N = 73$	Tangible Emotional Parenting	Availability ratings	Depressive symptoms	Tangible support Parenting support
2. Krause, 1986	Elderly community residents, $N = 351$	Tangible Informational Support to others Emotional (empathy, love, trust)	Number of providers	Depressive affect Positive affect Somatic depressive symptoms	Support to others (buffered effects of network crisis) None None
3. Hirsch & Reischl, 1985	High- and low-risk adolescents, $N = 48$ (high-risk subjects have disabled or depressed parent)	Cognitive guidance Emotional support Tangible assistance Confidant Peer contact	Number of people who provided each type following family stress Intimacy rating Number of activities with peers	Depression	Peer contact Confidant (low risk only) Peer contact Cognitive guidance, associated with higher depression (high risk only)

349

TABLE 13.5. *Continued.*

Work Stress

Authors	Sample	Support Components Assessed	Assessment Method	Outcome Variables	Support Components Predictive
1. Russell, Altmaier, & Van Velzen, 1987	Public school teachers, $N = 316$	Guidance Attachment Social integration Reliable alliance Reassurance of worth Opportunity to provide nurturance	Adequacy ratings	Burnout	Reassurance of worth
2. Constable & Russell, 1986	Army nurses, $N = 310$	Guidance Attachment Social integration Reliable alliance Reassurance of worth Opportunity to provide nurturance	Adequacy ratings	Burnout	Reassurance of worth
3. Ross, Altmaier, & Russell, in press	University counseling centers staff members, $N = 169$	Guidance Attachment Social integration Reassurance of worth Reliable alliance Opportunity to provide nurturance	Adequacy ratings	Burnout	Reassurance of worth Social integration
4. Cronin-Stubbs & Rooks, 1985	Critical care nurses, $N = 296$	Affirmation Aid Affect (love and respect)	Adequacy × Number of source types	Burnout	Affect

Transition to Parenthood

Authors	Sample	Support Components Assessed	Assessment Method	Outcome Variables	Support Components Predictive
1. Cutrona, 1984	First-time mothers, $N = 85$	Guidance Attachment Social integration Reliable alliance Reassurance of worth Opportunity to provide nurturance	Adequacy ratings	Postpartum depressive symptoms	Guidance (2 weeks postpartum) Social integration (8 weeks postpartum)
2. Stephens, 1985	Low SES pregnant women, $N = 311$	General support Pregnancy support Instrumental	Number of confidants and frequency of confiding Perceived emergency and child care aid	Alcohol consumption	Pregnancy support
3. Lenz, Parks, Jenkins, & Jarrett, 1986	Mothers of 6-month-olds, $N = 155$	Instrumental	Number Frequency Helpfulness of instrumental supporters	Number of postpartum illnesses	Number of instrumental supporters
4. O'Hara, 1986	Married pregnant adults, $N = 99$	Instrumental Emotional from spouse and closest confidant	Adequacy ratings	Postpartum major/minor depression	Instrumental and emotional support from spouse only

TABLE 13.5. *Continued.*

Authors	Sample	Transition to Parenthood			
		Support Components Assessed	Assessment Method	Outcome Variables	Support Components Predictive
5. Giblin, Poland, & Sachs, 1987	Urban pregnant adolescents, $N = 57$	Tangible aid from mother	Dichotomous availability rating	Self-esteem	Tangible aid from mother
		Child care assistance			Child care
			Number of expected sources	Pleasure with pregnancy	Positive pregnancy attitudes of peers
		Emotional support from baby's father	Adequacy rating	Number of prenatal clinic visits	Emotional support from baby's father
		Positive attitudes by peers regarding pregnancy	Adequacy rating		
6. Boyce, Schaeffer, & Uitti, 1985	Unmarried adolescent mothers, $N = 89$	Network tangible support	Number of supporters	Positive affect	Helpfulness of baby's father
		Network emotional support	Adequacy ratings	Negative affect	None
		Helpfulness of baby's father	Adequacy ratings	Perinatal complications	None
		Helpfulness of family and friends	Adequacy ratings		

Transition to Parenthood

Authors	Sample	Support Components Assessed	Assessment Method	Outcome Variables	Support Components Predictive
7. Paykel, Emms, Fletcher, & Rassaby, 1980	Postpartum women, $N = 120$	Confides in spouse Confides in other Helpfulness of spouse	Adequacy ratings	Depressive symptoms	Confiding in spouse Confiding in other Helpfulness of spouse
8. Norbeck & Tilden, 1983	Pregnant women, $N = 117$	Emotional/informational Tangible	Adequacy × Number of source types	Pregnancy complications Emotional disequilibrium (anxiety, depression, self-esteem)	Tangible Emotional/Instrumental
9. Wandersman, Wandersman, & Kahn, 1980	Expectant women and their spouses, $N = 90$	Marital instrumental Marital cohesion, consensus, affection Group support Network support	Frequency of support Adequacy ratings Participation in parenting group Adequacy rating	Well-being Parenting confidence	Marital cohesion Marital cohesion
10. Cutrona, 1988	Childbearing adolescents, $N = 128$	Guidance Attachment Social integration Reliable alliance Reassurance of worth Opportunity to provide nurturance	Adequacy ratings	Postpartum clinical depression	Reliable alliance

with a confidant and integration into a peer group. For the offspring of normal parents, intimacy with a confidant and social integration buffered the effects of family stress on level of depression. However, no buffering effects were found for the offspring of either the depressed or the disabled parents, with some kinds of support seeming to increase their depressive symptoms. Adolescents who face both family strife and the mental or physical health problems of a parent may be overwhelmed in a way that exceeds the buffering capacities of supportive interactions with others.

The results for the elderly and adolescent samples who faced network problems were quite different. For the elderly, only the opportunity to give support to others prevented depressive symptoms (Krause, 1986). For the adolescents (offspring of normal parents only), intimacy with a confidant and integration into a peer group helped them cope with family problems. Although the nature of the network crises faced by the participants in the two studies may have been quite different and the components of support assessed were not identical, the developmental characteristics of the elders versus those of the adolescents may also have contributed to the differences in results. Whereas mature adults are in a position to offer assistance to their friends and relatives who are in need, the adolescent has much more limited resources. Indeed, the only option available to the adolescent when problems arise in his or her family may be the consolation of involvement with individuals outside the family. Little is known about developmental differences in coping with life events, but this would seem to be a fruitful avenue for investigation (Compas, 1987).

WORK STRESS.   In our conceptual framework, work stress was classified as a threat in the achievement domain. However, stress in the workplace can take many forms, including interpersonal friction, job ambiguity, task overload, negative evaluation of performance, and boredom (Pearlin, 1983). Four studies investigated the contribution of specific components of social support in withstanding the pressures of work stress.

In a study of 316 public school teachers, Russell, Altmaier, and Van Velzen (1987) assessed all six of Weiss's social provisions (guidance, reliable alliance, social integration, attachment, reassurance of worth, and opportunity to provide nurturance) as predictors of "burnout," a syndrome of emotional exhaustion, depersonalization, and decreased feelings of accomplishment (Maslach & Jackson, 1981). They also studied the source of support (co-workers, supervisor, family, and friends), and the results showed that only reassurance of worth and supervisor support predicted lower levels of burnout. A similar study of hospital nurses was conducted by Constable and Russell (1986), who also assessed Weiss's six social provisions and source of support. As was found for the teachers, only reassurance of worth and support from supervisors were found to predict lower levels of burnout. A third study conducted by our research group (Ross, Altmaier, & Russell, in press) determined the degree to which each of Weiss's six provisions predicted level of burnout in a national sample of doctoral-level therapists employed in university counseling centers. The results were similar but not identical to those obtained for nurses and teachers, in that both reassurance of worth and social integration emerged as significant predictors of burnout. The final study of social support and work stress was conducted by Cronin-Stubbs and Rooks (1985). In this investigation, 296 critical care nurses were examined regarding the extent to which affirmation, aid, and affect support predicted level of burnout. Only affect support (a combination of love and esteem items) predicted lower levels of burnout.

There was a high degree of consistency regarding the optimal component of social support required for job stress. Reassurance of worth or esteem support emerged in all four studies as an important resource for individuals facing employment-related stress, suggesting that self-esteem is placed at particular risk by the kinds of stressors that occur in the workplace. Both nursing and teaching are professions that require intensive personal giving for relatively little monetary compensation or societal appreciation. Thus, input (from supervisors in particular) that helps individuals maintain sight of the value of their contribution and that of their profession may be especially important.

TRANSITION TO PARENTHOOD.   More studies were found that dealt with the transition to parenthood than with any other single event. Dealing with pregnancy, childbirth, and caring for an infant are challenging events that involve both physical discomfort and the acquisition of a new social role. In this context, we predicted health-protective effects for support that facilitates problem-focused coping and integration into a new role-relevant network.

In a longitudinal study of 85 first-time mothers, Cutrona (1984) assessed all six of Weiss's social provisions (guidance, reliable alliance, social integration, reassurance of worth, attachment, and opportunity to provide nurturance) during pregnancy as predictors of postpartum depressive symptoms. Guidance seemed to be important in the first two weeks after delivery, but social integration became the most important by eight weeks postpartum. In another longitudinal study, O'Hara (1986) assessed instrumental and emotional support from one's spouse and a confidant as predictors of diagnosable major or minor depression after delivery. Both instrumental and emotional support from one's spouse (but not from the confidant) were associated with a lower incidence of postpartum depression. However, in another study of postpartum women (Paykel, Emms, Fletcher, & Rassaby, 1980), both confiding in the spouse and in another person predicted lower levels of depressive symptoms following childbirth, as did perceived helpfulness of the spouse.

Norbeck and Tilden (1983) studied emotional/informational and tangible support early in pregnancy and found that emotional/informational support was associated with less emotional disequilibrium (anxiety, depression, poor self-esteem) late in pregnancy and that tangible support was associated with fewer complications of pregnancy. In a study comparing the effects of four kinds of marital support (instrumental, cohesion, consensus, affection), network support, and participation in a support group for new parents, Wandersman, Wandersman, and Kahn (1980) found that both psychological well-being and confidence in the parenting role were predicted by marital cohesion only. Lower alcohol consumption was associated with pregnancy support (confiding about pregnancy) but not general support (confiding about other issues) or instrumental support in a sample of 311 low-socioeconomic-status women (Stephens, 1985). Frequency and perceived helpfulness of instrumental support predicted the number of maternal illnesses in the first six months after delivery, according to Lenz, Parks, Jenkins, and Jarrett (1986), who found that women with high levels of instrumental support contracted fewer illnesses.

In a sample of 57 pregnant urban adolescents, tangible aid from mother, availability of child care assistance, emotional support from baby's father, and positive attitudes of peers toward pregnancy predicted three different outcomes (Giblin, Poland, & Sachs, 1987). Self-esteem was associated with tangible support from mother and availability of child care assistance. Pleasure with pregnancy was associated with positive attitudes toward pregnancy by peers, and number of prenatal clinic visits was associated with high emotional support from the baby's father. In a study of 89 unmarried adolescent mothers, helpfulness of the baby's father predicted positive affect, but helpfulness, tangible support, and emotional support of other network members did not predict young mothers' outcomes (Boyce et al., 1985). In an ongoing longitudinal study of 128 adolescent mothers (Cutrona, 1988), all six of Weiss's social provisions (guidance, reliable alliance, social integration, attachment, reassurance of worth, and opportunity to provide nurturance) from each of three sources (baby's father, parents, and friends) were assessed six weeks postpartum as predictors of later postpartum depressive symptoms. Reliable alliance (instrumental support) from the young mother's parents and the baby's father were the only significant predictors of depression six months after delivery.

To summarize, instrumental support was most consistently associated with positive outcomes for individuals undergoing the transition of pregnancy and childbearing. All 10 studies assessed some aspect of instrumental support, and 8 discovered a significant association with mental or physical health. Although a few studies looked at informational and tangible support separately (Boyce et al., 1985; Cutrona, 1984, 1988; Giblin et al., 1987; Norbeck & Tilden, 1983), most combined these two kinds of instrumental support into a single index that included assistance with child care, financial assistance, and advice on various aspects of infant care. The evident importance of instrumental support in the transition to parenthood is consistent with our prediction that events involving challenge (i.e., controllable events with a potential for gain or growth) would show the highest relative need for support that facilitates problem-focused coping.

Our second prediction, that role transitions would be aided by a sense of integration into a group of individuals who would validate the new role, was tested in only three studies (Cutrona, 1984, 1988; Giblin et al., 1987). Social integration predicted adjustment in two of the three studies (Cutrona, 1984; Giblin et al., 1987). Further tests of this association are required.

Emotional support was tested as a predictor of outcomes in nine of the studies we reviewed. Emotional support was a significant predictor in five of the nine studies (Giblin et al., 1987; O'Hara, 1986; Paykel et al., 1980; Stephens, 1985; Wandersman et al., 1980). Thus, although the results are not as consistent as are those for instrumental support, there is evidence that emotional support (e.g., acting as a confidant) is also valuable to individuals undergoing the transition to parenthood.

In contrast with the studies we reviewed concerning other kinds of events, studies of the transition to parenthood more frequently assessed not only type of support but also source of support. Support from the baby's father was more often associated with positive maternal outcomes than was support from any other source (Boyce et al., 1985; Cutrona, 1988; Norbeck & Tilden, 1983; O'Hara, 1986; Wandersman et al., 1980). This pattern was found for both instrumental and emotional support in all but one study that assessed multiple sources of support (Paykel et al., 1980). Thus, it is important to consider not only the optimal component of support required to maintain morale in the face of specific stressors but also who in the social network is the most effective source of support.

EVALUATION OF FIT OF THE THEORETICAL MODEL

According to our formulation, desirability, controllability, and life domain (assets, relationships, achievement, and social roles) are the dimensions of life events that determine the strains, challenges, and needs that in turn determine which types of socially supportive behaviors will most likely lead to good health outcomes. Controllability was the dimension thought to have the greatest influence on social support needs. We predicted that uncontrollable events would require relatively greater levels of emotional support, with an emphasis on emotional support that comforts, fosters acceptance, and draws attention to the degree to which one is loved. Because uncontrollable events often involve a loss or harm to a valued object or life domain, we predicted that support in the specific domain in which the loss occurred should help replace what was lost. We hypothesized that loss of assets would be associated with a need for tangible support, loss of a relationship with a need for attachment or social integration, loss in the achievement domain with a need for esteem support, and a loss of a social role with a need for social integration that validates or confirms remaining roles.

We believed that controllable events would require relatively greater levels of instrumental support, to help prevent or solve problems. Information, advice, feedback on plans for action, and emotional support that encourages and expresses confidence in instrumental competence (esteem support) seemed to be the most valuable types of support for controllable events. To a lesser degree than for uncontrollable events, we predicted that support in the specific domain of the event would be important. This input would not be a permanent replacement but, rather, would be either a temporary replacement of lost assets or the provision of sufficient resources to find a permanent solution.

Our analysis of the empirical literature revealed that the findings for approximately two-thirds of the life events studied were consistent with our theoretical model. Controllability and domain were relatively good predictors of the social support components associated with positive outcomes. Among the one-third of events that did not fit the proposed model, none was completely inconsistent with our predictions; rather, the typical pattern was one of underinclusiveness. That is, at least one of the predicted components was significantly associated with the outcome variable, but additional components of support not derived from the model were also predictive.

First, life events that yielded findings consistent with the model included financial strain, caregiving, victimization, smoking cessation, network stress, work stress, and transition to parenthood. For uncontrollable events, emotional support plus the component predicted by the domain in which the event occurred emerged as the best predictors of positive outcomes. Thus, adjustment to financial strain was consistently predicted by emotional support and tangible assistance (replacement of assets). The results for caregiving and victimization were consistent with our predictions, in that emotional support was beneficial to both stresses (although less consistently to crime victims). Domain had little effect on type of support needed, but the precise domain threatened by these events may not have been well represented in our conceptual scheme. For crime victims, especially those who suffered physical assaults, fear and mistrust may be the primary aftereffects of the event. For caretakers of demented elderly relatives, loss of freedom and the heartbreak of watching a loved one deteriorate seem to be the most relevant. These events suggest that the event categorization scheme needs to be further developed.

For controllable events, three of the four stressors generally followed the predicted pattern in which positive outcomes were associated with instrumental support and esteem support (expressions of belief in one's competence). We also predicted that the domain in which the event occurred would influence the support components needed, although not as strongly as for uncontrollable events. The results less consistently supported the specific influence of domain. Thus, for smoking cessation, both the spouse's instrumental efforts to aid abstinence and esteem support were associated with longer abstinence. For work stress, reassurance of worth (esteem support) was by far the most consistent predictor, although surprisingly, instrumental support did not predict more positive outcomes. In the case of network stress, in which someone else experienced the problem, the opportunity to provide support (i.e., to engage in instrumental behavior) predicted more positive outcomes, as did integration into a social network (compensation for the harm done to other components of one's network). Finally, among women experiencing the transition to parenthood, the most consistent predictor of positive outcomes was instrumental support. Fairly consistent support was also found for the contribution of social integration (facilitation of a new role identity).

In regard to findings that were less consistent with the model, the primary source of inconsistency appeared to be the fact that some events significantly affect several domains of an individual's life. We attempted to classify each life event within a single life domain and based our predictions on the needs associated with that domain. However, for four events (unemployment, medical illness, military combat exposure, and bereavement), several domains appear to have been affected, and the resulting needs for social support were broader than predicted. Unemployment entails losses in the domains of income, relationships with co-workers, sense of achievement, and social role. Tangible support was beneficial to the most deprived unemployed workers (Ullah et al., 1985), but beneficial outcomes were also associated with social integration and reassurance of worth, which would be expected from the nonfinancial losses that result from unemployment.

For medical illness, not only physical capacity but also income, contact with others, and a sense of achievement may be lost, and consistent with this broader view of resulting social needs, tangible support, social integration, and esteem support predicted more positive outcomes. Vietnam War veterans were at risk for losing their physical health, relationships with others, a sense of achievement, and an acceptable social role when they returned from combat. Thus, virtually all components of social support were associated with better outcomes for returning combat veterans (Keane et al., 1985). Finally, although bereavement is an uncontrollable event in the domain of relationships, as Stroebe & Stroebe (1983) described, the loss of a spouse (or other primary relationship) also entails the loss of those forms of support that he or she provided. This view is consistent with our finding that bereaved individuals benefit from a wide range of support components.

Overall, our review of the empirical literature suggests that for some events, certain kinds of social support can help achieve optimal adjustment but that for other events, a broad range of social support components are required for recovery. Clearly, a means to distinguish among these classes of events is needed, although we already have some clues to this distinction. That is, when the stressful event involves the loss of a key source of social support (e.g., the spouse), there will be support deficits in those areas of support that the lost individual previously provided (Stroebe & Stroebe, 1983). When a person's capacity to function in a wide range of life domains is impaired, as in the case of medical illness or unemployment, needs associated with each of those domains will be created.

In this regard, the case of the returning Vietnam veterans presents a challenging scenario to analyze. For Vietnam veterans, the traumatic experiences of combat changed their views of themselves and the society to which they returned. Thus, an overly simplistic view would be that they were psychologically damaged in a way that prevented successful functioning in multiple life domains. Such a model would apply more broadly to all categories of mentally ill individuals and does not differ fundamentally from our argument regarding physical and economic disabilities that impair performance across life domains. However, a second component of the Vietnam War veterans' experience was the societal devaluation and rejection that they faced, which prevented their successful integration into multiple life domains. This model would apply to all societally devalued groups, such as racial or cultural minorities.

These formulations are admittedly speculative. The next step in this endeavor must be to devise empirical methods to assess the demands, challenges, and needs that result from specific events. Such methods must permit characterization of single events as having consequences in multiple life domains. Although the stress taxonomy we propose appears to have heuristic value, we present it only as a starting point that needs to be refined further.

Many studies combined psychologically distinct components in their measures of support. A need suggested by our findings is for greater specificity in the assessment of social support components. In particular, we encourage researchers to distinguish between tangible and informational forms of instrumental support and between expressions of caring and of respect for competence as distinct types of emotional support. Although these dimensions may correlate with one another, our results suggest that their patterns of correlations with other variables are not identical and that one influence on their associations with health outcomes is the particular life event in which they are provided.

REFERENCES

Abramson, L. Y., Seligman, M. E. P., & Teasdale, J. P. (1978). Learned helplessness in humans: Critique and reformulation. *Journal of Abnormal Psychology, 87,* 49–74.

Arling, G. (1987). Strain, social support, and distress in old age. *Journal of Gerontology, 42,* 107–113.

Barrera, M., Jr. (1986). Distinctions between social support concepts, measures, and models. *American Journal of Community Psychology, 14,* 413–445.

Barrera, M., Jr., & Ainlay, S. L. (1983). The structure of social support: A conceptual and empirical analysis. *Journal of Community Psychology, 11,* 133–143.

Barrera, M., Jr., Sandler, I., & Ramsay, T. (1981). Preliminary development of a scale of social support: Studies on college students. *American Journal of Community Psychology, 9,* 435–447.

Beck, A. T., & Emery, G. (1985). *Anxiety disorders and phobias: A cognitive perspective.* New York: Basic Books.

Billings, A. G., & Moos, R. H. (1981). The role of coping responses and social resources in attenuating the stress of life events. *Journal of Behavioral Medicine, 4,* 139–157.

Bloom, J. R. (1982). Social support, accommodation to stress and adjustment to breast cancer. *Social Science and Medicine, 16,* 1329–1338.

Bolton, W., & Oatley, K. (1987). A longitudinal study of social support and depression in unemployed men. *Psychological Medicine, 17,* 453–460.

Boyce, W. T., Schaefer, C., & Uitti, C. (1985). Permanence and change: Psychosocial factors in the outcome of adolescent pregnancy. *Social Science and Medicine, 21,* 1279–1287.

Brandt, P. A., & Weinert, C. (1981). The PRQ—A social support measure. *Nursing Research, 30,* 277–280.

Bromet, E., Parkinson, D., & Schulberg, H. C. (1980). *Three Mile Island: Mental health findings.* Pittsburgh: Western Psychiatric Institute.

Brookings, J. B., & Bolton, B. (1988). Confirmatory factor analysis of the Interpersonal Support Evaluation List. *American Journal of Community Psychology, 16*, 137–147.

Brown, G. W., Andrews, B., Harris, T., Adler, Z., & Bridge, L. (1986). Social support, self-esteem and depression. *Psychological Medicine, 16*, 813–831.

Brown, G. W., & Harris, T. (1978). *Social origins of depression*. London: Tavistock.

Brown, M. A. (1986). Social support during pregnancy: A unidimensional or multidimensional construct? *Nursing Research, 35*, 4–9.

Bruhn, J. G., & Philips, B. U. (1984). Measuring social support: A synthesis of current approaches. *Journal of Behavioral Medicine, 7*, 151–169.

Bulman, R. J., & Wortman, C. B. (1977). Attributions of blame and coping in the "real world": Severe accident victims react to their lot. *Journal of Personality and Social Psychology, 35*, 351–363.

Caplan, G. (1974). *Support systems and community mental health*. New York: Human Sciences Press.

Cobb, S. (1976). Social support as a moderator of life stress. *Psychosomatic Medicine, 38*, 300–314.

Cobb, S. (1979). Social support and health through the life course. In M. W. Riley (Ed.), *Aging from birth to death: Interdisciplinary perspectives* (pp. 93–106). Boulder, CO: Westview Press.

Cohen, S., & Hoberman, H. M. (1983). Positive events and social supports as buffers of life change stress. *Journal of Applied Social Psychology, 13*, 99–125.

Cohen, S., & McKay, G. (1984). Social support, stress, and the buffering hypothesis: A theoretical analysis. In A. Baum, J. E. Singer, & S. E. Taylor (Eds.), *Handbook of psychology and health* (Vol. 4) (pp. 253–267). Hillsdale, NJ: Erlbaum.

Cohen, S., Mermelstein, R., Kamarck, T., & Hoberman, H. M. (1985). Measuring the functional components of social support. In I. G. Sarason & B. R. Sarason (Eds.), *Social support: Theory, research, and applications* (pp.73–94). The Hague: Martinus Nijhoff.

Cohen, S., & Wills, T. A. (1985). Stress, social support, and the buffering hypothesis. *Psychological Bulletin, 98*, 310–357.

Compas, B. E. (1987). Coping with stress during childhood and adolescence. *Psychological Bulletin, 101*, 393–403.

Constable, J. F., & Russell, D. W. (1986). The effect of social support and the work environment upon burnout among nurses. *Journal of Human Stress, 12*, 20–26.

Coppotelli, H. C., & Orleans, C. T. (1985). Partner support and other determinants of smoking cessation maintenance among women. *Journal of Consulting and Clinical Psychology, 53*, 455–460.

Coyne, J. C., & Lazarus, R. S. (1980). Cognitive style, stress perception, and coping. In I. L. Kutash & L. B. Schlesinger (Eds.), *Handbook on stress and anxiety* (pp. 144–158). San Francisco: Jossey-Bass.

Cronin-Stubbs, D., & Rooks, C. A. (1985). The stress, social support, and burnout of critical care nurses: The results of research. *Heart and Lung, 14*, 31–39.

Cutrona, C. E. (1984). Social support and stress in the transition to parenthood. *Journal of Abnormal Psychology, 93*, 378–390.

Cutrona, C. E. (1988, April). *Social support and the incidence of major and minor de-*

pression among childbearing adolescents. Paper presented at the annual meeting of the Midwestern Psychological Association, Chicago.

Cutrona, C. E., & Russell, D. (1987). The provisions of social relationships and adaptation to stress. In W. H. Jones & D. Perlman (Eds.), *Advances in personal relationships* (Vol. 1). Greenwich, CT: JAI Press.

Cutrona, C. E., & Troutman, B. R. (1986). Social support, infant temperament, and parenting self-efficacy: A mediational model of postpartum depression. *Child Development, 57,* 1507–1518.

Dimond, M. (1979). Social support and adaptation to chronic illness: The case of maintenance hemodialysis. *Research in Nursing and Health, 2,* 101–108.

Dimond, M., Lund, D. A., & Caserta, M. S. (1987). The role of social support in the first two years of bereavement in an elderly sample. *The Gerontologist, 27,* 599–604.

Dohrenwend, B. S., & Dohrenwend, B. P. (1978). Some issues in research on stressful life events. *Journal of Nervous and Mental Disorders, 166,* 7–15.

Dohrenwend, B. S., & Dohrenwend, B. R. (1981). Life stress and illness: Formulation of the issues. In B. S. Dohrenwend and B. P. Dohrenwend (Eds.), *Stressful life events and their contexts* (pp. 1–27). New York: Prodist.

Duncan-Jones, P. (1981a). The structure of social relationships: Analysis of a survey instrument (Part I). *Social Psychiatry, 16,* 55–61.

Duncan-Jones, P. (1981b). The structure of social relationships: Analysis of a survey instrument (Part II). *Social Psychiatry, 16,* 143–149.

Fava, G. A., Munari, F., Pavan, L., & Kellner, R. (1981). Life events and depression: A replication. *Journal of Affective Disorders, 3,* 159–165.

Folkman, S., & Lazarus, R. S. (1980). An analysis of coping in a middle-aged community sample. *Journal of Health and Social Behavior, 21,* 219–239.

Folkman, S., & Lazarus, R. S. (1984). If it changes it must be process: A study of emotion and coping during three stages of a college examination. *Journal of Personality and Social Psychology, 48,* 150–170.

Frankel, B. G., & Turner, R. J. (1983). Psychological adjustment in chronic disability: The role of social support in the case of the hearing impaired. *Canadian Journal of Sociology, 8,* 273–291.

Gersten, J. C., Langner, T. S., Eisenberg, J. G., & Orzek, L. (1974). Child behavior and life events: Undesirable change or change per se? In B. S. Dohrenwend and B. P. Dohrenwend (Eds.), *Stressful life events: Their nature and effects* (pp. 159–170). New York: Wiley.

Giblin, P. T., Poland, M. L, & Sachs, B. A. (1987). Effects of social supports on attitudes and health behaviors of pregnant adolescents. *Journal of Adolescent Health Care, 8,* 273–279.

Gore, S. (1978). The effects of social support in moderating the health consequences of unemployment. *Journal of Health and Social Behavior, 19,* 157–165.

Gotlib, I. H. (1984). Depression and general psychopathology in university students. *Journal of Abnormal Psychology, 93,* 19–30.

Grant, I., Sweetwood, H. L., Yager, J., & Gerst, M. S. (1981). Quality of life events in relation to psychiatric illness. *Archives of General Psychiatry, 38,* 335–339.

Heitzmann, C. A., & Kaplan, R. M. (1988). Assessment of methods for measuring social support. *Health Psychology, 7,* 75–109.

Heller, K., Swindle, R. W., Jr., & Dusenbury, L. (1986). Component social support processes: Comments and integration. *Journal of Consulting and Clinical Psychology,* *54,* 466–470.

Henderson, S., Duncan-Jones, P., Byrne, D. G., & Scott, R. (1980). Measuring social relationships: The Interview Schedule for Social Interaction. *Psychological Medicine,* *10,* 723–734.

Hirsch, B. J. (1980). Natural support systems and coping with major life changes. *American Journal of Community Psychology, 8,* 159–172.

Hirsch, B. J., & Reischl, T. M. (1985). Social networks and developmental psychopathology: A comparison of adolescent children of a depressed, arthritic, or normal parent. *Journal of Abnormal Psychology, 94,* 272–281.

Holmes, T., & Rahe, R. (1967). The Social Readjustment Rating Scale. *Journal of Psychosomatic Research, 11,* 213–218.

House, J. S. (1981). *Work stress and social support.* Reading, MA: Addison-Wesley.

House, J. S., & Kahn, R. L. (1985). Measures and concepts of social support. In S. Cohen & S. L. Syme (Eds.), *Social support and health* (pp. 83–108). New York: Academic Press.

Husaini, B. A., & Neff, J. A. (1980). Characteristics of life events and psychiatric impairment in rural communities. *Journal of Nervous and Mental Disease, 168,* 159–166.

Husaini, B. A., & Neff, J. A. (1981). Social class and depressive symtomatology: The role of life change events and locus of control. *Journal of Nervous and Mental Disease, 169,* 638–647.

Jacobson, D. E. (1986). Types and timing of social support. *Journal of Health and Social Behavior, 27,* 250–264.

Kahn, R. L. (1979) Aging and social support. In M. W. Riley (Ed.), *Aging from birth to death: Interdisciplinary perspectives* (pp. 77–91). Boulder, CO: Westview Press.

Kahn, R. L., & Antonucci, T. C. (1980). Convoys over the life course: Attachment, roles, and social support. In P. B. Baltes & O. Brim (Eds.), *Life-span development and behavior* (Vol. 3) (pp. 253–286). New York: Academic Press.

Kahn, R. L., Wethington, E., & Ingersoll-Dayton, B. (1987). Social support and social networks: Determinants, effects, and interactions. In R. P. Abeles (Ed.), *Life-span perspectives and social psychology* (pp. 139–165). Hillsdale, NJ: Erlbaum.

Keane, T. M., Scott, W. O., Chavoya, G. A., Lamparski, D. M., & Fairbank, J. A. (1985). Social support in Vietnam veterans with posttraumatic stress disorder: A comparative analysis. *Journal of Consulting and Clinical Psychology, 53,* 95–102.

Kessler, R. C., & Essex, M. (1982). Marital status and depression: The importance of coping resources. *Social Forces, 61,* 484–507.

Krause, N. (1986). Social support, stress, and well-being among older adults. *Journal of Gerontology, 41,* 512–519.

Krause, N. (1987). Chronic financial strain, social support, and depressive symptoms among older adults. *Psychology and Aging, 2,* 185–192.

Lazarus, R. S. (1966). *Psychological stress and the coping process.* New York: McGraw-Hill.

Lazarus, R. S. (1981). The stress and coping paradigm. In C. Eisdorfer, D. Cohen, A. Kleinman, & P. Maxim (Eds.), *Models for clinical psychopathology* (pp. 177–214). New York: Spectrum.

Lazarus, R. S., & Folkman, S. (1984). Coping and adaptation. In W. D. Gentry (Ed.), *The handbook of behavioral medicine* (pp. 282–325). New York: Guilford.

Lenz, E. R., Parks, P. L., Jenkins, L. S., & Jarrett, G. E. (1986). Life change and instrumental support as predictors of illness in mothers of 6-month-olds. *Research in Nursing and Health, 9,* 17–24.

Lovett, S. B., Gallagher, D. E., Benedict, A. T., & Kwong, K. L. (1986, November). *Caregiver stress, self-efficacy and social support.* Paper presented at the annual meeting of the Gerontological Society of America, Chicago.

Maddison, D., & Walker, W. L. (1967). Factors affecting the outcome of conjugal bereavement. *British Journal of Psychiatry, 113,* 1057–1067.

Mallinckrodt, B., & Fretz, B. R. (1988). Social support and the impact of job loss on older professionals. *Journal of Counseling Psychology, 35,* 281–286.

Maslach, C., & Jackson, S. (1981). *Maslach Burnout Inventory Manual.* Palo Alto, CA: Consulting Psychologists Press.

McRae, R. R. (1984). Situational determinants of coping responses: Loss, threat, and challenge. *Journal of Personality and Social Psychology, 46,* 919–928.

Mermelstein, R., Cohen, S., Lichtenstein, E., Baer, J. S. & Kamarck, T. (1986). Social support and smoking cessation and maintenance. *Journal of Consulting and Clinical Psychology, 54,* 447–453.

Miller, F. T., Bentz, W. K., Aponte, J. F., & Brogan, D. R. (1974). Perception of life crisis events: A comparative study of rural and urban samples. In B. S. Dohrenwend and B. P. Dohrenwend (Eds.), *Stressful life events: Their nature and effects* (pp. 259–273). New York: Wiley.

Mitchell, R. E., & Hodson, C. A. (1983). Coping with domestic violence: Social support and psychological health among battered women. *American Journal of Community Psychology, 11,* 629–654.

Norbeck, J. S., Lindsey, A. M., & Carrieri, V. L. (1981). The development of an instrument to measure social support. *Nursing Research, 30,* 264–269.

Norbeck, J. S., Lindsey, A. M., & Carrieri, V. L. (1983). Further development of the Norbeck Social Support Questionnaire: Normative data and validity testing. *Nursing Research, 32,* 4–9.

Norbeck, J. S., & Tilden, V. P. (1983). Life stress, social support, and emotional disequilibrium in complications of pregnancy: A prospective, multivariate study. *Journal of Health and Social Behavior, 24,* 30–46.

O'Hara, M. W. (1986). Social support, life events, and depression during pregnancy and the puerperium. *Archives of General Psychiatry, 43,* 569–573.

Paykel, E. S. (1974). Life stress and psychiatric disorder: Applications of the clinical approach. In B. S. Dohrenwend and B. P. Dohrenwend (Eds.), *Stressful life events: Their nature and effects* (pp. 135–149). New York: Wiley.

Paykel, E. S. (1979). Causal relationships between clinical depression and life events. In J. E. Barrett (Ed.), *Stress and mental disorder* (pp. 71–86). New York: Raven Press.

Paykel, E. S., Emms, E. M., Fletcher, J., & Rassaby, E. S. (1980). Life events and social support in puerperal depression. *British Journal of Psychiatry, 136,* 346–399.

Pearlin, L. I. (1983). Role strains and personal stress. In H. B. Kaplan (Ed.), *Psychosocial stress: Trends in theory and research.* (pp. 3–32). New York: Academic Press.

Pearlin, L. I., & Johnson, J. S. (1977). Marital status, life-strains, and depression. *American Sociological Review, 42,* 704–715.

Pearlin, L. I., & Schooler, C. (1978). The structure of coping. *Journal of Health and Social Behavior, 19,* 2–21.

Popiel, D. A., & Susskind, E. C. (1985). The impact of rape: Social support as a moderator of stress. *American Journal of Community Psychology, 13,* 645–676.

Rahe, R. H., Pugh, W. M., Erickson, J., Gunderson, E. K. E., & Rubin, R. T. (1971). Cluster analyses of life changes. I. Consistency of clusters across large navy samples. *Archives of General Psychiatry, 25,* 330–332.

Redfield, J., & Stone, A. (1979). Individual viewpoints of stressful life events. *Journal of Consulting and Clinical Psychology, 47,* 147–154.

Robbins, J. M., & DeLamater, J. D. (1985). Support from significant others and loneliness following induced abortion. *Social Psychiatry, 20,* 92–99.

Rose, J. A. (1986). *An intensive investigation of social support in the elderly.* Unpublished doctoral dissertation, University of Iowa, Iowa City.

Ross, R. R., Altmaier, E. M., & Russell, D. (in press). Job stress, social support, and burnout among university counseling center staff members. *Journal of Counseling Psychology.*

Ruch, L. O. (1977). A multidimensional analysis of the concept of life change. *Journal of Health and Social Behavior, 18,* 71–83.

Russell, D. W., Altmaier, E., & Van Velzen, D. (1987). Job-related stress, social support, and burnout among classroom teachers. *Journal of Applied Psychology, 72,* 269–274.

Russell, D., & Cutrona, C. E. (1984, August). *The provisions of social relationships and adaptation to stress.* Paper presented at annual meeting of the American Psychological Association, Toronto.

Russell, D., Cutrona, C. E., Rose, J. A., & Yurko, K. (1984). Social and emotional loneliness: An examination of Weiss's typology of loneliness. *Journal of Personality and Social Psychology, 46,* 1313–1321.

Schaefer, C., Coyne, J. C., & Lazarus, R. S. (1981). The health-related functions of social support. *Journal of Behavioral Medicine, 4,* 381–406.

Seligman, M. E. P. (1975). *Helplessness: On depression, development, and death.* San Francisco: Freeman.

Skinner, H. A., & Lei, H. (1980). The multidimensional assessment of stressful life events. *Journal of Nervous and Mental Disorders, 168,* 535–541.

Solomon, Z. (1985). Stress, social support and affective disorders in mothers of pre-school children—A test of the stress-buffering effect of social support. *Social Psychiatry, 20,* 100–105.

Stephens, C. J. (1985). Identifying social support components in prenatal populations: A multivariate analysis of alcohol consumption. *Health Care for Women International, 6,* 285–294.

Stokes, J. P., & Wilson, D. G. (1984). The Inventory of Socially Supportive Behaviors: Dimensionality, predictors, and gender differences. *American Journal of Community Psychology, 12,* 53–70.

Stroebe, M. S., & Stroebe, W. (1983). Who suffers more? Sex differences in health risks of the widowed. *Psychological Bulletin, 93,* 279–301.

Strogatz, D. S., & James, S. A. (1986). Social support and hypertension among blacks and whites in a rural, southern community. *American Journal of Epidemiology, 124,* 949–956.

Tardy, C. H. (1985). Social support measurement. *American Journal of Community Psychology, 13*, 187–201.

Tetzloff, C. E., & Barrera, M., Jr. (1987). Divorcing mothers and social support: Testing the specificity of buffering effects. *American Journal of Community Psychology, 15*, 419–434.

Thoits, P. A. (1982). Conceptual, methodological, and theoretical problems in studying social support as a buffer against life stress. *Journal of Health and Social Behavior, 23*, 145–159.

Thoits, P. A. (1983). Dimensions of life events that influence psychological distress: An evaluation and synthesis of the literature. In H. B. Kaplan (Ed.), *Psychosocial stress: Trends in theory and research* (pp. 33–103). New York: Academic Press.

Thoits, P. A. (1986). Social support as coping assistance. *Journal of Consulting and Clinical Psychology, 54*, 416–423.

Turner, R. J., Frankel, B. G., & Levin, D. (1983). Social support: Conceptualization, measurement, and implications for mental health. In J. Greenley (Ed.), *Research in community and mental health* (Vol. 3, pp. 67–111). Greenwich, CT: JAI Press.

Ullah, P., Banks, M., & Warr, P. (1985). Social support, social pressures and psychological distress during unemployment. *Psychological Medicine, 15*, 283–295.

Vaux, A., Riedel, S., & Stewart, D. (1987). Modes of social support: The Social Support Behaviors (SSB) Scale. *American Journal of Community Psychology, 15*, 209–237.

Wandersman, L., Wandersman, A., & Kahn, S. (1980). Social support in the transition to parenthood. *Journal of Community Psychology, 8*, 332–342.

Weiss, R. S. (1973). *Loneliness: The experience of emotional and social isolation.* Cambridge, Mass.: MIT Press.

Weiss, R. S. (1974). The provisions of social relationships. In Z. Rubin (Ed.), *Doing unto others* (pp. 17–26). Englewood Cliffs, NJ: Prentice-Hall.

Weiss, R. S. (1976). Transition states and other stressful situations: Their nature and programs for their management. In G. Caplan & M. Killilea (Eds.), *Support systems and mutual help: Multidisciplinary explorations* (pp. 213–232). New York: Grune & Stratton.

Wethington, E., & Kessler, R. C. (1986). Perceived support, received support, and adjustment to stressful life events. *Journal of Health and Social Behavior, 27*, 78–89.

CHAPTER 14

The Role of Social Environments in Social Support

BARTON J. HIRSCH, ALEXIS ENGEL-LEVY, DAVID L. DU BOIS,
AND PATRICK H. HARDESTY

Northwestern University

Northwestern University

University of Illinois at Urbana-Champaign

University of Louisville

This chapter will examine what Bronfenbrenner (1979) referred to as the *mesosystem* of the social environment. A mesosystem analysis focuses on linkages between settings, such as work and family, and is particularly suitable for research on social networks and social support. Mesosystem analysis enables us to discover how social networks are developed, how individuals cope with multiple role demands during periods of life stress, and how we can best combine multiple role involvements in pursuit of a satisfactory quality of life. We address each of these issues.

This chapter is divided into three sections. The first section is concerned with early adolescence, a time of many life changes. Our concern is with the school/nonschool context of networks and support, and especially with the transformation of in-school acquaintances to out-of-school friends. Race and gender differences are given prominent attention. The second section focuses on work/nonwork dimensions of support and particularly the work-marriage mesosystem. We consider how network support and rejection affect women's ability to manage both marriage and job, and also examine how work/nonwork segmentation can have deleterious consequences on empowerment within the workplace. The third section is concerned with how interconnections between network members ("density") may affect access to support and coping resources.

EARLY ADOLESCENCE AND THE SCHOOL–NONSCHOOL ECOLOGY OF PEER SUPPORT

The transition from elementary school to junior high school is a major developmental event that heralds the end of childhood and the beginning of adolescence.

As with any fundamental life change, it offers an opportunity for growth as well as the risk of psychological dysfunction. The quality of peer social support may have an important bearing on adaptive outcome. Peer support has been linked repeatedly to adolescents' well-being (e.g., Cauce, 1986; Epstein, 1983; Greenberg, Siegel, & Leitch, 1983; Hartup, 1983; Hirsch & Reischl, 1985), and there is growing evidence that positive peer ties facilitate adjustment to the new secondary school environment (Berndt, 1989; Fenzel & Blyth, 1986; Simmons & Blyth, 1987). Nevertheless, comparatively little is known about the specific processes that underlie this link.

In our own research, we have been especially interested in the adaptive value of supportive ties with school friends that extend to nonschool settings. In school, peers can offer useful support in dealing with academic tasks or other school requirements, can provide pleasant socializing interactions, can be a source of emotional support in the face of stressful experiences with teachers, and so on (cf. Asp & Garbarino, 1983). Positive ties with peers in school can also enhance a sense of community and social integration. Extending supportive school-based ties to nonschool settings is also expected to be beneficial, as it makes support available in a wider variety of settings and is likely to foster stronger bonds that increase the value of supportive exchanges.

There are several reasons to expect that nonschool peer ties are essential during early adolescence: Conflict with parents may peak at this time (Offer, 1969), thus making it an especially important time to have peer friends who can be relied on for support in nonschool settings. Interactions with peers outside school may also facilitate the exploration of new social identities, a fundamental developmental task of adolescence (Douvan & Adelson, 1966). Finally, the transition to junior high school may disrupt young adolescents' ability to rely on school as the primary setting for maintaining and establishing friendships, so that nonschool contact with peers becomes even more important.

As a first step toward addressing these issues, we obtained questionnaire data on the school–nonschool peer ties and self-esteem of a cross-sectional sample of approximately 300 junior high school students (a more complete description of the sample is reported in DuBois & Hirsch, 1989). In the remainder of this section we present three areas of findings from this research: (1) the school–nonschool ecology of peer ties, as it is both perceived by students and reflected in their self-reported friendship behavior; (2) race differences in the pattern of school–nonschool ties; and (3) the relation of school and nonschool friendship ties to psychological well-being.

The School–Nonschool Ecology of Peer Ties

Consistent with earlier research (Blyth, Hill, & Thiel, 1982), our findings indicate that both school and nonschool peer ties are salient features of the typical adolescent's social network. Almost all of the sample reported talking to most of their school friends during the school day. The great majority also reported seeing most of their school friends outside school either almost daily (55%) or once per week (29%). Moreover, students placed a premium on school friendships that extended to nonschool settings. Over 75% of the students reported that they felt closer to school friends whom they also saw outside school than they did to other school friends, and a similar proportion indicated that they knew more about those school friends with whom they had developed nonschool ties (Hirsch & DuBois, 1989).

Almost all children (89%) reported having at least one close friend in their neighborhood, and 26% of the sample indicated a relatively large number (six or more) of close neighborhood friends. It appears that there was considerable overlap between school and neighborhood friendships. Nearly two-thirds of the sample reported that they attended the same school as did almost all (44%) or at least half (21%) of their neighborhood friends. Less frequent contact was reported with nonschool neighborhood friends. Only about half (46%) reported getting together with nonschool neighborhood friends as often as once per week. Ties with nonschool neighborhood friends may play a more important role in peer networks in other communities with more of a split between public and private schools or where school boundaries bisect neighborhoods.

Do in-school and out-of-school contacts play different roles in the friendship development process? As a first step in exploring this question, we asked students about the circumstances under which they had met and become close with most of their close school friends, as well as their best school friend. As shown in Table 14.1, almost half of our sample chose being in a class together as the

TABLE 14.1. Percentage of Breakdowns of Primary Circumstances for Developing Different Features of School Friendships[a]

Circumstance	Most School Friends	Best School Friend
Meeting:		
In a class together	47.6	47.3
In a school-run activity	1.6	1.1
In an activity run by someone other than the school	2.1	1.6
By hanging around with same friend(s)	20.3	14.9
By living in same neighborhood	9.1	15.4
Through families who knew one another	3.2	3.2
Other	16.0	16.5
Becoming close:		
During classes	28.9	25.3
During the regular school day, but outside classes	13.9	8.4
In school-run activities	1.6	1.6
In activities run by someone other than the school	2.7	2.6
Dyadic meetings outside school	26.2	38.9
With other friends outside school	18.7	15.3
Other	8.0	7.9

[a] These data were obtained from seventh graders and ninth graders (approximately two-thirds of the entire sample). Figures are percentages and, owing to rounding, may not add to 100.0 for an item. *Source:* Hirsch & DuBois (1989).

primary reason they had met most of their friends, compared with only about a third that chose living in the same neighborhood or hanging around with the same friends (Hirsch & DuBois, 1989). A similar breakdown was found for the circumstances for meeting the best school friend. However, when asked about the circumstances under which they had developed close ties with friends, a nonschool circumstance was chosen by almost half (most school friends) or more than half (best school friend) of the sample. Among nonschool circumstances, dyadic and group meetings with friends outside school were much more likely to be chosen than were afterschool activities run by the school or someone else. Dyadic meetings were a particularly popular choice in the case of the best school friend. The overall pattern of findings suggests that school is one of the principal means for meeting new friends, whereas nonschool contact is often used to turn these acquaintanceships into close, supportive friendships. Nonschool activities that are relatively informal and private (e.g., home visits) appear especially well suited to fostering close peer ties. These conclusions fit well with the hypothesis that adolescents' friendships commonly progress from relatively formal school-based contacts to relatively unstructured nonschool activities and that this progression is associated with increased intimacy and support (Hirsch & DuBois, 1989).

If having access to peer social support in both school and nonschool settings is important, then we need to understand why some adolescents are unable to establish nonschool ties with peers or do so only with difficulty (see Hirsch, 1985, for a case study that illustrates this situation). We had our sample complete a 17-item questionnaire that we had developed to measure the degree to which a variety of person and environmental factors inhibited nonschool contact with school friends.

A principal components analysis of the responses to these items identified four components (see DuBois & Hirsch, 1989, for details). The items for each of the components are presented in Table 14.2. The identification of a social skills component is consistent with the literature that emphasizes social skills deficits as a source of difficulty in adolescent peer relations (e.g., Adams, 1983; Argyle, 1985). Many of these items relate to confidence and perceived skill in initiating nonschool contact with school friends. The other three types of obstacles are related to features of the social or physical environment (home conflict, moral concerns, competing activities). These findings suggest that there are situational, as well as more person-focused, obstacles to nonschool contact and that they may significantly restrict the degree to which school-based friendships can be broadened to include interaction outside school.

Our conversations with adolescents in pilot interviews provided anecdotal evidence that friends often recognize situational obstacles (e.g., living too far away) and take them into account in useful ways. For example, friends can make an effort during the school day to tell friends whom they do not see outside school about the nonschool activities of their mutual peer group. Interestingly, this kind of supportive behavior seemed to occur less often when social skill obstacles were indicated. It seemed that these obstacles were more likely either not to be acknowledged or to be attributed to negative traits (e.g., conceited) or those perceived to be hard to accommodate (e.g., shyness). Thus, failing to see school

TABLE 14.2.   Principal Components of Obstacles to Nonschool Contact with School Friends

Social Skill Problems

I'm not sure what to ask them to do.
I'm afraid they won't want to if I ask.
I do not like to do the same things outside school as they do.
I'm not sure how to go about asking.
I'm not popular with their other friends.
I don't know them well enough.
There is never a good time to ask.
They don't ask me to.
I'm not good enough at the things they like to do outside school.

Competing Activities

I have too many other things to do outside school.
I already do a lot of things with friends who do not go to this school.
I already do a lot of things with my family.
I see enough of them during the regular school day.

Home Conflicts

I live too far away from them.
I would be embarrassed for them to come to my house.

Moral Concerns

My parents do not allow me.
I have different opinions than they do about drugs and alcohol.

friends outside school may be less damaging when situation-related obstacles are salient.

The findings presented thus far have delineated several features of the school/nonschool ecology of peer ties during early adolescence. We next explored the extent to which these features were salient across different groups of students. Particularly noteworthy among our findings in this area was the pattern of race differences which emerged. We turn now to consider these findings.

Race Differences in School–Nonschool Friendships

We found several differences between black and white adolescents in their school–nonschool peer relationships (see DuBois & Hirsch, 1989). For example, blacks reported significantly more social skill and competing activities obstacles to nonschool activity than did whites. In predominantly white schools, the minority status of blacks may make them more likely than whites to confront race as an additional barrier to developing friendships and extending them beyond the school setting. In addition to the literature indicating relatively few cross-race friendships during early adolescence (Epstein, 1986; Schofield, 1981), there also is evidence to suggest that cross-race contact with peers is particularly rare in nonschool contexts (e.g., home visits) (Patchen, 1982). Consistent with this idea, we found that although over half of the sample (57%) reported having a close cross-race school friend, only 28% reported having a close cross-race school friend whom they frequently saw outside school (DuBois & Hirsch, in press). Although the black students in our sample may have had a generally more difficult time extending school-based friendships to nonschool settings, a somewhat different picture emerged when activity with only the best school friend was considered. Blacks not only reported more frequent in-school activity with their best school friend than did white males, but black males also reported more frequent structured nonschool activities (e.g., group activities organized by adults) with this friend than did whites (DuBois & Hirsch, 1989). Minority students may tend to become more involved with their best school friend, who is probably of the same race (Epstein, 1986), in response to limited access to other students as friends who can be seen both in and out of school.

We also found differences between blacks and whites in regard to neighborhood friendship ties (DuBois & Hirsch, in press). Compared with whites, blacks reported a greater number of close neighborhood friends as well as more frequent contact with neighborhood friends who did not attend their school. Just as the minority status of blacks in school may have increased the amount of time they spent with a same-race best school friend, it may also have heightened their reliance on the neighborhood as a source of peer friends. Our finding of relatively extensive neighborhood ties in the peer networks of black children may also reflect a more general pattern of especially well-developed kinship and friendship networks in black communities (Stack, 1974).

Our findings with regard to race differences in school–nonschool peer ties are only preliminary and exploratory. However, they do suggest that there may be important differences among groups of adolescents in patterns of school–nonschool peer ties.

School–Nonschool Peer Ties and Psychological Well-being

These analyses focused on whether the association between self-esteem and the frequency of nonschool activity with the best school friend varied according to other aspects of this friendship. We examined both structured nonschool activities (e.g., afterschool activities organized by adults) and unstructured nonschool activities (e.g., visiting the friend's home).

One hypothesis was that nonschool activity might be especially important to self-esteem when the friend was seen infrequently during the school day. We explored this possibility in a series of multiple regression analyses that tested the degree to which each nonschool activity scale interacted with level of in-school activity in predicting self-esteem (see DuBois & Hirsch, 1989, for details). These analyses revealed significant or nearly significant interactions for both measures of nonschool activity. These interactions showed a clear tie between nonschool activity and self-esteem only for those students who reported very low levels of in-school activity.

We also expected that nonschool contact with the best school friend would be most important to self-esteem when the friend was perceived as being supportive and helpful. Using an index of the perceived supportiveness of the best school friend, we found significant interactions of supportiveness with both nonschool activity scales on self-esteem. Frequency of nonschool activity was related positively to self-esteem among students reporting high levels of perceived support for the friendship. In contrast, correlations with self-esteem were negative among students reporting low levels of perceived support. The correlation between unstructured nonschool activity and self-esteem remained significant after removing level of in-school activity. Thus there may be distinct benefits to establishing nonschool ties with school friends who are regarded as supportive. This may be especially true in the case of relatively unstructured nonschool activities (e.g., visiting a friend's home) that facilitate close, informal dyadic interactions.

We next looked at the extent to which race, gender, and grade level were associated with differences in the relation of self-esteem to school–nonschool activity. Our primary aim was to begin considering how the benefits of school–nonschool friendship contacts might differ according to various dimensions of the developmental–ecological context. These analyses revealed a strong interaction between gender and structured nonschool activity in predicting self-esteem. The frequency of this type of activity with the best friend was significantly correlated with self-esteem among boys, but not among girls. The correlation remained significant after controlling for level of in-school activity, suggesting a distinctive role for these contacts among boys. For boys entering adolescence, structured nonschool activities (e.g., intramural sports) may provide valuable opportunities to elaborate and demonstrate competencies in domains such as athletics and group leadership. In view of the emphasis that traditional sex roles place on males to develop skills in these sorts of performance-related domains, it would not be surprising if participation in the kinds of nonschool peer activities that seem likely to foster such competencies were, in turn, closely related to self-esteem among boys of this age. Although these findings highlight the potential developmental importance to boys of nonschool contacts, it is worth noting that we might well have found significant effects for girls had we focused on those aspects of nonschool interactions (e.g., emotional intensity) more relevant to the developmental issues salient to them. In summary, these findings suggest that the adaptive value of extending school-based peer ties to nonschool settings may depend on several different factors, including the degree to which these ties are perceived as supportive, the level of contact that already occurs during school, and the extent to which the types of nonschool activities that do take place facilitate adaptation to key developmental tasks.

In the next series of analyses, we investigated the degree to which self-esteem was linked to the level of obstacles reported by students. The most striking finding in these analyses was a race-by-gender difference in the prediction of self-esteem by means of social skill obstacles. The negative correlation was remarkably strong among black girls ($r = -.77$), significant among boys of both races (for whites, $r = -.45$, for blacks, $r = -.39$), and not significant among white girls. As we mentioned earlier, minority students in predominantly white schools may experience race as an additional barrier to developing friendships and extending them to nonschool settings. Black girls may face a particularly difficult situation. Because they have less access than do black boys to cross-race dating (cf. Petroni, 1971), black girls may miss out on close cross-sex friendships and also achieve a lower status in same-sex friendship groups in which being regarded as attractive to boys is important to popularity (cf. Schofield, 1981). Thus, the social environment of a predominantly white school may offer black girls relatively few opportunities to engage in peer activities important to adolescent self-esteem. In this context it would not be surprising if the self-esteem of black girls were unusually dependent on their social skills (DuBois & Hirsch, 1989).

Future Directions

Given the paucity of research on school–nonschool friendships and the complex set of issues that are introduced by this ecological perspective, it is important to consider how these findings can be used to help guide the direction of future work in this area. To this end, we now offer some tentative conclusions regarding our findings.

Most adolescents seem to have extensive contact with peer friends both inside and outside school. However, school and nonschool contacts seem to play different roles in the friendship development process. Peers who become friends often first become acquainted during classes or other parts of the regular school day, whereas acquaintanceships are more likely to turn into close, supportive friendships outside school in relatively private, informal interactions. Although developing friendships along these ecological lines appears to be common, both person- and situation-related obstacles can make it difficult to have nonschool interactions. The adolescents most affected by these obstacles may find themselves unable to form close, multiple-setting peer ties to the extent that they would like.

The degree to which extending friendship ties from school to nonschool settings is beneficial to psychological well-being may depend on specific features of the friendship. Our findings suggest that both the supportiveness of the friendship and the level of contact in school may be important moderating factors in this regard. The special significance that structured nonschool activities seemed to hold for boys suggests that the degree to which nonschool interactions are relevant to developmental issues is another important consideration. Although nonschool contacts may be beneficial to psychological well-being only under certain sets of circumstances, when these conditions do apply, the contribution of nonschool contacts to well-being appears to be distinct from that of contacts occurring in school.

These tentative conclusions and hypotheses offer several promising avenues for future research. Longitudinal studies of peer friendships among early adolescents could be used to assess the progression of school and nonschool activities that most commonly characterize the development of close, supportive ties at this age. One could also examine the specific person- and situation-related obstacles that tend to be most problematic at various points in the friendship development process. Among situational obstacles, for example, factors related to school structure—such as the absence of an intact peer group across classes—may be problematic for initiating acquaintanceships. On the other hand, constraints that are tied to nonschool settings, such as living in different neighborhoods, may become more salient as the focus of activity shifts to relatively unstructured, informal contacts occurring outside the regular school day. Investigation into these issues could help schools and communities facilitate supportive ties among young adolescents. In doing so, it would be desirable to identify and target those students who are likely to benefit most from increased support in school or nonschool contexts. Our findings suggest that it may be fruitful to consider a number of different factors in making this determination, including features of the peer network and of the developmental–ecological context.

School–nonschool peer relationships during adolescence can also be considered from a broader, life-span perspective. If there are benefits to extending school-based friendships to nonschool settings during early adolescence, are multiple-setting relationships desirable at other stages of the life cycle? The parallel between school–nonschool and work–nonwork ecologies provides an interesting example that we will explore in the next section.

SOCIAL NETWORKS AND THE QUALITY OF WORK–NONWORK LIFE

In turning to consider adults rather than adolescents, and work rather than school, various new issues emerge to affect the social ecology. In particular, although there is usually little need to segment school and nonschool life among adolescents, among adults there often is. Indeed, compartmentalization is frequently suggested as a vehicle for preventing work stress from leading to burnout (e.g., Howard, Rechnitzer, & Cunningham, 1975; Pines, Aronson, & Kafry, 1981). Thus, adults may well consider more extensively the desirability of segmentation, with some shift in the goals or outcomes of interest (i.e., containing work stress vs. social network development). When we studied the nature of work–nonwork life, we discovered an even more differentiated picture.

Our initial exploration of these issues came during our involvement with a hospital nursing service. We were contacted initially by a nurse who had been employed by a large hospital to alleviate work stress among their nurses. We agreed to collaborate with her in considering the application of social network and support research to her efforts. In the course of our consultation, we conducted a workshop for nurse managers on social support and collected data on their work and nonwork social networks (see Hirsch & David, 1983, for details).

In studying the nurses' networks, it became clear that their work and nonwork ties were segmented in two ways. First, they rarely saw one another (or other nursing staff) outside the hospital. Consistent with much of the popular and professional literature, the nurses indicated that by doing so they hoped to keep work stress out of sight and, they hoped, out of mind. Second, there were almost no ties between their work associates and members of their nonwork social network—technically referred to as the work–nonwork boundary density of their network (boundary density is discussed more generally in the next section).

Although such segmentation may have been useful for controlling work stress, it seemed counterproductive for achieving other important goals. In particular, during workshop discussions we found that the nurses' principal work goal was to empower or enhance the status of nursing as a profession in the hospital. Several earlier field studies, however, documented the importance of multifaceted network ties to achieving political or work goals in conflictual situations (Kapferer, 1969; Mayer, 1966; Wheeldon, 1969). By contrast, these nurses' interactions with co-workers focused almost entirely on their work tasks. Their relationships with co-workers lacked the added strength that comes from forming richer and more varied ties with other people. Thus, regardless of what factors may have led to the development of such segmented networks, there may well be other deleterious consequences. This line of thinking is consistent with (and was influenced by) Kanter's (1977) thesis that work–nonwork segmentation, though often appearing to serve workers' interests, may instead often serve latent organizational objectives, to the detriment of the workers' well-being.

Indeed, the nurses generally agreed that physicians usually did not avoid socializing with one another outside the hospital. It is not unreasonable, then, to hypothesize that the multisetting ties formed among physicians enhance and reinforce the power of their profession. The nurses' segmented networks, on the other hand, may serve the interests of the status quo rather than their goal of empowering nursing.

Thus the meaning of multisetting ties can differ considerably for adolescents and for adults. For adolescents, the extension of school-based friendships to nonschool settings provides a vehicle for expressing their emerging interests away from the adult hierarchy at school. But the nurses' developmental objectives were quite different. Instead of fostering self-expression outside their organizational setting, they sought to acquire more power within it. Analyzing the nurses' multisetting ties required incorporating ideas and concepts relating to power, rather than focusing on social development, as was the case with the adolescents. In both instances, however, a concern with social roles and the quality of life were important to studying the impact of multiple environments on social support.

We followed this initial foray into the linkage between social support and work–nonwork life with a more systematic series of empirical studies. We especially wanted to consider more carefully the relation of social networks to the quality of both work and nonwork life. The remaining findings reported in this section are based on questionnaire responses from a random sample of approximately 250 married women nurses (see Hirsch & Rapkin, 1986a, 1986b).

Work and Nonwork Support and Rejection

Numerous studies have linked support for the work role with psychological well-being (e.g., French, Caplan, & Van Harrison, 1982; House, 1981). Few studies, however, have considered in depth the relation of work and nonwork support. Support for nonwork social identities may be especially important to women for two reasons. First, women are more likely than men are to be socialized to expressive roles emphasizing emotional nurturance and support (Belle, 1982; Bernard, 1981; Gilligan, 1977; Gove, 1984; Parsons & Bales, 1955; Vanfossen, 1981). General emotional support is necessary in order not to become burned out from the expressive role. This is particularly relevant to women engaged in care-giving occupations (Belle, 1982), such as nursing. Second, women are particularly vulnerable to interrole conflict between family and work, as well as overload from both sets of responsibilities (Haw, 1982). Married employed women thus need both "general" social support and support for their work role. Both support and rejection (negative interactions) need to be assessed as these may be independent dimensions (Fiore, Becker, & Coppel, 1983; Rook, 1984).

The quality of interactions with network members across role domains is also of interest. There is a general consensus that whether the husband supports his wife's working is critical to her experience of marital and job conflict (Andrisani & Shapiro, 1978; Berkowitz & Perkins, 1984; Holahan & Gilbert, 1979; Lewin & Damrell, 1978). Her supervisor's support is also known to affect job satisfaction and mental health (House, 1981), and female friends are a traditional source of support as well (Bernard, 1981; Rubin, 1985). Nonetheless, there have been no research designs that assessed positive and negative interactions among several key network members.

In order to understand the empirical relation of these different network dimensions, we constructed a questionnaire that addressed positive and negative interactions regarding both work and general domains for each of five key network members: supervisor, closest co-worker, closest friend outside work, spouse, and next closest adult family member (in our sample, typically the mother). As can be seen in Table 14.3, four factors characterized the interactions with each network member: work support, work rejection, general support, and general rejection (Hirsch & Rapkin, 1986b).

These findings begin to reveal the importance of distinguishing positive and negative network interactions regarding different spheres of life. Although the four factors are not surprising given the item pool, other solutions also would not have been surprising but were not obtained. Specifically, it would have been equally plausible if a work factor and a general factor had emerged with bipolar loadings for support and rejection on each. Another plausible two-factor solution would have been defined by a support factor and a rejection factor, with each factor having items from both work and general domains. The solution that emerged, therefore, was not forced by the nature of the items. We shall turn now to consider in what ways these four network variables are related to how well nurses manage both job and marital roles.

TABLE 14.3.   Principal Components Analysis (Promax Rotation)
of Nurses' Relationship Items

Network items	Factor			
	I	II	III	IV
Factor I: Work support				
Helps me handle stressful days at work	.69	−.11	.16	.09
Supports me when I am upset by a patient	.76	−.03	.03	.05
Encourages me to pursue things that excite me at work, or to try out new ideas	.75	−.07	.02	−.03
Is helpful when I am having a problem with a co-worker or physician	.80	−.04	.00	.01
Respects me as a professional; acknowledges my work skills	.57	.28	.03	−.12
Is sympathetic to my values and ideals about nursing	.67	.20	.03	−.09
Helps me to do a better job by lending a hand or giving training or advice	.77	.09	−.13	−.02
Helps me to set priorities for balancing my job with my nonwork life	.59	−.14	.18	.00
Factor II: Work rejection				
Competes with me for job status and recognition	−.14	.49	.26	−.05
Criticizes the way I do my job in a way that isn't helpful	−.10	.66	.16	.00
Refuses to take my career seriously when I want them to	.10	.60	−.16	.06
Puts me down when I question work rules or procedures	−.06	.76	.09	−.06
Makes things difficult for me when a nonwork matter conflicts with my work schedule	−.05	.62	−.05	.12
Fails to understand that my work can be boring or stressful	.20	.48	−.15	.22
Minimizes my job performance; fails to give me the recognition I deserve	.07	.70	.01	.06
Undermines my efforts to be the kind of nurse I really want to be	.09	.64	−.02	.01
Factor III: General support				
Knows how to make me laugh; a lot of fun to spend time with	.09	−.03	.65	.13
Seems to know the right thing to say or do when I'm distressed	.21	−.06	.61	.15
I feel that this person really likes and cares about me	.02	.24	.70	−.11
I confide in this person about really personal matters	.05	−.11	.78	.00
I feel particularly close to this person	−.04	.08	.84	−.05
Factor IV: General rejection				
Acts cold, aloof, or nasty to me	−.03	.27	.15	.46
Has a depressing outlook; makes me feel down	−.02	−.04	.10	.72

TABLE 14.3. *Continued.*

Network items	Factor			
	I	II	III	IV
Gets me really upset, annoyed, or irritated	−.08	.01	.01	.81
Expects his/her priorities to be my priorities; refuses to understand that other aspects of my life are important to me	−.05	.18	−.01	.65
Hurts my feelings	.07	.01	−.08	.77

Source: Hirsch & Rapkin (1986b).

Social Networks and Profiles of Marital and Job Satisfaction

Our focus in this phase of the research was on the quality of marital and job life. We had several reasons for considering satisfaction with each role as important criteria of success in managing roles. As noted by symbolic interaction theorists, our conception and evaluation of self is linked to our roles (Stryker, 1980). Critical aspects of our self-esteem are therefore based on role satisfaction. On a social ecological level, the extent of such satisfaction reflects whether we have been able to find a niche in the world that is personally satisfying and socially viable (Hirsch, 1981). Given the importance of role satisfaction to self-esteem and social integration, it is not surprising that higher marital or job satisfaction has been repeatedly linked with better mental health (Kasl, 1978; Seagraves, 1980). Moreover, the perceived quality of the role appears to be a better predictor of well-being than is mere status occupancy, that is, whether or not one is married or employed (Hirsch & Rapkin, 1986a; Renne, 1971).

Using cluster analytic procedures, we identified five different profiles of marital and job satisfaction (see Hirsch & Rapkin, 1986a, for details). Those women in the first cluster had the best profile: extremely high satisfaction with both marriage and job. The women in Clusters 2 and 3, on the other hand, were highly dissatisfied with one of their major social roles and were at best moderately satisfied with the other. Cluster 2 nurses were dissatisfied with their job and moderately satisfied with their marriage; Cluster 3 nurses were somewhat satisfied with their job but extremely dissatisfied with their marriage. Cluster 4 represented an "improved" version of Cluster 2: somewhat satisfied with their job but more satisfied with their marriage. Cluster 5 had a very positive profile, with extremely high job satisfaction, but in contrast with Cluster 1, only moderate marital satisfaction.

We were now in a position to study how support and rejection were related to the profiles of marital and job satisfaction. As can be seen in Table 14.4, the clusters never differed significantly on any of the co-worker variables and differed on only one of the best friend variables (general rejection). However, significant differences were obtained on all four supervisor variables. With respect to supervisor support, Groups 1 and 5 consistently received more than did Groups 2 and 4; for supervisor rejection, Group 4 reported more than Group 1.

TABLE 14.4.   Profile Differences on Social Network Variables

Measures	Group 1	2	3	4	5	F	p<	Newman–Keuls
			Closest co-worker					
General support								
M	3.69	3.48	3.85	3.55	3.73	.96		
SD	.88	.97	.90	.79	.66			
General rejection								
M	1.43	1.47	1.73	1.58	1.52	1.75		
SD	.56	.43	.49	.41	.40			
Work support								
M	3.75	3.48	3.56	3.56	3.79	1.72		
SD	.80	.76	.65	.64	.56			
Work rejection								
M	1.22	1.35	1.38	1.31	1.26	1.35		
SD	.26	.36	.41	.34	.32			
			Work supervisor					
General support								
M	3.03	2.38	2.19	2.53	2.94	6.48	.001	3,2,4<5,1
SD	.85	.85	.53	.93	.77			
General rejection								
M	1.67	2.08	1.97	2.09	1.96	2.66	.04	1<4
SD	.62	.74	.85	.83	.79			
Work support								
M	3.59	2.97	3.15	3.01	3.49	6.27	.001	2,4<5,1
SD	.76	.67	.65	.90	.74			
Work rejection								
M	1.37	1.72	1.73	1.76	1.59	3.05	.02	1<4
SD	.41	.57	.71	.78	.74			
			Best friend					
General support								
M	4.11	4.26	4.12	4.16	4.21	.42		
SD	.55	.57	.73	.58	.53			
General rejection								
M	1.38	1.62	1.72	1.67	1.50	4.00	.004	1<4,3
SD	.45	.45	.59	.45	.46			
Work support								
M	2.45	2.54	2.19	2.48	2.60	.56		
SD	1.14	1.03	.76	.98	1.03			
Work rejection								
M	1.12	1.15	1.26	1.19	1.13	1.60		
SD	.19	.22	.37	.26	.25			
			Spouse					
Work support								
M	3.45	3.06	2.33	3.29	3.45	5.50	.001	3<2,4,1,5
SD	1.12	1.13	.65	.91	.85			
Work rejection								
M	1.19	1.41	2.02	1.39	1.36	13.17	.001	1,5,4,2<3
SD	.26	.37	.75	.37	.42			

TABLE 14.4. *Continued.*

Measures	Group					F	$p<$	Newman–Keuls
	1	2	3	4	5			
	Adult family member							
General support								
M	4.33	3.91	3.88	4.22	4.37	4.09	.003	3,2<1,5
SD	.55	.65	.74	.67	.46			
General rejection								
M	1.59	2.21	1.91	1.92	1.77	4.39	.002	1,5<2;1<4
SD	.64	.90	.64	.59	.55			
Work support								
M	2.69	2.26	2.00	2.35	2.67	2.54	.05	3<5,1
SD	1.10	.96	.76	1.01	1.03			
Work rejection								
M	1.20	1.31	1.13	1.20	1.18	.98		
SD	.33	.32	.22	.25	.30			

Note: $df = 4,230$. Ns for groups: $1 = 60$, $2 = 18$, $3 = 15$, $4 = 69$, $5 = 73$.
Source: Hirsch & Rapkin (1986a).

We found strong differences for both spouse variables and particularly the spouse work rejection variable.[1] Group 3 reported both less work support and more work rejection from the spouse than did any of the other groups. With respect to interactions with the next closest adult family member, we obtained significant results for three of the four variables. Groups 1 and 5 tended to have better ties than did Groups 2 and 3.

These findings suggest that interactions with several network members have an important impact on the quality of marital and work life. All four supervisor variables significantly differentiated the marital and job profiles, as did three of the four adult family member variables. The two spouse variables were also related to the profiles. The level of the husband's work rejection was clearly more important than was the level of his work support. The greater importance of the husband's response is consistent with earlier studies that indicated that the marital role is ranked as more important than the occupational role (Lopata & Barnewolt, 1984). The husband's response may be particularly important to women, as cultural norms currently do not unambiguously sanction married women (particularly with children) to work outside the home. Norms for men are obviously different, raising questions as to whether a wife's response to her husband's paid work would have the same impact on him.

Although a husband's responses have been presumed to be critical to managing multiple roles, the underlying processes have not been clearly specified. Our findings indicate that the negative effect of the spouse's work rejection appears to be contained in the marriage. The Newman–Keuls test for spouse work rejection differentiated only the most maritally dissatisfied women from the other groups.

---

[1] General support and rejection from the spouse were omitted from these analyses, owing to their conceptual and empirical similarity to the measure of marital satisfaction.

It did not differentiate groups with contrasting levels of job satisfaction. Correlations among the entire sample (disregarding cluster membership) also indicated that spouse work rejection was strongly related to less marital satisfaction but more weakly related (albeit significantly) to job satisfaction. These findings suggest that the primary means by which a husband's work rejection impedes a woman's ability to manage multiple roles is by decreasing her marital satisfaction. The husband's work rejection is also associated with decreased job satisfaction, but this process appears to be of secondary importance.

The clusters were differentiated on the supervisor variables primarily on the basis of their job satisfaction scores. Supervisor variables were also more strongly correlated with job than with marital satisfaction (correlations with the latter, again, were weaker, although usually still significant). Bronfenbrenner's (1979) distinction between the microsystem and mesosystem helps clarify the nature of these findings. The microsystem refers to a particular social domain (e.g., work), whereas the mesosystem refers to linkages among different microsystems (e.g., marriage and work). Interactions with a role partner were associated with both role satisfaction within that domain (microsystem), as well as role satisfaction in other domains (mesosystem linkage). The supervisor findings were consistent with the spouse findings in suggesting the greater potency of microsystem over mesosystem effects on women's marital and job satisfaction.

Future Directions

We began this section by considering that nurse managers had severely segmented their work and nonwork social networks, in contrast with the adolescents, for whom there was considerable overlap between school and nonschool friendships. Certainly one area worth pursuing in future research is stability and change in the social ecology of networks over the life course. Of particular relevance may be periods of fundamental change in primary social environments and the roles that are assumed in them, such as the school-to-work transition that typically occurs in late adolescence or early adulthood. Bronfenbrenner (1979) referred to these shifts in role and environment as *ecological transitions* and emphasized the developmental significance of the individual's evolving understanding of and capacity to influence the social ecology. This question of what processes contribute to developing and maintaining a supportive network at different stages of life needs to be further understood, for both theory and application.

We suspect that both person and environment factors are worth investigating. One factor, already identified in the obstacles that adolescents reported to nonschool contact with school friends, is probably competing activities. Among adults, family demands are quite strong and friendship networks more stable, which (other things being equal) may reduce outside contact with those who are seen extensively during the workday. There also are occupational differences in this area, for "recreational" contact outside the workplace is considered essential in some lines of work. Both personal preference and environmental press may vary over the life cycle.

For logistical reasons, we limited our assessment of role-specific support and rejection to the work role. There is certainly good reason to extend this approach to assess other role-specific network interactions. For example, support and rejection items could be created for marital and parental roles, and role satisfaction profiles could be constructed for other roles as well.

SOCIAL NETWORK DENSITY

In prior sections we considered social networks in relation to multiple social environments, but focusing on ties within and beyond a particular organizational role involvement. In this section, we will instead highlight how the social environment can be conceptualized as relationships among social network members. Our emphasis will be on studies examining relationships among network members from different spheres of life, especially family and friends. This aspect of networks is typically considered to be a structural characteristic, and it provides an alternative vehicle for examining the impact of multiple social environments. Just as we earlier saw that whether or not organizationally based ties extend beyond the organizational setting had different meanings for adolescents (school) and adults (work), here, too, we will show that network structure has a complex relation to psychological well-being.

We begin with two sociological studies of network density that pertain to the relation between social networks and multiple role involvements. The density of a network is defined as the proportion of actual to potential ties among network members. Because density is usually assessed via self report, we thus will be dealing with perceived density.

The initial sociological interest in density can be traced to a concern with whether there has been a breakdown of "community" in industrialized society. Durkheim (1902/1960) argued that mass urbanization disrupted community ties, eventually leading to individual anomie and depression. Belonging to a high-density network, with many interconnections in the network, presumably would simulate the traditional society or *gemeinschaft* of the past and contribute to healthier adjustment.

In a large, demographically heterogeneous sample, Fischer (1977) found a much more complex pattern of findings. Higher-density networks were more common among those with low socioeconomic status (SES) and were associated with greater satisfaction with the social support of that group. Among more affluent individuals, however, greater support satisfaction was found in lower-density networks, which were also more typical of this SES group. It is important to note that because of the covariation between network size and density, high-density networks are usually drawn from one or two contexts (i.e., denser networks tend to be smaller and less diverse). Interestingly, these conditions occur most frequently among those of lower SES who may have limited access to participation in a variety of social domains. As Wellman (1981) pointed out, highly dense networks may be advantageous for those from lower-SES groups, because they enhance the ability of the powerless to conserve and control existing intra-network resources and to mobilize help quickly. On the other hand, individuals from higher-SES groups with greater social and economic resources can more easily afford to organize their lives across various contexts. This allows them to take advantage of diverse social roles, which often leads to less dense, wider-range networks. Although the tightly knit community of less affluent individuals may be adaptive in the stabilizing function it performs, a similar network config-uration for a high-SES person might reflect an overreliance on relationships in one or two domains, despite opportunities to participate in a wider range of ac-tivities with others.

The density–SES interaction was detailed in a study by Kadushin (1982) of the incidence of stress reactions among high- and low-SES Vietnam veterans. High-SES combat veterans living in large metropolitan areas had lower stress reactions if their networks were characterized by dense clusters with lower overall density across the entire network. These clusters could be thought of as small, intercon-nected groups within a larger network with little or no overlap between members from different groups. Whereas high-SES, metropolis-dwelling veterans had bet-ter adjustment in networks of this sort, those living in small cities and rural ar-eas, regardless of SES, fared better in networks with a high overall density. Kadushin explained this complex interaction in terms of differences in roles in which city versus rural individuals participate. High overall density may be help-ful only to the extent that it can simulate the *gemeinschaft* of the past, in which stable community norms and shared emotional support among a tightly knit group contributed to a general sense of well-being. Because this type of structure in which "everyone knows everyone else" is less common in the city, well-being may be achieved through involvements in a variety of domains. Opportunities for diverse roles are available in low-density networks composed of several different clusters, whereas high-density large-city networks may reflect a lack of available resources needed to cope with city life. Furthermore, the dense clusters may also provide some sense of community (cf. Hirsch, 1979). The studies by Fischer (1977) and Kadushin (1982) suggest that the association among density, SES, and adjustment is largely related to how well individuals are able to carry out roles in important domains, which in turn depends on additional ecological variables.

The construct of boundary density emerged in several studies as a useful analytic tool for examining connections across specific life spheres. Boundary density measures the extent to which members of different segments of an indi-vidual's network are interconnected. It is defined as the ratio of actual to poten-tial relationships existing across the specified life spheres. Most of the studies we will review focus on the (perceived) boundary density between family and friends.

In a study of recent younger widows and of mature women returning to col-lege, Hirsch (1980) found that a less-dense boundary between nuclear family and friends was associated with better mental health. Low boundary-density networks for these women may be adaptive in that they offer flexibility to articulate new role involvements, much in the same manner as low-density networks appeared to contribute to positive outcomes for the urban affluent in Kadushin's (1982) study. Both the widows and the returning students (in Hirsch, 1980) needed to intensify their involvement in nonfamily roles at this time. The widows typically already had strong ties to their children and thus needed to look outside the family to fill the social void left by their husband's death. The returning students now considered school and an eventual career, in addition to their family, to be important parts of their life.

Social networks differed considerably in their capacity to serve as support systems for intensified nonfamily involvements. In high boundary-density networks, the greater involvement of friends with children may have led friendships to concentrate on child- or family-related events and topics. Access to and support for nonfamily involvements were not as readily available. By contrast, a less dense or more segmented family–friend boundary encouraged the separation of family and nonfamily roles and activities, thereby providing a structural resource for focusing on nonfamily interests among friends.

A study by Wilcox (1981) of divorced women also highlighted the potential importance of network structure for the management of complex role changes. Pre- to postseparation differences were found in the networks of successful versus unsuccessful adjusters. Unsuccessful adjusters, as compared with successful adjusters, had a significantly higher preseparation overlap with their spouse's network. Many of these friendship ties were eventually lost, leading to a substantially greater turnover in the composition of their network. Moreover, after separation, the networks of unsuccessful adjusters contained a higher proportion of relatives than did the networks of successful adjusters. Having a network dominated by relatives produced as much stress as support, because interactions with them tended to include a lot of commentary on the failure of the marriage. These negative interactions probably impeded the development of new roles; furthermore, access to alternative sources of support for these roles was limited by the women's comparative absence of friends in their postseparation networks.

Another study of divorced mothers pointed out the importance of role orientation in mediating the relation between network structure and adaptation (McLanahan, Wedemeyer, & Adelberg, 1981). On the basis of interviews regarding current and past role orientation, women were categorized as either "stabilizers" (those who wished to maintain the primacy of their predivorce roles of wife or mother) or "changers" (those who wished to establish a new primary career role). Dense family of origin networks tended to be more adaptive for stabilizers, whereas loose, extended networks composed of more friends and of family who had no ties with these friends were better for changers. However, even if a stabilizer continues to fulfill her preferred role of mother, she may confront stressors difficult to cope with in kin-dominated, high-density networks. Wilcox and Birkel (1983) found that divorced women from such networks were more likely to say that they would rely on themselves when faced with a family problem but would turn to their families if suffering from depression. These women thus might place themselves at a particular disadvantage, given their risk for both family problems and depressive symptoms during the divorce transition. Looser networks containing nonfamily members give the divorcée opportunities to discuss family problems with peers who may offer more objective assistance. They also provide access to information regarding professional and self-help groups for addressing the particular emotional needs of divorced women (Wilcox & Birkel, 1983).

Further evidence of the complexity of the relation between density and adjustment was found in two studies of family–friendship boundary density. In each study, this boundary density was associated with more successful adjustment for one group but less successful adjustment for the other. The first investigation (Hirsch & Reischl, 1985) focused on three groups of high-risk and normal adolescents: adolescent children of a depressed parent, adolescent children of a parent with rheumatoid arthritis, and adolescent children of parents free of disorder ("normal" parents). An examination of the boundary density between an adolescent's friends and parents provided a unique vantage point from which to consider differences in social adaptational processes among individuals varying in vulnerability to psychological dysfunction because of family circumstances. Although there were no between-group differences in the mean levels of density, adolescents with a depressed parent reported more symptomatology when they were from high boundary-density networks, whereas boundary density was associated with less symptomatology among adolescents from normal families.

When we interpreted these data, we concentrated on the importance of shame and defenses against shame in the social transactions of adolescence. Adolescents can be quite uncomfortable with the experience of being different. This discomfort may be especially pronounced when they perceive their (depressed) parent as different in a negative way. The more frequent and more personal is the contact that their friends have with this parent, the more the adolescents may need to defend against being ashamed of that parent and the greater their conflicting feelings about that parent are likely to be. Increased symptomatology may be regarded as one manifestation of the adolescents' inability to cope with the resulting heightened ambivalence about the parent. In addition, adolescents with a depressed parent may worry about whether difficulties at home may make them unable to have friends over or about how their parents may behave toward their friends. These circumstances can lead to concern that their friendships may be jeopardized, as well as anxiety about how they themselves are perceived by their friends.

The social and personal adaptations of adolescents from normal families responded to different opportunities and constraints. Being less troubled by concerns about how they or their parents would be perceived, these adolescents could use linkages between friends and parents to integrate life spheres. A denser friend–parent boundary density may have helped them manage both distance and connectedness with parents, an important element of individuation in adolescence.

The second investigation was of recent mothers of full-term or very low birthweight, premature infants (Zarling, Hirsch, & Landry, 1988). Unlike previous studies, which may have introduced method bias by relying on self-report measures of both adjustment and network structure, Zarling and colleagues (1988) used observers' ratings of maternal sensitivity as the outcome measure. Nevertheless, their findings appear to parallel those of Hirsch and Reischl (1985), as they found a group-by-density interaction in the prediction of adaptive outcome. For mothers of very low birthweight babies, a higher boundary density between the mother's family of origin and the mother's friends was related to less maternal sensitivity, whereas a similar configuration was linked to greater sensitivity for mothers of full-term infants. To account for these findings, we once again need to consider how the impact of a particular network structure reflects specific life circumstances.

When a healthy infant is born, network members typically come together to celebrate the birth and offer support to the new parents. The roles of network members are unambiguous, and the greater network interconnectedness can facilitate positive communications about mother and infant.

The birth of a premature infant with medical complications, on the other hand, confronts the mother and her social network with an uncertain situation. Happy gatherings may be postponed or avoided, with the network members left unsure of their roles. Intranetwork communications, which are more likely to occur in denser systems, may reinforce the network's sense of helplessness and confusion over how to be helpful. The mother's anxiety and discomfort may increase with her exposure to such networks. Furthermore, if the network members find it difficult to provide positive support, they may instead reinforce a maternal role identity that the mother finds uneasy or negative. For example, many women noted that their own mothers often "felt sorry" for them or that friends implied that the infant would be "slow." Denser networks may thus inadvertently exacerbate the mother's fears and sense of failure or helplessness.

Although findings from Zarling et al (1988) are consistent with those of Hirsch and Reischl (1985), Kazak (in press) reported somewhat different results. This sample included parents of retarded institutionalized adolescents and young adults, and a matched group of parents of offspring without disabilities. Group-by-density interactions on parental mental health were not tested. Among parents of the disabled group, a lower family–friend boundary density in the parent's network was associated with less parental symptomatology, as in the two earlier studies, but the relation was not significant in this instance. This finding suggests that the effect of family–friendship boundary density is strongest during life transitions and weakens for more chronic stressors.

These studies of the family–friendship boundary density suggest that the adaptiveness of a particular network structure depends on its congruence with values, goals, and the needs of individuals in their specific life circumstances. Similar concerns are relevant when considering other types of network boundary density. For example, Hirsch and David's (1983) study of nurse managers (discussed earlier in this chapter) revealed both the benefits and the costs of low work–nonwork boundary density.

Future Directions

The adaptiveness of a particular network configuration varies according to both individual and environmental characteristics. High-density networks appear to be associated with positive outcomes if there is either identification with traditional values or the adoption of superordinate goals across the network. More generally, the adaptiveness of density may vary depending on the perceived desirability of the event or life circumstance. The rationale here is that more interconnections among network members will result in more exposure throughout the network to the event or circumstance. The more sustained attention will tend to amplify the network members' emotional responses. For positive events, this can lead to enhanced celebration and can facilitate involvement in and satisfaction with new roles. However, unremitting attention to negative or ambivalent circumstances can lead to increased anxiety and self-doubt, resulting in diminished satisfaction. The network's own sense of helplessness or confusion over how to be helpful may also increase in the latter circumstances, leading to a still greater rise in anxiety.

Individuals do not always agree with their network about the desirability of a life event or new life circumstance. When network members perceive a change as being undesirable, they may not only refuse to provide support, but they may also oppose it. In denser systems, this conflict is more likely to be contagious and reverberate through the network.

The level of density required for positive adjustment therefore varies to the extent that relevant values and roles can be reinforced within that network. Higher-density networks with greater overlapping ties seem suited to support traditional roles (e.g., wife and mother) or identities consistent with the tasks of normal development (e.g., individuation from the family during adolescence). However, the systems dynamics that we discussed earlier may make it more difficult to articulate new roles under conditions of substantial person–network or intranetwork conflict, or of highly ambiguous or negative circumstances. In such situations, individuals in dense networks may have to rely more on those network members who are not linked with other network members (although there may be few of them or they may not be adequate for the task); alternatively, it may be necessary to recruit new network members.

Individuals in lower-density systems are likely to have more diverse relationships that allow for the expression of a wider array of interests and values (see especially Hirsch, 1979). This may permit a smoother and less drastic reorganization of their lives when required. They may merely have to change the extent of their already existing commitment or identification with particular activities or relationships, rather than needing to create entirely new ones. Such persons may regard these changes as less threatening and so pursue them more confidently, as they have a greater backlog of actual experiences that indicate that these alternatives can be viable and satisfying (Hirsch, 1980).

Low-density systems may accordingly enable one part of the network to serve as a support system against stresses affecting other parts of the network. Few ties with network members, however, may diminish one's sense of overall connectedness and integration. Perhaps a lower-density network characterized by several dense clusters most effectively promotes personal growth and enhances adaptation without sacrificing a sense of community (Hirsch, 1979).

Given this conceptualization, further research is required to elaborate the values, goals, and priorities of both the subjects and the members of their network (cf. Reischl & Hirsch, 1989). Longitudinal research is also needed to chart the nature of network responses to life transitions and to clarify the underlying causal processes (Hirsch & Jolly, 1984, consider a number of conceptual issues bearing on such research).

CONCLUSIONS

In this chapter we examined how research on the social environment at the level of the mesosystem might further our understanding of social networks and social support. At present, few such studies have been conducted. Rather, the social sciences have tended to segment the study of the social environment and only recently have begun to address the interrelationship of these domains. We suggested several concepts and methods that might be useful to such research. Throughout, we urged that future investigations study both the person and the environmental context.

We do not believe that studying the environment need result in neglecting the person. On the contrary, a more differentiated knowledge of the environment can lead to a richer understanding of the person. In the personality domain, we referred repeatedly to the importance of considering an individual's goals and values as these develop over the life course. We also invoked a gamut of traditional personality variables, ranging from social skills to defense mechanisms. For an overall framework, we found it useful to draw on social–structural versions of symbolic interactionism (e.g., Stryker, 1980). In recent statements regarding this approach, roles are not considered to be fixed immutably by the environment but, rather, to be fluid constructions shaped by both individuals and social structures. This perspective provides many useful concepts that can facilitate the study of the self as reflected by and embedded in the social environment. It also is suitable for examining the interplay of these factors during life transitions.

The studies we reviewed also reflect a concern with the position or perspective of social network members and how this affects the availability, perception, or provision of support. Few other studies, however, attend to how specific network members are in turn affected by still other network members and by organizations. The more systems-oriented focus of ecological research complements and extends the findings of studies limited to the dyad.

In short, more studies are needed of the developmental ecology of persons and their social network. We look forward to the next generation of research on this topic.

REFERENCES

Adams, G. (1983). Social competence during adolescence: Social sensitivity, locus of control, empathy, and peer popularity. *Journal of Youth and Adolescence, 12,* 203–211.

Andrisani, P., & Shapiro, M. (1978). Women's attitudes toward their jobs: Some longitudinal data on a national sample. *Personnel Psychology, 31,* 15–34.

Argyle, M. (1985). Social behavior problems and social skills training in adolescence. In B. H. Schneider, K. H. Rubin, & J. E. Ledingham (Eds.), *Children's peer relations: Issues in assessment and intervention* (pp. 207–224). New York: Springer-Verlag.

Asp, E., & Garbarino, J. (1983). Social support networks and the schools. In J. Whittaker & J. Garbarino (Eds.), *Social support networks: Informal helping in the human services* (pp. 251–297). New York: Aldine.

Belle, D. (1982). The stress of caring: Women as providers of social support. In L. Goldberger & S. Bresnitz (Eds.), *Handbook of stress: Theoretical and clinical aspects* (pp. 496–505). New York: Free Press.

Berkowitz, A., & Perkins, H. W. (1984). Stress among farm women: Work and family as interacting systems. *Journal of Marriage and the Family, 46,* 161–165.

Bernard, J. (1981). *The female world.* New York: Free Press.

Berndt, T. (1989). Obtaining support from friends during childhood and adolescence. In D. Belle (Ed.), *Children's social networks and supports* (pp. 308–331). New York: Wiley.

Blyth, D., Hill, J., & Thiel, K. (1982). Early adolescents' significant others: Grade and gender differences in perceived relationships with familial and nonfamilial adults and young people. *Journal of Youth and Adolescence, 11,* 425–450.

Bronfenbrenner, U. (1979). *The ecology of human development.* Cambridge, MA: Harvard University Press.

Cauce, A. (1986). Social networks and social competence: Exploring the effects of early adolescent friendships. *American Journal of Community Psychology, 14,* 607–628.

Douvan, E., & Adelson, J. (1966). *The adolescent experience.* New York: Wiley.

DuBois, D. L., & Hirsch, B. J. (1989). *School/nonschool friendship patterns and self-esteem in early adolescence.* Manuscript submitted for publication.

DuBois, D. L., & Hirsch, B. J. (in press). School and neighborhood friendship patterns of blacks and whites in early adolescence. *Child Development.*

Durkheim, E. (1902/1960). *The division of labor in society* (2nd ed., G. Simpson, Trans.). New York: Free Press.

Epstein, J. L. (1983). The influence of friends on achievement and affective outcomes. In J. L. Epstein & N. Karweit (Eds.), *Friends in school: Patterns of selection and influence in secondary schools* (pp. 177–200). New York: Academic Press.

Epstein, J. L. (1986). Friendship selection: Developmental and environmental influences. In E. Mueller & C. R. Cooper (Eds.), *Process and outcome in peer relationships* (pp. 129–160). Orlando, FL: Academic Press.

Fenzel, L., & Blyth, D. (1986). Individual adjustment to school transitions: An exploration of the role of supportive peer relations. *Journal of Early Adolescence, 6,* 315–329.

Fiore, J., Becker, J., & Coppel, D. (1983). Social network interactions: A buffer or a stress. *American Journal of Community Psychology, 11,* 423–440.

Fischer, C. S. (1977). *To dwell among friends: Personal networks in town and city.* Chicago: University of Chicago Press.

French, J., Caplan, R., & Van Harrison, R. (1982). *The mechanisms of job stress and strain.* New York: Wiley.

Gilligan, C. (1977). *In a different voice: Psychological theory and women's development.* Cambridge, MA: Harvard University Press.

Gove, W. (1984). Gender differences in mental and physical illness: The effects of fixed roles and nurturant roles. *Social Science & Medicine, 19,* 77–91.

Greenberg, M. T., Siegel, J. M., & Leitch, C. J. (1983). The nature and importance of attachment relationships to parents and peers during adolescence. *Journal of Youth and Adolescence, 12,* 373–386.

Hartup, W. (1983). Peer relations. In P. Mussen (Ed.), *Handbook of child psychology: Vol. 4. Socialization, personality, and social development* (4th ed.). New York: Wiley.

Haw, M. (1982). Women, work and stress: A review and agenda for the future. *Journal of Health and Social Behavior, 23,* 132–144.

Hirsch, B. J. (1979). Psychological dimensions of social networks: A multimethod analysis. *American Journal of Community Psychology, 7,* 263–277.

Hirsch, B. J. (1980). Natural support systems and coping with major life changes. *American Journal of Community Psychology, 8,* 159–172.

Hirsch, B. J. (1981). Social networks and the coping process: Creating personal communities. In B. Gottlieb (Ed.), *Social networks and social support* (pp. 149–170). Beverly Hills, CA: Sage.

Hirsch, B. J. (1985). Adolescent coping and support across multiple social environments. *American Journal of Community Psychology, 13,* 381–392.

Hirsch, D. J., & David, T. G. (1983). Social networks and work/nonwork life: Action-research with nurse managers. *American Journal of Community Psychology, 11,* 493–507.

Hirsch, B. J., & DuBois, D. L. (1989). The school/nonschool ecology of early adolescent friendships. In D. Belle (Ed.), *Children's social networks and supports* (pp. 260–274). New York: Wiley.

Hirsch, B. J., & Jolly, E. A. (1984). Role transitions and social networks: Social support for multiple roles. In V. Allen & E. van de Vliert (Eds.), *Role transitions* (pp. 39–51). New York: Plenum.

Hirsch, B. J., & Rapkin, B. D. (1986a). Multiple roles, social networks, and women's well-being. *Journal of Personality and Social Psychology, 51,* 1237–1247.

Hirsch, B. J., & Rapkin, B. D. (1986b). Social networks and adult social identities: Profiles and correlates of support and rejection. *American Journal of Community Psychology, 14,* 395–411.

Hirsch, B. J., & Reischl, T. (1985). Social networks and developmental psychopathology: A comparison of adolescent children of a depressed, arthritic, or normal parent. *Journal of Abnormal Psychology, 94,* 272–281.

Holahan, C., & Gilbert, L. (1979). Interrole conflict for working women: Career versus jobs. *Journal of Applied Psychology, 64,* 86–90.

House, J. (1981). *Work stress and social support.* Reading, MA: Addison-Wesley.

Howard, J., Rechnitzer, P., & Cunningham, D. (1975). Coping with job tension—Effective and ineffective methods. *Public Personnel Management, 4,* 317–325.

Kadushin, C. (1982). Social density and mental health. In P. Marsden & N. Lin (Eds.), *Social structure and network analysis* (pp. 147–158). Beverly Hills, CA: Sage.

Kanter, R. M. (1977). *Work and family in the United States: A critical review and agenda for research and policy.* New York: Russell Sage.

Kapferer, B. (1969). Norms and the manipulation of relationships in a work context. In

J. C. Mitchell (Ed.), *Social networks in urban situations* (pp. 181–244). New York: Humanities Press.

Kasl, S. (1978). Epidemiological contributions to the study of work and stress. In C. Cooper & R. Payne (Eds.), *Stress at work* (pp. 3–48). New York: Wiley.

Kazak, A. E. (in press). Stress and social networks in families with older institutionalized retarded children. *Journal of Social and Clinical Psychology.*

Lewin, E., & Damrell, J. (1978). Female identity and career pathways: Post-baccalaureate nurses ten years after. *Sociology of Work and Occupations, 5,* 31–54.

Lopata, H., & Barnewolt, D. (1984). The middle years: Changes and variations in social role commitments. In G. Baruch & J. Brooks-Gunn (Eds.), *Women in midlife* (pp. 83–108). New York: Plenum.

Mayer, A. (1966). The significance of quasi-groups in the study of complex societies. In M. Banton (Ed.), *The social anthropology of complex societies* (pp. 97–122). A.S.A. Monographs 4. London: Tavistock.

McLanahan, S., Wedemeyer, N., & Adelberg, T. (1981). Network structure, social support and psychological well-being in the single-parent family. *Journal of Marriage and the Family, 43,* 601–611.

Offer, D. (1969). *The psychological world of the teenager.* New York: Basic Books.

Parsons, T., & Bales, R. (1955). *Family, socialization, and interaction processes.* New York: Free Press.

Patchen, M. (1982). *Black-white contact in schools: Its social and academic effects.* West Lafayette, IN: Purdue University Press.

Petroni, F. A. (1971). Teen-age interracial dating. *Transaction, 8* (11), 54–59.

Pines, A., Aronson, E., & Kafry, D. (1981). *Burnout: From tedium to personal growth.* New York: Free Press.

Reischl, T., & Hirsch, B. (1989). Identity commitments and coping with a difficult developmental transition. *Journal of Youth and Adolescence, 18,* 55–70.

Renne, K. (1971). Health and marital experience in an urban population. *Journal of Marriage and the Family, 33,* 338–350.

Rook, K. (1984). The negative side of social interaction: Impact on psychological well-being. *Journal of Personality and Social Psychology, 46,* 1097–1108.

Rubin, L. (1985). *Just friends: The role of friendship in our lives.* New York: Harper & Row.

Schofield, J. W. (1981). Complementary and conflicting identities: Images and interaction in an interracial school. In S. R. Asher & J. M. Gottman (Eds.), *The development of children's friendships* (pp. 53–90). Cambridge, England: Cambridge University Press.

Seagraves, R. (1980). Marriage and mental health. *Journal of Sex and Marital Therapy, 6,* 187–198.

Simmons, R., & Blyth, D. (1987). *Moving into adolescence: The impact of pubertal change and school context.* New York: Aldine.

Stack, C. B. (1974). *All our kin: Strategies for survival in a black community.* New York: Harper & Row.

Stryker, S. (1980). *Symbolic interactionism: A social-structural version.* Menlo Park, CA: Benjamin/Cummings.

Vanfossen, B. (1981). Sex differences in the mental health effects of spouse support and equity. *Journal of Health and Social Behavior, 22,* 130–143.

Wellman, B. (1981). Applying network analysis to the study of support. In B. H. Gottlieb (Ed.), *Social networks and social support* (pp. 171–200). Beverly Hills, CA: Sage.

Wheeldon, P. (1969). The operation of voluntary associations and personal networks in the political processes of an interethnic community. In J. C. Mitchell (Ed.), *Social networks in urban situations* (pp. 128–180). New York: Humanities Press.

Wilcox, B. L. (1981). Social support in adjusting to marital separation: A network analysis. In B. H. Gottlieb (Ed.), *Social networks and social support* (pp. 97–115). Beverly Hills, CA: Sage.

Wilcox, B. L., & Birkel, R. C. (1983). Social networks and the help-seeking process: A structural perspective. In A. Nadler, J. D. Fisher, & B. M. DePaulo (Eds.), *New directions in helping. Vol. 3. Applied perspectives on help-seeking and receiving* (pp. 235–255). New York: Academic Press.

Zarling, C., Hirsch, B., & Landry, S. (1988). Maternal social networks and mother–infant interactions in fullterm and very low birthweight, preterm infants. *Child Development, 59,* 178–185.

PART FOUR

Social Support Applications and Interventions in Clinical and Community Settings

The ultimate goal of social support research is to understand enough about how support works to be able to help people who lack it or who have a high level of stress and need adequate support. In this part the chapters illustrate how research ranging from the laboratory to the clinic to the community and even the battlefield can help achieve this goal. Despite their different topics, all the chapters emphasize that before we can achieve this goal we must know much more about the interactions between the supporter and the supported and the meanings they convey to each.

A neglected aspect of social support research is the effect on support provision of the prospective recipient's coping and his or her self-presentation of that coping. Chapter 15 examines this issue and considers the possible consequences of various types of self-presentation. It describes an experimental study in which confederates—some of them cancer patients—were portrayed using several different coping styles. The most positive responses and support were given to those confederates who displayed both some distress and some coping efforts. Although many other aspects of interactions between victims and potential helpers remain to be clarified, investigations of this type are an important tool for aiding victims, as well as offering information about supportive interactions.

Social relationships may hinder optimal health outcomes for those who are chronically ill, especially if they reinforce comfort-enhancing but noncompliant behaviors. Chapter 16 deals with both this Negative Functional Effects Model and a Positive Functional Effects Model in which the support provider reinforces health-promoting behavior. The chapter reviews the role of social support in the treatment of children and adolescents with asthma or insulin-dependent diabetes mellitus and the role of social relationships for adults with respect to their personal habits and health behaviors in several conditions: noninsulin-dependent diabetes mellitus, coronary heart disease, and back pain. The complex relationships the authors discovered point to a need for a systematic evaluation of the possible positive and negative effects of interventions, such as support groups and training for family members.

Evaluations of a stress-protective effect from social support often use the summation of major stressful life events over time as a measure of stress. If stress is evaluated by means of categories of events rather than summed events, the potential effect of social support in certain situations could be better predicted. Social support may be a positive resource, a burden, or a neutral element; the conservation of resources model described in Chapter 17 helps forecast which of these outcomes is likely for particular stressful situations. This chapter studies two categories of highly stressful events, illness and war, and describes the appropriate social support intervention strategies for each.

Work on social support interventions has been plagued by assumptions of homogeneity regarding the social support process, its delivery, and its benefits, to an even greater degree than has the entire area of social support research. Chapter 18 argues that in order to be effective, support interventions should be appropriate to the individual's specific life tasks. Reciprocity of social support in relationships also is essential. Without such reciprocity, the central goal of social support—its esteem-enhancing aspects and its restorative effects on role functioning—is not likely to be achieved. Support programs must incorporate reciprocal elements of social relationships, and they must reinforce rather than ignore existing social structures.

CHAPTER 15

The Role of Coping in Support Provision: The Self-presentational Dilemma of Victims of Life Crises

ROXANE COHEN SILVER, CAMILLE B. WORTMAN, AND CHRISTINE CROFTON

University of California, Irvine

State University of New York, Stony Brook

Prospect Associates, Ltd.

People who are suffering or are under severe stress appear to have a special need for close, supportive interactions with others (Coates, Wortman, & Abbey, 1979). Moreover, evidence is accumulating to indicate that such close social ties lessen the destructive impact of negative life events on physical and mental health (see Cohen, 1988; House, Umberson, & Landis, 1988; or Kessler, Price, & Wortman, 1985, for reviews). Yet, in our own research and practical experience, we have been confronted with evidence suggesting that victims of life crises sometimes have difficulty gaining the support they desire and need (DeLongis, O'Brien, Silver, & Wortman, 1990; Lehman, Ellard, & Wortman, 1986; Wortman & Lehman, 1985)[1]. For example, cancer patients report experiencing problems with others as a function of their disease, such as friends acting uncomfortable in their presence (Peters-Golden, 1982; see Wortman & Dunkel-Schetter, 1987, for a review). Such negative reactions appear to cancel out the benefits of positive support attempts (see, for example, Barrera, 1981; Porritt, 1979). In fact, research that compared the relative impact of positive and negative social exchanges found negative responses from others to be even more detrimental to well-being than positive responses are beneficial (Fiore, Becker, & Coppel, 1983; Pagel, Erdly, & Becker, 1987; Rook, 1984).

Approximately a decade ago, Wortman and her associates developed a theoretical model to account for the support problems that people seem to encounter following a life crisis (see Coates et al., 1979; Coates & Wortman, 1980; Wort-

---

[1] We use the term *victim* merely to reflect someone who has experienced a stressful life event over which he or she has little or no control. It is not meant to imply inferior status or to convey that the person views himself or herself as passive and helpless in the face of the event.

man & Dunkel-Schetter, 1979). Drawing from theoretical work in social psychology, as well as from practical experience with victimized populations, this model highlighted how vulnerability engendered by contact with victims of stressful life events may interfere with the effective provision of support. It was suggested that reactions to a person in need of support are a function of a conflict between (1) the feelings of vulnerability and helplessness that are evoked in potential helpers during an interaction and (2) beliefs about appropriate reactions to display when interacting with people who have experienced life crises (e.g., optimism and cheerfulness). Wortman and her colleagues argued that this conflict may result in behavioral responses, such as avoidance and displays of discomfort, that are unintentionally harmful to people who have suffered negative life events.

Until this point, this model focused primarily on ways in which the support provider's negative feelings may interfere with the effective provision of support. However, victims of stressful life events are not passive recipients of support provision. Because support is an interactional process, it is important to consider behaviors of the support recipient that may minimize the support provider's feelings of vulnerability and helplessness and may elicit responses that are truly supportive. In fact, relatively limited research attention has been paid to recipient variables that may influence the provision of support (Dunkel-Schetter, Folkman, & Lazarus, 1987; Wortman & Dunkel-Schetter, 1987). Some notable exceptions include the study of such recipient characteristics as gender and race (e.g., Riley & Eckenrode, 1986) and such dispositional variables as social skills (e.g., Heller & Swindle, 1983; Sarason, Sarason, Hacker, & Basham, 1985) or support-seeking orientations (e.g., Eckenrode, 1983; Mitchell & Trickett, 1980).

In this chapter, we attempt to establish a link between our work on coping with life crises (Silver & Wortman, 1980; Wortman & Silver, 1989) and our work on social support, by suggesting that how a person copes with a life crisis is likely to be a powerful determinant of the support he or she receives. In earlier work, we reported that those who express difficulties in coping with a stressful life event may elicit more rejection from others than do those who appear to be coping well (see Coates et al., 1979). The implications of these findings are distressing, as they suggest that those in greatest need of social support may be least likely to get it. A few subsequent studies offered evidence that the way a person copes with problems is associated with the amount of social support that he or she receives (Billings & Moos, 1981; Dunkel-Schetter et al., 1987). Surprisingly, however, this variable has received relatively little attention from theorists interested in support provision. If they want to maximize their chances of obtaining effective support, what should victims of life crises convey about how they are coping with their problems?

We believe that victims of life crises are faced with a dilemma regarding how to present their situation to others. If they display their distress and report difficulties in coping, they may drive others away. But if they fail to exhibit their distress, they may not signal a need for support. Are there ways in which the individual can present himself or herself so as to convey need without initiating negative feelings from potential support providers? Are there conditions under which distress can be expressed so as to elicit sympathy (cf. Coates et al., 1979) rather than avoidance? As early as 1959, Goffman identified the importance of self-presentation in facilitating effective social interactions and satisfactory social relationships (see Baumeister, 1982; Jones & Pittman, 1982; and Schlenker, 1980, for more recent discussions). In this chapter, we propose that victims of stressful life events can shape the support interaction by means of their self-presentations of how they are coping. First, we present a brief overview of our theoretical approach, illustrating how victims of stressful life events can unintentionally initiate feelings of vulnerability and helplessness in others. Next, we describe the process through which these feelings may interfere with the effective provision of support. Third, we consider possible self-presentations regarding how one is coping that may be expressed to potential support providers, and review the possible consequences of each. In particular, we note the probable social costs of seeking support by displaying signs of distress. Then, drawing from theory and research, we offer a potential solution to the self-presentational dilemma we have identified, and describe an experiment designed to test our ideas. In the concluding section of the chapter, we consider the implications of our analysis for subsequent research and theoretical development in this area.

THE VICTIMIZATION PERSPECTIVE

Earlier papers argued that a victim's plight is a powerful stimulus in its ability to arouse negative feelings in others (Coates et al., 1979; Dunkel-Schetter & Wortman, 1982; Wortman & Dunkel-Schetter, 1979; Wortman & Lehman, 1985). Based on social psychological work on victimization, these papers maintained that contact with others who are suffering may shatter a person's sense of invulnerability. That is, an individual's initial reaction to another's victimization is often a sharp sense of his or her own vulnerability (i.e., a sense that "it could have been me"). Learning that a friend or associate has lost a loved one or developed a life-threatening illness forces outsiders to acknowledge that such outcomes can happen to anyone at any time (Wortman, 1983).

As a result of increased contact with victims of life crises (see Wortman, Abbey, Holland, Silver, & Janoff-Bulman, 1980), we became aware of another source of negative affect among potential support providers: feelings of helplessness. When interacting with a person who has experienced a life crisis, it is common to feel overwhelmed by the magnitude and the scope of his or her problems (see Chesler & Barbarin, 1984). For example, when a cancer patient reveals that her prognosis is poor, she is in constant pain, her finances are in chaos, her husband is anxious, and her children are "acting out" in school, what can one possibly say or do to help? In fact, the more in need the victim appears to be and the more distress he or she consequently conveys, the more that others' feelings of helplessness are likely to be heightened. Personally, we found it difficult to engage in conversations with individuals who conveyed that they were distressed and overwhelmed by their problems, and we preferred spending time with those who were able to maintain a more optimistic perspective on their situation. It occurred to us that because of our own feelings of discomfort and helplessness, we were probably devoting most of our time and attention to those individuals who were least in need of them.

People may be more inclined to help another if they believe that such help will lead to concrete improvements in that person's situation. Conversely, efforts to help that result in no noticeable change are likely to be frustrating and upsetting (see Brickman et al., 1982; Chesler & Barbarin, 1984; Coates & Wortman, 1980). Moreover, if a potential support provider feels unable to do anything to alleviate the problem, he or she may be particularly likely to derogate the victim. In fact, in a study of 20-minute telephone conversations between distressed and nondistressed college students (Dunkel-Schetter, Silver, & Wortman, 1989), we found that the more helpless subjects felt when interacting with a person perceived to be distressed, the more they reported negative feelings toward and rejection of the target. Derogating distressed individuals by attributing negative feelings and fears to their own inadequacies in coping with the crisis can relieve the potential support provider's sense of personal responsibility for being unable, or even unwilling, to help (Dunkel-Schetter & Wortman, 1982).

Although people may harbor negative feelings toward those who have experienced life crises, they are likely to believe that they should not express these feelings to the victim directly. To the contrary, they are likely to assume that for the victim's benefit, they must act cheerful and encouraging (see Wortman & Lehman, 1985). But these discrepant feelings may be immobilizing, and such conflict and indecisiveness may result in unintentional avoidance of the victim. If they do find themselves in contact with someone who has experienced a life crisis, potential support providers may feel confused and uncertain about how to behave or what to say. Their attempts to be cheerful and to provide reassurance are, accordingly, unlikely to be convincing. Despite their best intentions, their interactions with the victim may be characterized by awkwardness and tension. Such discomfort might be expected to "leak out" nonverbally during the interaction or to result in inconsistencies between verbal and nonverbal behavior (see Wortman & Lehman, 1985, for a more detailed discussion).

There is evidence that victims of negative life events are nonetheless acutely aware of the discomfort that their distress creates for potential support providers, and consequently they withhold expressions of it. Several researchers have reported that distressed individuals hide their needs and negative feelings from members of their social network so as not to burden, upset, or scare them off, as well as to ensure that others do not form an impression of them as weak or needy. For example, almost 90% of the cancer patients that Dunkel-Schetter (1984) interviewed admitted that they sometimes kept their thoughts and feelings to themselves, usually because of their fears regarding how outsiders might react. More than three-quarters of the cancer patients interviewed by Meyerowitz, Yarkin-Levin, and Harvey (1988) reported having times when they would have liked to discuss their reactions to their illness with friends and family, but did not do so (see also Meyerowitz, Watkins, & Sparks, 1983). Similarly, Chesler and Barbarin (1984) found that parents of cancer patients limited their self-disclosures, even to their close friends. Koch (1985) discussed how many siblings of cancer patients withheld expressing their needs and feelings, even to their parents. Finally, Parkes and Weiss (1983) reported that because they feared social ostracism, bereaved individuals often hid their grief from others.

CONVEYING DISTRESS: SOCIAL VERSUS PERSONAL CONSEQUENCES

Our analysis suggests that in attempting to cope with their difficulties, victims may unwittingly exhibit behaviors that are upsetting to others and that lead others to respond in ways that are not supportive. Thus, there appear to be social costs in conveying distress to potential support providers. Indeed, victims seem to be aware of these social costs and so may withhold their distress for strategic purposes. However, it is widely believed among researchers and health care professionals that it is therapeutic for victims to express their feelings of distress (see Wortman & Silver, 1987). There also is evidence that victims desire opportunities to discuss their feelings and concerns and perceive these discussions to be beneficial (see, for example, Lehman, Ellard, & Wortman, 1986). Such interactions may aid the victim in achieving cognitive clarification (Clark, 1988) or in finding meaning in the experience (Silver & Wortman, 1980). In fact, a lack of opportunities to communicate distress may intensify the strain of the victimization (see Silver & Wortman, 1980). Thus, if victims maximize their chances for personal adjustment by openly expressing their distress, they may risk alienating their social network. In our own longitudinal study of coping with the loss of an infant to Sudden Infant Death Syndrome (SIDS), we found that the more distress the parents felt over the death, the more they wanted to talk to others about their feelings. However, the more they did so, the more they felt others were trying to suppress this ventilation. Over time, such suppression by outsiders increased the parents' distress (see DeLongis et al., 1990).

This suggests that victims face a difficult choice in deciding what to reveal about their victimization, and how they are coping with it, to potential support providers. Undoubtedly, the circumstances surrounding most victimizing experiences and one's reactions to them are complex and multifaceted. The victim must choose which aspects of his or her experience to share with others, and this choice is likely to have important consequences for the support received. Yet, beyond the aforementioned evidence that individuals under stress are sometimes strategic in their self-presentations, even among intimates (cf. Ginsberg & Brown, 1982; Kleck, 1968b), we know very little about the interpersonal consequences of particular types of disclosures. Because signals of distress may be necessary for outsiders to know that social support is needed or even desired (Ginsberg & Brown, 1982; Tait & Silver, 1989), it is unlikely that overly positive self-presentations will result in offers of support. So, although the general tendency of victims of negative life events might be to withhold their negative feelings from others, securing support may sometimes require highlighting, or even exaggerating, their needs (see, for example, Voysey, 1972). Surprisingly, we have been unable to locate any research that has systematically investigated this question: Are there any ways that individuals can convey their distress so as to elicit effective support from outsiders, rather than avoidance or rejection?

THE SELF-PRESENTATIONAL DILEMMA OF SUPPORT-SEEKING

Although a number of authors have noted the self-presentational concerns of victimized individuals and the impression management strategies they adopt to improve their social interactions (see, Albrecht & Adelman, 1987; Jones et al., 1984; Kleck, 1968b; Voysey, 1972; Wright, 1983), none have offered solutions to the self-presentational dilemma of support-seeking that we have identified. Logically, there are several possible ways a victim might present distress in an interaction with a potential support provider. We shall consider each of these alternatives and review the limited available evidence suggesting their likely consequences.

Positive Coping Self-presentation

When interacting with a victim of life crisis, outsiders' feelings of vulnerability and helplessness may be minimized if the victim conveys that he or she is coping well. For this reason, individuals who present themselves as coping effectively with a victimization, despite its stressful aspects, may be unlikely to elicit derogation and rejection from others. However, our society also insists on the presence of distress following negative life events (see Wortman & Silver, 1987, for an expanded discussion). Labeled the "requirement of mourning" by Dembo, Leviton, and Wright (1956), it is hypothesized that outsiders are motivated to insist on the presence of suffering in any individual whom they deem to be in an unfortunate position (see also Jones et al., 1984; Wright, 1983). If, however, that person appears not to be suffering, then others will "devaluate the unfortunate person because he or she ought to suffer" (Dembo et al., 1956, p. 21). Wright (1983) suggested that such a phenomenon may be due to outsiders' imagining how they might feel in the same situation, imagining their own distress, and projecting this onto the victim, as well as to the outsiders' need to preserve and elevate their own superior status. There is evidence that outsiders indeed expect individuals who have experienced a negative life event to go through a period of intense distress (see Wortman & Silver, 1987, 1989, for reviews). At this point, however, it is not clear how support provision is affected by the failure to express distress following a victimization.

Although the research is limited, there is some laboratory evidence that individuals who adopt a positive coping stance in response to a victimization are not derogated or disliked by outsiders. In a study that explored self-presentations among the handicapped, Hastorf, Wildfogel, and Cassman (1979) demonstrated that an open acknowledgment of one's disability fosters positive feelings in outsiders, and a desire for future interaction. Interestingly, these investigators employed a manipulation in which a handicapped confederate, while acknowledging that the handicap was a significant one, nonetheless stated that he had "learned to accept the inconveniences" (p. 1792). The results of a similar study (Bazakas, 1978/1979) suggested that acknowledgment of a disability leads to favorable impressions (less discomfort, more positive affect, less personal distance) *only* when the disabled individual portrays himself or herself as coping well with the limitations. In a study conducted in our own lab (Coates et al., 1979), rape victims who maintained, six months after the rape, that they had been able to "put the rape behind them," continued to feel happy, and reported feeling "very fortunate that I have so much to look forward to in my life" (p. 38) were rated as significantly more attractive than were victims who reported having continuing difficulty adjusting to the rape. Similarly, a study that manipulated coping portrayals following two recent negative life events (rejection by law school and breakup of a relationship) found that individuals who presented themselves as coping well were rated as significantly more attractive than were those who reported distress following the events, and no less attractive than individuals who reported experiencing no negative life events (Winer, Bonner, Blaney, & Murray, 1981).

There is even some evidence that individuals who portray themselves as well-adjusted to their victimization are preferred to and evaluated more positively than individuals who have not been victimized at all (see Kleck, 1968a; Kleck, Ono, & Hastorf, 1966, Study 1), although they may elicit some signs of nonverbal discomfort. Like media portrayals of "supercopers" (cf. Wood, Taylor, & Lichtman, 1985), such individuals might be viewed as deserving special respect and admiration for having "risen above" their victimization.

Individuals who indicate that they are coping well with their victimization may generate positive responses from outsiders because this self-presentational stance may minimize the outsiders' feelings of discomfort. Nonetheless, such positive self-presentations are unlikely to signal a need for support. Moreover, to the extent that such a portrayal is simply strategic (i.e., the public expression is intentionally discrepant from one's private experience; cf. Tait & Silver, 1989), it may lead the victim to feel alienated from the social environment and to doubt the validity of any positive responses that he or she receives (Coates & Wortman, 1980).

Poor Coping Self-presentation

Victims may communicate a need for support by stressing the difficulties they are encountering or by highlighting the negative aspects of their situation (see Dunkel-Schetter & Wortman, 1982; Jones et al., 1984). As we noted, however, the victimization model postulates that expressions of distress may enhance feelings of vulnerability and helplessness in potential support providers and consequently lead to rejection. In fact, a body of research on depression has provided evidence consistent with this view. This work has systematically examined self-presentations of distress by manipulating the presence or absence of a target's depression and then observing the reactions of others. In general, this research has found that exposure to or interactions with depressed individuals leads to derogation, rejection, and/or discomfort in others (see Gurtman, 1986, for a review). Unfortunately, in some of this research, the individual's behavior during the interaction (e.g., amount of inappropriate self-disclosure; cf. Coyne, 1976) is confounded with his or her expressed affect (see Coates et al., 1979, for a further discussion of this point). The study of rape victims conducted by Coates et al. (1979), described earlier, was designed to eliminate this type of confound. In that study, all aspects of the rape victim's experience and behavior were held constant. Nonetheless, women who conveyed poor coping following the rape experienced more derogation and rejection from observers than did those who appeared to be coping well (see Winer et al., 1981, for a comparable finding). Taken together, these results suggest that highlighting one's distress is a risky strategy to employ when seeking support.

Providing No Information About Distress

If a positive portrayal of one's coping fails to signal a need for support, and a negative portrayal appears to elicit negative feelings and result in rejection, might providing no information regarding distress solve the dilemma? We think not.

The Coates et al. (1979) study of rape victims described above also included a "no information regarding distress" control group. Subjects exposed to this condition failed to rate this target as significantly more attractive than the distressed target. In fact, she was rated as significantly more maladjusted than was the victim who reported that she was coping well. Similarly, in a study of interactions with disabled persons, nondisabled individuals who were given no information about the handicapped person's adjustment to his disability exhibited a number of behavioral signs of discomfort (Kleck et al., 1966, Study 2). We suspect that when individuals are given no direct evidence about how a victim is coping, they may be likely to respond according to their stereotypes of victims (see Jones et al., 1984) or myths about the adjustment process following negative life events (see Wortman & Silver, 1987, 1989). Unless they are provided with evidence to the contrary, outsiders may assume that the victim is suffering anyway (i.e., the requirement of mourning). In fact, Wright (1983) offered numerous examples of unsolicited assistance being forced on disabled individuals who neither needed nor desired it. Even if displays of distress are not obvious during an initial interaction, outsiders might assume that such distress nonetheless exists and will "leak out" in subsequent interactions (Wortman & Silver, 1987, 1989).

As Albrecht and Adelman (1987) pointed out, potential providers of support themselves are often faced with a dilemma about whether or not to provide support, particularly if they feel that it might be upsetting to the victim. In the absence of direct signals of need, outsiders may be reluctant to offer assistance, fearing their attempts will be rejected or perceived as intrusive. The general uncertainty about what to say or do in response to another's victimization (Dunkel-

Schetter & Wortman, 1982; Peters-Golden, 1982; Wortman & Lehman, 1985) may add to this reluctance. Thus, unless victims communicate their needs explicitly, potential support providers may misjudge the extent or types of support desired.

"Balanced" Coping Self-presentation

As we described above, the self-presentational dilemma faced by the individual who desires support concerns how to convey his or her distress to others so as to encourage support provision without exacerbating feelings of discomfort. There is unlikely to be an easy solution to this problem. Other than perhaps minimizing the presentation of the victimization's negative features to a potential support provider, there may be little a victim can do to decrease the feelings of vulnerability that may be evoked in the interaction. In fact, we expect that whether or not feelings of vulnerability are elicited in an outsider is likely to depend on factors outside the victim's control, such as the outsider's probability of encountering a similar problem.

However, as we noted earlier, we obtained data in our laboratory indicating that following an interaction with a distressed target, greater rejection of the target is accompanied by increased feelings of helplessness among outsiders (Dunkel-Schetter et al., 1989). This suggests that the rejection of and negative responses toward an individual who has experienced a life crisis might be reduced if the outsider's feelings of helplessness in alleviating the victim's distress were minimized. In contrast to perceptions of vulnerability, we hypothesize that the degree to which encounters with victims arouse feelings of helplessness in others may, to some extent, be modifiable by victims themselves. For example, to the extent that a victim appears to be taking steps to alleviate his or her own distress, that is, by taking "responsibility for the solution" (cf. Brickman et al., 1982), the outsider's sense of responsibility for doing so may be attenuated. Consequently, feelings of helplessness may be less likely to be elicited, even in the face of signs of distress.

Such a "balanced" self-presentation, in which the disclosure of distress is simultaneously accompanied by clear signals that the person is engaging in coping efforts on his or her own behalf, is both intuitively and theoretically appealing. Unfortunately, we have been able to find little empirical research that pertains to the likely consequences of such a stance. Nonetheless, the limited evidence we have uncovered suggests that such a self-presentational strategy may be effective. Experiment 3 of the Hastorf et al. (1979) report that we described above exposed nondisabled subjects to videotapes of two disabled confederates. One acknowledged that his handicap was a significant one and stated that he had learned to accept its inconveniences, but he did so while exhibiting obvious nonverbal signs of discomfort (i.e., clasping his hands tightly together, avoiding eye contact, running his hand through his hair). The second confederate neither acknowledged his condition nor signaled any signs of distress. Although the investigators had predicted otherwise, 65% of the subjects chose the distressed confederate when asked to select a partner for a subsequent session of the study. The authors speculated that although some subjects acknowledged that the confederate appeared uncomfortable with his condition, they nonetheless "may have chosen the nervous confederate because he was *trying* to cope with his handicap" (p. 1795, italics in original). Unfortunately, this hypothesis was not tested directly.

In the only other study we were able to locate that offers data relevant to our hypothesis (Dunkel-Schetter et al., 1987), middle-aged community residents were interviewed monthly over a six-month period about stressful events they had experienced during the previous month. Results indicated that those individuals who reported using problem-focused coping strategies to deal with their situation (e.g., endorsing such active problem-solving items as "I knew what had to be done, so I doubled my efforts to make things work" or "I made a plan of action and followed it," and cognitively reconceptualizing the problem so as to make it more solvable) received greater amounts of social support from a larger number of sources in their network. The authors speculated that the use of such strategies may have provided cues to network members that support was both needed and desired and may have made support providers feel more comfortable offering aid. Nevertheless, the data were correlational in nature, and the researchers noted that their results are also consistent with the interpretation that social support influenced the ways in which the individuals coped.

Thus, although the available data are suggestive, up to this point the interpersonal impact of a balanced self-presentational stance (i.e., offering signals of distress along with evidence of coping efforts) has not been subjected to any direct empirical study. Nor has it been compared with any alternative self-presentations. For example, are outsiders likely to focus on the negative affect expressed in a balanced portrayal and to derogate or reject the victim despite his or her attempts to cope? Or will such a balanced self-presentation be viewed favorably? How might such a stance be received when contrasted with a positive coping self-presentation or with one in which no information is provided about distress? Clear answers are unlikely to be obtained outside a controlled setting. So with these questions in mind, we designed a laboratory experiment in which we could manipulate and compare, in the context of an interaction between a victim and a nonvictim, these four possible self-presentational strategies.

THE STUDY

In our study, we hypothesized that the self-presentation of how one is coping with a stressful life experience constitutes a major determinant of a potential help provider's feelings and behavior toward a person who has been victimized. Specifically, we predicted that individuals who indicate that they are coping poorly with a negative life event will intensify others' negative feelings, and hence will elicit more derogation and avoidance from potential support providers than will those who convey a more balanced view of how they are coping, or those who indicate that they are coping well. We were particularly interested in how others would react to a balanced portrayal of the victimizing experience. As noted above, we felt that this alternative may be a possible solution to the self-presentational dilemma faced by victims of life crises, as it allows for the expression of distress and thus signifies the need for support; yet it does so in a way that may minimize feelings of helplessness on the part of the support provider.

In order to test these hypotheses, a number of conditions had to be met. First, we felt that it was important to structure our study around a live encounter between a subject and a person who had been through a victimizing experience. Live encounters make it possible to examine a wide range of dependent measures. Many of the early studies on victims were based solely on questionnaire measures designed to assess the victim's attractiveness (see Wortman, 1976, for a review). Because these early studies did not involve an actual interaction between the parties, there was no possibility of exploring the behavior of the subject during the interaction. The victimization perspective predicts that the prospect of interacting with someone who has been victimized will elicit conflicting feelings. An individual is likely to experience negative affect yet be motivated not to display these feelings out of concern for the victim. In order to test this model, it is essential to supplement self-report evaluations of a target with an assessment of a wide range of behaviors during the interaction. Moreover, as Gurtman (1986) pointed out, rejection of distressed individuals may take one of two forms: attempts to distance oneself (e.g., avoidance) and affectively based negative evaluations. Each may differ in the extent to which it is under a respondent's conscious control, and each may also be differentially affected by experimenter demand. In fact, a number of studies have demonstrated a discrepancy between signs of behavioral discomfort and evaluative ratings of a target (e.g., Gotlib & Robinson, 1982; Kleck, 1968a; Meyerowitz et al., 1988). For all of these reasons, we included a variety of behavioral and evaluative measures in our investigation.

Second, we felt it was necessary to select a truly serious victimizing experience. In order to determine whether the self-presentation regarding the victimizing experience could alter likely negative feelings and behaviors in the outsider, it was important to select a life crisis that would engender such negative feelings. For our study, we decided to focus on cancer. Cancer appears to exert a dark, negative influence on the public imagination (Sontag, 1978). The limited data that are available (see Dunkel-Schetter & Wortman, 1982, for a review) indicate that cancer indeed makes other people feel uncomfortable. Although systematic investigation is rare, several reports suggest that cancer patients are often subjected to negative behaviors from others, ranging from discomfort and avoidance to blatant social ostracism—for example, being the only one at a party to receive plastic eating utensils (see Dunkel-Schetter & Wortman, 1982; Peters-Golden, 1982). We also chose to study reactions to cancer because of this disease's prevalence. The American Cancer Society (1988) reports that one out of every five deaths in the United States is caused by cancer and that the disease strikes approximately three out of four American families. In view of these statistics, our results should have wide-ranging applicability to a problem that touches many people's lives. Finally, because we had worked for several years with cancer patient self-help groups (see Wortman et al., 1980), we felt that we were knowledgeable enough about this disease to develop stimulus materials and manipulations that would be credible.

A third requirement for the design was that respondents be exposed to actual cancer patients, rather than to confederates who pretended to be cancer patients. We noted earlier that victimized individuals, such as cancer patients, may be treated differently by nonvictims. If so, they may adopt subtle changes in their behavior to cope with others' negative reactions. It is also possible that a victimized status may affect behaviors in ways that are unknown to confederates who are not familiar with the role. For example, individuals with spinal cord injuries often shift their weight from side to side during an interaction to prevent the development of pressure ulcers. A confederate attempting to play the part of a spinal cord injured person may not be aware of this mannerism, which might affect others' reactions. Because of our contacts in the cancer community, we anticipated that we would be able to recruit and involve cancer patients in the study with relatively little difficulty.

Fourth, the study had to be designed so as to permit a clean and unconfounded manipulation of the victim's self-presentation. In order to assess the impact of the cancer patient's self-presentation about how he or she was coping with the disease, it was necessary to select a paradigm that would allow us to vary this self-presentation while holding constant other information about the disease. In the present design, we accomplished this by asking respondents to listen to a taped interview with a female cancer patient prior to interacting with her. The tapes were spliced so that the target person's description of herself and her illness was identical for all respondents, and only her self-presentation of coping was varied.

Overview of the Study

In this study, the respondents were asked to participate in an interaction with a female cancer patient. Before the interaction, the target's self-presentation was experimentally varied by asking the subjects to listen to a tape-recorded interview with her. The patient provided some information about her background (marital status, work, children), discussed her illness, and provided information about how she was coping with her disease. The segment of the tape dealing with coping was experimentally varied to convey good coping, a balanced portrayal of the patient's coping efforts, poor coping, or no information about the target's coping. In addition, a control condition (no disease) was included in which the target provided the background information only. Following the presentation of the tape, a face-to-face interaction was arranged between the target person and the subject. The dependent variables included questionnaire ratings of attraction to the target person and distress following the interaction, observer ratings of the subject's nonverbal signs of comfort during the interaction, and measures of interpersonal distance and desire for future interaction.

Procedure

Eighty undergraduates from a midwestern university participated in this experiment in order to fulfill a requirement in introductory psychology.[2] The sample (N = 16 per cell) was composed of slightly more females than males. The subjects were scheduled for individual sessions of an experiment that supposedly involved the acquaintance process. They were told that the study was part of a larger program of research on first impressions. We explained that most earlier studies had been based on interactions between college students but that in this study, we wanted to examine the first impressions created by a more diverse group of people. The subjects were told that many different types of people had been recruited to participate in the study, including some adults from the Chicago area who led normal, everyday existences, such as teachers, housewives, or salespeople, and some who had had unusually stressful or difficult lives—for example, parents of retarded children, spouses of alcoholics, or victims of illness or accidents.

The subjects were told that they would be meeting with an adult from the Chicago area who had already participated in the study once before. To prepare for this meeting, the subjects were asked to listen to a tape-recorded conversation between the adult, or target person, and an interviewer that had supposedly been made during the target person's first session. The subjects were told that after listening to the tape, they would be asked to complete a questionnaire regarding their impressions of the target person. We explained that following the presentation of the tape and questionnaire, they would meet the target person and participate in a brief "get acquainted" session and then answer a few questions about their meeting.

Manipulation of Independent Variables

The independent variables were manipulated through the tape-recorded conversation between the target person and an interviewer. In fact, this conversation followed a prearranged script that had been prepared by the investigators in collaboration with cancer patients. In all conditions, the conversation began with a general discussion centering on such topics as the target person's work, family, hobbies and interests, and plans for the future. After approximately 15 minutes, the manipulations were introduced. They began in response to a question about the target person's health. There were five experimental conditions: four cancer conditions (good coping, balanced coping, poor coping, and no information about coping) and a "no-cancer" control condition. In each of the cancer conditions, the target person revealed that she had Hodgkin's disease. Hodgkin's disease was

---

[2] Data from 9 additional subjects were discarded from the analyses, 7 due to their expressions of suspicion, and 2 because close relatives had died from cancer during the previous year. Also, 16 additional subjects were run in a condition of this experiment that is not relevant to the issues considered here and therefore will not be discussed in this report (see Crofton, 1981).

chosen because although it is a serious form of cancer that has debilitating symptoms, it is not intrinsically mutilating. Hence, for a given target person, we could experimentally vary whether or not subjects believed her to have Hodgkin's disease.

Table 15.1 provides excerpts of material from the good, balanced, and poor coping scripts. In the "good coping" condition, the target person expressed an optimistic view of her illness and appeared to be coping well. In the "balanced coping" condition, she conveyed distress about what was happening to her but indicated that she was trying her best and acknowledged some limited success at coping. In the "poor coping" condition, she displayed distress about what was happening to her and appeared to have difficulties coping with her circumstances. In the fourth cancer condition, she conveyed no information about her coping. In the no-cancer control condition, the target person presented herself as a healthy individual. The subjects in this condition heard only the "acquaintance" part of the discussion, followed by a brief statement from the target person alluding to her good health.

Confederates

Four confederates served as target persons for the study. All were female and ranged in age from their mid-thirties to early fifties. Two of these women were cancer patients and two were not. The cancer patients were recruited through a local chapter of Make Today Count, an organization dedicated to the self-help and emotional support of cancer patients. Noncancer confederates were recruited through an advertisement in the newspaper. Each confederate recorded a tape for each condition, and each confederate was paired with four subjects per condition. During the live interaction with the subject, confederates were blind to the subject's experimental condition. The use of both cancer and noncancer confederates enabled us to examine the impact of disease status on our findings, and the use of multiple confederates allowed us to examine the generality of the findings with different individuals.

Pretesting of Tapes

To ensure that the manipulations were perceived as intended, the tapes were pretested. Undergraduate subjects in groups ranging in size from 10 to 20 heard each confederate's version of each tape and then answered questions regarding the confederate's health status and coping. This pretest revealed that as expected, the confederates in the "good coping" condition were perceived as being significantly happier and more optimistic, as having a more positive outlook, as being better adjusted, and as coping better than were confederates in the "balanced coping" condition. The confederates in the "balanced" condition were rated significantly higher on each of these variables than were the confederates in the "poor coping" condition. As we hoped, there were no significant differences among any of these conditions on such variables as friendliness, warmth, ease in conversation, sincerity, or amount of suffering, suggesting that we had not inadvertently confounded coping ability with the target's personal qualities or her degree of suffering. All subjects correctly perceived the disease condition. As expected, those confederates portraying a cancer patient were rated as suffering significantly more than were the confederates portraying a healthy person. There were no systematic differences between the confederates who had cancer and those who did not, nor among individual confederates.

Dependent Measures

The following dependent measures were included in the study:

1. *Questionnaire ratings of attraction to the target person.* After listening to the tape recording, but before meeting the confederate, the subjects were asked to complete a questionnaire designed to assess their rating of the target person's attractiveness. Using seven-point scales, the subjects rated the target person on each of eight different items designed to measure attraction, such as how likable the target was and whether the subject would admit the target to his or her circle of friends. These items were summed to create a composite measure of attraction.

2. *Measure of interpersonal distance.* After the subject listened to the tape and completed the questionnaire measure of attraction, the experimenter took him or her into an adjoining room to meet the target person. The experimenter asked the subject to bring in his or her own chair. The distance, in inches, that the subject sat from the target person was measured following their meeting.

3. *Observers' rating of subject's comfort during the interaction.* The experimenter asked the confederate and the subject if they would like tea or coffee before beginning the second part of the study. The confederate was instructed to respond positively to this request. At this point, the experimenter excused herself to get the coffee and began timing the interaction. This five-minute interaction was rated surreptitiously by two observers who were seated behind a one-way mirror. Each experimental session was rated by a different pair of observers who also received course credit for their participation in the study. The observers were told that the study involved first impressions. They were not able to hear the conversation, and they were not told anything about the participants involved in the conversation. They were asked to focus primarily on the subject, who was seated facing them. Following the interaction, they were asked to rate the subject, using seven-point scales, on 14 different adjectives or phrases designed to assess his or her comfort during the interaction. The scale included such items as how much the subject enjoyed talking to the target person, how comfortable the subject seemed, and how interested he or she

TABLE 15.1. Excerpts of Material from Tape-recorded Interviews Designed to Convey Good, Balanced, and Poor Coping

Interview Question	"Good Coping" Script	"Balanced Coping" Script	"Poor Coping" Script
What kinds of things have you been feeling?	My reaction to having cancer has changed from the fear, the panic, that I originally experienced to an attitude of acceptance. I now value my life a lot more than I ever did before. . . . I feel much more aware of the good things in my life—like family and friends who love me—than I ever did before I discovered the cancer. Now I am determined to live to the fullest what time I have left.	Some days, I feel that it was a random thing, you know, cancer just *happens*; it just strikes someone. Other days I feel like I really need to have someone to blame—I mean, why did it have to happen to *me*? So . . . I just go on trying to deal with these problems and trying to make the best of what-ever time I have left.	I guess I feel really cheated, cheated out of a lot of the best experiences, the best times of my life. I mean, it's totally unfair that I have to put up with these prob-lems—hospital visits and doctor's appointments and X-ray treatments . . . and worst of all, worrying constantly, just worrying, over the least little pain or cough. . . . With all the problems associated with the treatment, it's hard for me to enjoy life or feel hopeful about anything.
What does your treatment involve?	Oh, another side effect is that the treatments have caused most of my hair to fall out. After my first se-ries, it took a couple of months for it to grow back in decently. So, since I've been undergoing this therapy, I've managed to find several wigs that are reasonably priced and attractive. Here again, I feel very lucky that the draw-backs associated with radiotherapy are ones that can be remedied.	Another embarrassing side effect is that the treatments have caused most of my hair to fall out. After my first series, it took a couple of months for it to grow back in de-cently. It's true that this isn't the worst thing that could happen to me—I mean, I can always wear wigs. But still, the fact that I *have* to wear them, if I want to look like a normal woman, can really drag my spirits down. I try to console myself with the fact that wigs at least provide a means of dealing with my situation. It's *something* I can do.	The treatments have another em-barrassing side effect. They have caused most of my hair to fall out, and it took a couple of months for it to grow back in decently. This has been extremely damaging to my feelings of attractiveness. I can wear wigs, of course, but they are often uncomfortable and inconve-nient, and, as any woman knows, it's just not the same as having your own hair.

412

How has your family been affected?

I have had to consider the possibility that I may not live long enough to enjoy my children's maturity . . . to see them graduate from college and begin careers, or start families of their own. This knowledge has served the purpose of intensifying and improving the time I spend with them now. Having gone through the experience of cancer has helped me to relate to people in a much more rewarding and productive way.

Sometimes it is difficult for me to be around my children. This is only because I'll look at them and happen to think of their graduation from college, or their weddings, which I'm afraid I won't see. Sometimes these thoughts crowd into my mind, and I end up reacting poorly towards people, even people I love. In some ways, I feel cheated and jealous because others don't have to put up with Hodgkin's disease, and I do. On the other hand, sometimes that same pain enables me to be more sensitive and understanding towards another's problems and actually draws me closer to them.

Lately, when I look at my children, I can only think that I may not be around to see them graduate from college or get married and start families of their own. It's difficult for me to relate to people who used to be my friends because I know that they will enjoy these things—retirement with their husbands, watching their children mature—and I'm afraid that I won't.

How are you handling your situation?

I act as if any encounter that I have with a person is of the highest importance—I try to focus in on them and really be caring. This has really raised my awareness and improved the quality of my life.

Some days, I feel depressed and hopeless about my situation, while on other days, I can work through things and set aside the grief. On those days, I feel halfway optimistic and happy just to be alive. I guess all I can do is keep on trying.

All of these things make it hard for me to have a positive attitude about anything. I feel depressed about my situation, and getting through most days is a struggle.

seemed in the interaction. The observers' ratings, which were highly correlated, were pooled for the analysis. A composite rating of observer-assessed comfort was created by summing the observer ratings into a single score.

4. *Self-report of distress following interaction.* At the end of the five-minute period, the experimenter returned with the coffee and told both participants that the experiment was over because the project supervisor had not shown up. They were told that they need only complete a brief questionnaire before they left. The subject then completed a 10-item self-report measure of distress (e.g., discomfort, anxiety, depression, anger) following the interaction. Each of these items was rated on a seven-point scale, and they were summed to create a composite measure of distress.

5. *Desire for future interaction.* Following the interaction, subjects were informed that the study would be continuing for the next several weeks. They were told that we wanted to study relationships as they developed over time and that we would like them to volunteer for additional sessions with the target person each week. They were informed that how they spent the time during their meetings was up to them and that we would be asking them some questions about the way the relationship was developing over time. The subjects were asked to volunteer for any number of one-hour sessions, up to 20.

Debriefing

At the conclusion of the study, all the subjects were fully debriefed. Because the experimental procedures had relied on deception at many points, great care was taken to construct a debriefing that was thorough and honest and that attempted to anticipate and respond to the subjects' feelings and reactions. Virtually all the subjects expressed strong interest in the study and positive feelings about having participated in it.

Results and Discussion

The results of the study are summarized in Table 15.2, which lists the means for each of the major dependent measures. A number of conclusions can be drawn from the pattern of findings that we obtained. First, our results provide clear evidence that the subjects responded less favorably, across a wide range of indicators, to the target who presented herself as coping poorly. In comparison with the good and balanced copers, the subjects reported significantly less attraction to the poor coper, sat farther away from her during the interaction, reported significantly more distress following the interaction, and expressed less willingness to interact with her in the future. The observers also detected significantly more nonverbal signs of discomfort in subjects who interacted with poor copers than they did in subjects who interacted with balanced copers.

Table 15.2. Reactions to Cancer Patients' Self-presentations

	Control (No Cancer)	Cancer Patient			
		No Information on Coping	"Good" Coper	"Balanced" Coper	"Poor" Coper
Self-report of Attraction to Target[1]	2.69[a]	2.67[a]	2.74[a]	2.52[a]	3 .59[b]
Distance Sat from Person (inches)	28.75[a]	50.25[c]	41.94[b]	42.31[b]	55.31[d]
Observers' Rating of Subject's Comfort with Target[1]	2.67[a]	3.72[c]	3.53[c]	3.03[b]	3. 58[c]
Self-report of Distress Following Interaction[1]	2.50[a]	3.19[b]	3.09[b]	3.16 [b]	3.60[c]
Self-report of Desire for Future Interaction[2]	7.56[d]	1.19[a]	3.06[b]	5.63 [c]	1.25[a]

Note: Means that do not share superscripts are significantly different at the $p < .05$ level.
[1] Mean composite ratings on 7-point scales; higher number = less attraction, more discomfort, greater distress.
[2] Mean number of hours desired.

Thus, we have again demonstrated what by now appears to be a rather robust finding: Individuals who convey that they are coping poorly with a victimization are likely to elicit unfavorable responses from nonvictimized others. A unique feature of our study, in comparison with previous studies on coping with victimization (e.g., Coates et al., 1979; Winer et al., 1981), is that it included a broad range of outcome variables. In fact, we found that the rejection exhibited toward targets was multifaceted, taking the form of behavioral avoidance, nonverbal signals of discomfort, and relatively negative evaluations of them. Although we did not ask the confederates to rate perceptions of support explicitly, it is unlikely that they would have felt supported during an interaction in which such conflicting signals were conveyed. This provides further evidence for the distressing conclusion offered by Coates et al. (1979) that "in their darkest moments, victims may find only social isolation and ostracism" (p. 48).

As we had expected, providing no information about how one is coping appears not to be a viable solution to the self-presentational dilemma of support-seeking. Although those individuals who took this stance were rated as highly as were the targets in the other four experimental conditions on self-report measures of attractiveness, their interaction partners demonstrated significant behavioral avoidance in the interaction and expressed little willingness to engage in future interaction with them. In fact, the subjects were no more willing to interact with victims who provided no information than they were with victims who displayed poor coping. We suspect that the confusion and uncertainty about how to respond to a victim may be intensified if the victim fails to provide any information about his or her needs. Moreover, in the absence of evidence to the contrary, people may assume that distress is being concealed and will "leak out" in subsequent interactions.

We expected the subjects to react quite favorably to the targets who conveyed either positive or balanced coping self-presentations, and our results illustrate that this was indeed the case. In 9 out of 10 comparisons, the responses to confederates who portrayed positive or balanced coping were significantly more favorable than were responses to poor copers. Moreover, those confederates who presented positive and balanced coping presentations experienced significantly less avoidance than did cancer patients who offered no information regarding coping. Despite this fact, even positive and balanced copers elicited significantly more discomfort, distress, and avoidance (on four out of five dependent measures) than did those confederates who portrayed a healthy (no-cancer) role.[3] Thus, it is important to recognize that although discomfort and avoidance by others may be minimized by a particular coping self-presentation, the mere existence of the victimization appears to be sufficient to elicit these negative reactions to some degree. That is, there appears to be no self-presentation that is effective in making potential support providers feel as comfortable as they would be if they were interacting with a person without cancer.

Interestingly, despite the clear expression of distress by the balanced coping target, the positive coping self-presentation was not preferred to the balanced coping stance on any of the five major dependent measures. On the contrary, the observers rated those individuals who interacted with balanced copers as exhibiting significantly fewer nonverbal signs of discomfort during the interaction than did those individuals who interacted with good copers. In addition, the subjects expressed significantly more interest in future contact with the balanced coper than with the good coper. There are several possible factors that may underlie this pattern of results. First, the nonverbal discomfort exhibited in interactions with the positive coper may be a signal that the subjects felt the target was disingenuous. The presence of positive affect in a situation in which suffering is expected (i.e., the requirement of mourning) may simply lead others to see the positive self-presentation as a strategic concealment of distress. If so, the subjects may have expressed little desire for subsequent interaction with this target because they expected the distress to be revealed in future encounters. In contrast and as predicted, a balanced portrayal of coping appeared to allow the person to disclose a considerable amount of distress with few apparent negative consequences.

IMPLICATIONS OF OUR ANALYSIS

In this chapter, we have argued that victims' self-presentations may have important effects on the provision of support by others. We presented evidence that in a

---

[3] It is noteworthy that the only measure on which the groups did not differ was the self-report of attraction. In fact, on average, subjects did not evidence much derogation or rejection of any target person on this measure. The attraction ratings of all the cancer patients except the poor copers were as high as those of the healthy target, and even the poor copers received a composite rating that was around the midpoint of the seven-point scale. Perhaps because of the subjects' self-presentational concerns, such measures are not as sensitive to feelings of discomfort as are nonverbal or behavioral measures.

live interactional setting, others' reactions to victims of life crises are strongly influenced by the victim's coping portrayal. In fact, our results suggest that given a victimized status, a positive or balanced portrayal of one's coping efforts can lead to relatively favorable responses from others. In the final sections of this chapter, we would like to move beyond this particular study to consider the more general issues raised by our findings. In so doing, we will explore the ramifications of each of these coping portrayals for both support providers and recipients. Although our ideas are somewhat speculative, they suggest a variety of avenues to explore in subsequent research on this topic.

Possible Solutions to the Self-presentational Dilemma: Positive Versus Balanced Coping

A Positive Coping Portrayal

We noted earlier that a positive self-presentational strategy may be unlikely to signal to potential providers that support is desired or needed. However, even if it does elicit aid from outsiders, we nonetheless feel that there are a number of drawbacks to the positive self-presentational stance that may ultimately limit its effectiveness.

In some cases, a positive coping portrayal may be strategic in that it is intentionally implemented and is discrepant from the victim's true feelings. Earlier, we discussed several reasons why victims might attempt to hide their distress and present themselves as coping well. However, there will undoubtedly be times or situations in which such a strategy will be difficult to maintain. In fact, this is most likely to be true as distress increases and as the effort and energy needed to conceal one's distress and to maintain a positive self-presentation are less available. In such instances, positive coping portrayals may be unconvincing, and distress may "leak out" nonverbally. Support providers may thus receive ambiguous or mixed messages, leading to discomfort and confusion about whether or how to offer assistance.

Another disadvantage of strategically positive self-presentations is that they fail to permit validation of the victim's true feelings (Coates & Wortman, 1980). Others cannot convey an understanding of what the victim is going through if his or her negative feelings are strategically concealed. Thus, such a strategy is likely to result in feelings of alienation and estrangement from others. Moreover, even if others respond favorably to the victim's strategic portrayal, the support received may have little meaning, especially if victims are aware that they had to distort their true feelings in order to get it. In fact, the greater the discrepancy between a person's coping portrayal and his or her true feelings, the less value any support received is likely to have (cf. Jones & Wortman, 1973). A further consequence of hiding one's negative feelings from others is that it may make such feelings less accessible to self-reflection and cognitive processing.

Our discussion suggests that the strategic concealment of distress may have negative consequences for both parties in the interaction. But what if a person's portrayal of positive coping actually reflects his or her underlying feelings? Even in this circumstance, we feel this portrayal is unlikely to facilitate the receipt of effective support. As noted earlier, independent of whether or not a positive coping portrayal is accurate, others may be skeptical and doubt its veracity. In fact, members of the social network may experience feelings of alienation in the presence of such presumed dishonesty. Others may also come to devalue or react judgmentally toward anyone who appears not to evidence sufficient distress following a life crisis (cf. Dembo et al., 1956). Moreover, outsiders may experience discomfort in the face of victims' positive coping portrayals, whether or not they are veridical, because such portrayals set unrealistically high standards for others. When they are confronted by individuals who convey positive coping with life's greatest tragedies, nonvictims may feel ashamed or inadequate for experiencing distress in response to more minor difficulties.

In addition to the problem that such high standards may create for nonvictims, individuals who present a positive coping stance may lead members of their social network to expect that they will continue to cope well. If their distress continues or perhaps increases over time, however, victims may not be able to meet these high expectations. Unfortunately, in such cases, any deviations from a positive stance may be met with negative reactions from others, who have come to expect positive coping (Silver, Hawkins, & Urbanowicz, 1990).

A Balanced Coping Portrayal

At least as operationalized in our research, there appear to be few costs associated with the balanced coping portrayal, in which distress is shared and coping efforts are highlighted. In fact, our study suggests that victims may be likely to get maximal support if they can adopt such a coping stance toward their victimization, at least in initial encounters. Displays of confusion and distress are possible as long as they are counterbalanced by evidence that the individual is making coping efforts on his or her own behalf. If individuals appear to be taking steps toward managing the instrumental demands placed on them or appear to be trying to regulate their emotions by employing certain self-help tactics, potential support providers may be more likely to add their own support and aid. Thus, by minimizing the support provider's feelings of helplessness in the face of distress, the victim can maximize the likelihood that support will be forthcoming. In addition, a balanced self-portrayal may influence not only whether support is offered in response to cues of distress but also the type of support that is provided. In the presence of active efforts at problem-solving on the victim's part, outsiders may be less likely to become overinvolved in the problem, to offer advice, or to engage in other behaviors that are typically viewed as unhelpful (see Coyne, Wortman, & Lehman, 1988; Lehman et al., 1986; Wortman & Lehman, 1985).

We believe that victims may thus benefit most by conveying that although they are distressed by what is happening to them, they are attempting to cope through their own efforts. Support providers may then try to reinforce the belief that active coping efforts can affect subsequent outcomes. If they do not have to take full responsibility for a victim's well-being, support providers may feel less threatened and hence may be able to provide more effective assistance (cf. Coyne et al., 1988). In addition, a balanced self-presentation allows others to offer support, not because of any perception of deficiency of effort on the victim's part, but simply as supplemental assistance. Such a stance is thus likely to foster respect, rather than derogation, from members of the support-seeker's social environment.

From the victim's perspective, validation of one's feelings and concerns is possible only if such issues can be shared openly with others. Thus, another important advantage of the balanced coping portrayal is that victims may obtain benefits from having the opportunity to express their feelings freely. For example, sharing one's distress in the presence of a supportive other is likely to facilitate adjustment through the development of empathic understanding, which Thoits (1986) has argued is a necessary condition for support provision to be effective. As noted earlier, open discussion can also foster the development of cognitive clarity or help the victim find meaning in a negative life event. Victims may erroneously assume that by sharing their problems, and the extent to which they are struggling to overcome them, they will convey weakness to others. To the contrary, our data provide no evidence that such negative judgments will be made. Because it appears to provide the individual with the opportunity to obtain the benefits of sharing distress without negative social consequences, the balanced coping stance has much to recommend it.

DIRECTIONS FOR FUTURE RESEARCH

We have demonstrated that in initial encounters between victims and potential support providers, the self-presentational coping stance taken by the victim can play an important role in the support provider's reaction. However, we still know very little about the ways in which the support process is affected by the self-presentation of coping efforts. Next, we will consider possible limitations to the conclusions we have drawn and will identify issues needing further theoretical and empirical attention.

Factors Influencing the Role of Coping in Support Provision

The Nature and Stage of the Relationship

First and foremost, it is important to consider how the findings and processes we described may be influenced by the degree of intimacy that exists between the victim and the potential support provider. In our research, we concentrated on how victims were judged and evaluated by relative strangers during an initial meeting. There are several reasons why it is important to understand the dynamics of initial encounters between victims and nonvictims. Through the course of their experiences, victims typically encounter a wide range of strangers and acquaintances who may have a considerable impact on their lives, such as health professionals, employers, or co-workers. In close relationships, victims are afforded many opportunities to identify and correct any misunderstandings that may occur. But they may have only a few moments to present themselves and their problems to important strangers (Coates et al., 1979). Moreover, there also is evidence that following a life crisis, people retreat from their former social network and form new ties (see Silver et al., 1990, for a review). These new ties may be particularly important in facilitating effective adjustment following such events, and our analysis may be relevant to the formation of these ties.

Nonetheless, we know very little about the role of self-presentation in the context of an ongoing relationship. In initial encounters, outsiders appear to tolerate the distress conveyed in a balanced coping portrayal. Over time, however, continuing displays of distress may be upsetting to others, regardless of the self-presentation of coping efforts. In fact, there is evidence that over time, outsiders become increasingly rejecting if the distress does not abate, despite signs that the victim is trying (Winer et al., 1981). Ongoing distress, even when accompanied by continuing coping efforts, may be even less tolerable to intimates for whom the victim's distress has important negative implications (Coyne et al., 1988; Silver et al., 1990). In close relationships, the balanced self-presentation may also set up expectations for continuing effort and eventual positive coping. Thus when such expectations appear to be violated by ongoing signs of distress, this may lead to frustration and, ultimately, to the ineffective provision of support (Silver et al., 1990).

In addition, the extent to which the self-presentational concerns we identified will hold in relationships among individuals who share the same victimization (i.e., similar others) is not known. However, there is evidence that derogation following a self-portrayal of poor coping may be unlikely among similarly distressed individuals (Hunsley, Silver, & Lee, 1989), suggesting that a balanced coping portrayal may be unnecessary.

The Nature of the Victimizing Experience

The study described in this chapter examined the role of self-presentational strategies in one victimizing experience—cancer. In subsequent research, it is important to consider the extent to which the processes we described are influenced by specific characteristics of the victimizing experience, such as how it was caused, its prevalence (and hence likelihood of occurrence), or its severity. Are potential support providers less tolerant of distress in lung cancer patients, whose behavior may have contributed to their disease, than in patients who apparently played no causal role in the development of their illness? Are they more threatened by displays of distress if the life crisis is one that they expect to encounter? For example, is an elderly woman, who anticipates becoming widowed herself, more compassionate or more rejecting in the face of a widowed friend's distress? Are individuals less tolerant of displays of distress in reaction to minor life problems than of equivalent displays in the face of a more serious difficulty? Or are they more tolerant of distress because the problems themselves are less threatening and upsetting?

The Nature, Source, and Timing of the Distress Conveyed

Victimizing experiences also appear to differ in the kinds of emotional reactions they are most likely to engender in victims, and perhaps in providers. Unexpected, untimely events, such as the death of a child or the death of a young spouse (cf. Wortman & Silver, 1987), may be particularly likely to evoke feelings of anger and outrage. Especially when the incident has occurred through no fault of the victim and has come about through the negligence of others, it may be accompanied by feelings of bitterness and rage. Potential support providers may experience more discomfort when interacting with victims who express bitterness and resentment than with those who express sadness or depression. It is unclear what the impact of a balanced coping portrayal will be in such cases.

In addition to the type of distress, the manner in which distress is conveyed may influence the processes we described. Are support providers more capable of tolerating another's distress if it is conveyed in a controlled manner? Previous research suggests that there is considerable variability in how distress is likely to be expressed, with some people remaining calm and composed and others crying uncontrollably (see Silver & Wortman, 1980, for a review of this literature). Is it especially important for victims who are unable to control their distress to present a balanced coping portrayal, or are they likely to elicit avoidance and rejection in any case?

Others' discomfort in the face of distress, particularly when it is uncontrolled, may also be strongly influenced by characteristics of the victim (i.e., gender, status, etc.), independent of any self-presentational strategies that he or she may employ. For example, it is possible that displays of distress from males will evoke more discomfort than equivalent displays from females. It may also be discomforting to be confronted with displays of distress from those in a superior social role, such as one's boss. Moreover, it may be particularly troubling to encounter displays of distress from those on whom one depends for support and guidance, such as one's parents (see Silver et al., 1990, for a further discussion of these issues).

Finally, the extent to which distress is tolerated by potential support providers may depend on the length of time that has elapsed since the onset of the victimizing experience. There is a great deal of evidence in the stress and coping literature that outsiders hold a number of assumptions about the time course of adjustment following stressful life events. As we have detailed elsewhere (see Wortman & Silver, 1987, 1989), it is expected that shortly after the crisis, individuals will respond with intense distress that will abate after a relatively brief period of time. This suggests that signs of distress may be tolerated in the early period following the event, but may not be tolerated for very long.

Additional Research Questions

Until now, we have focused on the impact of the victim's self-presentation on the potential support provider. However, we view the processes discussed in this chapter as transactional and dynamic (cf. Coyne et al., 1988). Therefore, it is important to consider how such processes unfold as the interaction progresses. Several surveys, described earlier, suggest that victims are aware of the discomfort they elicit in others and so take steps to reduce it. However, such surveys fail to clarify whether victims are accurate perceivers of any discomfort created. At this point, it is unclear whether victims are overly sensitive to their status and perceive rejection, regardless of others' behavior toward them (cf. Kleck & Strenta, 1980). Alternatively, they may reinterpret or minimize the presence of any discomfort that is conveyed. This matter could be clarified by controlled research that experimentally manipulated support providers' behaviors and examined victims' reactions to them. It would also be useful to study later stages in the interactional sequence to determine the strategies that victims employ to deal with others' negative reactions. Several studies have reported that outsiders' well-intentioned attempts to provide support are frequently perceived as unhelpful (see, for example, Davidowitz & Myrick, 1984; Helmrath & Steinitz, 1978; Lehman et al., 1986; Maddison & Walker, 1967; Peters-Golden, 1982). What self-presentational strategies, if any, do victims use to deal with such unhelpful social responses, and how does that influence the kinds and amounts of support they subsequently receive?

Another issue of major theoretical importance, but not addressed in our research, is the consequences of the self-presentational stances for victims themselves. Undoubtedly, individuals are sometimes aware of the extent to which they are concealing their distress or are presenting themselves in a more favorable light for others' benefit. But such behavior may not always occur as a result of conscious deliberation and in fact may become automatic or overlearned (see Arkin, 1980; Jones et al., 1984). Moreover, in the absence of any obvious cues, people may come to believe their own self-presentations (Arkin, 1980; Rhodewalt, 1986). In future studies, it will be important to determine how victims are affected by the coping portrayals they display to others. For example, do cancer patients who adopt a balanced coping stance, and hence emphasize that they are trying to cope with their problems, come to see themselves as more efficacious? If so, does this facilitate their adjustment to their illness, or to a recurrence?

In conclusion, an examination of the links between coping portrayals and support processes seems to be a promising focus of inquiry. The experiment we reported suggests that victims' self-presentations about how they are coping can indeed shape others' responses. Although much more research is needed, we suspect that coping portrayals exert a powerful influence on the course of the interaction and on the nature and quality of support received. We hope that the foregoing analysis will encourage research that will further elucidate the role that coping portrayals may play in the effective provision of support.

REFERENCES

Albrecht, T. L., & Adelman, M. B. (1987). Dilemmas of supportive communication. In T. L. Albrecht & M. B. Adelman (Eds.), *Communicating social support* (pp. 240–254). Newbury Park, CA: Sage.

American Cancer Society (1988). *Cancer facts and figures.* New York: American Cancer Society.

Arkin, R. M. (1980). Self-presentation. In D. M. Wegner & R. R. Vallacher (Eds.), *The self in social psychology* (pp. 158–182). New York: Oxford University Press.

Barrera, M. (1981). Social support in the adjustment of pregnant adolescents: Assessment issues. In B. Gottlieb (Ed.), *Social networks and social support* (pp. 69–96). Beverly Hills, CA: Sage.

Baumeister, R. F. (1982). A self-presentational view of social phenomena. *Psychological Bulletin, 91*, 3–26.

Bazakas, R. (1979). The interpersonal impact of coping, dependency, and denial self-presentations by the disabled in his interactions with the nondisabled. (Doctoral dissertation, New York University, 1978). *Dissertation Abstracts International, 39*, 4001-B.

Billings, A. G., & Moos, R. H. (1981). The role of coping resources in attenuating the stress of life events. *Journal of Behavioral Medicine, 7*, 139–157.

Brickman, P., Rabinowitz, V. C., Karuza, J., Jr., Coates, D., Cohn, E., & Kidder, L. (1982). Models of helping and coping. *American Psychologist, 37*, 368–384.

Chesler, M. A., & Barbarin, O. A. (1984). Difficulties of providing help in a crisis: Relationships between parents of children with cancer and their friends. *Journal of Social Issues, 40* (4), 113–134.

Clark, L. F. (1988). *Stress and the cognitive–conversational benefits of social interaction.* Unpublished manuscript, Purdue University, West Lafayette, IN.

Coates, D., & Wortman, C. B. (1980). Depression maintenance and interpersonal control. In A. Baum & J. E. Singer (Eds.), *Advances in environmental psychology: Vol. 2. Applications of personal control* (pp. 149–182). Hillsdale, NJ: Erlbaum.

Coates, D., Wortman, C. B., & Abbey, A. (1979). Reactions to victims. In I. H. Frieze, D. Bar-Tal, & J. S. Carroll (Eds.), *New approaches to social problems* (pp. 21–52). San Francisco: Jossey-Bass.

Cohen, S. (1988). Psychosocial models of the role of social support in the etiology of physical disease. *Health Psychology, 7*, 269–297.

Coyne, J. C. (1976). Depression and the response of others. *Journal of Abnormal Psychology, 85*, 186–193.

Coyne, J. C., Wortman, C. B., & Lehman, D. R. (1988). The other side of support: Emotional overinvolvement and miscarried helping. In B. H. Gottlieb (Ed.), *Marshaling social support: Formats, processes and effects* (pp. 305–330). Newbury Park, CA: Sage.

Crofton, C. (1981). *Attitudes towards victims of life-threatening disease.* Unpublished master's thesis, Northwestern University, Evanston, IL.

Davidowitz, M., & Myrick, R. D. (1984). Responding to the bereaved: An analysis of "helping" statements. *Research Record, 1*, 35–42.

DeLongis, A., O'Brien, T., Silver, R. C., & Wortman, C. B. (1990). *The interpersonal dimensions of coping: The role of social relationships and support of emotional expression following a traumatic event.* Manuscript submitted for publication.

Dembo, T., Leviton, G. L., & Wright, B. A. (1956). Adjustment to misfortune: A problem of social–psychological rehabilitation. *Artificial Limbs, 3*, 4–62.

Dunkel-Schetter, C. (1984). Social support and cancer: Findings based on patient interviews and their implications. *Journal of Social Issues, 40* (4), 77–98.

Dunkel-Schetter, C., Folkman, S., & Lazarus, R. S. (1987). Correlates of social support receipt. *Journal of Personality and Social Psychology, 53,* 71–80.

Dunkel-Schetter, C., Silver, R. C., & Wortman, C. B. (1989). *The effects of mood on social interaction: Mediators of rejection of distressed individuals.* Unpublished manuscript, University of California, Los Angeles.

Dunkel-Schetter, C., & Wortman, C. B. (1982). The interpersonal dynamics of cancer: Problems in social relationships and their impact on the patient. In H. S. Friedman & M. R. DiMatteo (Eds.), *Interpersonal issues in health care* (pp. 69–100). New York: Academic Press.

Eckenrode, J. (1983). The mobilization of social supports: Some individual constraints. *American Journal of Community Psychology, 11,* 509–528.

Fiore, J., Becker, J., & Coppel, D. B. (1983). Social network interactions: A buffer or a stress. *American Journal of Community Psychology, 11,* 423–439.

Ginsberg, S. M., & Brown, G. W. (1982). No time for depression: A study of help-seeking among mothers of preschool children. In D. Mechanic (Ed.), *Symptoms, illness behavior, and help-seeking* (pp. 87–114). New York: Prodist.

Goffman, E. (1959). *The presentation of self in everyday life.* Garden City, NJ: Doubleday.

Gotlib, I. H., & Robinson, L. A. (1982). Responses to depressed individuals: Discrepancies between self-report and observer-rated behavior. *Journal of Abnormal Psychology, 91,* 231–240.

Gurtman, M. B. (1986). Depression and the response of others: Re-evaluating the re-evaluation. *Journal of Abnormal Psychology, 95,* 99–101.

Hastorf, A. H., Wildfogel, J., & Cassman, T. (1979). Acknowledgment of handicap as a tactic in social interaction. *Journal of Personality and Social Psychology, 37,* 1790–1797.

Heller, K., & Swindle, R. W. (1983). Social networks, perceived social support and coping with stress. In R. D. Felner, L. A. Jason, J. Moritsugu, & S. S. Farber (Eds.), *Prevention psychology: Theory, research and practice in community intervention* (pp. 87–103). New York: Pergamon.

Helmrath, T. A., & Steinitz, E. M. (1978). Death of an infant: Parental grieving and the failure of social support. *The Journal of Family Practice, 6,* 785–790.

House, J. S., Umberson, D., & Landis, K. (1988). Structures and processes of social support. *Annual Review of Sociology, 14,* 293–318.

Hunsley, J., Silver, R. C., & Lee, C. M. (1989). *Anticipating meeting a peer: Cognitive processes in distressed and nondistressed women.* Manuscript submitted for publication.

Jones, E. E., Farina, A., Hastorf, A. H., Markus, H., Miller, D. T., & Scott, R. A. (1984). *Social stigma: The psychology of marked relationships.* New York: W. H. Freeman.

Jones, E. E., & Pittman, T. S. (1982). Toward a general theory of strategic self-presentation. In J. Suls (Ed.), *Psychological perspectives on the self* (Vol. 1, pp. 231–262). Hillsdale, NJ: Erlbaum.

Jones, E. E., & Wortman, C. B. (1973). *Ingratiation: An attributional approach.* New York: General Learning Press.

Kessler, R. C., Price, R. H., & Wortman, C. B. (1985). Social factors in psychopathology: Stress, social support, and coping processes. *Annual Review of Psychology, 36,* 531–572.

Kleck, R. (1968a). Physical stigma and nonverbal cues emitted in face-to-face interaction. *Human Relations, 21,* 19–28.

Kleck, R. E. (1968b). Self-disclosure patterns of the nonobviously stigmatized. *Psychological Reports, 23,* 1239–1248.

Kleck, R., Ono, H., & Hastorf, A. H. (1966). The effects of physical deviance upon face-to-face interaction. *Human Relations, 19,* 425–436.

Kleck, R. E., & Strenta, A. (1980). Perceptions of the impact of negatively valued physical characteristics on social interaction. *Journal of Personality and Social Psychology, 39,* 861–873.

Koch, A. (1985). "If only it could be me": The families of pediatric cancer patients. *Family Relations, 34,* 63–70.

Lehman, D. R., Ellard, J. H., & Wortman, C. B. (1986). Social support for the bereaved: Recipients' and providers' perspectives on what is helpful. *Journal of Consulting and Clinical Psychology, 54,* 438–446.

Maddison, D., & Walker, W. L. (1967). Factors affecting the outcome of conjugal bereavement. *British Journal of Psychiatry, 113,* 1057–1067.

Meyerowitz, B. E., Watkins, I. K., & Sparks, F. C. (1983). Quality of life for breast cancer patients receiving adjuvant chemotherapy. *American Journal of Nursing, 83,* 232–235.

Meyerowitz, B. E., Yarkin-Levin, K., & Harvey, J. (1988). *On the nature of cancer patients' social interactions.* Unpublished manuscript, Vanderbilt University, Nashville, TN.

Mitchell, R. E., & Trickett, E. J. (1980). Task force report: Social networks as mediators of social support. *Community Mental Health Journal, 16,* 27–44.

Pagel, M. D., Erdly, W. W., & Becker, J. (1987). Social networks: We get by with (and in spite of) a little help from our friends. *Journal of Personality and Social Psychology, 53,* 793–804.

Parkes, C. M., & Weiss, R. S. (1983). *Recovery from bereavement.* New York: Basic Books.

Peters-Golden, H. (1982). Breast cancer: Varied perceptions of social support in the illness experience. *Social Science and Medicine, 16,* 483–491.

Porritt, D. (1979). Social support in crisis: Quantity or quality? *Social Science and Medicine, 13A,* 715–721.

Riley, D., & Eckenrode, J. (1986). Social ties: Subgroup differences in costs and benefits. *Journal of Personality and Social Psychology, 51,* 770–778.

Rhodewalt, F. T. (1986). Self-presentation and the phenominal self: On the stability and malleability of self-conceptions. In R. F. Baumeister (Ed.), *Public self and private self* (pp. 117–142). New York: Springer-Verlag.

Rook, K. S. (1984). The negative side of social interaction: Impact on psychological well-being. *Journal of Personality and Social Psychology, 46,* 1097–1108.

Sarason, B. R., Sarason, I. G., Hacker, T. A., & Basham, R. B. (1985). Concomitants of social support: Social skills, physical attractiveness and gender. *Journal of Personality and Social Psychology, 49,* 469–480.

Schlenker, B. R. (1980). *Impression management: The self-concept, social identity and interpersonal relations.* Monterey, CA: Brooks/Cole.

Silver, R. C., Hawkins, J. D., & Urbanowicz, B. A. (1990). *Can intimates really help? The role of the relationship in support provision following stressful life events.* Unpublished manuscript, University of California, Irvine.

Silver, R. L., & Wortman, C. B. (1980). Coping with undesirable life events. In J. Garber & M. E. P. Seligman (Eds.), *Human helplessness: Theory and applications* (pp. 279–340). New York: Academic Press.

Sontag, S. (1978). *Illness as metaphor.* New York: Farrar, Straus, & Giroux.

Tait, R., & Silver, R. C. (1989). Coming to terms with major negative life events. In J. S. Uleman & J. A. Bargh (Eds.), *Unintended thought* (pp. 351–382). New York: Guilford.

Thoits, P. A. (1986). Social support as coping assistance. *Journal of Consulting and Clinical Psychology, 54,* 416–423.

Voysey, M. (1972). Impression management by parents with disabled children. *Journal of Health and Social Behavior, 13,* 80–89.

Winer, D. L., Bonner, T. O., Blaney, P. H., & Murray, E. J. (1981). Depression and social attraction. *Motivation and Emotion, 5,* 153–166.

Wood, J. V., Taylor, S. E., & Lichtman, R. R. (1985). Social comparison in adjustment to breast cancer. *Journal of Personality and Social Psychology, 49,* 1169–1183.

Wortman, C. B. (1976). Causal attributions and personal control. In J. Harvey, W. Ickes, & R. F. Kidd (Eds.), *New directions in attribution research* (Vol. 1, pp. 23–52). Hillsdale, NJ: Erlbaum.

Wortman, C. B. (1983). Coping with victimization: Conclusions and implications for future research. *Journal of Social Issues, 39* (2), 195–221.

Wortman, C. B., Abbey, A., Holland, A. E., Silver, R. L., & Janoff-Bulman, R. (1980). Transitions from the laboratory to the field: Problems and progress. In L. Bickman (Ed.), *Applied social psychology annual* (Vol. 1, pp. 197–233). Beverly Hills, CA: Sage.

Wortman, C. B., & Dunkel-Schetter, C. (1979). Interpersonal relationships and cancer: A theoretical analysis. *Journal of Social Issues, 35* (1), 120–155.

Wortman, C. B., & Dunkel-Schetter, C. (1987). Conceptual and methodological issues in the study of social support. In A. Baum & J. E. Singer (Eds.), *Handbook of psychology and health: Vol. 5. Stress* (pp. 63–108). Hillsdale, NJ: Erlbaum.

Wortman, C. B., & Lehman, D. R. (1985). Reactions to victims of life crises: Support attempts that fail. In I. G. Sarason & B. R. Sarason (Eds.), *Social support: Theory, research, and applications* (pp. 463–489). Dordrecht, Netherlands: Martinus Nijhoff.

Wortman, C. B., & Silver, R. C. (1987). Coping with irrevocable loss. In G. R. VandenBos & B. K. Bryant (Eds.), *Cataclysms, crises, and catastrophes: Psychology in action (Master Lecture Series, Vol. 6)* (pp. 189–235). Washington, DC: American Psychological Association.

Wortman, C. B., & Silver, R. C. (1989). The myths of coping with loss. *Journal of Consulting and Clinical Psychology, 57,* 349–357.

Wright, B. A. (1983). *Physical disability—A psychosocial approach* (2nd ed.). New York: Harper & Row.

CHAPTER 16

The Functional Effects of Social Relationships on Chronic Illnesses and Disability

ROBERT M. KAPLAN AND MICHELLE T. TOSHIMA
University of California at San Diego

THE RELATIONSHIP BETWEEN SOCIAL SUPPORT AND PHYSICAL HEALTH

A growing body of data suggests that social support may be an important determinant of health outcomes. In this chapter, we consider the relationship between social support and physical health. We will briefly review the epidemiological data linking social support to mortality. Then we will discuss the evidence that social support is relevant to self-care and health outcomes in chronic disease conditions, both evidence that social support enhances health outcomes and evidence that social relationships prolong and reinforce physical dysfunction.

The Epidemiology of Social Networks and Health Outcomes

Epidemiology is the study of the determinants and distribution of disease. The hallmark of epidemiological methodology is the prospective/longitudinal cohort study. Major investigations, such as the Framingham Heart Study, attempted to establish prospective predictors of mortality in a random sample from the general population. For example, the Framingham Study began with 5,127 participants who had no visible signs of heart disease. Each participant was given a physical examination and a detailed interview that included life-style and demographic characteristics. Each participant was then followed every other year (Kannel, 1987). Other major epidemiological investigations have used similar methodologies.

Most epidemiological studies were started some years ago before formal measures of social support had been developed. Nevertheless, simple measures of social network appeared to predict health outcomes in a variety of studies. The

---

Supported in part by Grant HL-34732 from the National Heart, Lung, and Blood Institute.

Alameda County Population Monitoring Study, for instance, demonstrated that a simple measure of social network was a significant predictor of longevity. The measure included marital status, number of close family and friends, church membership, and group affiliation. Men with weak social networks were nearly 2.5 times as likely to die within a defined time period as were men with extensive networks. Women benefited even more from established social networks (Berkman & Breslow, 1983).

Similar results were obtained in Tecumseh, Michigan, where 2,754 men and women were studied. In this investigation, men who were married, who attended church, and who participated in voluntary organizations and community activities were significantly less likely to die within a 10-year period than were men who were disconnected. The Tecumseh Study did not show similar relationships for women (House, Robbins, & Metzner, 1982). In contrast with the findings of Berkman and Breslow (1983) and House and colleagues (1982), in the Durham County, North Carolina, Study (Blazer, 1982), no consistent pattern of increased mortality rates was associated with a progressive decrease in social support. Rather, there appeared to be a threshold effect in which only those individuals, either male or female, who were at the extreme end of the continuum in terms of the least amount of social support, had increased mortality rates. The Evans County, Georgia, Study (Schoenbach et al., 1986), reported findings similar to those of the Durham County Study. The relationship between social support and mortality did not suggest a gradient of risk. Rather, those individuals with the fewest ties were at increased risk for mortality. The findings reported were significant for older white males only, and the data for blacks and white females, though in the expected direction, were weak and nonsignificant. In the Honolulu Heart Study, social support was not related to mortality or incidence of cardiovascular disease (Reed, McGee, Yano, & Feinleib, 1983).

Several studies have suggested that the combination of high stress and low social support are particularly strong predictors of negative outcome. For example, 142 women in the Framingham Heart Study had more cardiovascular disease if they worked in clerk or clerical roles and had unsupportive spouses (Haynes & Feinleib, 1980). A study of Swedish workers revealed that cardiovascular disease was excessive for workers who had low social support, perceived their jobs to be stressful, and felt they had little control over their work environment (Welin et al., 1985). One study of myocardial infarction patients classified the survivors according to social isolation and stress and then followed them prospectively. Those who experienced low stress and were socially connected had one-fourth the rate of mortality of those who were under high stress and were isolated (Ruberman, Weinblatt, Goldberg, & Chaudray, 1984). Despite these strong results, some studies have not shown a relationship between social support and health outcomes (Cohen & Syme, 1985).

It is difficult to compare these studies, as they used different definitions of heart disease. Some used myocardial infarction; some used mortality; and some used softer diagnoses such as self-reported chest pain. The populations also varied greatly from study to study, as did definitions of social support. The measures of social support were usually crude. Some of the studies merely recorded the presence of a spouse or participation in group activities. In addition, they often did not consider the degree of satisfaction associated with these relationships. Nevertheless, these studies generally show a relationship between social relationships and longevity (Davidson & Shumaker, 1987). These findings have intrigued epidemiologists and supported the notion that friends and family are assets to health. Yet, the epidemiological studies provide few clues to why social relationships enhance health.

It is important to point out that epidemiological studies use different independent and dependent variables than do psychological investigations. For the former, support is usually a simple enumeration of network size, and "health" is most often mortality. Yet, epidemiological studies provide the basis for many arguments that social support protects against illness. However, the relationship between network size and mortality is not necessarily related to the association between social support satisfaction and disability. At best, the epidemiological studies have stimulated interest in the relationship between social support and health; yet the epidemiological data provide only a very small piece of the puzzle. To follow up on the suggestive evidence from epidemiological studies, we need to focus on a wider array of health outcomes and learn more about social interactions among the infirmed.

Social Support in Health

Health is a much broader concept than mortality, as observed in epidemiological studies. The World Health Organization defines health as a complete state of physical, social, and mental well-being, which includes absence of a disability, freedom from symptoms, and a general state of wellness. A wide variety of studies identify a relationship among social support, coping, and physical disability (Wallston, Whitcher-Alagna, DeVellis, & DeVellis, 1983). For example, family, friends, and other social contacts can ease the emotional stress resulting from injuries incurred in automobile accidents (Porritt, 1979). Burn victims experience higher self-esteem and general life satisfaction if they have support from friends and family (Davidson, Bowden, & Tholen, 1979). Patients with kidney disease who have support from spouses and cohesive families have a higher morale and fewer changes in social functioning during hemodialysis than do those with less support (Dimond, 1979). Finlayson (1976) reported that males have better outcomes following myocardial infarction if they have support from their spouses. Without reviewing the literature in detail, suffice it to say that many studies suggest a social support–health outcome connection. The complex relationships among adaptations to chronic illness, self-care, and the social environment have not been described as well. In the following sections, we will explore some of these issues in relation to specific chronic illnesses.

Several researchers have discussed the main effects of social support. Cohen and Wills (1985), as did most others, emphasized the effects of social support as a buffer of life stress. However, they described a main effect in which a "beneficial effect of social support could occur because large social networks provide persons with regular positive experiences and a set of stable, socially rewarded roles in the community'' (p. 311). Thoits (1985) described a main effect of social support as by-products of more abstract processes. Social relationships may provide a sense of identity, a source of positive evaluation, or a sense of self-efficacy. Our emphasis in this chapter is on main effects, specifically the impact of social environment on health. We refer to this as a Functional Effects Model, which is more exact than the descriptions of main effects (Cohen and Wills, 1985; Thoits, 1985).

As Thoits (1985) indicated, the main effects of social support have been studied less often than have its buffering effects. Several studies have demonstrated that the social environment has some functional or reinforcing effects on health behavior. Social environments may be satisfactory, but they may also reinforce detrimental behaviors. For example, teenagers with insulin-dependent diabetes mellitus must adhere to a very strict regimen of diet, exercise, and insulin injections. Yet, teenaged diabetics who are highly satisfied with their social support system tend to be in very poor control of their condition (Kaplan, Chadwick, & Shimmel, 1985). In effect, the enjoyable social life of a teenager provides interpersonal satisfaction that may conflict with the strict diabetic regimen.

Interrelationships Between Illness and the Social Environment

The Functional Effects Model suggests that the social environment can affect health outcome. Conversely, illness causes modifications in the support environment. Diseases such as asthma and cancer are common stimuli for change. For example, cancer patients may be ''victimized'' by family members and friends. That is, these potential support group members may believe falsely that the disease is contagious, or they may feel uncomfortable visiting the patient (Wortman & Dunkel-Schetter, 1979). Disturbances in marital relationships often follow the diagnosis and treatment of serious conditions such as cancer. Some studies even suggest that children rebel against their cancer-stricken parents because the genetic components of cancer place the offspring at increased risk (Lichtman, Taylor, & Wood, 1986). Yet for some patients, life-threatening illness may actually clarify and enhance interpersonal relationships (Taylor, Whitman, & Wood, 1984).

The chronically ill may have a greater-than-average need for various forms of social support. For example, a person who is no longer able to meet certain responsibilities in the home may need instrumental support from caregivers and housekeepers. Although the chronically ill may need many kinds of social support, they may have difficulty obtaining adequate support. Chronic illnesses may produce feelings of alienation and estrangement from family members and friends. Frequently, misconceptions about the infectious nature of a condition can reduce the amount of available support. For example, diseases such as AIDS may discourage contact with others.

The Functional Effects Models

Social relationships may have different functions for the chronically ill than they do for other members of the population. We will review several cases in which caring social relationships may hinder health outcomes, when a support giver, out of empathy or concern, reinforces a behavior that is incompatible with optimal health outcomes. For example, patients in some chronic illness groups may need to follow regimens that are difficult, painful, or burdensome, and a caring and empathetic support giver may reinforce comfortable but noncompliant behaviors. That is, he or she may place immediate comfort over the long-term consequences of noncompliance. This is most likely to occur when the support giver believes that any suffering should be avoided. For example, if the spouse of a male cardiac patient believes that exercise is harmful, she may discourage activity, because of inadequate information about the condition or because of enduring beliefs. We conceptualize these as functional effects of social support. Functional effects may have a positive influence on health outcomes, however, only if the support giver reinforces appropriate health behaviors. When support givers reinforce maladaptive health behaviors, functional effects may have a negative influence, and so we feel it is important to distinguish between a "Positive Functional Effects" and a "Negative Functional Effects" model.

CHILDHOOD ILLNESSES

The effect of social support on the health of children has remained a relatively unexplored area. However, a growing body of epidemiological research suggests that the social determinants of disease and disability are as important in childhood as they are in the adult years. It has become increasingly clear that families play a crucial role in the development of health behavior and that family support is particularly relevant (Haggerty, Roghmann, & Pless, 1975). Several studies have discussed the family determinants of health. For example, family characteristics influence the utilization of child health services (Roghmann & Haggerty, 1973), specific illness outcomes (Plionis, 1977), and resiliency in stressful periods (Hansen & Johnson, 1979). Although the information is somewhat limited, several lines of evidence suggest that children benefit from supportive social environments. Poverty and insufficient resources remain the best predictor of serious childhood illness (McCormick, 1983). Other evidence indicates that parental separation and divorce have more severe consequences for a child when his or her relationship with the estranged parent is weakened. Children who are satisfied with their social support may adjust better to parental divorce than may those who are less satisfied (Sandler, Wolchik, & Braver, 1985). Illnesses are specific stresses for children and their families. In the next section, we will consider the effects of specific childhood illnesses.

Asthma

Asthma is the leading cause of children's limited activities and disabilities (Newacheck, Halfon, & Budetti, 1986). According to 1982 data, asthma accounted for 190,000 hospitalizations for children under the age of 15, with the average length of stay being 3.9 days (Cropp, 1985). It has been estimated that asthma is the major cause of time lost from school due to a chronic illness. Asthmatic children account for 20% to 25% of all school days lost because of a chronic condition (Evans, in press).

The role of the family in asthma has been a topic of considerable speculation. For many years, psychiatrists and pediatricians were misled by early psychoanalytic interpretations of the asthma syndrome. For example, French and Alexander (1941) believed that asthma represented the incompatible conflict between maternal attachment and sexual–genital wishes. Further, they suggested that asthmatic wheezing was the suppressed cry and solicitation of the mother. Although there is no systematic evidence supporting the psychoanalytic models, for many years these ideas had a substantial impact on pediatricians (Creer, 1982; Renne & Creer, 1985).

Negative Functional Effects

Several psychoanalysts believe that mother–child relationships are atypical when the child is asthmatic. Sandler (1965) went as far as to suggest that the mothers of asthmatic children take away their love in order to maintain discipline. However, systematic studies evaluating the relationship between asthmatic children and their parents have consistently failed to show any atypical relationship between asthmatic children and their mothers (Gauthier et al., 1978). Some residential treatment programs for asthmatic children are based on the belief that parental overconcern is bad for asthmatic children. In other words, they ascribed poor outcomes to negative functional effects. Many years ago, Peshkin (1930) stimulated residential treatment programs by presenting some evidence from a self-selected group of 41 children with severe asthma. He argued that 23 of 25 children who were separated from their parents improved, whereas the 16 children who remained with their parents did not improve. Peshkin even went so far as to advocate "parentectomy," the planned separation of child from parent, as a treatment for asthma.

Unfortunately, the data did not clearly support parental separation as the best treatment for asthma. There was some evidence that separated children were well behaved in residential treatment centers. However, over the years, behavioral problems in the centers became more common (Creer, Ipacs, & Creer, 1983). Renne and Creer (1985) argued that some of the patients in early residential treatment centers were from first-generation Jewish families and may have used asthmatic symptoms to manipulate their parents. However, the benefits of parental separation were not clear. In one systematic study, Purcell and colleagues (1969) separated parents and children for two weeks. The results suggested that separation helped children with emotional precipitants for asthmatic problems but had little effect on children with no emotional precipitants. Even for those who benefited, the strength of the effect was relatively weak.

Positive Functional Effects

Improvements in behavioral observation techniques have facilitated our understanding of families with asthmatic children. Recent studies found that some families overattend to the asthmatic child and give less attention to other family members (Creer & Leung, 1982). Such observations often lead to systematic interventions that help not only the asthmatic child but other siblings.

The benefits of family therapy have received some support in recent years (Liebman, Minuchin, & Baker, 1974; Lask & Matthew, 1979). In the families of children with severe asthma, studies uncovered dysfunctional family relations (Liebman, Minuchin, & Rosman, 1976). The goal of family therapy is to improve family function, so that the parents, the asthmatic child, and his or her siblings are better able to manage the child's symptoms at home, reduce exposure to precipitous factors, and ameliorate the disease's physiological manifestations. In a controlled study of 20 severe, chronic asthmatics, ages 6 to 15, Gustafsson, Kjellman, and Cederblad (1986) demonstrated that family therapy consisting of psychological and educational methods and components produced functional improvements in the children, in comparison with those in the control group. Over a 3.5-year period, these improvements were evaluated by the percentage of predicted peak expiratory flow (a measure of pulmonary function), compliance with medication requirements, and a general pediatric assessment, as well as significant reductions in Beta-2 agonist and steroid usage and functionally impaired days (e.g., staying home from school and restricting activities). There were also fewer hospitalizations and emergency room visits, although these changes were not statistically significant. Although the sample size was small, family therapy seems to improve severe bronchial asthma in children. The findings support the notion that overinvolved parents are actually "harmful" to the asthmatic child. Through instruction techniques and breathing exercises, as well as an understanding of the role that asthmatic symptoms play in the family system, the family changed its support network, and the result was a positive influence on the disease.

In summary, the family's effect on asthma in children has been the source of study and speculation for many years. The findings suggest that the family unit, a child's primary source of social support, significantly influences the asthmatic child. The most common belief is that parents harm asthmatic children and may even provoke asthmatic symptomatology through overprotection and overconcern. These findings support a Negative Functional Effects Model. It is interesting that there are very few studies on the positive role of social support for asthmatic children. Supportive families may be important to obtaining healthful behaviors and medication compliance. The Gustafsson study suggests that the negative family influence can be made a more positive one through therapy. Future work should investigate both the benefits and the consequences of parental involvement with asthmatic children.

Insulin-dependent Diabetes Mellitus

Diabetes mellitus is a major cause of dysfunction, disability, and death throughout the Western world. Diabetes is a heterogeneous disorder that is only partially understood. Two principal forms of the condition are recognized: insulin-dependent diabetes mellitus (IDDM) and non-insulin-dependent diabetes mellitus

(NIDDM). In this section, we will consider IDDM, which typically develops during childhood. Formerly, this condition was known as juvenile diabetes. In IDDM, the body's insulin-producing cells become dysfunctional, and so in order to survive, patients with this condition must receive injections of insulin. Before 1922, when insulin was first discovered, the disease was universally fatal. But with supplemental insulin, individuals survive, and it is estimated that there are now between 200,000 and 250,000 children being treated for this condition (Johnson, 1980).

Adolescents with IDDM must adopt a complex life-style that includes a special diet, exercise, and a strict medical regimen. Studies suggest that most diagnosed adolescents understand that they must comply with this difficult regimen but fail to do so for a variety of reasons. Surviving a normal adolescence is, in itself, a monumental task. And for the adolescent with diabetes, the ordinary frustrations of youth are compounded by the frustration and anxiety associated with an unrelenting chronic disease. Peer acceptance is particularly important to adolescents. Bamber (1974) found that "looking foolish" and "feeling rejected" were two of adolescents' major fears. Two-thirds of a diabetic sample in Sullivan's study (1979) said that they enjoyed eating with their friends, and one-half said that they felt embarrassed when they had to refuse food. One-third of the sample admitted that they would rather eat "something they shouldn't" than to tell someone that they had diabetes. One-third also felt that their nondiabetic friends would like them better if they did not have diabetes and that they would enjoy school more if they did not have diabetes. One-seventh of the sample reported having friends who deliberately tempted them to eat food that they should not. Several researchers concluded that peers may be the best models for adolescents with diabetes (Marble, 1978). Simonds (1979) argued that diabetic adolescents' compliance would improve if they could "identify with other diabetic youths who are successfully following a treatment program" (p. 551). He recommended slightly older diabetics as particularly helpful models.

Negative Functional Effects

The Negative Functional Effects Model might predict that peer influence could have negative consequences for the health outcomes of IDDM youths; that is, peers may reinforce behaviors that are incompatible with control of the condition. In one study of diabetic adolescents, Kaplan, Chadwick, and Schimmel (1985) randomly assigned 21 IDDM patients to one of two groups. One group participated in daily social learning exercises designed to improve social skills and the ability to resist peer influence. The second group spent an equal amount of time learning medical facts about diabetes care. Four months after the intervention, biochemical measures of diabetes control favored the social skills intervention. Several variables were significantly correlated with the diabetes control, including self-reported compliance with diabetes regimens and attitudes toward self-care.

One of the unexpected findings in the Kaplan et al. (1985) study was a significant correlation showing that social support satisfaction, as measured by the Sarason Social Support Questionnaire (SSQ), was associated with poor diabetes control as measured by a biochemical test. In addition, a measure of a problem-solving skill known as the Means–Ends Problem-solving (MEPS) Test (Spivak, Platt, & Shure, 1976) was administered to the participants. This test is designed to measure problem-solving ability, ability to orient, and ability to take action to solve problems. Some investigators have used the MEPS as a measure of social skill. Interestingly, the MEPS scores were significantly correlated with poor control of diabetes. The measure of diabetes control, HBA_1, is scored so that higher values indicate poor control. Thus the findings revealed that those youths who have the poorest control of their diabetes also had the highest scores on the MEPS measure (Chadwick, 1986; Kaplan & Chadwick, 1988).

These results may underscore the effect of the diabetic adolescent's social milieu. The diabetic youths with the poorest control are perceived as being so content with their environment that they have no need to change. Another explanation may be that they are so involved in a nondiabetic social network of peers that practice unhealthful behaviors that they are too distracted to change. Research has indicated that people become more aware of their bodily sensations when they are bored and less aware when they are fully occupied with a task (Pennebaker & Brittingham, 1982). Those diabetic youths who are less adept socially and less satisfied with their social network and have a small or minimal network of peers thus may transmit their social isolation into greater awareness of their metabolic condition. Withdrawal appears to be associated with a heightened awareness of symptoms (Baum, Aiello, & Davis, 1979).

In addition to peers, family support is unquestionably important to the management of diabetes. In one study, the investigators developed the Diabetes Family Behavior Checklist (DFBC), a 16-item scale designed to help understand the role of the family in managing IDDM. The scale evaluates the supportive and nonsupportive behaviors of family members that may influence adherence to the diabetic regimen. Positive and negative behaviors are scored separately. A field test with 54 adults and 18 adolescent patients showed that for adults, but not for adolescents, items reflecting negative components of support were correlated with changes in adherence to the diabetic regimen. The more negative social influences there were in the family, the lower was the prospective (six months) adherence to glucose testing, diet, and regular insulin injections (Schafer, Mc-Caul, & Glasgow, 1986). These results might be regarded as partially supporting the Functional Effects Model. The model would predict that reinforcing positive behaviors should improve adherence, but this prediction was not confirmed. However, the results implied that negative support was associated with poor adherence.

Positive Functional Effects

Not all research shows the effects of social environment to be damaging to diabetic youths. Hanson, Henggeler, and Burghen (1987) found that social competence was not significantly correlated with biochemical measures of diabetes control; however, they did discover an interaction between stress and social competence for diabetes control. Subjects were divided into high, medium, and low social competence groups, and they were also classified by high, medium, and low stress. For those in the low-stress group, high social competence was associated with the poorest level of diabetes control. Conversely, for the high-stress group, social competence was associated with good control of diabetes. Jacobson and colleagues (1986) reported that adjustment to diabetes was strongly correlated with self-esteem, locus of control, behavioral symptoms, and social functioning. In order to assess diabetes adaptation, they administered the Diabetes Adjustment Scale (DAS) (Sullivan, 1979), which includes four scales derived through factor analysis: attitudes toward diabetes, independence, peer relationships, and family relationships. These self-report scores were substantially correlated with self-esteem ($r = .70$), locus of control ($r = .60$), and self-reported symptom intensity ($r = .60$). It appears that the positive influences in the Jacobson et al. study (1986) contradict the negative influences reported by Kaplan et al. (1985).

Two issues are worthy of more detailed consideration. First, the Jacobson et al. study (1986) compared self-report measures with one another. Indeed, other studies have shown high correlations between self-reported adjustment to diabetes and social competence. However, the Kaplan study's results were in the opposite direction when biochemical measures of diabetes control were considered. Another interesting difference between the two studies is the participants' age. The Kaplan study focused on adolescents who were 14 or more years old, whereas the mean age in the Jacobson study was 12.8 years. Although the ages were similar, the transition from preadolescence to adolescence was associated with significant changes in independence and susceptibility to peer influence. Hanson and colleagues (1987) discovered that compliance with the diabetic regimen was correlated with parental support and that parental support declined as preadolescents became teenagers. It would be interesting to evaluate the differences in correlates of social influence for preadolescent versus adolescent youths.

In summary, studies of childhood illnesses have produced inconsistent findings. Studies of childhood asthma often concluded that overconcerned parents can have detrimental effects on health behaviors. The data on insulin-dependent diabetes indicate that youths who are satisfied with their peer relationships may actually have poorer control of their condition. These findings are in accordance with the Negative Functional Effects Model. Some studies also showed that negative family support may be associated with poor adherence to the diabetic regimen. Future studies will need to separate the effects of emotional support and concern and the social reinforcement of aspects of the regimen.

SOCIAL SUPPORT AND HEALTH OUTCOMES IN ADULTS

Most chronic illnesses occur during adulthood. In the United States, medical care costs have risen to account for nearly 11% of the gross national product. But the causes of death have changed remarkably since the turn of the century. In 1900, heart disease accounted for about 45% of all deaths, and infectious diseases, such as influenza and tuberculosis, also accounted for significant percentages of deaths. In the 1980s, cardiovascular (heart and circulatory system) diseases caused more than 70% of all deaths. The days when infectious diseases were the major killers in the industrialized world appear to be over. AIDS, although rapidly increasing in incidence, still accounts for a very small percentage of all deaths. Today, the major challenge is from the increasing incidence of chronic illnesses. The leading causes of death are heart disease, cancer, stroke, chronic obstructive lung disease, and diabetes, each of which may be associated with a long period of disability. In addition, personal habits and health behaviors may be linked to both the development and the maintenance of these conditions (Kaplan, 1985). In the following sections, we will explore some of the relationships between social support and adaptation to various chronic illnesses.

Non-Insulin-dependent Diabetes Mellitus (NIDDM)

Diabetes mellitus is a major public health problem that affects between 8 million and 12 million Americans. Approximately 90% of the individuals have Type II diabetes (NIDDM category). Although insulin or oral hypoglycemic medications may be used to manage this condition, in most cases they are not necessary for survival. Instead, the American Diabetes Association (1984) now recommends diet and exercise as the primary treatment for diabetes. Between 60% and 90% of patients with Type II diabetes are overweight, and losing weight results in the condition's improvement in a significant number of cases (Kaplan & Atkins, 1985). The consequences of poor management of diabetes, however, can be severe. Complications include blindness, amputations, and diseases of the kidneys, heart, and central nervous system. In current medical practice, virtually all patients with Type II diabetes are advised to make life-style changes, such as ingesting fewer calories, exercising more, and, in some cases, adhering to a regimen of insulin or oral hypoglycemic drugs. Because Type II diabetes typically has its onset in the fifth decade of life or later, changing one's life-style is often difficult. The role of social relationships in the predisposition to obesity (and diabetes) and in the achievement of life-style changes is therefore of considerable theoretical and practical importance.

Negative Functional Effects

The literature on social support and sex differences states that husbands receive more emotional support from their spouses than do wives. Men generally view their wives as confidants, whereas women frequently approach their children and other family members for emotional support (Kohen, 1983; Lowenthal & Haven, 1968). In the case of the diabetic patient, Heitzmann and Kaplan (1984) investigated the role of social support in NIDDM patients and found an interaction between sex and social support as measured by the Sarason Social Support Questionnaire. Male patients who expressed more satisfaction with their social supports had poorer metabolic control than did males with lower social support satisfaction scores. Female patients, on the other hand, exhibited the opposite pattern. Those females with high social support satisfaction scores had better metabolic control than did female patients who expressed less satisfaction with their social supports. These results may mean that social support is indeed quite different for males and females, and the Negative Functional Effects Model may explain the sex differences. With NIDDM—a disease that is largely managed by diet—the individual in the household responsible for purchasing and preparing food plays a crucial role as "gatekeeper" of the food, and in most instances, the female is considered the gatekeeper. Thus the supportive, involved wife of the male NIDDM patient may be reinforcing behaviors that do not achieve better diabetic control, by preparing foods that, though tasty, may ultimately lead to poorer metabolic control. The female NIDDM patient, on the other hand, may be reinforced by a supportive husband, children, or friends to follow through with the prescribed regimen. Subsequently, the female patient may be more apt to prepare the proper foods, not only for herself, but also for the entire family.

In a study of a different group of NIDDM patients, Kaplan and Hartwell (1987) studied 32 men and 44 women with a confirmed diagnosis of diabetes. Again, control of diabetes, as measured by the glycosylated hemoglobin assay, was significantly correlated with social support satisfaction for women but was negatively correlated with social support satisfaction for men. In addition, for women, the network size was significantly correlated with failure to attend sessions and with failure to complete a diet or exercise diary. For these women, the network size was not significantly correlated with weight loss, which was the program's goal. For men, the network size was correlated with increases in weight, cholesterol, and triglycerides over an 18-month period. These findings highlight some of the differences between social support satisfaction and network size. A social support network can buffer stress and provide a reinforcing social environment. However, as demonstrated in this study, a large social support network can also interfere with the successful alteration of health habits, particularly when the health behaviors differ from those of the patient's reference network.

The Functional Effects Model may explain the differential effects of social network size on men and women. Most of the studies of chronically ill adults have focused on older individuals in traditional sex role relationships. Women with large networks, therefore, may miss more sessions because of their obligations to family members (e.g., sick children), whereas men may not be burdened by such obligations. Moreover, because women may be more prone to engage in self-care activities and to be more responsive to illness (Wingard, 1984), they may be more inclined to seek assistance from the network to change their behavior. Conversely, men, with their greater tendency toward unhealthful life-styles (Wingard, 1984), might seek support for not conforming to the prescribed regimen. Although highly speculative, we suggest that environmental effects may have important influences on diabetic patients.

Positive Functional Effects

Regimen adherence and metabolic control may be related to family interactions, because (1) family members are often asked to share in the responsibility for implementing regimen requirements and (2) family routines can be disrupted by the diabetic patient's treatment regimen. Thus, the behaviors of family members may interfere with or facilitate adherence, whereas emotional stress or support in the family may influence metabolic control. Edelstein and Linn (1985) examined the perceptions of adult diabetic males concerning their family environment and how this influenced diabetic control. A combination of three variables, namely, achievement orientation, organization, and control, were identified as helpful in controlling the disease. Diabetic men in good control had families that valued achievement, had little conflict, and were not rigidly organized. Interestingly, there was no difference in perceptions of family environments between diabetic men and age-matched controls with other chronic illnesses.

The Diabetes Family Behavior Checklist (DFBC) was developed and validated on a group of IDDM patients to assess the impact of supportive and nonsupportive behaviors in the family on adherence to the diabetic regimen (Schafer, McCaul, & Glasgow, 1986). More recently, Glasgow and Toobert (1988) adapted the DFBC to measure family influences on the NIDDM patients' adherence. In particular, they concentrated on adherence to medication taking, glucose testing, exercise and diet. In this case, the endorsement of items reflecting negative components of support did not predict regimen adherence for the 127 adult NIDDM patients. The study revealed that family supportive behaviors in one aspect of the diabetic regimen did not correlate with supportive behaviors relevant to other self-care activities. This study identified one of the difficulties in evaluating the Functional Effects Model. That is, support members may reinforce one aspect of the regimen while not reinforcing other aspects. Furthermore, support for different aspects of self-care are not correlated.

Coronary Heart Disease (CHD)

Heart disease remains the major cause of death and disability in the Western world. There are many types of heart disease, and so adaptations to differing manifestations of disease may require different coping skills. Two common types of heart disease, myocardial infarction (MI) and cardiac arrest, have an abrupt onset and typically require hospitalization. Patients who have ongoing heart disease may require one of two types of traumatic intervention: (1) coronary artery bypass surgery, which revascularizes the coronary arteries, and (2) coronary angioplasty, which dilates the coronary arteries. Other patients have serious heart disease that is manifested through symptomatic angina pectoris. This typically includes severe chest pain and may require hospitalization if it becomes frequent, severe, or unstable. In general, heart procedures are stressful and often require a period of adaptation and rehabilitation followed by other life-style changes.

Although patients are commonly hospitalized for heart disease, the critical period comes after they are discharged. A coronary event often creates considerable fear and anxiety, and when the patient is released from the hospital to the home, his or her family may not be fully equipped to cope with the uncertainties and stresses of these conditions. It was suggested, however, that supportive environments enhance health outcomes following a cardiac event (Davidson & Shumaker, 1987).

Negative Functional Effects

Several studies have provided support for the Negative Functional Effects Model, which found that the involvement of supportive but overconcerned family members may lead to poorer health outcomes. In one study, congestive heart failure patients who were not working 3, 6, or 9 months after their hospitalization were reported to have more overprotective families than did those patients who resumed working during the same time period (Lewis, 1966). Garrity (1973) studied first-time MI patients and found that the more concerned the patient's family was, the fewer hours the patient worked at a job, independent of the heart attack's severity. These findings imply that the patient's family, though concerned, is interfering with his or her recovery. Furthermore, the actions of family members may actually be harming the patient by not allowing him or her to exercise and thus strengthen the heart muscle/tissue. Presumably the family members are supportive and want to see the patient recover, but their personal beliefs about the patient's frailty may lead to the reinforcement of sedentary behaviors.

Positive Functional Effects

Positive social influences were also documented. Significant others in the support environment may encourage adhering to the medical regimen and the adoption of appropriate health behaviors. A related positive functional effect is gained through modeling. That is, members of the support environment may model appropriate coping skills and health behaviors (Pearlin & Aneshensel, 1986). Thus, if a network member makes these changes at the same time, the outcome may be enhanced through mutual encouragement, mutual modeling, and a reduction in the perceived difficulty of making the changes. Another mechanism accounting for the benefits of social support is stress buffering; that is, adaptation may be made easier by having network members absorb some of the stress.

Some studies have confirmed the positive functional effects of a social support network. An intervention study with hypertensive patients (Caplan, Robinson, French, Caldwell, & Shinn, 1976) found that lectures alone did little to help patients control their blood pressure. But lectures in conjunction with social support and encouragement were significantly more effective. Social support was also found to aid in the maintenance of desirable health behaviors, such as weight loss, in postcoronary patients (Finnegan & Suler, 1984). In addition, dropout rates from CHD rehabilitation and intervention programs were also shown to be correlated with the amount of perceived social support in female hypertensive patients (Williams et al., 1985). Thus, perceived social support may either encourage or reduce attrition in such programs.

Miller and colleagues (1985) examined specific prescriptive factors (diet, medication, exercise, smoking cessation, and other life-style changes) leading to optimal health functioning in post-MI patients. They found that adherence to medical regimens after recovery from an initial MI is generally low but varies according to the prescription component. Patients readily adopted those behaviors requiring minimal life-style changes, such as taking medication. Conversely, they were less apt to make more complicated changes, such as altering their dietary patterns or participating in a regular exercise program. Of particular interest was the finding that the attitudes and perceived beliefs of significant others toward the prescribed changes correlated strongly with the patients' actual adherence to the regimen. These findings parallel those found in the diabetes compliance literature.

There is also some evidence for the buffering model, suggesting a link between social isolation and mortality in the CHD patient. Ruberman and colleagues (1984) reported that mortality from myocardial infarction was associated with social isolation and high levels of stress. In fact these two factors increased the risk of mortality more than four times in post-MI males.

In summary, social support was indicated to be an important variable in adapting to cardiovascular disease (Davidson & Schumacher, 1987). Several mechanisms seem to account for the effects of social support networks on health outcomes, of which the Stress-buffering Model and the Positive Functional Effects Model have received considerable attention in the research literature. However, to date, few empirical studies have addressed the contribution of overconcerned spouses and family members in reinforcing maladaptive or inappropriate behaviors that lead to worse health outcomes.

Back Pain

Nearly 80% of all Americans have disabling back pain at some point in their life. Back pain affects all social classes, men and women, and is common in both industrialized and developing nations. Disability associated with back pain affects nearly every family in the country (Nachenson, 1976; National Center for Health Statistics, 1977), and back disorders are the most common cause of disability for people under the age of 45 (National Center for Health Statistics, 1977). Furthermore, the impact of low back pain on the economy is remarkable. Nearly $14 billion are spent annually on the treatment of back pain, and $9 billion are spent on compensation to the afflicted (Akeson & Murphy, 1977). In some industries, the incidence of low back pain is about 50 per 1,000 workers per year, and heavy industries lose about 1,400 workdays per 1,000 workers each year. Although most episodes of back pain heal spontaneously within about two weeks, those afflicted may then have a greater incidence of chronic back pain. Chronic pain is defined as pain that lasts for six months or more.

Clinical approaches to the management of back pain emphasize different patterns of interaction between patients and their support network. Physical therapy approaches often emphasize reassurance from spouse and family. In contrast, behavioral approaches often require modification of the social environment.

Negative Functional Effects

According to operant approaches to pain management, individuals experiencing pain engage in *pain behaviors*. Pain behaviors can include changes in physical activity, reduction or avoidance of work, frequent use of pain medications, and communication of pain through facial expression. The operant model suggests that these natural behaviors, which are responses to acute pain, may be strengthened through reinforcement. Over time, therefore, they may have reinforcing consequences, including attention from a spouse or friend, avoidance of undesirable tasks, and use of narcotic drugs.

Various intervention programs based on operant principles have been described in the literature. Of particular interest is the role of social support network members in managing chronic pain. There are three basic "family" treatment approaches being used in multimodal treatment centers. The transactional approach promotes awareness of the ways in which patients use pain for psychological gain. In this approach, the goal of the therapy is to get the patient to discontinue his or her manipulative behavior. A systems theory approach assumes that certain types of social support network systems are organized in such a way that the patient's sick role behavior maintains the homeostatic balance. Therapy focuses on changing the structure of network organizations so that the patient no longer needs to play the sick role. Lastly, in the behavioral approach, supportive network members are trained to praise and encourage well behaviors such as walking and exercise, while minimizing their attention to pain behaviors. Although many pain programs use methods from several different "family" treatment approaches, most programs emphasize these behavioral approaches.

Several reports show that these programs are efficacious (Roberts & Reinhardt, 1980). In one study, pain patients were led to believe they were being observed by either their spouse or a ward clerk. Those with a solicitous spouse rated their pain significantly higher when they believed that their spouse was observing. The treatment was designed to extinguish these responses. Cooperation between spouses and family members is required to make this treatment work. Inpatient treatment is used when families do not cooperate, but generalization outside the hospital may be difficult when the spouse is not an agent in the treatment (Keefe & Gill, 1986). Several follow-up studies of pain treatment programs indicate that social support involvement in treatment is essential to its long-term success. In one study (Hudgens, 1979), 24 families who completed a behaviorally oriented program were assessed six months to two years later. The results showed that five of the six patients who had not maintained their treatment gains did not have adequate social supports at the time of follow-up.

Most studies indicate that family or supportive network members can contribute to the maintenance and treatment of pain behaviors. It appears that when family members are appropriately supportive and have learned not to reinforce pain behaviors, pain patients have a higher likelihood of long-term success. In summary, these studies demonstrate that it is possible to affect the social support network system in a way that promotes the reduction of pain behavior.

The pain literature clearly supports the Negative Functional Effects Model. In a majority of cases, it appears that the concerned, caring supportive members often reinforce pain behaviors, by doing tasks for the patients when they grimace and moan, or by allowing the patients to remain largely sedentary. As a result, the patients are reinforced for not getting well. Thus, chronic pain patients often remain disabled and unable to cope with the pain.

Positive Functional Effects

It is interesting that coping with pain has been described as analogous to coping with stress. Some investigators believe that cognitive factors similar to those that help individuals cope with stress may also help patients cope with pain (Turk & Rudy, 1986). In other words, pain is conceptualized as stress. According to these models, supportive interactions, availability of a confidant, and general warmth and acceptance may help rather than inhibit pain tolerance. To date, few systematic studies have compared the efficacy of interventions contrasting supportive and operant approaches to the management of pain. The few controlled studies evaluating the operant approach suggest that these interventions are associated with better outcomes than are waiting list controls or supportive relaxation interventions (Linton & Gotestam, 1985). As with other chronic illnesses, there is some conflict between advocates of supportive care and advocates of approaches that modify interpersonal relationships within the support network.

CONCLUSIONS

The effects of social support on various health outcomes may be complex. Table 16.1 summarizes the results of the studies we have reviewed. Only three of the studies found consistently positive benefits of social support for patients with a chronic illness. Seven studies found that overconcern or other aspects of social relationships can have a damaging effect on health outcomes. Six studies found inconsistent results, or either benefits or detriments for particular subgroups.

Among those studies showing benefits for social support, two of three were intervention studies. In one case, family therapy produced positive outcomes in four of six measures for children with asthma (Gustafsson et al., 1986). In addition, lectures including a social support component helped achieve better blood pressure control among patients with hypertension (Caplan et al., 1976).

The most common type of study suggesting a negative effect from social relationships includes some functional measure of outcome. These studies range from evaluations of asthma (Peshkin, 1930) to returning to work after a heart attack (Garrity, 1973) to functioning for patients with back pain (Roberts & Reinhart, 1980). Evidence from these studies showed that concerned family members may reinforce sick role behaviors and that strengthening sick role behaviors may be incompatible with optimal health status. Studies with mixed results tended to use biochemical measures or scales of adherence and treatment dropout.

How can we synthesize the results of these studies? First, we must evaluate the role of caring and concern. According to the Stress-buffering Model, genuine family concern may help chronically ill patients cope with difficult illnesses. On the other hand, evidence supporting the Negative Functional Effects Model suggests that caring and concern might reinforce behaviors that are not compatible

TABLE 16.1. Social Support Influences and Chronic Disease

Source	N	Population Group	SS Measure	Dependent Measure	Finding
			Negative Functional Effects—Childhood Asthma		
Peshkin (1930)	41	25 asthmatic children separated from parents; 16 asthmatic children remaining with parents	Living with parents or away from parents in a residential center		23 of 25 children separated from their parents improved, whereas 16 children who remained with their parents did not improve.
Purcell et al. (1969)	25	13 asthmatic children with emotional precipitants; 12 asthmatic children with no emotional precipitants	Living with family or with substitute parental figure in the child's home	• Peak expiratory flow rate (PEF) • Clinical exam • Medication intake • Daily history of Sx	Children with emotional precipitants improved on all 4 measures when separated from their families. Children with no emotional precipitants showed little change.
			Positive Functional Effects—Childhood Asthma		
Gustafsson et al. (1986)	20	Severely asthmatic children	Family functioning	• Predicted PEF • Clinical exam • Compliance with meds • Inpatient days • Emergency visits • Functionally impaired days	Family therapy consisting of psychological and educational methods improved the function of asthmatic children in 4 of the 6 dependent measures.
			Negative Functional Effects—Insulin-dependent Diabetes Mellitus		
Kaplan et al. (1985)	21	Type I diabetics	Social Support Questionnaire (Sarason SSQ)	Hemoglobin A1 (HbA1)	Social support satisfaction was positively correlated with HbA1. The higher the HbA1, the poorer the metabolic control.

Study	N	Sample	Social Support Measure	Outcome Measure	Results
Chadwick (1986)	21	Type I diabetics	Means–Ends Problem-solving (MEPS) Test	Hemoglobin A1 (HbA1)	MEPS was used as a measure of social skill. MEPS scores were significantly correlated with poor control of diabetes. Those with good social skills (high scores on the MEPS) were in the poorest control of their diabetes.
Schafer et al. (1986)	72	Type I Diabetics: 54 adults, 18 adolescents	Diabetes Family Behavior Checklist (DFBC)	Summary of self-care: activities questionnaire (e.g., diet, glucose testing, insulin)	For the adult patients, higher levels of nonsupportive family behaviors were related to poorer adherence to the diabetic regimen. For the adolescent patients, there were no consistent patterns.
Positive Functional Effects—Insulin-dependent Diabetes Mellitus					
Hanson et al. (1987)	104	Type I Diabetics	Social competence	• Biochemical measures, including HbA1 • Self-report of diet, insulin, glucose testing, hypoglycemia	Social competence was not significantly correlated with control of diabetes. In addition, parental support was significantly correlated with self-reported adherence to the diabetic regimen.
Negative Functional Effects—Non-Insulin-dependent Diabetes Mellitus					
Heitzmann & Kaplan (1984)	37	Type II Diabetics	Social Support Questionnaire (Sarason SSQ)	Hemoglobin A1	Males with satisfactory social supports had poorer metabolic control. Conversely, females with high social support satisfaction scores had better metabolic control.

TABLE 16.1. *Continued.*

Source	N	Population Group	SS Measure	Dependent Measure	Finding
Negative Functional Effects—Non-Insulin-dependent Diabetes Mellitus, *continued*					
Kaplan & Hartwell (1987)	76	Type II diabetics	Social Support (Sarason SSQ)	Hemoglobin A1	Diabetic control was significantly correlated with social support satisfaction for females but was negatively correlated with social support satisfaction for males.
Positive Functional Effects—Non-Insulin-dependent Diabetes Mellitus					
Edelstein & Linn (1985)	97	Type II diabetics	Family Environment Scale	• Hemoglobin A1 • Fasting Blood Glucose • Fasting Triglyceride • Cholesterol	Diabetic males in good control had families that were oriented toward achievement, were not strictly organized, and had little conflict.
Neutral Functional Effects—Non-insulin-dependent Diabetes Mellitus					
Glasgow & Toober (1988)	127	Type II diabetics	Diabetes Family Behavior Checklist (DFBC)	• Medication intake • Glucose testing • Exercise • Diet	Family behaviors, either supportive or nonsupportive, did not predict adherence to the diabetic regimen. Supportive behaviors in one aspect of the regimen do not correlate with supportive behaviors in other self-care activities.
Negative Functional Effects—Coronary Heart Disease					
Lewis (1966)	91	Congestive heart failure patients	Patient's perception of spouse/family attitudes (e.g., rejection, overprotection, no change)	Occupational work after hospitalization	Patients who were not working 3, 6, or 9 months following hospitalization were reported to have more overprotective families than did those patients who resumed working during the same period.

Study	N	Sample	Measures	Outcome	Results
Garrity (1973)	58	First-time MI patients	Patient's perception of the amount of family concern	Occupational work following MI	The more concerned the patient's family was, the fewer hours the patient worked at a job, independent of the heart attack's severity.
Positive Functional Effects—Coronary Heart Disease					
Caplan et al. (1976)		Hypertensive patients		Blood Pressure	Lectures and social support were effective in controlling blood pressure. Lectures alone, however, did little to help control blood pressure.
Williams et al. (1985)	359	Hypertensive patients	Dimensions of emotional and instrumental support	• Dropout from tx • Blood pressure	For females, but not for males, the amount of perceived support was negatively correlated with dropout from treatment and poor blood pressure control.
Miller et al. (1985)	141	Post-MI patients	Patient's perception of significant others' beliefs about the medical regimen	Regimen adherence (e.g., medications, diet, exercise, smoking cessation)	Attitudes and perceived beliefs of significant others toward prescriptive components were strong correlates of actual regimen adherence.
Negative Functional Effects—Back Pain					
Roberts & Reinhardt (1980)	26	Back pain patients	• Spouse/family interaction with the patient • MMPI of spouse	• Pain behavior responses • Daily activity diary • Medication use	A program designed to reward "wellness" behavior and ignore "pain" behavior reduced the patient's pain complaints. Also, the spouse's personality characteristics were related to outcome. Elevated hypochondriasis and hysteria scales of the spouse's MMPI predicted poor prognosis.

with optimal functioning. The Positive Functional Effects Model emphasizes that caring family members may have a positive effect, but only if they reinforce appropriate health behaviors. To date, very few studies attempted to separate these functions.

The results of these studies should not be interpreted negatively with regard to intervention. Indeed, several studies revealed that social support interventions may actually enhance health outcomes. The Functional Effects Model suggests that successful interventions are those that turn negative social influences into positive ones. In cases in which family members reinforce sick role behaviors, behavioral interventions might result in supportive interactions that ultimately improve the patient's functioning (Roberts & Reinhart, 1980).

In addition to clinical implications, the Functional Effects Model offers ideas for future research. First, it is clear that network size, as measured in epidemiological studies, is insufficient. Several examples have demonstrated that networks of equal size can have both positive and negative influences. Similarly, satisfaction may not be entirely sufficient as a measure. A social environment can have negative influences, even though it provides satisfaction.

How can we interpret some of the complex interactions between social support and health outcomes? To date, few studies have addressed the role of social support for the chronically ill, but several directions for future research should be considered. These include: (1) There is a major movement to create support groups for the physically ill, with such groups typically directed by lay leaders. The groups include those for patients with illnesses ranging from cancer to chronic lung disease to arthritis. The risk and potential benefits of these groups should be evaluated. (2) There is evidence from several studies that social support enhances mental health outcomes. On the other hand, family studies of chronic disease conditions have often found that family members must be retrained to avoid overconcern, reinforcement of sick role behaviors, and the like. Few studies have attempted to separate the benefits versus the risks of unconditional love and concern from family members. (3) Many current interventions imply that we do understand the impact of family interactions on health behaviors. At present, however, few systematic studies, such as those reported by Creer and associates in *Asthma,* have documented the relationship among interaction patterns, health behaviors, and health outcomes.

In summary, epidemiological studies clearly link the availability of a support network to positive health outcomes, but there are many conflicts in the literature about the benefits and consequences of supportive social relationships. The Functional Effects Model may help explain some of these inconsistencies.

REFERENCES

Akeson, W. H., & Murphy, R. W. (1977). Low back pain. *Clinical Orthopedics, 2,* 129.

American Diabetes Association. (1984). *The physicians' guide to Type II diabetes (NIDDM) diagnosis and treatment.* New York: American Diabetes Association.

Bamber, J. H. (1974). The fears of adolescents. *Journal of Genetic Psychology, 125*, 127–140.

Baum, A., Aiello, J. R., & Davis, G. E. (1979). *Open stress, withdrawal, and health.* Paper presented at the annual meeting of the American Psychological Association, New York.

Berkman, L. F., & Breslow, L. (1983). *Health and ways of living: Findings from the Alameda County Study.* New York: Oxford University Press.

Blazer, D. G. (1982). Social support and mortality in an elderly community population. *American Journal of Epidemiology, 115*, 684–694.

Block, A., Kremmer, E., & Gaylor, M. (1980). Behavioral treatment of chronic pain. The spouse as a discriminative cue for pain behavior. *Pain, 9*, 243–252.

Broadhead, W. E., Kaplan, B. H., James, S. A., Wagner, E. H., Schoenback, V. J., Grimson, R., Heyden, S., Tibblin, G., & Gehlback, S. H. (1983). The epidemiologic evidence for a relationship between social support and health. *American Journal of Epidemiology, 117*, 521–537.

Caplan, R., Robinson, E. A. R., French, J. R., Caldwell, J. R., & Shinn, M. (1976). *Adhering to Medical Regimens.* Paper presented to the Institute for Social Research, Ann Arbor, MI.

Chadwick, M. W. (1986). *Using social skills training in health education: A pilot study with adolescents.* Unpublished master's thesis, San Diego State University.

Cohen, S., & Syme, S. L. (1985). *Social support and health.* San Diego: Academic Press.

Cohen, S., & Wills, T. A. (1985). Stress, social support, and the buffering hypothesis. *Psychological Bulletin, 98*, 310–357.

Creer, T. L. (1982). Asthma. *Journal of Consulting and Clinical Psychology, 50*, 912–921.

Creer, T. L., Ipacs, J., & Creer, P. P. (1983). Changing behavioral and social variables at resident treatment facilities for childhood asthma. *Journal of Asthma, 20*, 11–15.

Creer, T., & Leung, P. (1982). The development and evaluation of a self-management program for children with asthma. In *Self-management education programs for childhood asthma* (Vol. 2). Bethesda, MD: National Institute for Allergic and Infectious Disease.

Cropp, G. J. A. (1985). Special features of asthma in children. *Chest, 87*, 55–62.

Davidson, D. M., & Shumaker, S. A. (1987). Social support and cardiovascular disease. *Artherosclerosis, 7*, 101–104.

Davidson, T. N., Bowden, L., & Tholen, D. (1979). Social support as a moderator of burn rehabilitation. *Archives of Physical Medicine and Rehabilitation, 60*, 556.

Dimond, M. (1979). Social support and adaptation to chronic illness: The case of maintenance hemodialysis. *Research in Nursing and Health, 2*, 101–108.

Edelstein, J., & Linn, M. W. (1985). The influence of the family on control of diabetes. *Social Science and Medicine, 21*, 541–545.

Evans, R. I. (in press). School-based health education for children with asthma. In J. Okene & S. Shumaker (Eds.), *Adoption and maintenance of behaviors for optimal health.* New York: Springer.

Finlayson, A. (1976). Social support networks as coping resources: Lay help and consultation patterns used by women in husband's post-infarction careers. *Social Science and Medicine, 10*, 97–103.

Finnegan, D. L., & Suler, J. R. (1984). Psychological factors associated with maintenance of improved health behaviors in postcoronary patients. *Journal of Psychology, 119*, 87–94.

French, T. M., & Alexander, F. (1941). Psychogenic factors in bronchioasthma. *Psychosomatic Medicine Monographs* (No. 4). Menasha, WI: George Banta.

Garrity, T. F. (1973). Vocational adjustment after first myocardial infarction: Comparative assessment of several variables suggested in the literature. *Social Science and Medicine, 7*, 705–717.

Gauthier, Y., Fortin, C., Drapeau, P., Breton, J. J., Gosselin, J., Quintal, L., Weifnagel, J., & Lamarre, A. (1978). Follow-up study of 35 asthmatic preschool children. *Journal of the American Academy of Child Psychology, 17*, 679–694.

Glasgow, R. E., & Toobert, D. J. (1988). Social environment and regimen adherence among type II diabetic patients. *Diabetes Care, 11*, 377–386.

Grant, I., Patterson, T. L., & Yeager, J. (1988). Social support in relation to physical health and symptoms of depression in the elderly. *American Journal of Psychiatry, 145*, 1254–1258.

Greydanus, D. E., & Hoffman, A. D. (1979). Psychological factors in diabetes mellitus. *American Journal of Diseases of Children, 133*, 1061–1066.

Gustafsson, P. A., Kjellman, N-I. M., & Cederblad, M. (1986). Family therapy in the treatment of severe childhood asthma. *Journal of Psychosomatic Research, 30*, 369–374.

Haggerty, R. J., Roghmann, K. J., & Pless, F. B. (1975). *Child health and the community*. New York: Wiley.

Hansen, D. A., & Johnson, V. A. (1979). Rethinking family stress theory: Definitional aspects. In W. R. Burr, R. Hill, F. I. Nye, & I. L. Reiss (Eds.), *Contemporary theories about the family*. New York: Free Press.

Hanson, C. L., Henggeler, S. W., & Burghen, G. A. (1987). Social competence and parental support as mediators of the link between stress and metabolic control in adolescents with insulin-dependent diabetes mellitus. *Journal of Consulting and Clinical Psychology, 55*, 529–533.

Haynes, S. G., & Feinleib, M. (1980). Women, work and coronary heart disease: Prospective findings from the Framingham Heart Study. *American Journal of Public Health, 70*, 133–141.

Heitzmann, C. A., & Kaplan, R. M. (1984). Interaction between sex and social support in the control of Type II diabetes mellitus. *Journal of Consulting and Clinical Psychology, 52*, 1087–1089.

House, J. S., Robbins, C., & Metzner, H. L. (1982). The association of social relationships and activities with mortality. Prospective evidence from the Tecumseh Community Health Study. *American Journal of Epidemiology, 116*, 123–140.

Hudgens, A. (1979). Family-oriented treatment of chronic pain. *Journal of Marriage and Family Therapy, 5*, 67–78.

Jacobson, A. M., Houser, S. T., Weitlied, D., Wolfsdorf, J. I., Orleans, J., & Vieyra, M. (1986). Psychological adjustment of children with recently diagnosed diabetes mellitus. *Diabetes Care, 9*, 323–329.

Johnson, S. B. (1980). Psychosocial factors in juvenile diabetes: A review. *Journal of Behavioral Medicine, 3*, 95–116.

Kannel, W. B. (1987). New perspectives on cardiovascular risk factors. *American Heart Journal, 114*, 213–219.

Kaplan, B. H., & Cassel, J. C. (1975). *Family and health: An epidemiological approach.* Chapel Hill, NC: Institute for Research in Social Science.

Kaplan, R. M. (1985). Behavioral epidemiology, health promotion, and health services. *Medical Care, 23*, 564–583.

Kaplan, R. M., & Atkins, C. J. (1985). Behavioral management of Type II diabetes mellitus. In R. M. Kaplan & M. H. Criqui (Eds.), *Behavioral epidemiology and disease prevention.* New York: Plenum.

Kaplan, R. M., & Chadwick, M. W. (1988). Training sozialer kompetess Bei Typ-I-Diabetes. In F. Strain, R. Holzl, & M. Haslbeck (Eds.), *Verhaltensmedizin und Diabetes Mellitus.* Berlin: Springer-Verlag.

Kaplan, R. M., Chadwick, M. W., & Schimmel, L. E. (1985). Social learning intervention to promote metabolic control in Type I diabetes mellitus: Private experiment results. *Diabetes Care, 8*, 152–155.

Kaplan, R. M., & Hartwell, S. L. (1987). Differential effects of social support and social network on physiological and social outcomes in men and women with Type II diabetes mellitus. *Health Psychology, 6*, 387–398.

Keefe, F. G., & Gill, K. M. (1986). Behavioral concepts in the analysis of chronic pain syndromes. *Journal of Consulting and Clinical Psychology, 54*, 776–783.

Kohen, J. A. (1983). Old but not alone: Informal social supports among the elderly by marital status and sex. *The Gerontologist, 23*, 57–63.

Lask, B., & Matthew, D. (1979). Childhood asthma. A controlled trial of family psychotherapy. *Archives of Diseases of Childhood, 55*, 116–119.

Leavy, R. L. (1983). Social support and psychological disorder: A review. *Journal of Community Psychology, 11*, 3–21.

Lewis, C. E. (1966). Factors influencing the return to work of men with congestive heart failure. *Journal of Chronic Diseases, 19*, 1193–2013.

Lichtman, R. R., Taylor, S. A., & Wood, J. D. (1986). Research on the chronically ill: Conceptual and methodological perspectives. In A. Baum & J. Singer (Eds.), *The handbook of environmental psychology* (Vol. 5, pp. 43–74). Hillsdale, NJ: Erlbaum.

Liebman, R., Minuchin, S., & Baker, L. (1974). The use of structural family therapy in the treatment of intractable asthma. *American Journal of Psychiatry, 121*, 535–540.

Liebman, R., Minuchin, S., Baker, L., & Rosman, B. (1976). The role of the family in the treatment of chronic asthma. In P. J. Guerin (Ed.), *Family therapy theory and practice* (pp. 309–324). New York: Gardner.

Linton, S. J., & Gotestam, K. G. (1985). Controlling pain reports through operant conditioning. *Perceptual and Motor Skills, 60*, 427–437.

Lowenthal, M. F., & Haven, C. (1968). Interaction and adaptation: Intimacy as a critical variable. *American Sociological Review, 33*, 20–30.

Marble, A. (1978). Careful treatment of diabetes: Methods and rewards. *Comprehensive Therapy, 4*, 32–39.

McCormick, M. C. (1983). The contribution of low birth weight to infant mortality and childhood morbidity. *New England Journal of Medicine, 312*, 82–90.

Miller, P., Wikoff, R. L., McMahon, M., Garrett, M. J., & Ringel, K. (1985). Indicators of medical regimen adherence for myocardial infarction patients. *Nursing Research, 34,* 268–272.

Nachenson, A. L. (1976). The lumbar spine: An orthopedic challenge. *Spine, 1,* 59–71.

National Center for Health Statistics. (1977). *Limitation of activity due to chronic conditions.* Washington, DC: Department of Health and Human Services, Series 10, No. 111.

Newacheck, P. W., Halfon, N., & Budetti, P. (1986). Prevalence of activity limiting chronic conditions among children based on household interviews. *Journal of Chronic Diseases, 39,* 63–71.

Pearlin, L. I., & Aneshensel, C. S. (1986). Coping and social supports: Their functions and applications. In L. Aiken & D. Mechanic (Eds.), *Applications of social science to clinical medicine and health policy* (pp. 417–437). New Brunswick, NJ: Rutgers University Press.

Pennebaker, J., & Brittingham, G. (1982). Environmental and sensory cues affecting the perception of physical symptoms. In A. Baum & J. Singer (Eds.), *Advances in environmental psychology: Environment and health* (Vol. 4, pp. 115–136). Hillsdale, NJ: Erlbaum.

Peshkin, M. M. (1930). Asthma in children: Role of environment in the treatment of a selected group of cases: A plea for a "home" as a restorative measure. *American Journal of Diseases of Children, 39,* 774–781.

Platt, J. J., Spivack, G., Altman, D., & Peizer, S. (1974). Adolescent problem-solving thinking. *Journal of Consulting and Clinical Psychology, 42,* 787–793.

Plionis, E. M. (1977). Family functioning and childhood accident occurrence. *American Journal of Orthopsychiatry, 47,* 250–263.

Porritt, D. (1979). Social support in crisis: Quantity or quality? *Social Science and Medicine, 13A,* 715–721.

Purcell, K., Brady, K., Chi, H., Muser, J., Mulk, L., Gordon, N., & Means, J. (1969). The effect on asthma in children of experimental separation from the family. *Psychosomatic Medicine, 31,* 144–164.

Reed, D., McGee, D., Yano, K., & Feinleib, M. (1983). Social networks and CHD among Japanese men in Hawaii. *American Journal of Epidemiology, 117,* 384–396.

Renne, C. M., & Creer, T. L. (1985). Asthmatic children and their families. *Developmental and Behavioral Pediatrics, 6,* 41–81.

Roberts, A., & Reinhardt, L. (1980). The behavioral management of chronic pain: Long-term follow-up with comparison groups, *Pain, 8,* 151–162.

Roghmann, K. J., & Haggerty, R. J. (1973). Daily stress, illness, and use of health services in young families. *Pediatric Research, 7,* 520–526.

Ruberman, W., Weinblatt, E., Goldberg, J. D., & Chaudray, B. S. (1984). Psychosocial influences on mortality after myocardial infarction. *New England Journal of Medicine, 311,* 552–559.

Sandler, I., Wolchik, S., & Braver, S. (1985). Social support and children of divorce. In I. G. Sarason & B. R. Sarason (Eds.), *Social support: Theory, research, and applications* (pp. 371–389). The Hague: Martinus Nijhoff.

Sandler, L. (1965). Child-rearing practices of mothers of asthmatic children. *Journal of Asthma Research, 2,* 215–256.

Schafer, L. C., McCaul, K. D., & Glasgow, R. E. (1986). Supportive and non-supportive family behaviors: Relationships to adherence and metabolic control in persons with- Type I diabetics. *Diabetes Care, 9*, 179–185.

Schoenbach, V. J., Kaplan, B. H., Fredman, L., & Kleinbaum, D. G. (1986). Social ties and mortality in Evans County Georgia. *American Journal of Epidemiology, 123*, 577–591.

Simonds, J. F. (1979). Emotions and compliance in diabetic children. *Psychosomatics, 20*, 544–551.

Singer, N. J. & Baum, A. (Eds.), *The handbook of environmental psychology*. Hillsdale, NJ: Erlbaum.

Spivack, G., Platt, J. J., & Shure, M. D. (1976). *The problem-solving approach to adjustment*. San Francisco: Jossey-Bass.

Sullivan, B. J. (1979). Adjustment in diabetic adolescent girls: I. Development of the diabetic adjustment scale. *Psychosomatic Medicine, 41*, 119–126.

Taylor, S. E., Whitman, R. R., & Wood, J. V. (1984). Attributions, beliefs about control in adjustments to breast cancer. *Journal of Personality and Social Psychology, 46*, 489–502.

Thoits, P. A. (1985). Social support and psychological well-being: Theoretical possibilities. In I. G. Sarason & B. R. Sarason (Eds.), *Social support: Theory, research, and application*. The Hague. Martinus Nijhoff.

Turk, D. C., & Rudy, T. E. (1986). Assessment of cognitive factors in pain: A worthwhile enterprise? *Journal of Consulting and Clinical Psychology, 54*, 760–768.

Wallston, B. S., Whitcher-Alagna, S., DeVellis, B. M., & DeVellis, R. F. (1983). Social support and physical health. *Health Psychology, 2*, 367–391.

Welin, L., Svardsudd, K., Ander-Peciva, S., Tibblin, G., Tibblin, B., & Larsson, G. (1985). Prospective study of social influences on mortality. *Lancet, 2*, 915–918.

Williams, C. A., Beresford, S. A. A., James, S. A., La Croix, A. Z., Strogatz, D. S., Wagner, E. H., Kleinbaum, D. G., Cutchin, L. M., & Ibrahim, M. A. (1985). The Edgecome County high blood pressure control program: III. Social support, social stressors, and treatment dropout. *American Journal of Public Health, 75*, 483–486.

Wingard, D. L. (1984). A sex differential in morbidity, mortality, and lifestyles. *Annual Review of Public Health, 5*, 433–458.

Wortman, C. B., & Dunkel-Schetter, C. (1979). Interpersonal relationships and cancer: A theoretical analysis. *Journal of Social Issues, 35*, 120–155.

CHAPTER 17

Social Support During Extreme Stress: Consequences and Intervention

STEVAN E. HOBFOLL AND MARY ANN PARRIS STEPHENS
Kent State University

Social support has received enormous attention as a source of resistance in combating the negative effects of stress. Indeed, reviews indicate that people who have socially supportive relationships are less likely to experience a wide range of negative physical and psychological health consequences (Cohen & Wills, 1985; Sarason & Sarason, 1985). The question most often addressed in these studies pertains to the positive effects of social support, that is, whether it directly aids well-being or whether it is particularly beneficial under high-stress conditions (Cohen & Wills, 1985; Wilcox, 1981). This emphasis is based on two preconceptions, (1) that social support has a positive effect and (2) that the effect of social support does not depend on the nature of the stressor, only its intensity.

Some researchers, however, have wondered whether social support has such a wide-reaching positive effect (Hobfoll, 1985a; Hobfoll & London, 1986; Riley & Eckenrode, 1986; Rook, 1984); surely not all social ties are supportive. In part, the belief that social support is a social panacea, able to meet the demands produced by all stressors, has been promulgated as an artifact of research that uses total stress scores (i.e., adding together disparate events to obtain an aggregate score). Because the standard method of ascertaining the degree to which people confront stressors is the stressful life events list method, which presents events ranging from the most benign to the most devastating (Dohrenwend, Krasnoff, Askenasy, & Dohrenwend, 1978; Holmes & Rahe, 1967; Sarason, Johnson, & Siegel, 1978), what are observed are the stress reactions to a disparate group of demands.

When the life events method is applied to the study of the stress-limiting effects of social support, it often is found that social support has an overall positive effect (Cohen & Wills, 1985; Sarason & Sarason, 1985). Such a finding, however, is actually the summation of social support's positive, negative, and neutral influence on the individual events. These studies thus indicate that social support has a positive effect when people face multiple stressors, but they offer no information about the nature of that effect in regard to a particular stressor.

A problem arises when one searches for alternatives to the life events list method, as there has been little theory or research regarding categories of events. Without categories of events, researchers would be forced to examine social support's effect on every event. Events could, however, be categorized. Then the effectiveness of social support for different kinds of stressors could be compared. In this chapter, we will discuss the special properties of one broad category of stress, the major stressors, and how social support is likely to interact with stress-related demands during highly stressful circumstances. We will concentrate on stress related to illness and to war. It is even unfortunate that *social support* is the term that has been coined, as our argument will be that the supportiveness of social ties waxes and wanes as stressful events are confronted and take their toll on the resources of those involved. We will explore the positive and negative effects of social support on both the provider and the recipient of support. Finally, we will draw up a blueprint for social support interventions for people confronting major life stressors.

THE CONCEPTS OF SOCIAL SUPPORT AND STRESS

Social support has been defined in many ways, perhaps the most common one being that social support is a vague notion about what people who are socially connected receive. In another sense, social support is seen as a commodity that is transferred in the commerce of social interaction that is intended to aid the recipient.

In one of the first conceptualizations of social support, Gerald Caplan (1974) suggested that social support aids individuals by providing feedback, validation, materials, and a sense that they can master their environments. More recent theory-driven research by Irwin and Barbara Sarason and their colleagues (Sarason, Shearin, Pierce, & Sarason, 1987), suggests that social integration and attachment to significant others are the central ingredients in social support. Their research highlighted the attachment to significant others, a point of view that is consistent with Bowlby's (1980) thinking on the importance of primary social attachments throughout life. House (1981), in contrast, focused more on the actual transaction of emotional concern, instrumental aid, and information that represents social support.

Hobfoll and Stokes (1988) argued that because there is evidence that both social integration and supportive exchanges offset the negative effects of stressors, social support should be defined to reflect both axes. Thus, we define social support as those social interactions or relationships that provide actual assistance or a feeling of attachment to a person or group that is perceived as caring or loving. Social support defined in this way encompasses both social connectedness and supportive interactions. Measurements of social support should then reflect either or both of these elements and should make clear what aspect of support they are assessing. Being the products of social interactions, we should expect both costs and benefits.

Stress is most commonly defined as an imbalance between stressors or demands, on one hand, and coping capacity or resistance resources, on the other hand (Cohen, Kamarck, & Mermelstein, 1983; Gentry & Kobasa, 1984; Lazarus & Folkman, 1984; Wilcox & Vernberg, 1985). According to the balance perspective, when demands outweigh coping capacity, stress follows. When coping capacity outweighs resources, an underload ensues that is also stressful. Hobfoll (1988) contended that this approach to stress is tautological and that research does not support some of the model's basic tenets.

If demands are defined as internal or external events that challenge resources (Lazarus & Folkman, 1984; McGrath, 1970), then stressful events can be known only when they challenge individuals' coping capacity. Coping capacity or resources, in turn, are those internal or external qualities or mechanisms that counteract the effects of stressors or demands. Thus, the balance model leaves us without any anchor point: A is defined by virtue of B, and B is defined by virtue of A. Without a clear anchor point, both demand and resources may be known only after the fact. We cannot know beforehand what will constitute a demand or a resource. If, for example, a potential coping resource does not ameliorate the negative effects of stressors, then according to this model, it is not a resource.

In addition, the balance model does not indicate what will result in a demand; it does not indicate whether the demand will be internal or external, positive or negative events, hassles or major stressors. Demand is purely the perception thereof. Again, this may be determined only after the fact and even then only by relying on idiographic accounts: that is, was it demanding as perceived by individual X? This kind of open-ended approach does not reflect our current knowledge about what kinds of experiences are stressful, as research strongly implies that undesirable events are those perceived as stressful (Thoits, 1983). People generally agree on which events are undesirable (Dohrenwend et al., 1978). Further, by not demarcating a border between internal thoughts and external events, researchers are apt to study symptoms of neurosis rather than reactions to stressors (Dohrenwend, Dohrenwend, Dodson, & Shrout, 1984). So, for instance, being irritated in traffic is seen as a stressor, whereas it may be a symptom of high-trait anxiety. This latter problem also applies to definitions of stress as "that which the individual perceives as stressful or uncomfortable" (Lazarus & Folkman, 1984; Houston, 1987), as such definitions are after the fact and fail to distinguish between a response to the environment and a response to internal psychopathology.

Finally, the balance model postulates that underload is also stressful. However, there is little evidence that underload is stressful on other than a physiological level. After some 30 years of stress research, underload has not received much more than anecdotal support (Hobfoll, 1988).

THE CONSERVATION OF RESOURCES MODEL

Hobfoll (1988) offered another stress model, termed the *model of conservation of resources.* This model is argued to be more comprehensive and less tautological and better reflects the current empirical evidence than does the popular balance perspective. The model of conservation of resources defines stress as a reaction to the environment in which there is a perceived threat of a net loss of resources, a perceived net loss of resources, or a perception that an investment of resources is not producing a net gain. Although personal perceptions are important to this model, they are seen as having broad social consensus, a view that differs markedly from more idiographic approaches that rely on individual perceptions of stressfulness (Cohen et al., 1983; Lazarus & Folkman, 1984; McGrath, 1970).

Resources, then, are the single unit of the model, and unlike demands and coping capacity in the balance model, resources are also clearly defined: resources are those objects, personal characteristics, conditions, or energies that are valued by the individual or group or that serve as a means for attaining these objects, personal characteristics, conditions, or energies. These resources may thus be measured before stress by the individual or by a social referent group. Most resources are seen as culturally valued, and so normative data may be gathered concerning the value of loss or gain of resources. Again, rather than envisaging individual perceptions as the *primum mobile,* the model suggests that social groups share values.

According to this model, stress occurs when individuals judge their environment as causing a loss of resources or when they are not gaining resources following an investment of other resources. This is an action view of stress that stems from the underlying assumption that individuals strive to construct a world in which they are protected, comfortable, loved, and esteemed. It envisions people as not passively waiting for stressors to occur but as actors who monitor their environment and seek to improve their situation, or at least to minimize any deterioration of their situation. This action view also distinguishes the conservation of resources model from other stress models that are reactive approaches (i.e., begin from the point of reactions to stressful occurrences).

Such a view is consistent with Epstein's (1980, 1984) cognitive—experiential self-theory that postulates that everyone unwittingly develops a personal theory of reality that structures their experiences and guides their behavior. The basis for constructing this theory, says Epstein, is to maintain a favorable level of pleasure and self-esteem and to assimilate daily reality. Underlying this theory is the assumption that individuals invest not only in their goals but also in an approach to life that preserves their cognitive schema. The model of conservation of resources would further have it that these schemata are similar for people in similar social groups (e.g., families, cultures). Both models regard as stressful those circumstances that disturb the maintenance of pleasure or positive self-regard or the value system that underlies them.

Another important aspect of the conservation of resources model is what it says about resource investment. Because the loss of resources is counteracted mainly by the investment of other resources (e.g., money, favors, self-esteem), resources tend to diminish as a result of the process of coping itself. In this way, the conservation of resources model regards the process of investing resources as the essence of coping. Self-esteem, for instance, may be used to offset a sense of loss owing to unemployment, but if the loss sequence cannot be turned around, self-esteem itself will be lost (Pearlin, Lieberman, Menaghan, & Mullan, 1981). In this way, the process of investing resources is also envisaged as possibly contributing to further stress; that is, using resources engenders costs. Schönpflug (1985) demonstrated this principle experimentally in sophisticated laboratory analogues of stressful life events.

The model of conservation of resources also outlines how specific resources, such as social support, may aid stress resistance. First, by providing a feeling of attachment, social support limits the sense of loneliness that emerges without such ties. In addition, social support prevents a feeling of losing other resources. By being connected to a social network that offers esteem, love, and affection, people are likely not to feel that their efforts to maintain family and friendship ties, to provide financially for their families, and to fulfill their families' needs have gone unrewarded. Social support may also directly prevent or limit resource loss and thereby insulate people from stressful circumstances. So, for example, people display social cues and reminders encouraging health care and maintenance, thereby preventing an array of problems that might otherwise occur.

Social support may act in two more ways after there is a loss. First, it may provide resources that are lost. So, money, for instance, may be replaced and the loss of a loved one may be counteracted by the provision of love, attention, and caring for the needs of the bereaved. Such replacement of resources may be direct, as in the case of receiving money when cash is needed, or it may be indirect or symbolic, such as receiving love that promotes esteem when a job loss has lowered one's self-esteem.

Second, following a loss, social support may help implement other latent resources. People often have a resource that they fail to use but that social support may foster, enhance, or make usable. An example is moving a couch. One may have the strength to lift a couch, but not the leverage to move it. Even a weak, but willing, other can provide the balance necessary to implement fully that strength. Similarly, supporters may remind people that they have a strong sense of mastery or the necessary skills to overcome their problems and may guide them in using these potential resources.

THE NATURE OF MAJOR STRESSORS

The model of conservation of resources postulates that stress follows a loss of resources. When reviewing common-event lists (Dohrenwend et al., 1978; Sarason et al., 1978), we might question whether minor hassles are stressful because they represent loss, although the conservation-of-resources model does suggest that even minor hassles are stressful to the extent that they represent or cause loss. Arguing this point, however, would require more space than available here and would be somewhat tangential to the purpose of this chapter. We need argue only that major stressor events clearly are loss events. Loss of a job, loss of a loved one, serious illness, rape, and forced retirement are a few examples of these. Indeed, a review of event lists shows that all those events that receive high weighting (i.e., are judged as being highly stressful) constitute a loss or the threat of a loss. Major stressors frequently are not circumscribed events but are more accurately depicted as sequences of events in which multiple losses occur. In discussing divorce, for instance, Wilcox (1986) described how it produces a loss of companionship, income, and child care assistance in a linked sequence.

Still another property of major stressors is that they are prolonged and often irrevocable. When one loses one's job, for instance, it may be months before one finds a suitable new job. The death of a loved one and a mastectomy are events that may not be reversed, no matter what efforts are made. Because major stressors evolve in sequences and are prolonged or irrevocable, they draw on resources for prolonged periods. Recall that coping depletes those resources that are used for resistance. In the case of social support, it appears that only the most robust social networks may continue to provide effective social support in such circumstances, as the use of support drains the resource reservoir (Mitchell & Hodson, 1986; Riley & Eckenrode, 1986).

Recent discussion of resources proposed that they are most effective when they fit situational needs (Cohen & McKay, 1984; Hobfoll, 1985b, 1986). Because both the nature of the stressors and the available resource pool change after stressors appear, fit must also be seen as evolving. That is, resources that aid stress resistance at one time may become burdens at another. This is especially true for major stressors, as they are the ones most likely to change interpersonal relationships, destabilize environments and alter the way that people view themselves and their world. This is a qualitative difference between minor and major stressors; perhaps one definition of major stressors is that they challenge the stability of the individual's presumptive world (Janoff-Bulman & Timko, 1987).

Social support is a potentially valuable resource in the face of major stressors. After stressful events people turn to those closest to them as a source of strength. It is those closest to us who carry our burdens when we are incapable; who offer a shoulder on which to cry, shelter from adversity, and solace from grief. Significant others share their resources to help those for whom they care through these most difficult periods of life. Yet we also know that this is an ideal and not always a reality. On one hand, it is usually those most intimate who are willing to confront the obligation and stress of the caregiver role. However, crises often happen to families or social groups, making resource demands on the whole group and thus leaving no one strong enough to support the others. Moreover, it is often those who would most likely provide support who are the cause of the major stress, through death, divorce, or illness. In such cases the cause of the stress also results in an absence of support sources.

ILLNESS AS A MAJOR STRESSOR

One of the greatest and most common stressors is physical illness, as it threatens both the victim and his or her social network. The loss for the individual involves independence, social mobility, capacity to work, exposure to pain, and threat of disfigurement and death. For those close to the victim, the threats are potential loss of a loved one, loss of the relationship as it was, and loss of one's own independence owing to caregiving demands. Confronted with illness, people especially need supportive actions to help meet instrumental and emotional needs. As illness is often long term, this creates an unusual demand on supportive relationships, as both intensity and chronicity are likely to deplete resources and test the limits of the supportive social systems. To illustrate the model of conservation of resources, we will first examine the illness of a child and how it stresses the mother-caregiver.

In the first study, Israeli mothers of children receiving medical care were interviewed at the time of their first encounter with the medical facility. The children were being seen either for a minor ailment (e.g., cold, influenza without complications, sore throat) or for a possibly serious illness. The latter group included the mothers of children who were hospitalized for high fever, convulsions, and meningitis and outpatients who were being seen for neurological, heart, and asthmatic disorders. Over the year the children remained well (controls), were ill and became well (acute illness), or remained ill (chronic illness). We assessed the women's sense of mastery over their future, the support they generally and recently received, their intimacy with significant others, and their discomfort in seeking aid.

At the time of their initial contact with the medical system, women who had a high sense of mastery experienced less psychological distress (a combined measure of anxiety and depression) than did women with a low sense of mastery (Hobfoll & Lerman, 1988). Women who generally received social support—measured in terms of their usual receipt of supportive interactions—also had less initial psychological distress than did women who generally lacked supportive interactions. However, when controlling for levels of generally received support, the women who had greatest psychological distress received the most supportive interactions at that time (i.e., recent support). These findings are illustrated in Figure 17.1. Although social support contributes to better stress resistance, the support system is being called upon during the process, with those in the most distress seeking the most support at that time.

At the time of follow-up, one year later, both mastery and intimacy with spouse were found to be related to psychological distress, so that the women with high mastery and high intimacy experienced the lowest psychological distress. It was also found at follow-up that high-mastery women used both aspects of social support (intimacy and supportive interactions) more effectively than did the women who lacked these resources. Specifically, the low-mastery group were either not affected or were negatively affected by social support, whereas the high-mastery group gained particular benefit from the social support they received.

For the women whose children were initially well and remained well and the women whose children were ill and became well, the more social support they generally received through supportive interactions, the lower their levels of psychological distress were. For the women whose children were chronically ill, however, the more supportive interactions they had, the more psychologically dis-

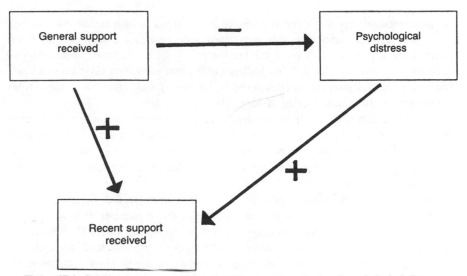

Figure 17.1. Relation between general and recent support received and psychological distress.

tressed they were. The reversal of the effects of supportive interactions again suggests an overtaxed system, in which obtaining support itself may become a burden. In this regard, although requesting support continues to be necessary, the debt people feel they owe others and the degree to which they feel they are intruding on others' lives represent an ever-heavier albatross when the stressors are chronic.

These complex findings can be summarized as indicating that social support has a mixed effect. Women with more intimate and giving supportive ties experience lower levels of psychological distress than do those who lack such relationships. Women who are low in mastery and women who have chronic major stress, however, may find social support to be an added burden. Further evidence from this study indicates that as chronic stress continues, personal and social resources (i.e., intimacy and comfort seeking aid) that normally ensure the receipt of supportive interactions no longer contribute to the receipt of supportive acts (Hobfoll & Lerman, 1989). This means that the continued need for social support depletes both the value of the support received and the ability of other resources to help mobilize supportive interactions.

In regard to the model of conservation of resources, it appears that social support aids stress resistance but that the fit between stressor and resource changes as the stress changes. It also appears that not only the positive contributions of social support become depleted, but the resources that contribute to social support (i.e., intimacy, discomfort in seeking aid) also are drained. Socially supportive interactions initially provide sustenance amidst the heavy emotional and instrumental demands placed on mothers, but as the stressors continue, the support itself becomes a burden.

These findings also provide insight into how intimacy both contributes to supportive acts and has an independent positive effect. In this regard, women with intimate relations receive more supportive interactions, which results in less psychological distress, and their intimacy itself independently contributes to lower psychological distress. This point further buttresses the conceptualization of social support suggested by Hobfoll and Stokes (1988) that envisions support as a combination of social integration (measured as intimacy) and supportive interactions (measured as the actual receipt of support).

Other research also points to the draining of caregivers' resources when meeting the needs of a chronically ill family member. In the next study we will detail the role of social relations in patients' recovery from a serious illness, such as stroke, as well as the impact that giving support has on caregivers to chronically ill children and older adults.

Stephens, Kinney, Norris, and Ritchie (1987) investigated the positive and negative effects of interactions between geriatric stroke patients and their family members after the patients' discharge from a rehabilitation hospital. Recovering from the disabling effects of a stroke is often a long process with an uncertain outcome, in which functioning is often severely impaired. Most patients never fully recover, and many become quite dependent on family and friends for assistance and emotional support. The loss of resources is great, in that many of these individuals have lost not only their ability to function physically but also important elements of being an adult, a sense of independence and self-reliance.

For patients in such a crisis, it is not difficult to understand how instrumental support (e.g., provision of care, transportation, shopping) might be helpful during their recovery. Such support may provide direct relief from fatigue and the inability to meet one's basic personal care needs. In contrast, expressive support may operate more subtly and indirectly by enhancing feelings of self-worth. Encouragement, attention to concerns, affection, and empathic listening are examples of this kind of support. Although it might seem obvious that both emotional and instrumental support are beneficial, this is not necessarily the case. Social support, it must be recalled, occurs within a network of social interactions, and such interactions are not consistently positive. Although family members may intend that their interactions with patients be supportive, the patients may perceive these interactions as unnecessary or unwanted. Even the most supportive relationships may sometimes be characterized by negative exchanges. So, too, the act of providing support itself may be loaded with unwanted obligations and feelings of dependence on the part of the patient (Fisher, Nadler, & DePaulo, 1983). Thus, family members may not only provide social supports, but they may be associated with social problems as well.

Because support may be characterized by both positive and negative aspects, Stephens and her colleagues assessed positive and negative interactions in two domains of support, instrumental (e.g., receiving needed or wanted aid with personal care vs. receiving unneeded or unwanted aid with personal care) and expressive (e.g., receiving helpful suggestions vs. receiving unwanted advice). Although the findings of this study indicated that negative interactions were reported less often than were positive ones, only the negative interactions were related to the patients' psychological adjustment. Moreover, patients reporting more social problems in their family networks also had a lower morale and more psychiatric symptoms than did those reporting fewer family problems even when the levels of patients' physical and mental impairments were controlled.

A closer examination of the negative interactions revealed that only negative interactions associated with expressive functions, and not those associated with instrumental aid, predicted poor psychological adjustment. In other words, positive emotional interactions and positive and negative instrumental interactions did not affect psychological well-being. It is not likely that these findings could be attributed to the distressed patients' creating conflict with their family members, as the patients reporting and those not reporting social problems did not differ in the amount of positive interactions they experienced. This also indicates that the distressed patients were not simply being more negative.

The fact that the patients' reported problems with instrumental aid were not related to psychological adjustment may be linked to the degree of the patients' functional dependence on others. Thus the assistance judged as negative might actually have been needed and so might have been perceived as a kind of "necessary evil." Alternatively, even inadequate instrumental aid may have been interpreted as a sign of love and caring and therefore was overlooked. Further, individuals may have restricted their negative feelings about instrumental aid for fear of being cut off, leaving them unable to survive or resulting in their institutionalization.

Perceptions that others were not meeting their emotional needs or were sometimes intrusive may reflect the patients' sense of helplessness in the fulfillments of their emotional needs. This personal impotence increases the importance attributed to family ties. The impact of family problems is further magnified owing to the failure of negative interactions to conform to expectations of involvement with family. In this regard, the patients may have had an idealized image of how their families should react to their plight. It often is difficult for the family to respond to such idealized norms (Bar-Tal, Bar-Zohar, Greenberg, & Herman, 1977). Thus, when problems do occur, they are especially salient and their effects are magnified. In addition, these negative interactions may reflect more general conflict and tension in the family network during a major life crisis.

When we applied the conservation of resources model, it became clear that the patients had suffered tremendous functional and personal losses as a result of their stroke. Negative interactions represented even more losses for the patients, because their expectations of recovering their losses and recuperating were not met. However, the fact that the negative interactions associated with expressive needs were related to poorer psychological adjustment, whereas those involving more tangible and direct assistance were not, illustrates the accounting of net losses. The patients were acutely aware of their losses, in terms of both their physical limitations and the dependency that these limitations imposed on them. Although instrumental aid may have been judged as negative at times, because it might have served as a reminder of important losses, such aid produced a gain of resources by enabling patients to complete many basic tasks in their daily living. Thus, losses and gains of resources may have offset each other, and thus did not influence the patients' psychological well-being. In contrast, feelings that one's emotional life was negatively affected by others further contributed to the patients' already great sense that their personal autonomy and their own value in the relationship had been jeopardized. That is, their emotional losses made them more sensitive and increased their mental health problems.

In the next study, Kinney and Stephens (1987) were interested in the cumulative debilitating effects of daily stressors on ongoing care for an older family member with a dementing illness, primarily Alzheimer's disease. In addition, they examined the possible buffering effects of small satisfactions or gains against the deleterious effects of the stressors. In their role as caregivers, these individuals expended a great deal of personal energy and time (often four or more years) in helping a family member whose dementing illness was gradually rendering them totally helpless, both physically and mentally.

The caregivers were mostly spouses and adult daughters of patients. These caregivers assessed both positive and negative daily events in several areas, including events associated with the patients' inability to participate in personal care activities (e.g., bathing, grooming) and in other daily activities (e.g., transportation), the patients' behavior (e.g., interactions with others, personal habits), their cognitive–emotional status (e.g., affect, degree of confusion), and the caregivers' social networks (e.g., help and understanding from family and friends).

Two striking patterns were detected. First, the events most strongly related to the caregivers' psychosocial well-being (anxiety, depression, hostility, somatization, and negative interpersonal relations) were not the tasks involving aid to patients in daily activities. Rather, those stressors involved in witnessing a loved one's declining behavioral and cognitive functioning were the most powerful predictors of emotional and social distress among caregivers. The next strongest predictor of caregivers' distress was the low levels of social support given to them for fulfilling their caregiving responsibilities.

Again, the emotional aspects of support the caregivers provided were more critical than instrumental ones in determining the psychosocial toll on the caregivers. There are several possible explanations. On one hand, those stressors associated with the patients' behavioral and cognitive limitations may have been especially symbolic to caregivers, in that they were constant reminders of the loss of an important adult relationship, such as with a spouse or a parent. Not only did dealing with problems related to the patients' aggression, wandering, inappropriate affect, and loss of memory remind the caregivers that their loved one's personality had changed dramatically and permanently, but it also reminded the caregivers of this person's inability to offer significant support in return. On the other hand, it might be the unpredictability of these problems that created a stressful situation. Although assisting patients in daily activities might tax one's personal resources, such activities usually can be scheduled. Behavioral and cognitive problems, in contrast, can occur at almost any time, thus requiring the caregivers' constant vigilance. Thus the loss of predictability and control over one's daily activities might have proved to be the source of stress.

Although exposure to ongoing stressors had a debilitating effect, those caregivers receiving help and understanding from family and friends in their caregiving efforts received both emotional and tangible gains that helped alleviate some of the daily stress of giving care. If, as the conservation of resources model suggests, providing support also drains resources, it is an important finding that when supporters are supported in their efforts, they are aided in their own stress resistance. Social support is not a bottomless well, but must be refilled.

As we already mentioned, this study analyzed the role of uplifting events as well. But rather than providing a buffer from stress, uplifting events were, in fact, predictors of poor psychosocial adjustment among caregivers. Those caregivers reporting more uplifting events in caregiving, especially uplifts connected to instrumental aid to the patient, also demonstrated more emotional distress. It is interesting to speculate on the nature of these associations.

It is possible that the appraisal of events as uplifting represents a form of coping with an inescapable and chronically stressful situation, including avoidance strategies and attempts at positive reappraisal (Lazarus & Folkman, 1984; Kobasa, 1979). That is, caregivers may have been attending only to the positive aspects of giving care and overlooking the negative, for example, recognizing the good feelings from being helpful and ignoring the physical exhaustion that accompanies such help. Or some caregivers might have initially regarded an event as stressful, but because the negative emotions that followed were too painful, they thus evaluated such events as being more positive, in order to make the losses more psychologically tolerable. Although such emotion-focused strategies may be effective in managing emotional responses to the immediate stressful situation, this cognitive "hocus-pocus" does not change the actual mounting losses. It appears that these actual losses inevitably determine the outcome.

Supporting this argument, other research (Stephens, Norris, Kinney, Ritchie, & Grotz, 1988) also indicated that caregivers engaging in some forms of emotion-focused coping strategies experience greater psychological and social distress. Thus, the caregivers' efforts to cope with a highly stressful situation by either selectively attending to it or changing its meaning do not appear to contribute to good mental health. Where there is a real expenditure of personal resources over long periods of time, cognitively transforming real losses into imagined gains or avoiding dealing with the fact that real losses have occurred does not appear to be psychologically beneficial. This finding supports the environmental emphasis of the conservation of resources model, which theorizes that objective loss and gain must be emphasized and that perceptions are not the sine qua non of stress.

WAR AS A MAJOR STRESSOR

The contribution of social support to stress resistance during extreme stress is also illustrated in the study of war, the ultimate stressor. Individuals have little control over their lives during war, and they and their loved ones are threatened with death, serious injury, and the loss of valued circumstances (e.g., freedom, security). Discussions of social support's effects on combatants is as old as military history. David and Jonathan in the Bible developed a friendship of love evolving from their joint efforts in battling the Philistines. The British regimental system relies on forces selected from the same geographic areas, as they are likely to have common bonds well before their entry into battle, for example, men fighting with men whose fathers were comrades. Winston Churchill's speeches during World War II were famous for rousing the British people's flagging spirits and a shared belief in ultimate victory. There has also been much discussion of the additional wound that Vietnam veterans received on coming home to a lack of support for their efforts to serve their country. However, there has been little empirical investigation of the effects of social support on withstanding the extreme stress of war. For the combatants, social support is necessary to secure their safety and to fight off the feeling of chaos and impending doom that accompanies battle. For the loved ones at home, social support is a resource that can aid their efforts to face life's ongoing demands despite the threatened loss of loved ones and the actual loss or severe injury of loved ones.

Hobfoll and London (1986) examined the effects of having loved ones suddenly mobilized into military roles. They interviewed Israeli women whose close male relatives were mobilized during the 1982 Israel–Lebanon War, in regard to their sense of self-esteem and mastery, their intimacy with friends and family, and the amount of support they received during the first week of the war. Their reactions were measured by assessing their anxiety and depression.

Mastery and self-esteem were found to be related to lower levels of psychological distress among these women. Both intimacy with friends and amount of support received, however, were related to greater levels of psychological distress. Women who were high in self-esteem and mastery, in particular, were negatively affected by the availability of social support, assessed as intimacy and supportive interactions. The debriefing revealed that those women who had intimate ties and who exchanged support thus exposed themselves to the stress of others, what we called a *pressure-cooker effect* and what Riley and Eckenrode (1986) termed *stress contagion*. That is, when discussing prospects of the war, having social support meant that women would be privy to rumor mills and to unceasing discussion of events about which they could do nothing. For the high-mastery, high-self-esteem women, such an approach to stress resistance was antithetical to their preferred style, which was more action oriented. Further, social psychological findings pertaining to decision making in groups indicated that those groups were more likely to draw extreme conclusions, termed *risky shifts*, than were individuals (Myers & Lamm, 1976). So, by having social support, these women were likely to be part of a social environment that drew the most negative conclusions based on news reports and rumor mills. Rather than limiting their sense of threatened loss, social support exaggerated this sense of loss, by both sharing the threatened and actual loss of others and projecting exaggerated potential losses.

For a second group of young Israeli women, possessing intimate ties characterized by affection and openness was not found to affect their anxiety, anger, or behavioral adjustment one year following the major period of fighting. Possessing intimate ties was an effective resource, however, for men who were themselves likely to be involved in the fighting (Hobfoll, London, & Orr, 1988). For this second group of women, the war-related stressors were past, and whatever psychological sequelae remained were not affected by social support. In contrast, the men were still likely to be called for duty in Lebanon. It is also likely that they carried the stressfulness of war-related events with them in their memories, as, unlike the women, many of them had been in combat. Witnessing such horrible events is known to have a long-term intrusive effect on memory (Horowitz & Solomon, 1975). Social support appeared to be an important resource for alleviating this personal conflict which continued long after the physical conflict had ceased. Such findings support the research on medical stress (Hobfoll & Lieberman, 1987; Hobfoll & Walfisch, 1984) and general stressors (Brown & Harris, 1978), which concluded that having a few confidants is critical to stress resistance.

Studies of the experience of Israeli combatants also indicated how social support aids individuals confronting extreme stress and how the kind of social support that is effective changes. This process is illustrated in a study of Israeli soldiers who fought in the Israel–Lebanon War, based on a sample of all those men who broke down in combat and a matched sample of men in the same combat zones who did not break down (Solomon, Mikulincer, & Hobfoll, 1986). When men confront more intense battle conditions, their stress increases; the consequences of this may be seen in their resultant breakdowns, termed *combat stress reaction* (CSR). This investigation showed that as the battle intensity increased, the incidence of CSR increased as well. Greater social support from buddies, junior officers, and noncommissioned officers helped offset this effect, however. In part, social support was seen as aiding stress resistance because it limited the feelings of loneliness that preceded CSR.

Both instrumental and emotional support were important in this context. Instrumental support ensured safety and organization amidst the inevitable chaos of battle. Emotional support helped sustain the group's morale and prevented individuals from feeling cut off from or overwhelmed by the real threats around them. Here we can observe how instrumental support helped limit the objective threat and how emotional support helped limit the subjective threat.

Family support, in contrast, seemed to be a burden on soldiers during combat (Solomon & Benbenishty, 1986). Soldiers' family ties are symbolic of what they and their families will lose if they are seriously wounded or killed. When they return home, however, family support becomes an important resource (Solomon, Mikulincer, & Hobfoll, 1987). At this time, social support from family was found to limit the incidence and severity of the soldiers' posttraumatic stress disorder.

These findings concerning war again illustrate that social support is effective to the extent it meets the individual's current needs. Far from being a social cure-all, it acts as a resource, a burden, and a neutral element, depending on the nature of the loss and the extent to which what is being lost may be replaced by social support or whether such support symbolizes further potential loss. Thus for women who are awaiting word from the front, social support increases their sense of loss. For women who have already dealt with their losses, social support has no apparent effect. For men who are confronting losses that may be prevented or limited by social support, the value of this resource is realized. Perhaps this points to the obvious, that social relationships have strong effects but that these effects depend on the nature of those relationships and the circumstances in which they are being asked for help. Although this is obvious, it is far from the rose-colored perception of support that was envisaged in the early phases of the social support literature.

INTERVENTION EFFORTS BASED ON SOCIAL SUPPORT

Traditional treatment following exposure to extreme stressors has focused on intervention for those who develop severe emotional disorders and who come to the attention of treatment providers. This approach does not emphasize prevention or community outreach. In addition, by waiting until the full-blown disorder is revealed and by treating the victims as patients, traditional treatment methods may actually exacerbate the chronicity of the disorder. Drug treatment and traditional psychotherapy are unlikely to be the treatment of choice for the majority of those exposed to extreme stressors, as we shall see in this section. Further, many people who do not develop extreme reactions or who do not come to the attention of mental health service providers nevertheless can benefit from greater attention than the traditional hospital-based programs provide.

Professional intervention aimed at exploiting the principles of social support to alleviate the consequences of extreme stress has not been well developed. One of the only systematic areas of study concerning the effects of professional intervention using social support on reactions to extreme stress focuses on CSR. Israel has, unfortunately, been a living laboratory for such research (Milgram, 1986; Spielberger, Sarason, & Milgram, 1982). These intervention efforts have tended to combine principles of crisis intervention (Miller & Iscoe, 1963) with principles of social support, but we shall see that crisis intervention is itself conceptually related to social support (see also Killilea, 1982, regarding this point).

During the Israel–Lebanon conflict, soldiers who broke down in combat-related conditions either were sent to treatment centers in Israel where they received traditional psychiatric care, or they were treated in frontline mental health units near the scene of battle but protected enough to afford safety. Traditional treatment consisted of psychotherapy, chemotherapy, and personal visitation. Psychiatric treatment in Israel resembles that in North America; the training of mental health professionals relies on English-language literature; and many of the professionals were trained in North America. In addition, owing to the positive regard in which soldiers are held, those receiving treatment receive the best that the society can provide.

Frontline treatment, in contrast, followed the regimen first set by the American psychiatrist Salmon during World War I (Salmon, 1919), who emphasized the importance of proximity, immediacy, expectancy, and community in treating psychiatric casualties of traumatic stress. These principles were translated into treatment by providing care close to the time and place of the precipitating event, by giving soldiers a clear message that they would soon return to their units, and by keeping them in the military community rather than releasing them to the civilian community. Although this strategy was used in this case by professional mental health workers, it relies much more on the nonpsychiatric approaches and expectancies typically found in social support, that is, (1) one-to-one contact, (2) no labeling of disorders, (3) an everyday rather than a medical setting, (4) expectations of continuing daily routines, (5) "naive" expectancy of full recovery, and (6) contact near the time of the event.

During the Israel–Lebanon War the choice of traditional psychiatric versus frontline treatment modalities was determined solely by logistics at the time of evacuation. This led to the possibility of comparing the effectiveness of the two methods (Solomon & Benbenishty, 1986). The researchers found that soldiers treated at frontline units returned to their army units significantly more frequently than did those treated traditionally. The sooner that the soldiers were treated, the more likely they were to return to their units than were soldiers who were treated longer after the time of the stressor events. Further, the more clearly the soldiers understood that their therapists expected them to return to their units, the more likely they were to return.

The significance of returning to the unit clarifies the importance of frontline treatment. Of those returning to their units, only 38% had PTSD one year after the cease fire. Of those who did not return to their units, 74% had PTSD one year later, even though the original severity of their disorder did not differ from that of those who returned to their units. Seen in another way, 71% of soldiers who had none of these three principles applied to their treatment experienced PTSD one year later, whereas a much lower 40% who had all three principles applied to their treatment had PTSD.

The prolonged consequences of PTSD may be seen in a separate set of data that indicates that 59% of Israeli soldiers who broke down in combat during the 1973 Yom Kippur War were judged unfit for combat for the 1982 Lebanon conflict, compared with 25% of a matched (for age and time of induction) control group who did not originally have a psychiatric breakdown (Solomon, Oppenheimer, & Noy, 1986). This indicates how severe and prolonged the effects of CSR are. However, we should also point out that only 1% of the 1973-CSR group who were later judged fit for combat had a psychiatric breakdown in 1982, a figure not much different from that for breakdown in the control group (0.67% breakdown). This latter finding may be interpreted as indicating that those who psychologically recover from CSR are not psychologically fragile when faced with stressors similar to those that originally contributed to their breakdown. This is an important point because otherwise it would be possible to conclude that social support–based intervention was only masking the severity of initial responses or, worse, contributing to even more severe and delayed responding.

The principles of proximity, immediacy, expectancy, and community also were applied to two civilian disasters in Israel, a terrorist attack on a bus and a bus accident. In the first instance, no data on the effects of the intervention were reported, but the intervention is clearly detailed. In the second instance, some limited evaluative data are available. In 1978 two buses of Egged (pronounced Eg-ged) (the Israel bus cooperative whose staff have shares in the company) were attacked by terrorists while on a company outing. Eighteen people were killed and 25 were wounded. Egged immediately put into operation a crisis intervention model based on emerging principles of social support in which the company was organized as a therapeutic community (Zafrir, 1982). This intervention was based on the following principles: (1) the need to rely on existing social systems in aiding victims, (2) the need to organize social support from people in their own environment, and (3) the need to encourage contact with undamaged social structures, including family and friends, work, school, and social organizations.

These principles were translated into action immediately after the attack. First, the community reorganized its business structure into a support community by establishing emergency headquarters in Haifa and Tel Aviv, the principal evacuation points. In addition, special centers were set up in crisis areas and the main hospitals to which the survivors were admitted. These centers were staffed by professional, paraprofessional, and volunteer personnel from Egged. Immediately these centers began to list Egged members and their families involved in the incident, locate the survivors and the injured, aid in identifying the dead, coordinate the transportation of family members, and provide emotional and material help to the injured and bereaved. Members of the cooperative circulated through hospitals with the message that "Egged is here at your service."

The day following the attack, members of the cooperative continued accumulating information to identify the dead, to help inform families, and to aid in funeral arrangements. They also arranged transport to funerals (in the hundreds) and helped during the traditional week of Jewish mourning. During and following this period, Egged continued to provide transportation and contact among family members who, in many cases, were at separate treatment sites.

Egged managers were organized as surrogate fathers for children losing a father in the attack. Professional staff also coordinated the contact of children and adults with local therapeutic agents in their home communities. When they returned home, the Egged contact was transferred to Egged members in the local community, who continued to be supervised by professional mental health staff. From the time of the incident, schools and institutions also helped mobilize home-based support and rehabilitation.

Perhaps it is less important to mention also that psychotherapy and group therapy were arranged when warranted. Rather, it is the more simple, human touches of this intervention that are remarkable. Parties on Jewish festival days continued to be held for children, for instance, when family disruption might have caused them to be set aside. Presents were given to all hospitalized children; personal birthday gifts were given to children at the appropriate time for months following the incident; arrangements were made for the children to go to summer camp; transportation was organized for injured children; volunteers were provided for night duty for those whose injuries required this; and members of Egged who had been wounded in the Yom Kippur War and who had been successfully rehabilitated visited the injured. Overall, members of the cooperative were guided in how to convey the messages of social acceptance, joy that individuals survived, and a feeling that Egged shared their grief and responsibility for their recovery.

In the second incident, in June 1985, a bus filled with schoolchildren stalled on a railroad crossing and was struck by a train. Nineteen junior high school children and three adults were killed, and many others were injured seriously. Here as before, the principles of social support and crisis intervention were brought to bear on the problem (Toubiana, 1986, cited in Milgram & Hobfoll, 1986).

The principle of *proximity* was applied by insisting that all children attend school after the incident and that even truants be brought to school. Parents were also called and told that even if their child was upset or exhibiting minor illness, the school was the best place for him or her to be. *Immediacy* was translated into organizing the intervention to start the day after the accident. The event was discussed in the classrooms in place of normal routines. Students were encouraged to talk about the deceased, dedicate poems and pictures, participate in erecting a temporary monument at the school, and visit the injured. *Expectancy* was translated into the official theme enunciated by teachers and counselors alike, "Such events happen, but rarely. All will grieve and we will not forget this event. Some of your reactions may persist for a while; they are normal and you will recover fully soon." Finally, the principle of *community* was apparent in the school that was chosen as the site of intervention and in the repeated encouragement to school personnel and children that they must help one another recover. Because the school year was coming to a close, a decision was also made to organize a summer activity program in which children scoring high on symptom checklists could be further supervised and counseled. This would also maximize the children's sense of a stable community. Over half the age-peers of the victims participated in this program.

In evaluating their efforts, Toubiana reported that only three of the children from the school (other than the victims) approached local mental health facilities after the school-based intervention. This might indicate the success of the program, or it might indicate that traditional care remained taboo for the children. The initial follow-up of the children did not lead Toubiana to believe that this incident produced more than low-level psychiatric fallout. Unfortunately, those who have been so creative in applying social support intervention in cases of extreme stress have typically not reported good data to support the success of their programs (Gottlieb, 1988), and these two interventions are cases in point. Nonetheless, a qualitative process analysis is possible, and clearly these two civilian interventions implemented principles that more careful research has shown to be effective.

Finally, we will discuss briefly a program currently under way to aid primary supporters of back-injured patients (Hofien, 1986). In this intervention, spouses of recent severely back-injured patients have been targeted for intervention. Knowledge that they too are under considerable stress and are expected to be the principal supporter for their spouse led to a design in which spouses are trained in social support. This program is examining the effect of both providing support to spouses and training them how best to provide social support. Randomly assigned to one of three experimental conditions, the spouses receive social support and hear tapes that model and explain quality support, or hear tapes that model and explain quality support, or hear taped medical information (control). This intervention is based on empirical work like that by Stephens and colleagues (1987), which indicates that the supporters themselves need support, and findings by Lehman, Ellard, and Wortman (1986), which show that people often know in theory what support to provide but are ineffective in translating this into action. This intervention will examine whether lowering supporters' stress levels and modeling support provision enhances the support providers' effectiveness. It is unfortunate that we do not yet have data from such well-controlled studies as this one, but a review of support-based interventions stated that this kind of information should be soon in coming (Gottlieb, 1988).

A BLUEPRINT FOR INTERVENTION

The model of conservation of resources may be used to create a blueprint for intervention for victims of extreme stress (Hobfoll, 1988). Such a framework could help in both planning social support–based intervention and evaluating these efforts. In this section we will try to draw up such a blueprint, basing our thinking on the model and on empirical findings concerning social support during highly stressful circumstances.

Evaluation of Loss

First, the model demonstrates that the nature of the loss must be considered. This raises questions as to whether social support could counteract the loss or prevent further loss. Is it even possible that certain gains could be made with the help of social support? Group discussions by professionals and key informants who have experienced the relevant stressful circumstances could make these assessments, or questionnaires designed to determine the nature of the loss for individuals could evaluate them empirically. It is also important to consider at this point whether the loss should be confronted or whether it could be reinterpreted as a challenge (Kobasa & Puccetti, 1983). Some losses are so intense that they must be accepted, but even then, some aspects of the challenge awaiting victims may help them reframe what has occurred. So too, the loss may be such that social support only magnifies its extent or prevents individuals from relying on more appropriate resources.

Intensity of Support-based Intervention

The next point we must consider is whether social support intervention can be intense enough to counteract the stress reaction. There is no evidence, for instance, that social support is a substitute for psychotherapy for deeply disturbed individuals, and the interventions detailed earlier tended to use social support as an addendum to individual treatment, or they incorporated principles of social support into professional intervention. Gottlieb's (1988) review of social support–based interventions described many social support interventions as being rather superficial. This conclusion may be compared with the far-reaching efforts outlined in the reports by Toubiana and Zafrir mentioned earlier. It is easy to see how support-based intervention could be applied superficially. What the research on natural support systems indicates, however, is that effective support is intensive and is usually supplied by the closest loved ones. One notable exception to this is the various self-help groups, but when they are successful, they may be using the strength of the group and good organization to substitute for what natural ties provide. In fact, there is little empirical information on such groups' effectiveness.

Evaluation of Other Resources

Social support often has been evaluated with tunnel vision, excluding other resources that are involved in the process. Research that has looked at social support in conjunction with other resources has found its effects to interact with personal characteristics (Hobfoll & Lieberman, 1987; Kobasa & Puccetti, 1983; Lefcourt, Martin, & Selah, 1984), economic factors (Parry, 1986), and physical constitution (Kobasa, Maddi, & Courington, 1981). Evaluating social support in isolation thus gives rise to simplistic questions and answers and prevents the reliable application of research to practice. Social support is but one resource, and its effectiveness clearly depends on its being exploited in an ecological context that considers person–resource–environment fit.

Timing

The design of social support interventions must also take into consideration that both the stressor sequence and the effectiveness of social support are dynamic processes. Initial social support–based efforts may need to be modified and even withdrawn, depending on the nature of the stress reaction and the demands placed on victims. As stressors continue, or in the case of the most extreme stressors, efforts must also be made to support the supporters. Work by Stephens (Kinney & Stephens, 1987; Stephens et al., 1987) clearly suggests that the supporter becomes increasingly fragile, and the loss model shows that this drain of resources is inevitable. Lehman, Wortman, and Williams (1987) also found that without supervision, social support is likely to be offered inappropriately. This in turn is likely to result in the support efforts' backfiring, further underscoring the importance of both the immediacy of professional supervisory involvement with natural support systems and a watchful eye on the reactions to efforts that have positive intentions.

Emotions and Cognitions Versus Action

The model of conservation of resources does suggest an important role for emotions and cognitions in stress resistance. However, it would be easy to overestimate their role in contrast with the contribution of actions. It is true that intimate, emotional support has generally been found to be the most important kind of support (Brown & Harris, 1978; Hobfoll, 1988); however, intimates are also the primary caregivers during major stress periods. Consequently, finding that intimacy is important implies that caregiving also is important. Organizing social support that addresses physical losses and that directly affects the source of the loss for crisis victims are salient areas of intervention. Examples of this type of intervention are the provision of shelter, food, and clothing; aid in finding work; help with child care; and assistance with shopping and home care. The study of Israeli combatants is another example, as it showed that both instrumental and emotional support were important.

Drain of Resources

Implicit in the model of conservation of resources is the thesis that when resources are summoned, they may be depleted. The research we cited indicates that this is true in the case of social support, for both the recipient and the provider of support. It is increasingly difficult for the recipients to continue asking for aid as they will come to feel that they are a burden on others. The support providers feel increasingly strained when called upon to help. They become more sensitive to stressors in their own lives, and as primary caregivers, they may have few chances for respite. Keeping this in mind, social support interventions should make sure not to overtax support systems. Supervising the support process, making psychological or medical expertise easily accessible to providers, and offering opportunities to relieve support providers are good ways to control the inevitable resource drain.

Environmental Versus Individual Intervention

There has been a tendency to envision social support as an interpersonal or even an intrapersonal process. Gottlieb (1985) argued that this denies the environmental aspect of social support. The conservation of resources model also emphasizes that many of the perceived losses are tangible. Interventions should keep this point in mind as well. In each of the interventions we discussed and in the studies that examined social support in natural circumstances, the context of the social support was critical. Interventionists should be aware of opportunities to alter settings in ways that make social support easier to provide, more effective, and more palatable. Normal school or work activities may need to be altered; the workplace may need to be moved outside its natural sphere of operations into the home; and treatment may need to be brought out of hospitals and community mental health centers and into the community.

Finally, when considering the design of social support interventions during major stress circumstances, one should remember that no one intervention effort is suitable for all situations, even if they concern similar stressors, because the interaction of persons, resources, and environments is too varied. The application of the preceding principles and familiarity with the literature on social support will, nonetheless, aid in designing the most effective interventions. As the literature on evaluations of social support interventions expands, it will offer additional insights.

FUTURE DIRECTIONS FOR GRADUATE TRAINING, SERVICE PLANNING, AND RESEARCH

The conservation of resources approach has implications for planning community programs and ultimately for clinically training psychologists. Rappaport (1981) has suggested that mental health is largely the product of being empowered and that resources are the basis of empowerment. The conservation of resources model makes a similar point, emphasizing the need to give resources to those who lack them and to facilitate the use of resources among those who have resources but lack the ability to apply them. The research discussed in this chapter suggests that emotional support and personal resources are critical to well-being and that instrumental support has less effect on the psychological outcome of either the support provider or the support recipient. This may be interpreted as meaning that the feeling of empowerment is more central to positive outcome than is the possession of material or instrumental resources. However, it should also be clear that there is some threshold of minimum material resources required for functioning. People who do not have this critical level of instrumental resources are likely to have difficulty meeting their basic survival needs (Hobfoll, Kelso, & Peterson, 1981).

We conclude that in addition to individually focused interventions, program planners should consider broad classes of stressors that target groups confront. For instance, a community mental health center that has many referrals of battered women could decide what resources these women will need to alter their circumstances, protect themselves and their children, and cope with their problems. Some resources are internal and may be handled by traditional methods such as psychotherapy, as might be the case for self-esteem. Legal assistance, shelter, and financial planning, however, are tangible resources that these women also require. By focusing on resources, the burden is taken off the individual alone and shared, at least in part, by the system.

Acquiring resources also speaks to the need to teach individuals those skills that enable them to gain resources. These are skills in finding a job, surviving bereavement and family dislocation, adjusting to physical disability, and managing a financial crisis. Such skills may be taught in advance or following the occurrence of major stressors. Behavioral psychology has much to contribute in this regard, and skills-training approaches have already shown promise in a wide variety of situations and settings (Danish, Galambos, & Laquatra, 1983). Nevertheless, skills training is an underutilized approach. The work on the benefits of social competency skills training is especially relevant to aiding individuals in mobilizing social support and best using what social support is offered (Gottlieb,

1988). In this respect, the work on major stressors points out that social support is managed by individuals and that personal traits such as mastery and self-esteem determine whether social support will be used efficaciously.

An understanding of the impact of the most extreme class of stressors, catastrophes, also points to the need for assembling intervention teams. Such teams are not necessary in every catchment area, but large cities and certainly each state should be able to call on emergency intervention teams when catastrophe strikes. Floods, large transportation accidents, radiation leaks, and other artificial and natural disasters are common enough to justify such standby teams. Examples of the use of such team approaches in Israel may serve as models for these efforts.

Such an approach also has implications for graduate training in psychology. Students need to be taught to evaluate and intervene on a psychological level, and they also need to be trained to evaluate and offer material and instrumental resources. Students should be trained to work with broader social systems than the individual and family, to be trained in governmental systems, agency administration, consultation, and negotiation. Indeed, because the skills for such an approach are so broad, no professionals in a single discipline will have all the required expertise for intervention. This means training in how to make and foster such contacts and practical experience working on intervention with multidisciplinary teams. Few agencies currently adopt such models.

Social support interventions following major stressful events have had a good record. Yet it is obvious that although research recommends a broad positive role for social support, the specific active ingredients of support and the circumstances in which they might be applied still have not been determined. To date, most of the naturalistic research on social support at best has pointed to probable causal paths. Intervention studies may contribute to further theoretical development, because they compare alternative approaches in order to assess causal models. In this regard, by examining the impact of a support-based intervention against, say, a no-intervention control, researchers can pinpoint social support's contribution. The model of conservation of resources could act as a heuristic backdrop for such model intervention studies and help programmatic research efforts yield more specific answers. Major life stressors will always occur; the question is whether mental health professionals will have more to offer than just calling in the National Guard for major disasters or recommending psychotherapy for personal crises.

Finally, we end with a word of caution. Despite social support's auspicious beginnings and its being heralded as a kind of social panacea (Caplan, 1974; Cobb, 1976; Dean & Lin, 1977), research on the role of social support and major stressors leads to a more modest impression. In this regard, social support will affect people positively to the extent that it meets a particular situation's environmental and personal demands. The model of conservation of resources suggests that this situation is represented by the extent to which social support counteracts or limits the effects of the loss of resources. Not all support can substitute for loss or prevent further loss, and not all individuals can always accept the support that could meet their needs. By having a general model to guide research, we also avoid having to study support for every situation, as we can look at general categories of loss and the loss-reducing properties of various kinds of social support. By using the conservation of resources and other models and comparing their heuristic value, we should also better understand the nature of stress and be more capable of offsetting its negative effects.

REFERENCES

Bar-Tal, D., Bar-Zohar, Y. B., Greenberg, M. S., & Herman, M. (1977). Reciprocity behavior in the relationship between donor and recipient and between harm-doer and victim. *Sociometry, 40,* 293–298.

Bowlby, J. (1980). *Attachment and loss: Vol. 3. Loss.* New York: Basic Books.

Brown, G. W., & Harris, T. (1978). *The social origins of depression: The study of psychiatric disorder in women.* New York: Free Press.

Caplan, G. (1974). *Support systems and community mental health.* New York: Behavioral Publications.

Cobb, S. (1976). Social support as a moderator of life stress. *Psychosomatic Medicine, 3,* 300–314.

Cohen, S., Kamarck, T., & Mermelstein, R. (1983). A global measure of perceived stress. *Journal of Health and Social Behavior, 24,* 385–396.

Cohen, S., & McKay, G. (1984). Interpersonal relationships as buffers of the impact of psychological stress on health. In A. Baum, J. E. Singer, & S. E. Taylor (Eds.), *Handbook of psychology and health* (Vol. 4, pp. 253–267). Hillsdale, NJ: Erlbaum.

Cohen, S., & Wills, T. A. (1985). Stress, social support, and the buffering hypothesis. *Psychological Bulletin, 98,* 310–357.

Danish, J. S., Galambos, N. L., & Laquatra, I. (1983). Life development intervention: Skills training for personal competence. In R. D. Felner, L. S. Jason, J. N. Moritsugu, & S. S. Farber (Eds.), *Preventive psychology: Theory, research and practice.* Elmsford, NY: Pergamon.

Dean, A., & Lin, N. (1977). The stress-buffering role of social support: Problems and prospects for systematic investigation. *Journal of Nervous and Mental Disease, 165,* 403–417.

Dohrenwend, B. S., Dohrenwend, B. P., Dodson, M., & Shrout, P. E. (1984). Symptoms, hassles, social support, and life events: Problem of confounded measures. *Journal of Abnormal Psychology, 93,* 222–230.

Dohrenwend, B. S., Krasnoff, L., Askenasy, A. R., & Dohrenwend, B. P. (1978). Exemplification of a method for scaling life events: The PERI life events scale. *Journal of Health and Social Behavior, 19,* 205–229.

Epstein, S. (1980). The self-concept: A review and the proposal of an integrated theory of personality. In E. Staub (Ed.), *Personality: Basic issues and current research* (pp. 82–132). Englewood Cliffs, NJ: Prentice-Hall.

Epstein, S. (1984). Controversial issues in emotion theory. In P. Shaver (Ed.), *Review of personality and social psychology: Emotions, relationships, and health* (pp. 64–88). Beverly Hills, CA: Sage.

Fisher, J. D., Nadler, A., & DePaulo, B. M. (1983). *New directions in helping: Vol. 4. Recipient reactions to aid.* Orlando, FL: Academic Press.

Gentry, W. D., & Kobasa, S. C. (1984). Social and psychological resources mediating stress-illness relationships in humans. In W. D. Gentry (Ed.), *Handbook of behavioral medicine* (pp. 87–113). New York: Guilford.

Gottlieb, B. H. (1985). Social support and the study of personal relationships. *Journal of Social and Personal Relationships, 2,* 351–375.

Gottlieb, B. H. (1988). Support interventions: A typology and agenda for research. In S. Duck (Ed.), *Handbook of personal relationships: Theory, research and interventions* (pp. 519–542). New York: Wiley.

Hobfoll, S. E. (1985a). The limitations of social support in the stress process. In I. G. Sarason & B. R. Sarason (Eds.), *Social support: Theory, research, and application* (pp. 391–414). The Hague: Martinus Nijhoff.

Hobfoll, S. E. (1985b). Personal and social resources and the ecology of stress resistance. In P. Shaver (Ed.), *Review of Personality and Social Psychology* (Vol. 6, pp. 265–290). Beverly Hills, CA: Sage.

Hobfoll, S. E. (Ed.). (1986). *Stress, social support, and women.* Washington, DC: Hemisphere.

Hobfoll, S. E. (1988). *The ecology of stress.* Washington, DC: Hemisphere.

Hobfoll, S. E., Kelso, D., & Peterson, W. J. (1981). Agency usage of skid row persons. *Journal of Alcohol and Drug Education, 26,* 832–838.

Hobfoll, S. E., & Lerman, M. (1988). Personal relationships, personal attitudes, and stress resistance: Mothers' reactions to their child's illness. *American Journal of Community Psychology, 16,* 565–589.

Hobfoll, S. E., & Lerman, M. (1989). Predicting receipt of social support: A longitudinal study of parents' reactions to their child's illness. *Health Psychology.*

Hobfoll, S. E., & Lieberman, Y. (1987). Personality and social resources in immediate and continued stress resistance among women. *Journal of Personality and Social Psychology, 52,* 18–26.

Hobfoll, S. E., & London, P. (1986). The relationship of self-concept and social support to emotional distress among women during war. *Journal of Social and Clinical Psychology, 12,* 87–100.

Hobfoll, S. E., London, P., & Orr, E. (1988). Mastery, intimacy, and stress-resistance during war. *Journal of Community Psychology, 16,* 317–331.

Hobfoll, S. E., & Stokes, J. P. (1988). The process and mechanics of social support. In S. Duck, D. F. Hay, S. E. Hobfoll, W. Ickes, & B. M. Montgomery (Eds.), *Handbook of personal relationships: Theory, research, and interventions* (pp. 497–517). London: Wiley.

Hobfoll, S. E. & Walfisch, S. (1984). Coping with a threat to life: A longitudinal study of self-concept, social support, and psychological stress. *American Journal of Community Psychology, 12,* 87–100.

Hofien, D. (1986). *Social support as a learned behavior.* Doctoral proposal, Tel Aviv University.

Holmes, T. H., & Rahe, R. H. (1967). The social readjustment rating scale. *Journal of Psychosomatic Research, 11,* 213–218.

Horowitz, M. J., & Solomon, G. F. (1975). Delayed stress response syndromes in Vietnam veterans. *Journal of Social Issues, 31,* 67–80.

House, J. S. (1981). *Work stress and social support.* Reading, MA: Addison-Wesley.

Houston, B. K. (1987). Stress and coping. In C. R. Snyder & C. E. Ford (Eds.), *Coping with negative life events: Clinical and social psychological perspectives* (pp. 373–399). New York: Plenum.

Janoff-Bulman, R., & Timko, C. (1987). Coping with traumatic life events: The role of denial in light of people's assumptive worlds. In C. R. Snyder & C. E. Ford (Eds.), *Coping with negative life events: Clinical and social psychological perspectives* (pp. 135–159). New York: Plenum.

Killilea, M. (1982). Interaction of crisis theory, coping strategies, and social support systems. In H. C. Schulberg & M. Killilea (Eds.), *The modern practice of community mental health* (pp. 163–214). San Francisco: Jossey-Bass.

Kinney, J. M., & Stephens, M. A. P. (1987, August). Appraisals of caregiving stressors and their relationship to caregiver well-being. In M. A. P. Stephens (Chair), *Family caregiving to dependent older adults: Stress, coping and adaptation.* Presented to the annual meeting of the American Psychological Association, New York.

Kobasa, S. C. (1979). Stressful life events, personality, and health: An inquiry into hardiness. *Journal of Personality and Social Psychology, 37,* 1–11.

Kobasa, S. C., Maddi, S. R., & Courington, S. (1981). Personality and constitution as mediators in the stress-illness relationship. *Journal of Health and Social Behavior, 22,* 368–378.

Kobasa, S. C., & Puccetti, M. C. (1983). Type A and hardiness. *Journal of Behavioral Medicine, 6,* 41–51.

Lazarus, R. S., & Folkman, S. (1984). *Stress, appraisal, and coping.* New York: Springer.

Lefcourt, H. M., Martin, R. A., & Selah, W. E. (1984). Locus of control and social support: Interactive moderators of stress. *Journal of Personality and Social Psychology, 47,* 378–389.

Lehman, D. R., Ellard, J. H., & Wortman, C. B. (1986). Social support for the bereaved: Recipients' and providers' perspectives on what is helpful. *Journal of Consulting and Clinical Psychology, 54,* 438–446.

Lehman, D. R., Wortman, C. B., & Williams, A. F. (1987). Long-term effects of losing a spouse or child in a motor vehicle crash. *Journal of Personality and Social Psychology, 52,* 218–231.

McGrath, J. E. (1970). A conceptual formulation for research on stress. In J. E. McGrath (Ed.), *Social and psychological factors in stress* (pp. 10–21). New York: Holt, Rinehart and Winston.

Milgram, N. A. (1986). An attributional analysis of war-related stress: Models of coping and helping. In N. A. Milgram (Ed.), *Stress and coping in time of war: Generalizations from the Israeli experience* (pp. 9–25). New York: Brunner/Mazel.

Milgram, N. A., & Hobfoll, S. E. (1986). Theories and practice in stress and coping: Generalizations from research on war related stress. In N. A. Milgram (Ed.), *Stress and coping in war: Generalizations from the Israeli experience* (pp. 316–352). New York: Brunner/Mazel.

Miller, K., & Iscoe, I. (1963). The concept of crisis: Current status and mental health. *Human Organization, 22,* 195–201.

480 Social Support During Extreme Stress: Consequences and Intervention

Mitchell, R. E., & Hodson, C. A. (1986). Coping and social support among battered women: An ecological perspective. In S. E. Hobfoll (Ed.), *Stress, social support, and women* (pp. 153–168). Washington, DC: Hemisphere.

Myers, B. G., & Lamm, N. (1976). The group polarization phenomenon. *Psychological Bulletin, 83,* 602–627.

Parry, G. (1986). Paid employment, life events, social support, and mental health in working class mothers. *Journal of Health and Social Behavior, 27,* 193–208.

Pearlin, L. I., Lieberman, M. A., Menaghan, E. G., & Mullan, J. T. (1981). The stress process. *Journal of Health and Social Behavior, 22,* 337–356.

Rappaport, J. (1981). In praise of paradox: A social policy of empowerment over prevention. *American Journal of Community Psychology, 9,* 1–26.

Riley, D., & Eckenrode, J. (1986). Social ties: Subgroup differences in costs and benefits. *Journal of Personality and Social Psychology, 51,* 770–778.

Rook, K. S. (1984). The negative side of social interaction: Impact on psychological well-being. *Journal of Personality and Social Psychology, 46,* 1097–1108.

Salmon, T. (1919). The war neuroses and their lesson. *New York State Medical Journal, 59,* 933–944.

Sarason, I. G., Johnson, J. H., & Siegel, J. M. (1978). Assessing the impact of life changes: Development of the Life Experiences Survey. *Journal of Consulting and Clinical Psychology, 46,* 932–946.

Sarason, I. G., & Sarason, B. R. (1985). Social support: Insights from assessment and experimentation. In I. G. Sarason & B. R. Sarason (Eds.), *Social support: Theory, research, and applications* (pp. 39–51). The Hague: Martinus Nijhoff.

Sarason, B. R., Shearin, E. N., Pierce, G. R., & Sarason, I. G. (1987). Interrelationships between social support measures: Theoretical and practical implications. *Journal of Personality and Social Psychology, 52,* 813–832.

Schonpflug, W. (1985). Goal directed behavior as a source of stress: Psychological origins and consequences of inefficiency. In M. Frese & J. Sabini (Eds.), *The concept of action in psychology* (pp. 172–188). Hillsdale, NJ: Erlbaum.

Solomon, Z., & Benbenishty, R. (1986). The role of proximity, immediacy and expectancy in frontline treatment of combat stress reaction among Israelis in the Lebanon war. *American Journal of Psychiatry, 143,* 613–617.

Solomon, Z., Mikulincer, M., & Hobfoll, S. E. (1986). Effects of social support and battle intensity on loneliness and breakdown during combat. *Journal of Personality and Social Psychology, 51,* 1269–1276.

Solomon, Z., Mikulincer, M., & Hobfoll, S. E. (1987). Objective versus subjective measurement of stress and social support: Combat related reactions. *Journal of Consulting and Clinical Psychology, 55,* 577–583.

Solomon, Z., Oppenheimer, B., & Noy, S. (1986). Subsequent military adjustment of combat stress reaction casualties: A nine-year follow-up study. In N. A. Milgram (Ed.), *Stress and coping in time of war: Generalizations from the Israeli experience* (pp. 84–90). New York: Brunner/Mazel.

Spielberger, C. D., & Sarason, I. G. (Eds.), & Milgram, N. A. (Guest Ed.) (1982). *Stress and anxiety* (Vol. 8). New York: Hemisphere.

Stephens, M. A. P., Kinney, J. M., Norris, V. K., & Ritchie, S. W. (1987). Social networks as assets and liabilities in recovery from stroke by geriatric patients. *Psychology and Aging, 2*, 125–129.

Stephens, M. A. P., Norris, V. K., Kinney, J. M., Ritchie, S. W., & Grotz, R. C. (1988). Stressful situations in caregiving: Relationships between caregiving, coping and well-being. *Psychology and Aging, 3*, 208–209.

Thoits, P. A. (1983). Dimensions of life events that influence psychological distress: An evaluation and synthesis of the literature. In H. B. Kaplan (Ed.), *Psychological stress: Trends in theory and research* (pp. 33–103). New York: Academic Press.

Wilcox, B. (1981). Social support in adjusting to marital disruption: A network analysis. In B. Gottlieb (Ed.), *Social networks and social support* (pp. 97–115). Beverly Hills, CA: Sage.

Wilcox, B. (1986). Stress, coping, and the social milieu of divorced women. In S. E. Hobfoll (Ed.), *Stress, social support, and women* (pp. 115–133). Washington, DC: Hemisphere.

Wilcox, B. L., & Vernberg, E. M. (1985). Conceptual and theoretical dilemmas facing social support. In I. G. Sarason & B. R. Sarason (Eds.), *Social support: Theory, research, and applications* (pp. 3–20). The Hague: Martinus Nijhoff.

Zafrir, A. (1982). Community therapeutic intervention in treatment of civilian victims after a major terrorist attack. In C. D. Spielberger & I. G. Sarason (Eds.), & N. A. Milgram (Guest Ed.), *Stress and anxiety* (Vol. 8, pp. 303–315). New York: Hemisphere.

CHAPTER 18

The Role of Social Support in Community and Clinical Interventions

KENNETH HELLER, RICHARD H. PRICE, AND JOHN R. HOGG

Indiana University

University of Michigan

Indiana University

The literature on social support touches an important theme in American society—a longing for increased interpersonal intimacy and social bonding. Loneliness and alienation have been cited as the by-products of a society that places a higher value on economically driven mobility and competition than on social embeddedness and human caring (Pilisuk & Parks, 1986). This societal theme received scientific credence with the publication of studies indicating that the socially enmeshed were at a lower risk of mortality than were the socially isolated (Berkman & Syme, 1979; Kraus & Lilienfeld, 1959). With the publication of early social support studies and their dissemination by prominent public health leaders (Caplan, 1974; Cassel, 1976; Cobb, 1976), the study of social support suddenly became a new major area of psychological research and inquiry.

Despite the voluminous literature indicating that those with support are generally better off than are those without it, there is still little consistent evidence that support, intentionally provided, can overcome an earlier lack of it (see Cohen et al., 1988, and Rook & Dooley, 1985, for a discussion of problems in support intervention research). The literature on social support interventions generally resembles the state of knowledge about psychotherapeutic interventions some 40 years ago. Like psychotherapy, the field of social support is plagued by "uniformity myths" (Kiesler, 1966) which carry implicit assumptions of homogeneity concerning the support process, how it is delivered, and who benefits from its administration. Although current social support theorists are beginning to distinguish among facets and components of social support (Barrera, 1986; Heller & Swindle, 1983; Thoits, 1982; Wethington & Kessler, 1986), refinements in thinking about social support components have not yet been extended to the interven-

Preparation of this manuscript was facilitated by Grants RO1MH41457 to Heller and P50MH38330 to Price, both from the National Institute of Mental Health.

tion literature. Social support intervention research has generally not kept up with the growing sophistication and refinements in the field. Programs seem to be applied indiscriminately to populations "at risk," without much thought as to whether the treatment provided meets in any way the specific needs of the targeted individuals. The end result is the kind of ambiguity that marked the early outcome research in psychotherapy. Both positive and negative findings are reported without a clear idea of the factors responsible for the effects that are found. The question "Is social support effective?" is as unanswerable as is the earlier question "Is psychotherapy effective?" Underspecified intervention programs, applied indiscriminately, are not likely to generate meaningful information.

A problem, then, when reviewing social support intervention research is the likelihood of obtaining equivocal, and difficult to interpret, results. Gottlieb (1988) reported finding no intervention studies illuminating the processes contributing to the optimization of support. He thereby concluded that "support group interventions and natural network interventions share the status of a 'black box,' appealing strongly to practitioners but leaving obscure the pathways to support afforded by different features of the natural and engineered social surround" (p. 530).

As Thoits (1985) noted, successful intervention programs require a theoretical understanding of the processes linking social support to particular outcomes. Following from this point of view, our task in this chapter will be to suggest parameters by which support effects are likely to be maximized. We will emphasize the macrostructures and regularities in community life within which support is embedded, in contrast with the interpersonal focus of much of the support literature. Although support does have interpersonal components, an interpersonal focus generally leads to interventions at the individual level. However, it is difficult for individuals to change their behaviors or to adopt new behaviors without appropriate social contexts that reinforce these changes. Support interventions may fail if they do not give enough attention to the regularities in social life in which support is embedded. Specifying these regularities means examining the social rules and customs that govern typical social interactions among men and women at different points in the life cycle.

THE DEFINITION AND SCOPE OF SOCIAL SUPPORT AND SUPPORT INTERVENTIONS

Social support theorists generally agree that social networks provide a number of supportive functions on which individuals draw as needed. These include a sense of social embeddedness, belonging, and attachment achieved through group membership; emotional esteem that demonstrates to the individual that he or she is valued by significant network members; an improved capacity for action, in that significant others can aid in coping by providing information or help in resolving problems; and the opportunity for reciprocity in social relationships. Most social relations can offer varying degrees of each of these resources and so serve multiple functions. At the same time, the individual's social learning history determines how these functions are actually carried out. For example, both wives and mothers provide emotional esteem and heterosocial bonding but do so for different life tasks in different stages of the life cycle.

Given the variety of functions served by social support and the different contexts in which support operates, definitions of social support vary considerably among different investigators. This diversity does not dismay us so long as theorists and researchers are clear about the processes on which they are focusing. Our own emphasis will be on esteem-enhancing social exchanges. We agree with Hamburg (1986) that among the fundamental human needs crucial to healthy development are reliable and predictable interpersonal relationships that create a sense of worth and belonging and that encourage the development of skills in coping with life tasks whose mastery earns respect from others.

We see social support as a process that involves an interaction among social structures, social relationships, and personal attributes (Heller & Swindle, 1983). Social structures such as schools, business organizations, neighborhoods, families, and voluntary associations provide the social context for developing social activities and relationships. The perception of support and the maintenance of supportive relationships depend on personal attributes and on the functions served by social activity (Heller, Swindle, & Dusenbury, 1986). A social activity or relationship is perceived as supportive if it fosters the development of competence, esteem, and a sense of belonging through the actual or anticipated exchange of tangible or psychosocial resources. Because not every relationship enhances esteem or competence, social support is not synonymous with social activity. Social relationships and activities also can undermine esteem, and unfortunately, too many of them do. Because relationships are embedded in social roles and structures, our definition also suggests that social support researchers must attend to social roles and structures as well as to social relationships.

Our choice of an exchange framework is meant to underscore the reciprocity of social relationships. Reciprocity serves to maintain relationships over time. Unreciprocated relationships thus are unlikely to persevere, and this explains why support attempts sometimes fail. Individuals need opportunities both to provide and to receive support in order to maintain equity in relationships. As much as we may feel sympathy for needy members of our network (e.g., aged parents, sick friends), these relationships will soon become burdensome unless these individuals were adequate providers of support in the past. For example, the obligation to care for aged parents is one way of restoring equity. Indeed, our motivation to do so is in large measure determined by the love and comfort they gave to us in previous relationships. Antonucci (1985) noted that support is best understood as a series of reciprocated social exchanges that occur over time, in which individuals build up a support "reserve" or "bank." "One does not need to pay back immediately or with the same type of support." However, it is expected that the account will be balanced over the life course (Antonucci, 1985, p. 120).

When individuals have no prior history of relationships (e.g., new friends, members of a newly formed support group), opportunities both to provide and to receive support are crucial for social bonding to occur. This is because reciprocity is one way in which relationships are defined. The opportunity to reciprocate contributes to self-worth and attachment to others (Thoits, 1985). In this regard, note the finding by DePaulo (1982) that people were more willing to ask for help from strangers when they believed that the provider would need their help in the future. However, reciprocity considerations exerted less influence on help-seeking behavior from family members with whom the seeker had already established a relationship. Yet, despite its theoretical importance, reciprocity is only now being recognized in the social support literature (Maton, 1988; Rook & Dooley, 1985; Shinn, Lehmann, & Wong, 1984; Shumaker & Brownell, 1984).

Social support is a by-product of role involvement and typically occurs indirectly as a benefit of social relationships (Thoits, 1985). There is a reciprocal relationship between social roles and social relationships. In part, social and familial networks define roles by conveying specific meanings and constructions regarding the nature of the role (e.g., men may become angry but should not cry; old people are treated with respect but are not expected to show competence). At the same time, roles define the parameters within which social relationships occur.

The access to psychosocial and material resources depends on their availability in the environment and on an individual's skill in being able to draw on them. Thus social support is a multifaceted construct that has both social and individual components (Heller & Swindle, 1983). The process of social support is reiterative and cumulative (Heller et al., 1986), changing over time in accordance with environmental demands and coping resources associated with different life stages or transitions.

The importance of viewing stressors and support resources in terms of life transitions was highlighted by Felner, Farber, and Primavera (1983), who saw life transitions as presenting a person with tasks that must be mastered for successful adaptation. These tasks are often specific to the life event, varying with the events and the personal and social resources that individuals bring to them. As individuals go through a transitional event, their life circumstances disrupt old patterns of behavior. They develop new expectations and so need new adaptations. In this context, individuals use network members in different ways to cope with shifting task demands.

It is important to specify the transitional life events and their associated task demands because social support resources are likely to be situation and domain specific (Swindle, Heller, & Lakey, 1988). This means that the perception of being supported is based on construals about the availability and utility of social resources in specific life situations. For example, Swindle and colleagues (1988) found that in work settings, the perception of support from co-workers and supervisors is more salient to work-related stress appraisals than is perceived support from spouse or friends. Thus, the amount of stress engendered by failing to receive a promotion might depend on how one's colleagues view the event and whether collegial esteem remains strong. The fact that one's spouse cares and provides esteem despite the job disappointment might be valuable, but not as relevant to stress reduction as is the esteem of one's supervisor and co-worker. The extent to which support resources can be substituted (wife esteem substituting for supervisor support in this example) still remains an unanswered question (Lieberman, 1986).

Not only is the need for support specific to life transitions and their associated task demands, but the modes of providing and receiving support also vary by gender, life stage, and social class. These variables largely describe the cultural circumstances in which supportive transactions take place, that is, the extent to which the social milieu structures the expression of support. As Mechanic (1974) stated, a person's ability to cope with environmental demands depends on the efficacy of the solutions that are culturally provided. Culture exerts its influence through a person's exposure to "preparatory institutions" (Mechanic, 1974, p. 33) and the ensuing socialization experiences. Gender, life stage, and social class are prisms through which social structures shape social experiences and behavior.

The theme of this chapter is that social roles and relationships—the vehicles through which supportive functions operate—are established over time in response to cultural demands and the stressors associated with life transitions. Therefore, an understanding of how social support can be enhanced by means of planned intervention requires considering separately the socialization experiences of men and women at different times in the life cycle in the context of environmental demands and resources available in different cultural settings.

We will use two different examples to illustrate how a group's culture can influence the expression of support. First, we will compare the expression of support in a Dale Carnegie public speaking course with the more familiar culture of a support group. In the second example, a former paratrooper describes the factors that influenced the friendships he formed during his basic training.

Support Group Functioning in Dale Carnegie Classes

Dale Carnegie classes have an historical focus on public speaking, communication, self-presentation, and motivating others to perform in a desired way. Carnegie's book, *How to Win Friends and Influence People,* though a popular bestseller, never was respected in academic circles. They saw the Dale Carnegie movement, with its network of franchised classes, as simply a money-making venture. Likewise, behavioral scientists never studied it seriously. Nonetheless, the Carnegie method has been a successful and influential approach to behavior change and social support for business and professional organizations. It is of interest because its assumptions about change principles differ markedly from those derived from more clinical, therapeutic traditions.

Before the first class begins, members are told that there will be no discussion of individual weaknesses or faults. Rather, personal strengths and positive thoughts will be emphasized because criticism "does more harm than good." The appeal is to "courage" and "resolve" for self-improvement and mastery.

The typical class is conducted as a series of public-speaking exercises with specific topics covered in small (roughly three-minute) speeches by class members. The speeches are preceded and/or followed by didactic material presented by a class instructor, who also offers suggestions for improvement to each speaker. However, the atmosphere after a speech is extremely supportive and morale boosting. There is much cheering and clapping before and after each speech, with the greatest amount of encouragement given either to those who are the most popular or to those who are the least skillful but have tried the hardest or improved the most. The support is given for effort and accomplishment and, because of the task focus, seems to be given and received with equal ease by both men and women. Receiving a standing ovation after a difficult speech is not uncommon and, as might be imagined, is a major source of encouragement and reinforcement.

Some speech topics are specifically designed to require emotional disclosure, but in the context of problem mastery. For example, a topic might be "My Most Fearful Moment," but the goal of the speech is not simple disclosure. Students are specifically instructed to end with a discussion of how they mastered (or could have mastered) the problem, or what they learned from the experience that would be useful in the future. Some individuals cry during their presentation of fearful experiences, but this show of emotion in a group focusing on problem mastery serves to bring the group closer together. In this setting it is permissible for men to show emotion because the focus is on mastery and control. Confronting emotions is seen as a tool for improving performance. The goal is not catharsis but control of emotional expression, and given this task focus, emotional expression is not considered a sign of weakness.

Both the franchised Dale Carnegie classes and more typical support groups are extremely popular, and using the criterion of consumer popularity and satisfaction, both appear to be meeting the needs of certain groups. Individuals who join these groups generally report benefiting from participation, although the groups' focus and tasks vary considerably.

Support groups generally emphasize coping with a commonly experienced stressor and use principles loosely derived from the psychological literature, such as the value of group process and self-disclosure. Dale Carnegie classes specifically avoid excessive disclosure of negative experiences and feelings of personal inadequacy, stressing instead strengths, confidence building, and positive thoughts. Negative experiences are used only as a vehicle for achieving empathy with the audience and mastering stress.

There are several reasons that both Dale Carnegie classes and support groups are successful, despite their different contents. Each comes from a different tradition (business vs. therapeutic helping), and each serves a different constituency. Furthermore, each is oriented to different life tasks. The Dale Carnegie classes are directed to achievement in business and successful interpersonal relations in business and professional organizations. They assume an organizational structure with social and behavioral norms with which the individual must learn to deal. The class lessons are designed to improve interpersonal functioning in that cultural milieu. Support groups, on the other hand, link individuals experiencing similar life stressors. The support group creates a setting for sharing common experiences among individuals who otherwise would have to cope alone with particular stressful events. Friends and family are usually available to such persons, but these would-be providers of support often experience tension in their interactions with distressed individuals (Lehman, Ellard, & Wortman, 1986) and so are not always helpful.

Friendship and Support Among Male Paratroop Recruits

The following material was prepared after an interview with a college student (A. M.) who had three years of experience as a medical corpsman in a paratroop division. A. M. was asked to describe the formation of friendships among men in the army, and the factors that facilitated or interfered with friendship development.

A. M. distinguished between ordinary friends with whom contact was likely to be temporary and closer friends or "buddies" with whom friendship was likely to last for some time, even after termination from the service. From the start of basic training, men made friends almost immediately, but these were likely to be the temporary friendships of people being thrown together facing a common stressor. Basic training was rough, and most men initially felt terrified. Friends were made almost immediately with men with whom one came into closest contact, for example, a roommate, or almost anyone with whom the initial experience was shared. Men talked about what was going on—the common experience—but avoided sharing much about their personal backgrounds, other than obvious factual information like where they were from. The men were afraid but never talked about their fears, other than more impersonal statements like "that was rough." There was talk about the demands of the situation and what would be required to overcome those demands. There was basic support in the sense of helpfulness in getting men to comply with demands, because if one person "screwed up," everyone would be punished. In this sense, the men "rooted" for one another, but it was clear to A. M. that many people were just "looking out for themselves," could not be trusted, and might take advantage of others if they could. It was also clear to everyone that friendships formed in basic training would be over in eight weeks, when the men moved to their next assignment.

This same basic pattern continued in the next stage, which for A. M. was training as a medic. There was less pressure, and men could relax more and get to know one another more personally. Friendships were more selective but still temporary because there would be another assignment in 12 weeks. With more free time, men began to form cliques based on only one or two characteristics (similarities) that they had in common. For example, people from a given geographical area might hang out together; the "weak" teamed up, as did the "strong" or the "arrogant." There was a "partying" group and a nonpartying group. Friendships were not really close, and A. M. did not keep up with any of the men he met here if they had no subsequent contact. Not only were the friendships not close, but there were many instances of men taking advantage of one another, and so it was not an atmosphere that encouraged trust. Men were friends because they were thrown into contact with one another and did similar things. Once separated, the friendships did not survive.

Moving to the final combat unit again required new adjustments. There was hazing and initiation rites that the new members of the unit had to endure. Friends were basically people that you hung out with and did things with. Talk with friends was still not personal. In A. M.'s judgment, 60% was shoptalk, 20% talk about women, and less than 20% personal talk. There were many acquaintances with whom to share activities, but still only a few friends. Friendships developed slowly among people who found similarities among them and who enjoyed one another's company. You slowly began to recognize who you could trust and these were people who "did not do you wrong." Being done wrong meant being taken advantage of or being used by someone who first appeared as a friend.

Friends comforted one another about shared stressors and looked out for one another, helping one another get prepared. However friends really did not share fears or feelings about possible failures. It was not "macho" to do so. Friends might admit to being "a little afraid" after a jump or a combat simulation, but they otherwise did not express their fears. You could see the fear in the behavior of the men, but they did not talk about it. It was permissible to talk about their feelings toward women, particularly if one was trying to recover from an unhappy or failed romantic experience. It was also acceptable to talk about feelings about the ill health or death of a parent, but not about personal fears or inadequacies, or anything that would reflect badly on one's competence (with the exception of a failed romance).

By the second year, the main topic of conversation with friends shifted to plans the men began to make about what they would do when they got out of the service. Friends listened to one another's plans, offering encouragement and advice as appropriate. Friends still did not share feelings of failure, serving instead as sources of encouragement.

The themes that emerged are that close male friends in the army shared similar stressful experiences and knew that they shared similar feelings by learning to "read" one another's feelings, but for the most part, they did not discuss their feelings. Close friends also learned that they could count on and trust one another, which meant not being taken advantage of or betrayed for personal gain. A. M. judged that friendships developed in this way (and he listed only three close friends from his army days with whom he still keeps up) are more likely to be lasting than are ordinary civilian friendships.

The purpose of this example is to illustrate that friendship and support are often gender and situation specific. The early socialization of many males in our culture de-emphasizes negative self-disclosure and sharing of emotion. Army life exaggerates these tendencies, calling for self-control, discipline, and suppression of fears, in order to facilitate performance in combat situations. Men are specifically trained to concentrate on the task at hand and to withhold what would be considered "interfering" emotion in the face of extreme stress and real threats to personal safety. It is difficult to know how typical the task demands of this setting are for men. Men can be socialized to respond more emotionally if they are in social environments that emphasize empathy training and reinforce emotional expression. So we are not suggesting that men are incapable of emotional disclosure, only that it is probably not a common element of their normal socialization. Furthermore, the army example suggests that in many male-dominated settings, emotional expressiveness may not be normative and thus may be a poor basis on which to build an intervention program.

We chose the Dale Carnegie and paratroop examples to demonstrate the concept of cultural conduciveness and the power of setting-specific norms in shaping social expectations and behavior. Each setting has unique elements and supportive features that enable friendships to form within the parameters of existing social norms. Those interested in designing supportive interventions should consider factors such as these, which define the social structure within which support is embedded.

Gender, social class, and age can be viewed as markers for an individual's location in the social structure, as they influence an individual's likelihood of obtaining prestige, power, and responsibility (Bengtson, Kasschau, & Ragan, 1977) and so define likely socialization experiences. Cultural pressures and opportunities generally vary according to particular points in the life cycle and are different for males and females. Along with ethnicity and class, these factors help determine the norms for expected behavior.

Socioeconomic status is another factor to be considered when designing support interventions. Access to material resources may have substantial implications for the need for support, the likelihood of recruitment and participation in support interventions, and the capacity to reciprocate when support is offered. In addition, cultural, educational, and stylistic differences associated with class differences may influence receptivity to support programs.

PRISMS OF SOCIAL SUPPORT: GENDER, SOCIAL CLASS, AND LIFE STAGE

Gender Influences on the Expression of Social Support

Research indicates that male same-sex interactions are considerably less intimate than are female same-sex interactions. Yet it is unclear what psychological mechanisms are responsible for this common finding. Are men simply less emotionally sensitive, unable to perceive the emotional nuances of many situations, or are they simply less capable of expressing themselves emotionally?

Reis, Senchak, and Solomon (1985) found that men and women use similar criteria for rating the intimacy of situations. They were equally willing to label the intimacy of interactions and responded with equal selectivity in the choice of partners with whom to share intimate interactions. Furthermore, men and women showed equal capabilities to respond intimately when put in a role-playing situation in which they were required to do so. Yet, even though they have the capacity and sensitivity to respond more intimately, men generally do not do so. Their same sex interactions were rated as involving less intimacy than similar same sex interactions of women. There was one exception to this general finding: Men responded more intimately and reported less loneliness when they interacted with women (Wheeler, Reis, & Nezlek, 1983).

Several implications for intervention flow from this research. If the goal is to provide emotional support or intimacy, support interventions for men and women targets might benefit from using women as the support providers. However, if the goal is to effect some change in behavior unrelated to increases in intimacy, then support provided by women might be less crucial. For example, for a male heart attack victim to discuss with a female nurse his fears of incapacity might be helpful, whereas new healthful exercises and routines might be learned better from a patient volunteer who had recovered from a similar condition.

Other research on help giving and receiving listed several conditions in which receiving aid from others may be seen as a threat to self-esteem. Help from a similar other can activate a negative social comparison process that can lead to feelings of inferiority and dependency (Fisher & Nadler, 1982). This is especially true for high self-esteem individuals, those who already think favorably of themselves. Fisher & Nadler found that high self-esteem individuals view aid from similar others as threatening but that those with low self-esteem did not.

Social support thus may produce negative effects under some conditions. For example, support groups of similar peers may activate negative social comparisons and may make some participants uncomfortable, for instance, if the competence of some of the members threatened the esteem of others. The key to the success of a support group is the opportunity it provides for reciprocity. Members take turns being helpers and "helpees" and thus should have opportunities for both positive and negative comparisons.

Still, even with reciprocity, in some circumstances support group participation can threaten esteem. For example, whereas women see help seeking as a way of sustaining interpersonal relations, men are more likely to see help seeking as a threat to their competence and independence (DePaulo, 1982). Thus, men may refuse to participate in such group activities or may withdraw from them in order to avoid appearing incompetent to themselves or to others. Asking for help from attractive, compared with unattractive same-sex companions poses a greater threat to esteem and more negative social comparison (DePaulo, 1982). Thus, the typical way of setting up a support group, which emphasizes the participants' attractiveness and similarity, is likely to increase the initial threat to esteem.

One possibility is to set up supportive groups on the basis of shared activity rather than simply as a way of receiving help. Thoits (1985) argued that support effects seem to be the benefits that individuals gain from role involvements rather than the benefits purposely offered to role partners as aid. Thus interventions can be helpful if they create a setting from which targeted persons can extract support.

In summary, we believe that social support interventions for men should not be based on an expectation of shared emotional disclosure, as this is not typically how men interact with one another. Men can be helped to prepare for an impending stressor or can be helped to deal with ongoing stress, but the emphasis should probably be on common action or tasks. For similar reasons, support groups for men should probably emphasize action steps, but in a way that minimizes competition, because men already have a strong competitive social comparison norm. Trust among men in a group should not be expected immediately, but the group might be structured to allow friendships and trust to develop slowly on the basis of being together or of participating in tasks together. Requiring men to admit to fears or anxieties in the presence of other men could make the group seem threatening and could lead to resistance or flight. In other words, we believe that support for men should come from groupings based on similarity and proximity in order to develop trust and then on action to learn skills to overcome stressors. In those instances in which emotional disclosure is necessary (e.g., fear of impending death, disfigurement, or incapacity), it may be important for the support provider or confidante to be a woman with whom the man has a private, one-on-one conversation.

Emotional disclosure can be prompted by a male model (e.g., a person who already has experienced the stressor and who can be open about his fears), but such a person needs to be a high-esteem model so that his emotionality will not be denigrated. Even here, what should be expected is a covert rehearsal of fears rather than their open expression, because it is not clear that most men would feel safe expressing their fears to someone with whom they do not yet have a trusting, noncompetitive relationship. Men who enter therapy do engage in emotional self-disclosure, but there is a self-selection process in operation, such that most men do not use opportunities to engage in therapeutic activity. Because some men do feel comfortable with emotional disclosure, it is easy to be misled into believing that the structure of the task is not an impediment, when in fact it might be.

The Mediating Role of Social Class

There is evidence that self-help groups are more attractive to middle-class individuals, because their mode of operation is more congruent with middle-class life-styles. The same is true for professionally developed support groups, as they attract motivated individuals who are comfortable reaching out and sharing emotional experiences with similar others. On the other hand, both Vachon, Lyall, Rogers, Freedman-Letofsky, & Freedman (1980) and Minde et al. (1980) reported similar findings concerning support group failures among, respectively, widows and parents of premature infants. The greatest number of dropouts and the least frequent group attendees came from those in the lowest social classes and those with the greatest number of preexisting problems. These findings are consonant with other reports of difficulty in involving low-income clients in either prevention or treatment activities (Gottlieb, 1983). Yet, indigenous support in low-income neighborhoods does occur (Garbarino & Sherman, 1980; Jason et al.,

1988; Shinn, 1987), so the factors that distinguish successful from less successful programs for low-income individuals need careful thought. Although typical support group formats may be inappropriate to low-income citizens, they do use and benefit from indigenous support. The task is to explicate the structure most appropriate to their ongoing life-style. For example, Pilisuk and Minkler (1980) described how supportive linkages were developed among isolated older adults by building on their few points of social contact at free-food distribution centers and blood pressure clinics.

Low-income persons may feel disadvantaged in group discussion skills, a common ingredient in formal support groups (Gottlieb, 1983), or they may feel out of place among dissimilar others. They may prefer to minimize stressful experiences rather than to emphasize the emotional upheaval associated with these experiences, or to take direct action, because earlier experience may have convinced them of the uncontrollability of such events. Another possibility is that structured activities may be more useful than group discussion, because the former is more likely to involve modeling concrete steps that might either help solve or avoid problems. We still, however, know little about effective coping among different social-class groups. Natural helping networks may sometimes be characterized by self-disclosure. But problem minimization or simple reassurance also may be normative in response to chronic uncontrollable stressors that are fairly common among the poor.

Social Support and Life-stage Transitions

Schulz and Rau (1985) distinguished between life events that are statistically or temporally normative and those that are not. Statistically normative events are those that happen to most individuals in a particular cultural group, and temporally normative events are those that occur within a predictable but limited age range. Thus, entering first grade, graduating from high school, marriage, birth of a first child, retirement, and widowhood are events that are both statistically and temporally normative. They are expected events, and they occur to most individuals at specific times in their life cycle. Because they are anticipated, people can prepare for the changes in coping required, and they usually can obtain support from their network members.

Schulz and Rau also noted that it is more difficult to obtain indigenous support for nonnormative events. Events that are unexpected or that occur to only a small number of individuals (e.g., accidental injury or death, cancer, widowhood at an early age, being fired from a job) are more difficult to cope with and are less likely to be associated with effective indigenous support. Network members have little experience with nonnormative events, and fewer institutionalized coping resources are available. For example, although for older women, being widowed is normative and produces little network disruption, among younger women or among men, being widowed is nonnormative and so can be expected to produce a more difficult adjustment. Thus, intervention is more likely to be needed for nonnormative events for which adequate coping and indigenous support are less likely to be available. However, even normative events may be problematic if basic social competencies and supportive networks are absent.

In general, normative tasks during the life cycle include friendship development and being accepted as a peer group member; learning gender-appropriate occupational and life skills; choosing a mate and learning appropriate behavior for a heterosexual dyadic relationship; providing guidance, emotional, and financial support to children; achieving a productive and satisfying life status; building social and community ties beyond the dyadic unit; maintaining old ties and developing new ones as family and friends are lost through migration or death; and maintaining status and esteem during occupational decline and retirement. How one deals with these tasks, and whether support interventions are needed, depends on individual skills and competencies and on the solutions provided by cultural mores and available social structures.

Support Available to Children and Adolescents

Children and adolescents have a fundamental need to develop a sense of esteem and self-worth (Hamburg, 1986). Children learn and maintain esteem in several ways—first, by learning age-appropriate, graded tasks and performing them competently and then by learning through the actions of others that one is loved and belongs to an appropriate social unit. These functions are most frequently performed by members of the child's indigenous network, primarily composed of family members and friends. Parents are children's initial source of support (Boyce, 1985); however, peers enter the picture early. Cauce and Srebnik (in press) reported that junior high school students see parents, siblings, and boy and girl friends as providing emotional support (i.e., they cluster together on an "emotional closeness" or "intimacy" dimension). However, by late adolescence, peers and family become differentiated as providers of intimacy and affection.

Family members become somewhat less crucial to maintaining esteem in adolescence, as the individual usually has the skill and freedom to tap other sources of esteem and acceptance, such as peers and adult nonfamily members. Peers are used for socializing and setting norms and can be sources of both support and stress. Conforming to the social group is important and is a major source of peer pressure. For example, adolescents value good looks, athletic ability, and monetary status, and so conformity to group norms in these areas is one way of achieving status. Intervention at this age level, therefore, must respect peer norms while offering opportunities to develop competence and mastery, as well as structures that provide a sense of belonging and approval.

Using Price's typology (1979), one can think of intervention possibilities in terms of setting selection, setting modification, and setting creation. Setting selection might be linking an adolescent to a new setting if it existed. But for this to be a viable option, the individual will need to learn how to act in the new setting. Setting modification might, for example, be developing prosocial alternatives in existing schools and teen centers. Setting creation can be more challenging because it means creating new social settings to which members can become attached, which they then are willing to maintain over time.

Consider, as an example, the factors that lead teenagers to join antisocial gangs. Family factors might include support from family members that denigrates esteem or, simply, no support from family members. Under these circumstances, adolescents are likely to turn to peer groups and gangs to win esteem. Gangs determine the standards for appropriate conduct and the opportunities that will be available to individual members to achieve esteem.

Social conduciveness for gang formation occurs when they are the primary source of social control and socialization in a given neighborhood. Suttles (1972) argued that gangs provide social structures otherwise missing in slum neighborhoods. The police and schools, which are the usual sources of social control and socialization, no longer function adequately in these neighborhoods, and the gangs are, in a sense, a "vigilante solution" in the absence of more adequate social structures. Youngsters in slum neighborhoods see lawlessness all around them, and the textbook morality taught by the schools does not match the reality that prevails. Gangs replace symbolic morality with "street knowledge" that is a more realistic guide to social behavior (Suttles, 1972). Gangs give members influence over the environment not available to them as individuals (McMillan & Chavis, 1986). But gangs mainly provide territorially based competencies. They are less effective in helping their members master the outside world. Gang rules and standards of conduct that apply to the neighborhood are rarely acceptable elsewhere (Suttles, 1972), and so gang members find it hard to negotiate social relationships in the outside world, such as with potential employers.

The Guardian Angels, an organization set up as a crime-deterrent force, is an example of an organization that offers the same sense of support and belonging as do gangs, while at the same time creating prosocial roles that teenagers value (Berkowitz, 1987). The Angels can be considered as a new social structure that was created and nurtured, almost single-handedly, by Curtis Sliwa, the group's charismatic leader. Another example of a program to create new social roles for teenagers is the Youth Action Program, a youth-run community service organization developed by Dorothy Stoneman, a former teacher in East Harlem, New York City. Operating out of a windowless two-story building, the Youth Action Program has several different projects, including a young people's block association that has transformed a vacant lot into a park and garden and a youth patrol that makes its rounds in housing projects to cut down on crime. Another project, the Home Away from Home Network, finds homes for teenagers who have family problems.

The following material from a Youth Action Program brochure explains how this program supports teenagers and, at the same time, provides opportunities for reciprocity, nonjudgmental adult role models and an appreciation of teenagers' strengths.

The basic premise of the Youth Action Program is that young people can be a strong force for good in their communities. They have a clear perception of what is wrong in the world and vivid ideas for constructive change; they lack only the confidence and skills needed to carry them out. The role of YAP's adult staff is to draw out the young people's ideas and to give the personal support and technical assistance necessary to realize them.

The process of youth governments is central to our concept. Each project is governed by a core group of leaders, while the overall program is governed by a policy committee consisting primarily of young people. Critical decisions about staffing, program policy, budget, and community action are in the hands of the policy committee.

Although this program has not been rigorously evaluated, the teenagers themselves believe that they have acquired significant skills and a sense of self-esteem. In the words of one of the participants:

Working in YAP, we learned from the meetings and discussions the decisions we had to make. We learned group dynamics, how to deal with people and problems. We were empowered because the program was based on our ideas. We got a sense of pride, of importance, something teenagers in East Harlem don't get anywhere else. (Freddy Acosta, a YAP founder, age 24)

Other, less dramatic examples of supportive opportunities available to teenagers include those provided by adult identification figures outside the family (e.g., teachers, family friends, employers) who can serve as role models. These individuals can encourage independence from the family or can help adolescents identify areas of personal competence. By their example, they advocate prosocial values and demonstrate that one can find an esteemed place in society. Because they take a personal interest in the adolescent and have some success in life, adolescents can identify with them. They demonstrate the importance of bonding to esteem-enhancing, positive models.

An example of a setting change strategy with supportive components might be a job training and employment program in a business organization. Because having adolescents work in a menial job in a corporation (such as the mail room) can be counterproductive if the teenagers view such jobs as a dead end and their supervisors show no personal interest in them, several businesses have instead established summer programs for adolescents as business apprentices, with an expeditor or advocate who smooths the way and helps the teenagers adjust to the new business environment. What is important in these programs is a structure that will allow the individual to demonstrate personal competencies and, by performing useful tasks, to be socially needed.

Creating new settings with new norms can be effective in teaching competency skills and helping establish a purpose in life. Summer camp experiences, wilderness challenge groups, or special retreats for adolescents all are examples. The problem with new settings is that new values may dissipate once the individual is back in the home environment. Thus there need to be avenues that encourage new friends to stay together. If elements of the new setting cannot be incorporated into the adolescents' ongoing social life, they are unlikely to maintain their new prosocial friendships.

The support intervention designed by Felner, Ginter, and Primavera (1982) illustrates the creation of a new supportive setting in an existing social institution, which thereby enhances support by making changes within a regular, ongoing social structure. The goal of the project was to reduce the stress associated with the transition to high school for low-income urban adolescents, by decreasing the complexity of the transition and increasing the supportiveness of the school setting. Homeroom teachers expanded their roles to include counseling activities with the youngsters and outreach and linking activities with their families. At the same time, the students' daily life was restructured to establish a stable peer support system. All project students were assigned to classes so that they took their academic subjects with other project students. The goals of these changes were to "facilitate the development of a peer support system, enhance the student's sense of belonging and increase the perception of the school as a stable, well organized and cohesive setting" (Felner et al., 1982). The findings of the research indicated that compared with matched control group youngsters, the project students had clearer expectations and higher levels of teacher support. The project participants also had better school attendance, reported more stable self-concepts, and had higher grade point averages at the end of the year.

Life Tasks and Support Interventions in the Transition to Adulthood

Children face a number of life tasks as they move into adulthood. For example, as young people enter the occupational world, one major task is learning the skills needed to achieve some level of occupational status. There are social tasks to be learned as well. For most young people, these are choosing a mate, learning to live in a close heterosexual dyadic relationship, and accepting personality differences and differences in gender role expectations. The dyadic unit is strengthened as the partners learn to negotiate marital tasks such as choosing whether to have a family and maintaining and supporting new family members. The marital pair also needs to build and maintain social ties beyond the dyadic unit and often may have to establish ties in a new community. People usually get help with these tasks from family members and old friends who are retained as the dyadic unit grows stronger. However, given the mobility of young people in today's society, for many the transition to new friends is a challenge.

Individuals may have difficulty with these problems of transition because they may lack the skills necessary to negotiate and solve life tasks or they are in settings that impede the development of new friendship links. For example, the group culture may not be conducive to reaching out to others, or individuals may choose to join an inappropriate social group or may be considered outsiders for reasons beyond their control, such as their ethnicity or socioeconomic status. There are several intervention possibilities that can smooth the transition into young adulthood. Many communities have classes in marital relationship, child rearing, and family relations, but usually those who are most needy do not go to these classes. So the problem is how to bring the intervention to the individual or to his or her social circle. Intervention possibilities include outreach by significant community organizations, such as business organizations, civic clubs, health departments, and churches (Maton & Pargament, 1987). The concept of a visiting home aide is probably more common in other countries than it is in ours, but the basic idea is to bring newcomers into a new social circle and, at the same time, to train them in whatever social skills and social expectations are needed to fit into the group. The idea is to reach out to needy others rather than requiring them to take the first step to establish social relationships or to ask for help. The outreach visitor can also smooth the transition and introduce the newcomer to members of other social groups or social institutions.

Research by David Olds (1988) provides an example of outreach support to deal with a major life transition. In the Prenatal/Early Infancy Project, Olds and his colleagues devised a program to mobilize social support by using the strategy of a nurse visiting the home. The target population in Olds's study was low-socioeconomic-status (SES) pregnant teenagers about to have their first child. These characteristics had direct implications for these women's needs and the type of support to which they would most likely respond. Because these teenagers were pregnant, they needed child care skills and nutritional resources both during their pregnancy and after delivery. And because they were young, they had fewer social and material resources available. Furthermore, because they were poor, they were at highest risk for health problems, for both themselves and their offspring. Their class status also meant they had less contact with and less trust in the formal health system. Finally, because it was their first child, they were more receptive to external support efforts.

The support intervention strategy that Olds and his colleagues designed was to respond to these needs. The intervention included parent and health education to introduce the teenagers to caregiving. Olds's intervention also was designed to recruit the informal support of boyfriends, family, and other friends. The teenagers were asked to name others whom they could "count on" for help. These friends and relatives in their social network were encouraged by the intervention staff to offer both emotional and material support for maintaining health behaviors, such as quitting smoking and losing weight. The intervention also linked the family to the community's health and human service system. In addition, Olds formed a local steering committee to promote cooperation among agencies and to provide legitimacy for the social support intervention, thereby illustrating that supportive interventions themselves need institutional support.

The study compared mothers visited at home with two randomly assigned control groups of mothers who received free transportation to local clinics and physicians' offices and/or developmental screening by an infant specialist, but no home visits. The results indicated that the program mothers were more likely to give birth to heavier infants who were seen less frequently in hospital emergency rooms. Also, the program mothers reported that their babies' fathers had a greater interest in their pregnancies. The mothers were more likely to be accompanied to the hospital by a support person, and they were less likely to abuse or neglect their child. Mothers who were visited by a nurse also were more likely to return to school and to gainful employment and to have fewer subsequent pregnancies (Olds, Henderson, Chamberlin, & Tatelbaum, 1986; Olds, Henderson, Tatelbaum, & Chamberlin, 1986, 1988).

Entering the work force for the first time is an important social transition for most adults, and it has both positive and negative effects. Having a job can be esteem-enhancing, but work can also be esteem-denigrating if the job offers little opportunity for personal control or creative expression. The psychological impact of work can also influence social interactions in nonwork settings. For example, when examining the influence of work on family life, Piotrowski (1979) found that boring, undemanding work with little opportunity for control led husbands in blue-collar families to withdraw from participating in the family. On the other hand, if a husband's work was filled with conflict, a pattern of tense family interaction was the result.

Men and women experience different amounts of negative spillover from family to work life. When children are sick, or there is some other problem in the family, men tend to experience little change in their work role, but women with small children feel considerable stress (Crouter, 1984). Kraus and Geyer-Pestello (1985) interviewed a number of working women with families and asked them about their satisfaction with pay, their commitment to their work, and their general sex role orientation. Kraus and Geyer-Pestello found that those women who said they were deeply committed to their work were much more satisfied with their jobs and were less depressed than were those women whose commitment to their work was less. Having young children in the home was a stressor for only those women with a traditional sex role orientation. These more traditional women engaged in more solitary child care activities and shared the task of child care less with others. Apparently, for these mothers, a traditional sex role orientation made them less comfortable with receiving social support in the form of child care and left them feeling that the combination of job and mother role demands was more stressful.

The role of an advocate or mentor has taken on new importance as women begin entering the work force. Mentor relationships among younger and older males in work organizations have existed for some time and are viewed as important to both a young person entering a career and the senior member of the relationship, who can derive satisfaction from observing the younger colleague's development. Kram (1983) studied junior managers and their mentors and found several predictable stages in the mentor relationship. Early in the relationship, the younger member tended to be in an initiation phase, in which the work of the senior partner was admired. Later, this initiation changed into a phase of cultivation, in which the senior member made sure that projects were assigned to the young person and offered advice and guidelines. Still later, as the younger person became more independent, the relationship became characterized by mutual acknowledgment and appreciation.

Although women need equal levels of support, it is not clear that mentor relationships in work settings are equally available to them. Davidson and Cooper (1983), in an extensive survey of male and female managers in England, found that women managers experienced different stressors than men did. The women believed themselves to be disadvantaged in promotions, stereotyped by others, and under pressure to outperform the opposite sex. They also reported feeling prejudice from both men and women in their organizations, and an absence of positive mentors. One wonders whether the support and advice given to a female manager by a male mentor would have the same effect and credibility as that offered by a female mentor, who presumably appreciates some of the difficulties of the female executive role.

Another major workplace stressor is unemployment, because work provides a major role identity for many individuals. To deal with the stresses felt by unemployed persons looking for jobs, Caplan, Vinokur, Price, and van Ryn (in press) devised an intervention program to help the unemployed search for jobs and to help them sustain their efforts in the face of inevitable setbacks. The participants were recruited from unemployment lines and were those who expressed a willingness to take part in a training program designed to help them find jobs. The program began with trainers engaging in behaviors designed to establish trust. That is, the trainers engaged in moderate levels of self-disclosure in which they described a previous period of unemployment, their feelings during that time, and ultimately their success in obtaining a new job. The trainers demonstrated their expertise, or "expert-power," by describing the training program and showing how it was based on behavioral science findings. Once the preconditions of trust and expertise were in place, the unemployed participants were more receptive to the training program and to the trainers' efforts to help in their search.

It was assumed that both skill in job-seeking activities and the motivation to carry them out were critical to effective job-seeking behavior. The program taught the participants a variety of skills, including identifying jobs that matched their experience, skills, and background; searching one's social network for job leads; and self-presentation skills in preparing and presenting résumés and in job interviews.

In addition to teaching skills, the program was aimed at motivating the participants to continue seeking a job despite rejections. The training program taught the participants to regard rejections as an inevitable part of the job-search process. At the same time, the trainers and fellow trainees reinforced and supported the participants' effort and achievement.

The program also prepared the participants for setbacks in their job search after completing the training program. The participants were taught to anticipate situations in which setbacks were likely, to use alternative methods for overcoming dysfunctional responses to setbacks, and to acquire skills needed to cope more effectively with temporary reversals. Finally, the intervention was designed to increase the participants' social support, from both trainers and peers in the program.

This program was evaluated in a randomized field experiment with 928 participants. The results indicated that those who participated in the experimental condition obtained better jobs in terms of earnings and job satisfaction. Even those who were not reemployed as rapidly were better motivated to continue seeking work. There was also some evidence indicating that the intervention may have alleviated some of the negative mental health consequences of losing a job.

Although we have emphasized the supportive elements of the Caplan et al. (in press) program, there are other crucial elements in the program as well. The program promoted job search skills, and the participants were taught to deal with the frustration of being rejected during the job application process. Our own view is that these are valid elements in a support program because the development of competence and esteem are crucial ingredients in supportive programs. The goal of supportive behavior is competency and esteem enhancement achieved through an interpersonal transaction. Most individuals achieve esteem through the practice of normal role behaviors, such as working at a job. So we should pay more attention, as did Caplan et al. (in press), to restoring or enhancing normal role functioning.

Friendship and Life Tasks in the Later Years

Demographic trends show that the population of the United States is aging (Morrison, 1983). However, patterns of aging among different social groups reveal the heterogeneity of the aged population (Bengston et al., 1977). Age does not eradicate sex, race, class distinctions, or differences in personality and temperament. Furthermore, age adds a social stratum to society to the extent that age differences are defined as real, and older persons are assigned to status and role categories on the basis of their age. Rosow (1985) noted that individuals lose institutional roles when they grow older (e.g., forced retirement at age 65) and find that their contribution to society is devalued, not on the basis of personal attributes or behavior, but because age has moved them to the role of a nonparticipant in society. In preindustrial cultures, the elderly are considered to be the bearers of traditional wisdom and thus are accorded a great deal of respect and status. In quickly changing technological societies, however, the generation of new knowledge often is more important than the accumulation of wisdom. In addition, when families no longer live together as intergenerational units, the elderly are consulted less often about their knowledge of child care or family relations (Heller, Price, Reinharz, Riger, & Wandersman, 1984). The dilemma is that if the elderly continue to be excluded from useful social participation, it will be difficult to make up their loss, because the birthrate has been declining since about 1960. Thus, there will be fewer younger workers on whom society can depend, as the currently working population ages and retires.

We suspect that society will react to these demographic changes in a number of ways. We already see older persons returning to the labor force after they retire, albeit in different capacities. In some cases, the elderly are performing unskilled part-time work that previously had been reserved for teenagers (e.g., part-time employment as retail clerks or in fast-food restaurants). Some businesses have moved to voluntary rather than mandatory retirement so that valued employees can stay on as needed. However, given the shift toward more sophisticated technology and the technical knowledge required of future employees, it is unlikely that many older workers will have the educational background to be successfully retrained in newer work skills.

In discussing loneliness among the elderly, Revenson (1986) distinguished between feelings of desolation that result from interpersonal loss (e.g., death of a spouse) and loneliness that results from other causes, such as the lack of social skill in initiating and maintaining friendships or the dissipation of social ties through role loss. These distinctions, along with those associated with gender and social class, are important because different interventions are implicated in each case. For example, support groups and widow-to-widow programs might be appropriate for widows, but generally have not been successful with widowers (Barrett, 1978; Silverman, 1988). Similarly, widows might resist social skills training if they interpreted such efforts as a public announcement that they were "looking for a man," but training of this sort might seem perfectly suitable for elderly individuals relocating to a new living arrangement, such as a nursing home. Indeed, people in nursing homes often stay in their own rooms because they find their new environment overwhelming. Training in institutional procedures and in dealing with other patients who might be disruptive (Berger & Rose, 1977), while at the same time encouraging links to intact patients and to staff, can help increase these persons' perceived control and reduce their feelings of loneliness.

Loneliness associated with role loss can be more difficult to overcome, as there often are societal barriers that prevent the maintenance of productive social roles in what usually are considered the "retirement years." However, the loss of work roles and status does not mean that the elderly need to be socially unproductive. Although people lose institutional roles with age, they can retain informal roles for a much longer period of time (Rosow, 1985). Informal roles depend on networks of friendships and voluntary activities that tie individuals to social institutions. Berger & Neuhaus (1977) referred to these as "mediating structures" that stand between the individual and the larger institutions of public life. The challenge for society will be finding ways for older citizens to perform useful social roles in neighborhood, family, and voluntary social organizations—roles that convey a sense of continued competence and esteem.

Wolff (1987) described a program, in Massachusetts, whose goals are to focus on prevention and empowerment, combat stigmatization and ageism and to engage older persons in self-help and advocacy. Elements of the program included starting a chapter of the Gray Panthers to strengthen advocacy efforts, establishing a cooperative food-buying club, finding employment opportunities for the elderly in the child care field, and training the elderly to lead peer self-help groups in their own communities. Evaluation data were not provided in this report, but all these program components are promising initiatives. By encouraging the maintenance of useful social roles and mutual help opportunities, they suggest alternative support structures that can challenge the tendency of helping services for the elderly to foster "unilateral dependency" (Estes, 1979; Wack & Rodin, 1978; Wolff, 1987).

CONCLUSIONS

Our emphasis in this chapter has been on social structures that determine the opportunities available to express support. We do not deny the importance of personality processes in influencing an individual's ability to gain access to and maintain supportive relationships (Heller, 1979; Heller & Swindle, 1983). But individual differences sometimes seem more important than is warranted, partly because of measurement problems (Shinn, in press). Questionnaire measures, which are the most common way of assessing support, often reflect stable individual differences (Sarason, Sarason, & Shearin, 1986). But that does not mean that support should be viewed exclusively in terms of individual perceptions. Supportive behaviors occur in social contexts that have structural regularities. The timing and expression of support are determined by cultural factors such as social roles and socialization experiences. We therefore believe that in order to be successful, intervention programs must pay more attention to those features of social settings that encourage the development of supportive social ties (House, Umberson, & Landis, 1988; Rook, 1984). We need to recognize that most individuals achieve esteem through the practice of normal role behaviors in reciprocal relationships, and so we should encourage procedures that restore or enhance reciprocal role functioning.

This chapter examined role transitions that vary by gender, social class, and life stage. Our analysis is motivated by the belief that in order to be useful, support interventions should be appropriate to specific life tasks. Social support is extracted from normal role involvements, and there are any number of ways to restore or enhance role functioning, and so ethnographic studies that precede intervention would be valuable. The research we described demonstrated how support may be embedded in ongoing social life, by reinforcing rather than bypassing existing social structures.

We think that interventionists would find it useful to concentrate on social structures and relationships that foster competence, esteem, and a sense of belonging. Programs of this sort might use "support groups" or "confidants," but feelings of competence, esteem, and belonging also can be created in other than confiding relationships. Engaging in shared activities, being socially useful, providing for others, and demonstrating mastery of a stressful life transition all are activities likely to draw support from others. These reciprocal characteristics of social relationships are the elements which must be incorporated into support programs.

REFERENCES

Antonucci, T. C. (1985). Personal characteristics, social support, and social behavior. In R. H. Binstock & E. Shanas (Eds.), *Handbook of aging and the social sciences* (pp. 94–128). New York: Van Nostrand Reinhold.

Barrera, M., Jr. (1986). Distinctions between social support concepts, measures and models. *American Journal of Community Psychology, 14*, 413–445.

Barrett, C. J. (1978). Effectiveness of widows' groups in facilitating change. *Journal of Consulting and Clinical Psychology, 46*, 20–31.

Bengtson, V. L., Kasschau, P. L., & Ragan, P. K. (1977). The impact of social structure on aging individuals. In J. E. Birren & K. W. Schaie (Eds)., *Handbook of the psychology of aging* (pp. 327–353). New York: Van Nostrand Reinhold.

Berger, P. L., & Neuhaus, R. J. (1977). *To empower people: The role of mediating structures in public policy.* Washington, DC: American Enterprise Institute for Public Policy Research.

Berger, R. M., & Rose, S. D. (1977). Interpersonal skill training with institutionalized patients. *Journal of Gerontology, 32*, 346–353.

Berkman, L. F., & Syme, S. L. (1979). Social networks, host resistance, and mortality: A nine-year follow-up study of Alameda County residents. *American Journal of Epidemiology, 109*, 186–204.

Berkowitz, B. (1987). *Local heroes.* Lexington, MA: Heath.

Boyce, W. T. (1985). Social support, family relations, and children. In S. Cohen & S. L. Syme (Eds.), *Social support and health* (pp. 151–173). Orlando, FL: Academic Press.

Caplan, G. (1974). *Support systems and community mental health.* New York: Behavioral Publications.

Caplan, R. D., Vinokur, A. D., Price, R. H., & van Ryn, M. (in press). Job seeking, reemployment, and mental health: A randomized field experiment in coping with job loss. *Journal of Applied Psychology.*

Cassel, J. (1976). The contribution of the social environment to host resistance. *American Journal of Epidemiology, 102*, 107–123.

Cauce, A. M. & Srebnik, D. S. (in press). Peer networks and social support: A focus for preventive efforts with youth. In L. Bond, B. Compas, & C. Swift (Eds.), *Primary prevention of psychopathology: Prevention in the schools.* Hanover, NH: University Press of New England.

Cobb, S. (1976). Social support as a moderator of life stress. *Psychosomatic Medicine, 38*, 300–314.

Cohen, S., Lichtenstein, E., Mermelstein, R., Kingsolver, K., Baer, J., & Kamarck, T. (1988). Social support interventions for smoking cessation. In B. H. Gottlieb (Ed.), *Marshaling social support: Formats, processes and effects* (pp. 211–240). Newbury Park, CA: Sage.

Cohen, S., & McKay, G. (1984). Social support, stress and the buffering hypothesis: A theoretical analysis. In A. Baum, J. E. Singer, & S. E. Taylor (Eds.), *Handbook of psychology and health* (Vol. 4, pp. 253–267). Hillsdale, NJ: Erlbaum.

Crouter, A. C. (1984). Spillover from family to work: The neglected side of the work–family interface. *Human Relations, 37*, 425–442.

Davidson, M., & Cooper, C. (1983). *Stress and the woman manager.* New York: St. Martin's Press.

De Paulo, B. M. (1982). Social–psychological processes in informal help seeking. In T. A. Wills (Ed.), *Basic processes in helping relationships* (pp. 255–279). New York: Academic Press.

Estes, C. (1979). *The aging enterprise.* San Francisco: Jossey-Bass.

Felner, R. D., Farber, S. S., & Primavera, J. (1983). Transitions and stressful life events: A model for primary prevention. In R. D. Felner, L. A. Jason, J. N. Moritsugu, &

S. S. Farber (Eds.), *Preventive psychology: Theory, research and practice* (pp. 199–215). Elmsford, NY: Pergamon.

Felner, R. D., Ginter, M., & Primavera, J. (1982). Primary prevention during school transitions: Social support and environmental structure. *American Journal of Community Psychology, 10*, 277–290.

Fisher, J. D., & Nadler, A. (1982). Determinants of recipient reactions to aid: Donor–recipient similarity and perceived dimensions of problems. In T. A. Wills (Ed.), *Basic processes in helping relationships* (pp. 131–153). New York: Academic Press.

Garbarino, J., & Sherman, D. (1980). High-risk neighborhoods and high-risk families: The human ecology of child maltreatment. *Child Development, 51*, 188–198.

Gottlieb, B. H. (1983). *Social support strategies: Guidelines for mental health practice.* Beverly Hills, CA: Sage.

Gottlieb, B. H. (1988). Support interventions: A typology and agenda for research.In S. W. Duck (Ed.), *Handbook of personal relationships* (pp. 519–541). New York: Wiley.

Hamburg, D. A. (1986). *Preparing for life: The critical transition of adolescence.* Annual report to the Carnegie Corporation of America, New York.

Heller, K. (1979). The effects of social support: Prevention and treatment implications. In A. P. Goldstein & F. H. Kanfer (Eds.), *Maximizing treatment gains: Transfer enhancement in psychotherapy* (pp. 253–382). New York: Academic Press.

Heller, K., Price, R. H., Reinharz, S., Riger, S., & Wandersman, A. (1984). *Psychology and community change. Challenges of the future* (2nd ed.). Homewood, IL: Dorsey.

Heller, K., & Swindle, R. W. (1983). Social networks, perceived social support, and coping with stress. In R. D. Felner, L. A. Jason, J. N. Moritsugu, & S. S. Farber (Eds.), *Preventive psychology: Theory, research and practice* (pp. 87–103). Elmsford, NY: Pergamon.

Heller, K, Swindle, R. W., & Dusenbury, L. (1986). Component social support processes: Comments and integration. *Journal of Consulting and Clinical Psychology, 54*, 466–470.

House, J. S., Umberson, D., & Landis, K. (1988). Structures and processes of social support. *Annual Review of Sociology, 14*, 293–318.

Jason, L. A., Tabon, D., Tait, E., Iacono, G., Goodman, D., Watkins, P., & Huggins, G. (1988). The emergence of the Inner-City Self-help Center. *Journal of Community Psychology, 16*, 287–295.

Kiesler, D. J. (1966). Some myths of psychotherapy research and the search for a paradigm. *Psychological Bulletin, 65*, 110–136.

Kram, K. E. (1983). Phases of the mentor relationship. *Academy of Management Journal, 26* (4), 608–625.

Kraus, A. S., & Lilienfeld, A. M. (1959)., Some epidemiologic aspects of the high mortality rate in the young widowed group. *Journal of Chronic Disease, 10*, 207–217.

Kraus, N., & Geyer-Pestello, H. F. (1985). Depressive symptoms among women employed outside the home. *American Journal of Community Psychology, 13*, 49–67.

Lehman, D. R., Ellard, J. H., & Wortman, C. B. (1986). Social support for the bereaved: Recipients' and providers' perspectives on what is helpful. *Journal of Consulting and Clinical Psychology, 54*, 438–446.

Lieberman, M. A. (1986). Social supports—The consequences of psychologizing: A commentary. *Journal of Consulting and Clinical Psychology, 54*, 461–465.

Maton, K. I. (1988). Social support, organizational characteristics, psychological well-being, and group appraisal in three self-help group populations. *American Journal of Community Psychology, 16*, 53–77.

Maton, K. I., & Pargament, K. I. (1987). The roles of religion in prevention and promotion. In L. A. Jason, R. E. Hess, R. D. Felner, & J. N. Moritsugu (Eds.), *Prevention: Toward a multidisciplinary approach* (pp. 161–205). New York: Haworth Press.

McMillan, D. W., & Chavis, D. M. (1986). Sense of community: A definition and theory. *Journal of Community Psychology, 14*, 6–23.

Mechanic, D. (1974). Social structure and personal adaptation: Some neglected dimensions. In G. V. Coelho, D. A. Hamburg, & J. E. Adams (Eds.), *Coping and adaptation* (pp. 32–44). New York: Basic Books.

Minde, K., Shosenberg, N., Marton, P., Thompson, J., Ripley, J., & Burns, S. (1980). Self-help groups in a premature nursery: A controlled evaluation. *Journal of Pediatrics, 96*, 933–940.

Morrison, M. H. (1983, May). The aging of the U.S. population: Human resource implications. *Monthly Labor Review*, pp. 13–19.

Olds, D. L. (1988). The prenatal/early infancy project. In R. H. Price, E. Cowen, R. Lorion, & J. Ramos-McKay (Eds.), *Fourteen ounces of prevention: A casebook for practitioners* (pp. 3–17). Washington, DC: American Psychological Association.

Olds, D. L., Henderson, C. R., Jr., Chamberlin, R., & Tatelbaum, R. (1986). Preventing child abuse and neglect: A randomized trial of nurse home visitation. *Pediatrics, 78*, 65–78.

Olds, D. L., Henderson, C. R., Jr., Tatelbaum, R., & Chamberlin, R. (1986). Improving the delivery of prenatal care and outcomes of pregnancy: A randomized trial of nurse home visitation. *Pediatrics, 77*, 16–28.

Olds, D. L., Henderson, C. R., Jr., Tatelbaum, R., & Chamberlin, R. (1988). Improving the life-course development of socially disadvantaged mothers: A randomized trial of nurse home visitation. *American Journal of Public Health, 78*, 1436–1445.

Pilisuk, M., & Minkler, M. (1980). Supportive networks: Life ties for the elderly. *Journal of Social Issues, 36*(2), 95–116.

Pilisuk, M., & Parks, S. H. (1986). *The healing web: Social networks and human survival.* Hanover, NH: University Press of New England.

Piotrowski, C. S. (1979). *Work and the family system.* New York: Macmillan.

Price, R. H. (1979). The social ecology of treatment gain. In A. P. Goldstein & F. H. Kanfer (Eds.), *Maximizing treatment gains: Transfer enhancement in psychotherapy* (pp. 383–426). New York: Academic Press.

Reis, H., Senchak, M., & Soloman, B. (1985). Sex differences in the intimacy of social interaction: Further examination of potential explanations. *Journal of Personality and Social Psychology, 48*, 1204–1217.

Revenson, T. A. (1986). Debunking the myth of loneliness in late life. In E. Seidman & J. Rappaport (Eds.), *Redefining social problems* (pp. 115–135). New York: Plenum.

Rook, K. S. (1984). Promoting social bonding: Strategies for helping the lonely and socially isolated. *American Psychologist, 39*, 1389–1407.

Rook, K., & Dooley, D. (1985). Applying social support research: Theoretical problems and future directions. *Journal of Social Issues, 41*, 5–28.

Rosow, I. (1985). Status and role change through the life cycle. In R. H. Binstock & E.

Shanas (Eds.), *Handbook of aging and the social sciences* (pp. 62–93). New York: Van Nostrand Reinhold.

Sarason, I. G., Sarason, B. R., & Shearin, E. N. (1986). Social support as an individual difference variable: Its stability, origins, and relational aspects. *Journal of Personality and Social Psychology, 50,* 845–855.

Schulz, R., & Rau, M. T. (1985). Social support through the life course. In S. Cohen & S. L. Syme (Eds.), *Social support and health* (pp. 129–149). Orlando, FL: Academic Press.

Shinn, M. (1987). Expanding community psychology's domain. *American Journal of Community Psychology, 15,* 555–574.

Shinn, M. (in press). Mixing and matching: Levels of conceptualization, measurement, and statistical analysis in community research. In P. H. Tolan, C. Keys, F. Chertok, & L. Jason (Eds.), *Researching community psychology: Integrating theories and methods.* Washington, D.C.: APA.

Shinn, M., Lehmann, S., & Wong, N. W. (1984). Social interaction and social support. *Journal of Social Issues, 40,* 55–76.

Shumaker, S. A., & Brownell, A. (1984). Toward a theory of social support: Closing conceptual gaps. *Journal of Social Issues, 40,* 11–36.

Silverman, P. R. (1988). Widow to widow: A mutual help program for the widowed. In R. H. Price, E. Cowen, R. Lorion, & J. Ramos-McKay (Eds.), *Fourteen ounces of prevention: A casebook for practitioners* (p. 175–186). Washington, DC: American Psychological Association.

Stoneman, D. (1987). Youth Action Program. *Press Highlights,* 1280 Fifth Ave., New York, NY 10029.

Suttles, G. D. (1972). *The social construction of communities.* Chicago: University of Chicago Press.

Swindle, R. W., Heller, K., & Lakey, B. (1988). A conceptual reorientation to the study of personality and stressful life events. In L. H. Cohen (Ed.), *Life events and psychological functioning: Theoretical and methodological issues* (pp. 237–268). Newbury Park, CA: Sage.

Thoits, P. A. (1982). Conceptual, methodological, and theoretical problems in studying social support as a buffer against life stress. *Journal of Health and Social Behavior, 23,* 145–159.

Thoits, P. A. (1985). Social support and psychological well-being: Theoretical possibilities. In I. Sarason & B. Sarason (Eds.), *Social support: Theory, research, and application* (pp. 51–72). Dordrecht, Netherlands: Martinus Nijhoff.

Vachon, M. L. S., Lyall, W. A. L., Rogers, J., Freedman-Letofsky, K., & Freedman, S. J. J. (1980). A controlled study of self-help intervention for widows. *American Journal of Psychiatry, 137,* 1380–1384.

Wack, J., & Rodin, J. (1978). Nursing homes for the aged: The human consequences of legislation shaped environments. *Journal of Social Issues, 34,* 6–21.

Wethington, E., & Kessler, R. C. (1986). Perceived support, received support, and adjustment to stressful life events. *Journal of Health and Social Behavior, 27,* 78–89.

Wheeler, L., Reis, H., & Nezlek, J. (1983). Loneliness, social interaction, and sex roles. *Journal of Personality and Social Psychology, 45,* 943–953.

Wolff, T. (1987). Community psychology and empowerment: An activist's insights. *American Journal of Community Psychology, 15,* 151–166.

Author Index

Subject Index

abortion, 346–347, 348, 354
abusive relationships, 102
acceptance, latitude of, 167
Achenbach Child Behavior
    Checklist (CBC), 81, 82, 83
activity theory, 219
adaptation, 130
    social support predictors of,
        334–338
adequacy, of social support, 17,
    200. *See also* satisfaction
adherence to medical regimen,
    438–439
Adjective Checklist, 107
adjustment, 335, 341–342
    and negative interactions,
        462–465
    and network density, 384–387
    and received support, 16
    and social support, 84–85,
        120, 121
    to school, 83
adolescence, 347, 349
    coping in, 347, 354
    diabetes in, 433–436
    peer support in, 367–375
    social support in, 53,
        494–497
adult attachment, 102
adults, older, *see* elderly
affect:
    expression of, 339
    positive, 226–227
    in relationships, 111
affiliation, 113–114
    need for, 231
age:
    and social support, 118,
        184–186
    and social support reciprocity,
        18, 192–193
aging, longitudinal study of,
    234–235. *See also* elderly
AIDS, 263
Alameda County Population
    Monitoring Study, 428

alienation, 300
Alienation Test, 297–298
Alzheimer's disease, 259–260,
    464
anger, 84, 111
anxiety, 152, 161–162, 338,
    341, 460
    and early experience, 106
appraisal, 17
    of stress, 324–325, 485
appraisal support, 42, 44, 45,
    115, 321, 348
Arizona Social Support
    Interview Schedule
    (ASSIS), 271–272
arousal, 226–227
assessment:
    of children's social support,
        86–88
    historical origins of, 12–20
    of social support, 9–23
assumptive world, 201–202
asthma, 431–433, 444
attachment, 64–67, 109, 174,
    178, 321, 331, 335, 455
    in adulthood, 102–104
    exploratory behavior in,
        100–101
    and social support, 99,
        100–109
attachment behavior system, 100
attention, self-focused, 228–229
attraction, 99
available support, 17–19, 267,
    268, 269–275, 273–274,
    275–280, 283, 284, 285,
    286, 288–290
    and health, 285
    measurement approaches to,
        18–20

back injury, support for, 472
back pain, 441–443, 447
balance model, of stress, 456
Barr virus (EBV), 255, 256,
    258, 259, 260

Beck Depression Inventory,
    284, 297–298
belonging, 42, 44, 45. *See also*
    intimacy; social integration
belonging support, 222–223
bereavement, 260–261,
    280–281, 339, 344–345.
    See also loss
    support for, 277,
    withholding of feelings in,
        401
Berkeley Growth Study, 103
biological marker, 255
black adolescents, 371–372
black Americans, 190
    social support of, 184–185
blended family, *see* stepfamily
bonding, *see* attachment
buffering effects:
    of hardiness, 307
    reverse, 345
    of social support, 130, 220,
        222, 224, 284, 286, 310,
        333, 349, 441, 443–444
    of spouse, 13
burnout, 308, 350, 354–355
    in teachers, 354
    in therapists, 354–355
    in supporters, 275–279

cancer, 276, 277, 280, 336,
    341, 397, 400
    coping with, 407–411,
        414–416
    self-presentation in, 414–416,
        420–421
cardiovascular disease, 427–429
caregiving, 342, 358
    effects of, 260, 464–465
    for elderly, 220
    and immune function,
        259–260
    long term, 220
    stress of, 129–146, 220
causal modeling, *see* structural
    equation modeling

521

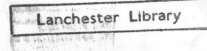